The Politics of War

The Politics of War

RACE, CLASS, AND CONFLICT
IN REVOLUTIONARY VIRGINIA

Michael A. McDonnell

Published for the

Omohundro Institute of

Early American History and Culture,

Williamsburg, Virginia,

by the

University of North Carolina Press,

Chapel Hill

The Omohundro Institute of Early American History and Culture is sponsored jointly by the College of William and Mary and the Colonial Williamsburg Foundation. On November 15, 1996, the Institute adopted the present name in honor of a bequest from Malvern H. Omohundro, Jr.

Library of Congress Cataloging-in-Publication Data
McDonnell, Michael A.
The politics of war : race, class, and conflict in revolutionary Virginia /
Michael A. McDonnell.
p. cm.
Includes bibliographical references and index.
ISBN-13: 978-0-8078-3108-3 (cloth : alk. paper)
1. Virginia—History—Revolution, 1775-1783—Social aspects. 2. Virginia—Politics and government—1775-1783. 3. Virginia—Race relations—History—18th century. 4. Virginia—Social conditions—18th century. 5. Social classes—Virginia—History—18th century. 6. Social conflict—Virginia—History—18th century. 7. United States—Militia—History—18th century. 8. United States. Continental Army—Mobilization. 9. United States—History—Revolution, 1775-1783—Social aspects. I. Omohundro Institute of Early American History & Culture. II. Title.
E263.V8M39 2007
975.5'03—dc22
2006020158

Parts of this book draw on my previously published work: "Class War? Class Struggles during the American Revolution," *William and Mary Quarterly,* 3d Ser., LXIII (2006), 305-344; "A World Turned 'Topsy Turvy': Robert Munford, *The Patriots,* and the Crisis of the Revolution in Virginia," *William and Mary Quarterly,* 3d Ser., LXI (2004), 235-270; "National Identity and the American War for Independence: A Reappraisal," *Australasian Journal of American Studies,* XX (2001-2002), 3-17; (with Woody Holton) "Patriot vs. Patriot: Social Conflict in Virginia and the Origins of the American Revolution," *Journal of American Studies,* XXXIV (2000), 231-256; "Popular Mobilization and Political Culture in Revolutionary Virginia: The Failure of the Minutemen and the Revolution from Below," *Journal of American History,* LXXXV (1998-1999), 946-981.

This book received indirect support from an unrestricted book publications grant awarded to the Institute by the L. J. Skaggs and Mary C. Skaggs Foundation of Oakland, California.

11 10 09 08 07   5 4 3 2 1

Maps by Rebecca L. Wrenn

In memory of my brother,
my father, and my grandfather.
James, Patrick, and Jim

Cymaint o Gariad a Chymaint o
Atgofion Ni'ch Anghofiwn fyth

Acknowledgments

Though this book is long enough already, it has been long in coming. It has also been an international affair, researched and written in England, Wales, Canada, the United States, South Africa, and now Australia. Over time and place, there are many to thank who have made the making of this book endurable, even enjoyable. The long list below is but a snapshot of the people who have made this book possible.

First I would like to thank the many staff and librarians of the diverse institutions in which I have had the pleasure to work, including Rhodes House Library in Oxford, the Alderman Library at the University of Virginia, the Virginia Historical Society, the Library of Virginia, the Swem Library at the College of William and Mary, the John D. Rockefeller, Jr., Library of Colonial Williamsburg, and the David Library of the American Revolution in Pennsylvania. Brent Tarter and John Kneebone at the Library of Virginia were especially welcoming and ready with advice and suggestions, and Nelson Lankford and Frances Pollard at the Virginia Historical Society made my stay there particularly fruitful. David Fowler at the David Library proved as adept at guiding me through the archives as he was at navigating the New Jersey Pine Barrens. While at Monticello, I had the good fortune to run into James Horn, who made that stay productive and enjoyable.

I have also benefited greatly from the optimism of many institutions that have supported my work, for which I am grateful. At Balliol College, I was funded by a Devorguilla Scholarship. My initial research in the United States was funded by a generous grant from the Social Sciences and Humanities Research Council of Canada. Along the way, I have also received welcome funding from the Virginia Historical Society, the David Library of the American Revolution, the Huntington Library, the Scouloudi Foundation at the Institute for Historical Research, University College, London, and from the Thomas Jefferson Memorial Foundation, at the International Center for Jefferson Studies, Monticello, Virginia. Most recently, my writing has benefited from the generous support of Richard Waterhouse and the School of Philosophical and Historical Inquiry and the University of Sydney.

The seeds of this project were sown long ago under the fortuitous stewardship of Joyce Appleby and James Henretta, who held successive visiting chairs at Oxford at a crucial moment, managing to save more than a few D.Phil. theses from early obscurity. From isolated beginnings, my own British "early American" crew began to form. Daniel W. Howe took up post-mid-thesis and provided encouragement, while Peter Thompson journeyed back across the Atlantic to shake up and shepherd several of us through the last crucial stages of our work. As he has done for others, Peter provided much-needed advice and suggestions as well as inspirational support, as he has continued to do since. While at Oxford, I was also fortunate to benefit from the friendship of Christopher Brown, William O'Reilly, and Sarah Knott as well as early readings of my work by J. R. Pole, Kathy Lloyd, Kurt Berends, and Tim Roberts.

After taking up post at the Department of American Studies at the University of Swansea, that early American community grew. In Swansea I ran into fellow early Americanist Steve Sarson, who has been a source of constant support and whose own work on the Chesapeake in the era of the Revolution has given me much food for thought and much pause to think. At Swansea I also benefited from the friendship, support, and advice of many—Alan Bilton, Duncan Campbell, Bev Evans, Emma Frearson, Angela Jones, Steve McVeigh, Phil Meling, Craig Phelan, Jon Roper, Nick Selby, and David R. Brewster-Taylor, whose good-humored jokes about Loudoun County kept me sane, and keen to make larger connections.

During my time at Swansea, I benefited immensely from the support provided by two different groups and networks of scholars. The lively and dynamic British Association for American Studies provided one congenial forum for collegiality and the presentation of work in progress, and their annual conferences really do rank among the best. Special thanks particularly to all those on the executive committee of the Association who provided critical support and a home away from home when I needed it. At the same time, and through BAAS, we realized that there were more than a few people in the United Kingdom working on early American topics, and, with the generous help of Tony Badger at Cambridge and Ron Hoffman of the Omohundro Institute of Early American History and Culture, we began meeting regularly to reap the rewards of generous and critical readings of one another's work with equally generous servings of good British ale. There are too many good people to thank here by name, but I am particularly grateful to Trevor Burnard, Francis D. Cogliano, Julie Flavell, Douglas Hamilton, Simon Middleton, Ken Morgan, Simon Newman, Betty Wood, and Natalie Zacek for their support and suggestions.

On various research trips to the United States, too, I have also benefited from the generosity of many who have taken me in, shared their research, and provided welcome advice on my work. Moreover, conference participants in at least seven different countries have helped shape and sharpen my analysis and provided good critical readings of several portions of this book. Among these are Terry Bouton, Seth Cotlar, Matthew Dennis, Konstantin Dierks, Marc Egnal, Emory G. Evans, Elizabeth Fenn, Sylvia Frey, Jack P. Greene, Robert Gross, Sally Hadden, Douglas Hamilton, C. Dallett Hemphill, Katherine Hermes, Don Higginbotham, Thomas Humphrey, Allan Kulikoff, Philip D. Morgan, Cassandra Pybus, Marcus Rediker, John P. Resch, Jeffrey H. Richards, Nancy L. Rhoden, David Rollison, Walter Sargent, Jon Sensbach, Billy Smith, Jennifer Spear, Robert C. H. Sweeny, Alan Taylor, Albert H. Tillson, Peter Way, Andy Wood, Peter H. Wood, and Alfred F. Young.

Most recently, I have benefited from the warm welcome I have had in Sydney, where conversations about and critical readings of my work by diverse colleagues have helped shape the final lines of interpretation. These include Saliha Belmessous, Andrew Fitzmaurice, Chris Hilliard, Maggie MacKellar, Cindy McCreery, Kirsten McKenzie, Penny Russell, and Ian Tyrrell as well as the many bright and brilliant students I've already had the honor of teaching over the past two years. But it especially includes the nucleus of the American History Reading Group in Sydney, composed of Frances Clarke and Clare Corbould (whose forthcoming books on Civil War sentimentality and black nationalism in the early twentieth century will soon transform those fields), Stephen Robertson (whose own class-based interpretation of child sex crimes in New York has just been published by the University of North Carolina Press), and Shane White (who is as indomitable a mentor as he is a prolific—and terrific—writer). My appreciation of their collective support is immense; nobody could ask for or expect better colleagues, and friends.

For the time they took to read more of my work than they probably desired, I also need to thank especially Edward Countryman for his critical insights into several chapters that formed the basis of articles, Robert Gross for his timely reading and comments on the entire manuscript, Thad W. Tate for helping me to put it all into perspective, and James Horn for marshaling it through the early stages of the Institute review process. Fredrika J. Teute, too, took her formidable pen to every page of the manuscript and provided challenging and stimulating comment on so many different aspects, and Gil Kelly worked heroically on the final version. I am grateful to have learned much from both.

For their intellectual, inspirational, or just plain extraordinary contributions to this book, I also must give special thanks to the following: Julian Gwyn, whose unwavering confidence in me from the start was undeserved. Trische Kell, who early inpsired in me a love of learning and pushed me to attempt, not to succeed, but to excel. Marie and Ray Raphael, for their grace and inspirational support under the most trying circumstances. Colleen and Rhys Isaac, who have been unfailingly enthusiastic in their support, whether it be in providing a warm welcome to Australia or a close reading of almost every word I have written. Sally Mason and Ron Hoffman, who have done the same for me in the United States (ensuring that I had at least one warm meal every trip) and whose close friendship and collaboration have been immensely reassuring. Thanks as well to Marjoleine Kars, who has provided timely support and constant good humor. And to Gretchen School, who has provided welcome relief from the raucous roar of Woody Holton (whose forthcoming book is much more than a sequel to this one). Woody has been a constant collaborator, provocateur, critic, cheerleader, and friend from the moment of our serendipitous meeting in the Library of Virginia to the final page proofs of this book. Therefore, any errors can be attributed to him.

There is, of course, a fine line between friends and intellectual collaborators. But there are several friends especially who have helped immensely by listening to my pleas not to talk about work while enjoying the views from hills and trails across at least three continents, or enjoying the surf in the freezing waters of South Wales (or the warmer currents of New South Wales). These include Bill, Anne, and Leela Ehrhart, Pete Carr, Gail Evans, Charles Fairchild, Emma Faulkner, Nick Francis, Craig Fraser, Danni Irvine, Eileen Lambourne, Cam MacKellar, Phil and Ceri Morgan, Mary and Pat Whalen, and Geoff Woodin.

And, finally, I owe a huge debt to my own family. This includes my extended family in Wales who helped me develop this project in ways only I could appreciate. And it also includes a deep affection for a growing family of in-laws in South Africa and London who have welcomed me with a warmth unsurpassed and who have been a model of patience with me. I can only say to them, where there is no lobolo, there is a book. This new world of braais, koeksoesters, and ubuntu has opened to me through Frances Thomas, who has steadfastly steered clear of being dragooned into proofreading duties but whose influence over every word of this book is immeasurable. It is impossible to express the appreciation I have for her, except to say that there can be no greater gift in the world than her unrepentant exuberant love.

It is a love and generosity of spirit that Frances has also shared with my immediate family too, through a particularly difficult period in all of our lives. Indeed, I owe especial thanks to my sister Jody and her partner, Paula, my Mum, Pam, and my grandmother, Cath, who have never questioned the value of what I've been doing, and provided unconditional support despite a series of devastating losses that have put everything into proper perspective. We all still mourn the recent loss of my grandfather and my brother, both of whose unfailing infectious enthusiasm will be sorely missed at the launch of this book, and of my father, who was always as keen to hear about the progress of this work as he was to hike together in the Drakensberg. It is to the memory of the three of them that this book is dedicated.

Contents

o

6

r 399

Abbreviations and Short Titles

AHR
    American Historical Review

Hening, comp., *Statutes at Large*
    William Waller Hening, ed., *The Statutes at Large: Being a Collection of All the Laws of Virginia* (1809-1823; rpt. Charlottesville, Va., 1969)

CWFL
    Colonial Williamsburg Foundation Library, Williamsburg, Va.

CWM
    Earl Gregg Swem Library, College of William and Mary, Williamsburg, Va.

DLAR
    David Library of the American Revolution, Washington Crossing, Pa.

JAH
    Journal of American History

LoC
    Library of Congress, Washington, D.C.

LiVi
    Library of Virginia, Richmond

MHVR
    Mississippi Valley Historical Review

Papers of Jefferson
    Julian P. Boyd et al., eds., *The Papers of Thomas Jefferson* (Princeton, N.J., 1950-)

Papers of Madison
    William T. Hutchinson et al., eds., *The Papers of James Madison* (Chicago, Charlottesville, Va., 1962-)

Papers of Mason
    Robert A. Rutland, ed., *The Papers of George Mason,* 3 vols. (Chapel Hill, N.C., 1970)

Papers of Pendleton
    David John Mays, ed., *The Letters and Papers of Edmund Pendleton, 1734-1803,* 2 vols. (Richmond, Va., 1967)

Papers of Washington
    W. W. Abbot et al., eds., *The Papers of George Washington* (Charlottesville, Va., 1976-)

Rev. Va.

William J. Van Schreeven et al., comps., Robert L. Scribner et al., eds., *Revolutionary Virginia: The Road to Independence,* 7 vols. (Charlottesville, Va., 1973–1983)

UVa

Alderman Library, University of Virginia, Charlottesville

Va. Gaz. (D and H)

Virginia Gazette (Williamsburg) (Dixon and Hunter)

Va. Gaz. (P and D)

Virginia Gazette (Williamsburg) (Purdie and Dixon)

Va. Gaz. (Pinkney)

Virginia Gazette (Williamsburg) (Pinkney)

Va. Gaz. (Purdie)

Virginia Gazette (Williamsburg) (Purdie)

VHS

Virginia Historical Society, Richmond

VMHB

Virginia Magazine of History and Biography

WMQ

William and Mary Quarterly

The Politics of War

Introduction

In Northumberland County in the lower Northern Neck of Virginia a dramatic and tragic incident unfolded in the midst of the Revolutionary war. On the day appointed for a draft of eligible males for service in the Continental army in September 1780 "a considerable body of men" gathered together at the county courthouse to "prevent the said draft being made." One witness reported that upward of 150 men, or almost 25 percent of the militia, had "formed themselves in a regular body, and were armed." Local officials sent out two captains with a detachment of men under a flag of truce to treat with the rebellious militia and try to persuade them to lay down their arms. But the delegation was also under strict orders to quell the mutiny any way they could—to "reduce" the mutineers "to order or submission." Ultimately, the officers persuaded the rioters to surrender and come in "on terms," and without their arms. But, as the militia marched back to the muster ground, one of them, Joseph Pitman, "passed with his firelock on his shoulder." Captain Edwin Hull took offense at Pitman's act of silent defiance and ordered him to "ground his fire arms." Pitman replied, "You ground your fire arms."

Neither could turn back from the brink. As a witness reported, "Both of them levelled their pieces . . . at each other, at the same instant and fired." Captain Hull died immediately; Pitman was wounded but survived. The encounter sparked a protracted and divisive conflict in Northumberland: Thomas Gaskins, Sr., the county lieutenant, reported to the governor that "almost the whole county was inflaim'd." Later, to Gaskins's surprise and horror, the situation worsened, and many men in the militia on whom he had counted to help suppress the insurgents "appeard in arms against us." Peace was not fully restored until the following spring.[1]

1. My account of the riot in Northumberland was drawn from the following sources: Pension Record of Edwin Hull, W14316 (which includes valuable depositions concerning his participation in the draft proceedings that led to his death); Lewis Lunsford to Robert Carter, Sept. 18, 1780, in William Jennings Terman, Jr., "The American Revolution and the Baptist and Presbyterian Clergy of Virginia: A Study of Dissenter Opinion and Action" (Ph.D. diss., Michigan State University, 1974), 201; Thomas Gaskins to Thomas Jefferson, Feb. 23, 1781, *Papers of Jefferson,* IV, 693. In Executive Papers, LiVi: "Advertizement," Sept. 18, 1780;

Uncovering this incident in the Virginia State Archives, the details of which are not published in any of the many sources pertaining to Virginia's Revolutionary history, came as something of a surprise to me. I had begun a study of Virginia during the Revolutionary crisis because I wanted to see how patriot leaders had pulled off what seemed like a successful revolution and military campaign in the midst of what I knew to be a large, restive, and potentially rebellious enslaved population. As I delved deeper into the archival records, however, I came across more and more references to incidents like the one in Northumberland in 1780. Though few were as richly detailed, it quickly became clear that sharp divisions existed in Revolutionary Virginia.[2]

Surveying the years of war and looking in some depth at mobilization

---

"Proceedings of Northumberland Court Martial Respecting Rioters," Sept. 16–26, 1780; Thomas Gaskins to Jefferson, Mar. 17, 1781; Gaskins to William Davies, Aug. 12, 1781; Gaskins to William Davies, Apr. 30, 1782. Northumberland had a militia force of about 630 in 1780–1781, of whom 538 were probably eligible for the draft. Thirty-nine were below the age of eighteen, and 77 were invalids fit for station duty only ("Return of Militia in 1780," General Return of Militia in November 1781, War Office Records, LiVi; Thomas Jefferson, *Notes on the State of Virginia,* ed. William Peden [Chapel Hill, N.C., 1954], 89). Edwin Hull was well connected to the local gentry, owned three hundred acres of land valued at £150, and owned up to eleven slaves, thirteen cattle, and two horses (Northumberland Land and Personal Property Tax Lists, 1782, LiVi).

2. For the most part, I focused my research on the more-settled counties of Virginia east of the Blue Ridge Mountains in regions more commonly known as the tidewater, the piedmont, and the southside. I began by using previously neglected local county court records, war office and executive records, and militia petitions to reconstruct the diverse wartime experiences of Loudoun and surrounding counties in northern Virginia, Cumberland and Powhatan counties in the central piedmont region, and the lower Northern Neck. These three areas had relatively complete records for the war years and differed in social structure and wartime experiences. The lower Northern Neck, exposed and vulnerable to oceangoing vessels, was in a constant state of siege during the war from both British and privateering plunderers. Cumberland and Powhatan, in the heart of piedmont Virginia, were left relatively at peace for the duration of the war except in 1781 when the British invaded and briefly marched through the community. Loudoun, in the upper Northern Neck and bordering the Blue Ridge Mountains on its western edge, never saw a redcoat in arms, but was continually called upon for help both to the north and south. Ultimately, these county-level studies provided a point of departure for studying Virginia society at war in general.

in several different counties across the state, I saw that the disaffection and discontent in Virginia at times reached critical proportions—most often, when patriot leaders tried to persuade, entice, or coerce men into military service. Beginning with the "minutemen" as early as 1775, continuing with the regular service throughout the war, and ending with militia call-outs in 1781, poorer laboring whites and middling farmers in Virginia refused to follow blindly and participate fully in a military effort orchestrated largely by their superiors. Yet, despite its extent and persistence, this resistance has not been placed in the foreground of the history of Revolutionary Virginia.

Intrigued by the level of disaffection I was finding in a wartime society long presented as comparatively unified, I was also keen to understand its nature. What brought men like Joseph Pitman and his neighbors to a point of defiance that risked civil war against other white men, when all of them lived in the midst of one of the highest concentrations of a volatile enslaved population? However sharp the dissatisfactions that spurred Pitman and his comrades to defy their "betters," was not the even greater threat of slave uprisings sufficient to mitigate those differences so that white patriots of whatever rank and status stood together against the British?

Recovering and understanding the nature of this discontent proved more difficult than delineating it. The "discontented"—small farmers, tenants, laborers, and indentured and convict servants—like enslaved Virginians, left very few written records of their own thoughts and experiences. Most Virginians, particularly those not of the top echelons of society, lived in an oral-aural world: perhaps as many as 75 percent of adults in the colony could not sign even their names. This means that the main sources for analyzing Revolutionary Virginia consist primarily of the writings of a very few, predominantly wealthy, men who often left self-conscious accounts and were reluctant to air their problems in public.[3]

Few gentlemen thus spent much time analyzing such discontent, and fewer still were willing to talk to each other about Virginia's internal problems. When they did talk about problems, most gentlemen dismissed incidents such as the one that took place in Northumberland County as self-interested disaffection or, more often, as isolated cases spurred on by a handful of pro-British loyalists, or tories, as they were derisively called. Many southerners were particularly scrupulous not to dwell on such divi-

3. On the predominantly nonliterate world of Virginia, see Rhys Isaac, "Dramatizing the Ideology of Revolution: Popular Mobilization in Virginia, 1774 to 1776," *WMQ,* 3d Ser., XXXIII (1976), esp. 357–364.

sions because of the enslaved population in their midst; such a large number made the appearance of harmony paramount. Most gentlemen thus wrote anxious but reassuring letters that have been taken at face value and not analyzed in light of the disaffection underneath. Therefore, their texts give the impression that white Virginians were very close to being united during the Revolutionary period, and rarely do they illuminate the sources of discontent.[4]

Ordinary Virginians seldom gave voice to their complaints in writing, at least in the early stages of the war, but their actions spoke loudly: and the records tell us when they did or did not turn out to fight. Just as congratulatory comments from patriot leaders tell us when support for the war was high, careful investigation, especially in admittedly scant county court records, reveals widespread discontent, threats of violence, and violent actions precipitated by the efforts of those in authority to recruit and mobilize certain segments of the population. By weighing this evidence carefully, we can discern patterns of resistance that speak to the motives and bring us closer to the mind-sets of Virginia's nonliterate majority. Matching the

4. George Mason to the Virginia Delegates in Congress, Apr. 3, 1781, Mason to George Mason, Jr., June 3, 1781, *Papers of Mason,* II, 682–683, 693–694. Cf. Emory G. Evans, "Trouble in the Backcountry: Disaffection in Southwest Virginia during the American Revolution," in Ronald Hoffman, Thad W. Tate, and Peter J. Albert, eds., *An Uncivil War: The Southern Backcountry during the American Revolution* (Charlottesville, Va., 1985), 180. Much of the account above of the Northumberland riot came, not from contemporaries, for example, but from the pension records of Edwin Hull, collected and recollected years after the event. As we shall see, a more subtle reading of the conflicts that wracked Virginia reveals, however, that, if many of the men labeled as tories were not prepared to fight for the patriots, neither were they prepared to die for the British. In times of war, of course, as we have learned again only too recently, the first casualty is usually a fair and adequate airing and representation of dissenting opinions and views. For a look at the language of loyalty, see Michael A. McDonnell, "A World Turned 'Topsy Turvy': Robert Munford, *The Patriots,* and the Crisis of the Revolution in Virginia," *WMQ,* 3d Ser., LXI (2004), 235–270. For a look at the extent of so-called loyalism in Virginia, see, especially, Evans, "Trouble in the Backcountry," in Hoffman, Tate, and Albert, eds., *An Uncivil War,* 179–212; Adele Hast, *Loyalism in Revolutionary Virginia: The Norfolk Area and the Eastern Shore* (Ann Arbor, Mich., 1982). Few people identified themselves as loyalists in Revolutionary Virginia. For that reason I have generally tried to avoid using what was most often an elite label of derision or condemnation.

terms of service with the success or failure of different attempts to mobilize the militia, for example, helps determine the conditions under which men would, or would not, risk their lives. By examining the experience of mobilization, then, we can begin to piece together its meaning for the different participants. The greater importance of the story of wartime mobilization is the insight it affords us into the normally inaccessible worlds of lesser-known Virginians who left few written accounts of their feelings about the war.[5]

• • • But, if this is a story told through the lens of wartime mobilization, it is also a story of a society at war—at war almost as much with itself as with Britain. For the tremendous demands of the Revolutionary war exposed existing social fissures even as the war created new ones—and most often those divisions were between whites. A careful examination of mobilization in local records, for example, reveals the ways in which Virginia's colonial political and social structure affected the state's response to the Revolu-

5. This is, of course, an application and extension of the methodology used by Rhys Isaac in *The Transformation of Virginia, 1740-1790* (Chapel Hill, N.C., 1982), esp. 323-359, but see also his "Dramatizing the Ideology of the Revolution," *WMQ*, 3d Ser., XXXIII (1976), 357-364. (Isaac drew on Clifford Geertz's influential work, *The Interpretation of Cultures* [New York, 1973]). In this respect, my work has been influenced not just by the insights of Isaac but by the works of the "new military" historians, beginning with John Shy, whose provocative essays are collected in *A People Numerous and Armed: Reflections on the Military Struggle for American Independence*, rev. ed. (Ann Arbor, Mich., 1990). The work of Charles Royster, Fred Anderson, Steven Rosswurm, and James Titus has been influential. See Royster, *A Revolutionary People at War: The Continental Army and American Character, 1775-1783* (Chapel Hill, N.C., 1979); Anderson, *A People's Army: Massachusetts Soldiers and Society in the Seven Years' War* (Chapel Hill, N.C., 1984); Rosswurm, *Arms, Country and Class: The Philadelphia Militia and the "Lower Sort" during the American Revolution* (New Brunswick, N.J., 1987); Titus, *The Old Dominion at War: Society, Politics, and Warfare in Late Colonial Virginia, 1775-1783* (Columbia, S.C., 1991). Some of these and other works of this school and their importance are surveyed in E. Wayne Carp, "Early American Military History: A Review of Recent Work," *VMHB*, XCIV (1986), 259-284; Don Higginbotham, "The Early American Way of War: Reconnaissance and Appraisal," *WMQ*, 3d Ser., XLIV (1987), 230-273. Cf. Robert A. Gross, *The Minutemen and Their World* (New York, 1976); Gregory T. Knouff, "'An Arduous Service': The Pennsylvania Backcountry Soldiers' Revolution," *Pennsylvania History*, LXI (1994), 45-74.

tionary war. The way patriot leaders organized for war and reacted to the demands of those they expected to fight it depicts a conservative, anxious, sometimes fearful group clinging to traditional notions of hierarchy, deference, and public virtue in an attempt to maintain its privileged position within an increasingly challenged and challenging social and political culture. Edwin Hull, the recruiting officer who died in the Northumberland confrontation, was only trying to maintain his own, and his state's, faltering authority. Hull was a member of the local gentry and tied to a cosmopolitan group of wealthy young men enthusiastically committed to the Continental cause. Though there were some exceptions, the paramount concern of Hull's peers was to win the war against the British without major disruptions to Virginia's social and political order. That meant fighting the war within a hierarchical structure whose base would be obeisant and disciplined soldiers.

This conception was at loggerheads with the new realities precipitated by the Revolutionary conflict. As the Northumberland incident indicates, ordinary Virginians went to war against Britain for reasons that could differ from those of patriot leaders, and the reasons they continued to fight, or not to fight, did not necessarily jibe with what their leaders surmised. Small farmers and planters, for example, consistently demonstrated their commitment to their farms, families, and local neighborhoods and put the protection of them ahead of provincial or Continental concerns. Poorer Virginians, in turn, often wanted to be paid, and paid a fair rate, for their services. In return for their wartime contributions, ordinary Virginians in general wanted to fight on their own terms and demanded returns for their sacrifices.

But, as the war progressed, one of the most interesting dimensions of these divisions was the fact they were not always simple conflicts between the patriot ruling class and the ruled. Under the pressure of wartime demands, for example, landholding Virginians resisted patriot leaders' efforts to persuade or coerce them into the army, in part by *joining* gentlemen to put more pressure on unpropertied Virginians to serve. By the end of the war, at least some middle-class Virginians adopted the same ideas about soldiers that many gentlemen held, believing that only the lower classes were "fit for common service," as one put it. In turn, some lower-class Virginians willingly gave up their independence to serve in the Continental army but demanded a high price for their services. They forced legislators to offer high bounties, and they forced their better-off neighbors to offer increasingly larger payments for serving as their substitutes. Both gentlemen and middling Virginians resented the demands lower-class Virginians made on them, and tensions between the three grew through the war.

Thus it was that, in increasingly demanding and insistent petitions, middle-class Virginians could simultaneously accuse their lower-class neighbors of "fleecing" them, while lashing out at wealthier neighbors for not bearing their fair share of the war. Indeed, what was almost as surprising as the growing number of complaints that reached the Virginia assembly, especially after 1776, was the increasingly complex articulation of particular middle-class rights and claims contained therein. And, as the demands of war grew, middling militia especially began to legitimate their claims and justify their grievances against poorer and richer Virginians alike on the basis of their own wartime sacrifices.[6]

• • • In the end, these complaints and claims revealed what was perhaps most startling in exploring wartime protests, resistance, and conflicts over the all-important question of who should serve: the fact that they were so often expressed in a kind of language of class and seemed to reflect class divisions. And in trying to explain and understand these patterns of resistance and the divisions and conflicts they engendered in Revolutionary Virginia, one thing became very clear: class seemed to be at least as important as race in thinking about mobilization and social relations within the new state.[7]

6. Significantly, slaveholding militia could also use those sacrifices to justify their continuing hold over the very lowest class of Virginians. Indeed, postwar proslavery petitions show that white militia used the rhetoric of wartime sacrifices and military service, however limited it might have been, to justify their claims to keep a tenacious hold on their property. In doing so, middling slaveholding militia, for the first time, used Revolutionary principles and their Revolutionary participation to legitimate the continued enslavement of black Virginians. Fredrika Teute Schmidt and Barbara Ripel Wilhelm, "Early Proslavery Petitions in Virginia," *WMQ*, 3d Ser., XXX (1973), 133–146.

7. Having begun my research under the sway of Edmund S. Morgan's powerful argument that the need for racial unity smoothed over class divisions in Virginia and created a shared commitment to racial slavery that was the basis of a cohesive white culture in the eighteenth century, I was hard pressed at first even to recognize divisions between whites, let alone make sense of them. Ironically, however, Morgan's analysis of seventeenth-century Virginia gave historians one of the most powerful and explicit class-based analyses of colonial society ever written (*American Slavery, American Freedom: The Ordeal of Colonial Virginia* [New York,

Such grievances were not always expressed in a consistent and coherent language of class or class-consciousness, but class still seemed the most useful way of understanding the conflicts that clearly divided the state.[8] At the very least, for example, careful reading of protests during the Revolutionary war reveals that, repeatedly, divisions occurred along the lines of propertyholding and socioeconomic status, and grievances were expressed in terms of the conflicting interests of different groups and the unjust or unequal effects of specific policies. The war made tremendous economic demands on people; how one reacted to them often reflected one's economic position.[9]

1976]); cf. T. H. Breen, "A Changing Labor Force and Race Relations in Virginia, 1660–1710," in Breen, *Puritans and Adventurers: Change and Persistence in Early America* (New York, 1980), 127–147.

8. Elites and others did not always use a specific language of class. But, as Keith Wrightson, David Cannadine, and others have shown, this was a period of transition in the kinds of language used by contemporaries to describe their view of society. At least three kinds of language were in use that would gradually merge into a "discourse of class" by the middle to end of the eighteenth century. They include an idea of society as a finely graded hierarchy of ranks (which had itself evolved from a medieval notion of the three estates); or comprising "sorts of people"—usually the "better sort" versus the "meaner sort" or "poorer sort" and, at least since the mid-eighteenth century, the "middling sort." Such languages overlapped in their use and were "conceptually muddled but admirably flexible," and each was used to characterize social relations and inequalities even as a more specific language and idea of classes were emerging in the eighteenth century. See, especially, Keith Wrightson, "Class," in David Armitage and Michael J. Braddick, eds., *The British Atlantic World, 1500–1800* (New York, 2002), 133–138. Cf. David Cannadine, *The Rise and Fall of Class in Britain* (New York, 1999), esp. chap. 1.

Significantly, historians of early America have long been comfortable with acknowledging elite perceptions of class and have spent a great deal of time of late demonstrating the various ways in which elites consciously strove to distance and distinguish themselves from other classes. Despite this, we have much more trouble acknowledging lower- and middling-class-consciousness. Surely, elites' constant striving to distance themselves from the rest of colonial society did not go unnoticed?

9. For a full explication of my use of class as a tool of analysis, see Michael A. McDonnell, "Class War? Struggles during the Revolutionary War in Virginia," *WMQ*, 3d Ser., LXIII (2006), 305–344. Here it might suffice to say that I view class as a process, not a set of predetermined categories, and particular sorts of relations may or may not be based on people's relationships to the means of production, but they

Perhaps this should not be so surprising. Though we often think of Virginia as a slave society, divided by white masters and black slaves, late-eighteenth-century Virginia was, in effect, a society with slaves. The "bulk" of the people were not slaveowners. Moreover, those who did own slaves commonly engaged only one or two slaves at most.[10] Indeed, enslaved Vir-

---

are at the very least influenced by material circumstances and economic inequalities. Defined this way, class can be used as a way of examining and interrogating relations between social groups, particularly wherein economic inequalities were marked. In this respect, see, especially, E. P. Thompson, "Eighteenth-Century English Society: Class Struggle without Class?" *Social History,* III (1978), 147–150, and the special forum, "Class in Early America," *WMQ,* 3d Ser., LXIII, no. 3 (April 2006). Modern work that takes this broader view of class has already forced us to think anew. Woody Holton, among others, has persuasively argued that, indeed, the coming of the American Revolution was very much a product of class conflict (*Forced Founders: Indians, Debtors, Slaves, and the Making of the American Revolution in Virginia* [Chapel Hill, N.C., 1999]). But class as a tool of historical analysis might be even more useful in studying the war itself, given the economic demands it imposed on different social groups. Cf. the large corpus of work by Rhys Isaac, who pioneered the way in making us rethink many of our commonly held assumptions about Virginia society and the Revolution, especially *The Transformation of Virginia.* See also Alan Kulikoff, "The Death and Rebirth of Class Analysis in Early American History," MS (2001). As will become clear, my debt to the work of Kulikoff in particular for his theoretical work and longer-term pespective is great. Cf. Allan Kulikoff, "Was the American Revolution as Bourgeois Revolution?" in Ronald Hoffman and Peter J. Albert, eds., *The Transforming Hand of Revolution: Reconsidering the American Revolution as a Social Movement* (Charlottesville, Va., 1996), 58–89; Kulikoff, *The Agrarian Origins of American Capitalism* (Charlottesville, Va., 1992), esp. chaps. 1–2; Kulikoff, "Revolutionary Violence and the Origins of American Democracy," *Journal of the Historical Society,* II (2002), 229–260.

10. George Mason to George Mason, Jr., June 3, 1781, *Papers of Mason,* II, 693. In 1988 John E. Selby concluded that, at war's end, "the typical white Virginia male was a small farmer" who "had access to no more than a couple of hundred acres, at most a slave or two, and some cattle." Just fewer than 50 percent of white males were small landowners, 10–20 percent were tenants (concentrated in the Northern Neck), and 20–30 percent were agricultural laborers or indentured servants. Of the farmers, even in slave-rich areas like the tidewater and the heart of the piedmont, as many as 30 percent of families worked their land without enslaved help. In some places this figure was much higher. (See Selby, *The Revolution in Virginia, 1775–1783* [Williamsburg, Va., 1988], 24.) There was, of course, much regional variation. In Loudoun County, for example, situated in northwestern Virginia but still to

ginians themselves formed but only the bottom of a hierarchical edifice that included male and female convict and indentured servants, apprentices, free wage-laborers and overseers, tenant farmers and nonslaveholding smallholders, poorer slaveholders and substantial landholders, and, finally, local and cosmopolitan elites who often held hundreds of Africans in bondage and owned thousands of acres throughout the colony. Even within some of these apparently monolithic social blocs, many, sometimes overlapping layers of differences helped complicate social relations both within and between different classes of Virginians. Ultimately, as any self-respecting gentleman, tenant farmer, or enslaved Virginian would know, this was a deeply divided and carefully defined hierarchical society in which social and economic inequalities were on conspicuous display.[11]

---

the east of the Blue Ridge Mountains, far fewer people owned slaves in 1784, and many of the rest owned only one or two. As late as 1790, the proportion of blacks in the county was only 21.2 percent (Stanley B. Parsons, William W. Beach, and Dan Hermann, *United States Congressional Districts, 1788–1841* [Westport, Conn., 1978], 28–31; Loudon County Tax Records, 1784, LiVi). Richard S. Dunn concluded that "a majority of the whites stood outside of the slave system at the time of the Revolution" ("Black Society in the Chesapeake, 1776–1810," in Ira Berlin and Ronald Hoffman, eds., *Slavery and Freedom in the Age of the American Revolution* [Charlottesville, Va., 1983], 67).

11. Precise statistics are not easy to come by and often vary, but the bulk of the literature thus far on the subject suggests a carefully delineated and hierarchic social structure: Isaac, *Transformation of Virginia;* Philip D. Morgan, *Slave Counterpoint: Black Culture in the Eighteenth-Century Cheaspeake and Lowcountry* (Chapel Hill, N.C., 1998). Even among African American communities, divisions were sometimes pronounced; see Ira Berlin, *Many Thousands Gone: The First Two Centuries of Slavery in North America* (Cambridge, Mass., 1988). Cf. Steven Sarson, "Landlessness and Tenantry in Early National Prince George's County, Maryland," *WMQ,* 3d Ser., LVII (2000), 585–594; Sarson, "Similarities and Continuities: Free Society in the Tobacco South before and after the American Revolution," in Eliga H. Gould and Peter S. Onuf, *Empire and Nation: The American Revolution in the Atlantic World* (Baltimore, 2005). The literature on indentured and convict servitude is well known (though often not incorporated into the larger picture), but there is a dearth of work on the extent of tenantry in eighteenth-century Virginia. Close study is revealing: Loudoun County probably had one of the highest proportions of tenant farmers in Virginia also. Overall, perhaps as many as 466, or 38 percent, of the 1,225 landholders in the county were tenants. Many tenant farmers, too, were not slaveholders, or owned only one or two slaves. Astonishingly, between 42 and 75 percent of white males in Loudoun might have been

Ultimately, the demands of the Revolutionary war threw these inequalities into bold relief, forcing us to recognize other kinds of divisions in Virginia. But the particular demands of war—for military service especially—made clear that control over labor was the basis of many of these emerging grievances and divisions. Smallholding farmers, for example—"self-working farmers" with few or no slaves to work for them—protested that their own labor was essential to their household independence. What they were most fearful of, they claimed, was that, should they be compelled to serve in the military for long terms of service, they might lose their independence by finding upon their return that their wives and children were forced to go about, as they put it, "abeging and aslaving." Elite Virginians, in turn, tried to target the lower sort for longer-term military service, in part because their labor was not seen as essential to the maintenance of a household. But, when the demands of the war—and the resistance of the lower sort to the appropriation of their own labor—forced the ruling class to expand its search for soldiers to more independent Virginians, smallholding farmers protested vigorously and sometimes violently, helping to cripple mobilization. Control over labor, then, emerged as the defining element in social relations during the war and was at the heart of class divisions in Virginia.[12]

---

landless. Selby claims that nearly three-quarters in the Loudoun area were landless, compared to half overall in Virginia. Loudoun County Personal Property and Land Tax Records, 1784, LiVi; Selby, *Revolution in Virginia*, 24. Cf. Willard F. Bliss, "The Rise of Tenantry in Virginia," *VMHB*, LVIII (1950), 429–430. For cosmopolitan versus local elites, see Darrett B. Rutman and Anita H. Rutman, *A Place in Time: Middlesex County, Virginia, 1650–1750* (New York, 1984), 128–163. For divisions among yeomen and slaveholders, see, especially, Stephanie McCurry, *Masters of Small Worlds: Yeoman Households, Gender Relations, and the Political Culture of the Antebellum South Carolina Low Country* (New York, 1995), 47–55.

12. Peter Linebaugh and Marcus Rediker, *The Many-Headed Hydra: Sailors, Slaves, Commoners, and the Hidden History of the Revolutinary Atlantic* (Boston, 2000); Kathleen M. Brown, *Good Wives, Nasty Wenches, and Anxious Patriarchs: Gender, Race, and Power in Colonial Virginia* (Chapel Hill, N.C., 1996), 321; McCurry, *Masters of Small Worlds,* 50. In this respect, scholarship on independents and dependents helps us appreciate that some of these struggles at least arose around deeply entrenched gendered notions of the household, and household independence in particular. As Kathleen Brown has reminded us, for wealthy planters in Virginia "independence" and authority emanated out from the home, or plantation. Elite planters at least dreamed of "hegemonic authority over compliant wives,

• • • Such claims and recognition of the nature of these important divisions between white Virginians compel us to also reconsider the influence exerted by the enslaved who constituted a powerful proportion of the fledgling state's population. That the strength of black Virginians' desire for their own freedom was critical in the Revolutionary equation became strikingly apparent from early on. Governor Dunmore's plan to free all slaves belonging to rebel masters and willing to fight for the king was prompted by the numbers of black Virginians keen to join his ranks. And from the first confrontation with Dunmore in April 1775 until Cornwallis's surrender of Yorktown in 1781, enslaved Virginians continued to remind free Virginians that dreams of liberty could not be confined.

Black bids for freedom thus played a fundamental role in shaping mobilization in Revolutionary Virginia. Rebellious enslaved Virginians, for example, did encourage the British to focus their efforts on Virginia at various moments throughout the war. And planters who owned large numbers of slaves often refused to serve when called upon for fear of leaving their plantations and families vulnerable to restive blacks who were often willing to threaten more than just to run to British lines. Slaveholding elites in the legislature were also happy to bend the rules to appease their slaveholding constituents' anxieties and ensure stability on the home front.

But, if slavery played a central role in the Revolutionary war, it was not always in the ways we might expect. At times, many nonslaveholding farmers seemed less concerned about threats from blacks and more concerned about their white neighbors' willingness to evade military service. They often complained that slaveholders were not bearing their fair share of the burden of war. Moreover, nonslaveholders were also quick to point out that military service was actually much more onerous for those without slaves, for they had no one to labor for them in their absence. Slaveholding was so divisive that Virginia legislators finally debated one revolutionary

---

children, and slaves and of unquestioned political leadership over less privileged men." Though political leadership might not have been so important, the dependence of household members was crucial to the independence of "masters of small worlds" too. These kinds of conflicts also demonstrate that slavery, race, and gender are important components of any explanation of wartime disunity in Virginia. But they also point to the fact that such explanations are insufficient without thinking about the ways in which class and perceptions of class intersected with race and gender and powerfully shaped what were or became class struggles during the Revolutionary conflict.

proposal: to lift the burden of service from the shoulders of middling Virginians, they considered taking slaves from the very wealthiest (who were seen to be shirking military service) to give to the very poor to entice them to enlist.

Enslaved Virginians, then, helped to cripple mobilization, yet slaveholding, particularly toward the end of the war, increasingly became the touchstone for class divisions among white Virginians. Indeed, even in the face of overt threats from within and without, whites did not unite and rally to the cause; living in a region of Virginia where enslaved blacks composed the majority of the population did not deter Joseph Pitman and his neighbors from risking civil war. There was no force, not even the constellation of fears and issues of race that often animated this slaveholding society, that was strong enough to overcome class interests and forge unity among Virginia's white population.

* * * If class as a tool of analysis enriches our understanding of the Revolutionary war in Virginia—and, in particular, the desperate struggles that wracked the state and undermined its ability to mobilize effectively—those struggles, in turn, enrich our understanding of the immediate consequences of such a massive failing. For, in the end, conflict within Virginia—between blacks and whites and within white society—profoundly shaped not only the course of the war but also its political settlement. Indeed, if the first half of this study takes as its theme the deep internal fissures exposed in Virginia by the unraveling of imperial authority, the second focuses on the transformation the Revolutionary experience wrought on those divisions and the critical influence the new social and political realities thereby exerted upon the reconstitution of authority.

In some sense, of course, this is a well-told tale. But emphasizing the conflicts that divided Virginians during the war complicates the well-known story of the Revolutionary transition from colony to Republic. For ordinary Virginians challenged the authority of patriot leaders at least as much as they did that of British officials. And it was often at the local militia musters that the real business of war was conducted. Only by looking carefully at these most meaningful transactions—the small politics of war—at this local level can we begin to grasp the larger political transformations taking place. How individuals and groups responded to the numerous demands on their time and their lives gives us great insight into how ordinary Virginians thought about their relationship to others. Thus it was that lower-class, middling, elite, and enslaved Virginians struggled against one another, developed strategies for protecting and defending their interests, and made claims and demands on one another amid the turmoil of the war. Read in this light, Joseph Pitman's refusal to defer to Edwin Hull was a refusal to continue to make sacrifices on terms dictated by his social superior. Hull's violent death symbolized the passing of an older political culture.

In a world of uncertain loyalties, wartime demands, and highly contingent circumstances, these conflicts were the crucible within which Americans forged a new political order. Challenges to the authority of gentlemen over military service signaled the rise of very different ideas about political and social relations that helped shape life in postwar Virginia. These ideas most immediately manifested themselves at the local level. As middling and lower-class Virginians resisted, evaded, and protested state laws compelling them to serve, officials responsible for carrying out these laws—militia officers and county court magistrates—were faced with hard choices. They could, like Edwin Hull, try to enforce the laws. Most, however, were unwilling to risk the wrath of their armed neighbors and instead adapted and ignored the laws when and where necessity dictated. Many officials resigned under such wartime pressure, leaving room for more popular replacements. Consequently, through a variety of means, by war's end the crucial prewar links between local and provincial elites had been broken, and many counties throughout Virginia enjoyed considerable autonomy from the intrusive legislation and demands of the state and Continental governments.

But the resolution of problems that took place at this local level foreshadowed and shaped the contours of the political settlement evolving at the state and national level. For the small politics of war—the very divisions that plagued wartime Virginia—were also at the heart of larger postwar political developments. Precisely because so many people refused to fight the war on terms proposed by elites, defended their interests, asserted new ways of thinking about how to organize society, and closed ranks at the local level, elites themselves in turn began thinking about new ways of organizing society and politics to protect a notion of society that some at least believed was increasingly under threat. This became particularly evident in many elites' responses to the massive tax resistance of the 1780s, in which thousands of farmers justified their refusal to pay taxes on the basis of their wartime military services and material sacrifices. The anxiety of elites found expression in a heightening of postwar political tensions among legislators, but it would also push some to radically rethink the nature and structure of government. The political settlement of 1787, then, resulted not so much from Washington's seamless leadership during the war, nor from the enlightened ruminations of some undoubtedly astute political thinkers and reformers. Rather, it reflected the messy, divisive, and challenging conflicts that had been endemic thoughout the war.

From the turbulence of a war that forced patriot leaders to rely upon an army of ordinary men arose a new world in which men of all ranks, free and unfree, believed it was their right both to express forcefully their ideas about governance and social relations—and act to assure that those ideas would be taken seriously. Yet the debates, dialogues, conflicts, and struggles that ensued were, in an important sense—and as they are today—equally if not more important in shaping politics in the new Republic than was their resolution. Ultimately, then, this is a story of how ordinary Virginians, free and unfree, directly and indirectly transformed a War for Independence into a Revolutionary war, fundamentally changing the course of their history and the new nation they created, for better and for worse.

PART ONE

The Ebullition of Patriotism

CHAPTER I *Mustering Patriotism*

THE PROBLEM OF POPULAR MOBILIZATION,

1774–1775

A few days before General Thomas Gage marched his redcoats into the Massachusetts countryside in 1775 and provoked the famous conflict at Lexington and Concord, George Gilmer of Albemarle County, Virginia—home of Thomas Jefferson—exhorted his neighbors to ready themselves for conflict. Parliament and the colonial assemblies had reached a tense impasse. The time had come to decide their fate. Invoking familiar imagery, Gilmer told his audience that either they could become "the voluntary and abject slaves of a wicked administration," or they could "live free as the air we breath." Gilmer said he had chosen freedom and was willing to fight and die for it. To prove it, he had armed himself—he had a "Tomahawk girt about me." Gilmer also tied the protection of his "Country" (Virginia) to that of the other colonies embroiled in the dispute with Parliament, exhorting, "never to bury the Tomahawk untill liberty shall be fixed on an immoveable basis thro the whole Continent." Gilmer's speech, and many others like it across the colonies, could be taken as evidence of an increasingly heated but united resistance to the latest British imperial measures.[1]

In the wake of the Boston Tea Party late in 1773 and the response of the British government, relations between Parliament and the colonies had deteriorated rapidly through 1774. More militant patriot leaders throughout the eastern seaboard circulated plans for a continental congress and an "Association" that included a boycott of trade between Britain and the mainland colonies. As the summer progressed, however, fears grew that more

1. Address of George Gilmer to the Albemarle County First Independent Company of Gentlemen Volunteers, [Apr. 18, 1775], *Rev. Va.*, III, 50, 52. Gilmer was a neighbor and physician to Thomas Jefferson and was active in provincial politics. For a short biography of Gilmer, see III, 50n.

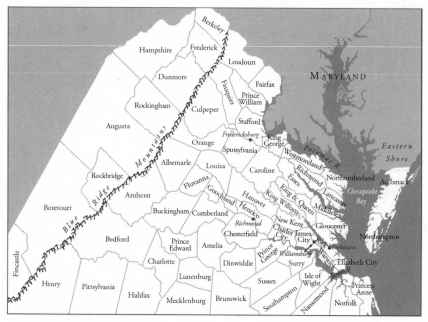

Map 1. Virginia, 1770s–1780s

than just economic resistance might be necessary to counter the British; indeed, the Boston Port Act was seen by some as an "invasion"—an "arbitrary and humiliating" attempt to make Massachusetts submit to the authority of Britain. One traveler in Virginia noted that his genteel hosts were "much exasperated" by the measures of Parliament and increasingly "talk as if they were determined to dispute the matter with the sword." Four months later, in early October 1774, "Nothing but War is talked of."[2]

But if, as Peyton Randolph (one of the most prominent patriot leaders) worried, matters seemed "to be hurrying to an alarming Crisis," Gilmer's address to his neighbors also revealed several problems. In the first place, Gilmer confessed that there was little in the way of a model martial tradition from which to draw. Gilmer was "too sensible" of his own "awkwardness" with the native American tomahawk he carried, and he was also unfamiliar with even the militia exercises that he and his neighbors by law were supposed to have been practicing regularly. Yet, in promising to make himself a master of the "necessary parade of war," Gilmer also revealed his anxiety about his own leadership abilities. Finally, his uncertainty and fears were only exacerbated by his worry that his neighbors were divided, and not at all as committed to the patriot cause as they ought to be. Gilmer urged them to put aside all "divisions" and ideas of "rancour and revenge" and stand united. On the eve of war, then, George Gilmer hinted that Virginians were unready for war and divided behind an altogether uncertain leadership.[3]

• • • Enslaved Virginians were perhaps the only group in the colony who listened to reports of the growing imperial crisis with as much interest as patriot leaders. Certainly, as rumors of war began to circulate and other colonies began to arm themselves in the summer of 1774, enslaved Virginians gave their patriot masters cause for concern. Fresh in the collective memory was the experience of the Seven Years' War. Very early in the

2. [Thomson Mason], "The British American, VII," *Va. Gaz.* (Rind), July 14, 1774, *Rev. Va.,* I, 184; May 30, Oct. 11, 1774, Nicholas Cresswell, *The Journal of Nicholas Cresswell, 1774-1777* (London, 1925), 19, 42. Cf. Prince George County Resolves, *Va. Gaz.* (P and D), June 30, 1774, *Rev. Va.,* I, 151; June 3, 1774, Jack P. Greene, ed., *The Diary of Colonel Landon Carter of Sabine Hall, 1752-1778* (Charlottesville, Va., 1965), II, 817-818.

3. Peyton Randolph to Members of the House of Burgesses, May 31, 1774, *Papers of Jefferson,* I, 111-112; Gilmer to the Albemarle County First Independent Company of Gentlemen Volunteers, [Apr. 18, 1775], *Rev. Va.,* III, 50-52.

war, enslaved Virginians were "very audacious on the Defeat on the Ohio." Blacks knew that war among whites presented opportunities for freedom. Governor Robert Dinwiddie found out about at least one slave conspiracy in Lancaster County in July 1755. Dinwiddie expected it. "The Villany of the Negroes on any Emergency of Gov't is w't I always fear'd." Dinwiddie thought "these poor Creatures imagine the Fr[ench] Will give them their Freedom." The threat of slave uprisings helped shape Virginia's wartime mobilization. The governor worried about the large number of enslaved Virginians in their midst but hoped still to "be able to defeat the Designs of our Enemies and keep these Slaves in proper Subject'n." In May 1756, Dinwiddie told the War Office that they could not possibly raise enough white soldiers to fight on the frontiers: "We dare not venture to part with any of our White Men any distance, as we must have a watchful eye over our Negro slaves, who are upwards of 100,000." The following August, Dinwiddie claimed that the colony's sizable enslaved population "alarms our People much and [they] are aff'd of bad consequences if the Militia are order'd to any great Distance from the pres't Settlem'ts." Though the Seven Years' War in America was carried out primarily on the far frontiers of Virginia, whites everywhere remained uneasy about the threat of "combinations of the Negro Slaves." Black dreams of freedom panicked white leaders, never more so than in the midst of war.[4]

The imperial dispute of the 1770s gave black Virginians further hope. Black rebelliousness continued apace with a rapid increase of African Americans in Virginia after the Seven Years' War and with each fresh report of a growing rift between Britain and its colonies. As the number of black Virginians approached that of whites, many enslaved Virginians had begun to expect an emancipation proclamation in the wake of conflict between Britain and its colonies. With expectations high among black Americans throughout the southern colonies, slave rebelliousness was on the increase just as the conflict between white colonists and royal authority came to a head. Amid rumors of British plans to employ enslaved Americans more generally against the white colonists, one South Carolinian recalled that fears ran high among planters, as it was well known that blacks "enter-

4. Peter H. Wood, "'Liberty Is Sweet': African-American Freedom Struggles in the Years before White Independence," in Alfred F. Young, ed., *Beyond the American Revolution: Explorations in the History of American Radicalism* (DeKalb, Ill., 1993), 154; James Titus, *The Old Dominion at War: Society, Politics, and Warfare in Late Colonial Virginia* (Columbia, S.C., 1991), 75–76.

tained ideas that the present contest was for obliging us to give them their liberty."[5]

Enslaved Virginians drew encouragement from Americans and Englishmen alike. Anxious patriots like Arthur Lee reported that one pamphlet circulating in Britain suggested that the way to put down rebellion in America was to "Proclame *Freedom* to their Negroes." The pamphlet, Lee told a Virginia correspondent, contained a "proposal for emancipating your Negroes . . . and arming them against you" and allegedly "meets with approbation from ministerial People." By late November 1774, according to James Madison, it was common knowledge that the British would take advantage of this situation: "If america and Britain should come to a hostile rupture I am afraid an Insurrection among the slaves may and will be promoted." Such rumors continued to stir the fires of rebellion in slave quarters and fear and anxiety in the great houses. As patriots denounced British coercive measures, enslaved Virginians plotted their own resistance to tyranny.[6]

In the face of black rebelliousness, Gilmer's admonishments to maintain a united front took on added meaning. Yet even in the face of these twin threats—from Britain as well as within—white Virginians themselves were still divided in their responses to British measures and to patriot leaders' calls for support. For, if black Virginians remembered the Seven Years' War as a moment of opportunity, many white Virginians recalled it as a catalyst for insecurity. Conflict had its costs. Middling Virginians in particular had suffered because of the Seven Years' War. Taxes to pay for it rose consider-

5. Wood, "'Liberty Is Sweet,'" in Young, ed., *Beyond the American Revolution,* 160; Peter H. Wood, "The Changing Population of the Colonial South: An Overview by Race and Region, 1685-1790," in Wood, Gregory A. Waselkov, and M. Thomas Hatley, eds., *Powhatan's Mantle: Indians in the Colonial Southeast* (Lincoln, Nebr., 1989), 38; John Drayton, *Memoirs of the American Revolution, from Its Commencement to the Year 1776, Inclusive; As Relating to the State of South-Carolina* (Charleston, S.C., 1821), I, 231.

6. Woody Holton, *Forced Founders: Indians, Debtors, Slaves, and the Making of the American Revolution in Virginia* (Chapel Hill, N.C., 1999), 140-141; James Madison to William Bradford, Nov. 26, 1774, *Papers of Madison,* I, 129-130. Cf. William Lee to Robert Carter Nicholas, Mar. 6, 1775, Worthington Chauncey Ford, ed., *Letters of William Lee, 1766-1783* (Brooklyn, N.Y., 1891), I, 144; Gerald W. Mullin, *Flight and Rebellion: Slave Resistance in Eighteenth-Century Virginia* (New York, 1972); Sylvia R. Frey, *Water from the Rock: Black Resistance in a Revolutionary Age* (Princeton, N.J., 1991).

ably at the start of the conflict and continued long after its end. Whereas Virginia's leaders normally raised revenue only through taxes on tobacco exports, the mounting costs of that war forced the Burgesses to rely more heavily on unfair and regressive poll taxes and land taxes. Both kinds of taxes protected the interests of the propertied in the assembly. Poll taxes were assessed on everyone, regardless of wealth, and land taxes were calculated by the number of acres owned rather than the value of the land. The Burgesses used the poll tax in particular to pay most of the cost of the war, expecting it to raise more than 55 percent of the total taxes in 1763–1765, 66 percent from 1766 through 1768, and 68 percent by 1769. This was on top of supplementary poll taxes levied in 1766, 1769, and 1772 and a tax of forty-six pounds of tobacco per poll levied to pay for Pontiac's War. Local and religious taxes for support of the Anglican Church and county government also added to the poll tax burden.[7]

High taxes only exacerbated economic problems in the colony and increased conflict among whites. The tobacco-based economy had been wobbly since the end of the Seven Years' War in 1763; a postwar recession had lasted until about 1766. A new tobacco crisis beginning in the fall of 1772 precipitated a deep recession in Virginia that lasted until the start of the new conflict in 1775. As tobacco prices fell by half in many places, the recession hit smaller farmers hardest. Squeezed by anxious merchants for the debts they had contracted in the more prosperous years between 1766 and 1772, specie-starved farmers had to sell property to pay judgments against them. By the spring of 1774, one-third of the families in Pittsylvania County had been brought into court for debts, and one merchant commented, "Our folks are so much indebted to the Merchants, that they hardly care which end goes foremost."[8]

On top of the financial problems that rocked the colony in the 1760s and 1770s, natural calamities also hit Virginia farmers hard in the early 1770s.

7. Robert A. Becker, *Revolution, Reform, and the Politics of American Taxation, 1763–1783* (Baton Rouge, La., 1980), 78–79.

8. Charles Yates to Samuel Martin, Apr. 2, 1774, Charles Yates Letterbook, UVa. On the economy and debt, see Holton, *Forced Founders,* 95–105; Allan Kulikoff, *Tobacco and Slaves: The Development of Southern Cultures in the Chesapeake, 1680–1800* (Chapel Hill, N.C., 1986), 118–161; T. H. Breen, *Tobacco Culture: The Mentality of the Great Tidewater Planters on the Eve of Revolution* (Princeton, N.J., 1985), chaps. 4, 5; Bruce A. Ragsdale, *A Planter's Republic: The Search for Economic Independence in Reolutionary Virginia* (Madison, Wis., 1996).

As the imperial conflict grew to a head in 1774, thousands of farmers were still reeling from a major "freshet" that swept down the major rivers of Virginia in the spring of 1771 but hit the less wealthy James River valley particularly hard, causing thousands of pounds worth of damage and killing as many as 150 people. More recently, a freak snowstorm and late frost in May 1774 added to the more immediate hardships of the common farmer in that year. The "Great Frost," as it came to be called, "killed all the fruite, all the wheat, Rye, Barley, Oats, etc., and the corn also"—the staples of smaller subsistence farmers. The "Destruction of the wheat by the late Frost," noted one wealthier planter who thought he had lost twenty-five hundred bushels himself, "must be severely felt." "It was really a solemnly looking scean," concluded one eyewitness years later.[9]

Perhaps more troubling for many middling to small farmers, the economic troubles of the 1760s and 1770s played out against a backdrop of a long-term decline of opportunity. From 1750 to 1775, Virginia's population grew from 130,000 to more than 400,000 as thousands of newcomers from all over the American continent, Europe, and Africa passed into Virginia's borders. Free families, indentured and convict servants, and newly enslaved Africans arrived en masse in a relatively short span. But natives and newcomers alike were finding it increasingly difficult to obtain—and hold on to—land. In the Chesapeake at large, landholding was on the decline. In Prince George's County in Maryland, the proportion of householders owning land decreased from 65 percent in 1705, to 56 percent in 1755, and down to only 45 percent in 1776, while the absolute number of households rose substantially from 459 in 1705, to 1,337 in 1755, and to 1,669 in 1776. Such patterns prevailed also throughout the older areas of Virginia. In ten counties where change can be documented over the late colonial period, the proportion of landowners decreased in seven, rising in only three. In Richmond County in the lower Northern Neck, the proportion of landowners slid from 65 to 41 percent, and in Accomack County on the Eastern Shore the proportion shrank from 48 to 33 percent. Even in the expanding southside (south of the James River), the proportion of landowners was also decreasing in some areas, as in Amelia County (from

9. Hening, comp., *Statutes at Large,* VIII, 493–503; *Va. Gaz.* (P and D), June 6, 1771; Robert Beverley to Landon Carter, June 9, 1774, Carter Family Papers, VHS; Chester Raymond Young, ed., *Westward into Kentucky: The Narrative of Daniel Trabue* (Lexington, Ky., 1981), 41–42. Cf. Louis H. Manarin and Clifford Dowdey, *The History of Henrico County* (Charlottesville, Va., 1984), 120.

76 to 55 percent), Halifax County (85 to 74 percent), and Lunenburg (78 to 61 percent).[10]

Moreover, where it can be measured, evidence suggests that tenants were increasingly subject to much shorter term tenancy agreements, making their landholding less certain. In Fairfax County, for example, the proportion of landowners remained stable between 1748 and 1770, but tenants on long-term leases fell from 42 to 12 percent of adult white males, as more went on short-term leases. Nor did western lands any longer hold out possibilities for smallholders and landless Virginians. The Proclamation Line of 1763 had halted any opportunities white Virginians might have had for gaining new lands. (And almost all of the good lands east of the Proclamation Line had already been granted by 1763.) Thus an ever-greater number of farmers found themselves without land or with a more uncertain claim to land as resistance to Britain intensified. Though some smallholders might have blamed the British for denying them access to western territories, many Virginians blamed wealthy land speculators for monopolizing what lands there were.[11]

As landowners and longer-term tenants diminished, so too did farmers allowed to vote, adding to the grievances of ordinary white Virginians. In Accomack County, for example, while the population rose from 979 adult white males in 1738 to 1,396 in 1768, landowning fell from 48 to 33 percent, and long-term tenancy fell from 20 to 18 percent, which reduced the electorate from 68 to 51 percent. The increase in short-term leases in Fairfax County had the effect of reducing the eligible electorate there from 66 to 35 percent of adult white males. In Loudoun County the electorate fell from 45 percent to 39 percent from 1761 to 1769 as the population grew from 779 to 1,213, so that the number of ineligible voters grew from 428 to 740. Overall, while perhaps two-thirds of adult white males could still vote in Virginia, "the level of enfranchisement declined nearly everywhere in the closing decades of the colonial era due primarily to a steadily increasing population coupled with stable or declining opportunities for owner-

10. Kulikoff, *Tobacco and Slaves,* 134–135; Dale Edward Benson, "Wealth and Power in Virginia, 1774–1776: A Study of the Organization of Revolt" (Ph.D. diss., University of Maine, 1970), 35, and chap. 1; John Gilman Kolp, *Gentlemen and Freeholders: Electoral Politics in Colonial Virginia* (Baltimore, 1998), 44–46; Holton, *Forced Founders,* chap. 1.

11. Kulikoff, *Tobacco and Slaves,* 134–135; Kolp, *Gentlemen and Freeholders,* 44–46; Holton, *Forced Founders,* chap. 1.

ship and long-term tenancy." Ordinary Virginians, then, were increasingly losing land, slipping into precarious short-term tenancy agreements, or becoming landless laborers on the eve of the Revolution. They were also losing the political voice to defend themselves.[12]

Losing land and political rights was even more alarming as the prospect of war loomed. In previous colonial conflicts, provincial elites raised soldiers by coercing and exploiting the poor, the needy, and the vulnerable. During the War of Jenkins's Ear (1739-1741), the Burgesses conscripted, or drafted, only "able-bodied persons, fit to serve his majesty, who follow no lawful calling or employment." Then, in the Seven Years' War, Governor Dinwiddie and the Burgesses fell upon the same expedient. Two years later they made their intentions clear when they exempted from the draft anyone who could vote.[13]

Certainly, by such means, Virginia's elite had also alienated Virginia's expanding population of the lower and laboring classes. Poorer Virginians listened with indifference, or even suspicion, to the new rumors of conflict that circulated in 1774-1775, scarred by their experience during the Seven Years' War. Some veterans of the previous war had been able to capitalize on opportunities presented by the earlier conflict—soldiers prospected for land while on expeditions, for example, and used their military warrants to claim land and settle in new western communities. But, for most

12. Kolp, *Gentlemen and Freeholders,* 44-49.

13. Titus, *Old Dominion at War,* 4, 59, 80, 98-99. Cf. Edmund S. Morgan, *American Slavery, American Freedom: The Ordeal of Colonial Virginia* (New York, 1975), 340. This was standard colonial practice. See Don Higginbotham, "The Military Institutions of Colonial America: The Rhetoric and the Reality," in Higginbotham, ed., *War and Society in Revolutionary America: The Wider Dimensions of Conflict* (Columbia, S.C., 1988), 19; E. Wayne Carp, "Early American Military History: A Review of Research," *VMHB,* XCVI (1986), 272. Cf. Alan R. Millet and Peter Maslowski, *For the Common Defense: A Military History of the United States of America* (New York, 1984), 7-8, 51-54, 79-80; John K. Mahon, *History of the Militia and the National Guard* (London, 1983), 20-22; Reginald C. Stuart, *War and American Thought: From the Revolution to the Monroe Doctrine* (Kent, Ohio, 1982), xiii-xv; John Shy, "The American Military Experience: History and Learning," in Shy, *A People Numerous and Armed: Reflections on the Military Struggle for American Independence,* rev. ed. (Ann Arbor, Mich., 1990), 277-280; Robert Middlekauf, *The Glorious Cause: The American Revolution, 1763-1789* (New York, 1982), 297-298; Eliga H. Gould, *The Persistence of Empire: British Political Culture in the Age of the American Revolution* (Chapel Hill, N.C., 2000), esp. 72-105.

Virginians who suffered through service then, the experience was bitter. The first land bounty offered in 1754 by Governor Dinwiddie amounted to only 200,000 acres in total, most of which was bought up by the officers of the men to whom the land was awarded, in exchange for needed cash (and much of this land ended up in George Washington's hands). The only other land bounty was given in the Proclamation of 1763, but only to officers, which was then qualified to mean British officers. Resentment grew apace during the imperial crisis as British authorities closed down the settlement of western lands, forcing the Burgesses to renege on their promises of securely titled land bounties. The smoldering legacy of the Seven Years' War was vividly expressed in one early report from the Northern Neck in 1774, where many poorer men had been drafted for service during that war. One diarist warned, "The lower Class of People here are in a tumult on the account of Reports from Boston, many of them expect to be press'd and compell'd to go and fight the Britains!" Increasing lower-class radicalism throughout the Atlantic world in the second half of the eighteenth century had helped sensitize Virginia's most vulnerable white community against another exploitative conflict.[14]

The lower classes not only suffered most during the Seven Years' War, but they were also hit hard by postwar taxes. Because most money was raised through poll taxes, the heavy demands for money hit the poorer sort—who had to pay as much as their wealthy neighbors—hardest. The Reverend James Maury from Louisa County complained as early as June 1756 that "taxes on taxes are multiplied" and were very burdensome to the "lower ranks of people," especially for those for whom "tobacco is the only medium of raising money." When the crops were bad, the poor "generally

14. Hening, comp., *Statutes at Large,* 661–662; Titus, *Old Dominion at War,* 47–48, 132–133; Holton, *Forced Founders,* 10–13, and chap. 1; Bernhard Knollenberg, *George Washington: The Virginia Period, 1732–1775* (Durham, N.C., 1964), 91–100; Titus, *Old Dominion at War,* 59, 80, 98–99; May 31, 1774, Hunter Dickinson Farish, ed., *Journal and Letters of Philip Vickers Fithian, 1773–1774: A Plantation Tutor of the Old Dominion* (1943; Williamsburg, Va., 1957), 111. For Atlantic lower-class radicalism, see, especially, Peter Linebaugh and Marcus Rediker, *The Many-Headed Hydra: Sailors, Slaves, Commoners, and the Hidden History of the Revolutionary Atlantic* (Boston, 2000), 211–247; Rediker, *Between the Devil and the Deep Blue Sea: Merchant Seamen, Pirates, and the Anglo-American Maritime World, 1700–1750* (New York, 1987), chap. 5; Jesse Lemisch, "Jack Tar in the Streets: Merchant Seamen in the Politics of Revolutionary America," *WMQ,* 3d Ser., XXV (1968), 371–407.

cultivate the meanest lands, so were their crops proportionally short." After the war, the burden of heavy taxes was exacerbated by the increasing scarcity of paper money as the Burgesses gradually withdrew the emissions of paper money from circulation. "Things wear but a gloomy aspect," wrote Peter Fontaine of Hanover County in July 1765. "The country is so excessively poor that even the industrious, frugal man can scarcely live, and the least slip in economy would be fatal. There is no money."[15]

As poorer Virginians and small farmers in the first postwar recession were pressed by the economic crisis and left politically emasculated by the loss of their land, some turned to violence to redress their grievances or resist creditors. One merchant wrote home asking for "a pair of Pistols" to carry in "a side Pockett," believing it to be "Dangerous in Traveling through our wooden Country Particularly at this time when the planters are pressed for old Ballances." Farmers were so overcome with debt suits —and the prospect of a jail term—because of the credit contraction that they turned on symbols of county authority. One man reported, "Scarcely a prison is allowed to stand, in some Countys the People have agreed to defend one another against the officers" of the court. The county courts especially were the focal point for an increasing number of attacks. In Richmond County, for example, radical vigilantes showed their contempt for the court in March 1771 in offering "an Insult of the most Extravagant Nature" by "daub'g" the court bench "with Tar and Dung in many places." When the new recession began in 1772, old wounds were reopened, and new conflicts between smallholders and gentry, debtors and creditors, and tenants and landlords emerged.[16]

Not all middling and poorer whites turned to violence; some turned inward. Many Virginians, for example, looked to the new evangelical message spread by Baptist and Methodist ministers in Virginia through the 1760s and 1770s. Both of these sects experienced a rapid rise in converts on the eve of the War for Independence. Devereux Jarratt later told Thomas

15. Becker, *Politics of American Taxation,* 83, 84.

16. William Allason to Bogle and Scott, July 29, 1764, and Allason to Alexander Walker, June 24, 1764, in Breen, *Tobacco Culture,* 165, 168–169; Gwenda Morgan, "Law and Social Change in Colonial Virginia: The Role of the Grand Jury in Richmond County, 1692–1776," *VMHB,* XCV (1987), 475, 478; Richmond Orders, Mar. 4, 1771, in A. G. Roeber, *Faithful Magistrates and Republican Lawyers: Creators of Virginia Legal Culture, 1680–1810* (Chapel Hill, N.C., 1981), 112; Holton, *Forced Founders,* 163.

Rankin that, during the 1760s and 1770s, it was the "common people" who "frequented the church more constantly, and in larger numbers than usual." In some sense, the remarkable growth of these congregations might be seen as a response to and escape from the "harsh realities of disease, debt, overindulgence and deprivation, violence and fear of sudden death, that were the common lot of small farmers." Baptist and Methodist congregations offered a more literal form of salvation to those feeling increasingly marginalized or unable to cope in an increasingly complicated and alienating mainstream social and economic white world. Instead, they could seek refuge in a "close, supportive, and orderly community" of the disciplined faithful. The ranks of the Dissenting congregations were filled mainly by the poor and unlearned, drawn also by the alternative value system found in evangelical fellowship, which was more egalitarian and consensual than the hierarchical and authoritarian world of slave-society Virginia.[17]

Baptists by and large eventually supported the patriot cause, but, for other religious groups, turning toward the spiritual often meant turning away from the secular and the worldly, including the growing political controversy. The Methodists in particular shied away from embroiling themselves in the patriot movement. Though Francis Asbury, the most prominent Methodist itinerant preacher in Virginia, started a diary only after hostilities began, his main concern was to stay out of politics. Embarrassed by the pro-Parliament writings of the leader of the Methodist revival, John Wesley, Asbury himself just prayed for peace. "Martial clamours," he wrote in late 1775, only "confuse the land," adding in early 1776 that those with a "martial spirit" had "lost the spirit of pure and undefiled religion." While not advocating loyalism, to those seeking salvation Asbury and other ministers heading the emerging "revival of religion" made it clear that they would not find it in the patriot movement.[18]

17. Elmer T. Clark, J. Manning Potts, and Jacob S. Payton, eds., *The Journal and Letters of Francis Asbury* (Nashville, Tenn., 1958), I, 208; Rhys Isaac, *The Transformation of Virginia, 1740-1790* (Chapel Hill, N.C., 1982), 161–177, quotes on 164, for estimates of the numbers of Baptist converts on the eve of Revolution, see 173; William Parks, "Religion and the Revolution in Virginia," in Richard A. Rutyna and Peter C. Stewart, eds., *Virginia in the American Revolution: A Collection of Essays* (Norfolk, Va., 1977), I, 38–56, esp. I, 44–46.

18. Rhys Isaac, "Preachers and Patriots: Popular Culture and the Revolution in Virginia," in Alfred F. Young, ed., *The American Revolution: Explorations in the History of American Radicalism* (DeKalb, Ill., 1976), 127–156; Oct. 8, 1775,

Yet even in the pulpits of the Anglican churches, gentlemen-patriots who dominated the parish vestries could not rely on wholehearted support for their stance against the British. Many Anglican ministers were reluctant to endorse resistance to the British government; some were happy to foment divisions among white Virginians. In Nansemond County, for example, the Reverend John Agnew of Suffolk Parish found a ready audience for his sermons preaching antipatriot propaganda. Perhaps with the burdens of the previous war still fresh in his mind, Agnew had been heard to say that the "the designs of the great men were to ruin the poor people; and that, after a while, they would forsake them, and lay the whole blame on their shoulders, and by this means make them slaves."[19]

Nervous newspaper reports and private correspondence show that patriot leaders in the colony were well aware of the range of opinions—and extent of dissent—among those they sought to govern. But, if the triple crises of the Seven Years' War, parliamentary coercion, and the economic downturn meant that they might not be able to rely on the wholehearted support of their neighbors, elites also increasingly fought among themselves. Some of these conflicts were caused by provincial legislative and political issues, but the imperial dispute initially at least looked to contribute to these divisions. The debate over Patrick Henry's Stamp Act resolves, for example, divided the Burgesses—so much so that Peyton Randolph, leader of the party that favoured moderation, exclaimed, "By God, I would have given 500 guineas for a single vote."[20]

Apr. 23, 1776, Clark, Potts, and Payton, ed., *Journal of Asbury,* I, 165, 181, 184, and cf. 211.

19. *Va. Gaz.* (D and H), Apr. 1, 1775. Daniel Trabue noted in his memoir that, in his home county of Chesterfield, the Baptists and Presbyterians supported the patriot movement, but the Anglican parson had told his father that "the people was Deluded by some of their Leaders," and warned that the "negros would also rise in Rebellion . . . if the people Did Rebel" and they would "suffer much by high Fines and Taxes, etc." Young, ed., *Westward into Kentucky,* 42.

20. Other men like Robert Munford must have experienced considerable but subtle anxiety as colleagues and kin edged toward more moderate or conservative viewpoints. Munford, later a moderate, early allied himself with Patrick Henry, being one of the three colleagues who had been "in Conclave" with Henry, "Consulting and preparing resolutions" upon the Stamp Act crisis in 1765. The young Munford, in his first appearance in the House of Burgesses, was labeled by Governor Francis Fauquier as one of the "Young, hot and Giddy Members" who spoke in

Divisions also emerged at the polls. Though competition for places in the House of Burgesses varied from region to region and time to time, there were worrying signs that contested elections were becoming the norm. An increase in voter "treating," the solicitation of "Interest," and making "promises" to voters seemed to some to be upsetting the more traditional and genteel manner of choosing virtuous representatives. Newspaper articles urged voters to "strike at the Root of this growing Evil" and "be influenced by Merit alone." Violence at the polls and accusations of outright bribery confirmed these views. It was as if some "Daemon" had "lately come among us to disturb the peace and harmony, which had long subsisted in this place." One prominent planter and politician, Robert Carter, actually decided to quit public life in the early 1770s rather than adjust to the "new system of politicks" that had begun, he believed, "to prevail generally."[21]

As the economic situation deteriorated and divisions multiplied, liter-

---

support of Henry's resolutions and thus must have been pained and perhaps embarrassed when his uncle Richard Bland and his mentor Peyton Randolph spoke out against them. Such divisions only caused greater anxiety among men who were already nervous about their legitimacy, authority, and unity in the face of resistance to Parliament. Rodney M. Baine, *Robert Munford: America's First Comic Dramatist* (Athens, Ga., 1967), 26–27; Marc Egnal, "The Origins of the Revolution in Virginia: A Reinterpretation," *WMQ,* 3d Ser., XXXVII (1980), 417; Edmund Pendleton to James Madison, Apr. 21, 1790, *Papers of Pendleton,* II, 565.

21. *Va. Gaz.* (P and D), Apr. 11, 1771; *Va. Gaz.* (Rind), Oct. 31, 1771; Gordon S. Wood, "Rhetoric and Reality in the American Revolution," *WMQ,* 3d Ser., XXIII (1966), 28; Louis Morton, *Robert Carter of Nomini Hall: A Virginia Tobacco Planter of the Eighteenth Century* (Williamsburg, Va., 1941), 52; Jack P. Greene, ed., *Diary of Carter,* II, 1006–1010, 1073, 1102–1103; Greene, *Landon Carter: An Inquiry into the Personal Values and Social Imperatives of the Eighteenth-Century Virginia Gentry* (Charlottesville, Va., 1965), 40–70. Cf. Richard R. Beeman, "Robert Munford and the Political Culture of Frontier Virginia," *Journal of American Studies,* XII (1978), 169–183, esp. 178–182. Munford's two plays, *The Candidates* and *The Patriots,* provide a vivid portrayal of that sense of crisis (Courtlandt Canby, ed., "Robert Munford's *The Patriots,*" *WMQ,* 3d Ser., VI [1949], 437–503). Cf. Beeman, "Deference, Republicanism, and the Emergence of Popular Politics in Eighteenth-Century America," *WMQ,* 3d Ser., XLIX (1992), 416–418; Wood, "Rhetoric and Reality in the American Revolution," *WMQ,* 3d Ser., XXIII (1966), 27–30, who also notes that the *Virginia Gazette Index, 1736–1780* (ed. Lester J. Cappon and Stella F. Duff [Williamsburg, Va., 1950]) registers an "astounding increase in essays on corruption and cost of elections" in the late 1760s and early 1770s (see I, 351).

ate gentlemen sometimes brought their differences out into the open, publicly challenging ruling class practices. An anonymous newspaper writer in 1770, speaking of the "desperation" that some were feeling because of mounting debts and the fear of debtor's prison and the loss of property, told the House of Burgesses that they must provide relief to jailed debtors: "Oppression will forever lessen the effect of authority in the hearts and minds of a free people." A "Planter in Caroline" wrote in November 1773 of the need for the Burgesses to do something about the falling price of tobacco and also asserted that the "great and learned Men" could have problems maintaining their authority: "If those who are chosen to represent and redress the Grievances [of] their Constituents remain silent on this Occasion, I am at a Loss to know what Use we have for such Men." If they did not correct the situation, "the present Situation of the Planters may, possibly, draw more fatal Consequences."[22]

Challenged by other Virginians and increasingly doubting their capacity to rule in the public sphere, many gentlemen in Virginia did indeed feel a "growing sense of impending ruin" that was tied to a belief that their public and private authority was coming undone. Given this perception, gentlemen responded to the imperial crisis with mixed emotions. On one hand, some of the colonial elite could welcome conflict with Britain as an opportunity to reconstitute or reassert and legitimize their claims as a unified planter class to authority in and over the colony. At the very least, wealthy planters hoped to present a united front to British coercive measures. In doing so, many gentlemen might have hoped, too, that the imperial crisis would galvanize popular support for the embattled ruling class. In diverse ways, then, resistance to Britain might arrest the crisis that seemed to engulf the ruling class by the 1760s and 1770s. Yet, precisely because many gentlemen felt such an acute sense of crisis, they embarked upon a program of increased resistance to Britain with trepidation.[23]

22. *Va. Gaz.* (Rind), June 7, 1770; *Va. Gaz.* (P and D), Nov. 4, 1773. Great planters themselves were suffering from the recession and debts. Even conservative estimates of the total debt owed by Virginians to British merchants on the eve of the Revolution put it at upward of two to three million pounds. See Lawrence H. Gipson, "Virginia Planter Debts before the American Revolution," *VMHB*, LXIX (1961), 259–260. Cf. *Va. Gaz.* (P and D), Nov. 6, 1766; Breen, *Tobacco Culture,* chaps. 4, 5; Holton, *Forced Founders,* 159–170.

23. See Wood, "Rhetoric and Reality in the American Revolution," *WMQ,* 3d Ser., XXIII (1966), 28; Benson, "Wealth and Power," 14–27; Isaac, *Transformation of Virginia,* 255; Breen, *Tobacco Culture,* esp. 160–203; Holton, *Forced Founders.*

••• When news came of the deliberations of the newly formed Continental Congress in 1774, then, patriot leaders in Virginia reacted with caution. Instead of unilaterally pushing ahead with the Continental recommendations, patriot leaders called unprecedented public meetings designed, as one said, to "feel how the pulse of the common people beat." Some meetings were discouraging and fulfilled patriots' worst expectations. At one in Richmond County in the Northern Neck in June 1774, a "vast concourse" of people attended, but only a "very few express any outward signs of approbation on the occasion," except a "few gentlemen." At another meeting in neighboring Westmoreland County, according to Dr. Walter Jones, "Many People" shared the opinion—"too common among [the] Vulgar"—that "the Law [resp]ecting Tea alone, did not concern them, because they used none of it." Instead, Jones worried, "many of the more depraved have Said, let the Gentlemen look to it."[24]

To counter such "prejudices," as another gentleman put it, and build a unified front, patriot leaders called more meetings and "endeavoured" to "Convince the People that the case of the Bostonians was the case of all America." In a bow to popular ritual, they arranged the hanging and burning of effigies of hated British opponents, and "some of the greatest men of the colony" attended to "encourag[e] the common people to a like steady adherence to the [proposed Association]." Patriot leaders also

---

For challenges to planters' private and public authority, see, especially, Kathleen M. Brown, *Good Wives, Nasty Wenches, and Anxious Patriarchs: Gender, Race, and Power in Colonial Virginia* (Chapel Hill, N.C., 1996), 321, 323–324; Kenneth A. Lockridge, "Colonial Self-Fashioning: Paradoxes and Pathologies in the Construction of Genteel Identity in Eighteenth-Century America," in Ronald Hoffman, Mechal Sobel, and Fredrika J. Teute, eds., *Through a Glass Darkly: Reflections on Personal Identity in Early America* (Chapel Hill, N.C., 1997), 330; Lockridge, *On the Sources of Patriarchal Rage: The Commonplace Books of William Byrd and Thomas Jefferson and the Gendering of Power in the Eighteenth Century* (New York, 1992); Rhys Isaac, "Communication and Control: Authority Metaphors and Power Contests on Colonel Landon Carter's Virginia Plantation, 1752–1778," in Sean Wilentz, ed., *Rites of Power: Symbolism, Ritual, and Politics since the Middle Ages* (Philadelphia, 1985); Isaac, *Landon Carter's Uneasy Kingdom: Revolution and Rebellion in a Virginia Plantation* (New York, 2004); Michael A. McDonnell, "A World Turned 'Topsy Turvy': Robert Munford, *The Patriots,* and the Crisis of the Revolution in Virginia," *WMQ*, 3d Ser., LXI (2004), 235–270.

24. David Wardrobe to Archibald Provan, June 30, 1774, *Rev. Va.,* II, 135–136; Dr. Walter B. Jones to Landon Carter, June 17, 1774, Sabine Hall Papers, UVa.

used the churches. The deist Jefferson was behind a proposal to declare a day of fasting and prayer "to electrify the people from the pulpit," as he confessed that he and others were "under conviction of the necessity of arousing our people from the lethargy into which they had fallen." Finally, patriot leaders in the assembly in the summer of 1774 tried to mitigate the effect of any trade boycotts by acquiescing to small farmers' demands to close the county courts when their fee bill expired "in order that none need be under any apprehension of distress by the merchants during their non-importation." That meant that no debtors could be brought to court for the duration of the boycott.[25]

However, popular public support was slow to develop. Though an extraordinarily large number of county resolutions made their way into the public papers in the summer of 1774, most were the products of a deliberate campaign by gentlemen leaders to exhibit a united front toward the British and encourage wider participation in the protests. The printed resolutions rarely represented the sense of an entire county. Only fifty-one people actually signed the Loudoun County resolves, for example, roughly less than 3 percent of the male population of "Freeholders and other inhabitants." One historian, at least, has concluded that the meetings that produced the

25. June 8, 1774, Greene, ed., *Diary of Carter,* II, 821; David Wardrobe to Archibald Provan, June 30, 1774, *Rev. Va.,* II, 135–136; "Autobiography," *Papers of Jefferson,* I, 105–106nn, 116–117nn; *Rev. Va.,* I, 104. Hard-pressed farmers hoped that the Association's nonexportation agreement would create at least a temporary rise in tobacco prices. But small farmers also demanded the closure of Virginia's courts to protect themselves from prosecution by their creditors until they could get a good crop in and a healthy price for it. With the courts closed, some merchants found it difficult to collect debts, and that by "some strange mode of reasoning" farmers believed it was "Patriotism not to pay anybody." Charles Yates to ———, July 21, 1774, to John Southwaites, July 25, 1774, to Samuel and William Vernon, Oct. 5, 1774, to Isaac Heslop, Feb. 20, 1775, Charles Yates Letterbook, UVa; William Allason to Walter Peter, July 1, 1774, "The Letters of William Allason, Merchant of Falmouth, Virginia," *Richmond College Historical Papers,* II (1917), 154.

For the general popularity of the court closure, see Holton, *Forced Founders,* chap. 4; George M. Curtis III, "The Role of the Courts in the Making of the Revolution in Virginia," in James Kirby Martin, ed., *The Human Dimensions of Nation Making: Essays on Colonial and Revolutionary America* (Madison, Wis., 1976), 136. Not all the patriot gentry were happy about closing the courts. See Edmund Pendleton to Ralph Wormeley, Jr., July 28, 1774, CWFL, and Beverley Randolph to Landon Carter, June 18, 1774, Landon Carter Papers, VHS.

county resolutions that summer were "stage-managed" by "a few politically powerful individuals," who drew up resolutions beforehand and appealed for ratification. Despite their thin support, these resolves, as was hoped, were interpreted as evidence of full popular—and united—support for the common cause by contemporaries on both sides of the Atlantic and subsequent historians alike.[26]

Yet a month after the formal Continental Association was agreed to by the gentry-dominated First Virginia Convention of August 1774, the patriot leadership still worried about the support of the people. William Lee was warning Richard Henry Lee that in every colony "incessant pains should be used to engage the yeomanry or people at large in the same spirit of opposition with the principal men." Though they would be met with "many obstructions from the slavish principles of some. . . . It is the part of the leaders to engage the Body of the people, step by step, till they have advanced too far to retract." Tellingly, in an address in the fall or winter of 1774–1775, "adapted to the understandings, and intended for the information of, the middling and lower classes of people," "Brutus" thought that old prejudices remained: "You are told that the present dispute . . . is concerning the duty on *tea*. . . . Some of you may now tell me it is a dispute with which you have nothing to do, as you do not make use of that commodity, and the duty cannot affect you." Brutus believed that many of his less wealthy neighbors saw the imperial dispute in distinct class terms, echoing the sentiments of the Reverend John Agnew. Many of his neighbors, he thought, believed that "the *high-minded gentlemen* are the occasion

26. Burr Powell, the son of one of the authors, Leven Powell, later suggested that it was a more intimate affair than imagined: "a large portion" of those who signed were Powell's own "neighbors and personal friends." Loudoun County Resolves, June 14, 1774, *Rev. Va.,* VII, 734; Burr Powell to R. H. Lee, Jan. 11, 1826, *WMQ,* 1st Ser., XII (1903–1904), 234; Richard R. Beeman, *Patrick Henry: A Biography* (New York, 1974), 55–56. Loudoun County had an estimated eligible fighting force (white males between sixteen and sixty) of sixteen hundred in 1776 ("The Number of Men of Military Age in Virginia, 1776," *VMHB,* XVIII [1910], 35). Just more than half of Virginia's sixty-five counties drew up resolutions, thirty-three of which are still extant. See *Rev. Va.,* I, 109–168, VII, 733–734, 737–738, for the majority of the resolutions. Cf. Westmoreland County Resolutions, June 22, 1774, and David Wardrobe to Archibald Provan, June 30, 1774, in Richard Barksdale Harwell, ed., *The Committees of Safety of Westmoreland and Fincastle: Proceedings of the County Committees, 1774–1776* (Richmond, Va., 1956), 36.

of the present confusion, and are bringing you into difficulties to support their extravagance and ambition." Brutus hoped his address would "reconcile the different opinions . . . respecting the necessity or propriety of resisting the enemies of American liberty."[27]

Given their awareness of these divisions below, patriot leaders were also uncertain how best to reassert their public authority on the parade ground. As militia and new companies of special minutemen mobilized in other colonies, Virginia's patriot leadership also considered its military options. Even if few gentlemen in Virginia expected or desired armed conflict with Britain, many agreed that at least an appearance of martial readiness was required. Such a strategy, pushing resistance into a new phase, would bolster the language of political resistance patriot gentlemen had employed ever more forcefully over the previous months. As important, however, if gentry-led mobilization could help in the confrontation with Britain, it could also help frighten rebellious slaves back into submission and galvanize the white population into support for patriot measures. Crucial to this reassertion of leadership was the resurrection of a manly, martial tradition, at the head of which gentlemen could command with authority.

The most obvious place for a martial and manly display of authority in the face of parliamentary intransigence was in the militia. In the militia many would-be gentlemen traditionally had tried to bolster their claims to status and authority. By securing commissions as officers in the militia, gentlemen believed they gained access to a third pillar—alongside their dominance of the courts and the Anglican parish vestries—for their claims to gentility and authority. Because the county court made appointments in the militia, gentry families traditionally monopolized the upper echelons of command. Appointments reflected social prestige and a carefully delineated county hierarchy.[28]

27. William Lee to R. H. Lee, Sept. 10, 1774, in Ford, ed., *Letters of William Lee,* I, 90–91; Brutus, "Address," [May 15, 1775], *Va. Gaz.* (Purdie), July 15, 1775, *Rev. Va.,* III, 126, 130. The exact date of this address is not clear. Though not printed by Purdie until July 15, 1775, and dated May 15, 1775, by the editors, it appears from internal evidence that it was written sometime between the end of October 1774 (after the First Continental Congress) and March 1775 (the Second Virginia Convention). The author refers to the First Continental Congress as having already met. My thanks to Brent Tarter at the Library of Virginia for helping to date this document.

28. Isaac, *Transformation of Virginia,* 104–110. Cf. Carp, "Early American Military History," *VMHB,* XCIV (1986), 271; Ronald L. Boucher, "The Colonial Mili-

But the militia itself was then more often than not neglected. Gentlemen who secured commissions were rarely interested in actual military service, and their authority over the militia was best served, not by frequent and rigorous mustering, but by the occasional voluntary—and social—gathering of friends and neighbors. Most officers knew little of their craft. The result was that the militia was persistently underprepared. Governor after governor complained about the officers of the militia. Governor Sir William Gooch complained in the 1740s that, if they could get the militia to the field, "scarce one Officer knows how to form . . . or to instruct them." Gilmer acknowledged that Virginians generally could not draw from experience or tradition. At the head of a new military unit, he promised that he would now exert himself to "make myself Master of the necessary parade of war." It would not be experience, but his neighbors' "esteem" that would make him more comfortable with his tomahawk and "animate me to its proper use."[29]

Yet Gilmer could be nervous about relying on his neighbors' esteem. Most ordinary white Virginians were only too happy to ignore the laws that insisted they enroll and train regularly in the militia, which meant time away from farms and families. Though Virginia's expanding frontier meant that western settlers maintained some vigilance, most Virginians in the eastern part saw little reason to maintain the militia. George Washington believed that years of uninterrupted peace had enervated the militia. Until the Seven Years' War, he wrote, most Virginians had "lived in the most profound, and Tranquil peace; never studying War nor Warfare." As a result, when Governor Dinwiddie arrived in the colony in 1756, he found the militia "in very bad Order" and of limited use. But even during the Seven Years' War, which was fought, for the most part, on Virginia's far-flung western frontiers, eastern militia often refused to train or serve, falling back upon traditional English rights and privileges. They might defend the country, but only in times of absolute necessity. Dinwiddie thought that, though as many as thirty-six thousand men were enrolled in the militia, few would actually do any duty beyond home defense: they were "chiefly Free-holders,

---

tia as a Social Institution: Salem, Massachusetts, 1764–1775," *Military Affairs,* XXXVII (1973), 125–127; Edmund S. Morgan, *Inventing the People: The Rise of Popular Sovereignty in England and America* (New York, 1988), 153–173.

29. Richard C. Bush, "The Militia of Northumberland County," *Bulletin of the Northumberland County Historical Society,* XXXI (1994), 24; Gilmer, address, [Apr. 18, 1775], *Rev. Va.,* III, 52.

who insist on th'r Privileges not to enlist or serve but on imminent danger."[30]

The neglect of the militia was all the more extraordinary because of the rapidly expanding enslaved community in Virginia. Traditionally, the militia was supposed to play one deadly important function: the policing of a large and restive enslaved population. Indeed, as Indians, enslaved and free blacks, and indentured and convict servants came to be excluded from the militia through the eighteenth century, the militia was increasingly used to guard against individual and collective uprisings from within. In an important sense, all across the colonies the militia more and more protected the propertied from the unpropertied. In Virginia, it most often was a pool from which to draw patrols for local vigilance against the expanding enslaved population. Though all members of the militia were liable for slave patrol duty, in reality, partly because the militia was so neglected, the duties usually fell to a smaller, usually poorer, self-selected group. In return for exemptions from mustering in the militia and, more important, from public, county, and parish levies, some whites chose to serve regularly in slave patrols to supplement their income. Patrolling and policing enslaved Virginians was not a community affair.[31]

30. Morgan, *American Slavery, American Freedom,* 112; Washington to John Campbell, January 1757, *Papers of Washington,* Col. Ser., IV, 90; Robert Dinwiddie to Halifax, Feb. 24, 1756, in Titus, *Old Dominion at War,* 77; Higginbotham, "Military Institutions," in Higginbotham, ed., *War and Society,* 30-31; Bush, "The Militia of Northumberland County," *Bulletin of the Northumberland County Historical Society,* XXXI (1994), 24; Titus, *Old Dominion at War,* 1, 75-77. Cf. Robert Dinwiddie to William Byrd III, July 22, 1755, Marion Tinling, ed., *The Correspondence of the Three William Byrds of Westover, Virginia, 1684-1776* (Charlottesville, Va., 1977), II, 616. For the origins of the English and colonial militia, see especially T. H. Breen, "The Convenanted Militia of Massachusetts Bay: English Background and New World Development," in Breen, *Puritans and Adventurers: Change and Persistence in Early America* (New York, 1980), 25-45. Virginia's early militia tradition is most ably discussed by William L. Shea, *The Virginia Militia in the Seventeenth Century* (Baton Rouge, La., 1983), while Titus, *Old Dominion at War,* is the best source on the militia during the Seven Years' War. For an account of the English militia tradition as it evolved in the middle of the eighteenth century, see Eliga H. Gould, *Persistence of Empire,* esp. 72-105; Gould, "To Strengthen the King's Hands: Dynastic Legitimacy, Militia Reform, and Ideas of National Unity in England, 1745-1760," *Historical Journal,* XXXIV (1991), 329-348.

31. James Kirby Martin and Mark Edward Lender, *A Respectable Army: The*

As Virginia moved toward war with Britain, then, the militia was in a deplorable state, existing only on paper (if at all), particularly east of the Blue Ridge Mountains. The Second Virginia Convention, in March 1775, stated the problem clearly: the "legal and necessary disciplining of the Militia has been much neglected . . . to the evident Danger of the Community in Case of Invasion or Insurrection." In this light, exhortations stressing the importance of a "well regulated Militia, composed of gentlemen freeholders, and other freemen," as "the natural strength and only stable security of a free Government," were only rhetorical gestures aimed at creating an ideal, not explaining the real.[32]

• • • Given the state of the militia and the uncertain level of popular support for the cause, Virginia gentlemen looked to one other elitist martial model, briefly tested in the Seven Years' War and also rooted in an Anglo-American tradition. Then a brief, dramatic, but ultimately unsuccessful attempt was made by the gentry to stir up popular support in the face of declining enthusiasm and poor morale. In the spring of 1756, an "Association of Gentlemen" was formed to help Washington in his campaign against the native Americans and in building forts in the backcountry. Led by Attorney General Peyton Randolph, the "Associators" were leading gentlemen serving at their own expense in an effort to inspire lesser men to enlist in the provincial army that was also forming. Governor Dinwiddie hoped the "Association" would "be of Service in animating the lower Class of our People."[33]

Military Origins of the Republic, 1763–1789 (Arlington Heights, Ill., 1982), 17; Sally E. Hadden, *Slave Patrols: Law and Violence in Virginia and the Carolinas* (Cambridge, Mass., 2001), esp. 24–32, 93–90; Philip D. Morgan, *Slave Counterpoint: Black Culture in the Eighteenth-Century Chesapeake and Lowcountry* (Chapel Hill, N.C., 1998), 307–308, 388–389.

32. George Mason, "Fairfax County Militia Plan 'for Embodying the People,'" [Feb. 6, 1775], Fairfax County Committee of Safety Proceedings, [Jan. 17, 1775], Fairfax County Militia Association, [Sept. 21, 1774], *Papers of Mason,* I, 210–211, 212, 215–216; "Address of George Gilmer," *Rev. Va.,* III, 51; Proceedings of the Second Virginia Convention, Mar. 25, 1775, *Rev. Va.,* II, 242, 244 n. 3, 374–375.

33. Fairfax County Militia Association, [Sept. 21, 1774], *Papers of Mason,* I, 211; Tinling, ed., *Correspondence of the Byrds,* II, 621; John Ferling, "Soldiers for Virginia: Who Served in the French and Indian War?" *VMHB,* XCIV (1986), 317; Titus, *Old Dominion at War,* 144; Douglas Southall Freeman, *George Washington: A Biography* (New York, 1948–1957), II, 198; Rhys Isaac, "Religion and Au-

So, in September 1774, more radical patriot leaders set in motion a voluntary movement to form "independant Compan[ies] of Voluntiers" to ready themselves against "hostile Invasion, or real Danger of the Community of which we are Members." As in 1756, the informal movement was also designed more to "rouse the attention of the public," "excite others by our Example," and "infuse a martial spirit of emulation" among all ranks of society than to actually provide a front line of defense.[34]

Membership in these companies was not actually open to all. Instead, the independent companies were to help gentlemen: that is, provide a nursery for officers. According to one declaration, they would "provide a fund of officers; that in case of absolute necessity, the people might be better enabled to act in defence of their invaded liberty." Indeed, the Fairfax volunteers saw their independent company as the first step in "putting the Militia . . . upon a more respectable Footing." Gentlemen would thus ready themselves first, train, and, if war came, go forth among the people and assume leadership in battle and in a more traditional military organization. The independent companies were designed by gentlemen for gentlemen and trusted freeholders, not for the common sort.[35]

Limited membership and the terms upon which these companies came together reinforced their social exclusivity. Membership was generally to be confined to "gentlemen of the first fortune and character," and many of the companies stipulated a maximum of one hundred individuals (though most were much smaller). The more material terms of enrollment seemed

---

thority: Problems of the Anglican Establishment in Virginia in the Era of the Great Awakening and the Parsons' Cause," *WMQ,* 3d Ser., XXX (1973), 30.

34. Fairfax County Militia Association, [Sept. 21, 1774], Fairfax County Militia Plan "for Embodying the People," [enclosure of Feb. 6, 1775], "Remarks on Annual Elections," [ca. Apr. 17-26, 1775], *Papers of Mason,* I, 210-211, 215, 229. It is of note that Spotsylvania County "recommended" raising a company only two weeks after James Madison had reported the conspiracy of enslaved Virginians in neighboring Orange County, noted above (see Spotsylvania County Committee Proceedings, Dec. 15, 1774, *Rev. Va.,* II, 197; Fairfax County Militia Association, [Sept. 21, 1774], *Papers of Mason,* I, 210-211).

35. Fairfax County Militia Association, [Sept. 21, 1774], Fairfax County Militia Plan "for Embodying the People," [enclosure of Feb. 6, 1775], "Remarks on Annual Elections," [ca. Apr. 17-26, 1775], *Papers of Mason,* I, 210-211, 215, 229. In Fairfax, at least, most of the initial members of the independent company did later become high-ranking militia officers (see Lund Washington to George Washington, Sept. 29, 1775, *Papers of Washington,* Rev. War. Ser., II, 64-65, 66n).

tailored to exclude less wealthy farmers, playing the role, in effect, of property qualifications for holding office in civil life. Among other accoutrements, each member had to provide his own "Blue, turn'd up with Buff" uniform complete with "Coat and Breeches and white Stockings" along with "a good Fire-lock and Bayonet" and six pounds of gunpowder, twenty pounds of lead, and fifty gun flints, "at the least."[36]

Because the new independent companies were established by gentlemen and for gentlemen and substantial yeomen alone, their organization was much more consensual and egalitarian than militia or regular provincial army units ever had been. Service was voluntary: "Subscribers" entered into a "bond," an "Association" that was "freely and voluntarily agreed" to. Unlike the militia or other regular military units, the members were bound to serve, not by law, but, rather, "by the sacred ties of virtue, Honor, and love to our Country" and "the words of Gentlemen."[37]

More striking were the provisions for the appointment of officers and their command. Officers were to be "of their own Choice," selected "from among our Friends and acquaintaince, upon whose Justice, Humanity and Bravery we can relie." One contingent specifically stipulated, "When a sufficient number of men were enlisted to form a company, they should choose the officers to command them." Members then promised to "obey the commands of the officers" that they themselves had "elected from the Inlisted Volunteers." They would pay "due submission" to such officers "for the Sake of Good-order and Regularity." But some associators went further and pledged to "adhere strictly" only "to such resolves which shall be entered into by a Majority of the Company."[38]

36. Fairfax County Militia Association, [Sept. 21, 1774], *Papers of Mason,* I, 211.

37. My account of the formation of the independent companies is drawn primarily from the following sources: Declaration of Subscribers to the First Independent Company of Dunmore County (n.d., but probably after January 1775), Dunmore County Committee of Safety Papers, VHS; Fairfax County Militia Association, [Sept. 21, 1774], Fairfax County Militia Plan "for Embodying the People," [enclosure of Feb. 6, 1775], "Remarks on Annual Elections," [ca. Apr. 17-26, 1775], *Papers of Mason,* I, 210-211, 215, 229; "Terms of Inlisting," [ca. April 1775], R. A. Brock, ed., "Papers, Military and Political, 1775-1778, of George Gilmer, M.D., of 'Pen Park,' Albemarle County, Va.," VHS, *Collections,* n.s., VI (1887), 82; William E. White, "The Independent Companies of Virginia, 1774-1775," *VMHB,* LXXXVI (1978), 152; "The First Independent Company of Dunmore," *VMHB,* XLIV (1936), 102-104.

38. Charles Dabney to William Wirt, Dec. 21, 1805, in William Wirt Henry,

Electing officers was a radical innovation in the military, unprecedented in the southern militia tradition. Yet, precisely because the companies were generally small and of the "better sort," associators permitted the election of officers and a more consensual style of leadership and direction. George Mason implied that such elections would be acceptable only if a company was composed of "gentlemen" of equal merit; if competition was limited to "equals," no one would feel "degraded" by doing duty "in the ranks" under someone else's command. Just as in electoral competition in the political arena among gentlemen, Mason believed, elections of military officers from among equals would not threaten anyone's perceived social status. And companies of gentlemen could leave regulations, rules, and even actions to a democratic vote, but by limiting membership patriot leaders made it clear that democracy was acceptable only for the preferred few. Such a martial arrangement was ideal for a besieged and anxious patriot elite. These units resembled elite gentlemen's clubs rather than formal military units, and in forming them gentlemen drew upon a hierarchical social ideal committed to government by the few. Such an organization reveals much about gentlemen's beliefs in a natural aristocracy on the eve of the War for Independence—and the limits of the rights of the people out-of-doors to participate in more democratic governance.[39]

• • • Patriot leaders hoped such an initiative would serve a threefold purpose: send a message of a united and defiant opposition to Britain, help rouse an apparently indifferent and divided population, and, finally, help gentlemen reestablish a unified, manly, and unchallenged authority over Virginia's black and white communities. But the gamble went horribly awry. Gentlemen, for example, continued to divide among themselves. As Continental resistance to Parliament heated up over the winter of 1774–1775, some patriot leaders pushed for wider mobilization. Patriots in Fairfax County drew up a plan for "Embodying the People" in early 1775, adapting their earlier plan of association of the volunteer company to a more general call to arms in the county. A month later, in March 1775, hot-headed patriots led by Patrick Henry pushed the members of the Second Virginia Convention to do the same. Supporting a proposal to put the

---

Patrick Henry: Life, Correspondence, and Speeches (New York, 1891), I, 251–252, and notes above.

39. Remarks on Annual Elections, [ca. Apr. 17–26, 1775], *Papers of Mason,* I, 231–232.

colony "into a posture of Defence," Patrick Henry rose to make his famous "Give me liberty, or give me death!" speech, arguing, "The war is actually begun." More conservative patriot leaders, however, opposed making what seemed to be a formal declaration of war. Robert Carter Nicholas had come to the convention to "have errours rectified, and not to alter or destroy the Constitution." After a long and heated debate, Henry's supporters narrowly passed the resolution. Even then, the convention recommended only that each county obey the militia law and form volunteer companies.[40]

The close vote over putting the colony into a posture of defense reflected continuing divisions among gentlemen over how far to push resistance. Patrick Henry represented one end of the patriot political spectrum; Robert Munford, the other. Munford, one of the "Young, hot and Giddy Members" who had acted with Patrick Henry in preparing resolutions against the Stamp Act, was also moderator of the county committee meeting in Mecklenburg that passed resolves in support of the Continental Association in July 1774. By the spring of 1775, however, he worried about where resistance was heading. Just after the Second Convention adjourned, Munford wrote to his friend William Byrd about the "unwarrantable measures that have been adopted with too much precipitation by our unwary countrymen": the militarism of some of his compatriots would actually lead to civil war. He told Byrd he had drawn up an address to the governor, for which he hoped to gain support among the more "moderate and prudent." Condemning therein the "spirit for warfare displayed by the last Convention," Munford, the county lieutenant of the militia of Mecklenburg, assured the governor of his allegiance; his militia, at least, would not "embody or arm" until "required" by the "constituent powers of the legislature or the commander in chief."[41]

40. Proceedings of the Second Virginia Convention, Mar. 23, 1775, *Rev. Va.,* II, 366–367, 368–369 n. 8; "Fairfax County Militia Association," [Sept. 21, 1774], and the Fairfax County Militia Plan "for Embodying the People," [Feb. 6, 1775], *Papers of Mason,* I, 210–211, 215–216; Rhys Isaac, "Dramatizing the Ideology of Revolution: Popular Mobilization in Virginia, 1774 to 1776," *WMQ,* 3d Ser., XXXVIII (1976), 379–380.

Throughout, I have used the terms "convention" and "assembly" interchangeably, as contemporaries often did when referring to any of the five extralegal Revolutionary conventions in Virginia that convened between 1774 and 1776. After Independence and the creation of a new constitution in 1776, the legislative body became known formally as the General Assembly.

41. Baine, *Robert Munford,* 26–27; Pendleton to Madison, Apr. 21, 1790, *Papers*

Munford was not the only one reluctant to follow the militants' lead, even if he was one of the few to voice his concerns. County leaders throughout the colony appeared to drag their heels. James Madison wrote in late November 1774 that independent companies were forming "in many counties" but hoped that they would become "a general thing thro'ought this province." Yet, even by April 1775, only a handful of independent companies had embodied themselves. Even after the Second Virginia Convention officially recommended raising them, few counties hastened to do so. No action appears to have been taken by any of the counties for whom we have committee records, and perhaps only two counties (Chesterfield and King George) later reported that they had formed their companies in response to the convention's recommendation. The Spotsylvania county committee had previously recommended raising a volunteer company; Fairfax, Prince William, Loudoun, Westmoreland, King George, and Caroline had more than likely done so. Dunmore County probably had formed a company before April, and Albemarle established one only by mid-April. Even in Patrick Henry's Hanover County, it seems that, though the company was enlisted in the fall of 1774, it was not actually embodied until late April 1775. The House of Burgesses in June 1775 concluded, "There were a few companies of Gentlemen formed, who were desirous of perfecting themselves in military exercise," but in total there were "not more than six or seven throughout the whole colony."[42]

------

of Pendleton, II, 565; Mecklenburg County Resolves, July 29, 1774, *Rev. Va.,* VII, 737, 738n; Robert Munford to William Byrd, Apr. 20, 1775, Tinling, ed., *Correspondence of the Byrds,* II, 806. For Munford's hesitations, see McDonnell, "A World Turned 'Topsy Turvy,'" *WMQ,* 3d Ser., LXI (2004), 235–270.

42. Madison to William Bradford, Nov. 26, 1774, *Papers of Madison,* I, 129; "Report of the Committee to Inquire into the Causes of the Late Disturbances and Commotions in the Country," June 1, 1775, in "The Proceedings of the House of Burgesses in Virginia" (Williamsburg: Alexander Purdie), in William Sumner Jenkins, comp., *Records of the States of the United States* (LoC, 1949), reel Va. Ib, reel 3, 1773–1781, 22–23, 24, 231–237; White, "Independent Companies of Virginia," *VMHB,* LXXXVI (1978), 151. White's list of volunteer companies is based on companies embodied through to June 1775. See Michael A. McDonnell, "The Politics of Popular Mobilization in Revolutionary Virginia: Military Culture and Political and Social Relations, 1774–1783" (D.Phil. thesis, University of Oxford, 1996), 35–36, for the lower figure. Based on White's list, the majority of counties in which companies were formed were in the lower piedmont, along either side of the fall line, from north to south. Outside of Amherst, no companies in southwest-

Nor were ordinary white Virginians much interested either. Even in the counties where independent companies had formed, membership remained limited. Despite the attempts of the Fairfax gentry to broaden popular support and the participation of the mechanics of Alexandria, a muster of both groups of volunteers there in March 1775 brought out only an estimated 150 men, or 15 percent of the able-bodied males of the county. In Dunmore County, of an eligible fighting population of approximately 800 males, only 87 enrolled—predominantly gentlemen, or at least well-to-do.[43] The independent company from Albemarle County was typical; the 23 men enlisted there represented fewer than 1.8 percent of the county's 1,314 eligible males. Of the 23, 15 were on the 1782 Albermarle county personal property tax lists, and 15 were on the land tax lists of that year (8 men were on only one list). Among them, they owned a total of 232 slaves (or an average of 15 each), 403 cattle (27 each), and 114 horses (or 8 each). They also owned a total of 14,594 acres of land, for an average of a substantial 973 acres. In Fairfax County, George Mason later boasted that the independent company always consisted "entirely of Gentlemen."[44]

---

ern Virginia appear to have been formed, and only a few came from the tidewater counties. See the following sources for evidence of the volunteer movement prior to April 1775: Feb. 25, 1775, Cresswell, *Journal,* 57; Charles Lee to Robert Morris, Jan. 27, 1775, *The Lee Papers,* I, 168, New-York Historical Society, *Collections,* IV (1871); Lord Dunmore to Dartmouth, Dec. 24, 1774, John C. Fitzpatrick, ed., *The Writings of George Washington from the Original Manuscript Sources, 1745-1799* (Washington, D.C., 1931-1944), III, 248n; Madison to William Bradford, Nov. 26, 1774, *Papers of Madison,* I, 129; Charles Dabney to William Wirt, Dec. 21, 1805, in Henry, *Patrick Henry,* I, 251-252.

43. Gilmer, "Address to the Albemarle County Independent Company," [Apr. 18, 1775], *Rev. Va.,* III, 50-51; Mar. 18, 1775, Cresswell, *Journal,* 58-59; White, "Independent Companies of Virginia," *VMHB,* LXXXVI (1978), 151; Fairfax County Militia Association, [Sept. 21, 1774], *Papers of Mason,* I, 211; Declaration of Subscribers from Dunmore County, [n.d.], Dunmore County Committee of Safety Papers, VHS. Fairfax had approximately one thousand men of military age in 1776 ("Number of Men of Military Age," *VMHB,* XVIII [1910], 34-35).

44. Autograph Diary and Revolutionary Memoranda of Dr. George Gilmer, VHS; George Mason to [Mr. Brent], Oct. 2, 1778, *Papers of Mason,* I, 434. The printed edition of the Gilmer papers lists twenty-four additional men, but these were taken from rolls drawn up at a later date (Brock, ed., "Papers of Gilmer," VHS, *Collections,* n.s., VI [1887], 69-140; Albemarle County Personal Property and Land Tax Records, 1782, LiVi). Estimates of the number of males eligible for military

Instead, most ordinary farmers were more worried about getting their crops in than joining independent companies. As late as April 18, 1775, one commentator wrote, "The Planters, especially the common sort of them, are in high Spirits, so that they think little about the political dispute." Rather than muster for resistance to British tyranny, "they are making great preparations for another Crop of Tobacco . . . they have their Plantations in great order and forwardness"—ready to reap the harvest of expected high prices from the last shipment before nonexportation would take place. Though patriot leaders had, in their resolve in the March convention, finally and officially thrown down the gauntlet to royal officials, the formation of independent companies failed to inspire many ordinary Virginians to support the movement.[45]

What was perhaps worse for patriot leaders, enslaved Virginians *were* inspired by the general uncertainty and divisions among whites. As early as November 1774, some enslaved Virginians had met and selected a leader "to conduct them when the English Troops should arrive." Impressed that "by revolting to them they should be rewarded with their freedom," they thought that such a time would be "very soon." Knowing that enslaved Virginians had their own networks of communication, James Madison worried that "such attempts should be concealed as well as suppressed" in order to "prevent the Infection." As tensions between whites heightened, blacks grew bolder. The same week Gilmer made his speech in the spring of 1775, white inhabitants of Chesterfield County—a mere four counties removed from Albemarle—were "alarm'd for an Insurrection of the Slaves."[46]

• • • Such a situation boded ill for patriot leaders. Though *reports* of the formation of independent companies might have served as valuable propaganda demonstrating unity and martial readiness, they only incensed royal officials. Governor Dunmore wrote to Lord Dartmouth, secretary of state for the colonies, on December 24, 1774, "Every county, besides, is now arming a company of men, whom they call an Independent Company, for

---

service in Dunmore and Albemarle Counties come from a manuscript list, "The Number of Men of Military Age in Virginia in 1776," LiVi, reprinted in *VMHB*, XVIII (1910), 34-35.

45. Robert Donald to Patrick Hunter, Apr. 18, 1775, in David John Mays, *Edmund Pendleton, 1721-1803: A Biography* (Cambridge, Mass., 1952), II, 354n.

46. Madison to William Bradford, Nov. 26, 1774, *Papers of Madison*, I, 129-130; Holton, *Forced Founders*, 140-141.

the avowed purpose of protecting their Committees, and to be employed against government if occasion require." Nicholas Cresswell, a British sympathizer caught in the midst of the rebellion, despaired that the phenomenon was even more general: "Independent Companies are raising in every County on the Continent."[47]

But, given the lack of substance behind such reports, patriot leaders risked prematurely provoking British officials, and especially the impetuous Governor Dunmore, into action. Virginians were ill prepared for a confrontation. Elite Virginians disagreed over the next step to take, middling whites seemed preoccupied with their estates, and black Virginians watched all with increasing anticipation. No wonder then that, a day before Lexington and Concord and three days before Governor Dunmore moved against the patriots in Virginia, George Gilmer stood "awkwardly" before his neighbors desperately exhorting them to rally behind patriot leaders and to inspire Gilmer himself to lead. Gilmer had charged to the head of the patriot movement in Virginia, but it was not clear whether anyone was following; nor was it clear he knew what he was doing.

47. Lord Dunmore to Dartmouth, Dec. 24, 1774, Fitzpatrick, ed., *Writings of Washington,* III, 248n; Oct. 24, 1774, Cresswell, *Journal,* 43–44.

Enslaved Virginians made the first bid for independence. Almost at the same time that armed white farmers in Massachusetts defied royal authority and began the American Revolution, enslaved black workers defied white authority and began the Revolution in Virginia. Especially along the James River, reports flew of blacks on the move against their white masters in mid-April 1775. The insurrection of slaves in Chesterfield County was only the start. In Norfolk, at least two slaves conspired to ignite an insurrection. In the capital, Williamsburg, "disturbances" by enslaved Virginians were reported. All along the James River, enslaved Virginians struck fear in the hearts of their white masters, and accounts from throughout Virginia magnified the problem. Tales of incipient insurrections hailed from Prince Edward County, southwest of Chesterfield. Much farther afield, in the lower Northern Neck, two slaves in Northumberland actually burned the house of a militia officer "with a parcel of Straw fixed to the end of a Pole" on the night of April 20.[1]

On that same night, Governor Dunmore made a fateful move to thwart the incipient rebellion of whites in his colony. Angry over exaggerated reports of militant patriots gathering in independent companies, he was unaware of the virtual conflagration that had engulfed the Massachusetts

---

1. Edmund Pendleton to George Washington, Apr. 21, 1775, *Papers of Pendleton,* I, 102; Woody Holton, *Forced Founders: Indians, Debtors, Slaves, and the Making of the American Revolution in Virginia* (Chapel Hill, N.C., 1999), 141; *Va. Gaz.* (D and H), Apr. 29, 1775, supplement; Jan. 9, 1776, Northumberland County Order Book, 1773–1783, LiVi. A later correspondent noted that in April and May of 1775 there had been many rumors throughout the colony of the "Negroes intending to Rise." See Edward Stabler to Israel Pemberton, May 16, 1775, Photostat Collection, CWFL; cf. *Rev. Va.,* III, 6; *Va. Gaz.* (Purdie), June 16, 1775; Edmund Randolph, *History of Virginia,* ed. Arthur H. Shaffer (Charlottesville, Va., 1970), 219; "Declaration of the Delegates," Aug. 26, 1775, *Rev. Va.,* III, 501.

countryside to the north. He gave final orders to a small group of royal marines to seize under cover of night what gunpowder there was in the provincial magazine that stood prominently on the town common in Williamsburg. Late that night and into the early morning of April 21, 1775, Lieutenant Henry Collins directed the removal of fifteen half-barrels of gunpowder from the magazine. An alert resident spotted the detachment as they finished, but Collins escaped with the gunpowder, unchallenged. Though no shot was fired that could be heard around the world, the American Revolution began in Virginia two days after the fire had been kindled in Massachusetts. Ultimately, the governor's seizure of the powder, together with enslaved Virginians' rebellions, precipitated a calamitous chain of events that led to armed conflict—and to Virginians' declaring their independence from Britain.[2]

Despite the speed of events in hindsight, for most of 1775 few whites on any side of the conflict either expected or even desired Independence as an outcome, though in retrospect it seems inevitable. Patriot leaders in particular found themselves in a difficult position after Dunmore's seizure of the powder. While anxious to capitalize on the propaganda value of the governor's provocations to raise support for the patriot cause, leaders also worried about internal convulsions—the threat not only from enslaved Virginians but also from some of their white countrymen, who might push the movement in more radical directions. In December 1775, the Louisa county committee revealed the nature of the problem. It offered thanks to two of its most prominent members, the ministers Thomas Hall and John Todd, not just for their efforts in "rousing those lethargic wretches, who would tamely submit to a deprivation of their rights and liberties, to a proper sense of their danger and duty" but also for "checking the wild irregular sallies of those who would aim at too much."[3]

The acknowledgments of the Louisa county committee at the end of 1775 mark a significant but often overlooked phenomenon in Revolutionary Virginia and point us toward one of the central problems of the Revolution that patriot leaders faced almost everywhere. In rallying popular support for conservative resistance to perceived parliamentary encroachments upon their rights and liberties, gentlemen in Virginia, like patriots elsewhere,

2. *Rev. Va.*, III, 4–5; John E. Selby, *The Revolution in Virginia, 1775–1783* (Williamsburg, Va., 1991), 1–2.

3. Louisa County Committee, Proceedings, Dec. 4, 1775, *Va. Gaz.* (D and H), Dec. 23, 1775.

had to challenge and undermine the constituted authority in the colony. However, in undermining the authority of the crown, patriot leaders also risked losing control over the patriot movement and losing their own authority over their compatriots. In rousing "lethargic wretches" to unite behind resistance to Britain the patriot leadership also literally and figuratively exposed its own already fragile authority to "wild irregular sallies" from within.

The acknowledgments of the Louisa committee also show that not all patriots in Virginia spoke with the same voice. In diverse places and at different times, other voices raised in the contest against Britain were not always articulated clearly in more traditional sources, and certainly not all were in agreement with the leading patriot gentry. When the actions and voices of ordinary Virginians, black and white, free and unfree, are taken into account—and we pay more careful attention to the sequence of events—a more complicated story of rebellion and revolution emerges. These voices were at their loudest in the first few months after the outbreak of open, armed conflict with royal forces in the colony, as Virginians of all ranks struggled to define the meaning, aims, and limits of resistance and revolution. This dissent was all the more potent because it emerged at a critical moment in the imperial crisis, when all authority was under challenge, and because at this particular moment patriot leaders themselves were divided. Conservative, moderate, and radical gentlemen in the colony struggled over the patriot agenda. For a few short months in the spring and early summer of 1775, the outcome of these struggles between Virginians was not at all clear. And, though more moderate gentlemen within the patriot leadership seemingly maintained a degree of control over the resistance movement, the consequences of these months of trial profoundly altered the military and, more especially, political landscape in Virginia.[4]

4. This Revolutionary crisis of authority can be seen more intimately through the eyes of moderates such as Landon Carter and Robert Munford. In this respect, see, especially, Rhys Isaac, *Landon Carter's Uneasy Kingdom: Revolution and Rebellion in a Virginia Plantation* (New York, 2004); Michael A. McDonnell, "A World Turned 'Topsy Turvy': Robert Munford, *The Patriots,* and the Crisis of the Revolution in Virginia," *WMQ,* 3d Ser., LXI (2004), 235–270. For other colonies, see Dirk Hoerder, "Boston Leaders and Boston Crowds, 1765–1776," in Alfred F. Young, ed., *The American Revolution: Explorations in the History of American Radicalism* (De-Kalb, Ill., 1976), 235–271; Pauline Maier, *From Resistance to Revolution: Colonial Radicals and the Development of American Opposition to Britain, 1765–1776* (New York, 1972); Ray Raphael, *The First American Revolution: Before Lexington and*

• • • The immediate reaction to Dunmore's seizure of the powder in Williamsburg set the tone of the problem that would dominate patriot politics for the next three months. In the capital, a crowd of angry and armed residents quickly gathered outside the Governor's Palace, just down the road from the magazine. They demanded that Dunmore return the powder and issued "continual threats" that, if it were not returned, they would kill the governor and anyone who helped him. Some, at last, were particularly agitated by rumors of a slave uprising. "Various reports" from "different parts of the country" had led them to believe that "some wicked and designing persons have instilled the most diabolical notions into the minds of our slaves." Disarmed by the governor at the very moment that enslaved Virginians might be plotting their demise, the crowd grew larger and angrier as the morning wore on. The governor was acutely aware that many of the crowd were armed, and the independent company of the city was among those gathered in protest.[5]

Intent on avoiding bloodshed, city and provincial officials, including the mayor, John Dixon, and the speaker of the House of Burgesses, Peyton Randolph, quickly asserted their authority and convened a meeting at the courthouse. Not willing to risk civil war and wanting to buy time while other gentlemen might be consulted and the Continental Congress convened, anxious patriot gentlemen in the capital reasserted a modicum of control. They calmed the crowd and carried a motion to assemble the Common Hall (equivalent to a city council) and prepare a remonstrance to present to the governor "in a decent and respectful manner." Randolph, Dixon, and others then met with the governor and presented the address of the Common Hall, to wit, that the townspeople were exasperated at his actions because of their timing in the midst of rumors of a slave uprising. Reluctant

---

Concord (New York, 2002). For New York, see Edward Countryman, *A People in Revolution: The American Revolution and Political Society, 1760–1790* (New York, 1981), esp. part 1. For Pennsylvania, see Steven Rosswurm, *Arms, Country, and Class: The Philadelphia Militia and the "Lower Sort" during the American Revolution, 1775–1783* (New Brunswick, N.J., 1987); Richard Alan Ryerson, *The Revolution Is Now Begun: The Radical Committees of Philadelphia, 1765–1776* (Philadelphia, 1978).

5. Peyton Randolph for himself and the Corporation of the City of Williamsburg to Mann Page, Jr., Lewis Willis, and Benjamin Grymes, Jr., Apr. 27, 1775, *Rev. Va.*, III, 64; *Va. Gaz.* (Purdie), Apr. 21, 1775, supplement; Municipal Common Hall to Governor Dunmore, Apr. 21, 1775, *Va. Gaz.* (D and H), Apr. 22, 1775; *Rev. Va.*, III, 5.

to challenge the governor's authority directly, they noted the inhabitants thought Dunmore's actions "extremely alarming" because they feared for the "internal security" of the town. The genteel delegation issued only a mild challenge to Dunmore in the end—"guardians of the city," the writers of the address "humbly" asked the governor to explain his actions.[6]

Dunmore was surprised that the address was "milder in terms" than he had expected, but he still felt affronted, and particularly "incensed" that the citizens of Williamsburg had flown to arms. Despite the mild terms of the address, he thought that the actions of the crowd were at worst treasonable, at best, "one of the highest insults, that could be offered to the authority of his majt'ys Governt." Their supplicating posture notwithstanding, the delegation came to the palace and presented its address "under the muskets of their independent company which they left only at a little distance from my house." Believing the delegation purposefully used the threat of the mob, Dunmore turned the tables on his visitors. First, he told them that he had seized the powder because he had actually heard of "an insurrection in a neighbouring county." Protesting the innocence of his actions, he gave his "word and honour" that, should it be needed upon any insurrection, he would deliver it "in a half hour." He was "surprised to hear that the people were under arms on this occasion" but that it was not "prudent to put powder into their hands in such a situation." Striking at their most vulnerable point, Dunmore linked the threat of a slave insurrection with the continued insult of the mob under arms. The governor was willing to help put down any slave insurrection—but only if white Virginians desisted in their threats to royal government.[7]

The delegation was chastened by the threat. Primed by reports of slave

6. Municipal Common Hall to Governor Dunmore, Apr. 22, 1775, *Va. Gaz.* (D and H), Apr. 22, 1775; *Rev. Va.,* III, 5; Peyton Randolph for himself and the Corporation of the City of Williamsburg to Mann Page, Jr., Lewis Willis, and Benjamin Grymes, Jr., Apr. 27, 1775, *Rev. Va.,* III, 64; *Va. Gaz.* (Purdie), Apr. 21, 1775, supplement. Civis later praised the "worthy inhabitants" who had helped calm those "who, in an unguarded moment, were for carrying things the farthest." *Va. Gaz.* (D and H), Apr. 29, 1775, supplement.

7. *Rev. Va.,* III, 5; Dunmore to General Gage, May 1, 1775, K. G. Davies, ed., *Documents of the American Revolution, 1770-1783* (Shannon, 1972-1981), IX, 110; Governor Dunmore's reply to the Municipal Common Hall, Apr. 22, 1775, *Va. Gaz.* (D and H), Apr. 22, 1775; Peyton Randolph for himself and the Corporation of the City of Williamsburg to Mann Page, Jr., Lewis Willis, and Benjamin Grymes, Jr., Apr. 27, 1775, *Rev. Va.,* III, 64; *Va. Gaz.* (Purdie), Apr. 21, 1775, supplement.

uprisings, the delegates were all too ready to believe Dunmore's explanation. Peyton Randolph later reported that the governor had told them of an alarm of insurrection "from the County of Surry, which at first seem'd too well founded." More willing to suppress an incipient slave revolt than openly instigate a conflict with the governor, Williamsburg officials quickly backed off. Though acknowledging that Dunmore's response was not "more explicit and favourable," the delegation hurried back to the waiting crowd and did its best to reassure them and get them to disperse.[8]

Despite Randolph's and other leaders' best efforts, however, they could not control the angry crowds. Though civilian patriot leaders appeared anxious about Dunmore's threats, militants in the Williamsburg vicinity were only further angered. Though the crowd dispersed after hearing what Randolph and his delegation had to report, a large group assembled again that evening upon hearing a rumor that royal soldiers from the *Magdalen* were advancing on the city. Town officials once more calmed the crowd and persuaded it to go home. The local independent company of volunteers then took the lead. Under more popular firebrands, including a young George Nicholas, the son of the colony's treasurer, and William Finnie, the son of a former keeper of the Raleigh Tavern, the volunteer company stayed throughout the crisis and kept a vigilant—and mischievously provoking—watch on Dunmore and his household. They spread word of Dunmore's actions throughout the nearby countryside, and they fueled rumors that Dunmore was not only fortifying the palace but also arming his own black servants and some Indian hostages he had brought back from his recent war against the Shawnees. More people poured into the town over the next day or two. Dunmore angrily reported that parties of "armed Men were continually coming into town from the adjacent Counties," offering "fresh insults." While Dunmore grew irritated, civilian officials fretted. Both recognized that the volunteer company had become an authority in its own right and appeared to have the support of the townspeople.[9]

8. Peyton Randolph for himself and the Corporation of the City of Williamsburg to Mann Page, Jr., Lewis Willis, and Benjamin Grymes, Jr., Apr. 27, 1775, *Rev. Va.*, III, 64.

9. John Pendleton Kennedy, ed., *Journals of the House of Burgesses of Virginia, 1773-1776* (Richmond, Va., 1905), xviii (hereafter cited as *JHB, 1773-1776*); "Report of the Committee to Inquire into the Causes of the Late Disturbances and Commotions in the Country," June 1, 1775, in "The Proceedings of the House of Burgesses of Virginia" (Williamsburg: Alexander Purdie), in William Sumner

Dunmore responded first. Two days after he seized the powder, exasperated by constant harassment, especially by the volunteer company, Dunmore ordered the arrest of Finnie and Nicholas, who he believed were the root of resistance to him. That civilian officials had allowed the tavernkeeper's son Finnie in particular "to go at large" and insult royal government was particularly galling. He went further. He would, "by the living God, declare Freedom to the Slaves, and reduce the City of Williamsburg to Ashes" if further "injury or insult" came to him or other royal officials. He would have "a Majority of white People and all the Slaves on the side of the Government" and would quickly "depopulate the whole Country." With civilian officials standing helpless, more militant patriots had pushed the governor to threaten outright war with the rebels and employ the power of their most potentially destructive opponents.[10]

Dunmore split the patriot ranks. While many formerly leading patriots stood paralyzed or tried to bridge the growing rift, many others used the opportunity to score a major propaganda victory over the governor. Newspaper accounts of the seizure emphasized fears of slave insurrections to whip up exasperation with the British and enthusiasm for the patriot cause. Most reprinted the address of the Common Hall to Dunmore and stressed patriot leaders' pleas to the governor to return the powder in the face of the "diabolical notions" in "the minds of our slaves." They contrasted the mild address of the supplicating patriots to the aggressiveness of the governor. Only the coldest-hearted white Virginians could fail to empathize with the "peculiar and critical" plight of the now defenseless capital city. Other, more private "loose Report[s]" of the events in Williamsburg also juxtaposed the governor's extraordinary seizure of the powder with rumors of "disturbances in the City, by the *Slaves*."[11]

Such reports had the intended effect. As news of Dunmore's threats spread amid rumors and authentic reports of slave uprisings, many hundreds, if not thousands, of white Virginians took up arms against the gov-

Jenkins, comp., *Records of the States of the United States* (LoC, 1949), reel Va. Ib, reel 3, 1773–1781, 231–237; Dunmore to General Gage, May 1, 1775, Davies, ed., *Documents of the American Revolution,* IX, 110. For Finnie and Nicholas, see *Rev. Va.,* V, 195; Selby, *Revolution in Virginia,* 46, 48, 62, 63, 283, 315.

10. *JHB, 1773–1776,* xviii; "Report on the Causes of the Late Disturbances," June 1, 1775, Jenkins, comp., *Records of the States,* 231–237.

11. *Va. Gaz.* (D and H), Apr. 22, 1775; *Va. Gaz.* (Pinkney), Apr. 21, 1775, supplement; Pendleton to George Washington, Apr. 21, 1775, *Papers of Pendleton,* I, 102.

ernor. Most men joined existing independent companies of volunteers or created their own. Whites in Chesterfield County, for example, threatened on one side by rebellious slaves and on the other by a governor who seemed determined to encourage such revolt, immediately raised a volunteer company and began training. In Hanover County, local leaders later reported that the governor's actions caused "commotions" that were "heightened and increased by his threatening to enfranchise the slaves," and county residents immediately formed a volunteer company. Angry farmers also raised volunteer companies in Henrico, Sussex, Nansemond, Essex, Louisa, New Kent, King William, Gloucester, and probably Amelia Counties as well as in the town of Falmouth in the days after the powder magazine incident. Within a few weeks, at least thirty-two volunteer companies were raised in whole or in part throughout Virginia. Thomas Jefferson, ruminating upon the previous two weeks, wrote in early May that "a phrenzy of revenge seems to have seized all ranks of people." Even Dunmore later admitted that he had smashed the hornet's nest: "My declaration that I would arm and set free such slaves as should assist me if I was attacked has stirred up fears in them which cannot easily subside."[12]

Like the volunteers in Williamsburg, the men joining the new indepen-

12. Thomas Jefferson to William Small, May 7, 1775, *Papers of Jefferson,* I, 165; Dunmore to Secretary of State, June 25, 1775, Davies, comp., *Documents of the American Revolution,* IX, 204. Cf. Roger Atkinson to Benson Fearon, July 22, 1775, Roger Atkinson Account Book, UVa; Testimony of Thomas Mitchell (Louisa), James Lyle and Robert Donald (Chesterfield), Archibald Ritchie (Essex), Archibald Bryce (Henrico), Archibald Govan, Thomas Evans, John Johnson, George Braikenridge (Hanover), in "Report of the Causes of the Late Disturbances," June 1, 1775, Jenkins, comp., *Records of the States;* George Hamilton to Gustavus Brown Wallace, June 5–6, 1775, Wallace Family Papers, UVa; Amelia County Committee Proceedings, May 3, 1775, *Va. Gaz.* (Purdie), May 19, 1775, supplement, *Rev. Va.,* III, 83; Sussex County Committee Proceedings, May 8, 1775, *Va. Gaz.* (Purdie), July 7, 1775, supplement, *Rev. Va.,* III, 107–108; New Kent County Committee Proceedings, May 3, 1775, *Va. Gaz.* (Purdie), May 19, 1775, supplement, *Rev. Va.,* III, 85; Officers of the Independent Companies in Williamsburg to the Norfolk Borough Committee, July 19, 1775, Gilmer Papers, VHS; Proceedings of the Gloucester County Committee, July 24, 1775, *Va. Gaz.* (Purdie), Aug. 4, 1775, *Rev. Va.,* III, 340; William C. White, "The Independent Companies of Virginia, 1774–1775," *VMHB,* LXXXVI (1978) 151; Election and Proceedings of the Mecklenburg County Committee, May 8, 1775, *Va. Gaz.* (Pinkney), June 1, 1775, *Rev. Va.,* III, 105.

dent companies looked and acted different from the gentlemen who had dominated the companies before Dunmore seized the powder, and different from civilian patriot leaders. In George Gilmer's Albemarle County, for example, membership in the volunteer company blossomed from the twenty-three who had originally signed on in or before April, to seventy-four present at a muster in June (and there was one report that nearly three hundred volunteers signed up following Dunmore's seizure). However, only twelve of the original company were present, and in the others' place stood an entirely different group of men. Of those whose property-holding can be traced, the average number of acres of land held by members of the company before April was 973; the June soldiers owned only 322 acres each. The new men also owned an average of 5 slaves, 10 cattle, and 3 horses, compared with 15, 27, and 8, respectively. Moreover, while all the men from the earlier muster for whom tax records are available owned slaves, one-third of the new group owned none at all. Gone were the white-stocking "gentlemen" volunteers. After April, descriptions of *"the damned shirtmen"* showed the majority to be wearing "an Oznaburg Shirt over their Cloathes, a belt round them with a Tommyhawk or Scalping knife." The members of the independent companies were no longer predominantly gentlemen but were more middling farmers. They looked like "a band of Assassins," according to one unfriendly report.[13]

The enlargement of the independent companies posed new problems, mainly of control and authority. Whereas gentlemen had previously dominated the resistance movement through the provincial conventions, the county committees, and even the independent companies, control slipped from their grasp after the powder incident. Even when they retained control, they came under intense popular pressure to take more radical action

13. Terms of Inlisting, Apr. 18, 1775, Gilmer Papers, VHS; "List of Volunteers Present at Muster, June 17, 1775," R. A. Brock, ed., "Papers, Military and Political, 1775-1778, of George Gilmer, M.D., of 'Pen Park,' Albemarle County, Va.," VHS, *Collections*, n.s., VI (1887), 85, and "Address to the Inhabitants of Albemarle," [fall 1775], 122; Albemarle County Personal Property and Land Tax Records, 1782, LiVi (property tax records from 1782 are available for thirty of the sixty-two new men, and land records for twenty-one); James Parker to Charles Steuart, June 12, 1775, "Letters from Virginia, 1774-1781," *Magazine of History*, III (1906), 159. Rhys Isaac, "Dramatizing the Ideology of Revolution: Popular Mobilization in Virginia, 1774-1776," *WMQ*, 3d Ser., XXXIII (1976), 379–383, provides an excellent description of the "popularization" of mobilization in the days and weeks immediately following Dunmore's raid on the magazine.

against Dunmore. If local officials in Williamsburg struggled with this problem immediately following Dunmore's seizure of the powder, the problem became more general as news of Dunmore's provocations spread and more and more ordinary Virginians joined local volunteer companies. As civilian officials in Williamsburg tried to rein in their militants, new reports of volunteer companies gathering around the colony panicked patriot leaders in the capital.

One of the largest gatherings of men took place in Fredericksburg, eighty-five miles north of Williamsburg. Within a week of the seizure of the powder by Dunmore, as many as fourteen companies from around the Northern Neck and northern piedmont area responded to a call from officers of the Fredericksburg volunteer company to rendezvous before marching to Williamsburg. There, thousands of men mustered, sent offers of assistance to Williamsburg, and began to "debate" the propriety of marching on the capital to "revenge the insult."[14]

The gathering tested the authority of patriot leaders. Some groups, like the volunteer company from Spotsylvania County, claimed they marched for Fredricksburg after they were directed to do so by their local civilian county committee. Others, like the Prince William volunteer company, spontaneously embodied and decided themselves whether to march. After receiving a letter from the Fredericksburg contingent asking for support, the officers of the Prince William volunteers "immediately called together this Company and had the *vote* put, whether they would march to *Williamsburgh* for the purposes mentioned in that Letter, which was carried unanimously." And, though the meeting at Fredericksburg was probably called and convened by more militant patriot leaders in the area, it quickly degenerated into a rather large campfire debate. At least 600 and possibly 2,000 "well armed" men met at Fredericksburg, reportedly both "Rich and poor." The volunteers formed an oversized "Council" of 102 men that met continuously for two or three days, debating whether to march on Williamsburg. Discussion was heated: "The propriety of such a step was

14. Randolph, *History of Virginia,* ed. Shaffer, 220; Charles Yates to Samuel Martin, May 11, 1775, Charles Yates Letterbook, UVa; Michael Wallace to Gustavus Wallace Brown, May 14, 1775, Wallace Family Papers, UVa; Peyton Randolph to Mann Page, Jr., Lewis Willis, and Benjamin Grymes, Jr., Apr. 27, 1775, *Rev. Va.,* III, 63–64; James Madison to William Bradford, May 9, 1775, *Papers of Madison,* I, 144–145; "Proceedings of a Council in Fredericksburg," Apr. 29, 1775, *Va. Gaz.* (Pinkney), May 11, 1775, *Rev. Va.,* III, 70–71.

warmly agitated and weighty arguments adduced both for and against it." Along the edges of the meeting, hundreds more volunteers held their own councils and debates, presumably reporting their results to their respective representatives at the main meeting. Following the precedent set in the independent companies, new volunteers demanded a vote for any actions contemplated. All volunteers, "Rich and poor," would have to have a say.[15]

In the end, the council in Fredericksburg sent three officers, along with men from other companies, down to Williamsburg to find out what was going on. The officers told the inhabitants of Williamsburg that they were dissatisfied with the town delegation's settlement with Dunmore; their volunteers were angry over Dunmore's actions and could not possibly "rest satisfied with his Excellency's answer to the address of the corporation of the city of Williamsburg" in which he had promised to give the powder back if they needed it. They were ready and willing to come to their assistance, with at least two thousand men "ready to march down upon a moment's notice."[16]

Officials in Williamsburg, however, quickly stopped the Fredericksburg contingent from marching on the capital. Afraid of further trouble with the governor, Peyton Randolph intercepted the officers and told them that "the

15. Testimony of Robert Gilchrist and Patrick Kennan of Caroline County, in "Report of the Causes of the Late Disturbances," June 1, 1775, Jenkins, comp., *Records of the States;* William Grayson to George Washington, Apr. 26, 1775, Peter Force, ed., *American Archives: Consisting of a Collection of Authentick Records, State Papers, Debates, and Letters and Other Notices of Publick Affairs* . . . (Washington, D.C., 1837-1853), 4th Ser., II, 395; Charles Yates to Samuel Martin, May 11, 1775, Charles Yates Letterbook, UVa; Michael Wallace to Gustavus Wallace Brown, May 14, 1775, Wallace Family Papers, UVa; Peyton Randolph to Mann Page, Jr., Lewis Willis, and Benjamin Grymes, Jr., Apr. 27, 1775, *Rev. Va.,* III, 63-64; Madison to William Bradford, May 9, 1775, *Papers of Madison,* I, 144–145; "Proceedings of a Council in Fredericksburg," April 29, 1775, *Va. Gaz.* (Pinkney), May 11, 1775, *Rev. Va.,* III, 70-71; Hugh Mercer et al. to William Grayson, Apr. 24, 1775, Force, ed., *American Archives,* 4th Ser., II, 395. Edmund Pendleton later "suppose[d]" that there were about one thousand men gathered in Fredericksburg (Pendleton to Joseph Chew, June 15, 1775, *Papers of Pendleton,* I, 110). The role and membership of the county committees is discussed in Dale Edward Benson, "Wealth and Power in Virginia, 1774-1776: A Study of the Organization of Revolt" (Ph.D. diss., University of Maine, 1970).

16. *Va. Gaz.* (D and H), Apr. 29, 1775; Peyton Randolph to Mann Page, Jr., Lewis Willis, and Benjamin Grymes, Jr., Apr. 27, 1775, *Rev. Va.,* III, 64.

people of Williamsburg" were, "unexpectedly," "quite peaceable." Randolph sent the officers back to Fredericksburg that same evening with a letter drawn up by himself and other civilian officials on behalf of the city. The letter related the events of the past week and emphasized their belief in Dunmore's pledge to give the powder back so soon as it was needed, provided that the armed citizens disperse peacefully. Randolph told the volunteers that Dunmore's honor was at stake, that he would not be *"compell'd"* to give back the powder but would "cheerfully" do so if peace was restored. Thus the volunteers ought to "desist" and disperse. Town officials thought it best if the matter was "quieted" immediately and the town and colony were restored to "perfect Tranquility." Randolph concluded, warning, "Violent measures may produce effects, which God only knows the consequences of."[17]

The Fredericksburg officers brought the letter back to their volunteers. Uneasy and unconvinced, the volunteers were persuaded to disband only when they met with Virginia's congressional delegation, on its way to Philadelphia to the Second Continental Congress. The delegation, like Williamsburg officials, appealed for calm and told the volunteers that they ought to give Congress a chance to deliberate before taking further action. In their printed resolution circulated by the Virginia newspapers, the volunteers were dispersing to avoid "the horrors of a civil war" and to "heal our mutual wounds . . . preferring peaceable measures whilst the least hope of reconciliation remains." Clearly dissatisfied, however, and contrary to Randolph's assurances of the governor's good faith, they declared his actions were "impolitic, and justly alarming to the good people of this colony," and tended "to destroy all confidence in Government and to widen the unhappy breach between Great Britain and her colonies." Dunmore's actions were "ill timed and totally unnecessary." Though it was publicly reported that the final determination of the council of one hundred was "read at the head of each company" and "was cordially and unanimously approved," private reports suggested that there was considerable disagreement. One observer noted that militants among the Fredericksburg volunteers still wanted to march; only with "some difficulty they were stopped from going to call the Govr. to Accot. and prevailed on to return to their homes." The volunteers in their public address also warned that, if the "violent and hostile proceedings of an arbitrary Ministry" were not brought to

17. Ibid.

an end, they would, "at a moment's warning . . . re-assemble, and, by force of arms" defend the "laws, the liberty, and rights" of Virginia—and "any sister colony."[18]

But, while the volunteers at Fredericksburg debated whether to march, Dunmore issued his own ultimatum, on April 28, the day after Randolph's appeal for calm. "In hourly expectation" of the appearance of more independent companies, Dunmore declared, "If a large Body of People came below *Ruffin's Ferry* (a place about thirty Miles from this City) that he would immediately enlarge his plan, and carry it into Execution." "More than once," the governor reportedly said, "he should not carry these plans into Execution unless he was attacked." Dunmore's first threat to arm enslaved Virginians against their masters might have been dismissed by some as impetuous. Dunmore's repeated declaration confirmed white Virginians' worst fears that he was serious about carrying out his threat if provoked. A few days later, Dunmore added the threat of native American attack to his challenge, raising the stakes further for men of property and those who had a "love of order." If the "present ferment" did not subside, Virginians would be well advised to consider the "dangers to which [they were] exposed from a savage enemy; who, from the most recent advices . . . are ready to renew their hostilities against the people of this country."[19]

Dunmore's repeated threats frayed the nerves of some patriot leaders but only energized militants. Showing less restraint than their counterparts in Fredericksburg, the rapidly expanding company of volunteers from Albemarle, after receiving advice from the leaders of the Fredericksburg volunteers to disband, were still "at a loss what to do." The county committee had told them that they were under civilian command and "should not be led to duty without the voice of the committee." However, on this occasion "no committee could be had, members not attending." The majority of the company therefore voted in favor of marching to Williamsburg. They

18. "Proceedings of a Council in Fredericksburg," Apr. 29, 1775, *Va. Gaz.* (Pinkney), May 11, 1775, *Rev. Va.,* III, 71; Charles Yates to Samuel Martin, May 11, 1775, Charles Yates Letterbook, UVa.

19. *JHB, 1773–1776,* xviii, and William Pasteur, deposition, June 14, 1775, 231; Royal Proclamation, May 3, 1775, *Va. Gaz.* (Pinkney), May 4, 1775, *Rev. Va.,* III, 81. On the governor's threats to use native American allies, see Chester Raymond Young, ed., *Westward into Kentucky: The Narrative of Daniel Trabue* (Lexington, Ky., 1981), 42; Dartmouth to Dunmore, July 12, 1775, Davies, ed., *Documents of the American Revolution,* IX, 45.

were determined "to demand satisfaction of Dunmore for the powder, and his threatening to fix his standard and call over the Negroes."[20]

The volunteers of Albemarle did not just sidestep the issue of civilian control; they also ignored the voices of moderation. When they voted to continue their march—despite being told to turn back by Williamsburg officials—two men in the company dissented. John Coles and David Rodes, two prominent and wealthy county committee members who had been and would remain staunch patriots, voted against marching for the capital on the grounds that it had not been sanctioned by their local county committee or by Williamsburg officials. They paid dearly for their hesitation. "The opinion of the Comp'y" was that they "ought to be drum'd out," and they unceremoniously were. Their treatment was meant to serve as "an example" precisely because they were from the traditional county elite. Ominously, the company believed that such behavior "might be of dangerous consequence" coming from such men and wanted to send out a warning to similar "people of such conspicuous characters" in the county. Coles's and Rodes's wealth and status and possible influence, then, became a liability. Employing the rhetoric and weapons of the hitherto gentry-led resistance movement—public ostracism—the volunteer company saw no need for deference, sending out a very public signal to rich and poor alike.[21]

20. "Resolutions of the Independent Company of Albemarle," [Apr. 11, 1775], Proceedings of the Independent Company of Volunteers, [Apr. 29, 1775], Albemarle County Committee Resolutions, [Apr. 1775], Gilmer Papers, VHS. Cf. *Rev. Va.*, III, 9, 71–72n; note by George Gilmer on the marching of the Albemarle Independent Company, *Rev. Va.*, III, 52n. Williamsburg officials redoubled their efforts to stop the volunteers, fearing the consequences. Robert Carter Nicholas, the treasurer of the colony and a patriot leader, allegedly "in a terrible panic," began "writing letters over all the country." An unsympathetic James Parker saw the irony in how Nicholas was now forced to try to quash rebellion in the colony. Parker wryly noted that the treasurer was finding it more difficult to extinguish a flame than kindle it. James Parker to Charles Steuart, May 6, 1775, "Letters from Virginia, 1774–1781," *Magazine of History,* III (1906), 158–159.

21. Significantly, the county committee, of which Coles and Rodes were members, tried to control the damage done by voting to exonerate the two men from any wrongdoing at a later meeting. Albemarle Committee to the Gentlemen Volunteers of the Williamsburg Independent Company, May 31, 1775, *Rev. Va.,* III, 177; Proceedings of the Independent Company of Volunteers, [Apr. 29, 1775], Albemarle County Committee Resolutions, [April 1775], Gilmer Papers, VHS. Cf. *Rev. Va.*, III, 69–70, 71–72n; Albemarle County Committee Proceedings, May 31, 1775,

Such independent action alarmed many prominent Virginians. Some worried that the volunteers were not under any civilian control. There was no clear chain of command either between county committees and provincial leaders or, sometimes, even between the county committees and the independent companies. With no central coordinating body such as the House of Burgesses or the extralegal conventions in session, the independence of the county committees and volunteer companies quickly contributed to rather than relieved the problems facing Williamsburg. In some places, the volunteers acted upon the recommendations of or in conjunction with the local county committee. Other groups of volunteers, such as those from Albemarle, were clearly acting more independently. Some listened to officers; others elected new officers each time they assembled. Most of the time, volunteers themselves decided what to do. They acted autonomously and democratically, asserting their own control over the developing situation. Dunmore himself summed up the problem with the volunteer companies: they had been raised "in defiance of any Authority" and therefore "pay no obedience to it, but assemble and act *as their Will directs* nor are they to be controlled even by the power which they are intended to support." Thus, at a critical juncture in the resistance movement, patriot decision making was almost entirely in the hands of militant patriots.[22]

Gilmer Papers, VHS. Coles and Rodes were both wealthy, owning, in 1782, 5,000 and 568 acres of land, respectively. Coles also owned 64 slaves, 86 head of cattle, and 45 horses. Rodes owned a more modest but not insubstantial 22 slaves, 28 cattle, and 12 horses (Albemarle County Personal Property and Land Tax Records, 1782, LiVi).

22. The independent company from Spotsylvania County repeatedly acted under the direction of its county committee, as had a company from Louisa. Because at this point the county committees were generally dominated by the traditional elite of the counties, cooler heads often prevailed when the committees exercised control over the volunteers. But many county committees, such as the Norfolk committee, specifically denied the volunteers were under their control. For Spotsylvania, see "Report of the Causes of the Late Disturbances," June 1, 1775, Jenkins, ed., *Records of the States;* for Louisa, see "Receipt" signed by Nathan Hill, Watson Family Papers, UVa. Norfolk County Committee Proceedings, May 4, 1775, *Rev. Va.,* III, 89; "Resolutions of the Independent Company of Albemarle," [Apr. 11, 1775], Gilmer Papers, VHS; Dunmore to Dartmouth, June 25–27, 1775, CO 5/1353, PRO (emphasis added); Royal Proclamation, May 6, 1775, *Va. Gaz.* (D and H), May 13, 1775, *Rev. Va.,* III, 100–101. Cf. Pendleton to Washington, Apr. 21, 1775, and Pendleton to William Woodford, May 30, June 14, 1775, *Papers of Pendleton,*

One such group was a large contingent of volunteers from Hanover County, led by the popular and hot-headed Patrick Henry. The Hanover volunteers resolved to act first and only later seek the county committee's approval. They joined up with the volunteers from Albemarle County as well as contingents from King William, Orange, and other neighboring counties. By early May, many volunteers had heard news of Lexington and Concord and considered themselves in a state of war with royal government already. Under Henry's leadership they decided to press on toward Williamsburg and demand retribution from Dunmore. Officials there, still desperate to avoid a confrontation, sent "messenger after messenger" to meet the volunteers and ask them to stop. Henry finally did pause, but only long enough to send out a small detachment of volunteers to seize the receiver general, Richard Corbin, and force payment for the powder. After that plan failed, Burgess Carter Braxton intervened and negotiated a settlement. In the end, Henry and his volunteers were satisfied with a promissory note from Thomas Nelson, Jr., a councillor, for the full value of the powder. After offering further protection to the inhabitants of Williamsburg, Henry agreed to persuade his men to disperse only when Robert Carter Nicholas wrote him that he had "no apprehension of the necessity or propriety of the proferred service."[23]

Though Nicholas had again prevented a clash of arms, it was too late; irreparable damage had already been done to provincial relations with Dunmore. Believing that upward of two thousand volunteers were about to de-

---

I, 102, 103, 109; testimony of Robert Gilchrist and Patrick Kennan of Caroline County, in "Report of the Causes of the Late Disturbances," June 1, 1775, Jenkins, comp., *Records of the States;* Caroline County Committee Proceedings, Apr. 29, 1775, *Rev. Va.,* III, 70. Cf. Margherita Marchione, ed., *Philip Mazzei: My Life and Wanderings,* trans. S. Eugene Scalia (Morristown, N.J., 1980), 216–217.

23. Madison to William Bradford, May 9, 1775, *Papers of Madison,* I, 144–145; James Parker to Charles Steuart, May 6, 1775, "Letters from Virginia," *Magazine of History,* III (1906), 158–159; testimony of Dr. William Pasteur before the Virginia convention, "Virginia Legislative Papers, 1774–1775," *VMHB,* XIII (1905–1906), 49–50; *Va. Gaz.* (Purdie), May 5, 1775, supplement; testimony of Archibald Govan, Thomas Evans, John Johnson, George Braikenridge of Hanover County, in "Report of the Causes of the Late Disturbances," Jenkins, comp., *Records of the States;* Hanover County Committee Proceedings, May 9, 1775, *Rev. Va.,* III, 111; William Wirt, *The Life of Patrick Henry,* rev. ed. (Hartford, Conn., 1832), 158; *Rev. Va.,* III, 7–9. Cf. Emory G. Evans, *Thomas Nelson of Yorktown: Revolutionary Virginian* (Williamsburg, Va., 1975), 47.

scend on the capital, the governor sent his wife and children aboard the H.M.S. *Fowey* off Yorktown and on May 1 appealed for reinforcements from General Thomas Gage and Admiral Samuel Graves in Boston. He also made clearer and more public his threat to arm the slaves to spread "Devastation wherever I can reach." It was already rumored that he had become more belligerent because he had been reinforced by numbers of enslaved Virginians who had begun to make their way to him. One newspaper account noted that "several negroes made a tender of their services" as the volunteer companies approached Williamsburg. Though Dunmore reportedly turned them away, one early historian who had firsthand accounts said that the governor began taking in runaway enslaved Virginians in retaliation for Henry's march. Reputedly, "Parties of negroes mounted guard every night" at the palace. Dunmore also fortified the palace and, upon hearing of Henry's maneuvers, ordered forty marines and sailors from the *Fowey* to the palace, swearing that he would fire upon the town "the very moment one hostile Virginian should enter it." When Henry asked the York county committee to stop Dunmore's retreat if necessary, Captain George Montagu of the *Fowey* threatened to attack Yorktown. Dunmore, fed up with Henry and his "deluded Followers," outlawed the patriot leader. He declared it treasonable to give aid or countenance to either Henry or "any other Persons concerned in such unwarrantable Combinations." The independent companies had put themselves in a "Posture of War," Dunmore complained, "exciting the People to join in these outrageous and rebellious Practices," and brought "great Terrour" to all who valued the "least Security for the Life or Property of any Man." Enslaved Virginians and militant patriots, then, brought the imperial crisis to a deadly impasse.[24]

• • • Some Virginians were quite content to capitalize on events to increase popular support for the patriot movement. Many planters and especially more radical patriot leaders thought that the governor's latest machinations would rouse all white Virginians to the dangers of further inaction.

24. Dunmore to General Gage, May 1, 1775, Davies, ed., *Documents of the American Revolution*, IX, 110; *Va. Gaz.* (Pinkney), May 4, 1775; John Burk, *The History of Virginia, from Its First Settlement to the Present Day* (Petersburg, Va., 1804–1816), III, 407, 409; *Rev. Va.*, III, 9; George Montagu to Thomas Nelson, Sr., May 4, 1775, *Rev. Va.*, III, 91; Royal Proclamation, May 6, 1775, *Va. Gaz.* (D and H), May 13, 1775, *Rev. Va.*, III, 100–101. Cf. *Va. Gaz.* (Pinkney), June 1, 1775.

Dunmore had forfeited the "Confidence of the People not so much for having taken the Powder as for the declaration he made of raising and freeing the Slaves," according to one gentleman. Another wrote about the "treachery" of the governor who had been held in high esteem until it was discovered he had been writing inflammatory letters to England, and worse: "You will see what Diabolical (horrible to relate) measures he fell upon by Robing the Magazine of powder, the Muskets of locks. . . . Stiring up the Negroes to Rebellion etc. etc." Henry called the powder incident a "fortunate circumstance" that would "arouse the people." "You may in vain mention to them the duties upon tea, etc. These things, they will say, do not affect them. But tell them of the robbery of the magazine, and that the next step will be to disarm them, and they will be ready to fly to arms to defend themselves."[25]

Many other prominent Virginians were taken aback by the speed at which relations between provincial leaders and the governor had deteriorated. They obviously worried that Dunmore might actually encourage enslaved Virginians to join him against their masters. But so too were they concerned about the effects of Dunmore's public threats on enslaved Virginians in general, which could provoke individual and collective rebellion among them or even a massive uprising. Others were simply desperate to avoid an outright conflict with royal authority. Finally, some moderates also feared that they might provoke Dunmore prematurely, before they knew whether they had the full support of their countrymen and other colonies. Patriots like Robert Carter Nicholas worried that they could not take on Dunmore and the weight of the British army on ther own. For all these reasons, many "Flegmatic" leading gentlemen were angered by "Mr. Henry's Manoeuvre" and were anxious to avoid making a bad situation worse. Henry's "rash disorderly action," noted one Williamsburg observer, "has lost him the Confidence and Esteem of most sensible moderate Men."[26]

25. Madison to Bradford, May 9, 1775, *Papers of Madison,* I, 145; Benjamin Waller, deposition, Committee on the Late Disturbances, report, June 14, 1775, *JHB, 1773–1776,* 232; Rawleigh Downman to Samuel Athawes, July 10, 1775, Rawleigh Downman Letterbook, 1760–1780 (transcripts from the LoC), CWFL; William Wirt Henry, *Patrick Henry: Life, Correspondence, and Speeches* (New York, 1891), I, 279. Cf. Gloucester County Committee Proceedings, Apr. 25, 1775, *Va. Gaz.* (Purdie), Apr. 28, 1775, *Rev. Va.,* III, 61.

26. Pendleton to Joseph Chew, June 15, 1775, *Papers of Pendleton,* I, 110; Ed-

Unusually, divisions among gentlemen over recent events found their way into newspapers, even in the very midst of the problems with Dunmore. Even before Henry's march, "Civis" appealed for calm: some had carried the "rage of patriotism" too far—"so far as even to occasion a tumult directed to that end." After Henry's march, a "True Patriot" in the *Virginia Gazette* thought Henry and his followers, through "misinformation, and their zeal . . . may have been precipitated into acts as pernicious in their consequences as they were intended to be salutary." But the anonymous writer was more concerned that no legal representative body had sanctioned Henry's actions. If Henry and his followers would not "revise their proceedings," then at least they must subject their "zeal" to the sound judgment of "a provincial or general congress" (presumably governed by more moderate patriots). If then their actions were to be found "derogatory to the line of conduct which ought religiously to have been adhered to," there must be "concessions and reparation, for damages, as may be perfectly consistent with sound policy and the strictest justice." Another newspaper address in the *Virginia Gazette* appealed to the "middling and lower classes of people" for continued support but criticized "rashness and violence" as potentially "destructive." Successful resistance to Britain would be achieved only by discouraging "every kind of violence" that would "disunite us, and . . . involve us in confusion" and by maintaining "peace, order, and the secuity of our property."[27]

Henry and his volunteers had clearly touched a nerve. Not only were their actions considered rash, but they had also threatened the sanctity of property. As early as the summer of 1774, the "British American" pointed out in the *Virginia Gazette* the dangers of resistance to the wealthy. "Even a slight commotion may expose part of your wealth to the ravages of the populace, or the plunder of a licentious army." Now the prophecy might come true. Certainly more conservative men saw Henry's actions as a precursor to an assault on any and all private property. The attorney general,

ward Stabler to Israel Pemberton, May 16, 1775, Photostat Collection, CWFL. Civis also worried about division in the patriot ranks, noting the good effect the powder incident had in engaging "the attention of us all," but worried that the response meant that the "effects it has produced in our minds seem not to be of the same impression." *Va. Gaz.* (D and H), Apr. 29, 1775, supplement.

27. *Va. Gaz.* (D and H), Apr. 29, 1775, supplement; *Va. Gaz.* (Pinkney), May 11, 1775; Brutus, "Address," [May 15, 1775], *Va. Gaz.* (Purdie), July 14, 1775, *Rev. Va.*, III, 126, 131, 132.

John Randolph, for example, had allegedly argued that the merchants of the colony would not meet in the capital as planned because they were not "such fools as to come to Williamsburg, with money in their pockets, when Patrick Henry, or any other set of men, might come and take their money from them." Asked whether he thus thought Henry would take any person's private property, Randolph answered, "He might as well do it as to have extorted the money in the manner he did from the receiver-general."[28]

Even many *patriot* gentlemen were uncertain whether to endorse Henry and his followers' actions. Henry himself believed many would frown upon his role in the march. Before he left to attend Congress, he wrote to Francis Lightfoot Lee justifying his conduct, as he expected "an Attempt may be made to condemn the Measure and misrepresent my Conduct." He was right. After divisive debate, the members of the Caroline county committee, for example, finally commended "the Zeal and good intention of the Party" led by Patrick Henry, "tho' they disapproved the measure"—a decision that "much pleased" the chairman, Edmund Pendleton. Pendleton and the Caroline county committee represented a third group of patriot sentiment. They were keen to maintain popular outrage against Dunmore in order to garner support for the patriot movement, but they were anxious to control it and maintain authority over the situation.[29]

28. [Thomson Mason], "The British American, VII," *Va. Gaz.* (Rind), July 14, 1774, *Rev. Va.,* I, 184; William Eaton to Alexander Purdie: A Public Deposition, *Va. Gaz.* (Purdie), July 21, 1775, *Rev. Va.,* III, 323. Another conservative, Ralph Wormeley, Jr., who had been shocked by the "wickedness and immorality" of the House of Burgesses in June 1775, was also alarmed at popular action: "When popular fury break forth, unrestrained by law, uncontrolled by authority, unopposed by force, it is not easy to say, to what excess, it will tower" (*Rev. Va.,* IV, 36).

29. Henry to Francis Lightfoot Lee, May 8, 1775, Paul P. Hoffman, ed., *Lee Family Papers, 1742-1795* (microfilm) (Charlottesville, Va., 1966); Pendleton to William Woodford, May 30, 1775, June 14, 1775, *Papers of Pendleton,* I, 103, 109. Pendleton summed up the range of feelings among patriot leaders at the beginning of June. "The Crisis of our Fate in the present and unhappy Contest seems approaching nearer than may be imagined by us," Pendleton told a correspondent. "In such times there will be as great Variety of Sentiments as Constitutions, among those who have the same end in view." He summarized them: "The Sanguine are for rash Measures without consideration, the Flegmatic to avoid that extreme are afraid to move at all, while a third Class take the middle way and endeavor by tempering the first sort and bringing the latter into action to draw all together to a

Patriot gentlemen like Pendleton strove to establish a middle ground over which they could still exercise some control. Landon Carter found himself in this position when a company of volunteers from his home county of Richmond wanted to march to Williamsburg, and, keen to assert his authority, he addressed them. Recognizing its treasonous nature, Carter first made it clear that he had not sanctioned the move to march on the capital but, in an effort to maintain his authority, assured the volunteers of his support. Clumsily reasoning that the powder was the colony's, he assured the company that they were marching only to recover "what is most essentially your own": the "whole world not arbitrarily bent on a flagrant injustice, must Commend you." But Carter sanctioned only what appeared inevitable, recognizing the danger in unleashing "the mob." A slippery slope beckoned, were the volunteers not carefully briefed and kept harnessed. "When you have made that recovery, Secure it the best you can, and be contented." Reasserting his authority and his fellow patriot leaders', Carter admonished: "It is not your business as you are to do anything more." How well Carter's plea went down among them is impossible to tell, though their willingness to risk their lives in recovering the powder probably gave them some justification to think that it was indeed their "business" as much as anyone else's, especially the reluctant Carter's. Carter himself no doubt believed that he had done his part. But the uneasiness and uncertainty his address betrays surely stemmed from his knowledge that sanctioning the subversion of royal authority was also opening the door to the subversion of his own.[30]

But the militants won the day. James Madison noted that, though the Virginia delegates would disapprove of Henry's actions, they had "gained him great honor in the most spirited parts of the Country." Letters of support from different counties quickly began to reach Henry and the *Gazette*. The committees of Spotsylvania, Albemarle, Louisa, Caroline, Culpeper,

---

Steddy, 'tho Active Point of defense." Pendleton to Joseph Chew, June 15, 1775, *Papers of Pendleton,* I, 110.

30. "Address to The Independent Company or Company of Volunteers of Richmond County," Apr. 28, [1775], Sabine Hall Papers, UVa. We don't even know whether the militant volunteers stuck around long enough to listen to Carter's advice. There is no reference to the event in the diary. Cf. Michael A. McDonnell, "The King is Dead! Long Live the King," *Australasian Journal of American Studies,* XXIV (2005–2006), 59–82.

Orange, and Hanover Counties all sent in their approval of the Hanover volunteers' action within a week of the event. In the newspapers, a "Ranger" quickly stifled any further discussion of the matter: no one could possibly condemn an action "which is agreed by a vast majority of, if not all the colony, to be at worst, but the ebullition of patriotism." Answering the anxiety of the True Patriot, who feared the "pernicious" consequences of Henry's actions on imperial relations, the Ranger warned more moderate patriots that it was equally or more "dangerous at this time to damp the spirit prevailing in the back counties, or circumscribe their actions within the line of meer prudence and circumspection." Gentlemen, caught between the need to maintain an apparently popular and united front and the need to maintain a modicum of control, were forced to yield—at least temporarily—to the torrent. Ranger's parting shot reminded patriot elites that the public opinion they had tried to manipulate was a two-way street.[31]

As new reports of the hostilities in Massachusetts flooded into Virginia and in the face of Dunmore's ever more vociferous threats, even Edmund Pendleton thought that the "Variety of Opinions on that Subject" made it "prudent to have it as little Agitated as may be, lest difference of Sentiment should be wrought into dissentions, very injurious to the common Cause." Jefferson inadvertently revealed the dynamic behind that thinking. Within a week of Henry's march, he confessed that resistance had spiraled out of control, so much so that "the utmost efforts of the more intelligent people hav[e] been requisite and exerted to moderate the almost ungovernable fury of the people." The "abler part" of the people had been "pushed" to support their rights in the field of reason, Jefferson protested to William Small, but "it was there alone they wished to decide the contest." The less able part of the people had carried the conflict too far. Dunmore's life had been saved only by "the intercessions of the principal people" who at length prevailed upon the volunteers "to return to their habitations." Jefferson thought it better not to expose any such divisions between the "abler part" of the people and the rest—and, in a rare move, struck out the offending passage from his final letter. The "ungovernable fury of the people" would

31. Madison to Bradford, May 9, 1775, *Papers of Madison*, I, 144–145; for committee declarations of approval and thanks, see *Rev. Va.*, III, 104, 110, 112–113, 118–119. Cf. *Rev. Va.*, III, 159–160, 172, 189, 208–209, 211, 277; "A Ranger," *Va. Gaz.* (Pinkney), June 1, 1775, *Rev. Va.*, III, 181; "A True Patriot," *Va. Gaz.* (Pinkney), May 11, 1775, *Rev. Va.*, III, 117.

now have to represent the united public opinion of the colony, including the views of his elite and more moderate patriot colleagues.[32]

• • • The extent to which the radicals had won the initiative became clearer when Dunmore made one last attempt to restore order in the colony. The governor had been instructed by London to convene a General Assembly to seek approval of a conciliatory resolution drawn up by the prime minister, Lord North. North proposed that Parliament give up its claims on the colonies if the assembly undertook to raise the required revenue itself. Perhaps hoping to take advantage of the public split in patriot ranks, Dunmore called an assembly of the Burgesses on June 1, 1775, and, though "still expecting every moment to be attacked," brought his wife and family to the palace. Hoping to further tame the volatile situation, the governor had the marines and sailors who had been stationed in Williamsburg since Henry's threatened descent removed, and, rather unusually, his council issued an address to the colony in preparation for the meeting of the Burgesses. The members of the council protested against the "licentious and ungovernable spirit that is gone forth" and asked people to consider the "probable consequences of such conduct." Reminding the Burgesses that they too had families and were propertyholders, the councillors enjoined them to take measures "most salutary and conducive for enforcing obedience to the laws" and to secure and "preserve the peace and good order of the community." Sensing a possible split between radical and conservative patriots, Dunmore and his council sought to secure conciliation by playing on the fears of the moderates.[33]

32. Pendleton to William Woodford, May 30, 1775, *Papers of Pendleton,* I, 103; Jefferson to William Small, May 7, 1775, *Papers of Jefferson,* I, 166–167n. The passage is struck out in the draft of the letter.

William Byrd described Virginia politics in a more negative but similar light. He told Sir Jeffrey Amherst on July 30, 1775, that, since his last letter to him, "Our countrymen have . . . gone from one step to another, 'till they have at last gone such daring lengths that tis now impossible to avoid a civil war. The violent, who are at present by far the most numerous, are in open rebellion, and the moderats are aw'd into silence, and have no opportunity to shew their alegiance." Marion Tinling, ed., *The Correspondence of the Three William Byrds of Westover, Virginia, 1684-1776* (Charlottesville, Va., 1977), II, 812.

33. *JHB, 1773-1776,* xxi–xxiii; Jefferson to William Small, May 7, 1775, *Papers of Jefferson,* I, 166–167n; *Rev. Va.,* III, 11–12; Selby, *Revolution in Virginia,* 41.

If this was the governor's thinking, the militants among the independent companies would again frustrate his attempts to bring quiet to the colony. A few days after the council's address, the Williamsburg volunteer company gathered and raised the stakes for the forthcoming meeting. Not only did the members reaffirm their pledge to maintain a close watch on the movements of the governor and his troops and oppose the "landing of any foreign troops in this country" as a "most dangerous attack on the liberties of this country," but they also declared that every member must *"oblige"* himself "to march, on the smallest warning, to any part of the continent, where the general cause of American liberty may demand their attendance." They drew upon the court of public opinion for their authority. Whenever action was needed, they would "consult their fellow countrymen in the different parts of this province"—rather than the county committees, or the provincial or Continental Congress. At least three other volunteer companies in the colony publicly concurred.[34]

On Thursday, June 1, 1775, the Burgesses met and, after an uneventful few days, adjourned on Saturday, June 3, until Monday. Almost immediately, trouble began again. That night, a group of men tried to break into the public magazine and were repelled by a rigged spring-loaded shotgun that wounded three. Though clearly trying to enter the powder magazine unlawfully, the blood of militants helped push moderates into more radical positions. The three newspapers assisted. Alexander Purdie's went so far as to reason that, if one of the men had been killed, the "perpetrator, or the perpetrators, of this diabolical invention, might have been justly branded with the opprobrious title of MURDERERS." John Dixon and William Hunter's paper claimed that there was a second spring gun

---

North's proposals were printed in the supplements to Pinkney's and Purdie's *Va. Gaz.* on Apr. 28, 1775, and in Dixon and Hunter's paper on Apr. 29, 1775; Governor's Council to the People of Virginia, May 15, 1775, *Va. Gaz.* (D and H), May 20, 1775. The Burgesses who sat in Williamsburg were effectively the same group that had met as the extralegal Second Virginia Convention. There had been no intervening elections. See Cynthia Miller Leonard, comp., *The General Assembly of Virginia, July 30, 1619–January 11, 1978: A Bicentennial Register of Members* (Richmond, Va., 1978), 105–107, 112–113.

34. Proceedings of a Meeting of the Williamsburg Volunteer Company, May 25, 1775, *Va. Gaz.* (Pinkney), May 25, 1775, *Rev. Va.*, III, 170; Albemarle Volunteers to Williamsburg Volunteers, June 1, 1775, *Va. Gaz.* (Pinkney), July 6, 1775, *Rev. Va.*, III, 180.

set at the magazine and accused Dunmore of contriving them. And John Pinkney's paper whipped up public anger by suggesting that Dunmore was involved in training officers throughout the colony in such deadly arts. The actions of the radicals, though unauthorized, helped again turn more moderate public opinion against the governor. Upon hearing of the affair, even the normally cautious Edmund Pendleton thought that, if Dunmore had ordered the trap, as his servants claimed, "he might well fear what he must have been conscious he deserved, Assassination."[35]

Outraged Williamsburg citizens then stormed the magazine and took what was left in it, and the town volunteer company mobilized once more amid rumors that Dunmore had again summoned reinforcements. The volunteers from Williamsburg and adjoining counties were "greatly alarmed" and "determined to attack the said Marines and Sailors if they should come" to the capital. Before leaders could meet with Dunmore, he himself fled in the middle of the night to an awaiting vessel. Dunmore had abandoned his conciliatory efforts because of the "heated and irascible temper" of the people, and his "house was kept in continual Alarm and threatened every Night with an Assault." He, his wife, and children were in "danger of falling sacrifices to the blind and unmeasurable fury which has so unaccountably seised upon the minds and understanding of great numbers of People." One observer noted that Dunmore would only return "provided the shirt men are sent away."[36]

The assembled Burgesses were angered; most of them, even conservative John Randolph, believed that Dunmore was in no real danger. However, to the last, they also tried to placate him, promising to "cheerfully" accede to "any measure that may be proposed proper to the security of yourself and family" if he would return, as this would be the "most likely means of quieting the minds of the People." Dunmore refused to budge, however, citing "commotions among the People, and their menaces and threats," which he suspected would end in "Crime." He would return only if the

35. *Va. Gaz.* (Purdie), June 9, 1775, supplement; *Va. Gaz.* (D and H), June 10, 1775; *Va. Gaz.* (Pinkney), June 8, 1775; Pendleton to Joseph Chew, June 15, 1775, *Papers of Pendleton*, I, 113.

36. *Rev. Va.*, III, 16; "Report of the Causes of the Late Disturbances," June 1, 1775, Jenkins, comp., *Records of the States;* Selby, *Revolution in Virginia*, 42–44; Dunmore to Dartmouth, June 25–27, 1775, C.O. 5/1373; *JHB, 1773–1776*, 206; James Parker to Charles Steuart, June 12, 1775, "Letters from Virginia," *Magazine of History*, III (1906), 159.

courts were reopened, he were reinstated with full powers of his office, and the independent companies were disarmed and dissolved. He refused to negotiate with patriot leaders under the threat of nearby armed citizens.[37]

In abandoning the seat of government Governor Dunmore laid the blame squarely on the shoulders of militants, but thereby lumped militants and moderates together, angering the latter. In response, the Burgesses formed a committee for inquiring into the "late disturbances and commotions in the country" and, in defense of themselves, justified the actions of the militants as solely a response to Dunmore's provocations. The House report shows the extent to which the militance of the independent companies had undergirded the radicalization of the resistance movement in Virginia. Angry with Dunmore's flight to the *Fowey,* perhaps concerned in light of reports of bloodshed to the north that this was a prelude to actual invasion, moderates began to justify the position that they now found themselves in, by supporting the militance of the crowd and the radicals that led it. Dunmore had in effect accused patriot gentlemen, regardless of their political positions, of raising and countenancing an armed mob and losing control of it. The Burgesses countered with a report that said all was quiet until Dunmore provoked the people. Gentlemen then did all they could to restrain them, as Jefferson had noted privately. Gentlemen of all political leanings pointed to the militance of the independent companies to justify themselves. Radicals like Jefferson used the heightened tensions to keep pressure on Dunmore and the crown, and moderates used Dunmore's actions to exonerate themselves from any wrongdoing in —and responsibility for—the impending collapse of royal government in the colony. Whatever the position, the tone of wounded innocence that the Burgesses could now employ made for good propaganda. Dunmore himself had stirred up the crowd, gentlemen patriots had done their best to calm and quiet it, but the governor still refused to be conciliatory. Having done as much as they felt that they could, the Burgesses adjourned on June 24. Two days later, Peyton Randolph issued a summons for a Third Virginia Convention to meet, in Williamsburg, beginning on July 17. Royal government in Virginia had come to an end.[38]

37. *JHB, 1773–1776,* 208, 214–215, 280.

38. See "Report of the Causes of the Late Disturbances," June 1, 1775, Jenkins, comp., *Records of the States,* 21–23, 36; *Rev. Va.,* III, 14–24; *Va. Gaz.* (Purdie), June 30, 1775.

CHAPTER 3 *Checking Wild Irregular Sallies*

PATRIOT LEADERS REASSERT CONTROL

The "rage of patriotism" abated little after Governor Dunmore fled the capital. With no formal government sitting in Williamsburg between the end of June and mid-July 1775, formal relations between Virginia and royal authority stood in limbo. While moderate and neutral Virginians stood anxiously sidelined, the volunteer companies filled the vacuum of authority. As they did, the momentum for outright war gathered force at speed from three sides. While enslaved Virginians continued to agitate for their own freedom in the midst of the ostensibly white conflict, news of major battles to the north flooded into the colony. Militants quickly moved to shore up their own position, in two ways. Volunteers continued to act offensively and independently, but they also began to demand a stricter accounting of allegiances. Already in arms against royal authority yet still concerned about their level of support, many volunteers demanded that others cast their lot with the patriot movement. Seeking to ensure support among their neighbors, militants radicalized resistance by closing the middle ground.

Yet, even as militants pushed the colony further into a posture of war, patriot gentlemen began to reclaim their control over the revolutionary situation. Meeting at the Third Virginia Convention in mid-July, a now badly divided group of patriot leaders argued over how best to prosecute and control the resistance movement. Fully aware of Continental as well as provincial developments, delegates to the convention heatedly debated their next moves. Dunmore's actions, combined with news of hostilities farther north, made further mobilization essential. But both unchecked militants and rebellious slaves made it imperative that the delegates reestablish some kind of law and order and governmental authority in the colony. Virginia's patriot leaders thus took strong steps to smother the flames of dissent in part at least by mobilizing for war with Britain.

• • • With Dunmore now at large and threatening invasion, the citizens of Williamsburg took defensive action that initiated a new phase in the resistance against Britain. They called a meeting and invited up to 250 men from several counties to come help guard the town against any "surprises" from Dunmore and from within: troops were needed to "assist the citizens in their nightly watches." The call for assistance flew around the colony. Indeed, with the flight of Dunmore offshore, there was another outpouring of militarism throughout the colony. "Mars the great God of Battle, is now honoured in every Part of this spacious Colony . . . here every Presence is warlike, every Sound is martial!" wrote one observer: "Drums beating, Fifes and Bag-Pipes playing, and only sonorous and heroic Tunes." "Volunteers presented themselves from every direction," a soldier recalled, and George Gilmer wrote a little later, "Every rank and denomination of people [is] full of marshal notions." As the Burgesses dispersed, volunteer companies from around the colony converged on the capital and set up camp on the edge of town to protect it from an invasion. The very element that had contributed most to the end of royal authority—the independent companies—now filled the void of authority left by the departing Burgesses.[1]

The volunteers quickly made trouble. Their lack of discipline was evident early on. Neither the volunteers themselves nor their officers seemed willing to defer to any authority. Thomas Jefferson was told that one of the elected commanding officers, a Captain Scott, though his "goodness and merit is great, fear[s] to offend, and by that many members are rather disorderly." Punishments were light, reflecting the principles of a volunteer

1. *Va. Gaz.* (D and H), July 1, 1775; Gilmer to Jefferson, [July 26 or 27, 1775], *Papers of Jefferson,* I, 238; recollection of one of Hugh Stephenson's recruits in Berkeley County, *Papers of Washington,* Rev. War Ser., I, 24n; June 6, 1775, Robert Greenhalgh Albion and Leonidas Dodson, eds., *Philip Vickers Fithian: Journal, 1775-1776, Written on the Virginia-Pennsylvania Frontier and in the Army around New York* (Princeton, N.J., 1934), 24; *Va. Gaz.* (Purdie), June 30, 1775, *Rev. Va.,* III, 218, 218–219 n. 4; John E. Selby, *The Revolution in Virginia, 1775–1783* (Williamsburg, Va., 1988), 47–48; William Reynolds to George F. Norton, July 16, 1775, William Reynolds Letterbook, LiVi; *Rev. Va.,* III, 322, 325n; *Va. Gaz.* (D and H), July 15, 1775. Cf. Extract of a letter from a Gentleman in Virginia to his Friend in Edinburgh, Scotland, Dated Middlesex, September 1, 1775, in Peter Force, ed., *American Archives: Consisting of a Collection of Authentick Records, State Papers, Debates, and Letters and Other Notices of Publick Affairs* . . . (Washington, D.C., 1837-1853), 4th Ser., III, 620-621. For Randolph's fears, see *Va. Gaz.* (Purdie), June 23, 1775.

army: the officers were subject to censure for disobedience; the troops, to a reprimand, confinement for two hours, or, at worst, expulsion. Nor were they particularly well trained. One observer noted that he had watched "one of your independent companies go through the *Prussian* exercise, as they called it. . . . But if I have any judgement, it is mere burlesque on all exercise." Most conspicuously absent—to many gentlemen—was the lack of a clear chain of command with centralized control.[2]

Almost immediately, with little to do in Williamsburg and hungry for action, the volunteers went on the offensive. On the very day the Burgesses adjourned, a group of young men broke into the governor's house and stole his arms and swords, which they redistributed to anyone in need. A little later, the volunteers raided the palace again, reportedly breaking all the locks to the doors, rooms, cabinets, and "private places" and stealing what remained of the governor's arms. Dunmore claimed this "inhuman robbery" had been done "in the face of day" under the nose of the son of the treasurer, probably George Nicholas.[3]

Volunteers also harassed Dunmore outside Williamsburg. When the governor put ashore at his estate in Porto Bello, about twelve miles above Yorktown, to eat and secure a new mast for the *Fowey,* a "body of men in Arms" chased them back to the *Fowey,* fired shots at one of the retreating servants, and seized the two ships' carpenters. Three days later, on July 10, the smaller, twenty-gun *Mercury* sailed into the York River to relieve the *Fowey,* an act that, to a nervous patriot elite, presaged further trouble. Wilson Miles Cary, naval officer of the lower district of the James, whom Dunmore described as "one of the most active and virulent of the Enemies of Government," used the occasion to spread an "allarm" that the British were bringing in more troops. That night, volunteers arrived at Yorktown from Williamsburg to reinforce the local independent company, and together they set up a camp behind the town within cannon shot of the two ships of war. According to one report, the volunteers boldly paraded in arms along the shore, flouting Dunmore's power, and challenged every boat or person

2. "Meeting of Officers at Williamsburg," July 18, 1775, R. A. Brock, ed., "Papers, Military and Political, 1775-1778, of George Gilmer, M.D., of 'Pen Park,' Albemarle County, Va.," VHS, *Collections,* n.s., VI (1887), 92-93; George Gilmer to Jefferson, [July 26 or 27, 1775], *Papers of Jefferson,* I, 237; Robert Washington to the Members of the Convention, [July 29, 1775], Force, ed., *American Archives,* II, 1750; *Rev. Va.,* III, 373.

3. Selby, *Revolution in Virginia,* 46; *Rev. Va.,* III, 223-224.

who came their way. They also prevented Dunmore's servants from procuring supplies on shore.[4]

If this impertinence was sufficient to irritate Dunmore, the volunteers soon gave the patriot civilian elite cause for concern as well. On July 19, the officers of the troops at Williamsburg wrote to the Norfolk Borough committee expressing their worry at a report that "you are some of you desserting the Glorious Cause," having been told that "there are Volunteers recruiting in opposition to the Continental plan." The officers in Williamsburg wanted to know whether this was true, so that they could "assist the proper side with all our force." The Norfolk Borough committee quickly assured them that their assistance would not be needed.[5]

Also, believing any period of delay "would be dangerous, and tend to defeat our purposes," the volunteer companies decided to "wait on" the receiver general, naval officers, and other collectors and procure and protect public money from leaving the colony. Should those officials refuse to comply, they were to be brought to camp to explain themselves. One unsympathetic observer later reported, "The Independent Companys are riding over all the Country to Seize what money is in the public offices." Though the officers did retroactively seek approval from the convention when it finally met in mid-July, they thought the "Circumstances of the case" required "immediate procedure," particularly since they had heard that one of Dunmore's officers had already sent a "very considerable sum of the Publick Money" to the *Fowey*. Even as they wrote to the convention, they threatened further unauthorized action. In a hasty postscript, they noted that a vessel belonging to a man-of-war had just carried off upward of nine hundred pounds from the naval office at Hampton. "From want of time," they ended hastily, "we can not give you our whole proceedings at present as intended." By the time the convention responded, the volunteers had commandeered a total of nine hundred pounds from Lewis Burwell, naval officer for the district of the upper James River, and "Twelve hundred dollars" in silver from Jacquelin Amber, collector of the port at Yorktown.[6]

---

4. *Rev. Va.,* III, 224–225; *Va. Gaz.* (D and H), July 8, 1775.

5. William Davies to the Officers of the Independent Companies at Williamsburg, July 21, 1775, and Officers of the Independent Companies at Williamsburg to the Norfolk Borough Committee, July 19, 1775, Gilmer Papers, VHS; *Rev. Va.,* III, 304–306.

6. *Va. Gaz.* (D and H), July 29, 1775; James Parker to Charles Steuart, Aug. 4,

The volunteers at Williamsburg continued to act independently, even after the Third Virginia Convention convened in Richmond on July 17. The officers of the volunteers, for example, appointed two of their number to "wait on" Richard Corbin, the receiver general, again and "demand a state of his public ac[coun]ts" and deliver any balance, or force him to bind his whole estate for the security of the balance. If he refused to comply, the delegated officers were to "call all the Volunteers in reach to assist in bringing him to the Incampment in Wm*bgh*." Corbin complied and assured the officers of his cooperation, but in his letter to Lord Dunmore he took notice of the "extraordinary" nature of this incident, which he thought had been precipitated by the officers' being "Struck with Suspicions of the most dreadful Nature."[7]

Other groups also helped radicalize resistance by pushing for a stricter accounting of allegiances among wavering patriots, polarizing the conflict within Virginia. Often they called for a public show of support for the volunteer companies and the patriot cause, and they ostracized those who were slow in showing their allegiance or even their approval. While many leading gentlemen wanted moderation, prudence, and caution, militants in the independent companies recognized that the Rubicon had already been bridged. Once engaged in the conflict, volunteers found it difficult to turn back, and put tremendous pressure on other white Virginians, rich and poor, to join them.

As resistance built, many more militant patriots still worried they did not yet have full popular support. In July 1775 George Gilmer, already fully committed to armed conflict, admonished his neighbors in a second address to put aside their differences and join the cause. He worried about the "divisions, discords, and discentions" among them and warned them to give up "every view of private Interest," "incline rather to forgive than revenge," and discourage all "private factions." Troubled on several fronts, in particular he tried to convince two different groups who held back from supporting the volunteers. Some apparently considered the actions already taken as too rash, because they were based only on conjectures of what the

---

1775, *Rev. Va.,* III, 375n; *Rev. Va.,* III, 404n; Officers to the Convention, July 26, 1775, *Rev. Va.,* III, 98–99.

7. Proceedings of the Officers of the Volunteer Companies in Williamsburg, July 29, Aug. 1, 1775, Richard Corbin to the Officers, July 29, 1775, Gilmer Papers, VHS; *Rev. Va.,* III, 375n.

governor planned to do. But he also addressed those who were as yet uninterested altogether in the patriot cause. "Let us all cheerfully embark in this common cause," he appealed, "for we are all equally concerned." He implied that some of the disgruntled had class differences in mind, but answered, "The honest industrious labourer who counts a cabin his dwelling a single cow and a small parcel of Land while his estate will be as essentially ruined as the man that has boundless possessions." Those who had not yet declared their support, for either reason, could expect retribution. "Our country crys aloud for us to let fall our just indignation on the head of every apostate to the grand american cause."[8]

Gilmer, an aspiring gentleman, tried to shame the uncommitted. Other volunteers used more violent means to keep their neighbors in line. Whereas the county committees had previously relied upon public ostracism and only occasionally the threat of crowd action during the political resistance movement, the volunteer companies were quick to use physical intimidation. Soon after Dunmore's seizure of the powder and the mobilization of the independent companies, for example, Philip Vickers Fithian recorded that one volunteer in his town was merely "backward this Morning in his Attendance with the Company of Independants." Accordingly, in a public ritual to reinforce the importance and authority of the group, a "File" was sent to bring him in before the company. The delinquent soldier originally "made some Resistance" but was "compelled at length" by his fellow soldiers. Perhaps having wavered, the "backward" volunteer "is now in great Fear, and very humble, since he hears many of his Townsmen talking of Tar and Feathers." Fithian, an onlooker himself, concluded that this rough justice was a compelling form of persuasion. "Tar and Feathers" were "mortifying Weapons," Fithian noted with some dread, and "with their necessary Appendages, *Scoff and Shame,* are *popular* Terrors, and of great Influence."[9]

The volunteer companies seemed particularly keen to maintain their respectability, even stooping to less than respectable means of enforcement. When John Sherlock from Accomack County, for example, was held up for "public contempt" by the county committee for his "most daring and insulting manner" against the patriots and the independent company in particular, he was first called before the civilian committee. Sherlock refused to appear and wrote an "abusive, insulting letter." The committee, "agreeable to

8. Gilmer, Address, July 1775, Gilmer Papers, VHS.
9. June 8, 1775, Albion and Dodson, eds., *Fithian Journal,* 25.

the rules of the [Continental] association," resolved to publish the proceedings in the public newspapers. Unsatisfied with such a solution, a number of men from the independent company went after Sherlock themselves. After a brief standoff at his house, Sherlock gave himself up to the volunteers and was "carried" to the courthouse. After a "solemn trial," the entire company "received from him, under the Liberty Pole, his recantation," particularly for "very imprudently" calling the independent company an "unlawful mob, and many other idle and foolish words." Yet Sherlock also had to ask for pardon from "each member of the said Company respectively" and, finally, to declare the company a "very respectable body of men."[10]

On more than one occasion the volunteer companies stepped in to prosecute suspect patriots after the local committee passed judgment. In Norfolk, the committee tried John Schaw, a merchant and local debt collector, for pointing out one of the volunteers, Alexander Main, to Dunmore's troops. Schaw had told the soldiers that the fifer ought to be apprehended for his "impudence" for "appearing in our presence habited in a hunting shirt." The British soldiers subsequently took Main into custody and confined him for some time. Though the committee extracted a public declaration of repentance from Schaw, the volunteers and townsmen apparently thought it insufficient. The following day the "populace" seized Schaw, "parading him . . . into town to the tune of Yankee Doodle, as played by the Fifer he had caused to be apprehended." Schaw escaped and found refuge in the home of a local alderman. Though "great persuasions were used with the people to disperse," they did so only when "three gentlemen" intervened and offered themselves as security for Schaw's appearance before the committee the following morning.[11]

The volunteers at Williamsburg were also quick to redress any grievances. One Joshua Hardcastle, an inhabitant of Williamsburg, found himself in hot water when he "exasperated" the volunteers in the city by "uttering expressions highly degrading the good people who compose the several companies now in this place." The volunteers themselves "waited upon"

10. *Va. Gaz.* (Pinkney), July 20, 1775, *Rev. Va.,* III, 236–237.

11. See *Virginia Gazette, or the Norfolk Intelligencer,* Aug. 16, 1775, *Rev. Va.,* III, 414–415, 420, 432–433. The actions of the "mob" almost precipitated the cannonading of the town by the British navy when Andrew Sprowle appealed to it for protection after he said that he would not appear before the committee without the protection of the British army and navy, because, by the actions of the crowd against Schaw, "it would appear the Committee has no Government of the Mob."

Hardcastle and "conducted" him to their camp. Here, in front of both officers and men, he was publicly examined and found guilty by the ad hoc and clearly extralegal tribunal. The officers voted between drumming him through the city, tarring and feathering him, and forcing him to make "public concessions," finally deciding that Hardcastle "should *only* ask pardon of all the officers and soldiers present, and give his promise that he never would be guilty of a like offence." Ominously, the volunteers also published their proceedings, not to justify their actions, but "as a warning to those who may hereafter sport with the great and glorious cause of America"—or at least with the independent companies.[12]

At least some of the independent companies were keen to enforce allegiance to the cause through participation with the volunteers. Many of those they targeted were prominent men. Charles Duncan, a merchant living in Blandford, complained in July 1775 that he and his partners wanted to remain neutral in the dispute with Britain and asserted that they had always complied with any regulations laid down by Congress and the Virginia conventions. They thought this was enough to guarantee their peace and safety. However, Duncan and his partners in Brunswick County had each been called upon by the commander of the volunteer company and told to enlist or face the "pain of incurring the Displeasure" of the entire company and be treated as "Enemies to the Country." The commander also threatened that, in such a case, the merchants would be "exposed to all the Violence, that may happen from the mistaken Zeal of men heated by Passion, and prejudice, and who treat with disregard the peaceable remonstrances of your Memorialist." Duncan concluded that they would be happy to comply with any laws or recommendations from the convention, but that now it was wrong to be "called upon, or compelled, by any Set of Men, under an assumed authority, either to enlist as Soldiers, or take part in any Military regulation." Militant volunteers, acting under their own authority, not only pushed the conflict with Dunmore to an extreme, but they also threatened to alienate any neutral or even sympathetic observers. Such actions raised the specter of civil war.[13]

12. *Va. Gaz.* (Pinkney), Sept. 7, 1775, *Rev. Va.,* IV, 72–73. Cf. Dale Edward Benson, "Wealth and Power in Virginia, 1774–1776: A Study of the Organization of Revolt" (Ph.D. diss., University of Maine, 1970), 221–229, 234–239; Emory G. Evans, *Thomas Nelson of Yorktown: Revolutionary Virginian* (Charlottesville, Va., 1975), 50.

13. [Aug. 9, 1775], *Rev. Va.,* III, 410, 412n. Cf. Proceedings of the Third Virginia

Unauthorized actions against unsympathetic, neutral, or even moderate patriots by armed men also carried a threat to men of status and property. Indeed, one of the most important manifestations of the volunteer companies' newfound independence was the leveling entailed by increased attacks on lukewarm patriots like prominent committeemen David Rodes and John Coles of Albemarle County. These men were hardly "tories." Rather, they were ostracized because they were not radical enough—regardless of who they were and what authority they represented. Significantly, a "Friend of Liberty" asked the people of Henrico County in June 1775 to guard against those "pretending the most zealous attachment and firmest adherence to the just cause of *America*" but who refuse "to enter themselves as volunteers." He hinted that "a few among" their leaders were lagging behind, "whose consciences accuse them of not having taken an active [military] part" in the cause thus far. Such persons should receive "every mark of discountenance and disesteem" and "be carefully observed in future, and not be suffered to enlarge upon that confidence already entrusted in them."[14]

With active—even radical—service in the independent companies rapidly becoming the touchstone of patriotism, men as prominent as William Byrd could no longer feel safe. Byrd had fallen under suspicion of the local committees and was "often threatened with Visits from the valiant Volunteers of some of the neighbouring Counties." He believed that he had received "many insults" and given "great offence" because he would not offer his services to command in the army. Reluctant to commit himself to outright war with Britain, Byrd worried about the direction resistance was taking, and particularly its more militant leadership. He worried about the civil war that might ensue and the "inevitable Ruin" many faced.[15]

Convention, Aug. 25, 1775, *Rev. Va.,* III, 490–491. For similar problems in Philadelphia, see Steven Rosswurm, *Arms, Country, and Class: The Philadelphia Militia and the "Lower Sort" during the American Revolution, 1775–1783* (New Brunswick, N.J., 1987), where this issue is carefully explicated in chap. 2.

14. "A Friend to Liberty," [June 22, 1775?], in Force, ed., *American Archives,* 4th Ser., II, 1056–1057. Daniel Trabue later recalled some volunteers also targeted Anglican ministers (see Chester Raymond Young, ed., *Westward into Kentucky: The Narrative of Daniel Trabue* [Lexington, Ky., 1981], 42–43).

15. William Byrd to Sir Jeffery Amherst, July 30, 1775, Marion Tinling, ed., *The Correspondence of the Three William Byrds of Westover, Virginia, 1684–1776* (Charlottesville, Va., 1977), II, 812; Byrd to Ralph Wormeley, Oct. 4, 1775, Worme-

Finally, many planters' worries about attacks on their property by the independent companies were only exacerbated by the large, restive population of enslaved Virginians in their midst. White fears were twofold: enslaved Virginians could at the very least take advantage of the upheaval to slip away; at worst they could turn on their masters and neighbors or join Dunmore. The governor, of course, had encouraged the call to arms of the summer of 1775 by his continual threats to arm Virginia's enslaved population. Many more militant Virginians had reacted with a show of arms and joined the volunteer companies. Many wealthier and, particularly, slave-rich planters, however, were not so sure of the best way to counter such a threat. Armed conflict could only lead to a greater threat from the enemy within. Indeed, more fearful of the consequences of opposing Dunmore outright, particularly in light of the rumors of slave uprisings and the actual threats of the governor, James Madison thought that "the Gentlemen below," in the tidewater counties on the York and James Rivers, "whose property will be exposed in case of a civil war in this Colony were extremely alarmed."[16]

They had good reason to worry about their property. The precipitous actions of the volunteer companies only encouraged the near anarchy that provided many opportunities for enslaved Virginians to fight or flee. Be-

---

ley Family Papers, UVa; James Earle to Thomas Ringgold, July 22, 1775, in Keith Mason, "Localism, Evagelicalism, and Loyalism: The Sources of Discontent in the Revolutionary Chesapeake," *Journal of Southern History,* LVI (1990), 30. Cf. Ronald Hoffman, *A Spirit of Dissension: Economics, Politics, and the Revolution in Maryland* (Baltimore, 1973), esp. 126–151; Michael A. McDonnell, "A World Turned 'Topsy Turvy': Robert Munford, *The Patriots,* and the Crisis of the Revolution in Virginia," *WMQ,* 3d Ser., LXI (2004), 235–270.

James Earle of Maryland feared that volunteers might attack "persons and property" who had become offensive from a "want of forwardness from the natural coolness and complexion of their minds." He was explicit about the consequences if armed men were allowed free rein to persecute those not in line with their thinking. He hoped that the Provincial Congress would "lay if possible a strong controulling power over the licentiousness of the people in all Cases that concern the Safety of persons and property." "If they are subject to the caprice and blind impulse of the Rabble," he warned, *"all all* is gone." Many gentlemen in Virginia were also coming to the same conclusion about the need for a "strong controulling power."

16. [Thomson Mason], "The British American, VII," *Va. Gaz.* (Rind), July 14, 1774, *Rev. Va.,* I, 184; Madison to William Bradford, May 9, June 19, 1775, *Papers of Madison,* I, 145, 153.

ginning with the arrival of "several negroes" who went to the Governor's Palace shortly after the powder magazine incident to "make a tender of their services," enslaved Virginians across the colony increasingly made their way to British protection over the summer of 1775. In June, one newspaper was full of advertisements calling for the return of enslaved Virginians who had run away from all parts of the colony. Jonathan, for example, a twenty-year-old with a "bold Countenance," ran away from his master in New Kent County and was subsequently seen in Yorktown, "intending to make his Escape out of the Colony."[17]

Many enslaved Virginians in the Norfolk region in particular tried to gain their freedom on board the British ships of war in the harbor. Though they were supposedly turned away, owners were "much disturbed" by the "elopement of their negroes" through July and August. One magistrate of Norfolk Borough declared in mid-August that the "notorious" practice had "of late . . . frequently happened, from the countenance shewn them by some enemies to this colony." The Norfolk county committee was convinced by the middle of August that Dunmore and other officers of the British ships of war had done much "in promoting a disaffection among the slaves" and had concealed them "for a considerable time on board their vessels." But enslaved Virginians were not just running away. The arrival of British troops from Saint Augustine in the Norfolk area in July 1775, for example, caused "exceedingly bad effects" upon the enslaved in the area, which it was feared would be "very much encreased by the arrival of these troops." Local officials in nearby Southampton County brought Phil and Mial, enslaved Virginians belonging to John Bailey, to trial "on suspicion of a conspiracy" on July 15.[18]

Rumors continued to fly that Dunmore was "tampering with the Slaves and that he has it in contemplation to make great use of them in case of a civil war in this province." The rumors were widespread. While delegates to the Third Virginia Convention were gathering, a Marylander wrote,

17. *Va. Gaz.* (D and H), June 17, 1775.

18. *Virginia Gazette, or the Norfolk Intelligencer,* Aug. 2, 1775, and Mayor Paul Loyall to Captain John Macartney, Aug. 14, 30, 1775; Proceedings of the Norfolk County Committee, Aug. 16, 1775, *Virginia Gazette, or the Norfolk Intelligencer,* Aug. 23, 1775; Norfolk Borough Committee to Peyton Randolph, July 31, 1775, *Rev. Va.,* III, 378, 381n; *Virginia Gazette, or the Norfolk Intelligencer,* Aug. 16, 1775; Court of Oyer and Terminer, [Aug. 10, 1775], Southampton County Order Book, 1772–1777, LiVi (reel 26), fol. 414.

"The governor of Virginia, the captains of the men of war, and mariners, have been tampering with our Negroes; and have held nightly meetings with them; and all for the glorious purpose of enticing them to cut their masters' throats while they are asleep." In North Carolina, one committee of safety instituted "Patroles to search and take from Negroes all kinds of Arms whatsoever" and worried in June and July about the "truly alarming situation," with the "Governor collecting men, provisions, warlike stores of every kind, spiriting up the back counties, and perhaps the Slaves." Many patriots in North Carolina believed the crown had promised "every Negro that would murder his Master and family that he should have his Master's plantation . . . the Negroes have got it amongst them and believe it to be true." Insurrections did actually occur across the Carolinas in July 1775.[19]

Enslaved Americans were not the only ones who challenged patriot planters' authority and threatened their property. Indentured and convict servants made bids for freedom too. Twenty-seven-year-old John Fleming and seventeen-year-old George Wassell ran away from their master in Williamsburg in early June. Robert Shaw and Andrew Ingles, two Scottish indentured servants, joined forces with Thomas Walsom, a convict servant, and made their escape from masters in Alexandria, also in early June. Some of them might have been trying to reach Dunmore in the hopes of offering their services to him. One convict servant named William Wells of Farnham Parish, in Richmond County, ran away on May 12 and tried to get on board some ships at Hobb's Hole (present-day Tappahannock), across the Rappahannock River. After that plan failed, he joined with two sailors, stole a boat, and set sail for Norfolk. Just after Dunmore fled Williamsburg, so too did the Englishman John Staunton and the Scotsman Andrew McGill. Their former master thought that the two servants would try to pass for sailors and get on board one of the nearby ships of war. Those in chains did not hesitate to band together to seek freedom, even if it meant crossing the color line. George Newton, a Yorkshire-born farmer who arrived in the colony as a convict servant in the spring of 1775, for example, escaped in Spotsylvania County with an enslaved Virginian named George. Their owner thought they might also have joined with a black Virginian named

19. James Madison to William Bradford, June 19, 1775, *Papers of Madison*, I, 153; "Extracts of a Letter from a Clergyman in Maryland to his Friend in England," Aug. 2, 1775, in Force, ed., *American Archives*, 4th Ser., III, 10; Jeffrey J. Crow, "Slave Rebelliousness and Social Conflict in North Carolina, 1775 to 1802," *WMQ*, 3d Ser., XXXVII (1980), 79–102 (quotes on 83, 84).

Tim, who belonged to John Tayloe. The runaways had announced that they were going to try to get on board some ship, and their owner thought they would probably try to get on board one of the British ships of war. Though neither servants nor slaves could be certain that Dunmore would welcome them, both groups quickly took advantage of any chance. Servants and especially enslaved Virginians had been the objects of both the governor's and patriot leaders' threats over the past couple of months, and neither watched events unfold passively. While not everyone in bondage was ready to make a bid for freedom, most watched, listened, and waited carefully for the right opportunities to present themselves.[20]

Finally, white and black bonded laborers were not the only ones watching the civil conflict unfold. Rumors had already been circulating that Dunmore was threatening to cooperate with the native Americans, and Dunmore himself warned Virginians to consider the "dangers to which [they] were] exposed from a savage enemy; who, from the most recent advices . . . are ready to renew their hostilities against the people of this country." By mid-June, Dunmore began to help realize the threat, using an agent stationed at Pittsburgh, John Connolly, to try to secure Indian support for the crown. The plan seemed to be working. James Wood, who had been negotiating with native American nations in the Virginia-Pennsylvania backcountry, had learned that an "English Officer" had told the Wyandots and Delawares to be on guard, as the "White People intended to strike them very soon" and that the Virginians in particular "would take the whole Country if they did not all join together against them." But the Ohio Indians needed no encouragement. Wood soon warned officials in Virginia that from "every discovery I was able to make the Indians are forming a General Confederacy against the Colony having been led to believe that we are a people quite different and distinct from the other Colonies."[21]

20. *Va. Gaz.* (D and H), June 10, 17, July 29, 1775; *Va. Gaz.* (Pinkney), June 22, 1775.

21. General Gage to Dartmouth, Sept. 12, 1775, K. G. Davies, ed., *Documents of the American Revolution, 1770–1783* (Shannon, 1972–1981), XI, 122; Journal of Captain James Wood, July 20, 28, 1775, Wood to Peyton Randolph, Aug. 18, 1775, *Rev. Va.*, III, 326, 363, 463, 465; Royal Proclamation, May 3, 1775, *Va. Gaz.* (Pinkney), May 4, 1775, *Rev. Va.*, III, 81; Selby, *Revolution in Virginia*, 56–58; Proceedings of the Third Virginia Convention, Aug. 22, 1775, *Rev. Va.*, III, 477; *Va. Gaz.* (D and H), Aug. 26, 1775. Wood's letter would reach the convention on August 22. The *Va. Gaz.* (D and H) modified Wood's alarm, noting that the Mingos, Wyandots, and Shawnees "appear to be friendly" and would come to the treaty at Pitts-

Anxious wealthy planters with much to lose watched these developments with growing apprehension. In the middle of June 1775, Philip Vickers Fithian noted that, even far off in the Shenandoah Valley, "slaves are running off daily." But anxiety over enslaved Virginians' absconding only exacerbated a gloomy and uncertain feeling that disorders were on the rise. Fithian noted, "Servants [were] skulking about, and pilfering—Horses, and many other things stolen weekly—Riots on many Occasions in most Parts of the Continent—And in every Place much Anxiety and Debt, and almost no Attention to Business." A little later, another commentator explicitly linked such disorders and anxieties to the martial preparedness of Virginians: "We are all in arms. . . . No person goes abroad without his sword, or gun, or pistols. The sound of war echoes from north to south. Every plain is full of armed men." The result of the rage militaire in Virginia was not all positive. "All is anarchy and confusion."[22]

On top of these internal problems, momentous news reached Virginia throughout late June and early July. Volunteers had been amassing in the countryside outside Boston since late April; almost ten thousand ringed Boston within a few weeks and remained there, keeping the British at bay. In mid-June, British commanders in Boston, fortified with recent reinforcements, including Generals William Howe, John Burgoyne, and Henry Clinton, took the offensive. On June 17, the British launched a massive frontal assault on hastily constructed patriot entrenchments on Breed's Hill, on the Charlestown peninsula near Boston. When the smoke cleared, the British had routed the patriot forces, but at a staggering cost. The British suffered more than 1,000 casualties, including 228 dead, among their force of 2,500 men. The Americans lost just more than 400 men, including 100 killed. Though they had lost the field, the patriot forces claimed a victory at the misnamed Battle of Bunker Hill. If previous skirmishes with the British had been uncertain, the scale of this battle made it clear to most that the British and the colonists were now officially at war.[23]

<hr />

burgh the following month, but that "many of the more western and south western tribes seem determined to take up the hatchet against us."

22. June 17, 1775, Albion and Dodson, eds., *Fithian Journal,* 31–32; "Extract of a Letter from a Gentleman in Virginia to His Friend in Edinburgh, Scotland, Dated Middlesex, Sept. 1, 1775," Force, ed., *American Archives,* 4th Ser., III, 620–621. Cf. Selby, *Revolution in Virginia,* 47.

23. Don Higginbotham, *The War of American Independence: Military Attitudes, Policies, and Practice, 1763–1789* (New York, 1971), 65–77; James Kirby Martin

At the same time that reports of the battle began to reach Virginia in late June, Virginians also learned that the Second Continental Congress had agreed to adopt the volunteer army around Boston on June 14. To ensure this new army would be a truly Continental army, the delegates in Philadelphia voted to raise ten companies of riflemen from Pennsylvania, Maryland, and Virginia to reinforce the volunteers. More important, however, they chose Virginian George Washington to head the new Continental army. Though Washington was one of the more experienced military veterans in the colonies, his appointment was primarily a result of New England delegates' desire to have a southern commander. By appointing Washington, New Englanders hoped to align more closely the southern colonies with the northern colonies. With a Virginian at the head, the open conflict with Britain in Boston took on a truly Continental character. It also put Virginia—ready or not—front and center in that conflict.[24]

• • • Delegates to the Third Virginia Convention, then, faced several pressing concerns. But, while Continental concerns weighed heavily on the minds of the delegates, many believed that equally serious problems confronted Virginia from within. They were particularly worried about Dunmore's threats to destroy their property and arm enslaved Virginians. Noting that the governor's forces had already "received and detained" many blacks, Richard Bland wondered aloud about Dunmore's threats to raze Williamsburg, "lay Waste the Country and emancipate our Slaves." But the delegates also addressed white Virginians. They received firsthand accounts of the maneuvers of the volunteer companies and the the seizures of public money from the receiver general, naval officers, and other collectors. A letter from the volunteers asked for permission to move offensively against loyalist forces said to be gathering in the Norfolk area. The militants in the volunteer companies also proposed their own solution to Dunmore's threats to harbor and arm enslaved Virginians. The volunteers at Williamsburg wanted to attack the governor and his troops immediately in order to eliminate the catalyst for black activism. Angered by reports that Dunmore's ships had "carried off a number of Slaves belonging to private Gentlemen" in the Norfolk and tidewater areas, they thought it "high time

and Mark Edward Lender, *A Respectable Army: The Military Origins of the Republic, 1763–1789* (Arlington Heights, Ill., 1982), 36–40.

24. *Va. Gaz.* (D and H), July 8, 1775; Higginbotham, *War of American Independence*, 84–85.

to establish the doctrine of reprisal, and to take immediate possession" of the governor himself, or at least "his property." Finally, several British merchants petitioned the convention for protection against the volunteer companies. The committee of Chesterfield County summed up these problems for the delegates. Unless the volunteer companies were put under some kind of civilian control, the colony could face much greater dangers than the British: the volunteer company might assume "an authority independent of any Military Controul by law established."[25]

The volunteers' most recent actions reminded delegates that the resistance movement was becoming unwieldy, dangerous, and potentially subversive and that their control over the "ebullition of patriotism" had slipped away. Mainstream civilian patriot leaders had, in effect, lost control of the movement—seen in the actions of the volunteers throughout the colony in driving Dunmore out and pushing Virginia into outright conflict but also in their unauthorized attacks on individuals, wealthy and poor, who failed to embrace the movement with enthusiasm and "warmth." Armed bands of men were continuing to take the law into their own hands, thereby radicalizing the resistance movement. The language used by many gentlemen suggests an awareness that they had toppled a hornet's nest, and it was impossible to predict the consequences. Even Jefferson had spoken of the "phrenzy of revenge" that "seized" the people, and the House of Burgesses confessed the great "difficulty there is in restraining an incensed multi-

25. Proceedings of the Third Virginia Convention, July 19, 1775, *Rev. Va.,* III, 323; Officers at Williamsburg to the Convention, Aug. 1, 1775, Brock, ed., "Papers of Gilmer," VHS, *Collections,* n.s., VI (1887), 109; Proceedings of the Third Virginia Convention, Aug. 5, 1775, *Rev. Va.,* III, 401 (cf. Aug. 11, 1775, III, 417–418, for a similar incident); memorial of Charles Duncan, [Aug. 9, 1775], *Rev. Va.,* III, 410, 412n; memorial of sundry merchants, and others, natives of Great Britain, Proceedings of the Third Virginia Convention, Aug. 25, 1775, *Rev. Va.,* III, 490–491; Chesterfield County Committee memorial, [prior to July 25, 1775], *Rev. Va.,* III, 339 (cf. Proceedings of the Bedford county committee, June 26, 1775, III, 230). Patriot leaders in Virginia faced the same problems as their counterparts in Massachusetts. Joseph Warren told Samuel Adams in late May: "The continent must strengthen and support with all its weight the civil authority here; otherwise our soldiery will lose the ideas of right and wrong, and will plunder, instead of protecting the inhabitants" (Massachusetts Provincial Congress to Continental Congress, May 16, 1775, in Force, ed., *American Archives,* 4th Ser., II, 620–621; Warren to Adams, May 26, 1775, in Higginbotham, *War of American Independence,* 83, 95).

tude." The movement was becoming too popular, driven by the radicals who courted popularity among their volunteers. The "confusion" created by the independent companies, then, the lack of proper militia laws to enforce patrolling and ready the colony against invasion, and anxieties over the "enemy within"—in short, fears over the near-anarchic conditions in Virginia in May and June 1775—were foremost in the minds of the men who gathered for the Third Virginia Convention.[26]

The delegates moved against the militants first. They stopped the volunteers from marching on Norfolk. They told them in no uncertain terms to act defensively and remain in Williamsburg. Rather than unleash the undisciplined volunteer companies in a volatile situation, many patriot leaders believed that they needed tighter control over them. Convening a committee of the whole to debate the seizure of public money, the convention resolved, "The Proceedings of the Officers of the voluntier Companies in Williamsburg . . . though they arose from the best Motives, cannot be approved"; they were to "desist from carrying their Resolutions into Execution." Shortly after the convention received Charles Duncan's memorial about coercion into volunteer companies, the delegates immediately wrote to the local commanding officer of the volunteer company in Brunswick County "requiring them to desist from a further prosecution of the Measures mentioned." Most delegates were anxious that any unprovoked attacks on neutral persons and private property might provoke a civil war.[27]

26. "A Ranger to a True Patriot," *Va. Gaz.* (Pinkney), June 1, 1775, *Rev. Va.,* III, 181; Jefferson to William Small, May 7, 1775, *Papers of Jefferson,* I, 165.

27. Proceedings of the Third Virginia Convention, July 28, 1775, *Rev. Va.,* III, 361, 367n; Peyton Randolph to the Officers of the Volunteer Independent Companies at Williamsburg, July 28, 1775, Brock, ed., "Papers of Gilmer," VHS, *Collections,* n.s., VI (1887), 107–108, and Officers at Williamsburg to the Convention, Aug. 1, 1775, 109; Robert W. Carter to Landon Carter, July 29, 1775, Sabine Hall Papers, UVa; Proceedings of the Third Virginia Convention, July 28, Aug. 5, 11, 1775, *Rev. Va.,* III, 361, 367n, 401, 417–418; Dunmore to Dartmouth, Sept. 24, 1775, Davies, ed., *Documents of the American Revolution,* XI, 132; "Resolution concerning Peaceable British Subjects Resident in Virginia," [Aug. 25, 1775], and Mason to Martin Cockburn, Aug. 22, 1775, *Papers of Mason,* I, 251, 253. The convention later toyed with the idea of drawing up a test oath but settled on a general declaration that patriot Virginians ought to treat all natives of Britain as friends, unless they acted otherwise. See Proceedings of the Third Virginia Convention, Aug. 10, 16, 19, 25, 1775, *Rev. Va.,* III, 413, 451, 467, 490–492; An Ordinance

More formally, and acting upon a congressional recommendation, the delegates resolved to try to harness the enthusiasm of the volunteer companies and raise and embody a "sufficient armed Force" for the "Defence and protection of this Colony." The convention specifically directed that such plans ensure that "proper Officers" were appointed, "under proper Regulations and Restrictions." Three days later, George Mason spelled out what was intended by the convention. The committee appointed was to "raise forces for immediate service—to new-model the whole militia—to render about one-fifth of it fit for the field at the shortest warning" and, significantly, "to melt down all the volunteer and independent companies into this great establishment." The committee was also to define the role of a central "Committee of Safety," which would oversee and "superintend" the forces raised, providing a more regular civilian authority over the new military organization.[28]

After almost six weeks of prolonged and rancorous debate, the convention accepted a three-tiered military establishment. First, the delegates formally resurrected the traditional militia service. Composed of all free white males, hired servants, and apprentices between the ages of sixteen and fifty, the militia was to muster and train once every two weeks (except in December, January, and February) and attend a general countywide muster twice a year. The county committees were to appoint all officers of the militia, effectively giving the committees the job that county courts had previously done. County lieutenants were ordered to hold regular courts-martial. The

---

for Establishing a General Test Oath, Aug. 19, 1775, Mason to Martin Cockburn, Aug. 22, 25, 1775, *Papers of Mason,* I, 246–247, 251. Cf. *Va. Gaz.* (Pinkney), Aug. 31, 1775, (Purdie), Sept. 1, 1775, and *Va. Gaz.,* (D and H), Sept. 2, 1775.

28. Proceedings of the Third Virginia Convention, July 18, 19, 1775, *Rev. Va.,* III, 315, 317–318, 319, 323–324; Mason to Martin Cockburn, July 24, 1775, *Papers of Mason,* I, 241. The members of the convention that met in the middle of July were ostensibly the same as those who had met in the Second Convention, and generally the same group who had met briefly as the House of Burgesses in June. The delegates were supposed to have been elected according to a recommendation of the Second Convention on its last day of session, Mar. 27, 1775; however, few elections appear to have been held (*Rev. Va.,* II, 386, III, 40, 139, 203). For a full analysis of the membership of the convention, see *Rev. Va.,* II, 366, 368–369, III, 303–304; for an analysis of the membership of the committee appointed to draw up the new military plans, see *Rev. Va.,* II, 97, 343–344, 356, 361–362, III, 48–49, 119, 330, 334, 339, 342, 351, 357, 360.

militia was generally to act as a reserve force in case of invasion and, when called out for service, would be under the same rules and regulations as the regular troops and receive the same pay. Finally, the militia would also be the first line of defense against insurrections of enslaved Virginians. The commanding officer was empowered to appoint patrollers as needed. Significantly, to try to curb rebellious slaves, the convention exempted all overseers of four tithables residing on a plantation from any militia service. While militant volunteers wanted to attack Dunmore to quiet rebellious slaves, the convention delegates chose a more defensive strategy of keeping a closer eye on enslaved workers at home.[29]

The convention then divided the colony into fifteen military districts for the purpose of organizing and recruiting a small "regular" force of troops. Each district had to provide one company of 68 full-time, paid men who would become professional soldiers for one year in the regular army, to be stationed in Virginia initially, for a total of 1,020 regulars. The convention undertook the appointment of field officers and delegated the appointment of company-grade officers to special military district committees. The creation of a force of regulars drew upon an older tradition of having a core provincial army to do the colony's bidding and provide a more stable and consistent defense. A semipermanent force would also send a clear and forceful message to enslaved Virginians contemplating insurrection or joining Dunmore. Soldiers in the regular force would be enlisted for as long as was felt necessary, but it was stipulated that, should the need exceed one year, any soldier might give three months' notice of leaving. Provisions for the soldiers anticipated that those who enlisted might be worse off than the average independent company volunteer. New enlistees, who were to be paid on a full-time basis, were to be given a musket and sufficient clothing, and recruiting officers were allowed to advance any sum, not exceeding one month's pay, as they "may think necessary" to recruit successfully. Moreover, "for the greater encouragement and further promotion of the service," any soldier maimed or disabled while in service would be

29. *Rev. Va.,* III, 406, 463, 466, 471, 476; Hening, comp., *Statutes at Large,* IX, 27–35. Other exemptions from militia duty included all members of the council and the Committee of Safety, the presiding officers of the convention, all clergy and Dissenting ministers, the president, professors, and students and scholars of the College of William and Mary, the keeper of the public jail, and all millers and persons concerned in the ironworks.

supported at the expense of the public upon discharge. If there were some advantages to serving in the new regular forces, new recruits also had to abide by seventy-three rules and articles for the "better government of the forces" that prescribed punishments and the terms of courts-martial for all disorderly acts and unsoldierly conduct, ranging from fines to whipping and to capital punishment for certain offenses.[30]

As well as their eastern defense, the convention delegates also tried to protect their western flank. Having received James Wood's warning about a possible attack by a "General Confederacy" of Indians on August 22, the convention immediately ordered two extra companies raised for the protection of the "western frontiers" to be stationed at Pittsburgh and also at Fort Fincastle and Point Pleasant in Virginia. The troops were to be raised from the West Augusta District and the western counties of Botetourt and Fincastle. To ensure the loyalty of the counties and veterans most immediately involved with the governor in Dunmore's War against the Shawnees in 1774, the convention also made provision for paying the militia for their services during that earlier conflict.[31]

The capstone of the convention's military plan, however, was the min-

30. The ordinances are printed in Hening, comp., *Statutes at Large,* IX, 9–35, 35–48, quotes on 12, 14, 35. The ordinance for the "better government of the forces to be raised" in Virginia was also passed on August 21 and was copied almost verbatim from the "Rules and Regulations" passed by Congress on June 30, 1775, which had been printed in the *Va. Gaz.* (D and H), on July 22 and 29, 1775 (Proceedings of the Third Virginia Convention, Aug. 21, 1775, *Rev. Va.,* III, 471; Hening, comp., *Statutes at Large,* IX, 35–48; Worthington Chauncey Ford et al., eds., *Journals of the Continental Congress, 1774–1789* [Washington, D.C., 1904–1937], II, 111–122; Mason to Washington, Oct. 14, 1775, *Papers of Mason,* I, 256). For an informed discussion of the establishment of the Continental army and its impact on the Virginia establishment, see Higginbotham, *War of American Independence,* 81–95. For a general discussion of "standing armies" in the ideological origins of the Revolution, see Lawrence Delbert Cress, *Citizens in Arms: The Army and the Militia in American Society to the War of 1812* (Chapel Hill, N.C., 1982), chaps. 1–4; Reginald C. Stuart, "'Engines of Tyranny': Recent Historiography on Standing Armies during the Era of the American Revolution," *Canadian Journal of History,* XIX (1984), 183–199; Bernard Bailyn, *The Ideological Origins of the American Revolution* (Cambridge, Mass., 1967), 61–64, 112–117.

31. Wood to Peyton Randolph, Aug. 18, 1775, *Rev. Va.,* III, 465; Proceedings of the Third Virginia Convention, Aug. 22, 1775, *Rev. Va.,* III, 477; Hening, comp., *Statutes at Large,* IX, 13, 61–71.

uteman service. The convention ordered the sixteen districts to each raise an additional battalion, or regiment, of five hundred "minutemen" who would train for twenty days immediately and twelve days at a time twice in the following year. The minutemen were to be provided with hunting shirts and leggings and receive pay only when training and in actual service. This minute service was to be at the heart of Virginia's defense, providing a force of eight thousand men, better trained and disciplined than the militia and ready to fight at a moment's notice in case of invasion or insurrection. The convention intended that the minuteman service replace the independent companies. As George Mason noted, "The volunteer Companys are all discharged and melted down in the plan for the Regiments of Minute-Men." Significantly, the delegates decreed that the volunteer companies should be disbanded on the last day of the convention.[32]

In the minute service, then, patriot gentlemen hoped to marshal the enthusiasm of the same men who had turned out in large numbers and with vigor in the independent companies that were still gathering strength. Virginia's leadership, encouraged by the spontaneous outpouring of popular enthusiasm since April 1775, wished to keep many of the better sort at the center of military resistance. George Gilmer hoped the new minuteman plan would be "on such footing as essentially to draw in Gent'n of the first property in the Colony" and immediately signed up himself. Indeed, George Mason gave instructions to his own son that it was "very contrary to my Inclination" that he should enter into the regular service and was "by all Means against it." Instead, the elder Mason wanted his son George to wait until the minuteman plan was completed, to which he would have "no Objection" to his son's entering. It was "the true natural, and safest Defence of this, or any other free Country"; as such, Mason wished "to see it encouraged to the utmost." Writing to George Washington after the

32. Hening, comp., *Statutes at Large,* IX, 16–27; Mason to Martin Cockburn, Aug. 22, 1775, *Papers of Mason,* I, 251; Proceedings of the Third Virginia Convention, Aug. 25, 1775, *Rev. Va.,* III, 488. Cf. Madison to William Bradford, July 28, 1775, *Papers of Madison,* I, 160. The minute service called for a rotating enrollment of eight thousand men, or just under one-fifth of the eligible male population. Sixteen men from each company were to be discharged every twelve months and others recruited in their stead (Hening, comp., *Statutes at Large,* IX, 22–23); Virginia's eligible fighting population has been estimated at forty-five thousand in 1776 (Hamilton J. Eckenrode, comp., *Virginia Soldiers of the American Revolution* [1912–1913; rpt. Richmond, Va., 1989], 4–5).

Third Convention had adjourned, Mason felt that the minuteman plan was "a wise one" that could furnish eight thousand troops ready for action in a short time "in whose Hands the Sword may be safely trusted."[33]

The gentlemen in the convention were, however, intent on ensuring that the new service could truly "be safely trusted." After noting that all the volunteer companies were "discharged and melted down" into the minuteman plan, George Mason also explained that "particular rules" had been "drawn up for the better regulation and Government of the Army; to which both the Minute-Men and Militia are subjected when drawn into actual Service." The committee responsible for the new military plan met amid the disturbances occasioned by the undisciplined volunteers at Williamsburg and the uncontrolled zealousness of their elected leaders. Consequently, the prescribed terms of service compelled men to train and serve for longer periods than in the independent companies. The rules and regulations for the governance of the regular forces were then applied to all troops in the field, with the primary aim of imposing strict discipline throughout all the ranks. The convention wanted the armed forces under proper subordination and under a clear hierarchy and chain of command. As a result, the delegates ended once and for all the popular election of officers of any rank. Though these terms of service followed Virginia's military tradition, they went against the precedent established in the independent companies. No longer would "subscribers" be allowed to come together as equals when and only when needed, elect their leaders, and determine their own course of action. The new volunteers, in short, would be subject to the same rules and regulations as the regular troops when they were training or called out on duty. The delegates chose order and discipline over liberty and enthusiasm.[34]

Finally, the convention asserted firm civilian control over the new armed forces. Indeed, if the seventy-three articles and rules for the "better government of the forces" were an insufficient guide for the conduct of both officers and soldiers alike, the convention also stipulated that in all things,

33. Gilmer to Charles Carter, July 15, 1775, Brock, ed., "Papers of Gilmer," VHS, *Collections,* n.s., VI (1887), 91, and Commonplace Book entry, [summer 1775], 90; Mason to Martin Cockburn, Aug. 5, 1775, Mason to Washington, Oct. 14, 1775, *Papers of Mason,* I, 245–246, 255–256. Cf. Gilmer to Jefferson, [July 26 or 27, 1775], *Papers of Jefferson,* I, 238.

34. Mason to Martin Cockburn, Aug. 22, 1775, *Papers of Mason,* I, 251; Hening, comp., *Statutes at Large,* IX, 9–53.

"not otherwise particularly provided for by this ordinance, and the articles established for their regulation," the troops were to be "under the controul, and subject to the order, of the general committee of safety." Thus all three branches of the military would now come under the direction of a central eleven-man Committee of Safety appointed by the Third Convention, which would oversee civil and military matters while the convention was adjourned. The committee had broad powers and was clearly created to prevent a repeat of the near-anarchic conditions of May, June, and July. The committee had sole power to direct the movement of the army and to call out the minutemen and militia into service, to call for assistance from other colonies, and to purchase any arms outside the colony. All officers in every branch of the armed forces were specifically ordered to obey the Committee of Safety; no military officers whatsoever could sit on it.[35]

In order to administer and enforce these new ordinances in a more orderly fashion, the convention turned its attention to the county committees —in some places themselves the source of the excess of zeal that so worried moderate patriot leaders. Given the important and controversial role the committees had assumed, convention members saw a need to make them more accountable and also to regulate them. Like the independent companies, the original county committees were voluntary and mostly unregulated. After the First Continental Congress recommended them as part of the Continental Association of 1774, at least thirty-three counties and three boroughs had formed committees by the end of 1774, and most had done so by April 1775. Not regulated in any way, the election of the committees differed from place to place. In many counties, local patriotic leaders were elected by spontaneous meetings originally designed to discuss the Continental Association. In most counties, many traditional local leaders were selected, but so too were others. As the size of the committees was not regulated, the number of members on them also differed significantly from place to place, from as few as thirteen to as many as seventy. The average number was about thirty.[36]

Already, some counties had demanded that new elections for county

35. Hening, comp., *Statutes at Large,* IX, 15–16, 35–53, 71–73; Proceedings of the Third Virginia Convention, Aug. 16, 1775, *Rev. Va.,* III, 451. The initial convention balloting for the committee revealed few surprises (III, 456–457, 460, 461).

36. Jack N. Rakove, *The Beginnings of National Politics: An Interpretive History of the Continental Congress* (New York, 1979), 51; Larry Bowman, "The Virginia County Committees of Safety, 1774–1776," *VMHB,* LXXIX (1971), 323–324.

committee members be called in light of the new situation. At least one committee dissolved itself just after Dunmore's seizure of the powder in April 1775 and called for a reelection of the committee. Inhabitants of Chesterfield County also complained that, when the first election was held on the recommendation of the Continental Congress, "Very Few had it in Their Power to Vote in the choice of the committee, at that time not well Understanding what they Ware to do, or the Intent of Associating." Therefore, the petitioners complained, "Some Persons Was by Then Few, Voted in, that we by no Means can think Propper," especially because they now realized that "the Committees are to Do business of much Greater Importance, then we Could possible then conceive." In what would quickly become a common refrain in the midst of the war, the petitioners played upon the real fears of the delegates to optimize their political leverage. Dissolving the old committee was the only way to quell the existing "Divisions amongst us." If granted their request, they could yet "all unite and be as one man in this Critical Time."[37]

Giving in to these demands and not wanting to alienate any freeholders, patriot leaders called for annual elections of the county committees in November of each year. The convention also trimmed the size of the committees to a maximum of twenty-one, hoping for a generally smaller and more select group. The ordinance stipulated that only freeholders who were entitled to vote were to elect "the most discreet, fit, and able men" to serve as the new committee.[38]

• • • The delegates left Richmond near the end of August believing that they had done as much as they could to secure the colony against external invasion and internal disorder, insurrection, and even civil war. They also presented a united front in their public proceedings, which was furthered by a "Declaration of the Delegates" passed unanimously on the last day and printed in the newspapers. But, if the newspapers in printing the proceedings gave the impression of a near unanimous group in its resolutions and ordinances, private letters and the unpublished minutes and papers of the convention suggest a different story, of prevailing "Partys and Factions." "We are getting into great Confusion here," George Mason reported after

37. Bedford County Committee Proceedings, Apr. 25, 1775, *Rev. Va.,* III, 60; Petition of the Freeholders and Inhabitants of Chesterfield County, Aug. 20, 1775, *Rev. Va.,* III, 469–470; Hening, comp., *Statutes at Large,* IX, 57–58.

38. Hening, comp., *Statutes at Large,* IX, 53–60.

two weeks. Robert Wormeley Carter concurred in a letter to his father, Landon Carter, on August 5: he was "greatly disgusted with our present proceedings." He complained that they were "of as many different opinions as we are Men." Five days later, he wrote that he was "most heartily tired" but warned that, with each passing day, he saw more clearly the "great necessity of honest men being Conventioners, as many deep Schemes appear to me to be laid which tend in my opinion towards the ruin of our Constitution." Even Dunmore had heard that the convention was plagued by dissent. Such divisions may account for the fact that the convention delegates took more than six long weeks to pass a total of seven ordinances—most of them concerning vital and pressing questions over military preparations.[39]

Despite Continental movements, patriot leaders in Virginia were still divided, mainly because of provincial concerns. Many of the divisions were over the size and composition of the troops to be raised. Some conservative and moderate delegates were reluctant to raise any troops; others wanted to raise many more in order to ensure that they and their property (including slaves) were safe. More militant delegates wanted to channel the energy of the volunteers into the new military units, with the popular Patrick Henry at their head. Others wanted to curb the volunteers entirely. The compromises reached at the convention would, in the end, please few.

At least some of the divisions stemmed from the general question of Patrick Henry's future role, echoing earlier debates about his conduct. In particular, there was heated discussion over who should lead the new troops, particularly the regular forces. Delegates believed that "the Contest" would be fought between the moderate Thomas Nelson, Jr., and Patrick Henry. When the issue first arose more formally, however, on August 3, the convention agreed to a resolution to raise one thousand regulars in two battalions and appointed William Woodford "first in Command" of the troops. Woodford was immediately responsible for a contingent that would be sent to the Norfolk area to restore peace, and Nelson was appointed as the second colonel, to lead a contingent based around Williamsburg. From experience, Woodford, a close friend and neighbor of Edmund Pendleton and a veteran of the Seven Years' War, could be counted upon

39. Mason to Martin Cockburn, Aug. 5, 1775, Mason to Washington, Oct. 14, 1775, *Papers of Mason*, I, 245, 255; Robert Wormeley Carter to Landon Carter, Aug. 5, 10, 1775, Sabine Hall Papers, UVa; Dunmore to Lord Dartmouth, Sept. 24, 1775, William Bell Clark et al., eds., *Naval Documents of the American Revolution* (Washington, D.C., 1964-), II, 195.

by the more moderate forces in the convention to work closely with them. Significantly, neither Nelson nor Woodford had served in the independent companies, and both were then sitting in the convention. Henry was still on his way back from the Continental Congress.[40]

But this first hasty resolution was either withdrawn or defeated, and the convention reconsidered the leadership question again two days later, on August 5. First, it separated civil and military offices by barring anyone who accepted a commission in the regular forces from serving as a member of the convention, Continental Congress, or Committee of Safety. Thus foreclosing the possibility that a popular man like Henry could join the two under one command, the convention then balloted for the colonels of the three regiments now seen as necessary. In the first ballot, for the colonelcy of the First Regiment, Hugh Mercer received 41 votes, Patrick Henry 40 votes, Thomas Nelson, Jr., 8 votes, and William Woodford 1 vote. In a run-off vote between Henry and Mercer, Henry won with a "Majority." Nelson was then elected colonel of the Second Regiment, but, perhaps because he would technically be under the command of Henry, he then withdrew altogether. Woodford was elected colonel of the Third Regiment after another decisive vote.[41]

If such proceedings left Carter complaining that the delegates were "undoing one day, what we did the day before," things would get worse. On August 9, the convention, sitting as a committee of the whole to discuss the committee's report on the ordinance for raising a sufficient force for the defense and protection of the colony, amended the number of regulars to be raised from 3,000 down to 1,020 men. Such a move eliminated the Third Regiment that Woodford had been appointed to command, but it also raised the question of command again more generally. Carter told his father he "cannot say who is to command" the reduced forces. Henry had accepted his appointment as soon as he returned on August 9 from Congress—just after the convention voted for the reduction in troops—but Carter thought, "As many of us are averse to him, some intend to bring on that matter again." Carter himself believed "it will be to no purpose" to do so, however, as Henry, just returned, would now be able to defend himself.

40. Robert Wormeley Carter to Landon Carter, July 29, 1775, Sabine Hall Papers, UVa; Proceedings of the Third Virginia Convention, Aug. 3, 1775, *Rev. Va.*, III, 393, 395; *Rev. Va.*, III, 119.

41. Proceedings of the Third Virginia Convention, Aug. 5, 9, 1775, *Rev. Va.*, III, 399–401, 409; *Rev. Va.*, III, 402–403.

Carter, a more moderate patriot yet accused by his own father of politicking, clearly became anxious. "I really fear trusting him," Carter wrote about Henry, "as he is very popular, and I know his principles."[42]

Any doubt over who was the overall commander in chief of the regular forces was finally resolved when the committee appointed to draw up the commission forms for the officers of the regular forces, minutemen, and militia reported. The committee printed the form of commission for the colonel of the First Regiment in its entirety, with Patrick Henry's name therein, and gave it to the convention as the proper commission for the "commander in chief of the regular forces." But, if Henry's final accession to power went uncontested in the convention chambers, the commission, the Committee of Safety, and the rules and regulations for the army made it clear that Henry's authority was limited and significantly circumscribed by the civilian powers of the colony. The commission clearly stated that the source of Henry's appointment was the delegates in convention. They gave Henry command of the First Regiment and made him "commander in chief of all such other forces" that might be ordered, by the convention, or Committee of Safety, to act in conjunction with them. The convention also empowered Henry to "resist and repel all hostile invasions, and quell and suppress any insurrections which may be made or attempted against the peace and safety of this his majesty's colony." But, equally, the commission stated that Henry had to promote "discipline and order among the officers and soldiers under your command, agreeable to such ordinances, rules, and articles, which are now, or hereafter may be, instituted for the government and regulation of the army." The commission also made it clear that Henry had to pay "due obedience to all orders and instructions which from time to time you may receive from the Convention or Committee of Safety." Henry was to "hold, exercise, and enjoy" his office "during the pleasure of the Convention, and no longer."[43]

42. Robert Wormeley Carter to Landon Carter, Aug. 5, 10, 1775, Sabine Hall Papers, UVa; Proceedings of the Third Virginia Convention, Aug. 9, 1775, *Rev. Va.*, III, 409; *Rev. Va.*, II, 216. For further divisions, cf. Proceedings of the Third Virginia Convention, Aug. 10, 17, 25, 1775, *Rev. Va.*, III, 413, 457–459, 488, 493; *Va. Gaz.* (Pinkney), Sept. 7, 1775.

43. Proceedings of the Third Virginia Convention, Aug. 21, 26, 1775, *Rev. Va.*, III, 471, 498, 499. For divisions over the number of men to be raised, see Robert Wormeley Carter to Landon Carter, July 29, Aug. 5, 1775, Sabine Hall Papers, UVa; George Mason to Martin Cockburn, Aug. 5, 1775, Mason to Washington, Oct. 14, 1775, *Papers of Mason*, I, 250, 251, 256; *Rev. Va.*, III, 394–395.

By the end of the convention, then, the moderates among the delegates appeared to have won the day and curbed and contained not just the independence of the volunteer companies but also one of their most popular leaders. George Mason told Washington some weeks afterward that it was only "after some Weeks" of meeting that the "Partys and Factions" that had generally prevailed in disrupting the proceedings of the meeting began to quiet as "the Bablers were pretty well silenced." In their place, a "few weighty Members began to take the Lead," and "several wholsome Regulations were made, and if the Convention had continued to sit a few Days longer, I think the public Safety wou'd have been as well provided for as our present Circumstances permit." In the end, the delegates also managed to paper over any and all divisions during the convention, presenting a united public front to their constituents and to the governor. But the barely muted divisions inside the convention only foreshadowed more explicit divisions outside the halls of assembly.[44]

44. Mason to Washington, Oct. 14, 1775, *Papers of Mason,* I, 255.

PART TWO

Movements for Independence

CHAPTER 4 *Plebeian* I*nfamy*

THE MINUTEMEN AND *Their* WORLD

A period of relative calm followed the adjournment of the Third Convention in August 1775, giving patriot leaders hope that their plans to shore up the defense of the colony and restore authority over the protest movement had worked. For at least a month after the convention adjourned, Dunmore was at bay in the Chesapeake battling only nature (at least one fierce storm from the Caribbean battered his small fleet and drove several ships on shore) and boredom as he awaited further instructions from London. In the meantime, white Virginians went about the business of recruiting. After a quiet September, Dr. Archibald Campbell of Norfolk reported in early October, "Our reguler Provincial Troops are . . . rised." Ten days later, another white Virginian noted, "The standing army of this Colony is compleated and station'd about two miles from Williamsburg." The newspapers of the colony reported the arrival of each company of soldiers and eagerly repeated rumors that more soldiers were on their way or about to arrive. Of the fifteen companies ordered to Williamsburg in August 1775, twelve arrived by October 21, and the remaining three (from Berkeley, Pittsylvania, and Augusta West districts, the three most distant) arrived by early December. Altogether, about a thousand men—or a complete contingent of the regular forces the convention ordered raised—gathered in and around Williamsburg in the late fall of 1775.[1]

We know very little about these early recruits. They were probably a mixed group, however. In the initial flush of patriotic enthusiasm, several

1. Archibald Campbell to St. George Tucker, Oct. 10, 1775, William Bell Clark et al., eds., *Naval Documents of the American Revolution* (Washington, D.C., 1964-), II, 395; James Freeland to John Tailyour, Oct. 20, 1775, *Rev. Va.,* IV, 246; *Rev. Va.,* IV, 274-275; Brent Tarter, ed., "The Orderly Book of the Second Virginia Regiment: September 27, 1775-April 15, 1776," *VMHB,* LXXXV (1977), 170-171, and nn. 44-46; *Va. Gaz.* (D and H), Oct. 7, 14, 21, 1775.

of these new recruits were undoubtedly drawn from the volunteer companies. They might have been younger sons of gentlemen and middling farmers, eager for battle and a chance to test their mettle. Though George Mason was against the idea, he thought his own son George might be attracted by the new army and have "a Mind to enter into the Service." But, following eighteenth-century tradition and Virginia's own experience in the Seven Years' War, most were undoubtedly young, single, and not particularly wealthy. For such men, even this short-term service promised some job security, a signing-on bonus of the first month's pay, clothes, and a musket.[2]

But, if the small regular force was raised with little fuss, recruiting for the larger and more important minuteman service quickly ran into problems. After an initial flurry of enlistments, reports began to circulate that recruiting was sluggish. James Freeland from Fredericksburg noted on October 20, 1775, "The Officers of The Minute men are much behind and by all accots will not be able to get the full compliment of men." Freeland thought that only one district had yet been recruited to full strength. Just over a week later, Archibald Cary from Chesterfield County confirmed the problem firsthand. His own battalion of minutemen was "not Yet Compleat," though he had already been given command of them. In fact, only half of his command had been raised. Based on his own experience and other stories, Cary worried that "few Battalions of Minute Men will be rais'd" at all. In mid-November, Fielding Lewis confirmed Cary's prophecy, telling George Washington that still only one battalion was complete and that there was "little prospect of the others being so."[3]

2. George Mason to Martin Cockburn, Aug. 5, 1775, *Papers of George Mason,* I, 245–246. No studies have been done of these first recruits, mainly because complete lists of soldiers are scarce. But see Richard C. Bush, "'Awake, Rouse Your Courage, Americans Brave': Companies Raised in Northumberland County for the Virginia Continental Line, 1776 and 1777," *Bulletin of the Northumberland County Historical Society,* XXIX (1992), 7–10; John Johnson to ———, Nov. 16, 1775, *Rev. Va.,* IV, 415.

3. James Freeland to John Tailyour, Oct. 20, 1775, *Rev. Va.,* IV, 246; Archibald Cary to Thomas Jefferson, Oct. 31, 1775, *Papers of Jefferson,* I, 249; Fielding Lewis to George Washington, Nov. 14, 1775, *Papers of Washington,* Rev. War. Ser., II, 372; Northhampton County Committee of Safety to the Continental Congress, Nov. 17, 1775, "Virginia Legislative Papers," *VMHB,* XIV (1906–1907), 253. Cf. John Page to the Chairman of the Lancaster District Committee (Landon Carter), Nov. 4, 1775, Sabine Hall Papers, UVa.

By all accounts, recruiting for the minute service went from bad to worse. Lund Washington told his cousin George in early December: "Our minute Scheme does not Equal the Conventions Expectation. [T]he people do not come readily into it." In early January, Robert Honyman, a physician from Hanover County who kept a diary through the war, concluded, "There never was more than half of them raised," the hopeful patriot actually overestimating the number. In all, by the end of October 1775, only 49 of 160 companies had been raised, and many of these were yet incomplete. Culpeper district battalion, for example, touted as the largest and best known of the minutemen units, raised fourteen companies. However, the officers were able to muster only about 350 men to march to Williamsburg in October 1775—the equivalent of just seven full companies.[4]

Explanations for the failure of the minute service varied, though many contemporaries believed that the terms of the service were the problem, not patriotic enthusiasm itself. Honyman noted that, from the start, "people disliked the plan." The Northampton Committee of Safety also complained that "people in general" were "averse to the minute service" in particular. Fielding Lewis was disgusted that his neighbors would not enlist, even though, he reported with some sarcasm, "all are ready they say to serve their Country."[5]

But George Gilmer, the same former officer of the Albemarle indepen-

4. Lund Washington to George Washington, Dec. 3, 1775, *Papers of Washington,* Rev. War. Ser., II, 479; Jan. 2, 1776, Diary of Robert Honyman, Jan. 2, 1776–Mar. 11, 1782, Alderman Library, UVa (microfilm) (cf. Mar. 17, 1776); Hening, comp., *Statutes at Large,* IX, 86–88; E. M. Sanchez-Saavedra, *A Guide to Virginia Military Organizations in the American Revolution* (Richmond, Va., 1978), 13; Sanchez-Saavedra, "'All Fine Fellows and Well-Armed': The Culpeper Minute Battalion, 1775-1776," *Virginia Cavalcade,* XXIV (1974–1975), 4–6. Sanchez-Saavedra's work does not distinguish between complete and incomplete companies; he also includes companies that were raised after December. The number of companies raised in whole or in part before the end of October was forty-nine, and from November to December only another nineteen were formed. For a full analysis of the raising of the minutemen companies, see Michael A. McDonnell, "Popular Mobilization and Political Culture in Revolutionary Virginia: The Failure of the Minutemen and the Revolution from Below," *JAH,* LXXXV (1998–1999), 946–981.

5. Jan. 2, 1776, Diary of Honyman; Northhampton County Committee of Safety to the Continental Congress, Nov. 17, 1775, in "Virginia Legislative Papers," *VMHB* (1906–1907), XIV, 253; Fielding Lewis to Washington, Nov. 14, 1775, *Papers of Washington,* Rev. War. Ser., II, 372.

dent company—and now a convert to the minutemen—believed that there were several problems and many different groups of dissatisfied whites in Virginia. In an illuminating address for his neighbors at the end of October, Gilmer summed up what he thought were the main causes of complaint about the minuteman service but also revealed other sources of discontent. He confirmed what others suspected: many former volunteers were dissatisfied with the particular terms of service in the new minuteman establishment. Others felt that the new service was simply too "burthensome," particularly while Virginia was not at the center of the war. Still others were concerned about the security of their families and farms, especially in view of enslaved Virginians' increased rebelliousness. Finally, much to Gilmer's frustration, many believed that "Gentlemen" or the "men of Fortune" ought to bear the expense and difficulties of defending the colony against Britain.[6]

Gilmer's remarkable speech revealed a number of divisions and problems in Virginia; but, most worrying for patriot leaders like Gilmer, that discontent was widespread and endemic through all ranks of white society. The failure of the minute service not only reflected those divisions, but the new military regulations actually contributed to them. At the very moment that the patriot leadership asked for the support of all white Virginians, Gilmer asserted, "Every denomination of the people seem backward." The problem was twofold: in resurrecting the militia and calling for more than eight thousand minutemen, leaders were asking for much greater support than previously. But, because they were more concerned with controlling the new armed services, the regulations they imposed on them alienated even some of their most ardent supporters. The consequences were dire.[7]

• • • Gilmer and other patriot leaders were particularly concerned about the drop in martial enthusiasm among their most loyal constituents—those who had fought in the volunteer companies a mere few months previous. Many white Virginians who had joined them in the spring and early summer apparently refused to sign on for the minute service as generally ex-

6. "Address to the Inhabitants of Albermarle," [fall 1775], R. A. Brock, ed., "Papers, Military and Political, 1775–1778, of George Gilmer, M.D., of 'Pen Park,' Albemarle County, Va.," VHS, *Collections,* n.s., VI (1887), 115–119, 122, 123, 125. The speech was written sometime after October 22, 1775, the date of Peyton Randolph's death, which Gilmer notes, but sometime before Dunmore planted his standard in Norfolk in mid-November.

7. Ibid., 123.

pected. Gilmer complained, "The Convention have altered the name Volunteers to that of Minute Men, and behold! what a wondrous effect it has had." "Out of near three hundred Volunteers" in Albemarle County alone, "so few" had joined the minutemen that "I am afraid to name them." Gilmer, like others in the colony, was surprised and embarrassed at the extent of the problem and the apparent change in attitude among those previously committed to the patriot cause. "We were once all fire, now most of us are become inanimate and indifferent."[8]

Though most of Gilmer's address was aimed indiscriminately at previous volunteers and nonvolunteers alike, he did address the specific concerns and complaints that he felt were keeping ex-volunteers out of the new minute service. From the point of view of Gilmer's neighbors, the minute service was much more burdensome than service in the independent companies. Ex-volunteers' biggest complaint was the amount of time required to train: twenty days initially, plus four days a month after that, and twelve days with a battalion twice more in the year. Small farmers, with little or no help around the estate, found this, in the words of George Gilmer, "a heavy duty." This was particularly heavy for middling and poorer farmers who owned no slaves. For many slaveholding planters, time away from the estate meant at worst lost profits; for a small farmer with no help—whose own labor sustained his family—the basic subsistence of the family was at risk. Hence many ordinary Virginians were particularly affected by calls for them to leave their farms for any duration, when they constituted the prime labor force. Moreover, training took place at some of the busiest periods of the farming year. Though the wealthy slaveholding elite who created the minutemen could rely on enslaved workers and other help in their absence, small farmers could lose an entire year's crop in several days' absence. The "One great Objection" of the inhabitants of Accomack to the minute service "Arises from the time of Encampment being such that it must unavoidably break in upon their whole years Business."[9]

8. Ibid., 122–125.

9. Ibid., 122–123, 125, 127; Hening, comp., *Statutes at Large,* IX, 20–21; Accomack County Committee of Safety to the Fourth Virginia Convention, Nov. 30, 1775, "Virginia Legislative Papers," *VMHB,* XIV (1906–1907), 258. For complaints that military service hit nonslaveholders harder, see Petition from Chesterfield County, in Proceedings of the Fifth Virginia Convention, May 7, 1776, *Rev. Va.,* VII, 47. For a full analysis of the impact of training on the farming year, see McDonnell, "Popular Mobilization," *JAH,* LXXXV (1998–1999), 946–981.

But ex-volunteers, like delegates to the convention, were also concerned about the leadership of the minutemen. The delegates to the Third Virginia Convention had quite abruptly and resolutely abandoned the experiment of allowing troops to elect their own officers, as part of the backlash against the independence of the volunteer companies. Gentlemen wanted to bring the armed services under greater civilian control. Yet some also wanted to curb the potentially subversive aspects of the popularization of the military; elections for officers could and did make a mockery of the traditional hierarchy of the militia, where officer rankings generally reflected power and status among the gentry in each county. Thus, they gave responsibility for appointing militia and minutemen officers to the locally elected county committees and the newly created district committees (of representatives from each county committee).[10]

In abolishing elections of officers by their own men, the delegates repudiated one factor in the success of the earlier mobilization. Many ex-volunteers, contemplating enlistment in the new minuteman service, felt aggrieved that the right to elect officers directly had been taken away from them, particularly when even Congress had recommended that all militia and minutemen officers below field officers be elected. Believing the committees were still dominated by wealthy planters and the county elite, many volunteers resented having officers imposed upon them by their supposed

10. Mason to Martin Cockburn, Aug. 22, 1775, *Papers of Mason,* I, 251; Hening, comp., *Statutes at Large,* IX, 9–35. Some gentlemen believed that this mode of appointing officers was still *too* popular. They wanted appointments back in the hands of the county courts, not elected county committees. See, for example, James Hendricks to Leven Powell, Apr. 5, 1776, Robert C. Powell, ed., *A Biographical Sketch of Col. Leven Powell, Including His Correspondence during the Revolutionary War* (Alexandria, Va., 1877), 84–85; Archibald Cary to Jefferson, Oct. 31, 1775, *Papers of Jefferson,* I, 249; Courtlandt Canby, ed., "Robert Munford's *The Patriots,*" *WMQ,* 3d Ser., VI (1949), 437–503. On popularity of new officers, see Hening, comp., *Statutes at Large,* IX, 86; June 3, 1775, Robert Greenhalgh Albion and Leonidas Dodson, eds., *Philip Vickers Fithian: Journal, 1775–1776, Written on the Virginia-Pennsylvania Frontier and in the Army around New York* (Princeton, N.J., 1934), 21; Albemarle County Deputies to John Ware [Sept. 1775], Gilmer Papers, VHS. Cf. Washington to John Hancock, Sept. 24, 1776, *Papers of Washington,* Rev. War. Ser., VI, 387–388. Some gentlemen wanted the central Committee of Safety alone to have power over appointments. See Pendleton to Woodford, Dec. 24, 1775, *Papers of Pendleton,* I, 140–141.

betters. In Northumberland County, there was "great excitement growing" among farmers because of the "desire" among the "leading men" there to "have their friends appointed" as officers. Ex-volunteers simply refused to serve under such appointed officers. George Gilmer, one of those appointed officers, understood the problem clearly. In order to persuade his neighbors to join him in the minutemen, he told them that he was "ready and willing to submit to the determination of such as are or intend to become minute men, whether I shall continue Captain or become a common soldier." Attempting to rouse popular enthusiasm and counter criticism, Gilmer's willingness to make this concession is significant.[11]

In the end, small farmers' discontent with the mode of appointing officers, in both the minutemen and the militia, was exacerbated by the convention's introduction of a hierarchical pay structure for the entire armed services. Whereas neither officer nor private was paid in the independent companies, in the new military establishment even the most junior officers were paid twelve times as much as privates (three shillings per day, as opposed to one-quarter shilling, or three pennies, per day). Captains of companies in the minute and regular services were paid twenty-four times as much as privates, and field officers (major through colonel) in the regulars between forty and one hundred times more than privates. Patrick Henry, colonel of the First Regiment, was paid almost forty pounds per month, compared to less than eight shillings for the privates under him. Colonels in the minute service were paid slightly less than Henry and Colonel William Woodford, but they would still receive sixty times the pay of their neigh-

11. Congress had made the recommendation to elect officers in a letter reprinted in the public newspapers (see *Va. Gaz.* [D and H], Aug. 5, 1775). Richard C. Bush, "The Militia of Northumberland County," *Bulletin of the Northumberland County Historical Society,* XXXI (1994), 29; "Address," Brock, ed., "Papers of Gilmer," VHS, *Collections,* n.s., VI (1887), 125. Cf. Nov. 19–20, 1775, Albion and Dodson, eds., *Fithian Journal,* 133–134. Virginia stood almost alone among the colonies in repudiating the concept of popular elections of officers at the company-grade level. For elections of officers elsewhere, see Don Higginbotham, "The American Militia: A Traditional Institution wtih Revolutionary Responsibilities," in Higginbotham, *War and Society in Revolutionary America: The Wider Dimensions of Conflict* (Columbia, S.C., 1988), 87: "Whereas in New England there was a tradition of electing militia officers, the conflict with Britain saw the extension of that practice, especially below field grade, to New York, New Jersey, Pennsylvania, Maryland, and southward."

bors. Officers and privates in the militia were, when called out on duty, subject to the same pay scale as the regulars.[12]

At a basic level, higher pay for officers meant more taxes to pay them. However, many farmers, particularly ex-volunteers, complained that this was unequal pay for what was ostensibly equal work. When the new forces were first established, "the People" in Loudoun County complained about the officers' wages as "being too high." Even the chairman of the Sussex county committee had criticized the delegates of the convention over the wages of the officers for the new forces, inadvertently helping to "inflame the minds of the people." Gilmer's Albemarle neighbors also denounced "any difference in the pay of an officer and soldier." In fact, some among them believed that, as in the volunteer companies, there should be "no pay at all" for officers or soldiers.[13]

Most gentlemen in the convention, of course, were persuaded that discipline and subordination demanded a wide pay disparity, that a much greater pay allocation for officers was absolutely vital to the maintenance of a rigid hierarchy, necessary for maintaining discipline. George Washington would argue later that better pay for officers was absolutely necessary to preserve a "decent" distance between an officer and his men. If an officer was in no way distinguished, his men would "consider and treat him as an equal; and . . . regard him no more than a broomstick." Without a proper distinction, an officer and his men would be "mixed together as one common herd" in which "no order, nor no discipline can prevail." Without proper pay, an officer could never "meet with that respect which is essentially necessary to due subordination." Charles Lee, a former British army officer, made the connection between pay and "distinctions" more explicit. Petitioning Congress for an increase in officers' pay, he explained: "Men who chuse to preserve the decent distance of officers, must have a decent subsistance, and without this distance no authority or respect can be expected." A little later, he reinforced the need for "distance" when he ordered his officers to "be particular in not associating with the Soldiers so far as to let them Make use of Familiarity." The ideas of professional officers were

12. Hening, comp., *Statutes at Large,* IX, 10, 21–23, 34.

13. Leven Powell to Sally Powell, Dec. 5, 1775, photocopy of original letter in private hands, VHS; *Va. Gaz.* (Pinkney), Nov. 20, 1775; "Address," Brock, ed., "Papers of Gilmer," VHS, *Collections,* n.s., VI (1887), 125–126. Cf. Lund Washington to George Washington, Feb. 29, 1776, *Papers of Washington,* Rev. War. Ser., III, 395–396.

apparently common knowledge among civilian gentlemen. "Such as have been already in the service," Gilmer explained, trying to counter his neighbors' complaints in the fall of 1775, "must know that without some distinction there can be no subordination."[14]

The language of these gentlemen contrasted sharply with that used to celebrate the virtue of the independent companies a few short months earlier. Gentlemen then had stressed the equality of each member of the volunteer companies, and, after Dunmore's seizure of the powder, they had been at pains to emphasize that white Virginians, "rich and poor," had taken up arms together to repel Dunmore's provocations. On mobilizing earlier in the year, Gilmer asked, "Did we not all indiscriminately mix together as Volunteers; was there ever any partiality or distinction shewn?" Yet now gentlemen expected ordinary Virginians, even well-to-do white ones, to recognize distinctions among themselves and show respect and subordination to officers appointed over them.[15]

The contest over military service and the complaints about the minute service reflected wider social issues. The convention delegates intended the minute service to channel the volunteers' enthusiasm for the cause. In an important sense, delegates linked the service to the militia and the citizen-soldier ideal. Delegates wanted the minutemen to be filled with independent, liberty-loving inhabitants yet also to serve as an institutional control over the passions of armed men. Shocked by the spectacle of bands of armed men roaming the countryside taking the law into their own hands in the summer of 1775, patriot gentlemen in the Third Convention were keen to direct them into a more disciplined and subordinate group, one more traditional in military—and social—organization. Officers would be

14. Washington to John Hancock, Sept. 24, 1776, *Papers of Washington,* Rev. War. Ser., VI, 110, 387–388; Charles Lee to Benjamin Rush, Oct. 10, [1775], *The Lee Papers,* I, 212, New-York Historical Society, *Collections,* IV (1871); General Orders, Apr. 3, 1776, "The Orderly Book of the Company of Captain George Stubblefield, Fifth Virginia Regiment, from March 3, 1776, to July 10, 1776, Inclusive," VHS, *Collections,* n.s., VI (1887), 159; "Address," Brock, ed., "Papers of Gilmer," VHS, *Collections,* n.s., VI (1887), 126, 128.

15. "Address," Brock, ed., "Papers of Gilmer," VHS, *Collections,* n.s., VI (1887), 122, 126. Compare, for example, the "instructions" of county lieutenant John Augustine Washington to one of his militia captains in the fall of 1775 with the "subscriptions" entered into the previous spring by the independent companies and noted in Chapter 1 (see John Augustine Washington to ———, Nov. 1775, Feinstone Collection, DLAR).

appointed, and only by other gentlemen. Rules and regulations, a carefully delineated hierarchy, and a centralized command were imposed. Discipline was paramount. Though explicitly military concerns seem to be at the forefront of efforts to reform the armed services, implicit concerns for the social order clearly were behind the way they reorganized.

For example, when the conflict began, many gentlemen hoped that deference would be sufficient to rouse popular enthusiasm and keep it under control, that the independent companies would "infuse a martial spirit of emulation" and "excite others by our Example." In other military matters, they hoped for ordinary Virginians' "implicit acquiescence and Concurrence" (as Cumberland officials put it) in whatever was recommended. As Gilmer noted with regard to the minutemen, the gentry wanted and expected ordinary Virginians to "sacrifice their own ease and interests to their country's wellfare." When appeals to deference failed to keep small farmers in check, gentlemen tried to reimpose their authority through a more traditional military establishment that reasserted their raw power through regulations reinforcing subordination, discipline, and hierarchy. In the midst of a colonial protest movement that was rapidly deteriorating into an outright rebellion, gentlemen had suddenly found that, in challenging royal authority, their own authority was rendered precarious by a volatile enslaved population, an uneasy lower class, and an uncertain middling group of farmers. In organizing for further conflict, gentlemen expected, and needed, obedience to a rule of law that sustained their authority.[16]

More explicitly, George Gilmer first invoked a deferential argument to justify distinctions for officers in the form of higher pay. He asked his neighbors, "Could a thinking, considerate soldier suffer a man who he admires, whose commands animate him to action, to be no ways distinguished?" Yet while officers were no longer elected, "admiration" was hardly the glue that bonded or "wedded" "thinking men" to their "superiors." Gilmer, obviously in frustration, then betrayed a mentality that must have prevailed among many gentlemen at this critical juncture. Realizing

16. "Address to the Inhabitants of the County of Cumberland," June 30, 1775, "Proceedings of the Committees of Safety of Cumberland and Isle of Wight Counties, 1775–1776," Virginia State Library Board, *Fifteenth Annual Report* (Richmond, Va., 1919), 16–17; George Mason, "Remarks on Annual Elections," [ca. Apr. 17–26, 1775], and Fairfax County Militia Association, [Sept. 21, 1774], *Papers of Mason,* I, 210, 229; "Address," Brock, ed., "Papers of Gilmer," VHS, *Collections,* n.s., VI (1887), 122–123, 125, 127.

that deference was not sufficient to justify the distinctions in rank that the convention had introduced, Gilmer invoked a more trenchant metaphor. Since "Time immemorial every head or chief has had marks of distinction and certain emoluments above those under him. The Custom is so prevalent with ourselves that every planter allows his Gang leader certain indulgences and emoluments above the rest of his slaves." In comparing the new military establishment with slavery, Gilmer in one breath infuriated his neighbors and betrayed the anxieties of many prominent planters about their lack of control over both their enslaved workers and their white inferiors.[17]

Gilmer could not have introduced a more revealing analogy in a colony in which approximately 40 percent of the population were enslaved, constantly reminding small farmers of what they were *not* supposed to be. It was precisely the same inequality, subordination, dependence, and involuntary service inherent in slavery that farmers were sensitized against in the military. Ordinary Virginians were having none of it. They refused to act deferentially, and they refused to act like enslaved Virginians, particularly when asked to make unequal sacrifices. They would serve only on their own "terms"—expressed in their wish, manifested most obviously in the independent companies, to "mix indiscriminately" with gentlemen, with "no partiality or distinction shewn," and march "promiscuously and on equal footing." George Washington himself perhaps best summed up the problems inherent in the clash of cultures between the gentry and yeomanry. Remonstrating against the idea of raising "volunteers" in Virginia a little later in the war, Washington claimed, "Those who engage in Arms under that denomination . . . are uneasy, impatient of Command—ungovernable and claiming to themselves a sort of superior merit generally assume not only the privilege of thinking, but to do as they please." In their demands for no differences in pay, or no pay at all, the inhabitants of Albemarle, along with those in other counties like Loudoun, demanded just that. They demanded, in short, not to be "tied down by the severest rules," as Gilmer told them they must, but instead to be "free to do and act as they please," especially while making sacrifices.[18]

The differences between the terms of service of the independent com-

17. "Address," Brock, ed., "Papers of Gilmer," VHS, *Collections,* n.s., VI (1887), 126.

18. Washington to Henry, Apr. 13, 1777, *Papers of Washington,* Rev. War. Ser., IX, 146–148.

panies—the volunteer companies—and the minuteman service were crucial for many potential enlistees. Gentlemen in the convention had indeed changed "the name Volunteers to that of Minute Men," but that was not all they changed. They had established rigid rules and regulations for the minute service, virtually identical to those in the regular service. They had also introduced more rigorous forms of discipline and control within all of the armed forces, including the minute service. Finally, they had ended the election of officers and established a hierarchical pay structure within the forces that would reinforce dramatically the distinctions between officers and men. Patriot leaders did succeed in creating distinctions with the new minute service; they were not, however, the kind of divisions patriot leaders had envisaged.

Patriot gentlemen had miscalculated, and their attempt to reassert control over zealous patriots and the military establishment had backfired, actually helping to end the rage militaire that had prevailed in Virginia during the spring and summer of 1775 and creating and exposing more divisions between Virginians. Patriot gentlemen helped quash the martial enthusiasm of ordinary Virginians and even angered many into neutrality or apathy. The minuteman plan had contributed to the demise of patriot enthusiasm for the cause and, at a crucial moment, had crushed a more popular movement.

As Gilmer feared, problems in the minute service had wide and dramatic repercussions. Patriot gentlemen across Virginia fretted about the lack of enlistments. They knew what was at stake. Not only would the colony's physical defense be jeopardized without a large force to counter Dunmore and threatened British invasions, but the very patriot movement was also in danger of collapsing. Fielding Lewis, noting the problems in the minute service in early November, told George Washington that Virginia was in the "greatest confusion." Gilmer climaxed his speech by pleading with his neighbors to put aside their differences and to overcome their specific objections, to "rouze what spirit resides in our constitutions" and "become . . . Minute men, or we shall not know who to call on in the moment of danger." If patriotic farmers hesitated, Gilmer implied, they would have a much harder time trying to mobilize other ordinary Virginians who were not yet convinced about the patriot cause.[19]

19. Fielding Lewis to Washington, Nov. 14, 1775, ibid., II, 372; "Address," Brock, ed., "Papers of Gilmer," VHS, *Collections,* n.s., VI (1887), 125.

• • • As a result the rest—and bulk—of Gilmer's speech was most clearly aimed at those yet unconvinced. The first four pages of his long address reiterated the patriot position in the imperial dispute, and Gilmer reminded his neighbors of the events leading to the present crisis and the attempts of Congress to settle the matter without recourse to arms. Gilmer tried to make the conflict personal. The admiralty laws, he asserted, gave a board of commissioners power to "forcibly" enter "your houses" and "break up and destroy all such furniture as he shall suspect to contain contraband." "Insolent" excise officers could "g[ou]ge" their orchards, and "almost every conveniency in life" could be taxed to support a "debauched nobility and pensioned sycophants." In short, their very farms were at the mercy of Parliament, "to be disposed of as they please." They were in imminent danger of attack as well. Boston had been attacked, and Dunmore threatened their own shores.[20]

Gilmer's words must have struck a chord with some of his neighbors, but only to increase their fears. In addition to the governor's threats, from about July 1775 onward rumors had been flying that the British planned to throw their weight against the southern colonies. To raise support for the patriot cause, the newspapers helped fuel these fears; they reported in October that, among other plans, the British were sending "commodore Shuldham, with a fleet of frigates, cutters, and tenders, to Virginia, to destroy the towns, and carry devastation to all the plantations upon the rivers." The propaganda campaign backfired. Such rumors were particularly rife in October 1775, just as recruiting for the minuteman plan began to stall. Many preferred to keep their heads low. Lund Washington in Fairfax County thought there was a class divide in the face of these threats. He could only believe that the "gentlemen" were "ready and willing to turn out and defend any mans property," but the "common people" were "most Hellishly freightned."[21]

20. "Address," Brock, ed., "Papers of Gilmer," VHS, *Collections,* n.s., VI (1887), 116, 125–128.

21. A Person of Credit in London, Extract, July 31, 1775, *Rev. Va.,* IV, 32; Virginia Delegates in Congress to the Virginia Committee of Safety, Oct. 6, 1775, *Rev. Va.,* IV, 169, 173n; *Va. Gaz.* (Purdie), Oct. 20, 1775; Resolution, Virginia Committee of Safety, Oct. 26, 1775, *Va. Gaz.* (Pinkney), Oct. 26, 1775; Oct. 23–24, 1775, Nicholas Cresswell, *The Journal of Nicholas Cresswell, 1774–1777* (London, 1925), 127; Lund Washington to George Washington, Oct. 29, Nov. 14, 1775, *Papers of Washington,* Rev. War. Ser., II, 258, 375. Cf. Jefferson to Francis Eppes, Oct. 10,

Rumors and reports that Dunmore or other British officers were cruising Virginia's inner waterways were particularly worrying in light of Dunmore's now apparently open door policy toward enslaved and indentured Virginians. Rumors continued to circulate that Dunmore was enlisting slaves, servants, and any other Virginians who might be willing to join his ranks against the patriots. Verified reports of servants' and enslaved Virginians' escaping to British ships only intensified fears. Rumors of insurrections compounded the problem. Early in September, Samuel Kemp, a schoolteacher in Caroline County, had to counter "infamous" reports that he "had endeavoured to exasperate the Negroes to rise and carry into Execution the Ministerial Measures." Many whites were on edge. Fearful for their lives, the safety of their families, and the loss of their property, smallholders and planters alike in affected areas refused to join the new minuteman service.[22]

Though a restive enslaved and indentured population might have kept farmers on their back foot, smallholders in Virginia also had other—perhaps more compelling—reasons for not joining the new minuteman plan. Gilmer complained that his neighbors had multiplied and exaggerated numerous misfortunes that might accrue from a "determined resistance" to Britain. Most simply had "no inclination to sacrifice their own ease and interests to the country's welfare." Yet Gilmer's speech reveals that farmers had very specific interests to defend, and they were often at odds with those of the patriot leadership. Underlying many of the complaints about the new minute service were more serious class resentments about the inequity of the new military establishment in general. Most obviously, at least some of Gilmer's neighbors thought that the new military establishment was unfair

1775, *Papers of Jefferson,* I, 247, Robert Carter Nicholas to Washington, Sept. 8, 1775, *Rev. Va.,* IV, 78–79; Francis Lightfoot Lee to Landon Carter, Oct. 21, 1775, Clark et al., eds., *Naval Documents,* II, 557.

22. *Va. Gaz.* (D and H), Sept. 23, 30, Oct. 21, 1775; *Va. Gaz.* (Pinkney), Oct. 26, 1775. Owners of both servants and slaves who ran away assumed they were headed toward Dunmore (see, for example, notice for John Greene, *Va. Gaz.* [D and H], Oct. 21, 1775). Other enslaved Virginians simply took advantage of the divisions among whites and the failing military establishment to make a bid for freedom— not necessarily to join Dunmore. In late September, William Byrd gave notice that two of his slaves, Michael and Aaron, had broken free from the Charles City jail, where they were under a sentence of death. Byrd feared that they were "daring and dangerous Villains, capable of attempting the most horrid Crimes." *Va. Gaz.* (D and H), Sept. 23, 1775.

and particularly oppressive to poorer Virginians; many had complained it was "calculated to exempt the gentlemen and throw the whole burthen on the poor."[23]

Indeed, while Gilmer never mentioned explicitly whether his neighbors were worried or even concerned about troublesome or rebellious enslaved Virginians, he did imply that slavery was at the heart of some of his neighbors' complaints—about *other* whites. The Third Convention had exempted all overseers of more than four slaves, for example, from any military service, even in the militia. Hundreds of petitioners would later claim that this exemption prompted many wealthy planters to "become Overseers that Otherways wou'd not, on purpose to Secure Themselves from Fighting in defense of their County as well as their own property." Whether true or not, even patriot leader Fielding Lewis worried that the minute service was failing because of "the young Gentlemen not setting a good example of inlisting." If they did join, it was only as appointed officers. Gilmer noted of his neighbors, "Some declare the Gentlemen have more at stake and ought to fight to protect it, but that none enter the service but as officers." Gentlemen were far too "fond of officers' places." Many of Gilmer's neighbors were furious and thought that, since the crisis was brought on by gentlemen, the "men of Fortune should bear the whole weight of the contest."[24]

Gilmer's neighbors might also have been angry because they knew they

23. "Address," Brock, ed., "Papers of Gilmer," VHS, *Collections,* n.s., VI (1887), 122, 127.

24. Petition of Inhabitants of Lunenburg County, [Apr. 26, 1776], *Rev. Va.,* VI, 474–475 (this and other, similar petitions are discussed in Chapter 6, below); Fielding Lewis to Washington, Nov. 14, 1775, *Papers of Washington,* Rev. War. Ser., II, 372; "Address," Brock, ed., "Papers of Gilmer," VHS, *Collections,* n.s., VI (1887), 122–123; *Va. Gaz.* (Purdie), Nov. 3, 1775, *Rev. Va.,* IV, 163–164. Cf. Woodford to the president of the convention, Dec. 4, 19, 1775, *Rev. Va.,* V, 50, 193; Woodford to John Page, Nov. 26, 1775, *Rev. Va.,* IV, 478; John Smith, on behalf of the Frederick County Volunteers, to the House of Delegates, Dec. 12, 1776, "Virginia Legislative Papers," *VMHB,* XVIII (1910), 29–31.

For one example of a gentleman's refusing to allow his son to enlist as a "common Soldier," see Francis Willis to Robert Carter, July 19, 1775, Carter Family Papers, VHS. Dixon and Hunter carried a piece in the *Va. Gaz.* noting that Mann Page, Jr., a delegate to the convention, had enlisted as a private in a company of minutemen that was captained by his younger brother. The editors had printed the notice as an example for others to "be regardless of what military station they serve their country in during the conflict" (*Va. Gaz.* [D and H], Oct. 7, 1775).

would have to pay even *more* than their fair share of the costs of conflict through new, and regressive, taxes. Many white Virginians were still recovering from the recessions of the 1760s and early 1770s, caused in part from the expense of the Seven Years' War, also paid largely by farmers through regressive poll taxes supplemented by taxes on the acreage rather than on the value of lands. Nor had Dunmore's War with the Shawnees in 1774 yet been paid for. George Mason originally calculated that the expense of Dunmore's foray was about £150,000, that Virginia's share of the expense of the Continental army was about £150,000, and that the expense of raising their own troops, including the minutemen, would be about £350,000. The Third Convention stipulated that this would be paid for again by unfair poll and land taxes. Moreover, many nonslaveholding Virginians would have to pay more for keeping slaveholders' property secure, as county courts still had to levy the costs of increased slave patrols in the face of heightened slave rebelliousness. By September 1775, one man claimed that white Virginians were already heavily burdened by such increases in local taxes. The "country labours" under a "heavy load of taxes to support its internal police." Ordinary white Virginians, even if not privy to talk of what George Mason admitted was an "enormous Sum," could clearly see that they had almost as much to fear from the architects of the new military establishment as they did from "Insolent" British excise officers.[25]

Many smaller farmers in Virginia were particularly anxious about taxes because of the increasingly debilitating effects of the patriot economic boycotts. At the same time as the Third Convention levied new taxes to pay for mobilization, the colonywide nonexportation agreement—which was scheduled to begin in September 1775—would soon prevent farmers from selling their crops and obtaining the wherewithal to pay such taxes, their rents, and other charges. The economic boycott also threatened the colony with shortages. Under the terms of the Continental Association, free Virginians had agreed to stop importing British manufactured goods in De-

25. Robert Beverley to Landon Carter, June 9, 1774, Carter Family Papers, VHS; Chester Raymond Young, ed., *Westward into Kentucky: The Narrative of Daniel Trabue* (Lexington, Ky., 1981), 41–42; "Galba," *Va. Gaz.* (Pinkney), Sept. 14, 1775; Mason to Martin Cockburn, Aug. 5, 22, 1775, to Washington, Oct. 14, 1775, *Papers of Mason,* I, 245, 251, 256; Robert A. Becker, *Revolution, Reform, and the Politics of American Taxation, 1763–1783* (Baton Rouge, La., 1980), 78–79, 82; "Address," Brock, ed., "Papers of Gilmer," VHS, *Collections,* n.s., VI (1887), 116, 125–128.

cember 1774. A primary purpose of this nonimportation plan was to exert pressure on Parliament by precipitating unemployment, and thus riots, in Britain. But the weapon that the patriot elite used to counter parliamentary legislation could also be turned against them via a blockade.[26]

Starting in 1775, Britain did blockade Virginia and the other rebel colonies to keep them from trading with foreign countries. Nonimportation and the British blockade were both successful. Britain shipped only about two thousand pounds worth of goods to the Chesapeake in 1775, and few ships carrying goods from other countries managed to slip past the British navy ships guarding the bay. Even as the nonimportation agreements began, in December 1774, Dunmore predicted the trade boycotts would split the patriot ranks: "The people . . . of fortune may supply themselves and their negroes for two or three years; but the middling and poorer sort, who live from hand to mouth, have not the means of doing so, and the produce of their lands will not purchase those necessaries." Dunmore thought such shortages would "ruin thousands of families" and make "the lower class of people . . . discover that they have been duped by the richer sort, who for their part elude the whole effects of the association, by which their poor neighbors perish." But patriots too were worried that the "troubles" the "poorer Sort of People and negroes" were already experiencing from the "extreme scarcity of goods" would only get worse.[27]

Shortages did get worse. Some of Gilmer's neighbors were in "great dread" over shortages of clothing, and others worried about the loss of "impliments" and other manufactured goods that would allow them to continue farming. Most people, however, were especially concerned with a looming shortage of salt by the fall of 1775, used to preserve meat and fish and fed to cattle, hogs, and sheep. One gentleman in Fredericksburg said that there "never was such a demand for that article" and that most "Plant-

26. William Lee to Richard Henry Lee, Jan. 17, 1775, Lee Family Papers, UVa; Richard Henry Lee to Washington, Sept. 26, 1775, Fielding Lewis to Washington, Nov. 14, 1775, *Papers of Washington,* Rev. War. Ser., II, 53, 372–373; William Lee to his brother, Dec. 13, 1774, in Richard Henry Lee, *Life of Arthur Lee* . . . (Boston, 1829), I, 210.

27. Dunmore to Dartmouth, Dec. 24, 1774, John C. Fitzpatrick, ed., *The Writings of George Washington from the Original Manuscript Sources, 1745–1799* (Washington, D.C., 1931–1944), III, 249; William Allason to Thomas B. Martin, Mar. 10, 1775, "Letters of Allason," *Richmond College Historical Papers,* II (1917), 164; United States Bureau of the Census, *Historical Statistics of the United States, Colonial Times to 1957* (Washington, D.C., 1960), 1176–1178.

ers this way do not know what to do for Salt." Another observer thought that the problem could become acute: "If no Salt comes in there will be an insurrection in the Colony."[28]

By October 1775, predicted shortages led to a decline in martial enthusiasm even among the more committed. One loyalist-leaning merchant in Norfolk was more explicit. "A few months ago, the people here, were all mad with Politicks," Andrew Watson wrote then, "but the numberless inconveniences, they have since felt, have much coold them, especially the lower Ran[k]." A few weeks later, Watson told his father, "Great many of the lower rank of people are already dissatisfied with the present measures." Watson believed that they needed only a British presence to prompt them to act against the patriot government. He was frustrated that Dunmore did not act more quickly: "There is no force here to unite them. The Government have been shamefully inactive."[29]

• • • As Watson hinted, the "numberless inconveniences" and the mounting burden of the conflict had another effect; in many cases the authority of patriot leaders was questioned. Even before the colony began to mobilize, for example, one man had complained about the county collection of money for the Virginia delegates in Congress: "Can't the poor dogs pay their own Expenses"? Shortly after the new military plans had been announced, Alexander Miller in Augusta County East had repeatedly and very publicly claimed that the members of the Continental Congress and the Virginia convention were not only seditious but "aiming at their own interest at the expense of this country" by living "at free cost" and receiving large sums "to defray those pretended expenses." He thought that the provisions laid out by the convention for the collection of money for

28. "Address," Brock, ed., "Papers of Gilmer," VHS, *Collections,* n.s., VI (1887), 118; Oct. 11, 1775, Cresswell, *Journal,* 164; James Freeland to John Tailyour, Oct. 20, 1775, *Rev. Va.,* IV, 246–247; Jan. 2, June 28, 1776, Diary of Honyman; William Cabell Diary, Nov. 26, 1775, VHS. Cf. John Page to Jefferson, Nov. 11, 1775, *Papers of Jefferson,* I, 259; "Galba," *Va. Gaz.* (Pinkney), Sept. 14, 1775; and Robert Nelson to Harry Nelson, Oct. 26, 1775, *Rev. Va.,* IV, 284, for an account of predicted shortages in North Carolina as well as Virginia. William Roscow Curle to the Fourth Virginia Convention, Dec. 12, 1775, *Rev. Va.,* V, 119; Westmoreland County Committee Proceedings, Mar. 26, 1776, *Rev. Va.,* VI, 253; *Va. Gaz.* (Pinkney), Sept. 7, 1775; *Va. Gaz.* (Purdie), Sept. 8, 1775.

29. Alexander Watson, Jr., to William Lloyd, Oct. 18, 1775, *Rev. Va.,* IV, 237; Alexander Watson, Jr., to Alexander Watson Sr., Nov. 10, 1775, *Rev. Va.,* IV, 373.

ammunition and other military expenses were designed only to benefit the local and colonial elite, in "making gentlemen of themselves." "Under various pretences," the wealthier elite "would take every half-bitt they had, and then leave them to shift as they could." As Miller reveals, economic anxieties were often interwoven with barely masked class resentments and brought to the fore in the new crisis. Gentlemen in the convention, together with the delegates to Congress had, consciously or unconsciously, simply ignored the economic reality of their less well off neighbors. Many farmers responded by refusing to join up in the fall of 1775, choosing instead to harvest what might be their last profitable crop. Some Virginians, like Miller, began to question the motives of the patriot leadership in creating such a potential disaster.[30]

Gilmer claimed that Albemarle County was rife with divisions, and he was angry that he had suffered "censure, and illiberal abuse" for "appearing active in the weighty affairs of my Country and County." But the problems were not confined to Albemarle: many "ungenteel reflections" had been "thrown out against the conduct of persons, in public business" as discontent over the appointment of officers, who should bear the cost of the war, and mobilization in general contributed to a climate of criticism throughout Virginia.[31]

This climate of criticism manifested itself more formally in the county committee elections that the Third Virginia Convention had scheduled for November 1775. In Cumberland County, twelve previous members were left off the new committee. Two of these had recently been appointed captains in the minute service and might have declined serving again, but, of the remaining ten, four were justices then serving on the Cumberland court bench. Of the new members, none was then sitting as a magistrate. Moreover, some of the most prominent men in the county lost electoral ground. The previous chair, George Carrington, fell back into sixth place in the voting, for example. Some inroads were made by less wealthy farmers. Three of the new members owned less than 220 acres of land. One of them, Bart-

30. *Va. Gaz.* (P and D), Oct. 4, 1774; *Va. Gaz.* (Purdie), Nov. 3, 1775, *Rev. Va.,* IV, 163–164. Cf. *Rev. Va.,* II, 385; *Va. Gaz.* (D and H), Feb. 17, 1776.

31. "Address," Brock, ed., "Papers of Gilmer," VHS, *Collections,* n.s., VI (1887), 125. See, for example, King and Queen County Committee, subcommittee proceedings, Dec. 9, 1775, *Va. Gaz.* (Purdie), Feb. 16, 1776, supplement, *Rev. Va.,* V, 92–93; Election of Convention Delegates in King and Queen County, May 21, 1776, *Rev. Va.,* VII, 212.

lett Thompson, launched an appeal against one of the local grandees of the county, Thomas Davenport, when he felt he had been unjustly left out of the new committee. Despite the support of one of the most powerful families in the county, the Carringtons, Davenport ultimately lost his seat in a battle that lasted until February 1776.[32]

In other counties, the less complete records are still suggestive. In Hanover County, where discontent over salt shortages was brewing, at least four prominent men were not reelected to the new committee, including the largest landowner in the county, Nelson Berkeley. Less well known and less wealthy men, who owned on average between five hundred and one thousand acres, replaced them. One farmer, Paul Thilman, was elected to the committee despite, and perhaps because of, being brought before the old body in 1774 for fomenting opposition to it. Thilman had violated the Continental Association, but he had also displayed "contemptuous Behaviour to many respectable Gentlemen" who questioned him about it. He had also attempted to "stir up a Party in Order to support me in such my Behaviour." Thilman had enough of a "Party" in the county to get him elected to the new committee.[33]

32. Turnout in the elections was low, probably reflecting the upheaval in which they took place. See Allan Kulikoff, *Tobacco and Slaves: The Development of Southern Cultures in the Chesapeake, 1680–1800* (Chapel Hill, N.C., 1986), 307; Nov. 27, 1775, "Proceedings of Cumberland and Isle of Wight Counties," Virginia State Library Board, *Fifteenth Annual Report* (Richmond, Va., 1919), 25; Cumberland County Court Records, Order Books, 1774–1778, LiVi. The three new members owning little land were Bartlett Thompson, who owned only £62 of land in 1782, Arthur Moseley, who owned land worth only £180, and Miller Woodson, who owned £212 worth of land. See Dale Edward Benson, "Wealth and Power, 1774–1776: A Study of the Organization of Revolt" (Ph.D. diss., University of Maine, 1970), 405–407, for a listing of committee members' wealth. Davenport owned 1,000 acres of land and was a justice of the peace. For the battle between Thompson and Davenport, see "Proceedings of Cumberland and Isle of Wight Counties," Nov. 27, Dec. 18, 1775, Feb. 5, 29, 1776, 25–27, 32; Cumberland County Land and Personal Property Tax Records, 1782, LiVi.

33. Hanover County Committee Proceedings, Nov. 12, 1774, *Va. Gaz.* (P and D), Dec. 15, 1775; Hanover County Committee Proceedings, undated, *Va. Gaz.* (Purdie), Nov. 17, 1775; Benson, "Wealth and Power," 305.

Gentlemen protested after the election that the "tellers of the Ballots . . . took upon themselves to exclude some who were chosen by the voice of the People and admit others who were not." Not only did they want the committee entirely dis-

In the tidewater joint district of Elizabeth City County and Hampton, hit hard by Dunmore's seaborne plundering, only seven men of the twenty-one new members had served on the thirteen-man committee elected the previous year. Of the twenty-one new men in Spotsylvania County, only eight can be identified as serving on the older committee. In Louisa County in the central piedmont, several prominent men lost places, and others were elected but with fewer votes than previously; at least six men had never before served as county officials. In Caroline County, a tavernkeeper rose from ninth to first place in the polling, and several prominent gentlemen lost votes. Perhaps more embarrassing, some of the inhabitants of Caroline County, Edmund Pendleton's home seat, contested the election altogether. They complained that the chairman of the committee, James Taylor, a convention delegate, had neglected to appoint anyone to superintend the elections. Because of this, the petitioners to the Fourth Virginia Convention complained that some people voted who "had no right to Vote." More suspiciously, the lists of voters were "immediately destroyed" by the incoming committee, which "put it out of the power" of the petitioners to inspect them. The convention, noting that Taylor and several other members of the committee were present at the elections and ought to have supervised them more closely, found for the petitioners and ordered a new election.[34]

---

solved, but they also wanted the convention to change the rules to prevent people like Thilman from getting elected, to wit, an ordinance passed "incapacitating any Person from holding any place of Trust in the Government after a breach of publick Faith or a manifest abuse of Power." Hanover County Petition, Proceedings of the Fifth Virginia Convention, May 25, 1776, *Rev. Va.,* VII, 260.

The impending salt shortages might have influenced the elections in Prince William County more directly. No record of the election exists, but the new committee immediately appointed a subcommittee to "fall on any possible method to procure a Temporary supply" of salt in order "to quiet the minds of the people and keep peace in the Country." The committee had been besieged by "complaints and clamours" from the inhabitants in many quarters to procure salt "at any event." With a popular mandate behind them, the committee felt justified in writing directly to Congress, over the head of the Virginia authorities, and in sending someone to Norfolk to purchase salt, even though it thought it was probably illegal to by the terms of the Association. Electioneering or actual turnover among members of the committee might have helped the new board take this provocative but popular measure. Prince William County Committee of Correspondence to the Members of Congress, Nov. 14, 1775, *Rev. Va.,* IV, 396.

34. Spotsylvania County Committee Proceedings, Nov. 16, 1775, *Rev. Va.,* IV,

Though it is impossible to measure accurately the changes that took place during the new elections in November, local gentlemen certainly felt threatened enough to complain loudly about the electioneering. In Landon Carter's Richmond County on the Northern Neck, for example, Carter and his genteel friends were "much disturbed" by the "infamous Proceedings of the Party" during the run-up to elections. Carter himself had had enough and declared that he would not run for the committee, but, instead, would retire "to domestic Tranquillity." Dr. Walter Jones hoped that the younger gentlemen would "exert themselves on the occasion" in his place. Carter's son might at least help "in preventing" further "Disgrace on the County." Jones himself had thought about staying out of the contest but finally could not resist opposing the "plebeian Infamy" that gripped their county.[35]

417, 420; Spotsylvania County Committee Minutes, Dec. 14, 15, 1774, *Rev. Va.,* II, 195, 196–198; Elizabeth City County and Hampton Town Committee Proceedings, Nov. 22, 1774, *Va. Gaz.* (Pinkney), Jan. 26, 1775, *Rev. Va.,* II, 173–174, and Nov. 23, 1775, *Va. Gaz.* (Purdie), Dec. 29, 1775, *Rev. Va.,* IV, 459; Benson, "Wealth and Power," 305–306; Kulikoff, *Tobacco and Slaves,* 308; Proceedings of the Fourth Virginia Convention, Jan. 5, 11, 1776, *Rev. Va.,* V, 344, 383. For a detailed analysis of the committee elections, see Benson, "Wealth and Power," 303, 304, 308.

35. Francis Lightfoot Lee also asked Landon Carter to run for the committee, warning, "This is not a time for men of abilities with good intentions to be only spectators." Lee told him, "If we cant do all the good we cou'd wish, let us at least endeavour to prevent all the mischief in our power." In the end, Carter stayed out of the contest, deeply embittered about the changes that had taken place on the committee. Walter Jones to Landon Carter, Oct. 14, 1775, Sabine Hall Papers, UVa; Francis Lightfoot Lee to Landon Carter, Oct. 21, 1775, Clark et al., eds., *Naval Documents,* II, 557; May 1, 1776, Jack P. Greene, ed., *The Diary of Colonel Landon Carter of Sabine Hall, 1752–1778* (Charlottesville, Va., 1965), II, 1030–1031. Lee later asked Carter whether he had "defeated all the party schemes in Richmond" (Francis Lightfoot Lee to Landon Carter, Nov. 20, 1775, Clark et al., eds., *Naval Documents,* II, 1086).

Farther up the Northern Neck, there were rumors from Fairfax that it had been "publickly said the Committee that the people had in view to chuse, were such as cou'd Scarcely write their names." A little later, loyalist Nicholas Cresswell reported with considerable sarcasm that the newly elected Loudoun County Committee, supposedly "the first men in the County," had met and "had two bowls of toddy, but could not find cash to pay for it." Lund Washington to George Washington, Dec. 3, 1775, *Papers of Washington,* Rev. War. Ser., II, 479–480, 481n (apparently, however, the Fairfax committee was returned with little alteration). For other elite com-

Though the records are not as clear as we would like, assertions of "plebeian Infamy" and the upheaval at the polls indicate an unprecedented level of discontent in Virginia at this critical moment. Traditional county leaders such as Landon Carter had good cause to be uneasy. The leadership of the counties—drawn from the parish vestries, the county courts, and militia officers—had never been subject to a popular vote. Since the county committees effectively replaced the courts during the final stages of the imperial crisis, and, since many gentlemen justices like Carter sat on the original county committees, the elections were a direct reflection of their authority. Further, the county committees were ostensibly at the center of the resistance movement—including the administration of militia appointments—the contested elections were also a sign of deep dissatisfaction with the patriot leadership.[36]

Indeed, taken together, the committee elections, the complaints of ordinary Virginians about the new military arrangement, and the failure of the minutemen reflected not just a decline of what enthusiasm there was for the patriot cause but also a widening rift in the social and political culture of the colony. The new military establishment, while designed to ensure the internal and external safety of the colony, reflected numerous assumptions patriot leaders held about the society that they believed they were protecting. These assumptions, particularly amid the growing demands of the new conflict, were challenged—by other Virginians, including more radical gentlemen, middling farmers, poor whites, and enslaved Virginians. The new military establishment, intended to cure the anxieties of many elites, pleased few people outside the convention doors and exacerbated rather than ameliorated the problem of control and authority in the colony. Despite moderates' best efforts to maintain an appearance of unanimity, what

plaints about the composition of the Loudoun County Committee, see James Hendricks to Leven Powell, Apr. 5, 1776, Powell, ed., *Biographical Sketch,* 84–85. For similar problems in Maryland, see Ronald Hoffman, *A Spirit of Dissension: Economics, Politics, and the Revolution in Maryland* (Baltimore, 1973), 149–150.

36. Hening, comp., *Statutes at Large,* IX, 57–58. The regulation of such elections was, in the context of Virginia's political culture, a radical innovation in itself. Moreover, the balloting for committee members was to be secret. For an analysis of the original county committees and the overlap in membership of the traditional ruling elite, especially burgesses and justices of the peace, see Benson, "Wealth and Power," 104–144; Jack P. Greene, "Foundations of Political Power in the Virginia House of Burgesses, 1720–1776," *WMQ,* 3d Ser., XVI (1959), 493–502.

emerges from Gilmer's speech and the widespread discontent over the new military establishment is a picture of a Virginia deeply divided: between those dictating the terms upon which the colony would fight, and those expected to bear the brunt of those terms.

• • • These divisions emboldened opponents of the patriot regime. The boldest opposition came from below. Though the delegates to the Third Virginia Convention had taken measures to reassert authority over workers on the plantations, the lack of support for the new military establishment encouraged defiance, and white indentured and convict servants in particular made the most of the circumstances. George Washington's estate, Mount Vernon, was one site of internal trouble. Lund Washington, managing his cousin's plantation in the general's absence, had hired out one indentured servant, a painter, sometime before August 20, 1775. By the end of September, Lund had heard nothing of the man, and he began to worry: "I fear he has intirely made his Escape." Indeed, the painter had made a bid for freedom. He tried to join Lord Dunmore's forces, who were by then harassing Virginia's extensive coasts by sea. Literally fighting for his freedom, the painter made his way south but was wounded and captured during a skirmish with patriot forces and was jailed in Williamsburg. Calling himself Joseph Wilson but admitting he was a servant of Washington's, the painter declared that he was "unwiling to be sent back." Lund thus instructed Fielding Lewis to sell him if he could to "some of the back people, after Whipg him at a Publick whiping Post."[37]

In asserting their own independence, white servants caused considerable anxiety among their masters, not only about losing valuable property but about the potential retribution from disgruntled workers. When Lund heard that the painter had made his way to Dunmore, he began to understand (if he had not done so before) the precarious position he was in be-

37. George Washington to Lund Washington, Aug. 20, 1775, Lund Washington to George Washington, Sept. 29, Nov. 5, Dec. 3, 1775, *Papers of Washington,* Rev. War. Ser., I, 337, II, 64, 66n, 306, 479. Dunmore had not yet made his well-documented Proclamation promising freedom to slaves and servants who would join him in fighting the rebels, but he was still accepting help from any quarter— "Dunmore wants Men," Fielding Lewis told Washington, pessimistic about the chances of getting the servant back (Fielding Lewis to Washington, Nov. 14, 1775, *Papers of Washington,* Rev. War. Ser., II, 372). Cf. *Va. Gaz.* (D and H), Sept. 23, 1775.

cause of his and his cousin's stance in the imperial dispute. Isolated on a large plantation, surrounded by bonded laborers (as many as eleven full-time white servants, an unknown number of temporary tradesmen, and fifty-seven black slaves at Mount Vernon alone), and his more "common" neighbors "Hellishly freightned," Lund began to grow uneasy about the possibility of an uprising precipitated by the promise or reality of British aid. In a show of bravado that betrayed his own anxiety and popular fears of an uprising, he boasted to cousin George, "If [the painter] comes up here and indeavours to Land at mt Vernon *Raising the rest,* I will shoot him, that will be some Satisfaction."[38]

Throughout the summer and fall of 1775, black Virginians, too, continued to make their way to British lines and rumored promises of freedom, and the newspapers printed a constant stream of notices from owners looking for them. Most owners assumed that they were heading for Dunmore's ships. Edward Hack Moseley of Princess Anne County thought that Daniel, who had taken two younger boys with him, was "lurking about Norfolk" or "gone to Hampton," where they might find refuge with Dunmore's forces. Similarly, a slave belonging to William Nutt of Northumberland County allegedly stole a thirty-foot boat from Thomas Pinckard of neighboring Lancaster County and made his escape. Pinckard believed the runaway would head to Norfolk, "where (from a report that has lately prevailed) he may expect to be harboured and protected." Many did reach Dunmore's ships. Tom, "a very black negro man" who stole himself from Francis Boykin in Isle of Wight County, "had been on board with Dunmore's crew" in the fall of 1775. In early November, Edmund Pendleton noted, some accounts put the number of enslaved Virginians with the gov-

38. Lund Washington to George Washington, Oct. 29, Nov. 5, 14, 1775, *Papers of Washington,* Rev. War. Ser., II, 258, 306, 375 (emphasis added); "A List of Tithables in Truro Parish, Fairfax County, July 1774," personal communication with John P. Riley, historian at the Mount Vernon Ladies' Association of the Union, Mount Vernon, Va. For other examples of runaway servants in the fall and winter of 1775, see the case of James Bryant, "purchased jointly as a School master," who might have been on his way to join Dunmore when he was caught after six days' absence in the summer of 1775. Similarly, see the cases of Thomas Bird, Isaac Fleetwood, Jeremiah Heath, and Matthew Killimare in early 1776. Killimare was sentenced to fifteen lashes after he was caught running away a second time in three months (Aug. 14, 1775, Feb. 12, Mar. 11, Apr. 8, 1776, Loudoun County Court Records, 1774-1776, LiVi).

ernor as at least one hundred. So many slaves reached Dunmore that the Virginia Committee of Safety complained that he had incited "an insurrection of our own slaves" in the Norfolk area. Unable to admit that enslaved Virginians might seek Dumore out, the committee accused him of capturing, seizing, and detaining many slaves in the area.[39]

Black and white resistance to patriot authorities both within the minute service and on plantations delighted the exiled governor. As recruiting for the minute service slowed dramatically in September and October 1775 and servants and slaves swelled his own ranks, Dunmore watched the situation unfold with growing confidence from a ship just off shore but grew impatient waiting for reinforcements or even some instructions from the metropolis. As the "well informed" governor sensed the divisions within the patriot movement and the declining enthusiasm for the new military establishment, he began to plot his own counterattack.[40]

To begin with, Dunmore pushed ahead with plans to launch a counteroffensive from the west. In August, he had met with an agent, Dr. John Connolly, who in turn had been busy meeting with tribal representatives in the Ohio Valley. Connolly believed that the British could use to their advantage the anxiety of many tribes over new Anglo-American settlements west of the Appalachians, and Dunmore sent him on to Boston to secure General Thomas Gage's permission to recruit formally French and Indian allies and launch an attack on Virginia from Detroit. By then, Dunmore expected reinforcements and planned to attack from the east and rendezvous

39. Notice for Daniel, *Va. Gaz.* (D and H); Aug. 26, 1775; Thomas Pinckard's notice, *Va. Gaz.* (D and H), Sept. 2, 1775; Pendleton to the Virginia Delegates in Congress, Nov. 11, 1775, *Papers of Pendleton,* I, 128; Tom, *Va. Gaz.* (Pinkney), Jan. 20, 1776; Resolution, Virginia Committee of Safety, Oct. 26, 1775, *Va. Gaz.* (Pinkney), Oct. 26, 1775; *Va. Gaz.* (D and H), Sept. 23, 30, 1775. For runaways, see notice for eighteen-year-old Ned, who ran away from James Edmonson of Essex County in mid-July and was "seen going down the country" (*Va. Gaz.* [Pinkney], Jan. 6, 1776). Wilson Miles Cary also lost two slaves from his estate in King and Queen County, Aaron and Johnny, when they escaped to Captain Matthew Squires's ship, the *Otter,* sometime in July 1775, where they were also joined by a "mulatto man" named Joe Harris, who belonged to Henry King of Hampton (*Va. Gaz.* [Purdie], Sept. 8, 1775). Cf. notice for Daniel and two younger boys, *Va. Gaz.* [D and H], Aug. 26, 1775; for Michael and Aaron, *Va. Gaz.* (D and H), Sept. 23, 1775; for Harry, *Va. Gaz.* (D and H), Sept. 30, 1775.

40. Virginia Delegates to the Virginia Committee of Safety, Oct. 6, 1775, *Rev. Va.,* IV, 169.

with Connolly in Alexandria the following spring and thus sever Virginia from the northern colonies.[41]

In the meantime, Dunmore began a series of raids along the eastern coasts of Virginia, to harass the patriots and test their strength. First, he had someone steal the great seal and crest of Virginia from the office of Thomas Nelson, secretary of the colony. Then, at the end of September, he ordered a raid on Norfolk by soldiers and marines under his command. They carried off the printing press and two employees of John Holt's newspaper, the *Virginia Gazette, or the Norfolk Intelligencer.* In one account, only fifteen royal troops carried out the raid, in front of two or three hundred spectators. The local militia colonel, Matthew Phripp, had reportedly called for help, but only thirty-five men turned out, and no one tried to stop the royal troops.[42]

Emboldened by the lack of opposition to this raid, despite conducting it in broad daylight, Dunmore ordered further raids. Confining his operations to the Norfolk and Princess Anne coastlines, he looked for military stores and in one operation destroyed seventeen cannon and brought back two from stockpiles that lay "up the Country." Learning that a substantial amount of gunpowder and arms were stockpiled at Kemp's Landing, near Norfolk, and that "a Grand Muster" of the Princess Anne District Minute Battalion was to take place there, Dunmore ordered an attack. Captain Samuel Leslie led about 130 men against an estimated 250–400 minutemen. The officers of the minutemen, learning of Leslie's approach, decided not to risk an ambush, which was possible, and ordered their men to dis-

41. John Connolly to Thomas Gage, Sept. 9, 1775, Deposition of William Cowley, Oct. 12, 1775, Frederick County, Maryland, Committee, Nov. 23, 1775, John Hanson, on behalf of the Committee of Frederick County, Maryland, to the Virginia Committee of Safety, Nov. 25, 1775, *Rev. Va.,* IV, 82–84, 202–203, 206n, 458, 471–472; Mason to the Maryland Council of Safety, Nov. 29, 1775, *Papers of Mason,* I, 258–259; Woody Holton, *Forced Founders: Indians, Debtors, Slaves, and the Making of the American Revolution in Virginia* (Chapel Hill, N.C., 1999), 162–163.

42. *Rev. Va.,* IV, 5–6; Address of the Common Hall of the Borough of Norfolk to Lord Dunmore, *Va. Gaz.* (Purdie), Oct. 13, 1775; Captain Beesley Edgar Joel, on board the *Otter,* to Joseph Wright, Oct. 25, 1775, *Rev. Va.,* IV, 278; *Va. Gaz.* (D and H), Oct. 7, 1775; Samuel Edwards to ———, Nov. 8, 1775, *Rev. Va.,* IV, 345; Dunmore to Lord Dartmouth, Oct. 5, 1775, K. G. Davies, ed., *Documents of the American Revolution, 1770–1783* (Shannon, 1972–1981), XI, 137. Phripp resigned his commission in anger at his men's behavior (see *Rev. Va.,* IV, 156).

perse. When Leslie returned along the same path, two militia captains with 70 men also refused to attack. Patriot leaders were mortified. "These brave Captains," as Edmund Pendleton sarcastically called them, "even restrained their Men from Marching with a Gentleman who offered to head them." Pendleton despaired of the "degrading and mortifying Accounts" and worried about the "bleeding Honor of Virginia." John Page told Thomas Jefferson, then sitting in Congress in Philadelphia, that the affair at Kemp's Landing was "disgraceful and cowardly."[43]

The Committee of Safety of the colony, on which Pendleton himself sat as president, decided to act quickly to restore order and authority in the Norfolk region by sending Colonel William Woodford to the area with his regiment of regulars. It also gave Woodford command of five companies of minutemen from the Culpeper district, perhaps the best-armed and best-recruited district in the colony, as well as two companies of minutemen from Princess Anne district. Woodford was to set up camp at a convenient place, call in any further help as he saw necessary, and protect and defend local patriot inhabitants and "attact, kill, or captivate all such as you shall discover to be in arms for annoying of those persons." The committee also wanted Woodford to stop and detain all enslaved Virginians who tried to get past him to Dunmore. If they were in arms, he was to consider them at war. Finally, the committee instructed Woodford to use his "judgment and discretion" against the local inhabitants and act against only those who took "an active part against us."[44]

A brief skirmish at Hampton in which Virginia troops drove off several British ships attempting to cannonade the town helped temporarily buoy

43. Dunmore to Lord Dartmouth, Oct. 22, 1775, Clark et al., eds,, *Naval Documents,* II, 574; *Va. Gaz.* (D and H), Oct. 21, 1775; Captain Samuel Leslie to William Howe, Nov. 1, 1775, in Clark et al., eds., *Naval Documents,* II, 844; Dunmore to William Howe, Nov. 30, 1775, *Rev. Va.,* IV, 495–496; Captain Beesley Edgar Joel, on board the *Otter,* to Joseph Wright, Oct. 25, 1775, *Rev. Va.,* IV, 278; Samuel Edwards to ———, Nov. 8, 1775, *Rev. Va.,* IV, 345; *Rev. Va.,* IV, 6–7; Proceedings of the Virginia Committee of Safety, Oct. 24, 1775, *Rev. Va.,* IV, 269; Pendleton to Virginia Delegates in Congress, Oct. 28, 1775, *Papers of Pendleton,* I, 125; John Page to Jefferson, Nov. 24, 1775, *Papers of Jefferson,* I, 265.

44. Virginia Committee of Safety to William Woodford, Oct. 24, 1775, *Rev. Va.,* IV, 270–271. The committee, noting that it had discussed the subject for "several days," publicly justified this offensive measure by citing Dunmore's seizure of enslaved Virginians and other property and the reports that he and his officers had been harboring runaway slaves (269).

patriot spirits, but Dunmore continued his provocations. Upon receiving a report that some volunteers from North Carolina had posted themselves at Great Bridge, just south of Norfolk, he himself collected 130 regulars, some volunteers from among Norfolk's loyalists, and a number of black volunteers and began to move against them on November 13. The bridge, which gave easy access to Norfolk Borough and Princess Anne County, was strategically important for both sides. Though Dunmore found no one actually guarding the bridge in the end, he received word that perhaps 200 or 300 patriot troops were gathered at Kemp's Landing, ten miles away, and began to advance. The patriot troops, under Colonel Joseph Hutchings, attempted to lay an ambush but fired too early. In turn, Dunmore ordered a charge and scattered the Virginians, who fled under the pressure.[45]

In light of the feeble defense, Dunmore entered Kemp's Landing in triumph. Elated, he finally planted the king's standard and began to reassert royal authority. On November 14, he declared the colonists in rebellion and issued an oath of allegiance to the king. He also initiated an "Association" of his own, which bound the signers to denounce the various extralegal committees, conventions, and congresses that had been formed and had "under various false pretences usurped the legislative and executive powers of Government." The oath denounced the authority of these bodies, and the Association pledged its signers to instead uphold the authority of the crown. Noting that the "armed Bodies of Men" that had collected had done so "without any legal authority," the associators had to pledge to "defend the passes into our country and neighbourhood to the last drop of our blood," even if it "must expose us to all the horrors of a civil war."[46]

But the governor did not stop there. Encouraged by the numbers of

45. Captain Samuel Leslie to William Howe, Nov. 26, 1775, Clark et al., eds., *Naval Documents,* II, 1148, Captain Matthew Squire to Samuel Graves, Dec. 2, 1775, 1240-1241, Dunmore to Lord Dartmouth, Dec. 6, 1775, 1309-1311; Dunmore to William Howe, Nov. 30, 1775, *Rev. Va.,* IV, 495; Pendleton to R. H. Lee, Nov. 27, 1775, to William Woodford, Dec. 1, 1775, *Papers of Pendleton,* I, 132-134. For another contemporary summary of events around Norfolk, see Jan. 2, 1776, Diary of Honyman. See John Page to R. H. Lee, Feb. 19, 1776, Paul P. Hoffman, ed., *Lee Family Papers, 1742-1795* (microfilm) (Charlottesville, Va., 1966), for a longer-term assessment of the battle's effect on the morale of white Virginians.

46. Dunmore to Sir William Howe, Nov. 30, 1775, *Rev. Va.,* IV, 496-497, Oath of Allegiance, Nov. 14, 1775, 395, Association of Loyal Virginians, Nov. 15, 1775, 403-404, Proclamation, Nov. 7, 1775, 334; Dunmore to Lord Dartmouth, Dec. 6, 1775, Clark et al., eds., *Naval Documents,* II, 1309-1311.

enslaved black Virginians and indentured and convict servants who had joined him over the previous weeks, he issued his now infamous Proclamation, which he had drawn up in November. As well as placing Virginia under martial law, the Proclamation declared "all indented Servants, Negroes, or others, (appertaining to Rebels,) free that are able and willing to bear Arms . . . for the more speedy reducing this Colony to a proper Sense of their Duty, to His MAJESTY's Crown and Dignity."[47]

47. Ibid.

CHAPTER 5 *The Burning of Norfolk*

PATRIOT LEADERS BECOME RELUCTANT

REVOLUTIONARIES

....

Dunmore had finally done it. He had finally turned his threats to free slaves into reality. His Proclamation immediately sent shock waves throughout the colony, adding to the rising confusion. Patriot gentlemen reacted with predictable outrage. One anonymous gentleman in Williamsburg wrote, "Whoever considers well the meaning of the word Rebel, will discover that the author of the Proclamation is now himself in actual rebellion, having armed our slaves against us, and having excited them to an insurrection." This was "treason against the State, for which such men as Lord *Dunmore,* and even Kings, have lost their heads." Some felt the governor's action was worse than treason; gentlemen in and out of the colony began to demonize him. Landon Carter, on behalf of the Richmond county committee, referred to the "diabolical tendency" of the Proclamation, and an anonymous writer in the *Virginia Gazette* told his readers in verse, "Not in the legions / of horrid hell, can come a devil more damn'd / In evils, to top D*****e."[1]

The "diabolical" effects of the Proclamation were only compounded ten days later when the full details of John Connolly's plot to stir up the Ohio Indians against the colonists were revealed. On November 25, the committee of Frederick County, Maryland, gave the Virginia Committee of Safety

1. Anonymous letter, Nov. 30, 1775, Peter Force, ed., *American Archives: Consisting of a Collection of Authentick Records, State Papers, Debates, and Letters and other Notices of Publick Affairs* . . . (Washington, D.C., 1837–1853), 4th Ser., III, 1387; Richmond County Committee Resolutions, Dec. 5, 1775, Sabine Hall Papers, UVa; anonymous, *Va. Gaz.* (Purdie), Nov. 24, 1775, *Rev. Va.,* IV, 464. The editors speculate that the author was probably John Page. Cf. Benjamin Harrison to Robert Carter Nicholas, Jan. 17, 1776, Paul H. Smith et al., eds., *Letters of Delegates to Congress, 1774–1789* (Washington, D.C., 1976–2000), III, 107.

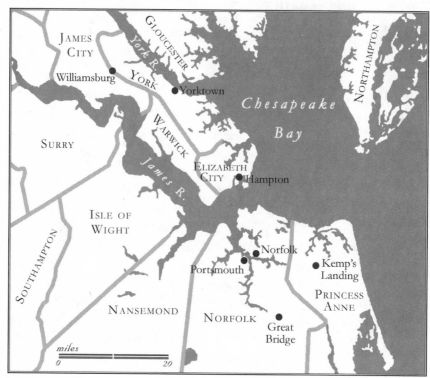

Map 2. The Norfolk Region

several documents intercepted when local militia there captured Connolly and several of his cohort. Connolly had been on his way to Detroit via the Pennsylvania-Virginia backcountry to begin implementing his plans. The "evil Designs" contained in the enclosures, as John Hanson put it, all pointed to the "raising an Army" from among the Ohio Indians and disaffected French settlers. But Connolly's plan included a plea to militia officers on the frontiers of Augusta County, Virginia, to join Dunmore's forces in exchange for confirmation of titles to their lands plus three hundred acres. If planters along the great rivers of Virginia did not have enough to worry about with Dunmore's ships plundering the shorelines and inciting insurrection among servants and slaves, they now had to consider the prospect of an army of French, Indian, and backcountry militia descending on the town of Alexandria.[2]

For most wealthy Virginians, even conservative planters, Dunmore had gone too far. The formal Proclamation made patriot converts of some reluctant, very prominent planters. William Byrd, for example, after offering his services to Dunmore in the summer of 1775, finally threw his lot in with the patriots—even offering his services in the patriot regular forces (as the volunteers had earlier demanded). So too did "most of the Council," who were determined to denounce the Proclamation publicly, the most prominent being the powerful Robert Carter. Moreover, Dunmore's actions pushed many moderate patriots into a more radical stance toward Britain. Robert Carter Nicholas, a cautious patriot, wrote of Dunmore's Proclamation that it was final proof that the governor was indeed the "executioner" of the "system of tyranny adopted by the Ministry and Parliament of Great Britain."[3]

2. John Connolly to Thomas Gage, Sept. 9, 1775, *Rev. Va.,* IV, 82–84, Frederick County, Maryland, Committee, Nov. 23, 1775, 458, John Hanson, on behalf of the Committee of Frederick County, Maryland, to the Virginia Committee of Safety, Nov. 25, 1775, 471–472; Mason to the Maryland Council of Safety, Nov. 29, 1775, *Papers of Mason,* I, 258–259. The plans were printed in the *Va. Gaz.* (Purdie), Dec. 22, 1775. Cf. Address of George Gilmer to Young Cornstalk Wolf and Shawnee Chiefs, [September] 1775, Gilmer Papers, VHS, for further evidence that gentlemen feared that the British were plotting with the native Americans against them; Deposition of William Cowley, Oct. 12, 1775, *Rev. Va.,* IV, 202–203, 206n, Virginia Indian Commissioners to Edmund Pendleton, Oct. 21, 1775, 250.

3. Archibald Cary to R. H. Lee, Dec. 24, 1775, Paul P. Hoffman, ed., *Lee Family Papers, 1742–1795* (microfilm) (Charlottesville, Va., 1966); undated notation in

Many patriot leaders also thought that the Proclamation had aroused the ire of all other white Virginians: "Men of all ranks resent the pointing a dagger to their Throats, thro the hands of their Slaves," wrote Archibald Cary; "nothing cou'd be more unwise than a declaration of that nature." And one man from the backcountry also felt that Dunmore's "Damned, infernal, Diabolical" Proclamation "deeply alarmed" the "Inhabitants of this Colony. It seems to quicken all in Revolution to overpower him however at every Risk." Richard Henry Lee asserted, "Lord Dunmores unparalleled conduct in Virginia has, a few Scotch excepted, united every Man in that Colony."[4]

Ultimately, Dunmore's Proclamation led to Virginia's independence, but not just because he angered prominent whites with his threat to free enslaved Virginians belonging to rebels. Rather, his Proclamation set off a complex chain of events that precipitated a major crisis for patriot leaders. For, however shocked, angered, and even invigorated most patriot leaders were, the Proclamation had diverse and unpredicted effects, in both white and black communities. Though many black slaves and white servants took up Dunmore's offer, many others could not or would not join him. Nor did white Virginians react with as much unanimity or outrage against Dunmore as patriot leaders believed, or hoped, they would. In some white quarters, the Proclamation did galvanize lukewarm planters into support for the patriot movement. In others, the offer to enslaved, convict, and indentured Virginians only contributed to a further deterioration in morale and many open defections to royal authority. Dunmore's new threats brought further division and confusion to the colony.

Coming on the tail of the failure of the minutemen, Dunmore's maneu-

---

hand of Ralph Wormeley, Jr., on William Byrd III to Ralph Wormeley, Jr., Oct. 4, 1775, Ralph Wormeley, Jr., Papers, UVa; John E. Selby, *The Revolution in Virginia, 1775–1783* (Williamsburg, Va., 1988), 66. Cf. Richmond County Committee Resolutions, Dec. 5, 1775, Sabine Hall Papers, UVa, for Landon Carter's reaction.

4. Archibald Cary to R. H. Lee, Dec. 24, 1775, Hoffman, ed., *Lee Family Papers;* Nov. 28, 1775, Robert Greenhalgh Albion and Leonidas Dodson, eds., *Philip Vickers Fithian: Journal, 1775–1776, Written on the Virginia-Pennsylvania Frontier and in the Army around New York* (Princeton, N.J., 1934), 135; John Hatley Norton to John Norton, [Dec. 9, 1775], Frances Norton Mason, ed., *John Norton and Sons, Merchants of London and Virginia: Being the Papers from their Counting House for the Years 1750 to 1795* (Newton Abbot, Devon, 1968), 391; R. H. Lee to Catherine Macauley, Nov. 29, 1775, James Curtis Ballagh, ed., *The Letters of Richard Henry Lee* (New York, 1911), I, 162.

vers actually met with considerable military success. In the end, the Proclamation did have the effect that Dunmore intended: it further weakened white planter authority in the colony vis-à-vis both black and white subordinates and contributed to an almost fatal collapse of the patriot movement. To shore up their deteriorating authority and prevent this collapse, patriot leaders finally took revolutionary action; they called for an even bigger, full-time professional army to stop Dunmore's progress, but, most importantly, and profoundly, they sanctioned the burning of Norfolk.[5]

• • • In the quarters of enslaved Virginians, the Great Emancipator's Proclamation had mixed results, which whites were often slow in perceiving. Dunmore had been sending out uncertain signals to enslaved Virginians for months. Though he had in May threatened to free enslaved Virginians, he also allegedly told some blacks who had offered to take up arms with him to "go about their business" and "threatened them with his severest resentment" if they tried to come back. In the interim, however, he had accepted the services of at least a few enslaved Virginians who made their way to his lines. When he finally published his Proclamation, it was clearly aimed as much at patriot whites as at all blacks, and he was looking for militarily useful allies. He was ready to give freedom only to those who could bear arms, and only to those owned by "Rebels." This was not the general emancipation proclamation that many blacks throughout the South had anticipated.[6]

Nor could all enslaved Virginians take advantage of the Proclamation — it was a risky business. In the week immediately following, rumors circulated that Dunmore had sent off a ship of runaway slaves to the notoriously harsher West Indies. Moreover, with Dunmore occupying only a small area around Norfolk, many potential black allies had to undertake long and dangerous journeys to join him and gain their freedom. Finally, white Virginians promised vengeance on runaway slaves, either by selling captured slaves themselves to the West Indies or by putting them to labor in the lead mines. In light of the risks, some enslaved Virginians hesitated. Many had extensive family and kinship ties in the local communities that they were loath to leave.[7]

5. John Page to Thomas Jefferson, Nov. 24, 1775, *Papers of Jefferson,* I, 265.

6. *Va. Gaz.* (Pinkney), May 4, 1775; Proclamation, Nov. 7, 1775, *Rev. Va.,* IV, 334.

7. White Virginians eagerly spread reports that Dunmore was selling captured

Yet, despite the risks and the rumors of poor treatment, hundreds of enslaved Virginians did escape their owners and join Dunmore. One report noted that, as soon as Dunmore made his Proclamation public, "about two hundred Slaves immediately joined him and were furnished with Arms." It was said enslaved Virginians were already "crouding to him" when he made his Proclamation, encouraging him to take such action. It was widely reported in the weeks after that "slaves flock to him in abundance." The newspapers reported Dunmore had recruited "about 2000 men, including his black regiment, which is thought to be a considerable part." Recently freed Virginians were said to be marching with the inscription "Liberty to Slaves" on their shirts. The governor himself reported that "the Negroes are flocking in also from all quarters," news of which he hoped would quell the rebellion almost immediately. Dunmore was in high enough spirits to suggest to his superior, General William Howe, that he needed only a "few more men" to march back to Williamsburg, "by which I should soon compell the whole Colony to Submit." Estimates of how many bonded black workers joined Dunmore immediately after his Proclamation vary, though by the governor's own reckoning, combined with historians' accounts, the number was probably between eight hundred and fifteen hundred.[8]

---

slaves. Once such treachery was made public, hoped Edmund Pendleton, the governor's "slave scheme" would be "at an end," as it would "stop his further increase of that Crew." See *Va. Gaz.* (Pinkney), Jan. 20, 1776; *Va. Gaz.* (Purdie), Jan. 12, 1776; Edmund Pendleton to Jefferson, Nov. 16, 1775, *Papers of Pendleton,* I, 131.

8. Committee of Northampton County to the President of the Continental Congress, Nov. 25, 1775, *Rev. Va.,* IV, 467, Dunmore to Sir William Howe, Nov. 30, 1775, 496; Pendleton to Richard Lee, Nov. 27, 1775, *Papers of Pendleton,* I, 133; *Va. Gaz.* (D and H), Dec. 2, 1775; Dunmore to Lord Dartmouth, Dec. 6, 1775, William Bell Clark et al., eds., *Naval Documents of the American Revolution* (Washington, D.C., 1964-), II, 1309-1311. Dunmore's letter was intercepted at sea on Dec. 17, 1775, turned over to Washington and Congress, and then printed in the *Va. Gaz.* (Purdie), Jan. 26, 1776 (see *Rev. Va.,* IV, 422, 499). For estimates of the number of enslaved Virginians who joined Dunmore, see Gerald W. Mullin, *Flight and Rebellion: Slave Resistance in Eighteenth-Century Virginia* (New York, 1972), 131-132; Woody Holton, *Forced Founders: Indians, Debtors, Slaves, and the Making of the American Revolution in Virginia* (Chapel Hill, N.C., 1999), 156; Sylvia R. Frey, "Between Slavery and Freedom: Virginia Blacks in the American Revolution," *Journal of Southern History,* XLIX (1983), 378; Benjamin Quarles, *The Negro in the American Revolution* (Chapel Hill, N.C., 1961), 31. For an important corrective to the numbers cited in these earlier accounts, see Cassandra Pybus, "Jeffer-

For as many enslaved Virginians as reached Dunmore, hundreds more tried to escape but failed, according to the newspapers. Edmund Ruffin of Prince George County noted that, sometime before December 23, six slaves in total had attempted an escape by boat. Two had been captured and jailed, but the four others were assumed to be in Dunmore's service, given that the boat was retaken quite far out from shore. Each of the escaped Virginians was relatively young and had skills that Dunmore might have found useful. Harry was a carpenter and wheelwright; Lewis was a wheelwright, wagonmaker, and "very good blacksmith." Apart from Lewis, the three other escapees were Virginia-born. Enslaved Virginians continued to band together to escape to Dunmore, seeking safety in numbers, not always successfully. Seven black Virginians belonging to four different masters were caught at Point Comfort, for example. Within three weeks of the Proclamation, Hampton officials complained that their jail was too full with the "Negroes we have from divers Quarters found going over to the Governor." They had become "too numerous" to hold safely, and conditions were dreadful. Many runaway Virginians died in captivity, and others refused to be captured. One belonging to William Smith "was Shot for refusing to surrender himself to the Troops when required." Given the risks in seeking refuge with Dunmore, enslaved Virginians who absconded during the Revolutionary war came closest of all to personifying Patrick Henry's rebellious cry of "Liberty or Death."[9]

Enslaved runaways helped Dunmore in diverse ways. Some caused a great deal of trouble behind patriot lines. Two women named Amy and Rachel belonging to Bennett Tomkins ran away in the midst of the crisis in the fall and committed robberies in York County. Other enslaved Virginians helped Dunmore in more specific but indirect ways. Caesar, described by patriots in Isle of Wight County as "a very great Scoundrel," had joined the governor at sea and was proving very valuable, an "Excellent pilot" and such a "fello they can't do well without."[10]

son's Faulty Math: The Question of Slave Defections in the American Revolution," *WMQ*, 3d Ser., LXII (2005), 243–264.

9. *Va. Gaz.* (Pinkney), Jan. 6, 1776; Committee of Safety, Dec. 24, 1775, *Rev. Va.*, V, 239; *Va. Gaz.* (Purdie), Jan. 12, 1776; Proceedings of the Fourth Virginia Convention, Jan. 17, 1776, *Rev. Va.*, V, 423, William Roscow Wilson Curle to the Virginia Committee of Safety, Dec. 3, 1775, V, 46; Proceedings of the Fifth Virginia Convention, May 9, 1776, *Rev. Va.*, VII, 78–79. Most masters assumed that runaways were heading for Dunmore. Cf. Mullin, *Flight and Rebellion*, 133.

10. Proceedings of the Fourth Virginia Convention, Jan. 17, 1776, *Rev. Va.*, V,

But generally Dunmore was interested in marshaling escaped slaves into more formal military units. As hundreds of blacks poured into his lines in the weeks after his Proclamation, he gained more confidence in his military position, forming the runaways "into a Corps as fast as they come in" and assigning them white officers. He had posted blacks, white volunteers, and twenty-five regulars at a stockade at Great Bridge (which they had taken earlier in the month), and they had thus far "defended it against all the efforts of the Rebels." In all, Dunmore reported with some satisfaction, "with the little Corps" he had under his command, "I think we have done wonders."[11]

Colonel William Woodford's defensive operations at Great Bridge were indeed severely hampered by local blacks' defiance. Within ten days of the Proclamation, he reported that the "principle Scotch Tories" in Norfolk "command Black Companys" and were rumored to have spoken "with great confidence of beating us with the odds of five to one." By December 4, he thought that the 250 estimated enemy troops who were occupying the fort at Great Bridge were "Cheifly Blacks." The reports were sufficient to force him to advise against any offensive operations and instead to call for reinforcements from the First Virginia Regiment, which was supposed to be guarding the Williamsburg region. The new black recruits on the British side were not so passive; a few, at least, were very active in exacting revenge on their former white owners. "Some blacks got over last Night," Woodford reported on December 4, "and set fire to the House Nighest the Bridge." At least five houses were burned down—"some of them Valuable" —as Woodford's men watched from the safety of their barricades.[12]

423, Thomas Pierce and Thomas Smith to Pendleton, Dec. 17, 1775, 170. Though women constituted only 12 percent of the runaway population throughout the colonial period, their numbers rose slightly during the Revolutionary war (Billy G. Smith, "Black Women Who Stole Themselves in Eighteenth-Century America," in Carla Gardina Pestana and Sharon V. Salinger, eds., *Inequality in Early America* [Hanover, N.H., 1999], 138, 148). Pybus, in "Jefferson's Faulty Math," *WMQ*, 3d Ser., LXII (2005), 243–264, notes that most of the hundreds of fugitives who fled to Dunmore were in family groups, despite the governor's promise to free only slaves who could bear arms for him.

11. Dunmore to Sir William Howe, Nov. 30, 1775, *Rev. Va.,* IV, 495–497.

12. Woodford to John Page, Nov. 26, 1775, *Rev. Va.,* IV, 477, Charles Scott to William Woodford, Nov. 26, 1775, IV, 476, William Woodford to the President of the Convention, Dec. 4, 1775, V, 49–50. Cf. Charles Scott to a Williamsburg Correspondent, Dec. 4, 5, 1775, in *Va. Gaz.* (Purdie), Dec. 8, 1775.

The next day, Woodford reported that a group of about twenty-six blacks and nine whites had discovered and fended off a party of almost fifty men he had sent out to scout the enemy's position at Great Bridge. The scouting party did, however, capture two black Virginians, who confirmed Woodford's fears. One man, George, who formerly belonged to Samuel Donaldson of Suffolk, reported that he had come through from Norfolk with a party of fifty-five black and two white men, leaving behind at least four hundred blacks in the town. At Great Bridge, George informed Woodford, there were already thirty whites and ninety blacks, and "all the blacks who are sent to the fort at the great Bridge, are supplied with muskets" and "strictly ordered to use them defensively and offensively." Significantly, George also told Woodford that the other black captive, Ned, had "entered as a Voluntier into the service."[13]

As Dunmore took advantage of black Virginians' desire for freedom, white Virginians finally came face to face with their worst nightmare. Dunmore's use of enslaved Virginians meant that armed blacks might now confront whites. In the Norfolk region especially, many enslaved Virginians took every opportunity to settle old scores. After one skirmish, recently freed men were "sent in pursuit" of those who had fled before the British. Two black soldiers discovered Colonel Joseph Hutchings, one of the patriot leaders, in a nearby swamp—one of the soldiers was Hutchings's own former bondsman. The irony of finding his recent master hiding in one of the favorite haunts of runaway black Virginians was probably not lost on the freedman. Hutchings tried unsuccessfully to shoot his former bondsman with a pistol; in return, he was slashed across the face with a sword and captured. It was a sign of things to come, or at least of what might yet come.[14]

As the story of Hutchings reminds us, whites felt threatened by black Virginians in a personal, intimate manner. In early December the *Virginia Gazette* noted that "some of Dunmore's bandits, about 12, mostly Negroes," raided the plantation of Benjamin Wells on Mulberry Island. "After threatening and abusing him in a most infamous manner, they robbed him of all his most valuable effects, and carried off two Negro women." In another instance, two wives of local patriot leaders in the Kemp's Landing area complained that an "ugly looking negro man, dressed up in a full suit of British regimentals, and armed with a gun," forced his way into their

13. Woodford to Pendleton, Dec. 5, 1775, *Rev. Va.*, IV, 57–59.
14. Pendleton to R. H. Lee, Nov. 27, 1775, *Papers of Pendleton*, I, 132–133.

house and began searching for the "dirty shirts" (patriots wearing hunting shirts). Though he left without doing the women any harm, he promised he would return. Dunmore was quite happy to encourage such behavior and used episodes like this to scare patriots into the loyalist fold. After the two women complained to Dunmore of the black Virginians' behavior, Dunmore agreed that it was a "provoking piece of insolence" but that it was to be expected "whilst this horrid rebellion lasts." Dunmore boasted, "There is no keeping these black rascals within bounds."[15]

• • • Enslaved Virginians were not the only ones to benefit from Dunmore's new official policy. Among the very lowest class of whites, Dunmore's Proclamation was perhaps even more welcomed. Dunmore had promised freedom not just to enslaved Virginians owned by patriots but also to indentured and convict servants who could escape their rebel masters and join him. Though there were few white servants in the coastal areas that Dunmore initially controlled, his Proclamation did have a material effect further afield. In the convict- and indentured-servant–rich Northern Neck counties, for example, many whites tried to escape to Dunmore, and more plotted their escape and waited for the right moment. Indeed, in some quarters, like George Washington's own estate, Mount Vernon, discontented and rebellious white servants caused almost as much anxiety as enslaved blacks.[16]

15. *Va. Gaz.* (D and H), Dec. 2, 1775; *Rev. Va.,* IV, 11. Dunmore's Proclamation had far-reaching effects outside Virginia. See, for example, *Pennsylvania Evening Post* (Philadelphia), Dec. 14, 1775; Peter H. Wood, "'Liberty Is Sweet': African-American Freedom Struggles in the Years before White Independence," in Alfred F. Young, ed., *Beyond the American Revolution: Explorations in the History of American Radicalism* [DeKalb, Ill., 1993], 170).

16. Dependent laborers of some sort made up almost 40 percent of the population in the Northern Neck. Included among these was a very large group of convict servants. More than twelve thousand were transported to Virginia between 1746 and 1775, with the Northern Neck constituting a "prime area" for their destination, as slaves did not fully meet the labor needs of the region. See A. Roger Ekirch, *Bound for America: The Transportation of British Convicts to the Colonies, 1718-1775* (Oxford, 1987), 115-116, 141, 156; David W. Galenson, *White Servitude in Colonial America: An Economic Analysis* (Cambridge, 1981), 85-86; Selby, *Revolution in Virginia,* 24; James Chapin Bradford, "Society and Government in Loudoun County, Virginia, 1790-1800" (Ph.D. diss., University of Virginia, 1976), 10-15. Cf. Aaron S. Fogleman, "From Slaves, Convicts, and Servants to Free Passen-

Lund Washington, already shaken by the escape of at least one indentured servant from Mount Vernon earlier that fall, was horrified to learn that Dunmore had actually gone through with his rumored plan. "Dunmore has at length Publishd his much dreaded proclamation." Lund was now more open about his uneasiness: "What effect it will have upon those sort of people I cannot tell." But Lund seemed more concerned about the white servants under his lash than the black slaves, or at least that white servants might stir up trouble in black quarters. "I think if there was no white Servts in this family I shoud be under no apprehension about the Slaves," he nervously told George Washington. He was "determined" that "if any of them Create any confusition to make and [an] example of him." Thus, as George Washington contemplated Independence in the fall of 1775, his own white and black unfree servants plotted and attempted to carry out their own bids for independence. One white servant at Mount Vernon told Lund, "There is not a man of them, but would leave us, if they believe'd they could make there Escape." Still not completely understanding the social forces unleashed by the resistance movement, Lund complained bitterly about his own rebellious "family": "And yet they have no fault to find[.] Liberty is sweet."[17]

What seemed to worry Lund Washington most was possible cooperation between white and black servants and slaves. Dunmore himself was not the only one to realize the chilling effect that the threat of a combined white and black uprising might have on white patriot activity. Several plans drafted in the autumn of 1775 indicated the idea, and fear, was widespread.

------

gers: The Transformation of Immigration in the Era of the American Revolution," *JAH*, LXXXV (1998-1999), 43-76. Fogleman finds evidence that the numbers of indentured and convict servants was growing in the period before the Revolution and that many were unhappy with their status and treatment. Indentured and convict servants made up the majority of the labor force in Lund Washington's neighboring county of Loudoun, where as late as the first federal census in 1790 the black population was still only 21.2 percent of the whole (Stanley B. Parsons, William W. Beach, and Dan Hermann, *United States Congressional Districts, 1788-1841* [Westport, Conn., 1978], 28-31; Selby, *Revolution in Virginia*, 24-25; Loudoun County Tax Records, 1784, LiVi).

17. Lund Washington to George Washington, Dec. 3, 1775, *Papers of Washington*, Rev. War. Ser., II, 479-480, 481n. Not all white servants sought freedom with Dunmore; some ran away and joined patriot forces see Richard Adams's notice for Ralph Chillingsworth, *Va. Gaz.* (Purdie), Jan. 5, 19, 1776, and notice for John Mahaney, Jan. 5, 1776.

Sir John Dalrymple, for example, recommended that indentured servants as well as the "bravest and most ingenious of the black Slaves" be recruited on the Pennsylvania side of the Delaware Bay as well as in towns like Annapolis and Baltimore in Maryland, and Alexandria and Fredericksburg in Virginia.[18]

Such plans were only fueled by the real fears of planters like Lund Washington and the reality of white and black cooperation. Charles White, a twenty-eight-year-old convict servant, was employed at Isaac Zane's Marlborough Iron Works in Frederick County, along with many other white and black workers. White, originally a stocking weaver, was disgruntled and had some strong political views of his own—he had said "some atrocious things in respect to the dispute between Great Britain and the colonies." White had also been stirring trouble among his coworkers. He had allegedly used "the most diabolical Practices to corrupt the Minds of his fellow Servants." What these "diabolical Practices" might have been were left unsaid in the newspapers, but Zane's outraged language might have had something to do with White's color blindness. When White finally ran away after Dunmore's Proclamation, he escaped with another English convict servant, James Leighton, and a "country born negro" named Will and headed for the coast. White was later captured at Fredericksburg, where he had boarded a British armed ship.[19]

18. Jonathan Boucher, an Anglican minister from Maryland, also proposed capitalizing on planters' worst nightmares, to keep rebellious planters' "fears perpetually awake, either by apprehensions of having their Slaves armed against them, or their savage Neighbours let loose on their Frontiers." Besides their slaves, both Maryland and Virginia planters had other "enemies in their bowells"—indentured servants—who should also be used. These whites were particularly disgruntled with their status, which could make them a potent force, "not a little to be dreaded." Sir John Dalrymple, "Project for Strengthening Howe's Operations in the north by a Diversion in the South," n.d., George Germain, first Viscount Sackville, 1776–1785, Papers, 1683-1785, William L. Clements Library, Ann Arbor, Mich.; Boucher to [Germain], Nov. 27, 1775, Germain Papers, in Sylvia R. Frey, *Water from the Rock: Black Resistance in a Revolutionary Age* (Princeton, N.J., 1991), 68; for similar plans in the southern colonies, see 66-69.

19. *Va. Gaz.* (Pinkney), Jan. 6, 1776; *Va. Gaz.* (D and H), June 18, Nov. 22, 1776. Cf. notice for Plim, *Va. Gaz.* (D and H), Sept. 23, 1775; Thomas Parramore and John Bowdoin, Jr., to the Committee of Safety, Apr. 23, 1776, *Rev. Va.,* VI, 449, for evidence of black and white cooperation before Dunmore's Proclamation.

Not only escaped convicts saw black Virginians as potential allies, and the problem was not confined to exposed coastal areas. Fincastle County in the southwestern corner of Virginia was in turmoil just after Dunmore's Proclamation. One man, John Spratt, had "damnd." his county committee and declared that he "Could and would raise one Hundred men for the King." Another man in the same county went further. John Hiell, a "Distiller and Planter" who owned perhaps as many as five hundred acres of land and who had lived in "very affluent Circumstances" in Fincastle County for twenty-eight years, tried to stir up cooperation between both white servants and slaves after the Proclamation. According to Hiell, "all his Neighbours and all the People up and down the river were for the King," but Hiell also told "a Servant man . . . that in about a month he and all the negroes would get their Freedom." Hiell said he did not act alone. Upon being summoned before the committee to answer for his transgressions, Hiell fled to Dunmore at Norfolk "at the request of some Hundreds of his County" to inform him that they were "ready to join" the governor as soon as he could "open a Communication with them."[20]

Another man, self-professedly "Born and bred a Gentlemen," also joined forces with enslaved Virginians. John Collett, originally from Philadelphia, had moved to Accomack County in 1773, where he had opened a store. Local patriots asked him to command troops in the county, but he declined to. He also turned down an offer from Dunmore to serve as a noncommissioned officer in the royal forces. However, Collett was not above helping Dunmore further his schemes for using blacks against their rebel masters. He was captured off Hampton in a ship bound for the Eastern Shore, "manned with 16 Negroes." Other whites also reportedly joined forces with recently freed blacks. Even after patriot troops had reoccupied Norfolk, white rebels in the area complained of the "lawless plundering" of "insidious Neighbours" and the "more savage Slave," who together had "ravaged" plantations, "invaded" "Bed-Chambers," stripped "Wives and Children . . . almost to Nakedness," and robbed them in the night. The Norfolk patriots

20. Fincastle County Committee Proceedings, Jan. 10, 1776, *Rev. Va.,* V, 376, 382n; Memorial of John Hiell, May 11, Nov. 23, 1785, AO 13/31, PRO. White Virginians were besieged on all sides by reports of cooperation between rebellious slaves and disgruntled whites. Reports emanating from Maryland were particularly worrying; see, in particular, Ronald Hoffman, *A Spirit of Dissension: Economics, Politics, and the Revolution in Maryland* (Baltimore, 1973), 147, 148.

felt vulnerable and wanted to get rid of the freed blacks entirely, fearing not only the destruction they caused but also the encouragement they gave to the pro-British.[21]

Not all whites, then, were horrified by Dunmore's Proclamation. Some embraced it, and patriotic whites certainly believed that it was not beyond the realm of the possible for even more of their neighbors to join forces with blacks. William Roscow Wilson Curle, head of the Hampton county committee, was terrified at the prospect of being left vulnerable to Dunmore's raiders. With the county jail overflowing with enslaved Virginians who had tried to escape, Curle had a palpable reminder at his doorstep of the extent of black Virginians' resolve to gain freedom. Worse, though, in Curle's mind, was the tenor of recent letters his committee had intercepted, which revealed "some of our most base, vile, secret and malicious Enemys," who, the Hampton committee believed, had formed "a diabolical Combination to do their Utmost" to undermine the patriot cause. Linking both black and white enemies in a literal and metaphorical sense, Curle concluded that, if their internal enemies continued "in our Land thus free; Virginians must be Slaves."[22]

Among free whites, then, Dunmore's military success, his occupation of Norfolk, and his Proclamation had a decidedly mixed effect. Indeed, Dunmore's actions helped fragment the patriot movement in several different ways. In the first place, whites outside the area immediately affected by Dunmore's Proclamation reacted ambiguously. The threat of trouble within Virginia's enslaved and servant quarters kept many free whites wary, and at home, as Dunmore predicted. Immediately after issuing his Proclamation, he speculated that news of black Virginians' making their way to his lines would have a salutary effect and "oblige the Rebels to disperse." White Virginians would have to go home "to take care of their families, and property." Though we have no idea how many men in the armed forces actually deserted after the Proclamation, it only added to the list of reasons farmers had compiled for not joining the minutemen. As enslaved Virginians grew bolder in the face of Dunmore's now public pro-

---

21. John Collett to Lord Dunmore, Dec. 20, 1775, *Rev. Va.,* V, 198, 204n, Patrick Henry to Pendleton, Dec. 23, 1775, 227, Petition of Inhabitants of Norfolk and Princess Anne Counties, [Jan. 8, 1776], 362–363, Proceedings of the Fourth Virginia Convention, Jan. 13, 1776, 396–397.

22. William Roscow Wilson Curle to the Virginia Committee of Safety, Dec. 3, 1775, *Rev. Va.,* V, 45.

nouncements, many middling farmers and smallholders stayed at home to keep an eye on their own slaves and to guard against the plundering of escaped slaves of other planters. Dunmore's Proclamation hardly led to a groundswell in martial enthusiasm; significantly, during all of November and December 1775, only nineteen more minuteman companies were formed in whole or in part.[23]

But Dunmore's Proclamation also made a more formal demand on the manpower of Virginians' newly raised militia. Patrick Henry, the commander of Virginia's troops, immediately wrote to all county lieutenants throughout the colony warning them of the Proclamation, "the Design and Tendency of which . . . is fatal to the publick Safety." Only an "unremitting Attention to the Government of the SLAVES may, I hope, counteract this dangerous Attempt. Constant, and well directed Patrols, seem indispensably necessary." As many counties stepped up their official slave patrols, more militia were needed for domestic duties. The overall effect of the Proclamation, thought one loyalist, was that it would bring many enslaved Virginians "to a violent Death" and keep "a number People employ'd in watching them, which indeed will distress the Colony."[24]

The Proclamation also tied up whites in another, more divisive way. Dunmore's offer forced many wealthy planters on larger plantations to keep their white employees closer to home to help keep an eye on their enslaved Virginians. The militia law of August 1775 allowed planters to do just that. The ordinance resurrecting the militia exempted from duty all overseers of four tithables or more on any plantation. Exemption from militia duty also exempted overseers from doing duty on militia slave patrols. The measure, designed to help keep the peace on large plantations, clearly favored the larger plantation owners. Not only would slaveholders have extra overseers

23. Dunmore to Sir William Howe, Nov. 30, 1775, *Rev. Va.,* IV, 496; Hening, comp., *Statutes at Large,* IX, 86–88; E. M. Sanchez-Saavedra, *A Guide to Virginia Military Organizations in the American Revolution* (Richmond, Va., 1978).

24. Patrick Henry for the Committee to the County Lieutenant of Westmoreland, Nov. 20, 1775, *Rev. Va.,* IV, 435–436, 442, John Johnson to James Balantine, Nov. 17, 1775, 426. The Virginia delegates to Congress pressed the assembly to adopt more rigorous controls over the enslaved population. Cf. Virginia Delegates to the Williamsburg Committee of Safety, Oct. 5, 1775, Hoffman, ed., *Lee Family Papers;* Francis Lightfoot Lee to Robert Wormeley Carter, [Dec. 2, 1775], Clark et al., eds., *Naval Documents,* II, 1237. The convention ordered the doubling of patrols as the holiday season approached (Proceedings of the Fourth Virginia Convention, Dec. 20, 1775, *Rev. Va.,* V, 201).

to aid in watching enslaved Virginians, but they also could find comfort knowing that the militia was patrolling the public roads, ferries, and rivers. Many planters took advantage of the loophole. Just more than a week after Dunmore issued his Proclamation, Robert Carter asked the militia colonel of Westmoreland County to take Robert Mitchell, his clerk and steward, off his list of eligible militia, because Carter wanted to make Mitchell an overseer. With a restive enslaved population of thirty-two on that estate, Carter believed he needed an extra hand at home.[25]

The loophole in the law and many planters' taking advantage of it did not escape the notice of those who had to shoulder the increased burden. Hundreds of militia later complained vociferously that many wealthy slaveholders had even designated themselves overseers to exempt themselves from militia duty. What was most grating was that many of these men, petitioners from Amelia County asserted, were "possessed of Considerable Property in Lands and Slaves." Moreover, many nonslaveholding militia resented having to share the burden of watching out for rebellious slaves at all. They particularly were unhappy that they might have to go out on more slave patrols. Even if they were not called on to patrol themselves, they, and everyone in the county, were responsible for paying the salaries of those who did. Increased slave patrols meant that the county tax burden was much higher. The resentment ran deep.[26]

The splits in white ranks were evident elsewhere. Significantly, many white Virginians, removed from Dunmore's waterborne reach, believed they had more pressing concerns than the governor and the threat from below. Indeed, that not all whites were as concerned about Dunmore's Proclamation as patriot leaders or slaveholders were can be seen not just in the continued falling enlistments but also in the unrest that erupted over salt. By the time of the Proclamation, earlier fears of shortages had grown into panic. The upper Northern Neck area seemed to be particularly hard hit. In the same week as the Proclamation, the Central Committee of Safety wrote to the Virginia delegates in Congress imploring them to get restrictions on imports of salt lifted, as "the Clamours of the people begin to be high on Accot. Of that Article, and we greatly fear the consequences if

25. Hening, comp., *Statutes at Large,* IX, 28; Robert Carter to John A. Washington, Nov. 23, 1775, Robert Carter Letterbooks, III, Robert Carter Papers, CWFL.

26. Petition of Amelia County Militiamen, [May 23, 1776], *Rev. Va.,* VII, 236–239.

some method cannot be fallen on to Supply their wants." Similarly, Prince William County reported being besieged by requests for salt, which was "not now to be had in this part of the Country." They wanted something done quickly to "quiet the minds of the people and keep peace in the Country."[27]

In early December—a few short weeks after Dunmore's Proclamation—the salt shortage did almost lead to civil war. The Hanover county committee reported on December 12, "Several persons have, of their own accord, gone about in a disorderly manner to search for salt, and have taken the same." The committee was forced to take heavy-handed measures against suspected salt hoarders to "preserve peace and good order, and to prevent riots and tumults." But the disorders spread to neighboring Henrico County, where "several companies of armed men" from the "upland" counties reportedly searched houses and seized salt. Significantly, some reports noted that the "poor and middling sort" of the lower counties who relied on salted fish for the mainstay of their diets were most in need. Some writers feared a class war. The "gentlemen in Henrico" who reported this warned, "If a stop was not put to such marauding, some among us may be induced to make opposition [which] may produce civil discord." A *Virginia Gazette* writer said that the salt riots confirmed Dunmore's year-old prophecy that the poor would rebel against the rich.[28]

27. Committee to the Delegates in Congress, Nov. 11, 1775, *Rev. Va.,* IV, 379, Prince William County Committee of Correspondence to the Members of the General Congress, Nov. 14, 1775, 396. Cf. Fairfax County Committee of Correspondence, Nov. 23, 1775, *Rev. Va.,* IV, 455-456. On the necessity of salt and the shortages, see Larry G. Bowman, "The Scarcity of Salt in Virginia during the American Revolution," *VMHB,* LXXVII (1969), 464-472; and see R. A. Brock, ed., "Papers, Military and Political, 1775-1778, of George Gilmer, M.D., of 'Pen Park,' Albemarle County, Va.," VHS, *Collections,* n.s., VI (1887), 119-120.

28. Hanover County Committee Proceedings, Dec. 12, 1775, *Rev. Va.,* V, 120; *Va. Gaz.* (D and H), Jan. 27, 1776; Dale Edward Benson, "Wealth and Power in Virginia, 1774-1776: A Study of the Organization of Revolt" (Ph.D. diss., University of Maine, 1970), 301-303; Edward Johnston to William Preston, Dec. 16, 1775, in Benson, "Wealth and Power," 302; *Rev. Va.,* IV, 13; "Virginian," *Va. Gaz.* (Pinkney), Dec. 9, 1775. Cf. Caroline County Committee Proceedings, Dec. 13, 1775, *Rev. Va.,* V, 132; *Va. Gaz.* (D and H), Jan. 27, 1776. For Dunmore's prophecy, see Dunmore to Dartmouth, Dec. 24, 1774, John C. Fitzpatrick, ed., *The Writings of George Washington from the Original Manuscript Sources, 1745-1799* (Washington, D.C., 1931-1944), III, 249.

The Proclamation complicated rather than unified white responses to these internal problems. Even Lund Washington admitted later that, when angry neighbors came to the plantation demanding salt, he "told the people I had none." The cousin of George Washington had actually hidden the general's stockpile of much-needed salt from his neighbors, because he feared the consequences of giving away or selling their extra salt, "knowg we cou'd not get more." In light of the troubled times and the threats and problems already experienced among enslaved and indentured workers on the estate, he felt he could not risk a shortage of the essential preservative. *"Our people* must have Fish." In the anxious climate following the Proclamation, Washington was torn between suppressing discontent among whites outside the plantation (and helping his neighbors) and keeping the peace on his own.[29]

• • • In the immediate area of Norfolk, Dunmore's actions were even more divisive, as thousands flocked to his standard. Many white Virginians were emboldened by his call to arms to declare openly their political sentiments for the first time since the conflict had begun. Indeed, many had demanded that the governor raise his standard. Dunmore told Lord Dartmouth, secretary of state for the colonies, that as early as the beginning of October he had been solicited by a "great number" of mostly "gentlemen" to erect the king's standard. They and "thousands" of others would flock to him if he could promise them some protection from patriot harassment in return. Their predictions rang true. Within a few days of the Proclamation, as many as three thousand men from the towns of Norfolk and Portsmouth as well as the counties of Norfolk, Princess Anne, Nansemond, and Isle

29. Lund Washington to George Washington, Feb. 8, 1776, *Papers of Washington,* Rev. War Ser., III, 271 (emphasis added). There were even problems among the regular troops because of the shortages. See Affidavit concerning John Dow, from Fielding Lewis and Charles Dick, Dec. 11, 1775, *Rev. Va.,* V, 110, Depositions of Captain Morgan Alexander and Corporals Charles Wood and Richard Partridge, Dec. 18, 1775, 181, John Richards to Edmund Pendleton, Dec. 14, 1775, 143, Proceedings of the Fourth Virginia Convention, Dec. 14, 1775, 138–139.

The idea that race and slavery did not bond whites together in a patriotic alliance of course goes against the majority of scholarship that began in its most explicit form with Edmund S. Morgan, *American Slavery, American Freedom: The Ordeal of Colonial Virginia* (New York, 1975), and that has found expression in Kathleen M. Brown, *Good Wives, Nasty Wenches, and Anxious Patriarchs: Gender, Race, and Power in Colonial Virginia* (Chapel Hill, N.C., 1996).

of Wight were reported to have come in and taken the oath of allegiance published by the governor. Instead of being angered by the Proclamation, as patriot leaders hoped, many white Virginians professed their loyalty to the crown. One patriot observer in Norfolk despaired, "Every Man in this County[,] Princess Anne and a great many from the Isle of White and Nansemond" had taken Dunmore's oath. In addition, "large bodies from the adjoining parts of Carolina" were "daily coming in to the Governor for Protection." This had "entirely changd. the face of affairs here which encourages them to think they can . . . withstand the whole United Force of the rest of the Colony." Dunmore was elated; he hoped to turn disgruntled and fearful whites against one another. He began to raise a loyalist regiment of five hundred troops, who, together with the hundreds of rebels' slaves flocking in to help, would be "enough to reduce this Colony to a proper sense of their duty." The patriot situation seemed so bad in the Norfolk region that Woodford thought that the number who had taken the oath to defend the governor was "if possible worse then the proclamation" that freed patriot slaves and servants.[30]

At the very least, Dunmore's success and his Proclamation helped overawe many potential patriots into neutrality. Indeed, for at least a few crucial weeks, the patriot situation in the Norfolk region looked grim. Dunmore's offensive exposed real cracks in the face of patriot claims of unanimity, much to the surprise and embarrassment of gentry leaders. Even William Woodford conceded little help would be forthcoming from frightened whites in the area. The committee had been empowered to call in help from the militia and minutemen of adjacent counties, "but from what I have seen of the People, none of them are to be depended upon (a few Gentlemen excepted)." James Imrie, a Scot living in Northampton County on the Eastern Shore, was perhaps typical. They were all "in a very terrible situation," he wrote in December. "We shall either be obliged to take up arms or be confined," though he himself was "determined to stand out the war, and, if possible, take up arms on neither side."[31]

30. Dunmore to Dartmouth, Oct. 5, 1775, K. G. Davies, ed., *Documents of the American Revolution* (Shannon, 1972–1981), XI, 137; Walter Hatton to Nathaniel Coffin, Nov. 21, 1775, Cary Mitchell to Colonel Cary Selden, Nov. 23, 1775, Dunmore to Sir William Howe, Nov. 30, 1775, *Rev. Va.*, IV, 447, 457, 496, Woodford to the President of the Convention, Dec. 4, 1775, V, 49–50, Woodford to John Page, Nov. 26, 1775, VI, 477.

31. William Woodford to the President of the Convention, Dec. 4, 1775, *Rev. Va.*,

Dunmore's success in the Norfolk region was testimony to the weakness of the patriot movement and to the divisiveness that the conflict with Britain had engendered among white Virginians. Many whites, especially poorer ones, had already had enough of shortages and were dismayed at the military demands placed upon them. What George Gilmer's speech in Albemarle County had nervously implied, loyalists in the Norfolk area openly celebrated and exaggerated. Observing that five hundred people in Princess Anne County took the governor's oath within a day and two hundred more later in Norfolk, one openly loyal resident in Norfolk, Neil Jamieson, noted with some relief, "Several of the Principal People concerned in the raising of the Poor people in Princess Anne County" had "been taken Prisoners." Not only Jamieson felt relieved, as the "poor people blame these Men much for obliging them to take up arms." Jamieson agreed with local reports that the "Principal Part of the people up in the Country" (outside the Norfolk coastal area) who were "in Low Circumstances" were "for Government, if they were at Liberty to declare their Sentiments." Another loyalist, Walter Hatton, thought that the recent engagement at Kemp's Landing, combined with the numbers of men who had flocked to take the royal oath, proved that "numbers" of men had been "forced to take up arms agt: their wills" in the militia.[32]

In the end, shortages and the divisive effects of the Proclamation gave Dunmore and his adherents cause for optimism. Neil Jamieson thought that even many people "up the Country" who were "lately in Opulent Circumstances" would "very soon be in a distrest Situation." Many merchants around Norfolk began to write to their business partners after the Proclamation urging them to send shipments of goods. The Virginians were so desperate and the situation looked good enough for Dunmore that some merchants felt they would "Never have such a Nother" chance "to Make Money by dry Goods in this Country." "Loose Not a Moment," Robert Shedden begged his brother on the same day, and send out "as Many

V, 49–50, James Imrie to John Hay, Dec. 16, 1775, V, 162, Woodford to John Page, Nov. 26, 1775, IV, 477. Cf. Charles Scott to Woodford, Nov. 26, 1775, *Rev. Va.,* IV, 477.

32. Dunmore's military success "has been cause sufficient for numbers who have been constrained to throw off the Yoke and boldly to Stand forth and confess themselves f[rien]ds of Govmt." Neil Jamieson to Messrs. Glassford, Gordon, Monteath, and Co., Glasgow, Nov. 17, 1775, Walter Hatton to Nathaniel Coffin, Nov. 21, 1775, *Rev. Va.,* IV, 423–424 447.

Goods in the Brig as She Will hold." While Dunmore thought he could soon crush the rebellion, merchants thought, "Now is the time to Strick a bold Strock."[33]

* * * Once it became evident that Dunmore's Proclamation did not galvanize their white neighbors as patriot leaders had hoped—indeed, that it provoked opposite responses—there was widespread panic. With Dunmore on the march and patriot forces unable to stop him, the loyalists' optimism was mirrored by patriot despair and anxiety. For many patriot leaders, the lack of support in the minutemen, Dunmore's Proclamation and the response to it, and his occupation of Norfolk precipitated a real crisis. Throughout the colony, but especially in exposed areas, local patriot leaders spoke up about their fears. Behind each message lay worries that their own county could as easily fall prey to Dunmore's depredations. Implicit in these concerns was also an uncertainty about the allegiances and the patriotism of their fellow white Virginians. Indeed, many believed they could be the next Norfolk.

Local leaders from the Eastern Shore and tidewater areas were among the first to register their concerns. The committee of Accomack County, on the Eastern Shore, for example, felt "much exposed" by recent events, and particularly by Dunmore's apparent control of the bay. They had not been able to raise enough minutemen, they could not expect help from Maryland, nor did they feel they had enough arms and ammunition to resist should Dunmore invade.[34] Farther down the Eastern Shore, their Northampton County counterparts were feeling even more exposed, and worried. The committee there wrote directly to the president of Congress for help: they expected an invasion, and they were highly vulnerable. Their enslaved population was "numerous," and "more than double the number of whites." They believed that, if Dunmore landed on their shores, few whites would "Attempt any resistance." Maintaining that such a people

33. Neil Jamieson to Edward and Rene Payne, Nov. 20, 1775, Robert Shedden to John Shedden, Nov. 20, 1775, *Rev. Va.,* IV, 438, 439. Patriot leaders at the local as well as provincial level worried as much about the ambiguous white response to Dunmore's Proclamation as they did about the black response to the governor's offer. See, for example, "Remarks on Lord Dunmore's Proclamation," *Va. Gaz.* (Pinkney), Nov. 23, 1775.

34. Accomack County Committee to the Delegates of the Fourth Virginia Convention, Nov. 30, 1775, *Rev. Va.,* IV, 498.

were not deserving of protection, the committee asked Congress yet to consider the consequences. Dunmore "would compel the People to take up Arms and lead them against the adjacent Counties. . . . The Slaves would croud to his Standard, and his Army become formidable in Numbers." He would also then possess half a million bushels of grain, which would provide the fuel for his growing army. Anxious that the patriot movement did not have the following that leaders believed it did, the committee conjectured what would happen to those who had "manifested their Attachments to the American Cause." They would first face the governor's "resentment," and then active patriots would "stand Censured by their County and at a future day be exposed to its Vengeance."[35]

Committee officials from Northampton linked Dunmore's success to their own unraveling authority. Not just the patriot cause but their own public authority were jeopardized. Dunmore's agents had already come along the coast and "insinuated to the fishermen and all the lower Class of People that they have nothing to fear, that no harm was intended against them." The governor and his agents were quick to take advantage of the divisions among whites, telling free whites that they were after only the "Committee-Men and other principal People"—those who had "advised them to take up Arms." The governor had exploited class tensions and "persuaded Many by these Means." Yet local patriots, at least, believed that Dunmore's campaign was aimed at the already converted. The committee members thought, "If Matters should soon come to an Extremity we should be exposed to the fury of the People." They had already "silently put up with several Enormities." If Dunmore invaded, "the people around us would deliver us up rather than be exposed to the fury of his Soldiers and Slaves." Fearing their less wealthy neighbors, even some of the patriot gentlemen of property "forbear openly to declare their Sentiments or take an active part." Though local patriots asserted that "Many Gentlemen here, in short, almost every Man of Considerable Property is well affected to the

35. The committee asked for support from Congress on behalf of the "common Interest." It was time "to encourage the friends of America and keep the disaffected in awe." Committee of Northampton County to the President of the Continental Congress, Nov. 25, 1775, *Rev. Va.,* IV, 467–468. The committee probably meant that the number of enslaved Virginians in the county was double the number of militia in the county. The federal census of 1790 put the black population of the county at about 54 percent of the total, or 3,244 slaves, 464 "other free persons," and 3,181 free whites (see *Rev. Va.,* IV, 473 n. 9).

American Cause," they stood alone. As a result, they concluded, "this Committee have very little Authority."[36]

Other exposed counties echoed the fears of the Eastern Shore. The county committee of Warwick, across the James River from Norfolk, Nansemond, and Isle of Wight Counties, pleaded for help and protection against their "calamitous State," as did the Hampton Committee of Safety. Further afield, members of the Fairfax county committee in northern Virginia, less exposed to Dunmore's waterborne force, were also worried. "It appears, not only from the public Papers, but Lord Dunmore's Assignation with *Conoly* that Alexandria was to be their place of rendezvous." The committee there was alarmed enough to issue instructions to its delegates to the upcoming convention, giving detailed suggestions for ensuring their own defense. Specifically, they wanted newly raised soldiers distributed evenly throughout the colony, not just sent southward to the Norfolk and lower tidewater areas, since their own part of the country had been left unguarded. This neglect pointed to the need for more "full and equitable Representation" on the Central Committee of Safety to stifle sectionally based divisions. Equal representation was "the only means to unite us and produce the most salutary Effects." Under the pressure of Dunmore's success and of rebellious slaves and servants, normally patriotic committees sent out warnings that all might soon not be well. In their complaints and concerns, the persistent localistic response of county officials only contributed to the deterioration of patriot authority at the provincial level.[37]

In marked contrast, in the dark weeks following Dunmore's Proclamation, the *private* correspondence of patriot leaders dropped off markedly, and what survives shows a fearful group. John Page, a member of the Central Committee of Safety, had told Jefferson in early November, a few

36. Committee of Northampton County to the President of the Continental Congress, Nov. 25, 1775, *Rev. Va.,* IV, 467–469.

37. Warwick County Committee to the Fourth Virginia Convention, Dec. 6, 1775, *Rev. Va.,* V, 67, William Roscow Wilson Curle to the Virginia Committee of Safety, Dec. 3, 1775, 45–46; John Dalton, William Ramsay, John Muir, John Carlyle, James Kirk, George Gilpin, and Richard Conway, Instructions of Fairfax County Committee to their Convention Delegates, Dec. 9, 1775, *Papers of Mason,* I, 260–261. Addressed to George Mason and Charles Broadwater, the Fairfax County delegates, the letter was read to the convention on Dec. 18, 1775 (*Papers of Mason,* I, 261n). Cf. Virginia Delegate to ———, extracted in *Va. Gaz.,* Oct. 16, 1775, Smith et al., eds., *Letters of Delegates to Congress,* II, 194.

days before the Proclamation was made public, that he thought, despite the shortages of salt, arms, and ammunition and unsuccessful skirmishes with Dunmore, that morale was still high. Two weeks later, he was despondent. Dunmore's victory in the region was total: "In short he has made a compleat conquest of Princess Ann and Norfolk and Numbers of Negros, and Cowardly Scoundrels flock to his Standard." Page also worried about the potential for anarchy. The Committee of Safety had adjourned before news reached it of the Proclamation, leaving it vulnerable. If Dunmore defeated Woodford and his small forces, "or should there be an Insurrection of the Negros," there was no one empowered to call in any assistance, except from the neighboring minute and militia companies. Because of their poor recruiting, such help was "at present in Fact none at all." Page was pessimistic. Had they had enough men and crushed Dunmore earlier (as volunteers had demanded in July), they might have been safe. Now Dunmore and his force "are so much reinforced that he is become not only very secure but formidable."[38]

The speaker of the convention, Robert Carter Nicholas, was also near panic. Two days after Dunmore's Proclamation, Nicholas issued a summons to delegates to meet at a Fourth Virginia Convention, beginning December 1, 1775. A week later, he pleaded for Continental help. Believing "Great Numbers" of both whites and blacks had joined Dunmore, Nicholas felt that the colony and individuals were at risk. With the British control over the bay, "no Man in the Colony is safe . . . as an Object of their Vengeance," meaning that many gentlemen and their riverside estates were unsafe. Many "Gentlemen" leaders had already been "taken by Surprize in their Beds"; others had fled. Nicholas thought the situation was bad enough for his colleagues in Congress to return home immediately: "No Country ever required greater Exertions of Wisdom than ours does at present."[39]

Patriot leaders *outside* Virginia were even more adamant about the need to stop Dunmore. George Washington, for example, urged Congress to "Dispossess Lord Dunmore of his hold in Virginia" as soon as it could, admitting to Richand Henry Lee late in December that, if Dunmore was not

38. John Page to Jefferson, Nov. 11, 24, 1775, *Papers of Jefferson,* I, 259, 265–266.

39. Summons to Reconvene the General Convention, Nov. 16, 1775, *Va. Gaz.* (Pinkney), Nov. 16, 1775, *Rev. Va.,* IV, 412, Robert Carter Nicholas to Virginia Delegates in Congress, Nov. 25, 1775, 470–471.

"crushed," he would become the "most formidable Enemy America has—his strength will Increase as a Snow Ball by Rolling; and faster." Washington, sensitized to the anxieties of his cousin at Mount Vernon, thought that Dunmore's success would also be far worse "if some expedient cannot be hit upon to convince the slaves and servants of the impotency of his designs." Charles Lee concurred and hoped that Norfolk would not become the next Boston. If it did, the threat from enslaved Virginians meant that Norfolk was a "place which in their hands will be infinitely more dangerous" than Boston.[40]

Francis Lightfoot Lee was also concerned about the Proclamation, but at least equally worried about the consequent effect that Dunmore's progress had on white society. He warned Robert Wormeley Carter, Richmond County delegate to the Fourth Virginia Convention, that Norfolk could be just the beginning of mass defections from the patriot cause. Many people in coastal areas and particularly the Eastern Shore could easily go the way of Norfolk and Princess Anne Counties. Indeed, it was likely that the people on the Eastern Shore, "from their exposed situation, and the number of their slaves, will thro' fear, be induced to follow the example of the other two Counties." He recommended sending a large force against Dunmore immediately, sequestering the estates of those who had taken arms against the cause, stepping up patrols, and burning "by the hangman" copies of the Proclamation. News of Dunmore's progress had given "concern to all the real friends of America; and subjects Your Countrymen to the sneers of its disguised Enemies and the lukewarm." "Fatal consequences may follow if an immediate stop is not put to that Devil's career."[41]

To arrest the progress of both internal and external threats, some patriot leaders wanted to use the crisis to strike a bold stroke of their own. Indeed, some military leaders and congressional delegates alike tried to use Dunmore's success to spur their compatriots to more decisive action. Francis Lightfoot Lee, an ardent and early proponent of Independence, was quick to play on patriots' fears over the loss of control of the movement and the loss of authority among their neighbors. It was time to "establish some kind

40. George Washington to R. H. Lee, Dec. 26, 1775, *Papers of Washington,* Rev. War. Ser., II, 610–613; Charles Lee to R. H. Lee, Dec. 18, 1775, *The Lee Papers,* I, 232–233, New-York Historical Society, *Collections,* IV (1871); Journal of the Continental Congress, Dec. 4, 1775, *Rev. Va.,* IV, 47.

41. Francis Lightfoot Lee to Robert Wormeley Carter, [Dec. 2, 1775], Clark et al., eds., *Naval Documents,* II, 1237.

of Government," since Dunmore, "by his proclamation, has utterly demolished the whole civil Government." A few days later, no doubt at Lee's urging, Congress took note of Dunmore's Proclamation, which had, by declaring martial law, torn "up the foundations of civil authority and government within" the colony. Accordingly, Congress recommended that, should they find it necessary, Virginia should "call a full and free representation of the people" and "establish such form of government, as in their judgment will best produce the happiness of the people and effectually secure peace and good order in the colony." In other words, Congress believed that Dunmore had provided justification enough for the ultimate rebellion. Only independence and the restoration of government would secure "peace and good order in the colony."[42]

Virginia's terrified leaders, however, were less than convinced that the time had come to push for Independence: the colony could barely muster the strength and authority to contain Dunmore's tiny force. The provincial Committee of Safety in particular stood paralyzed in the face of Dunmore's progress and refused to sanction any offensive action that might result in further losses. Mirroring divisions among civilian patriot leaders, some zealous officers believed they needed to act quickly. The popular ex-volunteer leader Charles Scott of Cumberland County, under William Woodford's command in the Second Regiment, argued for an immediate attack on Dunmore's forces at Norfolk before he could establish a proper beachhead or attract sufficient numbers of enslaved Virginians. But Woodford and his genteel civilian colleagues were less sure of the best way forward. Woodford told Scott to wait for more intelligence and then asked the Committee of Safety for guidance, which body in turn waited until the Fourth Virginia Convention before answering Woodford. After hasty deliberations on the first day, the delegates also counseled caution, and Pendleton told Woodford that they wanted him to "risk the success of your arms as little as possible, at this important crisis." In other words, in light of the Proclamation and its encouragement of enslaved Virginians, Pendleton and the committee felt that avoiding a further loss was much safer than a battle against Dunmore. Woodford was to send for reinforcements from

42. Francis Lightfoot Lee to Landon Carter, Dec. 12, 1775, Ludwell-Lee Papers, VHS; Francis Lightfoot Lee to Robert Wormeley Carter, [Dec. 2, 1775], Clark et al., eds., *Naval Documents,* II, 1237; Benson, "Wealth and Power," 310–311; Continental Congress Resolutions, Dec. 4, 1775, *Rev. Va.,* V, 47.

North Carolina and wait until the "numbers . . . in your judgment, give a moral probability of answering the purposes of your march."[43]

As Dunmore began to establish himself at Norfolk, most patriot leaders were fearful, unsure of their next move and unwilling to risk any further losses, and the delegates to the Fourth Virginia Convention reflected this uncertainty. Meeting in Richmond on December 1, the delegates immediately and unanimously elected Edmund Pendleton president of the body and adjourned to Williamsburg. They were less divided in their proceedings than at the previous meeting. Not only did they decide to keep the proceedings secret, but they also demanded that any letters intercepted by county committees come directly to the committee of safety "unopened."[44]

Then, for well more than a week, the delegates did nothing. Instead, they asked for returns of the armed forces and duly contemplated each letter sent by Woodford. What they read was not reassuring. Woodford was sure that he could not possibly call in any local reinforcements from the militia or minutemen, because most of them were disaffected. The governor's position was "very advantageous," and Woodford could find "no way to Attack them" and halt his progress. After four days of secret discussion, the delegates finally made one tentative move. In recognition of the desperate circumstances of Eastern Shore patriots, they ordered five hundred new troops raised solely for the defense of that peninsula. The delegates then went back into discussion for another four days, again little inclined to act with any conviction.[45]

• • • Finally, Dunmore helped patriot leaders out with a hasty and impetuous act. Just as the British were consolidating their position in and around Norfolk, Dunmore ordered an attack on Woodford's troops at Great Bridge —again. Though Woodford was in no position to act offensively against Dunmore, he did have a good defensive position. When Captain Samuel

43. Charles Scott to Woodford, Nov. 26, 1775, *Rev. Va.*, IV, 476, Woodford to John Page, Nov. 26, 1775, IV, 478–479, Proceedings of the Fourth Virginia Convention, Dec. 1, 1775, V, 33; Pendleton to Woodford, Dec. 1, 1775, "Declaration," Dec. 14, 1775, *Papers of Pendleton*, I, 134, 138.

44. See Proceedings of the Fourth Virginia Convention, Dec. 1, 6, 1775, *Rev. Va.*, V, 33, 65.

45. Woodford to the President of the Convention, Dec. 4, 1775, *Rev. Va.*, V, 49, Proceedings of the Fourth Virginia Convention, Dec. 6, 7, 1775, 65–66, 72.

Leslie marched out of the improvised British fort there in the early hours of December 9, the patriot Virginians could hardly believe their luck. Leslie led a charge of 280 of his best soldiers, including a strong contingent of "Volunteers and Blacks," straight into a fortified patriot breastwork. The rebel troops, numbering only 70 or 80 at the front line, held their fire until the British were almost upon them, then poured fire into their ranks. Three British officers and 14 regulars were killed almost immediately, and nearly 50 other men were wounded, of whom 15 were captured. The battle was over in less than thirty minutes, and the British retreated to their fort.[46]

Dunmore panicked, thought it best to withdraw to Norfolk and from there, despite the protests of many of its merchants, to the safety of his ships, believing Norfolk to be indefensible. A day later, a twenty-eight-gun ship under Captain Henry Bellew arrived in the Chesapeake Bay with three thousand stand, or sets, of arms, but too late for Dunmore to re-occupy Norfolk. Though Woodford was slow to take advantage of Dunmore's retreat, he moved into Norfolk after reinforcements arrived from Williamsburg and North Carolina. By December 14, Woodford's forces, including many regulars and militia from North Carolina under Colonel Robert Howe, stood at about twelve hundred men.[47]

The battle of Great Bridge broke the paralysis of patriot leaders. As soon as news of the battle and Dunmore's evacuation began to reach the doors of the convention, delegates started pushing through more offensive measures. Relieved that Dunmore had been chased back out to sea, patriot leaders with renewed determination set about ensuring that he would not repeat his manuevers. Their biggest concern was security, internal and external. Drawing on their own experience and from the letters from around the colony arriving soon after they had convened, most gentlemen in the convention believed that they needed a better army to neutralize Dunmore and thus restore some kind of order. As the Fairfax committee noted about the arming of the militia, it was too "dependant on a Contingency, we wish not to happen," that is, on *the Default of the People.*" Now, when the

46. See Woodford to the Fourth Virginia Convention, Dec. 9, 10, 11, 1775, *Rev. Va.,* V, 90-91, 98-99, 108-109, Proceedings of the Fourth Virginia Convention, Dec. 11, 12, 1775, 107, 114-115; Extracts of Letters of the Virginia Committee of Safety, Dec. 16, 1775, *Dunlop's Pennsylvania Packet, or, the General Advertiser* (Philadelphia), Jan. 1, 1776, *Rev. Va.,* V, 161.

47. Selby, *Revolution in Virginia,* 74.

"Sword is drawn, the Bayonet is already at our Breasts," they needed to make some more "immediate Effort" to ward off "the meditated Blow."[48]

Leading patriots cried out for greater protection by a paid, professional army. The committee of Accomack County, on the Eastern Shore, had not been able to raise even one company of minutemen for their own protection. Though they found "insuperable Difficulties in forming" their companies of minutemen, they believed they would have better luck enlisting men into regular army service. Those in need of a full-time occupation could help provide the mainstay of the regional defense force. The county committees of Warwick and Fairfax also pleaded for greater protection by regular soldiers. Fairfax recommended to the convention that it raise more regular soldiers, for the "Minute System is very inadequate to the Design." Regular soldiers could be permanently stationed anywhere the colony was "expos'd and vulnerable."[49]

Where the colony was most exposed and vulnerable, Robert Carter Nicholas made clear: the exposed river coasts that the British could attack most easily. Consequently, gentlemen and men of substantial property were most at risk. Nicholas also believed that the answer to Virginia's problems was "a greater Number of Regulars." "Neither Militia or Minutemen will do," he complained, for the "tolerable Security of this Country." Patriot leaders thus called for the end of reliance on a part-time unprofessional force; they wanted a larger regular army. It could protect vulnerable planters from Dunmore's depredations and incursions, overawe local whites into continued resistance, and intimidate local black and white slaves and servants into staying put.[50]

In December the convention thus resolved to raise another seven battalions of regular troops to augment the two from the summer of 1775, thereby conceding that the minuteman plan had failed. Yet, to avoid assuming the huge costs of such a full-time body of troops, the convention asked Con-

48. John Dalton, William Ramsay, John Muir, John Carlyle, James Kirk, George Gilpin, and Richard Conway, Instructions of Fairfax County Committee to their Convention Delegates, Dec. 9, 1775, *Papers of Mason,* I, 260.

49. Accomack County Committee to the Delegates of the Fourth Virginia Convention, Nov. 30, 1775, *Rev. Va.,* IV, 498, Warwick County Committee to the Fourth Virginia Convention, Dec. 6, 1777, V, 67; Instructions of Fairfax County Committee to their Convention Delegates, Dec. 9, 1775, *Papers of Mason,* I, 260.

50. Robert Carter Nicholas to Virginia Delegates in Congress, Nov. 25, 1775, *Rev. Va.,* IV, 470–471.

gress to take them all onto Continental pay, thus spreading the enormous costs across the colonies—and making it clear that the new troops were for local defense. In one stroke, the convention could provide a more adequate defense for the colony without risking further internal upheaval by imposing a greater financial burden on its citizens.[51]

Responding to the complaints of vulnerable patriots around the colony, and with Dunmore again at sea, the convention added the stipulation that the Committee of Safety station two regiments (or almost fourteen hundred men), when raised, between the Potomac and Rappahannock Rivers, two between the Rappahannock and the York, two between the York and the James, and two south of the James. The committee could move them "to repel the invasion or attacks of the enemy," but "the forces so ordered shall return to their respective stations so soon as the emergency shall cease." In ordering the dispersal of the troops and demanding that Congress pay for them, the convention members essentially demanded that the other colonies help pay for the local protection that militia and minutemen should have provided.[52]

But Congress would not pay for the extra soldiers for Virginia's defense, telling the convention that it would take only six extra battalions onto Continental pay. The convention quickly and sharply retorted that Virginia's "peculiar and exposed situation"—not just from foreign but also from "domestic" enemies—necessitated nine battalions of regular forces "at least," for a "tolerable Degree of Security." It hoped "Congress would have supposed them competent Judges of the number of Forces necessary to the security of this Colony." Congress ought to "without Hesitation have taken all the regular forces found necessary for their Defence into continental Pay."[53]

Thus, elite white Virginians were anxious enough about the threat from Dunmore to risk Continental harmony, even this early in the contest. The issue occasioned a "warm Debate" in Congress. "Almost every Colony" was

51. Proceedings of the Fourth Virginia Convention, Dec. 13, 1775, *Rev. Va.,* V, 128; Summons to Reconvene the General Convention, Nov. 16, 1775, *Va. Gaz.* (Pinkney), Nov. 16, 1775, *Rev. Va.,* IV, 412, Robert Carter Nicholas to Virginia Delegates in Congress, Nov. 25, 1775, 470-471.

52. Hening, comp., *Statutes at Large,* IX, 85-86, 95-96; *Lee Papers,* I, 375, NYHS, *Collections,* IV (1871).

53. Resolution of the Continental Congress, Dec. 28, 1775, *Rev. Va.,* V, 262, Proceedings of the Fourth Virginia Convention, Jan. 10, 1775, 372-373.

strongly opposed to the request from the Virginians, nor did Virginia delegates Benjamin Harrison and Thomas Nelson think it would pass. Harrison told Robert Carter Nicholas that he and the other Virginia delegates would "leave no Stone unturned to Carry the Point," but he wished "Congress had been treated with more Delicacy." "Every Country" could make the same argument. Congress could not, "In justice," pay for more Virginia troops without taking "at least twelve thousand men from the Different Colonies into pay that have been hitherto Refused."[54]

While willing to risk Continental harmony, Virginia delegates worked hard to achieve a consensus within their own ranks, and they did work more cohesively. In contrast to the previous convention, Archibald Cary told Richard Henry Lee, the "business of the Convention goes on as usual, Slowly," but, at least this time, "we are well agreed, as to what shou'd be done." Also in contrast to the divisions that wracked the Third Convention, there was very little disagreement over the elections of field officers to head the new regiments when raised.[55]

Delegates also moved against internal enemies. Within days of hearing of the governor's evacuation of Norfolk, they finally issued a response to Dunmore's Proclamation, offering a pardon to any enslaved Virginians who surrendered to William Woodford immediately. Acknowledging the restive mood of enslaved Virginians, their Declaration warned them against taking any further action. Noting that the Proclamation had given "encouragement to a general insurrection," the delegates announced that any enslaved Virginians who might be "conspiring to rebel or make insurrection" would suffer death. The convention then tried to shore up its Declaration by ordering county lieutenants throughout the colony to double up their slave patrols "during the ensuing holidays." Enslaved Virginians often used the Christmas period to visit kin and celebrate together, but patriot leaders recognized that they might use it to make other, more subversive, plans. The convention also repealed the exemption given to overseers in the militia, who now were ordered to do patrol duty.[56]

54. Benjamin Harrison to Robert Carter Nicholas, Feb. 13, 1776, Thomas Nelson to John Page, Feb. 13, 1776, Smith et al., eds., *Letters of Delegates to Congress*, III, 245, 248.

55. Cary to Lee, Dec. 24, 1775, Hoffman, ed., *Lee Family Papers;* Proceedings of the Fourth Virginia Convention, Jan. 11, 12, 1776, *Rev. Va.*, V, 383, 389-393.

56. Proceedings of the Fourth Virginia Convention, Dec. 13, 14, 20, 1775, *Rev. Va.*, V, 125-126, 139, 201; Hening, comp., *Statutes at Large*, IX, 89.

The delegates moved against disaffected whites too. A few days after hearing of Woodford's success at Great Bridge, they conceded that they had given a too "extraordinary and unexampled Indulgence" when they had exempted British immigrants from military service. Delegates believed that many of these people had sided with Dunmore and had persuaded others to do so. But they had also "excited our Slaves to Rebellion and some of them have daringly led them in Arms against our Inhabitants." The delegates now ordered them to share in "the common Defense" or leave the colony.[57]

In moving against internal enemies the delegates took an important though tentative step closer to Independence. Enlarging the army did, of course, widen the gulf between the colony and Britain. But by taking away a middle ground upon which loyalists or those yet undecided could at least perch uneasily, patriot leaders radicalized the resistance movement by polarizing allegiances. In some sense, they were following in the footsteps of militants in the volunteer companies who demanded a strict accounting of allegiances and tolerated no dissent. Delegates were surprised and angered that Dunmore had found so many ready converts—converts willing to subvert the social order to fight the patriot movement—and they were vehement. Shocked by events in November and early December, they would cross the Rubicon toward Independence in a final, tragically ironic act. In a conservative movement aimed at ensuring the sanctity of property, patriot leaders would stand by and do nothing to prevent the ultimate destruction of property: the burning of Norfolk.

• • • As news of Dunmore's withdrawal became clearer, the delegates ordered William Woodford on December 14 to round up any and all suspected loyalists who had borne arms against the patriots and send them to Williamsburg. On the same day, both Woodford and Robert Howe informed the convention that the patriot forces had occupied Norfolk; their assessments only fueled antiloyalist sentiment. Howe called the people there a "contemptible set of wretches" while Woodford assured the convention, "The Town of Norfolk deserves no favour." Woodford was particularly angry because three of his soldiers had that day been injured when someone fired on them, and he believed reports that the shots came from one of the houses in town. One day later, on December 15, in a letter quickly

57. Proceedings of the Fourth Virginia Convention, Dec. 19, 20, 1775, Jan. 20, 1776, *Rev. Va.,* V, 190–191, 198–200, 436–437.

published in the newspapers, he told the convention that he had "the worst opinion of the people here."[58]

Such sentiments had been building over the past several months. Archibald Campbell noted as early as October 10 that Norfolk had become a focus of anger among militant patriots. Zealous patriots in particular were angry because of the numbers of merchants there who they believed were sympathetic to Dunmore. Feelings were high: "Nothing less is talkd of by the Warm Patriots than destroying it, for fear it Should fall in to Lord Dunmore's hands." As Dunmore began to make successful raids in the area, rumors that the patriots intended the destruction of Norfolk reached fever pitch—even before Dunmore raised his standard. On November 11, the Central Committee of Safety issued a declaration countering "divers Reports" that claimed that the army sent to the Norfolk region was "empowered and directed to destroy the House and Properties of particular Persons" in the area.[59]

Such reports had some foundation in truth. More militant patriots were keen to suppress antipatriot activity in the area any way they could. At the end of October, even Jefferson told John Page, "Carthage must be destroyed"—"Delenda est Norfolk." Page, a member of the Committee of Safety, told Jefferson that was exactly what the townspeople feared: "The People at Norfolk are under dreadful Apprehensions of having their Town burnt." Page believed that patriots were as much to blame for loyalist action in the area as Dunmore. "Many of them deserve to be ruined and hanged but others again have acted dastardly for Want of Protection." Yet Page was sure of one thing, if the town continued to be a problem: "At all Events rather than the Town should be garrisoned by our Enemies and a Trade opened for all the Scoundrels in the Country, we must be prepared to destroy it."[60]

As commanders Howe and Woodford took control of the town and countryside in the wake of Dunmore's evacuation, they grew more irritated by what they saw but also gave civilian leaders the opportunity to vent their

58. Ibid., Dec. 14, 1775, *Rev. Va.,* V, 138, Robert Howe to Pendleton, Dec. 14, 1775, 141, Woodford to the President of the Convention, Dec. 14, 15, 1775, 142, 153.

59. Archibald Campbell to St. George Tucker, Oct. 10, 1775, in Clark et al., eds., *Naval Documents,* II, 395; A Declaration, by order of the Committee of Safety, Nov. 11, 1775, *Rev. Va.,* IV, 382.

60. Jefferson to John Page, Oct. 31, 1775, Page to Jefferson, Nov. 11, 1775, *Papers of Jefferson,* I, 251, 258–259.

anger and anxiety. Woodford and Howe presented the convention with two alternatives. On one hand, they could occupy and fortify the town against a return of the British. On the other hand, given Norfolk's strategic location, the sentiments of the inhabitants, and their past worrisome experience, the commanders wondered whether it would not be better to have the town "Totally distroy'd." Though they asked the convention to consider the question, they also tipped their own choice. Playing on the recent fears of an extensive civil war, Howe and Woodford had no doubt that the British would make the town a garrison as soon as any troops arrived. Destroying the town was the only way to avoid the "dreadful consequences" that might follow should the British repossess Norfolk.[61]

The convention never replied. Whether too wrapped up in debate in other matters, acquiescent, or simply too paralyzed at the thought of such destruction, the convention never advised on the matter, much to the military commanders' unease. Edmund Pendleton, at least, later told Woodford that the thought of "making a conflagration of our own Town, though too much the property of our enemies," was simply "too shocking to think of." Significantly, though, Archibald Campbell, a suspected loyalist, appeared before the convention as a deputy from town officials in Norfolk. He wanted to know what was to become of Norfolk, as there were many reports that the town would be plundered and then burned by patriot officials. The delegates referred his petition to a committee and then placed Campbell under house arrest in Williamsburg.[62]

On December 21, the twenty-eight-gun British frigate *Liverpool,* under Captain Henry Bellew, arrived in Norfolk harbor with 250 men on board. Woodford and Howe grew uneasy. They worried about the possibility of Dunmore's encircling them. They reiterated their arguments whether the town should be strongly fortified or destroyed. Playing on the fears of delegates, Woodford warned the convention that they could not risk de-

61. Howe to Pendleton, Dec. 14, 22, 1775, Woodford to Pendleton, Dec. 14, 15, 17, 1775, Woodford and Howe to Pendleton, Dec. 16, 1775, *Rev. Va.,* V, 141, 142–143, 153, 159–160, 173, 217.

62. Pendleton to Woodford, Jan. 16, 1776, *Papers of Pendleton,* I, 148; Woodford to Pendleton, Dec. 30, 1775, *Rev. Va.,* V, 287, Proceedings of the Fourth Virginia Convention, Dec. 16, 1775, 158. There is a possibility that the convention had at least sent its approval of the recommendations made by Howe and Woodford. On December 25, Howe wrote to Pendleton thanking him for a now missing letter and expressing satisfaction that "our proceedings are approved of" (see *Rev. Va.,* V, 243).

fending Norfolk. Because the enemy could surround them by water, any troops there would be lost. "The consequences may be fatal, not only to the Troops, but the cause." The convention, despite sitting the entire time, failed to respond.[63]

Just more than a week after these letters, the problem of Norfolk was solved. After Bellew's arrival, Virginia troops continued to spar with the British, taunting them from shore. Having had enough of Howe's men's open resistance, Bellew wrote to Howe warning that, if they did not desist from exercising in full view of the ships in the harbor, he would be forced into action against them. On New Year's Day 1776 patriot troops openly paraded in the streets of Norfolk with their hats fixed on their bayonets and used "other menacing actions." Some came down to the wharves and "used every mark of insult." By 3:00 P.M., Bellew had had enough and fired into the wharves and guardhouse of the patriots, triggering a hail of shot from other vessels in the harbor. Dunmore sent some men ashore to set fire to some warehouses on the lower side of the wharves that the rebels had used for cover when firing upon his ships. Again, men on the other British ships followed suit. As patriot and royal troops continued to exchange shots and insults, the fire became general and raged for days, much to Dunmore's surprise. At the end, Norfolk was a shell. One estimate noted that "seven eights of the Town is reduced to Ashes," another that it was "nine tenths," and still another put the worth of property destroyed at £176,426.[64]

But Dunmore was not responsible for the shocking destruction of Norfolk. A suppressed inquest and eyewitness accounts subsequently revealed that it was the Virginia troops that had fanned the flames in Norfolk and that had looted the burning town under the noses of commanders Woodford and Howe. If Woodford and Howe had tried to stop them, there is no record. Most evidence suggests that they condoned and acquiesced in what they believed was good for the defense of the colony. One patriot soldier on patrol near the lower wharves on the morning of January 2 reported that the fires set by Dunmore's troops were in "a great measure extinguished." However, he was astonished to find Virginia soldiers "with fire-brands in their hands, destroying the Houses of the inhabitants." One of the first to be burned was that of prominent loyalist James Parker. His mansion, com-

63. Robert Howe to the President of the Convention, Dec. 2, 1775, *Rev. Va.,* V, 217–218, Woodford to the President of the Convention, Dec. 22, 1775, 220.

64. See *Rev. Va.,* V, 15, 17. Captain Henry Bellew to Howe, Howe to Bellew, Dec. 30, 1775, *Rev. Va.,* V, 285.

plete with "marble chimnies and stone steps" along with "the best garden in that part of the country," was completely ruined. Yet even rebel properties were consumed. Joseph Hutchings, recently captured by his own slave, owned one of the wharves that the Virginia troops kept trying to burn even after the wind had blown Dunmore's fire out. John Calvert lost 7 houses, and Thomas Newton lost 9 tenements, 10 warehouses, 2 "elegantly furnished" mansions, and a "well furnished" shop. "Keep up the Jigg!" Virginia troops shouted as they burned their way through the town. One report later claimed that the troops were "drinking Rum" and "Crying out let us make hay while the Sun Shines." Even a "necessary house" of a prominent merchant was fair game. When asked whether this was deliberate, the soldiers cried, "Yes, damn them, we'el burn them all." And they did: a total of 1,331 buildings were burned.[65]

Fueled by stolen wine and rum, Virginia soldiers rioted through the streets of Norfolk looting shops and burning houses while their commanders looked on with indifference. Sarah Smith later reported that she had asked Howe—in front of Woodford—whether they intended to burn her house. Howe hesitated briefly and then answered in the affirmative. They intended to do more: after destroying Norfolk Borough, he said, "I believe we shall burn up the two Counties" of Norfolk and Princess Anne. Howe reportedly told another witness that he was too busy to interfere when told about the patriot arson. He was also supposedly unconcerned when told that even patriot homes were being burned. Woodford allegedly ordered a stop to the looting and burning on January 3, but no written order corroborates the claim.[66]

Instead, Woodford and Howe deliberately lied about the fire. While Dunmore claimed that the wind was blowing offshore and, therefore, the fire should not have spread farther than the first line of wharves, Howe and Woodford told the convention, "The wind favoured their design, and we believe the flames will become general." Howe added the next day that the Virginia troops tried to prevent the enemy from landing and setting more buildings on fire but that the wooden buildings "took fire immediately and

65. See *Rev. Va.*, V, 16–17; James Parker's Deposition to the Loyalist Commission, Mar. 9, 1784, PA-16.36, Parker Family Papers; Selby, *Revolution in Virginia*, 83; Deposition of John Roger, no. 3, Deposition of W. Goodchild, Sept. 19, 1777, Deposition of R. Jarvis, Sept. 30, 1777, Auditors' MS Item, no. 177, LiVi.

66. See *Rev. Va.*, V, 16; Deposition of S. Smith, Sept. 16, 1777, Auditors' MS Item, no. 177, LiVi; Selby, *Revolution in Virginia*, 83.

the fire spread with amazing rapidity." He thought that the whole town would be "consum'd in a day or two."[67]

Though the Virginia troops had destroyed more than 90 percent of the town, the convention delegates, after listening to a personal report from Colonel Howe (who had ridden to Williamsburg in haste after the conflagration), adopted resolutions that completed the destruction of Norfolk. On January 15, they ordered Norfolk evacuated and any "mills and entrenchments" still standing destroyed. On the following day, the convention also gave the committee of safety authority to consider "from time to time" whether Portsmouth should be either defended or destroyed as well. Finally, on the same day, the convention resolved that, before Howe and his troops evacuated Norfolk, they should take a list of the houses remaining in Norfolk and its suburbs, estimate their value, and, as soon as the inhabitants were evacuated as well, "cause all s[uch] Houses to be demolished as in his judgment may be useful to our Enemies." Once Dunmore "had done that horrid work, fit only for him," Pendleton could see no reason not to demolish the few remaining buildings so that they would not give any comfortable lodgings to their enemy. If there were any doubts about the propriety of their action, the convention allayed them by ordering the suppression of the resolves. The printer was instructed not to publish these three resolutions, which would not come to light until years after the end of the war.[68]

Howe appeared before the convention on January 13 and 17. Whether he admitted, publicly or privately, that patriot troops were involved or that he and Woodford had encouraged or acquiesced in such actions is not known. Regardless, patriot leaders did not hesitate to close ranks and cast the blame entirely upon Dunmore. We do know that Dunmore fought back with a report printed on the captured press he had on board with him.

67. Howe to Pendleton, Jan. 2, 1776, *Rev. Va.,* V, 319, Howe and Woodford to Pendleton, Jan. 1, 1776, 308. Cf. Woodford to Pendleton, Jan. 5, 1776, 346, and also Howe to Pendleton, Jan. 6, 1775, 355–356.

68. Council of War at Norfolk, Jan. 9, 1776, *Rev. Va.,* V, 368–369; Pendleton to Woodford, Jan. 16, 1776, *Papers of Pendleton,* I, 148; *Rev. Va.,* V, 19, Proceedings of the Fourth Virginia Convention, Jan. 15, 16, 1776, 405, 416, 417. Howe carried out the order to burn the rest of the buildings in Norfolk on Feb. 6, 1776. Adele Hast, *Loyalism in Revolutionary Virginia: The Norfolk Area and the Eastern Shore* (Ann Arbor, Mich., 1982), 59; Selby, *Revolution in Virginia,* 84; Howe to William Woodford, Feb. 9, 1776, in John Burk, *The History of Virginia, from Its First Settlement to the Present Day,* IV, cont. Skelton Jones and Louis Hue Girardin (Petersburg, Va., 1816), 111.

On January 18, the governor charged the provincial troops with the burning of Norfolk, and the Committee of Safety immediately ordered Howe to make a "Strict enquiry" into the "conduct of our Troops on that occasion" and transmit the depositions to it. No depositions have been subsequently found, and the question was still alive in 1777 when the assembly appointed commissioners to "Inquire into and Ascertain the Losses Sustained by the Late Inhabitants of the Borough of Norfolk." Their report placed the blame almost entirely on the patriot troops, but it was deliberately suppressed. (It was not made public for sixty years, and almost one hundred years would pass before historians brought it to public attention.)[69]

Neither Woodford nor Howe expressed much regret. Indeed, though the town was in a "very ruinous condition," with "seven eights of it being reduced to ashes," Howe considered it "as to its ultimate tendency, as greatly beneficial to the Public." Repeating the arguments of mid-December, Howe reminded the convention that "very few" of the inhabitants were patriots. Thus did gentlemen patriots become true revolutionaries. He and Woodford, part of the patriot elite, were satisfied that the burning of Norfolk was a necessary evil, to save the colony from ruin. Norfolk had been the base for Dunmore's depredations and a focal point for enslaved Virginians' aspirations for liberty. When Howe carried out the order to evacuate Norfolk and destroy the remaining buildings, he wrote with glee and relief: "We have removed from Norfolk, thank God for that! It is entirely destroyed; thank God for that also!"[70]

• • • Dunmore was taken aback by the actions of Woodford and Howe, particularly the rebels' "ill-judged and misapplied fury" in destroying not only valuable public property but also the property of those "who had never taken part in this contest." Sir John Dalrymple, afloat with Dunmore, believed he saw through the rebel plan. They had intended to destroy Norfolk from the beginning, "and indeed were so obliging as to assist us in it,

69. Of the 1,331 buildings burned, the General Assembly of Virginia later concluded that Dunmore's troops destroyed only 19 on the day of the naval bombardment, and 32 more buildings before they evacuated. The rest were burned by the Virginia or North Carolina troops. See Committee of Safety Resolution, Jan. 31, 1776, *Rev. Va.,* VI, 40, 41n; Hening, comp., *Statutes at Large,* IX, 328–330; *Rev. Va.,* V, 17, 19; Selby, *Revolution in Virginia,* 84.

70. Howe to Pendleton, Jan. 6, 1775, *Rev. Va.,* V, 355–356; *Rev. Va.,* V, 19, Proceedings of the Fourth Virginia Convention, Jan. 15, 16, 1776, 405, 416, 417.

by setting fire to the greatest part of the Town that was not in our reach." However, once the newspapers got hold of the story, Dalrymple thought, the rebels would take "the Inhumanity of the Action off their Shoulders" and put it "upon our own."[71]

Dalrymple was correct. The burning of Norfolk became a Continental cause célèbre, as patriot leaders used the affair to turn the tide of sentiment against the British. The Virginia newspapers repeated Howe's allegations that the wind had done most of the damage after Dunmore's troops had started the fires. Reports of Dunmore's shocking behavior flew up and down the Atlantic seaboard. By January 5, patriot leaders in New England had heard of the burning of Norfolk. Militants were overjoyed. Samuel Adams of Massachusetts thought that the burning would help convince all but the most cautious patriots that Independence was the only choice left for the colonists. He told James Warren that the sacking of Norfolk would "prevail more than a long Train of Reasoning to accomplish a Confederation, and other Matters which I know your heart as well as mine is much set upon." George Washington also thought that the combined effects of the burning of Norfolk and Falmouth, in Maine, would provide forceful "flaming Arguments" that would not "leave numbers at a loss to decide upon the Propriety of a Seperation."[72]

In Virginia, patriot leaders used the burning of Norfolk almost immediately as the primary justification for their own tentative first moves toward Independence. On the last day of the Fourth Virginia Convention, the delegates adopted a resolution that was tantamount to secession from the British Empire. They declared that Virginia's ports were now open to any nation for trade, except Britain, Ireland, and the British West Indies. They also recommended to Congress that it begin to find a way to allow exports from the colonies to overseas markets. Aware that farmers in Virginia were suffering from shortages, anxious to find a market for their wasting crops, and mindful that fighting a major war with Britain would require supplies of all kinds, patriot leaders in Virginia moved to establish free trade. In doing so, they announced to Britain that their special economic arrangement—and the basis for their colonial relationship—was over.

71. PRO, CO 5/1353, fol. 327, 5/40, fol. 126; *Rev. Va.,* V, 17.

72. Selby, *Revolution in Virginia,* 84; Washington to Reed, Jan. 31, 1776, *Papers of Washington,* Rev. War Ser., III, 228. Cf. John Page to Woodford, Jan. 2, 1776, in Burk, *History of Virginia,* IV, 110n; John Page to Richard Henry Lee, Feb. 3, 1776, Hoffman, ed., *Lee Family Papers.*

It was, in fact, a declaration of economic independence, taken, the delegates announced, only because of British provocations. In particular, they cited the British ministry's "open and avowed war" with Virginia, carried on with the "most unrelenting fury." The British themselves had forced the colonists to this renunciation of their economic relationship, not just by "exciting insurrections among our slaves, inviting the savages, and arming them against us" but also "by burning and destroying open and defenceless towns, contrary to the practices of war among civilized nations."[73]

73. Proceedings of the Fourth Virginia Convention, Jan. 20, 1776, *Rev. Va.,* V, 436-437.

CHAPTER 6 *The Spirit of Levelling*

MOVEMENTS FOR INDEPENDENCE,

JANUARY–MAY 1776

If patriot leaders had burned Norfolk in part at least to restore order throughout the colony, they had also inadvertently taken a step closer to Independence. Indeed, with the burning of the town and the opening of the colony's ports, Virginians stood uneasily poised between treason and Independence. Unable to turn back the clock but also fearful that they were ill equipped to take that final, fateful step, many patriot leaders stood paralyzed and simply waited for the much larger army they had called for to collect. Most hoped that the enlarged army would help keep peace within Virginia while much-hoped-for foreign alliances would keep the British at bay.

But, with patriot leaders vacillating over their next step and when to take it, many lower- and middle-class Virginians took initiatives of their own. Enslaved Virginians, for example, continued to take advantage of any and all opportunities that the conflict brought. Some white Virginians, on the other hand, continued indifferent to the conflict, but others grew impatient for quicker and greater change. Indeed, after December 1775, a new dynamic emerged among prominent groups of ordinary Virginians as, increasingly, many began to demand changes and show a keenness to wrest concessions from patriot leaders in return for their wartime support and sacrifices. Ultimately, ordinary Virginians pushed patriot leaders toward Independence. They did so in two ways: some of them vociferously advocated Independence for their own reasons; others by their independent actions worried prominent gentlemen into declaring Independence to restore formal order and authority in the colony.

• • • As the flames died down in Norfolk, patriot leaders waited anxiously for news about recruiting for the new army. Most hoped that an enlarged regular army would stabilize the situation and restore order, especially in the more exposed regions. Dunmore had only put back out to sea; he had not left the colony after he evacuated Norfolk. Many gentlemen felt vulnerable to attack from up the rivers, and the specter of Norfolk was never far from their minds. Moreover, slaveholders throughout Virginia, but especially along the riversides, were plagued by constant reminders that political separation from Britain was not the only "independence" contemplated by Virginians.

Indeed, enslaved workers continued to defy their masters' authority to seek their own independence. After the battle of Great Bridge and the fall of Norfolk, of course, many black dreams of liberty came to an end. For some, that loss was a direct result of the battle. At least thirty-four enslaved Virginians were taken prisoner at Great Bridge, and the Committee of Safety ordered most of them to be valued and sold in the West Indies. Some ended up as laborers in Virginia's own lead mines; one would die in jail. Others fell prey to the increased vigilance of patriots. When two runaways mistook a patriot ship for a British tender and inadvertently told those aboard of their "inclination to serve Lord Dunmore," they were captured and sentenced to death, "as an example to others." Any enslaved Virginians caught running away were given back to their owner only if that master could convey them to some interior part of the country. Unsuccessful runaways, then, lost not only their chance for freedom but also their local family and neighborhood connections. Reports like these gave many enslaved Virginians a reason to pause and take stock of their chances. Moreover, for black Virginians plotting their escape, Dunmore's evacuation from Norfolk meant that they were now unsure where they might find refuge with the British.[1]

Despite the decreased odds of success, enslaved Virginians continued to run away in the spring of 1776, adding to the anxieties of slaveholding white Virginians. Enslaved Virginians, for example, continued to take advantage of the unsettled situation in Norfolk. When patriot forces burned down the remaining buildings in Norfolk in February 1776, "two valuable Slaves" belonging to John Smith of Norfolk escaped and "entered into the Service of Lord Dunmore." Near the end of March, Edmund Pendleton

---

1. Proceedings of the Fourth Virginia Convention, Jan. 17, 1776, *Rev. Va.,* V, 423, 426 n. 15; *Va. Gaz.* (D and H), Apr. 13, 1776; July 12, 13, 1776, H. R. McIlwaine et al., eds., *Journals of the Council of the State of Virginia* (Richmond, Va., 1931–1982), I, 67, 71.

had heard that Dunmore was again amassing black troops and had "400 blacks at Portsmouth under Major Byrd." Perhaps because of the increased risks, those joining Dunmore in the spring appeared to Pendleton to be more militant. These former bondsmen, Pendleton believed, "have forgot the use of the hoe and ax and are the first Troops in America." Within a few weeks, Dunmore's forces were augmented further when a total of eighty-one slaves of John Willoughby, Sr., ran off from Willoughby Point, in Norfolk County, to join Dunmore.[2]

Eventually, Dunmore moved his forces to Gwynn's Island, at the mouth of the Piankatank River. Though not an ideal position, there were more than four hundred head of cattle there, and Dunmore could use the island as a base for naval operations. When he moved to Gwynn's Island, enslaved Virginians from the northern counties also got a chance to make a break for freedom. Not long after Dunmore moved there, eleven men from Landon Carter's estate stole as much ammunition, arms, and clothing as they could and made off in one of Carter's boats. They joined up with a group of enslaved Virginians from a nearby plantation and headed out into the bay to join Dunmore. An enslaved Virginian named Bristow, belonging to Rawleigh Downman, a planter from Lancaster County, also made his break for freedom when Dunmore was close by at Gwynn's Island. Bristow joined three or four other enslaved Virginians who made their escape via one of Downman's yawls.[3]

What was perhaps even more worrying to slave masters was that so many enslaved Virginians were acting collectively to make their escape. They did not just conspire with their fellow inmates on their own plan-

---

2. *Va. Gaz.* (D and H), Apr. 13, 1776. Cf. Proceedings of the Virginia Committee of Safety, Apr. 6, 1776, *Rev. Va.,* VI, 341; Petition of John Smith, May 21, 1776, *Rev. Va.,* VII, 214; Pendleton to James Mercer, Mar. 19, 1776, *Papers of Pendleton,* I, 160; for Willoughby, see *Rev. Va.,* V, 207.

3. "Diary of Col. Landon Carter," *WMQ,* 1st Ser., XX (1911–1912), 178–179; Petition of William Montague, Lancaster County Petition, [Nov. 5, 1778], Virginia Legislative Petitions, LiVi; July 12, 26, 1776, McIlwaine et al., eds., *Journals of the Council,* I, 67, 94. The Virginia troops in the vicinity captured the group of runaways, who were sent to the public jail and then put to work in the service of the state. Another three enslaved Virginians were caught trying to escape to Dunmore from Middlesex County sometime in June or July. Another man, Frank, a slave of William Kirby, was jailed in the early summer for "endeavouring to join lord Dunmore."

tations; they sought out like-minded rebels on other estates as well. At the end of March 1776, for example, another four enslaved Virginians attempted an escape from Stafford County. The four men—Kitt, two named Charles, and Harry—were owned by prominent planters George Brent, Robert Brent, Thomson Mason, and John Ratliff. The group conspired and stole on board a schooner lying at the wharf of Aquia warehouse in Stafford. Once on board, they put the schooner out into the Potomac River and tried to force the surprised crew to take them to Coan River in Northumberland, from where they could try to reach Dunmore or one of his ships. The crew eventually managed to steer them to Maryland, where all but one were captured.[4]

Some disaffected whites also continued to encourage and aid enslaved Virginians. Sometime in March, one white man in Northampton, a prisoner at large in the Eastern Shore county, had "thrown out" several "Hints of Lord Dunmore's extraordinary good treatment of the Negroes in his possession." As local patriot whites saw it, "Several" enslaved Virginians—"deluded Wretches"—took the information to heart and stole on board a vessel in order to escape to the governor. The group, perhaps numbering as many as thirteen, had been overtaken just out in the bay, heading toward the James River, and four of the enslaved were sentenced to death.[5]

Though leading gentlemen in the colony had publicly closed ranks, disaffected whites and rebellious blacks still constituted a nightmare scenario for propertied whites. Some whites actually tried to encourage enslaved Virginians not just to run away but also to rise up against their white masters. In March 1776, the county committee of Westmoreland hauled one Henry Glass before it to answer charges that he had said "many things disrespectful of Committees and their authority" back in January. But Glass's most heinous offense was that he had also said "many things to encourage the Slaves in Rebellion to their Masters." Under cross-examination, Glass freely acknowledged that he had "declared the slaves in the part of the Country he lived" were "ill used" and that "they would be justifiable to

4. Deposition of Ralph and John Grissoll, Apr. 2, 1776, *Rev. Va.,* VI, 305. Robert Brent's Charles and Kitt were both found guilty of felony and sentenced to hang; the other two were sentenced to be put into the pillory, each have an ear cut off, and each receive thirty-nine lashes (Stafford County Court Proceedings, Apr. 27, 1776, *Rev. Va.,* VI, 484–485).

5. Thomas Parramore and John Bowdoin, Jr., to the Committee of Safety, Apr. 23, 1776, *Rev. Va.,* VI, 449.

burn their Masters houses over their heads." This "was the least revenge they could take."[6]

While waiting for expected British reinforcements, the ever-watchful Dunmore continued to try to cultivate divisions between whites. Recognizing that his foothold in Norfolk had almost worked as he had planned, he entered into a propaganda war with the patriot committees around the colony. About the middle of January, he issued another proclamation, this time directed toward Virginians on the coasts. Described by the patriot press as an "artful invitation," the proclamation recommended that white Virginians on "the sea coast and rivers" remain at home, "take care of their plantations," and make some money by selling provisions "to the ships and army."[7]

Dunmore's strategy worked not just in vulnerable areas but also in the interior of the colony. Patriot leaders in Cumberland County, for example, felt compelled to draw up a set of resolutions condemning the fence-sitters in the their county and accusing "a Sett of Men among us" of filling people with the "most dreadful Apprehensions of the probable Issue of the present Contest." They were most concerned that such fears would disrupt any "Unanimity and Harmony" among them. In Sussex County, the committee accused one man, John Pettway, of trying to do just that. He reportedly claimed in church that the king was sending 100,000 troops over, and could send another 100,000 if needed. He had warned his neighbors that the patriots "could do nothing" and "were trifling in comparison."[8]

At the same time, Dunmore held out the prospect of a peaceful reconciliation. Relaying the contents of the king's speech to patriot leaders,

6. Westmoreland County Committee Proceedings, Mar. 26, 1776, *Rev. Va.,* VI, 253; Hening, comp., *Statutes at Large,* IX, 105-106.

7. See *Rev. Va.,* VI, 13; *Va. Gaz.* (Purdie), Feb. 2, 1776. Cf. Francis Lightfoot Lee to Landon Carter, Feb. 12, 1776, Paul H. Smith et al., eds., *Letters of Delegates to Congress, 1774-1789* (Washington, D.C., 1976-2000), III, 237. For one county committee response to this proclamation, see Sussex County Committee Resolution, Jan. 29, 1775, *Va. Gaz.* (D and H), Feb. 10, 1776.

8. Cumberland County Committee Proceedings, Feb. 5, 1776, *Rev. Va.,* VI, 56-57. The Cumberland committee drew from recent resolutions of Congress. See Jan. 2, 1776, Worthington Chauncey Ford et al., eds., *Journals of the Continental Congress, 1774-1789* (Washington, D.C., 1904-1937), IV, 18-19; Sussex County Committee Proceedings, Apr. 22, 1776, *Va. Gaz.* (Purdie), May 24, 1776, supplement. Cf. Loudoun County Committee, May 14, 1776, *Va. Gaz.* (Purdie), July 5, 1776, postscript.

Dunmore claimed that the king offered to allow any colony that submitted to the authority of the crown an immediate resumption of trade and commerce. He thus linked the idea of peace with the resumption of trade. Though the Patriot Committee of Safety rejected the overture, some Virginians were not so sure. The resumption of trade was not altogether an unpleasant idea for cash-starved farmers who had already felt the ill effects of the economic embargo. Many white Virginians across the colony were tired of shortages, worried about the crops they had on their hands, and stressed about the future taxes they would have to pay to support the enormous military establishment that patriot leaders had called out. Many believed that resuming trade with Britain was the best and easiest option to get out of the mess that they were in. On the same day the committee rejected Dunmore's peace overture, John Page told Richard Henry Lee that patriot leaders in Virginia were even more worried about morale in the colony. Page thought that, ever since the previous fall, morale had been low among whites, in part because they felt vulnerable and feared the British. The "County People and Militia," Page reported, were "without Arms." Yet some of them were hoping the conflict would end soon. Ordinary white Virginians were "lulled into a Stupid Security," Page believed, "by the Tales which flatter them with Peace."[9]

Given those concerns arising from below, as the new army recruits came in, the Committee of Safety made plans to deploy them around the colony, stationing them evenly on the different peninsulas to help protect the wealthy on the riverside from British raids and to guard against further slave uprisings or defections. With Norfolk and low morale in mind, patriot leaders also hoped that troops dispersed through the colony would inspire confidence in the patriot cause—or overawe dissidents, if need be. Early reports of successful recruiting buoyed patriot spirits, but they were tinged with worries. Edmund Pendleton noted on February 18 that the regulars were "raising fast." However, he also had to admit that "none of them

9. Dunmore to Richard Corbin, Jan. 27, 1776, Pendleton to Corbin, Feb. 19, 1776, *Rev. Va.,* VI, 29, 113; *Va. Gaz.* (Purdie), Mar. 1, 1776; *Rev. Va.,* VI, 116n; John Page to R. H. Lee, Feb. 19, 1776, Paul P. Hoffman, ed., *Lee Family Papers, 1742–1795* (microfilm) (Charlottesville, Va., 1966). Landon Carter confided in his diary that morale was generally low in Virginia, particularly among those in the more exposed lower parts of the country. "Many seem to be affraid" (Feb. 9, 1776, Jack P. Greene, ed., *The Diary of Colonel Landon Carter of Sabine Hall, 1752–1778* [Charlottesville, Va., 1965], II, 977–978).

[were] imbodied" or available yet for action. Not until mid-March did Virginians begin to feel more confident that the troops would be raised. Fielding Lewis, an army officer, reported in early March, "Our nine Regements are nearly compleat and our people seem to be fond of entring into the service."[10]

• • • But, just as patriot leaders began to breathe a sigh of relief, a new crisis arose that threatened the stability they hoped a large army would ensure. In early March 1776, officers and soldiers in the Virginia Line of the Continental army, stationed in Williamsburg, threatened a full-scale mutiny when they heard that civilian patriot leaders had snubbed Patrick Henry—whose "extensive popularity" many officers and soldiers believed was why the new troops had been raised with as much "expedition" as they had.[11]

A storm had been brewing over the leadership of the Virginia forces ever since Henry had been elected colonel of the First Regiment in contested circumstances during the Third Convention. Though radicals in the convention had in the end forced moderates to elect Henry as the commander of the first two regiments of regulars, moderates in turn, led by Edmund Pendleton at the head of the Committee of Safety, were able to neutralize Henry in the field. They had, for example, sent William Woodford's Second Regiment to the defense of Norfolk and kept Henry closer to home. They had also interpreted the ordinances issued by the Third Convention such that Woodford reported to and took orders from the Committee of Safety, rather than Henry, leaving the latter mostly in the dark about the military situation around Norfolk. The whole affair had left a bad taste in Henry's mouth, but his concern over the desperate situation in Virginia helped persuade him to stay on as colonel.[12]

10. *Rev. Va.*, VI, 5; John Robert Sellers, "The Virginia Continental Line, 1775–1780" (Ph.D. diss., Tulane University, 1968), 39–71; Pendleton to Nicholas Long and others, Feb. 18, 1776, *Papers of Pendleton*, I, 150; Fielding Lewis to Washington, Mar. 6, 1776, *Papers of Washington*, Rev. War. Ser., III, 418–419. Cf. Charles Lee to Washington, Apr. 5, 1776, *Papers of Washington*, Rev. War. Ser., IV, 43; Thomas Posey Memorandum Book, *Rev. Va.*, V, 393; Feb. 22, Mar. 17, 1776, Diary of Robert Honyman, Jan. 2, 1776–Mar. 11, 1782 (microfilm), Alderman Library, UVa.

11. *Va. Gaz.* (Purdie), Mar. 22, 1776.

12. In the end, Henry had been prevented from resigning or publicly complain-

When Congress had finally accepted six new Virginia regiments onto Continental pay at the end of December 1775, the question of leadership of the new forces arose again. Pendleton, a neighbor and good friend of Woodford's, hoped that the Virginia convention would not "intermeddle" in the choice of a general officer of the Virginia troops, but rather leave it up to Congress. Pendleton knew that propriety would probably compel the Virginia convention to name Henry as the major general commanding all the Virginia regiments, given his command and precedence in rank over Woodford. Pendleton, who thought Henry's actions back in May 1775 rash, was particularly vexed about the question; he hoped that Congress would choose someone else to lead the new forces.[13]

When the Fourth Virginia Convention did indeed fail to "intermeddle" and nominate Henry as the overall commander of the new forces, Henry was mortified. When the Committee of Safety gave Henry his new commission on February 28, which merely commissioned him as colonel of the First Virginia Regiment only, Henry gave it back "and retired" silently "without assigning any reason" for his refusal. The news of his resignation sent shock waves throughout the colony, but especially through Henry's own regiment. His men appeared to resent the insult almost as much as he did. When news reached them, they apparently went "into deep mourning." While the officers of the regiment took Henry to dinner, the men "assembled in a tumultuous manner" at camp and resolved never to serve under another commander, demanding their discharges at the same time. They threatened worse. Landon Carter heard that the troops "begot a presenting of Pieces" at some of the officers. Only when Henry and his brother-in-law William Christian spent the entire night visiting the men and mak-

---

ing only by the intercessions of Joseph Jones, convention delegate from King George County and committeeman-elect. In the midst of the crisis precipitated by Dunmore's Proclamation, Jones had counseled calm. Jones told Henry "to treat the business with caution and temper as a difference at this critical moment between our Troops wod. be attended with the most fatal Consequences." Jones acted as intermediary on a number of important occasions to calm trouble between Henry and the Committee of Safety. See Proceedings of the Fourth Virginia Convention, Dec. 22, 1775, *Rev. Va.,* V, 221, 225n; Jones to William Woodford, Dec. 13, 1775, Joseph Jones Letter, VHS; Pendleton to Woodford, Dec. 24, 1775, *Papers of Pendleton,* I, 141–142. Cf. Woodford to John Page, Nov. 26, 1775, Henry to Woodford, Dec. 6, 1775, Woodford to Henry, Dec. 7, 1775, *Rev. Va.,* IV, 478–479, V, 68, 77, 83n.

13. Pendleton to Woodford, Dec. 24, 1775, *Papers of Pendleton,* I, 141.

ing "extraordinary exertions" were the troops persuaded by his argument that he had resigned "from motives in which his honour alone was concerned." Though a general revolt was averted, it was not until mid-March that Richard Henry Lee took some satisfaction that "the mutinous spirit of our Soldiery" was "so well subdued."[14]

That was not quite the end of the matter, though, as Henry's supporters among his troops and officers made their feelings known, sparking a public debate among Virginians. "A Friend to Truth" tried to defend the Committee of Safety and warned that Henry's resignation might undermine its authority. On the other hand, "An Honest Farmer" in the same paper wrote that it was "envy" that "strove to bury in obscurity" Henry's "martial talents." Honest Farmer stressed Henry's popularity among the troops, and another correspondent nervously defended the army's patriotism. Many believed there would be "great discontent in the army" upon Henry's resignation, "by which our military operations would be retarded."[15]

Military operations were retarded. By early April, George Mason thought that, in light of the events, the new recruits had been raised "with surprizing Rapidity," but he was still not sure how complete they actually were. Virginia and Maryland were still "at present rather unprepared," and the levies of men were only complete "in a Manner." As late as mid-April, John Page warned that Virginia was still woefully ill prepared for conflict in part because "our People in some Places [are] discontented about Henry's Resignation."[16]

14. *Rev. Va.,* VI, 5; Continental Congress, Resolutions, Feb. 13, 1776, *Rev. Va.,* 89; Proceedings of the Virginia Committee of Safety, Feb. 28, 1776, *Rev. Va.,* 148, 150n; "A Friend to Truth," *Va. Gaz.* (Purdie), Mar. 15, 1776, supplement; Mar. 12, 1776, Greene, ed., *Diary of Carter,* II, 999; *Va. Gaz.* (Purdie), Mar. 1, 1776; R. H. Lee to John Page, Mar. 19, 1776, Smith et al., eds., *Letters of Delegates to Congress,* III, 408n. Cf. William Wirt, *The Life of Patrick Henry,* rev. ed. (Hartford, Conn., 1832), 208; Pendleton to Woodford, Mar. 16, 1776, *Papers of Pendleton,* I, 158–159. A little later, upward of ninety junior officers from Henry's regiment, Woodford's regiment, and the newly raised regiments also wrote a public address in support of Henry acknowledging his role in the resistance movement ("An Address to Patrick Henry," n.d., by the officers of the First, Second, Third, Fourth, and Fifth Regiments and of the Minute Service, Patrick Henry Papers, VHS).

15. "A Friend to Truth," *Va. Gaz.* (Purdie), Mar. 15, 1776, supplement, and "An Honest Farmer."

16. The damage to morale was widespread. Pendleton reported that Henry's resignation "has made much noise in the Countrey." Pendleton to Woodford, Mar.

Just how poorly prepared Virginia still was in March and April 1776 became glaringly apparent when General Charles Lee arrived in the colony. Congress had appointed Lee to take command of all the southern forces when it began to fear that the British would simply bypass Washington in Boston and make the southern colonies—with their rich resources and enslaved populations—their new focus. On the same day that Norfolk burned to the ground, Congress warned Virginia in particular that it could expect British reinforcements. Reports from the Virginia delegates in Congress and from New York put Virginia at the center of a British counterattack. The newspapers were full of reports about British troop ships leaving England for a major campaign in the southern colonies, fueling anxieties in Virginia.[17]

In this light Lee's arrival in Virginia at the end of March was a mixed blessing for patriot leaders. On one hand, local gentlemen felt reassured that Congress was keen to support them in their own conflict with the British. However, Lee not only exposed the holes in Virginia's defensive preparations, but he also angered patriot leaders with his own preparations. Lee himself thought that, if the British did come, they would make for Williamsburg, so he immediately rearranged Virginia's defense and called in all the regiments that the convention had carefully stationed on the different peninsulas. Lee agreed with the patriot leadership in Virginia about the need to maintain an effective defense and an intimidating presence of soldiers, but he was convinced that Virginians would have to abandon their local defense in the interests of the whole. The British would target Williamsburg for two reasons. Not only was it a "temptingly advan-

16, 1776, *Papers of Pendleton,* I, 158; Mason to Washington, Apr. 2, 1776, *Papers of Washington,* Rev. War Ser., IV, 18; John Page to [R. H. Lee], Apr. 12, 1776, Hoffman, ed., *Lee Family Papers.* The account books and proceedings for the Committee of Safety reveal that it was still handing out warrants for recruiting and commissions for officers well into April. See, for example, Proceedings of the Virginia Committee of Safety, Apr. 1, 1776, *Rev. Va.,* VI, esp. 296–297.

17. MS Journal of the Continental Congress, Jan. 1, 1776, *Rev. Va.,* V, 306; Joseph Hallett on behalf of the New York Committee of Safety to the New York Delegates in Congress, Feb. 4, 1776, *Rev. Va.,* VI, 50; Francis Lightfoot Lee to Landon Carter, Feb. 12, 1776, Smith et al., eds., *Letters of Delegates to Congress,* III, 237. Congress was convinced enough to send Lee to Virginia and to finally take Virginia's last three battalions onto Continental pay (see Continental Congress Resolution, Mar. 25, 1776, *Rev. Va.,* VI, 247, 250n. For gloomy reports of Virginia's readiness, see John Page to R. H. Lee, Feb. 19, 1776, Hoffman, ed., *Lee Family Papers.*

tageous situation" that commanded "two fine rivers, and a country abundant in all the necessaries for an army," but, more significantly, the occupation of Williamsburg would give the British military "an air of dignity and decided superiority" that "in this slave country" might be attended with important consequences by the impressions it would make in the minds of the Negroes. In other words, Lee was more concerned about preventing a general uprising of enslaved Virginians than preventing individual gentlemen's slaves from absconding to or being taken by the British.[18]

Lee's rearrangements had made the people in Williamsburg "very happy," but Pendleton feared it would be "very alarming to other parts" exposed to British plundering. Accordingly, he helped persuade the Committee of Safety to oppose Lee's efforts to centralize the troops. They acquainted Lee with "all local circumstances" and explained the convention's ordinance. The inhabitants of the colony were "badly armed," in part because they had given their "best arms" to the soldiers "intended for their immediate protection." These people, the committee warned, would be "more exposed than ever and may be exceedingly alarmed when the troops are called at a great distance from them while the measures of the enemy, or their intended place of Attack are altogether unknown." Though he had to concede and leave some of the northern soldiers at their posts, Lee was furious at the excuses given by the committee. In the end, he wondered why the convention "did not carry it still further, and post one or two men by way of general security in every individual Gentlemen's house."[19]

Lee's arrival also exposed Virginia's lack of preparedness—almost a year after war had actually broken out. For one thing, recruiting for the regular forces was still not complete. Colonel William Peachey, commander of the Fifth Regiment, told Lee that not all of his companies had yet assembled. He had not yet heard from his lieutenant colonel, nor from the rifle companies who were supposed to join him. Peachey confessed that all was "in

18. *Rev. Va.,* VI, 270n; *Va. Gaz.* (D and H), Apr. 6, 1776; Pendleton to Woodford, Mar. 16, 1776, Pendleton to James Mercer, Mar. 19, 1776, Pendleton to R. H. Lee, Apr. 8, 1776, *Papers of Pendleton,* I, 159, 160, 162; Charles Lee to Washington, Apr. 5, 1776, *The Lee Papers,* I, 378, New-York Historical Society, *Collections,* IV (1871).

19. Pendleton to R. H. Lee, Apr. 8, 1776, *Papers of Pendleton,* I, 162; Page to Charles Lee, Apr. 10, 1776, *Rev. Va.,* VI, 373; *Lee Papers,* I, 375, 409, NYHS, *Collections,* IV (1871). The inhabitants of Gloucester were among those unhappy with Lee's new plan. See Chair of the Committee of Gloucester to Charles Lee, Apr. 22, 1776, *Lee Papers,* I, 443–444, NYHS, *Collections,* IV (1871).

disorder." The Fifth Regiment was not the only battalion that had not yet embodied or assembled. Even the officers of the Ninth Regiment on the Eastern Shore had not yet assembled. After watching a muster of all the troops assembled in Williamsburg in early April, John Page lamented: "Our Army is but an handful of raw undisciplined Troops. . . . On a Review today there were only 500 Men fit for duty."[20]

Taking stock of the forces, arms, and artillery available, Lee was inundated with reports that made his heart sink. William Peachey also told Lee that what men he had were "very indifferently armed or accoutred, and no ammunition come to hand." Lieutenant Colonel Isaac Read of the Fourth Regiment told Lee that his men had "very few guns, and those not fit for service." George Mason also told Washington at about the same time that, though recruiting officers were still raising men, they were "very deficient" in arms for the new enlistees. Charles Lee wrote to John Hancock that the troops were "so extremely deficit in arms" that he had had to send an officer into the backcountry to try to purchase as many rifles as he could for the army. Lee thought the situation so poor that he felt compelled to equip at least two companies in each regiment with spears.[21]

Lee, an outsider, believed that Virginia was so unprepared because of the caution of some of the leading men. Of those on the Central Committee of Safety, Lee thought John Page, Thomas Ludwell Lee, and James Mercer were spirited enough, but he believed Pendleton, Richard Bland, Robert Carter Nicholas, "and Co." were dragging their heels. He told Washington that the Provincial Congress of New York "were angels of decision when compared to your countrymen." As he exposed the weakness of Virginia's defense, others in the capital came to agree with him. James McClurg, for example, told Jefferson that Lee had found them "worse prepared for defence than he expected." McClurg, like Lee, pointed an ac-

20. *Lee Papers,* I, 371, NYHS, *Collections,* IV (1871); General Orders, Apr. 4, 1776, Charles Campbell, ed., *The Orderly Book of That Portion of the American Army Stationed at or near Williamsburg, Va., under the Command of General Andrew Lewis, from March 18th, 1776, to August 28th, 1776* (Richmond, Va., 1860), 15; Page to R. H. Lee, Apr. 12, 1776, Hoffman, ed., *Lee Family Papers.*

21. John Page added that, as well as the lack of arms, the troops were also "wretchedly clothed, and without Tents or Blankets." *Lee Papers,* I, 371, 433, NYHS, *Collections,* IV (1871); Isaac Read to Charles Lee, Apr. 7, 1776, Charles Lee to Page, Apr. 21, 1776, *Lee Papers,* NYHS, *Collections,* I, 390–391, 437; Mason to George Washington, Apr. 2, 1776, *Papers of Mason,* I, 267; Page to R. H. Lee, Apr. 12, 1776, Hoffman, ed., *Lee Family Papers.*

cusing finger at Pendleton and the Central Committee of Safety. "The In-
dolence or Ignorance of Majority of our Committee, and their former General," McClurg asserted, "seem to be too glaring for concealment."[22]

• • • As cautious and indecisive gentlemen waited for their army to gather,
with their eyes more firmly fixed on internal security than on external defense, other groups of white Virginians began to grow as impatient as Lee.
Fed up with fighting a war on the terms dictated by cautious patriot leaders,
groups of farmers across Virginia also began to agitate for greater independence—both formally, from Britain, but also informally, from dependence
on the myopic policies of patriot leaders. The most dramatic illustration
of this took place in northwestern Virginia, in Loudoun County. Here, in
February 1776, an incipient internal rebellion that had been brewing for
months broke out in earnest. Ostensibly a protest over the payment of tenants' rents, this uprising was the product of months of unanswered wartime grievances and a newfound assertiveness among increasingly angry
Virginia farmers. Details of the uprising are scarce, but patriot gentlemen
in the capital took the matter very seriously. Within weeks, the Revolutionary government in Williamsburg, the Committee of Safety, sent troops to
quell the disturbances. Thus, five months before the American colonies declared their independence from Britain, Loudoun County in northern Virginia erupted into a heated *internal* confrontation pitting patriot gentlemen
against their less wealthy neighbors.[23]

By February 1776, like others around the colony, Loudoun farmers were
suffering from the conflict with Britain. Loudoun farmers, of course, had
already suffered through the same shortages that had affected most Virginians in the fall of 1775. At the end of November, Nicholas Cresswell
reported from Leesburg that there was a "Great disturbance for want of
Salt." A few days later, Lund Washington wrote from Mount Vernon that
"the people are run[nin]g mad about Salt." The salt shortage in particular was probably one of the crises on James Cleveland's mind when he
warned that, if the Revolutionary war continued much longer, the poor
people would be ruined.[24]

22. *Rev. Va.*, VI, 270n; *Lee Papers,* I, 377, 379, NYHS, *Collections,* IV (1871);
James McClurg to Jefferson, Apr. 6, 1776, *Papers of Jefferson,* I, 287.

23. Proceedings of the Virginia Committee of Safety, Mar. 20, 1776, *Rev. Va.,*
VI, 231.

24. Nov. 20, 1775, Dec. 4, 1776, Nicholas Cresswell, *The Journal of Nicholas*

The situation, however, actually worsened for many farmers, particularly tenants. There were more than three hundred tenant farmers in Loudoun, all of whom had to pay cash for their rents. Before the fall of 1775, tenants generally had few problems in raising their cash rents, asserting that they had benefited from a "very Flourishing" and "Growing Trade for Grain and Flower at Alexandria and other Ports" on both the Potomac and Rappahannock Rivers. But, as the export markets closed as a result of the nonexportation boycott beginning in September 1775, the tenants were soon left with no outlets for their produce. Some of the protesters explained after the riot that it was "so Notoriously Known" that those articles were now "Useless on our Hands." Even Richard Henry Lee later admitted that the price of farm produce had fallen to "a Pittance" after nonexportation began. Moreover, many tenants had contracted to pay gentlemen rent not only for land but also for slaves. After nonexportation, these slaves became a liability, for the tenants nevertheless had to continue to pay rent and taxes on them as well as feed and clothe them. Finally, the landlords had also apparently "bound the Tenants to pay all Land Taxe's," which would begin to mount in a costly, prolonged war. Without a steady income, tenants would be ruined.[25]

Cash was also becoming scarcer in the colony, making it even harder for tenants to pay their cash rents. The treasurer, Robert Carter Nicholas, acknowledged in early December that depreciation of the available paper

Cresswell, 1774-1777 (London, 1925), 132, 174; Lund Washington to George Washington, Nov. 24, 1775, Feb. 29, 1776, *Papers of Washington,* Rev. War Ser., II, 395–396 423, 424. Cf. R. H. Lee to Page, Mar. 18, 1776, Smith et al., eds., *Letters of Delegates to Congress,* III, 410.

25. Loudoun County Petition, [presented on June 8, 1776], *Rev. Va.,* VII, 325–326. Other tenants paid in produce either a fixed amount or a percentage of the crop. After nonexportation and the British blockade began, both tobacco and wheat fetched a "very low price" (Oliver Perry Chitwood, *Richard Henry Lee: Statesman of the Revolution* [Morgantown, W.Va., 1967], 137). Loudoun probably had among the highest proportion of tenant farmers in Virginia (Bliss, "Rise of Tenancy in Virginia," *VMHB,* LVIII [1950], 429–430; R. H. Lee to Henry, May 26, 1777, James Curtis Ballagh, ed., *The Letters of Richard Henry Lee* [New York, 1911], I, 299). My calculations of landholders and tenants in Loudoun, based on the 1784 tax lists (the nearest complete landholder lists), corroborate these findings. Cf. John E. Selby, *The Revolution in Virginia, 1775-1783* (Williamsburg, Va., 1988), 24, who claims that nearly three-quarters of the whites in the Loudoun area were landless, compared to half overall in Virginia.

money meant that the money emitted in the summer was already being discounted by 35 percent. A few days later, Nicholas asked the delegates in Congress to forward some paper so that they could print up more money: "You can hardly conceive how people are distress'd for want of small change." Less than a week later, James Imrie from the Eastern Shore told a Glasgow correspondent: "Cash was never scarcer. I am afraid it will be the longer the worse."[26]

Protests against paying rents began at Christmas in 1775, when annual rent payments were typically due. Individual tenant farmers simply refused to pay their rent, not only in Loudoun but in neighboring counties, "assigning for reason," Richard Henry Lee noted, "that they could not sell their produce." Individual protest quickly blossomed into collective action as many tenants who were withholding their rents attempted to "incite others to imitate their Example." By the end of December, landlords believed that there was already a concerted scheme not to pay rents. Tenant farmers not only refused to pay; they accused their landlords of wrongdoing: "They say it is Cruel in the Land Holders to expect their Rents when there is no market for the produce of the Land." They would pay their rents only if they could sell the crops they had harvested in the previous year; otherwise, they complained, it would be the "height of Injustice" to be forced to pay.[27]

Tenant farmers in Loudoun were not the only ones who insisted on making new demands. Since the conflict with Britain had broken out, many farmers insisted that they should not have to pay debts, since trade had stopped. Some, it was believed, did not pay because they could not pay. One merchant said he thought his debtors were "Honest men" who would pay their debts "as soon as they possibly can." The trade embargo had left many people throughout the colony in a "distrest Situation," and many farmers would "not be able to pay any debts, for some considerable time to come." Another merchant thought that the situation of many farmers had become so "desperate" that it was not uncommon "for the man that asks [for repayment of debts] to be knockd down or the like." "In short," the

26. *Rev. Va.,* V, 149n; Robert Carter Nicholas to the Virginia Delegates in Congress, Dec. 12, 1775, *Papers of Jefferson,* I, 271; James Imrie to John Hay, Dec. 16, 1775, *Rev. Va.,* V, 162.

27. R. H. Lee to Henry, [May 26, 1777], Ballagh, ed., *Letters of Richard Henry Lee,* I, 298; Henry Field, Jr., Memorial, [Nov. 18, 1776], Prince William County Petitions, LiVi; Lund Washington to George Washington, Dec. 30, 1775, *Papers of Washington,* Rev. War Ser., II, 621.

merchant summarized, "many people will not pay at any rate." On top of their refusal to pay debts, many farmers also began to refuse to pay the new taxes imposed by the Revolutionary convention. In mid-April, the Central Committee of Safety had to reissue a request—the third time it asked—for census returns from forty-three delinquent counties, or almost two-thirds of Virginia's whole. The returns were to go to Congress to help offset the costs of the war and would also be used by Virginia's leaders for the same purpose.[28]

In Loudoun, at least some landlords understood the tenants' plight and did not harass them for their rent. But other propertyowners commanded court officials to "distrain," or seize, their tenants' slaves, livestock, and other property. Tenants whose property was distrained would not only lose as much property as had to be auctioned off to pay the overdue rent—a substantial amount, given the scarcity of cash—but they also had to pay a commission to the sheriff and fees to attorneys and the county clerk. Nor was distrainment the landlords' only recourse. Some of them also threatened to evict delinquent tenants. Richard Henry Lee's rental agent told one Lee tenant "that he might rely" on the fact that Lee "would take possession of your Tenement very shortly." Finally, under the influence of the landlords, the patriot committee of Loudoun County also launched an effort to intimidate the leaders of the strike, who were "cited to appear before the Committee" in December 1775.[29]

Tenants fought back this time. They first made it clear that they would repel any attempts by landlords to collect their rents. The leaders of the rent strike, called "transgressors of the peace" by Lund Washington, had said

28. Neil Jamieson to Edward Payne, Nov. 20, 1775, George Rae to John Rae, Nov. 7, 1775, *Rev. Va.,* IV, 337–338, 438; Thomas Roberts to St. George Tucker, Oct. 20, 1775, William Bell Clark et al., eds., *Naval Documents of the American Revolution* (Washington, D.C., 1964–), II, 546; Notice of Census Returns, Feb. 15, 1776, *Va. Gaz.* (Purdie), Feb. 16, 1776, *Rev. Va.,* VI, 98, 100–101; Request for Census Returns from Delinquent Counties, Apr. 19, 1776, *Va. Gaz.* (Purdie), Apr. 19, 1776, postscript, *Rev. Va.,* VI, 424–425.

29. Lund Washington to George Washington, Dec. 30, 1775, *Papers of Washington,* Rev. War Ser., II, 621. In the spring of 1776, when seventy-three tenants presented a petition to the Virginia convention complaining about their situation, three justices were among the signers (see *Rev. Va.,* VII, 325–326); Lund Washington to George Washington, Dec. 30, 1775, Feb. 15, 1776, *Papers of Washington,* Rev. War Ser., II, 621, III, 317; Richard Parker to James Robison, Mar. 7, 1776, Hoffman, ed., Lee Family Papers.

they would "Punish the First officer that dare destrain for Rent." Then, when strike leaders learned that they were to be hauled before the patriot committee, they "said that they were not at all Intimidated by it." Indeed, they actually threatened to "turn the Committee out of the House."[30]

Though it was only in Loudoun County and the surrounding area that these acts of resistance reached an explosive climax, the developing confrontation there seems to have been but the tip of the iceberg. All across Virginia, a truly revolutionary situation was developing. No longer content with simply airing their grievances about the new military establishment and the prolongation of the war, small farmers began demanding some kind of compensation. What was different in Loudoun was that the tenants began to act in concert, found leaders, broadened their agenda, and curried some support from community leaders. Lund Washington told George that he had heard that some of the "first promoters" of the rent strike were "some of the Leadg men in Loudon."[31]

Tenants also began organizing collectively. Leaders of the uprising left no records, so we cannot know how they recruited participants. They probably worked the crowd at court day, where farmers from all over the county gathered to swap gossip as well as goods, and farmers also appear to have discussed their grievances at church on Sundays. Andrew Leitch, an army officer from Loudoun, fretted over the damage that "a few disappointed, carping creatures" with "dastardly souls" could do "if they can talk and hold forth amongst their honest, well-meaning neighbours." This would "work you more mischief in two or three church Sundays than a hundred virtuous and sensible citizens can, perhaps, eradicate in a year."[32]

Yet probably the most damage was done at militia musters. Certainly tensions ran high among farmers who had been pulled away from their work in order to train under appointed officers in the militia, only to be badgered to make an even greater sacrifice by joining the regular army. Indeed, the revolt seems to have taken a new, more outspoken turn in the midst of the fresh call for recruits to join the now enlarged regular army in January and February 1776. Officers no doubt used militia musters to

30. Lund Washington to George Washington, Dec. 30, 1775, *Papers of Washington,* Rev. War Ser., II, 621.

31. Ibid.

32. Leitch to Leven Powell, May 15, 1776, Robert C. Powell, ed., *A Biographical Sketch of Col. Leven Powell, Including His Correspondence during the Revolutionary War* (Alexandria, Va., 1877), 87.

drum up new recruits. But, if the farmers of Loudoun and elsewhere had grievances, the musters could also be used to share complaints and drum up support for collective resistance to unwanted measures.[33]

Two weeks after officers for the regular army were appointed, there was a militia muster in Leesburg on court day, February 12, 1776. Tenants who were angry at having to pay rents came together with farmers who were angry about the new military establishment. Their unhappiness and suspicion of patriot leaders' war policy was only exacerbated when it was revealed that day that the recruiting officers had turned up with no cash, not even paper money, to pay enlistment bounties. Nicholas Cresswell, a British native caught behind patriot lines, observed that they were "Enlisting men for the Rebel Army upon credit." With considerable sarcasm, Cresswell noted, "Their paper money is not yet arrived from the Mine." As recruiting officers tried to explain that not even paper money was available to pay the bounties and wages of recruits, landlords pressed their tenants to pay their rents. Farmers in Loudoun were having none of it. They first targeted the county court, closing it before any debt cases could be heard. "No business done," reported Cresswell. The militia muster was also broken up. Cresswell reported "Great confusion" that day.[34]

The protesters had also found a new leader in James Cleveland, a well-off but rough-lettered tenant farmer with a volatile temperament. Cleveland had recently done some work improving land in the west for the Washingtons, but, when he returned, George Washington accused him of being a spendthrift and told Lund Washington to pay Cleveland with the newly emitted paper money, despite the fact that the original contract called for

33. Officers appointed in the regular service had to raise a quota of men or risk losing their commissions. The officers, then, would have used the fortnightly militia musters to drum up enlistments for the regular service by putting pressure on the militia (Hening, comp., *Statutes at Large,* IX, 78–82, 89–90; Proceedings of the Virginia Committee of Safety, Feb. 3, 21, May 8, June 7, 1776, *Rev. Va.,* VI, 49, 122, 123n, VII, 69–70, 396; Jan. 29, 1776, Cresswell, *Journal,* 137).

34. Feb. 12, 1776, Cresswell, *Journal,* 138; Feb. 12, 1776, Loudoun County Court Records, 1774–1776, LiVi; Hening, comp., *Statutes at Large,* IX, 90. The bounty money did arrive soon after this muster. However, the new recruits in the Virginia Line of the Continental army would not be paid until June, and then only to the end of May, which, it was later reported, "gave rise to complaints which in several instances were just" (Proceedings of the Virginia Committee of Safety, Feb. 3, June 7, 8, July 2, 1776, *Rev. Va.,* VI, 49, VII, 396, 409, 680).

payment in sterling. Cleveland thus had good reason to be involved in the tenants' strike. Not only had he spent the growing season working for Washington in the Ohio Country instead of raising his own crops, but he also did not get paid as much as he contracted for. He was probably much pushed to pay the rents he himself owed. Whatever his motives, Cleveland, Lund claimed, had now "turn'd Politicion" and was "setg all Loudon to gether by the Ears."[35]

It was Cleveland who in February 1776 emerged at the "head of the Party" that had now broadened its protests to include mobilization in general. Lund Washington, watching events unfold from his cousin's plantation in neighboring Fairfax County, tried to summarize the protesters' grievances in Loudoun. He believed that they were still angry over patriot leaders' prosecution of the war. Echoing the complaints that arose over the abolition of the volunteer system and the erection of the minute service, Loudoun farmers now complained that the military establishment was too hierarchical: "The pay of the officers and Soldiers shoud be the same, or what woud be still better they should not be paid at all." Lund claimed that, in the words of "General" James Cleveland, there was "no inducement for a poor Man to Fight" in the regular military establishment, "for he has nothing to defend." Moreover, raising a more traditional army would inevitably lead to a prolonged and far more expensive war, which would be particularly hard on the less wealthy—those who had less, or "nothing to defend." Instead, the protesters wanted to act decisively, as they had in the independent companies: "Let us go and Fight the Battle at once, and not be Shilly Shally, in this way, until all the Poor, people are ruined." Some of the poor people the rioters had in mind, of course, were tenants, who composed between one-third and one-half of all landholders in Loudoun. While the war continued in Virginia, they asserted, the "Tennants should pay no Rents." The terse summary of the rioters' complaints by Lund Washington encapsulated many of the demands and grievances not just of tenants in Loudoun County alone but of many small farmers across Virginia. They supported

35. Mason to Washington, Dec. 21, 1773, *Papers of Mason,* I, 186–187; Donald Jackson and Dorothy Twohig, eds., *The Diaries of George Washington* (Charlottesville, Va., 1976–1979), II, 164; Washington to James Cleveland, Instructions, Jan. 10, [March 1775], Cleveland to Washington, May 21, 1775, *Papers of Washington,* Col. Ser., X, 230–233, 314–315, 365–367; Woody Holton, *Forced Founders: Indians, Debtors, Slaves, and the Making of the American Revolution in Virginia* (Chapel Hill, N.C., 1999), 178.

the patriotic cause, but not the means by which patriot leaders took to wage it.[36]

The growing frustration of the protesters in Loudoun and the broadening base of support worried patriot gentlemen everywhere. Lund Washington speculated that "the first Battle we have in this part of the Country will be in Loudoun, against General Cleveland." Rent collectors refused to go out and collect, and some demanded double and more what they usually charged because of the "troublesome times." Frustrated, Lund wrote from neighboring Fairfax County that he would have gone out and collected Washington's rents himself, "if I thought Mt. Vernon wou'd stand where it does, when I returnd." The mood continued to darken. Lund reported on March 7, "We have nothing new Stiring here all the talk is about the Tenants." At a general muster of the militia at Leesburg in late March Cresswell reported (again) that there was "Great confusion among them."[37]

By early March conditions in Loudoun were severe enough that the Committee of Safety in Williamsburg "feared" it might need to call in troops to "Quell" the "disturbances." Indeed, the actions of the committee show that it was, in effect, mobilizing for a different kind of conflict. First, the committee quietly moved the newly raised Loudoun company under Captain Charles West from the Third Virginia Regiment at Dum-

36. Lund Washington to George Washington, Feb. 29, 1776, *Papers of Washington,* Rev. War Ser., III, 395–396; Willard F. Bliss, "The Rise of Tenancy in Virginia," *VMHB,* LVIII (1950), 429; Selby, *Revolution in Virginia,* 24; A. Roger Ekirch, *Bound for America: The Transportation of British Convicts to the Colonies, 1718–1775* (Oxford, 1987), 182.

37. Lund was also clear about what ought to be done with him: he hoped that the "Consequence" of Cleveland's participation in this protest would be the "loss of his life." "Every Damn'd Vilian who meddles in matters he knows nothing off," Lund declared, perhaps in reference to Cleveland's long absence, ought to "get Hang'd." Lund Washington to George Washington, Nov. 5, 1775, Feb. 15, 29, Mar. 7, 1776, Valentine Crawford to George Washington, June 24, 1775, James Cleveland to George Washington, Nov. 16, 1775, *Papers of Washington,* Rev. War Ser., I, 28, II, 305–306, 382, III, 317, 395–396, 432–433; Mar. 22, 1776, Cresswell, *Journal,* 140; Leitch to Leven Powell, May 15, 1776, Powell, ed., *Biographical Sketch,* 86–87; Benson, "Wealth and Power," 346–347.

The problems might also have spread. In mid-February, Landon Carter wrote cryptically from Richmond County lower down on the Northern Neck that "Discord and secret Malice is again reviving" and that Virginians loved "the very Power of Oppressing each other" (Feb. 9, 1776, Greene, ed., *Diary of Carter,* II, 977–978).

fries, Prince William County, and brought in a company from Pittsylvania County, far down in the southwestern corner of piedmont Virginia. The Third Regiment would be the first used to put down the revolt. Since it was by no means certain whose cause the Loudoun troops would embrace, the committee thought it "inconvenient to have the Loudon Compy. in that regiment." To ensure that the Third Regiment would be ready to face an internal uprising, the committee also ordered all field officers in the battalion "into duty immediately" and to "repair to their Station at Dumfries." Moreover, on March 7, the committee redirected a newly raised company of regulars from Louisa County from Williamsburg to Dumfries and authorized a warrant for £175 for the immediate purchase of "Arms and Necessaries." At around the same time, a company of minutemen under Captain Simon Triplett was actually ordered to march into Loudoun.[38]

Finally, in the midst of the problems in Loudoun, Edmund Pendleton, taking no chances, wrote to the Maryland Council of Safety to establish a joint system of alarm along the Potomac River. The river was navigable by British "men of war" along its "great length . . . from its mouth to Alexandria," just downriver from Loudoun. Though General Henry Clinton had already left the Chesapeake Bay to go southward and the committee had heard of "no more naval arrivals," Pendleton and his colleagues still felt that there was a "probability of some attempts being made by the Enemy in that Quarter" that "make it prudent" to erect an early warning system. Whether by intelligence or intuition, the Committee of Safety doubted the allegiances of those involved in the uprising in Loudoun and felt that widespread discontent in that area could lead to another Norfolk.[39]

Yet, despite the committee members' fears, the protesters in Loudoun were not loyalists or even disaffected to the cause. The leaders of the protesters, Andrew Leitch believed, were only "wrong from chagrin and prejudice, and not from principles of dis[satisfaction] to their native country." For the most part, the participants of the uprising were "honest, well meaning" farmers driven awry by "disappointed, carping creatures." Some patriot leaders believed that the protesters had unpatriotic aims, but such

38. Proceedings of the Virginia Committee of Safety, Mar. 2, 5, 7, 20, Apr. 2, 1776, *Rev. Va.,* VI, 164, 171, 180, 231, 306. Cf. Benson, "Wealth and Power," 348.

39. Pendleton to the Maryland Committee of Safety, *Papers of Pendleton,* I, 157; Proceedings of the Virginia Committee of Safety, Feb. 21, Mar. 7, 1776, *Rev. Va.,* VI, 122, 180. Cf. Proceedings of the Virginia Committee of Safety, Mar. 6, 1776, *Rev. Va.,* VI, 175.

accusations were never substantiated. James Cleveland later claimed that he had been "misrepresented" by some of the members of the county Committee of Safety. Angry at this questioning of his patriotism, Cleveland had twice asked the committee to make a formal inquiry into his conduct, that he might "either be condemn'd or acquitted." "Knowg himself to be a Friend to his Country," Cleveland was very "unwillg to lay under the Censure he does."[40]

In the end, though Virginia teetered on the brink of civil war, the Committee of Safety's measures appear to have overawed the protesters in Loudoun. No reports of a battle with "General" Cleveland have surfaced. However, not until April 2 did the Committee of Safety feel that the situation had sufficiently "quieted" to return the Loudoun company to the Third Regiment at Dumfries. Even so, Andrew Leitch commiserated with Leven Powell as late as mid-May over the "torn and distracted condition" of the county. The "troublesome times," as Lund Washington put it, were slow to abate. They also held out fearful consequences for many of the local patriots involved. A Loudoun gentleman serving with the army in Williamsburg asked Powell about Loudoun as late as June 1776. Significantly, he used the language of the English Revolution: "How goes on the spirit of Levelling?" he asked. "Is all quiet?"[41]

40. There is no record of Cleveland's standing before the committee or the court. Patriot leaders in the county could not or would not bring him to answer for his role in the uprising. Cleveland apparently convinced either the committee or the court of public opinion in the county that "no part of his behaviour has been Criminal" or unpatriotic. Significantly, no one was "Hang'd" for participation in the Loudoun uprising. And, though patriot leaders reacted forcefully to the incipient rebellion, they did not even call the leader of the revolt to account (Leitch to Leven Powell, May 15, 1776, Powell, ed., *Biographical Sketch*, 87; Lund Washington to George Washington, Mar. 7, 1776, *Papers of Washington*, Rev. War Ser., III, 395–396). Cleveland was clearly interested in the imperial crisis. When he was working for Washington at the Great Bend of the Kanawha River, in May 1775, he asked Washington, "Pray let me know how Mattrs Stands be twen great Britton and a merica" (Cleveland to George Washington, May 21, 1775, *Papers of Washington*, Col. Ser., X, 366).

41. Proceedings of the Virginia Committee of Safety, Apr. 2, 1776, *Rev. Va.,* VI, 306; Leitch to Leven Powell, May 15, 1776, James Hendricks to Leven Powell, [June] 5, 1776, Powell, ed., *Biographical Sketch,* 87, 95; Lund Washington to George Washington, Feb. 15, 1776, *Papers of Washington,* Rev. War Ser., III, 317.

• • • The Loudoun County uprising revealed a new face of patriot support that patriot leaders could not ignore. Not only did the patriots among the protesters in Loudoun show that they were fed up with the posturing of patriot leaders and their inability or unwillingness to take decisive action against the British, but they also made it clear that they wanted something in return for their support of the resistance movement. Farmers in Loudoun, like soldiers in the army, made important demands on the patriot leadership at a critical moment in the conflict.

While the very fact of smallholders' making more demands of patriot gentlemen was itself new and radical, many smallholders and tenants also took it upon themselves to judge whether particular patriot policies were just. When James Cleveland argued that officers and soldiers should be paid the same or not at all, he was not simply seeking benefits for his class but very publicly articulating universal principles. But smallholders did not simply pass judgment on patriot policies; they were also increasingly likely to resist and protest against those policies collectively. In the fall of 1775 George Gilmer thought that some of his neighbors were making efforts to "delude the populace, to raise factions, or establish parties," and they had banded together to dissuade others from joining the minute service. In November 1775, after salt had become scarce, groups descended upon hoarders to seize salt that they redistributed among themselves. Aggrieved tenants had evidently held meetings by December 30, 1775, for the threats that Lund Washington repeated on that date—to beat up officers who distrained tenants' property and to overturn the patriot committee—were collective. By the end of February 1776, if not much sooner, participants in the uprising had chosen a leader, "General" James Cleveland. Even soldiers in the army had begun to act collectively to protest the loss of their popular leader. Put together, the facts that smallholders and tenants were making greater demands on gentlemen in authority, presuming to judge whether particular policies were "just," and doing all of this collectively make it clear that ordinary Virginians had developed a new "way of thinkg," as Lund Washington put it.[42]

42. "Address of George Gilmer to the Inhabitants of Albemarle," in R. A. Brock, ed., "Papers, Military and Political, 1775-1778, of George Gilmer, M.D., of 'Pen Park,' Albermarle County, Va.," VHS, *Collections,* n.s., VI (1887), 115, 123; King and Queen County Committee Proceedings, Dec. 9, 1775, *Rev. Va.,* V, 92-93; *Va. Gaz.* (Purdie), July 5, 1776, postscript, *Rev. Va.,* VII, 138; Lund Washington

But what was perhaps most extraordinary about this new "way of thinkg"—and what seemed to worry patriot leaders most—was that farmers pushed this new agenda at the very moment that unanimity was most required. Patriot leaders expected the threat from enslaved Virginians and Dunmore to solidify support for the patriot cause among white Virginians, yet many white Virginians saw instead an opportunity to pursue their own agenda. Mobilization gave farmers needed leverage to do so. Through their short but intense wartime experience, many farmers, tenants, and other Virginians came to see that their interests were markedly different from those of their patriot leaders.

Perhaps most unsettling for traditional leaders in the colony was the fact that ordinary Virginians and, in particular, middling farmers had come to assert themselves in more overtly political ways. The first signs had begun back in the fall of 1775, when farmers went to the polls to elect new committeemen in each county. But, most obviously, the growing politicization of small farmers actually contributed to the move toward Independence. Indeed, ideological developments and ordinary Virginians' politicization in the independent companies, protests against the minutemen, and serious divisions over who should bear the burden of war in the first place help to explain the popularity of Tom Paine's *Common Sense,* which appeared in January 1776 shortly after the minuteman controversy and in the midst of the problems in Loudoun County.

Though patriot leaders were slow to take notice of the pamphlet, many ordinary white Virginians quickly embraced the principles it contained. Significantly, farmers in Loudoun County in particular seemed taken by the arguments of Paine. Stranded Briton Nicholas Cresswell recorded the impact of *Common Sense* in Loudoun County. On January 15, 1776, he noted that Norfolk had been burned but made no comment about patriot reactions to the conflagration. Four days later, however, he noted, "A pamphlet called 'Commonsense' makes a great noise." The pamphlet was "full of false representations, lies, calumny, and treason," and he was thus chagrined to find that "the sentiments are adopted by a great number of people," particularly those "who are indebted to Great Britain." What seemed to have caught the interest of the people were the "principles" in *Common Sense* that advocated the subversion of "all Kingly Governments" and the erection of "an Independent Republic." Three days later, Cresswell re-

———
to George Washington, Dec. 30, 1775, *Papers of Washington,* Rev. War Ser., II, 621.

ported that there was "Nothing but Independence talked of" in the county. Paine's pamphlet stoked the fires of rebellion. "The Devil is in the people," he concluded with resignation.[43]

Yet political independence was not the only "principle" in Paine's pamphlet that farmers in Loudoun embraced. Indeed, ideas about popular sovereignty and egalitarianism that small farmers in Virginia had called for in their military organization and in their protests over the burden of the war were clearly expressed in *Common Sense,* which did more than any other document at the time to equate Independence and republicanism in the minds of the American people. This was as clear to Paine's detractors as it was to his supporters. Landon Carter claimed that *Common Sense* was the work of men who opposed the British monarchy—"Congress Republicans" and other "men of Republican turns."[44]

The central thesis of *Common Sense,* in effect, was the guiding principle of many ordinary Virginians who had struggled with the patriot leadership over the past year—that the common people possessed enough sense to govern themselves. Edmund Randolph observed many years later that it was "pregnant with . . . proud republican theories, which flattered human nature." This was the message that Landon Carter got when he heard reports about the popularity of *Common Sense.* Carter had heard "one definition . . . of Independency; It was expected to be a form of Government, that by being independt of the rich men eve[r]y man would then be able to do as he pleasd," echoing the fears and concerns of gentlemen like George Gilmer and George Washington over the "independence" of men serving in the armed forces.[45]

Common Sense showed Americans that republicanism would follow as an inevitable consequence of Independence. At the very least, most ordinary Virginians believed that Independence would give them a greater role

43. Jan. 15, 19, 22, 26, 1776, Cresswell, *Journal,* 135–136. Most historians acknowledge the decisive impact of *Common Sense* (see, for example, Paul A. Rahe, *Republics Ancient and Modern: Classical Republicanism and the American Revolution* [Chapel Hill, N.C., 1992], 575). However, the degree to which Paine's thoughts *reflected* a wider-spread point of view among the lower and middling sorts and was popular for this reason, rather than *advanced* a particularly new viewpoint, needs further examination.

44. May 3, June 14, 1776, Greene, ed., *Diary of Carter,* II, 1033, 1050.

45. Edmund Randolph, *History of Virginia,* ed. Arthur H. Shaffer (Charlottesville, Va., 1970), 233; Landon Carter to Washington, May 9, 1776, *Papers of Washington,* Rev. War Ser., IV, 236–237.

in the affairs of state: a new government would have to be better than the old one. Thus *Common Sense* helped articulate the desire of thousands of farmers in Virginia and other colonies to venture upon Independence as a bridge to a more inclusive, more responsive government. What made Paine's pamphlet so compelling, however, was that, though in many senses original, in its fundamentals it simply expressed what people were already thinking. Virginia in 1775 and early 1776 was fertile soil for a pamphlet that urged not just Independence from Britain but also the creation of a new form of government based on far different principles from the old.

Paine's pamphlet was popular not just in northwestern Virginia. Indeed, both its supporters and detractors were forced to cast aside any doubts about the popularity of *Common Sense* and its reflection of a more popular political ideology in Virginia within a few short weeks of its arrival. "The opinion for independency seems to be gaining ground," Fielding Lewis wrote George Washington in March 1776. "Indeed most of those who have read the Pamphlet Common Sence say it's unanswerable." Washington passed on the news to Joseph Reed of Pennsylvania, noting, "By private Letters which I have lately received from Virginia, I find common sense is working a powerful change there in the Minds of many men." Even Landon Carter was forced to admit, "There is abundance talked about independency . . . it is all from Mr Common Sense."[46]

• • • Ultimately, many ordinary Virginians showed the depth of their commitment to the main arguments of *Common Sense*—by actively pushing for real change. Elections for the Fifth Virginia Convention were held in the first weeks of April. Almost at the same time that Charles Lee described Virginia's patriot leadership as too indecisive, early reports about the election described freeholders as particularly determined. Josiah Parker wrote as the first results came in, "Our freeholders are all Mad, determined to have a New house altogether," and Robert Brent noted the general turmoil of the elections: "For many counties there has been warm contests for seats in our Approaching convention. Many new ones are got in."[47]

46. Fielding Lewis to Washington, Mar. 6, 1776, Washington to Joseph Reed, Apr. 1, 1776, *Papers of Washington,* Rev. War Ser., III, 418–419, IV, 11; Mar. 12, 28, 1776, Greene, ed., *Diary of Carter,* II, 999, 1006.

47. Josiah Parker to Landon Carter, Apr. 14, 1776, Sabine Hall Papers, UVa; Robert Brent to R. H. Lee, Apr. 28, 1776, Lee Family Papers, UVa.

Independence was clearly at the forefront of many of the contests. Those who held back from supporting Independence felt the sting of smallholders' resentment at the polls. Years later, Edmund Randolph recalled that the election of delegates for the convention that was to decide on secession "depended in very many, if not in a majority, of the counties upon their candidates pledging themselves . . . to sever . . . the colonies from Great Britain." Landon Carter for one believed that new men had been voted into the convention in order to secure Independence. It was with this "expectation," he lamented, that "they sent the men they did, in hopes they would plan such a form."[48]

Landon Carter had firsthand experience of the electioneering and the contests that Independence engendered. In Carter's own Richmond County, the two incumbents, Robert Wormeley Carter and Francis Lightfoot Lee, were "most shamefully turned out" after seven years of "faithful" service. Robert Wormeley Carter opposed Independence. Moreover, he was not prepared to campaign. He grumbled that he had "never ask'd but one man to vote for me since the last Election." He received only forty-five votes and complained that he was replaced by "pickd determined men." Francis Lightfoot Lee supported Independence, but he had been chosen to represent Virginia in the Continental Congress in the previous convention. Richmond County electors, it seems, were not prepared to miss out on having a say in the vote for Independence and the formation of a new government for the sake of Lee's honor. Landon Carter was surprised to find that "even relations as well as tenants all Voted against" Robert Wormeley Carter and Lee.[49]

Though political independence from Britain was at the forefront of many elections throughout Virginia, other important issues surfaced. Certainly, farmers' anger about the way the war was being waged seemed to have some influence on the outcome. One delegate, according to Carter, "actually in a most seditious manner, resisted the draughting the Militia by lot . . . and he got first returnd that way." Former burgess William Lyne of King and Queen County, who had in the fall been accused of undermining the minute service and provoking a mutiny, was also elected to the

48. Randolph, *History of Virginia,* ed. Shaffer, 234; Carter to Washington, May 9, 1776, *Papers of Washington,* Rev. War Ser., IV, 236–237, 240–241n.

49. Apr. 1, 1776, Robert Wormeley Carter Diary, CWFL; Apr. 1, 4, 1776, Greene, ed., *Diary of Carter,* II, 1008–1010.

Fifth Convention—the first Revolutionary convention the voters sent him to. Lyne's views about the minutemen apparently found favor among the electorate.[50]

Class tensions, made manifest by the problems in Virginia during mobilization, also announced themselves during the elections. Landon Carter was disgusted to hear that one man was elected after he had exclaimed "agst the Patrolling law, because a poor man was made to pay for keeping a rich mans Slaves in order." Such reports fueled Carter's anxiety that the coming of Independence would heighten class tension. More significantly, such reports showed that, at the moment when racial solidarity was most essential, white Virginians had difficulty surmounting class differences.[51]

Class tensions became prominent in other issues as well as military. Patriot Cuthbert Bullitt of Prince William County, for example, had got himself into hot water among patriot leaders when, early in November, he was heard to "censure the extravagance of the Convention, in allowing so great a salary, in many instances, to persons employed by them." He had also feared that this would prove the "greatest injury to the credit of the paper money of the colony." Details of the affair did not reach the public until a few weeks before the election, when the whole matter was aired in the pages of the *Virginia Gazette*. Bullitt's political views were popular enough among the electorate to get him elected in April. He replaced the long-serving Thomas Blackburn, who had actually called the tenants in his county "peasants."[52]

Anti-Scottish and antimerchant feeling among ordinary Virginians might also have played a role in the elections. Charles Barber McCarty and Hudson Muse were the candidates elected in Richmond County in place of Carter and Lee. Landon Carter described Muse as "a most silly though good natured fool," and McCarty as "a worthless, though impudent fellow."

50. Carter to Washington, May 9, 1776, *Papers of Washington,* Rev. War Ser., IV, 236–237, 240–241n; King and Queen County committee, subcommittee proceedings, Dec. 9, 1775, *Va. Gaz.* (Purdie), Feb. 16, 1776, supplement, *Rev. Va.,* V, 92–93; Election of Convention Delegates in King and Queen County, May 21, 1776, *Rev. Va.,* VII, 212.

51. Carter to Washington, May 9, 1776, *Papers of Washington,* Rev. War Ser., IV, 236–237, 240–241n.

52. *Va. Gaz.* (Purdie), Mar. 1, 1776; *Rev. Va.,* V, 167n, VI, 293, 299–300n; Robert Brent to R. H. Lee, Apr. 28, 1776, Lee Family Papers, UVa; Holton, *Forced Founders,* 203.

But McCarty might have endeared himself to his neighbors by accusing local Scottish merchant Robert Gilmour of price gouging during the Association, then challenging the local committee's acquittal of Gilmour. He also apparently pandered to populist sentiment by indicting all Scottish merchants for their duplicity during the resistance movement and exhorted his countrymen to "purge this sickly colony of such filth."[53]

Judging by the surprised comments of many gentlemen around the colony, the elections for the Fifth Virginia Convention were the most hotly contested since the imperial crisis had begun in earnest. Altogether, forty-eight seats, or 38 percent of the convention, changed from the Fourth to the Fifth meeting, the largest turnover since 1758 (another wartime election). Though some members of the previous convention were barred from re-election because they had taken up military posts and there were some retirements, voters probably changed at least thirty delegates. Such a sudden change was a dramatic turnaround from recent years. The previous elections for the Third and Fourth Virginia Conventions saw only a 4 percent change in composition. The previous lack of legislative change juxtaposed with the 1776 election makes the turnover all the more dramatic and significant. These facts, taken together with the results of the committee elections the previous fall and the pressing need for unanimity and harmony at that critical moment, speak volumes for the discontent of small farmers and ordinary Virginians on all sides of the political fence.[54]

53. Greene, ed., *Diary of Carter,* II, 1008–1009; Charles McCarty to John Pinkney, Dec. 15, 1774, *Va. Gaz.* (Pinkney), Jan. 19, Feb. 23, Mar. 9, 1775.

54. Even in counties where there were no changes, in many the incumbents had to overcome significant challenges to win their seats back. Henry Lee was "much push'd," as were conservatives Benjamin Harrison, Edmund Pendleton (who had been critical of Patrick Henry), and even George Mason (the chief architect of the new military establishment of August 1775)—who was only "with great difficulty return'd" in Fairfax County. There were also heated contests in the counties of King William, Essex, Fauquier (where there were five candidates), and Stafford, though little evidence is extant that sheds much light on why they were so contested (see Josiah Parker to Landon Carter, Apr. 14, 1776, Sabine Hall Papers, UVa; Richard Brent to R. H. Lee, Apr. 28, 1776, Hoffman, ed., *Lee Family Papers*). *Rev. Va.,* VI, 287–291; John G. Kolp, "The Dynamics of Electoral Competition in pre-Revolutionary Virginia," *WMQ,* 3d Ser., XLIX (1992), 660–661; Cynthia Miller Leonard, comp., *The General Assembly of Virginia, July 30, 1619–January 11, 1978: A Bicentennial Register of Members* [Richmond, Va., 1978]). In deducing whether

The many new faces at the convention led Landon Carter to worry that it "abounds with too many of the inexperienced creatures to navigate our bark on this dangerous coast; so that I fear the few skilful Pilots who have hitherto done tolerably well to keep her clear from destruction, will not be able to Conduct her with Common Safety any longer." Carter thought that "ambition" had "siezed so much ignorance, all over the Colony." And, though many of the members of the Fifth Convention were from older, genteel families, one qualitative comment made during the fall of 1776, when the same delegates were sitting as the assembly, suggests some inroads were made by the less wealthy in the spring 1776 elections. Roger Atkinson thought that the delegates were "not quite so well dressed, nor so politely Educated, nor so highly born" as members of "some Assemblies have formerly been," but they were "plain" and "full as honest, less intriguing, more sincere." Though it was a changed legislature, "yet upon the whole I like their Proceedings. . . . They are the People's men (and the People in general are right)."[55]

• • • As important as the legislative changes, freeholders advocating Independence made their voices heard around the colony, before, during, and after the elections. Jefferson told Thomas Nelson in mid-May that, before he left for Congress, he had taken "great pains to enquire into the sentiments of the people" about Independence. From his queries in his own piedmont neighborhood in the early part of the year, he felt safe in saying that "nine out of ten are for it." As the elections got under way, James McClurg in Williamsburg told Jefferson that such sentiments were not confined to the piedmont. "The Notion of Indepency seems to spread fast in this Colony," he asserted. Judging by the progress of the elections up to that point, McClurg believed that Independence would be adopted by a "Majority" of the next convention. A few days later, John Page thought that "almost every Man" near Williamsburg—"except the Treasurer"—was "willing to declare for independence." William Aylett, who had nearly

---

representatives were "new" or not, membership was checked back only to the elections of 1771. Thus, a few in this category might have seen legislative service, but before 1771.

55. Carter to Washington, May 9, 1776, *Papers of Washington,* Rev. War Ser., IV, 236–237, 240–241n; Roger Atkinson to Sammy ———, Nov. 20, 1776, Letter Book of Roger Atkinson, UVa. Though Atkinson was referring to the assembly that met in the fall of 1776, only the senators had been elected since that spring.

lost his election, wrote soon after the contest, "The people of this County almost unanimously cry aloud for independance."[56]

If delegates had still not got the message, freeholders made it clearer in a series of dramatic declarations of intent. In an auspicious move, freeholders began circulating "Instructions" to their delegates to ensure that they voted for Independence in the coming convention. In Cumberland County, the local committee took the lead and, following the elections, immediately adopted a set of instructions for their delegates. These they approved in committee, then got the general approval of "the People." Freeholders approved a set of instructions that committed their delegates to the convention "positively to declare for an Independency," to "abjure any Allegiance to his Britannick Majesty," and to "bid him a good Night forever." One day later, the Charlotte County Committee also presented a similar public letter of instructions for its new delegates to the convention to push for Independence. The following day, freeholders in James City County instructed their reluctant delegate, Robert Carter Nicholas, who had made it clear that he was against Independence. Instead of dumping Nicholas, voters in James City County elected him but then made him promise to push "towards dissolving the connexion between America and Great Britain, *totally, finally,* and *irrevocably.*" Finally, freeholders of Buckingham County also produced an "Address and Instructions" to their delegates, claiming that in the "great and leading questions" it was necessary to "take the sense of your constituents," which, they made clear, was for Independence. Their delegates were to "cause a total and final separation from Great Britain."[57]

56. Jefferson to Thomas Nelson, May 16, 1776, James McClurg to Jefferson, Apr. 6, 1776, *Papers of Jefferson,* I, 287, 292; Page to R. H. Lee, Apr. 12, 1776, William Aylett to R. H. Lee, Apr. 20, 1776, Hoffman, ed., *Lee Family Papers.*

57. Cumberland freeholders actually accused the king of ordering Dunmore to arm the slaves against them. Cumberland County Committee Instructions, Apr. 22, 1776, *Rev. Va.,* VI, 433–434; Charlotte County Committee to Delegates Paul Carrington and Thomas Read, Apr. 23, 1776, *Rev. Va.,* VI, 447 (the instructions were published in *Va. Gaz.* [Purdie] on May 10, 1776); Freeholders of James City County to Delegates Robert Carter Nicholas and William Norvell, Apr. 24, 1776, *Rev. Va.,* VI, 458, printed in Purdie's *Va. Gaz.,* Apr. 26, 1776; Address and Instructions of the freeholders of Buckingham County, [May 13, 1776], *Rev. Va.,* VII, 109–111.

Though the instructions of only four counties are extant, the practice was widerspread. A "Representation" from the committee of Augusta County East, for example, was sent directly to the convention arguing the need for "making the con-

Freeholders' instructions to their delegates did not just end with a demand for Independence. The instructions also laid out concerns of freeholders that lay behind their demand for separation. All four extant instructions make the need for the resumption of trade—a key demand of the rioters from Loudoun—the most important justification for Independence. A reopened trade would help bring in badly needed goods—goods necessary both to ease the shortages that plagued the patriot movement and to sustain the army. The instructions from Charlotte County also claimed that the resumption of trade was necessary to "enable us to pay the taxes . . . for carrying on a war." Trade, added the freeholders from Buckingham County, would "enable us to discharge the great burthens of the war, which otherwise may become intolerable."[58]

Patriot leaders in the Fourth Convention had declared their ports open to foreign nations, but freeholders believed that was not enough. They demanded foreign alliances that would guarantee that trade. As early as December 1775, when Virginians began to feel the adverse effects of shortages, reports circulated that the "King of France had declaird he would give the Americans any Assistance they should Require on Condision they would grant him a trade with them." But French diplomats had made it clear that they would not approve large-scale trade with Virginia and its neighbors while they remained colonies of Britain. The French were "exceedingly friendly" and happy to provide large supplies of arms and ammunition if they were not so "doubtful of the American submission to the claims of Parliament." Thus the only way to obtain trade with French merchants—the only way to put an end to the conflicts caused by nonimportation, nonexportation, and the war—was to declare Independence. The free-

---

federacy of the united Colonies the most perfect and lasting and of framing an equal free and liberal Government." Philip Mazzei in Albemarle County prepared instructions at the beginning of May, and Landon Carter in the Northern Neck reported that "Papers" were circulating everywhere for "poor ignorant Creatures to sign." They were "directions to their delegate[s] to endeavour at an independency." Proceedings of the Fifth Virginia Convention, May 10, 1776, *Rev. Va.,* VII, 87; *Rev. Va.,* VI, 444; Carter to Washington, May 9, 1776, *Papers of Washington,* Rev. War Ser., IV, 236–237. For a general assessment of the impact of such "other" declarations of independence, see Pauline Maier, *American Scripture: Making the Declaration of Independence* (New York, 1997).

58. Charlotte County Committee to Delegates Paul Carrington and Thomas Read, Apr. 23, 1776, Address and Instructions of the freeholders of Buckingham County, [May 13, 1776], *Rev. Va.,* VI, 447–448, VII, 109–112.

holders who instructed their delegates to the convention understood this connection perfectly. Declaring Independence, freeholders from Charlotte County asserted, would allow them to quickly "enter into a commercial alliance with any nation, or nations, friendly to our cause."[59]

Significantly, freeholders claimed that securing foreign alliances and declining Independence were also important for securing the allegiances of those who seemed keen to return to the British. Playing on the fears of those who worried about the lack of popular support for the patriot cause, the James City County freeholders warned that political and commercial alliances with foreign nations were absolutely essential because a "common lethargy" had seized many of them. "Faint advances toward peace, insidiously urged," they claimed, "have caught the ear of the credulous, and groundless hopes of accommodation deluded the timid." Echoing them, the freeholders of Buckingham also felt that the "prospects of reconciliation" had deluded the "ignorant, credulous, and unwary," into inaction.[60]

The arguments of freeholders in Buckingham and James City Counties help explain why some patriot leaders also pushed for Independence when they did. On several occasions in April 1776, John Page wrote from Williamsburg to Jefferson, now a Virginia delegate to Congress, that they must act decisively and declare Independence. Virginians would not be able to hold out much longer while they were constantly "tempted by peace and reconciliation." Moreover, Lee's arrival had made Virginians realize how deficient they were in the goods needed to carry on a full-scale war. They

59. The *Virginia Gazette* drove the point home: "The common toast among the French . . . is, *the independence of America;* until which is declared, they say our war with England can only be looked on as a domestic broil" (*Va. Gaz.,* [D and H], Apr. 6, 1776). See Thomas Peirce and Thomas Smith to Edmund Pendleton, Dec. 17, 1775, *Rev. Va.,* V, 171; Freeholders of James City County to Delegates Robert Carter Nicholas and William Norvell, Apr. 24, 1776, Charlotte County Committee to Delegates Paul Carrington and Thomas Read, Apr. 23, 1776, *Rev. Va.,* VI, 447, 458. For shortages of lead and powder, domestic efforts at producing them, and the French unwillingness to supply them unless the Virginians declared Independence, see Donald E. Reynolds, "Ammunition Supply in Revolutionary Virginia," *VMHB,* LXXIII (1965), 56–62.

60. Freeholders of James City County to Delegates Robert Carter Nicholas and William Norvell, Apr. 24, 1776, Address and Instructions of the freeholders of Buckingham County, [May 13, 1776], *Rev. Va.,* VI, 458, VII, 109–111. Cf. Charlotte County Committee to Delegates Paul Carrington and Thomas Read, Apr. 23, 1776, *Rev. Va.,* VI, 447.

were desperate, Page warned, not just for salt for the people, but for salt-peter, gunpowder, sulphur, arms, woolens, and linens for their growing army. The logic of separation from Britain was crystal clear to Page. All of Virginia's problems could be solved at once by finding a means of importing all the needed goods. In turn, he argued, "no Means can be so certain and can so fully answer our Purpose, as forming a commercial Alliance with France." A commercial alliance with France could be formed only if the colonies were independent.[61]

But, *unlike* the freeholders who prepared instructions, Page and others believed that Independence would solve other important problems in Virginia—they believed it would put a final end to the "rising disorders," as Francis Lightfoot Lee put it, that had plagued Virginia since the previous spring at least. Enslaved Virginians had, from the start, proved to be one source of "disorders." As early as January, Thomas Nelson, Jr., tried to goad his colleagues in Virginia by playing on their fears of insurrection. The British command of the sea, he warned, meant that, wherever their boats could reach, "Devastation will be spread." He was particularly worried about Dunmore's ability to stir up internal insurrection in Virginia. Though Dunmore was "lying still" for the moment, Nelson thought he was only cooking up "some Diabolical scheme, for our destruction." Francis Lightfoot Lee warned Landon Carter that the threat from enslaved Virginians, combined with expected British reinforcements and the Virgini-

61. James McClurg to Jefferson, Apr. 6, 1776, Page to Jefferson, Apr. 6, 1776, Apr. 26, 1776, *Papers of Jefferson*, I, 287, 288. Some ardent patriots tried to masculinize the argument for Independence. As early as January, Thomas Nelson, Jr., had begun to believe in the need for Independence. He was furious that some still entertained ideas of a reconciliation with Britain. He used gendered arguments to try to shame his colleagues in Virginia to ignore the prospects for peace and, instead, pursue commercial and military alliances. He told John Page in late January that they could not "form a connexion with any foreign power" while they still had a "womanish hankering after Great Britain." A few weeks later, he told Page that there were too many people in Congress and elsewhere who feared Independence, confederation, and foreign alliances. These ends, he asserted, were as "formidable to some . . . as an Apparition to a weak enervated Woman" (Nelson to Page, Jan. 22, Feb. 13, 1776, in Emory G. Evans, *Thomas Nelson of Yorktown: Revolutionary Virginian* [Williamsburg, Va., 1975], 54). Cf. R. H. Lee to Henry, Apr. 20, 1776, Smith et al., eds., *Letters of Delegates to Congress*, III, 563; Henry to John Adams, May 20, 1776, IV, 200; *Va. Gaz.* (D and H), Apr. 13, 1776.

ans' "want of Arms and good Genls will make this little army very formidable to you."[62]

Another source of disorder stemmed from farmers who were anxious to restore trade in order to pay taxes and rents and to procure badly needed goods. Patriots like Page believed that neither patriot-leaning farmers nor those in favor of reconciliation with Britain would suffer shortages much longer. Instead, they would do as they had shown signs of doing in the past. If the situation continued, ordinary Virginians would "give up the Authors of their Misfortunes, their Leaders," and "sacrifice them to a Reconciliation" in order to receive "a Trade equal to their wishes."[63]

A third source of disorders had arisen from the inability of Virginia's military forces to protect gentlemen and their property, in part due to the unwillingness of ordinary Virginians to serve in the armed forces on the terms laid down by patriot leaders. Gentlemen like Jefferson and George Mason became convinced that the most compelling reason for Independence was to procure badly needed civil and military supplies. Trade would not only placate reluctant patriots and suffering farmers, but it would also allow the army to protect Virginia more efficiently. In addition to securing a "regular Supply of military Stores," Mason believed that the object of a foreign trade alliance would lead to military alliances that would benefit more vulnerable colonies like Virginia. Tired of the constant alarms on the Potomac River, worried about the lack of local protection for the riverside plantations, and sure that Virginia could not protect itself, Mason argued that a foreign alliance ought at the very least to provide naval help to protect Virginia's trade and its coasts.[64]

Mason was particularly worried about the need for more military help, because in mid-April yet another British plan to act in concert with native Americans against the rebels was uncovered. On April 6, patriots cap-

62. Thomas Nelson, Jr., to Mann Page, Jan. 4, 1776, to John Page, Feb. 13, 1776, Smith et al., eds., *Letters of Delegates to Congress,* III, 30, 248–249; Francis Lightfoot Lee to Landon Carter, Feb. 12, Mar. 19, Apr. 9, May 21, 1776, III, 237, 407, 500–501, IV, 57.

63. Page to Jefferson, Apr. 6, 26, 1776, *Papers of Jefferson,* I, 287, 288.

64. Jefferson to John Page, May 17, 1776, *Papers of Jefferson,* I, 294; Mason to Washington, Apr. 2, 1776, Mason to R. H. Lee, May 18, 1776, *Papers of Mason,* I, 267, 271, 272. Cf. R. H. Lee to R. C. Nicholas, Apr. 30, 1776, Ballagh, ed., *Letters of Richard Henry Lee,* I, 184–185; R. H. Lee to Pendleton, May 12, 1776, Edmund Pendleton Papers, LiVi.

tured a British tender and intercepted dispatches from London and Dunmore that showed the British were still negotiating with native Americans against the patriots. At the end of April, Richard Henry Lee wrote to Robert Carter Nicholas that he had heard that the British were once again preparing to hold talks with the Indians at Detroit and Niagara in an attempt to persuade the "Savages" to "join in the war against us." Mason lived near Alexandria, the site earlier proposed as a rendezvous for a joint British–native American invasion. With the regular army on a better footing and with military help from a country like France, patriot leaders like Mason thought they would be freed from their dependence on full popular support for the movement.[65]

Finally, many patriot leaders believed that separation from Britain would allow them to suppress the more general crisis of authority in Virginia. Many gentlemen believed that the lack of a government—the House of Burgesses had not passed a law since 1773, county courts no longer tried civil suits, and so on—helped to foment disorderly actions such as the Loudoun rising. Not only were patriot leaders unsure of their jurisdiction and authority without a more formal government, but disaffected whites and blacks were keen to take advantage. Independence would allow patriot leaders to move for an immediate restoration of government—a government much like the one they had just repudiated. "To prevent Disorders in each Colony," Page asserted, "a Constitution should be formed as nearly resembling the old one as Circumstances, and the Merit of that Constitution will admit of." Page was adamant about the need for Independence. "For God's sake declare the Colonies independant at once," Page had pleaded with Jefferson, "and save us from ruin."[66]

Gentlemen who supported Independence used this argument to play upon the fears of those who did not. In April 1776, when delegate to Congress Francis Lightfoot Lee received a letter from Landon Carter reporting on the growth of "licentiousness" in Virginia, Lee argued that the only way to suppress it was to restore formal government. Carter had told Lee that he thought Independence would end in "Anarchy and confusion." Lee coun-

65. Mason to Washington, Apr. 2, 1776, Mason to R. H. Lee, May 18, 1776, *Papers of Mason*, I, 267, 271, 272; R. H. Lee to R. C. Nicholas, Apr. 30, 1776, Ballagh, ed., *Letters of Richard Henry Lee*, I, 184–185. Cf. R. H. Lee to Henry, Apr. 20, 1776, R. H. Lee to Pendleton, May 12, 1776, Smith et al., eds., *Letters of Delegates to Congress*, III, 564, 667.

66. Page to Jefferson, Apr. 6, 26, 1776, *Papers of Jefferson*, I, 287, 288.

tered that the reason "licentiousness begins to prevail in Virga." was that the "old Government" had been "dissolved, and no new one substituted in its stead." It was inevitable that without Independence and a new government, "Anarchy must be the consequence." Later, Lee told Carter that the convention that would meet in May 1776 should "make such an establishment, as will put a stop to the rising disorders with you, and secure internal quiet for the future." Lee also argued that the only way Rhode Island and Connecticut had preserved "order and quiet" was by maintaining their old colonial governments. New Hampshire and Massachusetts were "getting into the utmost disorder; but upon their assuming Government . . . they are restored to perfect harmony and regularity." If that convention failed to establish a regular government, Lee argued, "I dread the consequences," for they and the other southern colonies would soon "have violent symptoms to encounter." Though Lee was playing a propaganda game with Carter, it was clear that perceptions of disorder in Virginia were the playing pieces.[67]

Significantly, in the midst of their correspondence, Landon Carter had yet another firsthand experience of a direct challenge to patriot authority. On May 1, he wrote in his diary of one "G. R.," who had been called upon to help against a British ship coming up the river. The man refused with daring and unsettling insolence: "When asked to lend his firelock to go against the tender, [he] asked the People if they were such fools to go to protect the Gentlemen's houses on the river side; he thought it would be the better if they were burnt down." Carter was furious, but, since he had not stood for the county committee because of his disgust with the electioneering the previous fall, he could do little about G. R. Instead, Carter railed against the county committee for refusing to do anything about him. He had heard that "a Gentleman" had heard G. R. and had told the committee, but "no Notice was ever taken of it." For Carter, this was proof enough of what could be expected if Virginia declared Independence. Indeed, in his account, he interpolated his disappointment about the recent elections and paralleled G. R.'s defiance with the electorate's desire for change. Immediately after noting that the committee refused to take notice of G. R., Carter asserted, "The old deligates were left out, for this very Purpose and these new ones chose for this very Purpose of an intire independence in which no Gentleman should have the least share." "Hurray for Indepen-

67. Francis Lightfoot Lee to Landon Carter, Mar. 19, Apr. 9, May 21, 1776, Smith et al., eds., *Letters of Delegates to Congress,* III, 407, 500–501, IV, 57.

dancy, Sedition, and Confusion," Carter concluded. Rethinking the episode, Carter confided in his diary that, if he were still chair of the county committee, he might also have taken no notice of G. R.; to do so would have only created a conflict that he had no stomach to fight. This was a type of class warfare, and, if Carter or the committee took any action against G. R., they risked creating a more popular martyr. Through experience, he had learned that these types "only want to be taken notice of, that they may have some grounds to represent to those like themselves, what persecution they endure by resisting the rich or, as they call them, the Gentlemen."[68]

Carter might have told Francis Lightfoot Lee about his experience, for within a few weeks Lee told Carter that it was now essential to "put a stop to the rising disorders." It was particularly important, given the campaign the Virginians were fighting against the British and black troops, the threat of slave unrest, and also the increasingly obvious divisions among whites. Unanimity among whites was imperative: "The violent struggle we have to go thro' this summer, the hardships we must suffer, make it necessary to cultivate the utmost harmony among ourselves." As he had previously, Lee argued that Virginia should follow the example of other colonies for the sake of the reestablishment of internal law and authority as much as to counter the British. Even the conservative middle colonies "are going fast into Independency and constituting new Governmts. convinced of the necessity of it, both for the security of internal peace and good order; and for the vigorous exertion of their whole force against the common Enemy." Other pro-Independence gentlemen were also quick to make use of what Lee called Virginia's "rising disorders" in their arguments for final separation.[69]

If such arguments failed to persuade, some gentlemen tried to convince their foot-dragging colleagues that, in the face of popular support for Independence, there was now simply no alternative; they simply had to ride the tiger. General Charles Lee, commander of the Continental forces in the South, spent the election month of April 1776 in Virginia and came away

68. May 1, 1776, Greene, ed., *Diary of Carter*, II, 1030–1031.

69. Francis Lightfoot Lee to Landon Carter, May 21, 1776, Smith et al., eds., *Letters of Delegates to Congress*, IV, 57. Cf. R. H. Lee to Robert Carter Nicholas, Apr. 30, 1776, Smith et al., eds., *Letters of Delegates to Congress*, III, 608; Pendleton to R. H. Lee, Apr. 20, 1776, *Papers of Pendleton*, I, 164; John C. Miller, *Origins of the American Revolution* (Boston, 1943), 476; R. H. Lee to Henry, Apr. 20, 1776, Ballagh, ed., *Letters of Richard Henry Lee*, I, 177.

convinced that almost all white Virginians supported a declaration of Independence. The "spirit of the people . . . cry out for this Declaration,"
Lee told Patrick Henry early in May. Lee appealed to Henry's special relationship with the troops at Williamsburg. The "military in particular," he
said, "are outrageous on the subject." They would become "so dispirited
that they will abandon their Colours and probably never be perswaded to
make another effort" should the Virginia convention fail to declare for it.
Lee felt that a "man of your excellent discernment" would need not be told
how "dangerous" it would be to "dally with the spirit, or disappoint the expectations of the bulk of the People," warning, "may not despair, anarchy,
and finally submission be the bitter fruits?"[70]

• • • Thus, Independence was on the minds of many in the fall and spring
of 1775-1776, but diverse groups within Virginia, black and white, defined
Independence very differently. Lower- and middle-class patriotic whites
within the military wanted independence from authoritarian and unpopular officers. Middling farmers, like those contemplating joining the minutemen, wanted the independence to do "as they pleased." Others, like those
in Loudoun, wanted the independence to fight the British at once, on
terms more acceptable to working farmers, and not risk economic ruin.
Many aspiring whites, like Bartlett Thompson, wanted independence from
the traditional county elite and took the opportunity to challenge an older
hierarchy. Many of those outside the military simply wanted the independence to go about their own business and even resume trade with Britain. Other whites, as Landon Carter believed, wanted independence from
"the rich men" or, like the lower-class whites in Northampton, wanted
independence from the authority of their county committees. Still other
lower-class whites wanted independence enough to avoid being forced into
military service. Indentured servants, convict servants, and enslaved Virginians also wanted independence—from their masters. All of these Virginians, of course, posed a challenge to the patriot leadership, and particularly a challenge to their authority to govern the rebellious colony in lieu of
royal authority. Patriot gentlemen became convinced of the need for Independence, too, but many anxious patriots' vision was an Independence that
would help reestablish their splintering authority over other Virginians.[71]

70. Charles Lee to Henry, May 7, 1776, *Lee Papers,* II, 1–3, NYHS, *Collections,*
V (1872).
71. Many evangelicals wanted an Independence that included freedom of re-

By the time of the Fifth Virginia Convention on May 6, then, there was little doubt left that delegates would move for Independence. The newly elected president of the convention, Edmund Pendleton, set the agenda. If the Fourth Virginia Convention had focused on efforts to stop Dunmore's progress, the time had now come to restore order within the colony. "The Administration of Justice and almost all Powers of Government have been suspended for near two Years," Pendleton announced, warning that it was questionable whether "we can longer sustain the great struggle we are making in this situation." The delegates also had to beef up their defense by making further provision for their military and naval arrangements as well as for raising more funds for supporting them. They also had to secure the colony against further civil war among whites, Pendleton asserted, mainly by enacting further restrictive and punitive legislation against the "Enemies of America in this Colony." Finally, to secure internal peace in the colony, the delegates had to make every effort to procure "some Articles more immediately necessary for our People particularly Salt."[72]

All of this meant, of course, Independence. Debate on declaring Independence was, in the end, limited. Patrick Henry, speaking in support of the motion, told his colleagues that the "now apparent spirit of the people" had pushed him and others to the conclusion that Independence was inevitable. For the sake of unanimity, he put aside his belief that they needed to establish foreign alliances before they declared Independence. Robert Carter Nicholas, the only dissenting voice raised in the debate, still worried that they were not ready to declare Independence. He worried about the "competency of America in so arduous a contest." He claimed many others secretly shared his worries. Virginia's shaky performance thus far against a very small British force led by Dunmore, combined with more worries about the fear of slave insurrection and the loyalties of white Virginians, slowed Nicholas's enthusiasm. With more reports of much greater forces supposedly on the way from Europe, there is no doubt that many prominent planters in vulnerable areas did share his concerns. Most had to put their faith in Independence because they had no other choice at this

---

ligion, and some, like the Methodists, wanted a measure of independence from worldly intrusions. Many white women also looked for greater independence during the crisis. Some, according to Robert Munford, became more assertive about their own definition of masculinity. Others, like loyalist women, pitched in to try to defeat the patriots.

72. Proceedings of the Fifth Virginia Convention, May 6, 1776, *Rev. Va.,* VII, 27.

point. In the end, Nicholas did not oppose the vote for Independence but rather silently acquiesced, neither demanding a roll call vote nor willing to "contradict the general Voice."[73]

The following day, May 15, 1776, 112 present members of the convention unanimously agreed to a Declaration of Independence from Britain and instructed Virginia's delegates in Congress to declare the United Colonies free and independent states. Upon declaring Independence, they resolved, Congress ought to take "whatever measures may be thought proper and necessary . . . for forming foreign alliances and a confederation of the Colonies." The convention wanted control over the formation of its own government and thus reserved to itself the right to establish a government for "the regulation of the internal concerns of each colony." Then, apparently recognizing the arguments of both anxious patriot leaders and the demands of militant ordinary white Virginians, the delegates resolved to establish a Declaration of Rights and a government that would be "most likely to maintain peace and order in this colony and secure substantial and equal liberty to the people."[74]

73. *Rev. Va.,* VII, 146; Randolph, *History of Virginia,* ed. Shaffer, 250; Evans, *Thomas Nelson,* 56–58.

74. Proceedings of the Fifth Virginia Convention, May 15, 1776, *Rev. Va.,* VII, 143.

CREATING A NEW GOVERNMENT

If there was little disagreement among patriots by May 1776 about the need to declare Independence, there was much less agreement about "the form of Government" that Virginians should establish—a point made already by the testy and anxious Landon Carter. Carter, watching from the sidelines, believed that Independence was a foregone conclusion, but few people seemed to have given much thought to what kind of government they should create, and there seemed to be little consensus. "In vain," he had asked colleagues "what is design'd by" Independence and a new government. If the form of government was designed only "to Preserve Justice, Order, Peace, and freedom," then there were "few who would refuse" such a model. Worryingly for him, those who had circulated instructions for Independence could not or would not explain what they wanted in the new government. In Carter's eyes, this left the "ignorant representative"—the new men recently elected much to Carter's distaste—"to do what he pleases."[1]

Carter had reason to be worried. The Fifth Virginia Convention, with well more than a third of its members newly elected, appeared to be stacked with representatives with different—and competing—interests: from "plain" men to "Aristocrats," few of whom would have had much experience creating entirely new governments, even if they could agree on what kind of government they wanted. Expectations, and tensions, were high, a point reinforced when delegates had to decide who would lead the convention. Richard Bland of Prince George County nominated the past president of the convention and the Committee of Safety, moderate Edmund Pendleton. Given tradition, he should have been nominated to the powerful and prestigious position unanimously. But Thomas Johnson of

1. Landon Carter to George Washington, May 9, 1776, *Papers of Washington, Rev. War Ser.*, IV, 236–237.

Louisa County, an ardent supporter of Patrick Henry, stood to nominate the more radical Thomas Ludwell Lee. Though Lee could hardly have expected to carry the vote against Pendleton, the unprecedented challenge was a very public confirmation of the dispute between Henry and Pendleton and a sign of divisions to come.[2]

In the end, though the deliberations of the convention over the new form of government were kept secret, the final outcome clearly reflected the competing interests of the main protagonists in the Revolutionary drama. Perhaps unsurprisingly, conservative proponents of the paramount need of the new government to establish "peace and order" found a voice in the new government. But, surprisingly, delegates keen to "secure substantial and equal liberty" scored the most impressive victories. To the wonderment of almost all prominent patriots outside the convention, the final plan of government went much further than any of the extant written proposals in creating a truly popular government. Radicals in the convention, with the force of people "out of doors," had secured a generous Revolutionary settlement—at least for middling Virginians.[3]

• • • Landon Carter wanted as little change in the new government as possible. He was not alone. Edmund Pendleton also leaned toward tradition over innovation, and order and justice over liberty and a more democratic government. Pendleton and other prominent patriots were horrified by Thomas Paine's suggestion that only one popularly elected legislative body was necessary for good government. A unicameral legislature was far too democratic for most patriot leaders. And "a democracy," Pendleton told Carter Braxton on May 12, "considered as *referring determinations,* either

2. Roger Atkinson to Sammy [?], Nov. 20, 1776, Letter Book of Roger Atkinson, UVa; Thomas Ludwell Lee to R. H. Lee, June 1, 1776, Paul P. Hoffman, ed., *Lee Family Papers, 1742-1795* (microfilm) (Charlottesville, Va., 1966); Proceedings of the First Virginia Convention, Aug. 1, 1774, *Rev. Va.,* I, 222–223; Proceedings of the Second Virginia Convention, Mar. 20, 1775, *Rev. Va.,* II, 348; Proceedings of the Third Virginia Convention, July 17, 1775, *Rev. Va.,* III, 314; Proceedings of the Fourth Virginia Convention, Dec. 1, 1775, *Rev. Va.,* V, 33; Proceedings of the Fifth Virginia Convention, May 6, 1776, *Rev. Va.,* VII, 27. For Johnson's support of Henry, see *Rev. Va.,* II, 345, 359. Cf. Jack P. Greene, ed., *The Diary of Colonel Landon Carter of Sabine Hall, 1752-1778* (Charlottesville, Va., 1965), II, 1052–1053.

3. Proceedings of the Fifth Virginia Convention, May 6, 15, 1776, *Rev. Va.,* VII, 27, 143.

legislative or executive, TO THE PEOPLE AT LARGE, is the worst form (of government) imaginable." Pendleton was keen to replicate as closely as possible the English model of mixed government, balancing a strong executive with an upper and a lower chamber. "Of all others," Pendleton declared, "I prefer the true English constitution, which consists of a proper combination of the principles of honor, virtue, and fear."[4]

Pendleton's views counted. As president of the convention, he picked the committee to prepare a plan of government. When choosing members for other, less important committees, he made an effort to distribute assignments more evenly than ever before. Perhaps acknowledging the presence of more western counties and wanting an inclusive representation on the committees at this momentous time, Pendleton picked committee members from all over the colony, ensuring a wide range of interests. Yet, on the important issue of forming a new government, he went back to an older model of picking committee members. Though he included twenty-four counties plus the College of William and Mary and Williamsburg in the twenty-eight appointments he made, the committee was still top-heavy with tidewater spokesmen. Altogether, nineteen of the original twenty-eight committee members (or 68 percent) resided in counties on or below the fall line. Seven came from piedmont counties, and only two came from counties west of the Blue Ridge Mountains. Many of those residing outside the tidewater area had also recently removed or had extensive family connections with those in the east. A few days later, Pendleton told Jefferson that he hoped his plans for the committee were working and that the dependable George Mason "seems to have the Ascendancy in the great work" of forming a new government. With Mason taking the lead, the government would be "framed so as to Answer it's end, Prosperity to the Community and Security to Individuals."[5]

4. Edmund Pendleton to Carter Braxton, [May 12, 1776], *Papers of Pendleton*, I, 177. The text is taken from the *Examiner* (Richmond), Oct. 23, 1802, in an article on Ralph Wormeley. The editor of that newspaper stated that this letter was cited and printed in numerous Federalist publications in 1800.

5. Proceedings of the Fifth Virginia Convention, May 15, 1776, *Rev. Va.*, VII, 143; Pendleton to Thomas Jefferson, May 24, 1776, *Papers of Pendleton*, I, 180. Eight more members were added to the committee, presumably as they took their seats in the convention. Of these, four came from tidewater counties, one from the piedmont, and three from the western counties (see Proceedings of the Fifth Virginia Convention, May 16, 18, 21, 24, 27, 1776, *Rev. Va.*, VII, 158, 182, 208, 246, 273).

Along with their own ideas, the committee had a number of influential and formal proposals at their disposal, ranging across the political spectrum and differing in many details. On one side, like Landon Carter and Pendleton, many delegates wanted to keep government as similar to what they had had before as possible. Carter Braxton, who wrote perhaps the most conservative proposal for a new government, explained that the aim of those creating a new Constitution should be to look at the old government of Virginia, "and in a revolution," ask "how is its spirit to be preserved." "Tranquility and security," argued Braxton, were the preeminent objects of government. Arguing to preserve tradition over innovation and ensure stability, he called for triennial elections for representatives, who in turn would elect an upper house, or Council of State, of twenty-four men. Together, the representatives and the upper house would then elect a governor and a seven-man advisory council to help advise him. Braxton thus wanted to keep government quite substantially removed from the people, who would have their say only every three years, and then only to elect a lower house. The upper house, the privy council, and the governor—all of whom would keep a check on the lower house—would not be elected by popular vote and, significantly, would all serve for *life*. Lifetime terms, he asserted, would keep them free from worrying about their "popularity" so that they could serve with proper "impartiality."[6]

Braxton's ideas—which might have cost him his seat in the convention—were ridiculed by some patriot leaders. Richard Henry Lee called Braxton's plan for government a "contemptible little Tract," because of its "Confusion of ideas, aristocratic pride, contradictory reasoning with evident ill design." Yet Braxton was censured not so much because of the practicalities of his plan but rather because of its appreciative tone of the British constitution and its swipes at more popular plans. Like others, he had been troubled by the temper of the preceding months. His main priority was to reestablish order and authority in the colony. He had dismissed most other proposals because they "seem to accord with the temper of the times, and are fraught with all the tumult and riot incident to simple democracy." Looking around at events in Virginia over the past year, he worried that there would be too much leveling in a government entirely based on

6. "An Address to the Convention of the Colony and Ancient Dominion of Virginia; on the Subject of Government in General, and Recommending a Particular Form to Their Consideration, by a Native of That Colony," May 4, 1776, *Rev. Va.,* VI, 519, 523–524.

the votes of the people. The history of republics had shown "all the mischiefs which attend Agrarian laws and unjust attempts to maintain their idol equality by an equal division of property."[7]

Braxton was not alone. Patrick Henry, who called Braxton's plan a "silly Thing" and an "Affront and Disgrace to this Country," still worried that there were many supporters of the plan in the convention. He believed that they needed a more radical plan to counter that support in Virginia, "where there is among most of our opulent Familys, a strong Byass to Aristocracy." Significantly, though, most other patriot leaders who have left records agreed with Braxton about the need to preserve rather than innovate. Even the less moderate John Page argued that the best way to "prevent Disorders in each Colony" was to form a government "as nearly resembling the old one as Circumstances, and the Merit of that Constitution will admit of."[8]

Richard Henry Lee proposed one alternative—one that the committee perhaps relied upon more than any other. Lee in turn drew heavily from his New England friend John Adams, who had sent him a proposal back in November 1775, and then a revised version in January after he, Lee, and George Wythe had talked over the previous proposal. Though Lee censured Braxton's proposal, Lee himself was not looking to make too many radical changes either. He said that Adams's plan, which stressed a mixed government and which he liked very much, "with some variation, would in fact, be nearly the form we have been used to." In the end, the Lee-Adams proposal represented a moderate position among convention delegates. Even Patrick Henry approved. "I own my self a Democrat on the plan of our admired Friend, J. Adams," he wrote, as "the sentiments are precisely the same I have long since taken up."[9]

7. Ibid., 521, 522; Richard Henry Lee to Pendleton, May 12, 1776, Paul H. Smith et al., eds., *Letters of Delegates to Congress, 1774–1780* (Washington, D.C., 1976–2000), III, 667.

8. John Page to Jefferson, Apr. 6, 26, 1776, *Papers of Jefferson,* I, 287, 288; Patrick Henry to Adams, May 20, 1776, Robert J. Taylor et al., eds., *Papers of John Adams* (Cambridge, Mass., 1977–), IV, 200–201.

9. See *Papers of Jefferson,* I, 333; R. H. Lee to Robert Carter Nicholas, Apr. 30, 1776, Smith et al., eds., *Letters of Delegates to Congress,* III, 608; John E. Selby, *The Revolution in Virginia, 1775–1783* (Williamsburg, Va., 1988), 113. Boyd et al. give probably the best account of the different proposals for a plan of government (*Papers of Jefferson,* I, 333). R. H. Lee's proposal was written on April 10 and cir-

Though Richard Henry Lee regarded a unicameral legislature as the standard by which to measure how "democratic" a constitution was, he was unwilling to propose such a popular plan. Instead, following Adams, Lee prescribed a popularly elected lower house (without specifying the length of term). The elected delegates, in turn, would choose an upper house of twenty-four men, who would serve for seven years, ensuring some stability. Both houses would choose a governor and a twelve-man council, all of whom would serve for only one year. The governor would be chosen from among delegates in the upper and lower houses. The governor, with the advice of the council, would have the executive powers of government, appoint militia officers, and govern the militia. Judges would also be chosen by a joint ballot of both houses and continued during their good behavior. All other posts, like the secretary, lieutenant governor, commissary, attorney, and solicitor general, would be chosen septennially, and the treasurer annually, by joint ballot of the houses. Justices of the peace and sheriffs would be appointed by the governor with the consent of a majority of the council.[10]

In the end, Lee's plan really differed from Braxton's only in that the tenure of the governor, council, and upper house would not be for life. The key worry for most prominent delegates about a republican government was that, if the people were the basis of all authority, there could be no check on the people themselves. There was still a lingering suspicion among many gentlemen that, in the absence of a king and House of Lords, the new proposals placed too much power in the hands of the people—given that all appointments flowed from the elected representatives. Braxton's proposal that the lower house elect an upper house, council, and governor for life would ensure their future independence from popular demands and would solve that problem. Uncomfortable with life terms, Lee tried to ameliorate the problem by having the lower house elect the upper house for long, seven-year terms.[11]

Though Lee's plan did indeed come close to replicating the kind of government previously employed in Virginia, his plan was still too radical for some. On the only known copy of the original broadside of Lee's plan,

———
culated in Virginia shortly thereafter. It was printed in *Va. Gaz.* (Purdie), May 10, 1776.

10. Proposals for a Form of Government, Apr. 10, 1776, *Rev. Va.*, VI, 367–368; *Va. Gaz.* (Purdie), May 10, 1776.

11. Ibid.

someone registered his unease. "The choice in the people seems the basis of freedom. But yet it is at the same time the worm wch must destroy the happiness wch shd proceed from freedom." The writer worried about the power of ordinary men in a government that derived its power solely from the electorate. "Nothing is so easily corrupted as an ignorant Man, as soon as he gets an Idia, that he is the cornerstone in Public Happiness." Because of his impoverished situation, "an ignorant Man" could not be a proper judge of his leaders. "Activated by his circumstances, he regards not who keeps his foundation the fairest," the writer concluded, "but only who can give his poverty a good relish. And with that any lie will go down, to direct his choice."[12]

• • • On the surface, the "ignorant" men that the anonymous writer mistrusted seemed to have little direct say on the writing of the Constitution. However, direct and indirect evidence indicates that the people out-of-doors exerted considerable influence on the drafting of the Constitution, through their representatives and also through their instructions. At least one county's instructions for its delegates touched upon the form of government and made it clear where its sympathies lay. The freeholders of Buckingham demanded of their delegates that they help "cause a free and happy constitution to be established" and be unafraid to wipe the slate clean. They ordered their delegates to work toward a government in which everything found "inconvenient and oppressive" would be renounced and a "publick jealousy" fixed within the new Constitution as "an essential principle of its support." Though short on details, they made popular representation a priority, and, showing signs of Thomas Paine's influence, they advocated "full representation, free and frequent elections."[13]

Other ideas also reached the ears of the delegates. "Democraticus," for example, wrote a piece in the *Virginia Gazette* in early June arguing for annual elections to "check the aristocratick principle, which always inclines to tyranny." Keeping "the representatives dependent on the people," he argued, would be the best way of doing this. Democraticus also proposed rotating members of the assembly as well, which was the "sure and certain means of diffusing the government into more hands, and training up

12. See *Rev. Va.,* VI, 374. The broadside is lodged in the Chapin Library, Williams College, Williamstown, Mass.

13. Address and Instructions of the freeholders of Buckingham County, [May 13, 1776], *Rev. Va.,* VII, 109–111.

a greater number of able statesmen." Yet even Democraticus still believed that veto power in an upper chamber that was not directly elected was necessary to control any "overgrown popularity" or "arbitrary representative body." He proposed a novel form of election for the upper house, perhaps derived from experience with the county committees: that the upper chamber be composed of only twelve men, to be chosen by a committee in each county who would in turn be chosen by the people.[14]

But if freeholders did not advocate more specific, formal constitutional proposals, they did make appeals for the convention to remedy specific problems identified during the struggle with Britain. Indeed, the Fifth Convention saw the beginning of an unprecedented rise in petitioning among freeholders for specific changes in the laws. Such petitioning reflected an increased expectation that the new government, whatever form it took, had to be more responsive than the old government. Many also implied that those who were doing the fighting ought to be allowed a say in the contest. Taken together, through the recent election and their petitions, freeholders made it clear to delegates that they expected a fully representative new government.

Many of the men involved in the Loudoun protest, for example, legitimized their complaints by drawing up a petition for the Fifth Virginia Convention. They explained that they were suffering because of the cash rents they were still expected to pay. Whereas previously a flourishing trade and a good circulation of money had enabled them to pay their rents on a regular basis, the war had put an end to both. Though the petitioners left it up to the convention delegates to decide what kind of relief they could expect, the implication of their petition was clear. Either the convention had to order landlords to take a big loss on their rental incomes, or patriot leaders had to form commercial alliances to reopen trade so that tenants could pay their rents.[15]

Farmers in other parts of the colony also made similar demands. The instructions given to the Cumberland County representatives also demanded that the delegates find a solution to the problem of exports. Like tenants in

14. *Va. Gaz.* (Purdie), June 7, 1776. Cf. "E.F." in *Va. Gaz.* (Purdie), May 17, 1776.

15. Petition of Sundry Inhabitants of Loudoun County, [June 1, 1776], *Rev. Va.,* VII, 325–326. Though no other formal constitutional proposals are extant, there is no reason to think that the people out-of-doors did not make oral arguments to their representatives on court or election days.

Loudoun, they wanted the convention to do something about the surplus goods they had, which were now "perishing on our Hands thro a Stoppage of Trade." But, unlike Loudoun, farmers in Cumberland gave specific instructions about what to do. They noted with considerable foresight that, if the convention continued to emit paper money to fund the war without laying immediate taxes to support it, the paper money would depreciate. The war would be expensive and would require emissions of paper money "to so great Amount" that it would be ruinous to the public credit. Farmers in Cumberland thus proposed that the convention kill two birds with one stone with a new and radical idea: the convention could "remedy the Evil" of depreciating currency while helping farmers to use the produce that they could not export, by laying an immediate tax that could be payable in produce. Rather than emit more money, the instructions implied that the costs of the war could better be paid in provisions, which could be sold or be given to the increasing army. They thus told the delegates to work toward making the goods people had at hand—the fruits of their own labor—worth something.[16]

If farmers advocated very specific changes in their own interest, they also showed an awareness that they now had some leverage to see those changes effected. Indeed, petitions to the Fifth Convention generally took on a more demanding tone than previously. Several early petitions from inhabitants of western Virginia were typical. Petitioners from western Frederick County, for example, complained about the assessors whom the convention sent to repay expenditures from Dunmore's war at the end of 1775: the assessors were "utterly unacquainted with the Customs and Manners of the Inhabitants of this Wilderness" and had made countless errors and mistakes. They had ignored local valuations, they had undervalued for expensive wagoning, and they had underpaid soldiers. The assessors had, in short, taken hold of the "slightest Pretence, either for making deductions from or for taking from Your Petitioners, their just demands." Though the Frederick petitioners might not have expected any sympathy previously, they reminded the convention that their support for the new conflict was crucial. Many of them, they claimed, were already fighting in the new armed forces or being asked to advance supplies to the military. Ignoring

16. Cumberland County Committee Instructions, Apr. 22, 1776, *Rev. Va.*, VI, 433–434. Cf. Proceedings of the Fifth Virginia Convention, May 13, 1776, *Rev. Va.*, VII, 105, for a petition from Henrico County also asking that they might pay taxes in provisions rather than money.

their grievances, they warned, would have a direct effect on their support of the new conflict. The "greatest damp and discouragement . . . would thereby be thrown on the Cause of Liberty in this their quarter of the Colony."[17]

Petitioners from the newly settled area of Pendleton district in western Fincastle County also made clear demands in return for their support of the war. They told the convention that they had settled illegally on lands outside the "Limits hitherto Purchased by Government from the Indians." As the needs of the convention for troops grew in early 1776, the illegal squatters seized the opportunity. They had "form'd themselves into a Society" and even elected a local Committee of Safety "after the Pattern of the several Virginia Counties." Because they were not recognized and incorporated as a county, though, they were not "under the Immediate Direction of any regularly constituted Judicature" and thus were unable to "contribute their Mite to Support the glorious Cause." Instead, they remained "intirely inactive while their Brethren are brave bleeding in the Field." Their intent was clear: should the convention recognize their land titles and give them self-government as a county, they would join in the conflict with Britain.[18]

17. Petition of the Inhabitants of western Frederick County, [Dec. 7, 1775], *Rev. Va.,* V, 73–74. A similar petition was presented to the convention by inhabitants of Augusta County on Dec. 20, 1775 (see *Rev. Va.,* V, 201). The convention responded by appointing new commissioners on January 16 (Proceedings of the Fourth Virginia Convention, Jan. 16, 1776, *Rev. Va.,* V, 417).

18. Petition of the Committee of Pendleton district, West Fincastle County, Feb. 1, 1776, *Rev. Va.,* VI, 42. Some petitioners from western Fincastle County repeated their demands in a petition drawn up a few months later, warning the convention that they could not "but observe how impolitical it would be to suffer such a Respectable body of Prime Rifle Men, to remain (even) in a state of Neutrallity" at this point in the conflict—parenthetically warning that there was no guarantee that the committee could ensure such men would remain even neutral if they had no legal authority over them. These petitioners also warned that not acknowledging their claims would leave "an Opening to the wicked and Diabolical designs of the Ministry, as then this immense and Fertile Country, would afford a safe Assylum to those whose Principles are inimical to American Liberty" (Petition of the Committee of Western Fincastle County, June 20, 1776, *Rev. Va.,* VII, 565–566; cf. Petition of Inhabitants of the Western Part of Fincastle County, May 1, 1776, *Rev. Va.,* VI, 498). Both petitions were read to the House of Delegates on Oct. 8, 1776, and helped form the justification of the creation of three new counties out of Fincastle County: Kentucky, Montgomery, and Washington Counties (see *Rev. Va.,* VII, 567n; *Jour-*

Religious dissenters also made demands, asserting their rights to a full place in the new republic. In the middle of the Fifth Convention, Baptists from the church in Occaquon in Prince William County petitioned the delegates for greater rights. While the colony was "contending for the [civil rights and] liberties of mankind against the enslaving Scheme of a power[ful Enemy]," they began, it was vital that the "strictest unanimity" prevail. To achieve this, the convention would have to remove the "remainin[g c]ause of animosity and division," which for the Baptists and others meant granting them "several religious pri[vil]eges" that they had never enjoyed in Virginia before. They had not been allowed to "worship God in our own way, without interruption" nor been allowed to maintain their own ministers (and "no other"); nor had they been allowed to marry and be buried without paying the Anglican minister. Only when these rights had been granted would they "gladly unite with our Brethren of other denominations, and to the utmost of our ability, promote the common cause of Freedom."[19]

But, if Baptists were quick to make demands in return for their support of the war, militia told other Dissenters that they had no choice but to support the war. Militia from Frederick and Dunmore Counties claimed that the original ordinance for regulating the militia was unfair because of the exemption it gave to "Quakers and Menonists." Though they had a "tender regard for the Conscientious Scruples of every religious Society," they felt compelled to "represent the injustice of subjecting one part of the Community to the whole burthen of Government while others equally share the benefits of it." They felt conscientious objectors ought to be subjected to an extra payment in lieu of attending musters; and, if the militia was called into service, "they should be draughted in the same proportion as the Militia of the County." If they refused to serve or to provide able-bodied men in their places, they ought to be liable to the same fines as other militia. The petitioners went further, asking whether it might not be reasonable to allow everyone to make such an extra payment instead of attending musters if that is what they wanted. The petitioners also reminded the assembly that they could ignore their petition only at their own peril. The exemption

---

nal of the House of Delegates [Williamsburg, Va., 1776], 4; Hening, comp., Statutes at Large, IX, 257–260).

19. Petition of Baptists of Prince William County, May 19, 1776, Rev. Va., VII, 188–189. Signed by forty-seven people, the petition would be presented to the convention on June 20, 1776.

was "extremely impolitic as well as unjust in the present unsettled state of this Country." If the assembly did not rectify the problem, it would "greatly discourage the People in general from discharging the Duties of a Militia and other necessary impositions."[20]

Petitioners from Dunmore and Frederick Counties were insistent in enforcing the principle that all men were equally involved in the contest with Britain and should therefore bear an equal proportion of the burden of that contest. Other petitions drawn up in the spring of 1776 reinforced the same principle, at the same time echoing the earlier arguments of militants in the volunteer companies who demanded full participation as well as the more class-based complaints of those who felt the minute service was unfair. Hundreds of freeholders, militia, and other inhabitants of Lunenburg, Amelia, Chesterfield, and Mecklenburg Counties in the southside were among the first to make such complaints more explicitly, in April and May 1776. First, they made it clear that they had "hitherto Shown a readiness and Steadiness in Complying" with the previous resolves of the convention. However, they were angry that the new ordinance for raising troops in the colony had unfairly exempted overseers from serving in the militia and from being drafted for active duty. Such a measure, of course, created in the midst of the panic of December 1775, was designed to restore order and control upon larger plantations where slaves were agitating for their own independence. But the petitioners from Lunenburg felt that this benefited many slaveholding planters, because the ordinance stipulated that, for every four enslaved Virginians, a planter could designate one overseer. The petitioners believed that many wealthy planters had "become Overseers that Otherways wou'd not, on purpose to Secure themselves from Fighting in defense of their Country as well as their own property." More than a quarter of the militia from neighboring Amelia County also complained about this exemption. They felt that there were at least "Two Hundred and fifty Overseers"—or another quarter of the whole militia in the county—who were exempted from regular service in the militia. Not only were most of them "Strong healthy able bodied Men," but "Many of them [were] possessed of Considerable Property in Lands and Slaves." The petitioners felt it was unjust that these men were exempt, and they were also suspicious about their inclination for "Patrolling," which, the

20. Proceedings of the Fifth Virginia Convention, June 19, 1776, *Rev. Va.,* VII, 548–549; Petition of the Dunmore County Committee of Safety, July 23, 1776, LiVi.

petitioners felt, "we apprehend will be done but Slightly if intirely trusted to them."[21]

Class differences were clearly at the forefront of such complaints, and the petitioners did not hesitate to make them explicit. "Many of your Petitioners are poor men with Families that are Incapable of Supporting themselves without Our labour and assistance." It was therefore "extreamly hard and no ways equatable or Just that we Shou'd be obliged to leave our Families in such a Situation that if ever we should return again Woud find our Wives and Children dispers'd up and down the Country abeging, or at home aSlaving." "While the Overseers are aliving in ease and Affluance," they complained, the petitioners forced to do military duty away from home would be "quite unable to help" their families procure "the Necessaries of life."[22]

21. Petition of Inhabitants of Lunenburg County, [Apr. 26, 1776], *Rev. Va.,* VI, 475; Petition of Amelia County Militiamen, [May 23, 1776], *Rev. Va.,* VII, 236–237.

22. Petition of Freeholders and Sundry Inhabitants of Mecklenburg County, [May 13, 1776], *Rev. Va.,* VII, 114–115; Petition of Inhabitants of Lunenburg County, [Apr. 26, 1776], *Rev. Va.,* VI, 474–477; Hening, comp., *Statutes at Large,* IX, 28, 31, 89. Cf. Proceedings of the Fifth Virginia Convention, May 10, 1776, *Rev. Va.,* VII, 87, for a similar petition from Chesterfield County (the actual petition has never been found). Allan Kulikoff discusses the struggle over exemptions of overseers and its significance in "The American Revolution, Capitalism, and the Formation of the Yeoman Classes," in Alfred F. Young, ed., *Beyond the American Revolution: Explorations in the History of American Radicalism* (DeKalb, Ill., 1993), 80–119.

These petitions came from counties that had recently experienced a huge influx of enslaved Virginians. In the closing years of the colonial period, there was a massive increase of slave imports up the James River to counties further inland. The southern piedmont and southside counties also experienced the greatest growth in tobacco production, matching the increased reliance on enslaved labor. By the end of the war, one of the petitioning counties, Amelia, had the largest proportion of black inhabitants of any Chesapeake county, with well more than 60 percent. While farmers who had not benefited or could not benefit from the massive importation of slaves worried about their patriarchy if they served in the militia, planters who did take advantage of the prewar boom were clearly anxious about the new arrivals. The presence of so many new enslaved Virginians in the area clearly caused considerable anxiety among all inhabitants, but for different reasons. Richard S. Dunn, "Black Society in the Chesapeake, 1776–1810," in Ira Berlin and Ronald Hoffman,

Militia from Chesterfield County also made particular claims based on their interests as a class. Noting that the previous ordinance called for militia musters every two weeks, they complained that this requirement was now unnecessary and onerous. Not only had they learned the "the most essential parts of the Military exercise," but they now also had "an Army regularly trained" and, they might have added, for which they were paying. Under these circumstances, the militia ought to be called out only in defense against an invasion, and they ought not to be called "so frequently from their homes" unless absolutely "necessary." In their argument that the payment of taxes was sufficient sacrifice to secure their protection, the militia from Chesterfield adopted a transatlantic position. But, if they implied that a different—lower—class of men should do the fighting in the regular army in their place, they also lashed out at their wealthier, slaveholding neighbors, putting a local spin on their transatlantic position. They complained that fortnightly militia musters were particularly "burthensome" for "the poorer sort who have not a slave to labour for them" in their absence.[23]

Other petitions made similar class-based complaints. Hundreds of Spotsylvania militia, for example, did not hesitate to complain that they were subject to a "very great Hardship" in traveling some twenty to thirty miles to attend general, countywide musters, "which are Constantly appointed at the Courthouse in Fredericksburg," which was on one side of the county. Defying their commanding officer, they hoped the convention would pass an ordinance directing the muster to be held in the center of the county. Likewise, inhabitants of Cumberland County cited the hardships of militia musters and duty, given the large size of the county. The length of the county—up to seventy miles long—was a particular problem for poorer farmers. Attendance at general musters was generally "a grievance to the poorer Sort of people as they are Compell'd to take their Horses from the plough and to be absent for three Days together." Many militia, now forced

eds., *Slavery and Freedom in the Age of the American Revolution* (Charlottesville, Va., 1983), 58–59.

23. Proceedings of the Fifth Virginia Convention, May 7, 1776, *Rev. Va.,* VII, 47; Hening, comp., *Statutes at Large,* IX, 140; Eliga H. Gould, *The Persistence of Empire: British Political Culture in the Age of the American Revolution* (Chapel Hill, N.C., 2000), esp. 72–105; Gould, "To Strengthen the King's Hands: Dynastic Legitimacy, Militia Reform, and Ideas of National Unity in England, 1745–1760," *Historical Journal,* XXXIV (1991), 329–348.

into training and service for the first time in their lives, demanded concessions in return for that service. Some of these grievances seem petty to us now, but, for small farmers who had to labor for their subsistence and livelihood, one extra muster per month, or an extra day of traveling to that muster, could make or break that farm's prosperity for the coming year.[24]

Behind most of these petitions, of course, were implicit and explicit grievances of a more political kind. Petitioners from Cumberland, for example, were angry that wealthier legislators had neglected their interests when they drew up mobilization plans. But they were also more generally angry that their long-standing desire to divide the county had gone unheard for several years. They had petitioned to divide the county previously, they asserted, but to no avail. Thus "for a long Series of years" they had "labour under very great inconveniency arising form the Size of the County." Because of this, they complained that they lived without proper access to the law. Not only did the length of the county, up to seventy miles, stop some of them from attending militia musters, but it also hindered the collection of small debts or forced farmers into risking the loss of more money by trying to sue in the courts. Moreover, they could never obtain warrants without going so great a distance from home "as no Gentlemen will undertake the Office of a Justice of the peace." The size of the county also meant that the petitioners felt completely bereft of proper political representation. Because of the distances, they rarely could "fully enjoy their Votes at Elections as they cannot attend without injuring their Families." Consequently, "the Representatives of this County have not for Several Years past had the Voice of more than one half the Freeholders." And the Cumberland petitioners went further. The signers—who included only one member of the county committee—hinted darkly that they were oppressed by local leaders as much as the colonists were oppressed by ministers in Britain. A division of the county had been "neglected thro' the interest of a few interested individuals in power." Supplicating petitions for divisions of counties were common in the colonial period. These petitions demanded immediate action and came with implicit and explicit warnings. While they were fighting Britain for their rights and liberties, the suppression of their rights and liberties at home was unjust. The mention of militia musters re-

24. Petition of Freeholders and Inhabitants of Spotsylvania County, [June 8, 1776], *Rev. Va.,* VII, 404; Proceedings of the Fifth Virginia Convention, [June 20, 1776], *Rev. Va.,* VII, 562–563.

minded convention delegates that they now had some leverage to demand those rights.[25]

Starting with the Fifth Virginia Convention, then, freeholders increasingly asserted themselves through petitions. The number of petitions drawn up on diverse issues rose dramatically during the war, beginning in 1776. Though a more traditional form of communication, the new petitions drawn up in the spring and fall of 1776 were no less demanding than the instructions farmers gave to their delegates. Moreover, the petitions sent in to the Fifth Convention by freeholders indirectly asserted new principles—principles implicitly based on more egalitarian notions than previously and assuming a more representative and responsive republican government. The petitions also took on a new tone. Many of them sent in to the Fifth Convention in the spring of 1776 began or ended with an assertion of the petitioners' moral authority and legitimacy in asking for changes. The petitioners were always quick to point out their past and future support in the conflict with Britain. But implicit or explicit in their petitions was the warning that that support was contingent upon their views' being taken seriously by their representatives. Patriot leaders' authority, petitioners reminded the convention at their critical constitution-creating session, depended on the people.[26]

• • • Perhaps the written constitutional proposal that most reflected this sentiment was Thomas Jefferson's "Draft of a Constitution." Jefferson's plan, of all the written proposals extant, shows the influence of the people out-of-doors most directly. Jefferson called for the greatest changes between the old government and the new. His plan also put more power into

25. Proceedings of the Fifth Virginia Convention, [June 20, 1776], *Rev. Va.,* VII, 562–563. Other freeholders also used the imperial conflict to try to settle long-standing local grievances. See Petition of Sundry Inhabitants of Stratton Major Parish, King and Queen County, May 2, 1776, *Rev. Va.,* VI, 507, 510n. Cf. the petition of inhabitants of Newport Parish in Isle of Wight County to the Fifth Virginia Convention. They also asserted their right "to be Truly Represented in the Vestray, as that body of men have it in their power to give the greatest part of their Money away" ([June 2, 1776], *Rev. Va.,* VII, 333).

26. For an analysis of the role that instructions and petitions played in the minds of framers of the new state constitutions more generally, see Marc W. Kruman, *Between Authority and Liberty: State Constitution Making in Revolutionary America* (Chapel Hill, N.C., 1997), esp. 61–86.

the hands of the people than all the other plans. The house of representatives would have broad powers—to appoint the governor and privy council, to take over the prerogatives normally reserved to the king, and to appoint the delegates to congress, the treasurer, and the attorney general. This lower house would be elected annually. In another radical suggestion, Jefferson advocated representation in the house proportional to population, with no more than 300 representatives in total and no fewer than 125. Thus more populous western counties would be better represented. Additionally, Jefferson wanted to ensure that the new government had the clear support of at least most white male Virginians. Jefferson wanted the new form of government, after amendment by the convention, to be submitted to the people through county assemblies and be adopted only if two-thirds of the counties ratified it. Any alterations to these "fundamental laws and principles of government" could be made only by a popular vote of two-thirds of the counties.[27]

Though Jefferson had originally proposed to make appointments to the upper house, or senate, for life, his final draft proposal reflected a change in thinking. Nobody would be appointed for life in his final draft, and Jefferson was careful to severely limit the power of the upper house and of the governor. The lower house would have the power to appoint the governor and the senate, which would consist of no more than fifty members and no fewer than fifteen. But Jefferson imposed no property qualification for senators and stipulated a limited term of office. They were to serve three years, with one-third replaced annually; once having served, they were ineligible for a new appointment. Jefferson called his executive figure the "Administrator," thereby designating what he saw as the main role of the new governor. The administrator was to act for only one year and be eli-

27. Thomas Jefferson, Draft of a Constitution, [June 12, 1776], *Rev. Va.,* VII, 460–463. Jefferson sent a copy of his plan with George Wythe when Wythe left Philadelphia on June 13. Wythe passed it to Pendleton, who showed it to the committee before it ended its deliberations. Jefferson also included a lengthy preamble, much of it repeated verbatim in Jefferson's version of the Declaration of Independence, and an unequivocal statement that the legislative, executive, and judiciary offices would be kept separate. No one could hold office in more than one branch at a time. Jefferson then divided his lengthy plan into sections on the legislative, executive, and judicial branches, followed by a long list of private and public rights. At the county level, Jefferson maintained the appointment of magistrates by the administrator, but high sheriffs and coroners were to be elected by the freeholders, and sheriffs were to be allowed to serve only one year and then wait five years.

gible to serve again only after three years. Though Jefferson stipulated the governor have "the powers formerly held by the king," he severely circumscribed these. The administrator would have no power to veto legislative bills, and he would be liable for actions for private duties and wrongs. He would have no prerogative to dissolve, prorogue, or adjourn the assembly or to declare war or conclude peace. All of these prerogatives and others were now to be reserved to the legislature. A privy council appointed by the house of representatives would aid and advise the administrator.[28]

Though Jefferson's plan arrived in Virginia too late for the committee to use it as a starting point—and it was probably considered too radical by the committee to adopt wholesale—parts of it were incorporated into the plan of government that the committee produced. But even more striking were the significant alterations made to the final plan that went further than *any* of the extant written proposals in establishing a more representative government. Indeed, perhaps the best evidence of a more popular influence on the constitutional proposals can be seen by comparing the committee's first plan, drawn up principally by George Mason, with the actual final plan of government.[29]

Mason's original plan was in most important respects quite conservative. Like Jefferson's, Mason's plan separated the legislative, executive, and judiciary branches. It called for a lower house of assembly to be elected annually, but stipulated that representatives had to be at least twenty-four years of age and own at least one thousand pounds worth of land. The upper house would consist of twenty-four members elected by a unique electoral college of subelectors. The colony would be divided into twenty-four districts, and every county would be allowed to elect twelve deputies, or subelectors, who had to own an estate of at least five hundred pounds. The deputies would then choose by ballot for the upper house someone at least twenty-eight years old and owning at least two thousand pounds

28. Thomas Jefferson, Draft of a Constitution, [June 12, 1776], *Rev. Va.*, VII, 460–462. For Jefferson's original plan, including his provision to appoint senators for life, see Jefferson's First Draft, [before June 13, 1776], *Papers of Jefferson*, I, 337–345, 341.

29. Mason did have a full plan of his own, but the only extant version of it is the altered "Plan of Government" laid before the committee, between June 8 and 10. It is impossible to tell how much of this plan was solely Mason's and how much had been changed in the committee. For a full explanation of the proposals, see *Papers of Mason*, I, 295–299. Cf. John E. Selby, "Richard Henry Lee, John Adams, and the Virginia Constitution of 1776," *VMHB*, LXXXIV (1976), 387–400.

worth of land. To ensure stability, each year only six members of the upper house would be replaced in rotation. To ensure continuity, Mason wanted the present convention to elect the first group of members of the upper house, to serve until elections the following March. Thus did Mason and the committee try to bridge the gap between the proposals of Braxton and Richard Henry Lee. Members of the upper house, which had the power to reject legislation, would only be indirectly elected by the people, would be elected at arm's length, in districts, and would have to be very wealthy men, who would safeguard the interests of property. The governor and an eight-man council would be annually elected by joint ballot of both houses and be allowed to serve for only three years. The executive power would have the authority to prorogue or adjourn the assembly, the power of militia appointments and the government of the militia, and the appointment of justices of the peace.[30]

This original committee draft then went through a number of changes both in the committee and in the convention as a whole. The most obvious influence on the final draft of the Constitution came from Jefferson's late intervention, but other, more radical ideas also found their way into the final draft. Mason wrote about his troubles controlling the committee and the interventions of the convention as a whole when the plans were discussed. Indeed, even despite the weighting of the committee, Mason felt that there were too many interests at play. The committee was actually too "overcharged with useless Members" (a problem, he acknowledged, that was "not mended by the late Elections"). He worried that they would have a "thousand ridiculous and impracticable proposals, and of Course, a Plan form'd of hetrogenious, jarring and unintelligible Ingredients." Thomas Ludwell Lee also saw different conflicts and factions developing among convention members. There was a "certain junto, who never fail to exert themselves against every measure of sense and spirit." He also complained about "a certain set of Aristocrates," who were "by a thousand masterly fetches and stratagems" obstructing the more radical work of the convention. Years later, Randolph recollected that Mason had trouble controlling such conflicts. Randolph also noted that it was a "very large committee" that was charged with preparing a constitution, and many plans for it "dis-

---

30. "A Plan of Government," [June 8-10, 1776], *Papers of Mason,* I, 299–302. Mason might have drawn from his earlier speeches to the independent companies in advocating annual elections. His proposal was the only one to specifically suggest this. The proposal stuck.

covered the ardor for political notice rather than a ripeness in political wisdom." Even "the most expanded mind" of Mason, Randolph complained,
could not "secure itself from oversights and negligences in the tumult of
heterogeneous and indistinct ideas of government circulating in a popular
body unaccustomed to much abstraction."[31]

In the end, both "Aristocrates" and the popular "junto" scored important
victories in the final plan of government, reflecting the complexities of the
Revolutionary situation and the competing interests at play between those
keen to "maintain peace and order" and those advocating more "substantial and equal liberty to the people." For example, conservatives blocked
any kind of reform of the representational districts or of the suffrage. There
were proposals to do so. In Maryland, the people out-of-doors demanded
that anyone who bore arms in defense of his country ought to get the vote.
George Mason, living among discontented tenants in the upper Northern
Neck, wanted to extend the suffrage to those with long-term leases of seven
years. He also proposed reducing the property requirement to the simple
possession of a house, which would make white males liable for property
taxes, thus giving them, in Mason's eyes, the right to representation. But
Mason also revealed a more patriarchal view of society: he thought anyone
with at least three children should be allowed to vote. Jefferson proposed
an even bolder reform. Instead of lowering the property requirements for
voting, he suggested giving every adult male who did not own or had never
owned land fifty acres "in full and absolute dominion"—and entitle him to
vote and hold office. Lower-class whites would thus be given a stake in preserving society amid revolution.[32]

31. George Mason to R. H. Lee, May 18, 1776, *Papers of Mason,* I, 271; Thomas
Ludwell Lee to R. H. Lee, June 1, 1776, Hoffman, ed., *Lee Family Papers;* Edmund
Randolph, *History of Virginia,* ed. Arthur H. Shaffer (Charlottesville, Va., 1970),
252, 258. Jefferson later said that the Constitution had been fought over "inch by
inch" (*Papers of Jefferson,* I, 337). For the presence of a more radical faction, see
Randolph, *History of Virginia,* ed. Shaffer, 255; Pendleton to Jefferson, July 22,
1776, *Papers of Pendleton,* I, 188.

32. Proceedings of the Fifth Virginia Convention, May 15, 1776, *Rev. Va.,* VII,
143; Ronald Hoffman, *A Spirit of Dissension: Economics, Politics, and the Revolution in Maryland* (Baltimore, 1973), 169-172; John Parke Custis to George Washington, Aug. 8, 1776, George Bolling Lee Letters, VHS; A Plan of Government,
[June 8-10, 1776], *Papers of Mason,* I, 300; Jefferson, Draft of a Constitution,
[June 12, 1776], *Rev. Va.,* VII, 460-462, 464-466, 471n. Later in the war, in the
1780s, Jefferson finally addressed the problem of men who had to fight for the de-

But most convention delegates were unwilling to take the risk in the uncertain and Revolutionary situation. Many patriot leaders believed the lower classes, both white and black, were causing the most trouble for the patriot movement. Many gentlemen in the colony believed the disaffected were generally ill- and uninformed whites who had been led astray, and they were troubled by class-based criticisms of mobilization plaguing the resistance movement that stressed the burden imposed on poor people in particular. Moreover, many gentlemen worried about the "plebeian Infamy" that had beset committee elections the previous fall and the "spirit of Levelling" that they believed lurked behind the Loudoun County uprising. Thinking that lower-class and mainly propertyless Virginians were responsible for the disorders in the colony and knowing that the government now wanted to place heavier demands on them to serve in the army, at least patriot leaders were hesitant to extend the suffrage to any more of this volatile, potentially much more disaffected group. The "right of suffrage" in the final plan of government would "remain as exercised at present."[33]

The complex consequences of the struggles over the past year can also be seen in the provisions for local government. None of the extant proposals suggested changing county government or, in particular, the appointments of county court justices. The convention guaranteed the power of local elites and the authority of local magistrates by perpetuating the colonial practice of allowing the governor and council to issue commissions for the appointment of justices, militia officers, and other county officials on the recommendations of the county courts. Thus, these positions remained dependent on the self-nomination of the local courts themselves. Significantly, the only approved breach in the separation-of-powers clause was the provision that enabled justices of the county courts to sit in the assembly.[34]

---

fense of the state and pay taxes, yet were unrepresented in government. In his *Notes on the State of Virginia* he asserted that as much as a "majority" of men in the state, "who pay and fight for its support, are unrepresented in the legislature." The rolls of freeholders allowed to vote did not include even half of those on the rolls of the militia or half of taxpayers. Thomas Jefferson, *Notes on the State of Virginia,* ed. William Peden (Chapel Hill, N.C., 1954), 118.

33. Proceedings of the Fifth Virginia Convention, June 29, 1776, *Rev. Va.,* VII, 650–652.

34. Ibid., 650, 653–654. The governor and council would also have the power of removing any militia officer "on complaint of misbehaviour or inability." Judges could be removed for misbehavior subject to the determination of the General Court.

While following with tradition, these important provisions testified to the persistent localism of most elite Virginians, and particularly to their anxieties over their recent near loss of control over local politics. We know that more than a few gentlemen were shaken by their experience with the popularly elected county committees. Later in the war, for example, some gentlemen looked back to the time of the popular "rule of the committees" with some disgust. It was the patriot committees—"these little democracies"—that were satirized in Robert Munford's play, *The Patriots*. Munford, of course, had already suffered indignities from the popular independent companies. After throwing in his lot with the patriots, Munford continued to be disturbed by the popularization of the movement, especially as manifested in the county committees. In his play, written in early 1777 after the committees had been replaced by the reestablishment of the courts, Munford complained that committeemen had been elected only because they were popular. As a result, they could not be trusted as impartial judges. As Meanwell, a protagonist, lamented when the committees acted as a court, "Both property and characters lie at the mercy of those tribunals." Local affairs, then, would remain in the hands of appointed magistrates.[35]

Though local government and the suffrage remained intact, the most impressive victories at the convention were claimed by those advocating greater representation and a more responsive government. In the final draft of the Constitution, the preamble was almost verbatim from Jefferson's plan, and, following Jefferson, the committee called for the separation of the legislative, executive, and judicial powers. Significantly, elections for the assembly would be held every year. The assembly would meet at least once a year and comprise a lower and an upper house. The upper house would consist of twenty-four members, as Mason had suggested, but the convention stripped away Mason's plan for an electoral college as well as provisions set out in every other written plan to indirectly elect the upper house. Instead, the final draft called for direct election to the upper house. Gone too were Mason's property requirements for representatives. The

35. Courtlandt Canby, ed., "Robert Munford's *The Patriots*," *WMQ*, 3d Ser., VI (1949), 437–503, quotes from 450, 458. Cf. Meriwether Smith to Thomas Jefferson, June 25, 1779, *Papers of Jefferson*, III, 16, for another retrospective criticism of the popularity of the county committees. See also Michael A. McDonnell, "A World Turned 'Topsy Turvy': Robert Munford, *The Patriots*, and the Crisis of Revolution in Virginia," *WMQ*, 3d Ser., LXI (2004), 235–270.

governor would be elected annually by a joint ballot of both houses, as would eight members of the privy council, or council of state. The councillors could be chosen from the people at large, or from among standing members of the assembly, and two members of the council would have to rotate out of office every three years. A governor could serve for only three successive years, after which he would have to remain out of office for four years.[36]

Thus the final plan of government called for "full" and "frequent" elections and placed all power directly into the hands of the electorate. None of the extant proposals for a plan of government put so much power directly into the hands of enfranchised Virginians. The directly and annually elected lower house of the assembly was the most important part of government, but, incredibly, Virginia was the first state to mandate the popular election of the upper house as well as the lower house. Indeed, there would be little check on the more popular lower house by the upper house or the governor. Thus, propertied interests were unprotected from popular rule. With the lower house retaining most of the power, then, delegates to the convention formed a government that, while not quite as radical in form as in Pennsylvania, certainly came close to being a very democratic government.[37]

36. Proceedings of the Fifth Virginia Convention, June 29, 1776, *Rev. Va.,* VII, 650–652. Cf. Pendleton to Jefferson, Aug. 10, 1776, *Papers of Pendleton,* I, 197–198. The final plan also changed the name of the upper house to Senate and required that those elected also live in the district that they intended to represent and be over the age of twenty-five. Six of the twenty-four senators were to be rotated out of office every year (Proceedings of the Fifth Virginia Convention, June 29, 1776, *Rev. Va.,* VII, 650–654).

37. K. R. Constantine Gutzman, "Old Dominion, New Republic: Making Virginia Republican, 1776–1840" (Ph.D. diss., University of Virginia, 1999), 84, 88; Willi Paul Adams, *The First American Constitutions: Republican Ideology and the Making of the State Constitutions in the Revolutionary Era* (Chapel Hill, N.C., 1980), 267–268; Selby, *Revolution in Virginia,* 112. J. R. Pole, a leading scholar of the Virginia Constitution, concluded: "Virginia emerged from the debris of royal government with a firm foundation of legislative power. . . . All the principal powers were gathered into the hands of the two Houses of the legislature, [and] both of these were based on elections by freeholders" (*Political Representation in England and the Origins of the American Republic* [London, 1966], 292–293; cf. Jackson Turner Main, *The Sovereign States, 1775–1783* [New York, 1973], 158). In August, Pendleton told Jefferson that he thought the new Constitution would "require all

Significantly, the final product came as something of a surprise to some of the leading patriots. John Adams had composed *Thoughts on Government* with the more aristocratic temper of the southern colonies in mind. Indeed, he thought his plan would be "not popular enough" in New England, but "in the Southern Colonies . . . too popular." Afterward, he found that the Virginia Constitution was "remarkably popular, more so than I could ever have imagined, even more popular than Thoughts on Government." And Richard Henry Lee, who had supported a gubernatorial veto and seven-year terms for indirectly elected senate members and all executive officers except the governor, told Charles Lee assuringly that the Virginia government turned out to be "very much of the democratic kind."[38]

Such a result, however, was perhaps expected in light of the many different struggles leading up to the adoption of the new Constitution. In the first place, many small farmers, angry with the way the Revolution was being run, had elected men they believed would secure Independence and a more democratic form of government. Simultaneously, with rebellious slaves in mind as well as restive lower-class Virginians of dubious allegiance, many leading gentlemen began to see their own best interests in placating their middle-class neighbors. To shore up an uncertain alliance with middling Virginians, patriot leaders could afford to make the legislature more powerful and more representative. Indeed, retaining the colonial suffrage qualifications while making the legislature more representative and democratic, patriot leaders could with one stroke offer something to their middle-class neighbors while denying it to other Virginians. In doing so, they could believe that they were shoring up support for the patriot cause while restoring order and their authority.[39]

To reinforce this alliance, patriot leaders in the Fifth Convention also directly responded to many of the insistent complaints of freeholders who

the Attention of its Friends to prune exuberances and Cherish the Plant." Pendleton admitted that he wanted to make the election of senators for life, and "to have been chosen out of the people of great property to secure their Attachment." But this "seemed so disagreeable to the temper of the times I never mentioned it" (Pendleton to Jefferson, Aug. 10, 1776, *Papers of Pendleton,* I, 197–198).

38. Selby, *Revolution in Virginia,* 113; Richard Henry Lee to Charles Lee, June 27, 1776, James Curtis Ballagh, ed., *The Letters of Richard Henry Lee* (New York, 1911), I, 203.

39. At the same time, convention delegates also took measures to strengthen the new state, against both internal and external threats. See Hening, comp., *Statutes at Large,* IX, 102, 130.

sent in petitions. For example, the convention repealed the exemption for overseers in the militia, thus appeasing one of the largest and loudest groups of petitioners and suppressing one of the most damning complaints about mobilization. The delegates also repealed the military exemptions granted to Quakers and Mennonites. Thus, by 1776, almost all prewar exemptions from militia service had ended, including those for doctors, millers, tobacco inspectors, faculty and students at the College of William and Mary, and boat pilots. Even free blacks were supposed to be enrolled in the militia. The convention also reduced the number of private musters of the militia, further alleviating the demands made on middling Virginians. To counter complaints about their costs, the convention also reduced the number of delegates to Congress and reduced their expenses. Finally, the delegates in the Fifth Convention held over most of the other petitions presented in the session, keeping alive the possibility that they would be answered. Most of the petitions did eventually result in positive change.[40]

40. For overseers, pacifists, and private musters, see Proceedings of the Fifth Virginia Convention, June 15, 1776, *Rev. Va.,* VII, 504, 505; Hening, comp., *Statutes at Large,* IX, 139–140. For exemptions in general, Allan Kulikoff, *The Agrarian Origins of American Capitalism* (Charlottesville, Va., 1992), 156; John David McBride, "The Virginia War Effort, 1775–1783: Manpower Policies and Practices" (Ph.D. diss., University of Virginia, 1977), 43–44; Arthur J. Alexander, "Exemption from Military Service in the Old Dominion during the War of the Revolution," *VMHB,* LIII (1945), 163–171. The convention found the petition from Cumberland County reasonable, and, despite a series of counterpetitions, the assembly eventually divided the county in early 1777 (see *Rev. Va.,* VII, 564n). The petitioners from Pendleton district were also granted their wish later in the year, amid even greater manpower demands (see *Rev. Va.,* VI, 44n). And the petition from King and Queen County complaining about their vestry was presented to the Fifth Convention on June 15, 1776, held over until October 1776, whereupon new legislation was initiated that would result in a law correcting the situation in the spring of 1777 (see Proceedings of the Fifth Virginia Convention, June 15, 1776, *Rev. Va.,* VI, 504, 513–514n; Hening, comp., *Statutes at Large,* IX, 317–318). For the reduction of the numbers of delegates to Congress, see Proceedings of the Fifth Virginia Convention, June 20, 1776, *Rev. Va.,* VII, 557. For the convention's response to the Baptist petition, see below. Finally, the convention also made a promise to western squatters: that anyone who was settled on any unlocated or unappropriated lands in Virginia to which there was no other just claim would have preemption rights when the land was eventually granted. At the same time, the convention made it clear that claims to the lands by speculators would not be honored unless they were

Perhaps most significantly, though, the Virginia Declaration of Rights, which accompanied the Constitution, offered some fundamental protections for at least those in "a state of society." Principally authored by George Mason, the Virginia Declaration of Rights was one of the more revolutionary innovations of the day and influenced radicals everywhere in America and, later, France. For Virginians, it importantly softened the lack of changes to the county courts. Mason claimed in it that the power of magistrates was vested in the people, and thus at all times magistrates had to be amenable to them. No men were entitled to exclusive or separate emoluments and privileges from the community, except in return for public services, and no office, including of judge, magistrate, and legislator, was hereditary. Several clauses ensured the right of trial by jury and protection from excessive bail, fines, cruel and unusual punishments, and unwarranted searches and seizure. Finally, the Declaration held out the promise of future reform to freeholders. Government could be altered if it was found inadequate to provide for the "common benefit, protection, and security" of the people. If a majority of the community found it wanting, they had an "indubitable, unalienable, and indefeasible right, to reform, alter, or abolish it, in such manner as shall be judged most conducive to the publick weal." Mason, who wanted to include suffrage reform in his draft of the Constitution, also tried to leave the door open for future change here, too. Article 6 of the Declaration provided that elections for representatives ought to be free and that "all men, having sufficient evidence of permanent common interest with, and attachment to, the community, have the right of suffrage."[41]

More practically, the Declaration of Rights also shows the influence of the people out-of-doors in at least two other important respects. Dissenters, and particularly Baptists, had been vocal in their support for the patriot cause. The new government held out the promise of payback. Mason's first draft of the Declaration provided that "all Men shou'd enjoy the fullest Toleration in the Exercise of Religion, according to the Dictates of Con-

---

purchased from the Indians with the approbation of the Virginia legislature (see Proceedings of the Fifth Virginia Convention, June 24, 1776, *Rev. Va.,* VII, 593).

41. Final Draft of the Virginia Declaration of Rights, [June 12, 1776], *Papers of Mason,* I, 287–289. J. R. Pole notes that the Declaration of Rights was key to making the government in Virginia "weighted on the popular side" (*Political Representation,* 292–293). For the influence of the Declaration of Rights, see Selby, *Revolution in Virginia,* 103.

science." But toleration alone was inadequate in light of the sacrifices that Baptists and other Dissenters had said they were prepared to make in the growing conflict. James Madison made a bid to reward those sacrifices. He first proposed that they replace the provision for toleration with a clause that stated, "No man or class of men ought, on account of religion to be invested with peculiar emoluments or privileges." This would have ended the established church in Virginia. However, perhaps to disarm conservative opposition in the convention, he offered an alternative, including the clause, "All men are equally entitled to the free exercise of religion, according to the dictates of conscience." The Dissenters did not get disestablishment immediately, but they did get more than toleration.[42]

Enslaved Virginians also made an impact on the new Constitution. The power of enslaved Virginians' own rebellion was revealed in the controversy over the first line of the Declaration of Rights as proposed by George Mason, that all men were "born equally free and independant, and have certain inherent natural Rights." Thomas Ludwell Lee reported on June 1 that the report was delayed by the "Aristocrats . . . [who upon] finding that their execrable system cannot be reared on such foundations, have to this time kept us at bay on the first line, which declares all men to be born equally free and independent." Though the provision was "approved by a very great majority," the conservatives, led by Robert Carter Nicholas, were concerned that such a promise might lead to an open slave insurrection in an already overheated climate of rebellion and resistance. Nicholas believed it would be a "forerunner of . . . civil convulsion." More moderate men struck a compromise. The final version read that "all men are by nature equally free and independent, and have certain inherent rights, of which, when they enter into a state of society," they cannot be deprived. By making these subtle changes, the members of the convention could sidestep the issue by pointing out that enslaved Virginians were simply not members of civil society—and thus had no claim to the "inherent" but, now, not "natural" rights. Apart from this cautionary provision, enslaved Virginians, who had resisted and continued to resist white patriots in their conflict with Britain, were ignored in the new Constitution.[43]

42. First Draft of the Virginia Declaration of Rights, [circa May 20–26, 1776], Final Draft of the Virginia Declaration of Rights, [June 12, 1776], *Papers of Mason,* I, 278, 289, 290–291n.

43. Randolph, *History of Virginia,* ed. Shaffer, 253; Final Draft of the Virginia Declaration of Rights, [June 12, 1776], *Papers of Mason,* I, 287, 289n.

• • • Finally, the changes in the legislature and the turmoil over the last year help explain the election of the radical and popular Patrick Henry to the new position of governor. The delegates voted for the governorship on the same day they adopted the final plan of a new government, June 29, 1776. The balloting stood at sixty votes for Henry. Thomas Nelson, the president of the previous royal council, got forty-five, with one for John Page. The voting was unambiguous—Henry could have received more votes. Some more radical men in the convention might have voted for Nelson, in hope of attracting more conservative gentlemen into the fold, as Richard Henry Lee advocated when he campaigned for Nelson. Nelson's serving would dampen the fears of the conservatives, as he would possess "the knowledge, experience, and has already been in a dignified station."[44]

Given the enemies among other patriot leaders that Henry had made over the previous year and his relative lack of wealth, status, and prestige when compared to someone like Nelson, it is surprising that Henry did so well in the balloting. However, Henry's election was facilitated by two factors. In the first place, delegates could hardly ignore Henry's popularity among ordinary Virginians. His election as Virginia's first state governor —the man who angered conservatives and moderates with his militancy at the head of the volunteer companies, the man whose resignation from command of the regular troops threw the soldiery into "deep mourning"— would help shore up support for the new government among his followers.

At the same time, the delegates had just finished neutralizing the office of the governor in the new government. The final draft of the Constitution had stripped away virtually all of the executive's customary powers. The governor could, with the council, grant reprieves or pardons, but he could not prorogue, adjourn, or dissolve the assembly, as provided for in Mason's plan. More significantly, the governor had no power to veto any legislation. According to Jefferson, who also advocated a vastly weakened executive power, the governor would be a mere "Administrator." Henry himself agreed, complaining that without any power, and especially any veto, the governor would be "a mere phantom." Instead, real power lay in the legislature, and conservatives were more interested in retaining control

44. Proceedings of the Fifth Virginia Convention, June 29, 1776, *Rev. Va.,* VII, 654–655, 658–659n; R. H. Lee to Robert Carter Nicholas, Apr. 30, 1776, R. H. Lee to Pendleton, May 12, 1776, Smith et al., eds., *Letters of Delegates to Congress,* III, 608, 667. Cf. Emory G. Evans, *Thomas Nelson of Yorktown: Revolutionary Virginian* (Williamsburg, Va., 1975), 59.

there. When the convention reconvened as the first General Assembly in the fall of 1776, Edmund Pendleton was again elected speaker of the House. Indeed, with Henry out of the House, moderate and conservative patriot leaders might have believed that they would very easily have the run of the floor. Henry's election to the prestigious position of governor, then, served two badly needed purposes. By placing him at the head of the new government, patriots of all persuasions could hope to bolster popular support for the authority of the new regime. At the same time, more cautious patriots could also acquiesce in Henry's appointment because it removed him from the House and put him into what many thought would be a powerless position. Moreover, the convention then elected a conservative group of councillors to act as Henry's advisers. The hotspur was, once again, neutralized.[45]

45. Proceedings of the Fifth Virginia Convention, June 29, 1776, *Rev. Va.,* VII, 650–652; Thomas Jefferson, Draft of a Constitution, [June 12, 1776], *Rev. Va.,* VII, 462; Randolph, *History of Virginia,* ed. Shaffer, 256. Historians have generally concurred with these sentiments. Pole, for example, called the governorship "largely . . . a decorative and symbolic office" (see *Political Representation,* 284; cf. Emory G. Evans, "Executive Leadership in Virginia, 1776–1781: Henry, Jefferson, and Nelson," in Ronald Hoffman and Peter J. Albert, eds., *Sovereign States in an Age of Uncertainty* [Charlottesville, Va., 1981], 185–186). For the election of the more conservative group for the council, see Proceedings of the Fifth Virginia Convention, June 29, 1776, July 1, 1776, *Rev. Va.,* VII, 654–655, 659n, 667–668, 681.

PART THREE

The Limits of Allegiance

CHAPTER 8 *Fit for Common Service?*

MOBILIZATION PROBLEMS, 1776–1777

Even before delegates in the Fifth Virginia Convention could adjourn, there were obvious reminders that declaring Independence did not guarantee winning Independence. Though patriot leaders took bold steps to reassert authority over the Revolution, they could do little to control external threats and dangers. Dunmore continued at large, roaming the waters of the Chesapeake until the beginning of August. Even when he sailed north to join the British forces amassing at New York, rumors of his impending return at the head of a much larger British expedition haunted patriot leaders for the rest of the year. New state leaders also had to contend with a pan-Indian attack on their western flanks.

Pressed on all sides, state leaders struggled to balance the competing demands on their military abilities, particularly in choosing whether to put the needs of the new state ahead of the needs of the new union upon whose alliance they depended. That struggle was complicated by divisions among Virginians about just who ought to fight and on what terms. When middling Virginians showed an unwillingness to be deployed for all but the most necessary tasks, state leaders hoped they could encourage enough lower-class Virginians into the regular forces both for home defense and to aid General George Washington. But, as Washington's fortunes went from bad to worse between September 1776 and May 1777, lower-class Virginians refused to step forward in the numbers expected. Worried about the general "spirit of patriotism" in the state, patriot leaders in turn were forced to take other, ultimately more divisive measures to secure their defenses. Indeed, as lower-class Virginians increasingly came to be seen as most "fit for common service," ruling-class Virginians concluded that they had to *force* them into service to secure the loyalties of middling Virginians.[1]

1. Edwin Gray to James Gray, May 10, 1777, Ridley Family Papers, VHS; William Allason to Colonel Humphrey Brooke, Sept. 9, 1777, "The Letters of William

• • • Even as they were forming a new government, patriot leaders heard of new alliances forming on their western frontiers, and Governor Dunmore was still a threat on the eastern frontier. To shore up their defenses on both fronts, the convention delegates ordered 400 additional troops raised for western defense. The convention further authorized an additional 204 soldiers to join the Ninth Virginia Regiment of regulars stationed on the Eastern Shore to guard against further problems there. Finally, in order to more effectively protect Virginia's numerous waterways from predatory British attacks, the delegates also called for six troops of horse of 30 men each. Cavalry, they hoped, would respond quicker to attacks along the riversides. Significantly, the convention made it clear that all of these new troops were for the defense of Virginia only. The western troops, for example, were promised the same bounty and pay as Continental soldiers, but a final proviso to their contract stipulated that they would not be marched out of the colony without the "mutual Consent" of themselves and the governor.[2]

Before these new troops could be raised, Virginia's enemies exposed its vulnerability. The Fifth Convention had received numerous reports of a possible joint Creek-Cherokee Indian attack on the Virginia frontier. By late July, patriots from North and South Carolina had warned the Virginia government of Cherokee activity, and the new council immediately authorized an expedition. The two Carolinas were to attack the lower towns, and General Charles Lee and John Rutledge, president of the General Assembly of South Carolina, had asked Virginia to attack the upper, or Overhill towns (west of the Appalachians). Within days, new reports stated that the Cherokees had already initiated an attack against Virginia, some saying that they were going to try to cut off the all-important lead mines in Fincastle County. The council immediately authorized more troops and began preparing an expedition of twelve hundred against the Overhill towns. Council members were confident they could hold their own against the Overhill towns, but they dreaded a combination of all the Cherokees and feared the consequences should the "Creeks and other Nations . . . join them."[3]

Allason, Merchant, of Falmouth, Virginia," *Richmond College Historical Papers,* II (1917), 168–169.

2. Hening, comp., *Statutes at Large,* IX, 135–138, 141–142.

3. July 22, 26, Aug. 1, 1776, H. R. McIlwaine et al., eds., *Journals of the Council of the State of Virginia* (Richmond, Va., 1931–1982), I, 82, 95, 103–104; John

Within days, their worst fears were confirmed. On August 1, before any men marched westward, a report reached the council that a combined force of Creeks and Cherokees had "made an Iruption" into Fincastle County on the Holston River. Edmund Pendleton had heard that thirty or forty Virginians had been killed. The reports renewed fears of a pan-Indian alliance with the British as well. Pendleton noted that several of the raiding party had been killed and "on Examination had proved to be white men Painted." Though a small party of militia had beaten the raiders off in this instance, they had been told that this was only a "Detachment" from a much larger Indian force of six hundred Cherokees on their way toward the Virginia frontiers. Worse still, reports put Cherokee strength at twenty-four hundred fighting men in the different towns and stated that the Creeks and fifteen other "Northern Tribes" had joined with them against the new states. The council immediately began to mobilize militia from the counties west of the Blue Ridge.[4]

Almost at the same time, patriot leaders in Virginia struggled even to cope with Dunmore's now dwindling force. Dunmore, after fleeing Norfolk, cruised the bay for a while before settling on Gwynn's Island, in the upper bay, as a base of operations. Almost immediately, however, smallpox raged through his encampment, and his numbers shrank. Rumors of the problems there also helped deter new recruits, black and white, from joining him. Yet not until early July could Andrew Lewis, now commander of all the Virginia forces, muster enough men to guard Williamsburg while he launched an attack on Dunmore. In the end, he took ten companies, or about five hundred men, of the First and Second Regiments. Gathering up all available artillery from around the tidewater, Lewis poured a barrage

Page to the North Carolina Council of Safety, July 26, 1776, Page to John Hancock, July 27, 1776, H. R. McIlwaine, ed., *Official Letters of the Governors of the State of Virginia* (Richmond, Va., 1926–1929), I, 16, 18.

4. Within a month, commissioners at Fort Pitt appointed to treat with the northern Indians sent gloomy news, calling for a strengthening of that post with more men and ammunition. Edmund Pendleton to Thomas Jefferson, July 29, 1776, *Papers of Pendleton,* I, 189; Page to the North Carolina Council of Safety, Aug. 1, 1776, McIlwaine, ed., *Official Letters,* I, 22–23; Sept. 9, 1776, McIlwaine et al., eds., *Journals of the Council,* I, 151–152. The Cherokee threat came to an end by September, when a joint force of almost six thousand southern troops marched on the Cherokee towns and devastated Cherokee resistance (Tom Hatley, *The Dividing Paths: Cherokees and South Carolinians through the Era of Revolution* [New York, 1993], 193–200).

of fire into the British ships and island batteries before Dunmore could organize a defense. The governor himself was slightly wounded in the assault, which helped convince him that evacuation was the only safe action. His forces already weakened by smallpox, Dunmore confirmed his decision when news arrived that he could not expect reinforcements from General Henry Clinton, about to lay siege to Charleston. Dunmore once again took to the water.[5]

But Dunmore did not leave Virginia. For the next month, he cruised the Potomac River, mainly looking for fresh water and provisions. On one of these expeditions, near Dumfries, local militia taunted Dunmore's troops but hid in the woods when they actually landed. In retaliation, the British completely burned convention delegate William Brent's plantation. The incident enraged and worried vulnerable tidewater planters. Coming only a few weeks after declaring Independence and assuming a new government, the raid reminded white Virginians that they were still as vulnerable as ever—especially wealthy Virginians who held valuable riverside property. It also reminded wealthy Virginians that they were still very much dependent on their less well off neighbors.[6]

These tangible reminders of their vulnerability helped shape patriot leaders' thinking about state and Continental defense. Ironically, they were pushed into rethinking the balance between the two when Dunmore finally left the Chesapeake on August 5 because he had heard that British forces were regrouping and amassing at New York, to gather strength for a major assault. Thousands of reinforcements from Britain had also begun arriving in New York in early July. Eventually, General William Howe would

5. John E. Selby, *The Revolution in Virginia, 1775-1783* (Williamsburg, Va., 1988), 124-125.

6. Pendleton was furious with the local militia, especially those actually stationed at Brent's house, who he thought had acted irresponsibly. They had "departed from the Dignity of men," he told Jefferson, not just for running away when the British came on shore but also for their "Rude behavior" in provoking the enemy in the first place. Pendleton to Jefferson, July 29, 1776, *Papers of Pendleton,* I, 189; cf. Adam Stephen to Jefferson, July 29, 1776, *Papers of Jefferson,* I, 480–482; Selby, *Revolution in Virginia,* 126. Brent was a justice of the peace in Stafford, had served on the Committee of Safety, and would also later be a representative in the General Assembly (see *Papers of Mason,* I, xxxvii). Cf. entry of July 26, 1776, Jack P. Greene, ed., *The Diary of Colonel Landon Carter of Sabine Hall, 1752-1778* (Charlottesville, Va., 1965), II, 1065-1066; Sept. 18, Dec. 6, 1776, McIlwaine et al., eds., *Journals of the Council,* I, 166, 267.

have at his command about 32,000 men while his brother, Admiral Richard Howe, engaged seventy-three warships manned by upward of 13,000 seamen, or nearly 45 percent of the Royal Navy. Another detachment of 10,000 troops had been dispatched to Canada.[7]

To counter that coming British campaign northward, Congress looked to all of the states for help. Even before Dunmore had cleared the Chesapeake, Congress asked for two of the recently raised Continental regiments from Virginia, which Congress was paying for, to join the main army in the North against the amassing British forces as being more needed there. Patriot leaders in Virginia, however, shaken by their experiences against Dunmore, remained paranoid about the possible return of the British. Pendleton was among them and, like other patriot leaders, wanted the Virginia troops to remain. The council reluctantly agreed to send the two Virginia regiments, but only after protesting to Congress. Still nervous about popular support, the council worried about "the dispersed situation of our troops, [and] the number of navigable rivers, exposing our country to the ravages of the enemys fleet" as well as about a "great demand" for men and arms on the western frontier.[8]

Friction between state and Continental leaders was exacerbated later in September, as the situation in New York worsened. Congress ordered three more regiments of Continental troops from Virginia to march to New Jersey. With rumors rife of Dunmore's return to Virginia at the head of an enlarged army, patriot leaders were in a quandary. Keen to maintain Continental harmony, yet worried about home defense, Virginia's patriot leadership faced a difficult decision. In the end, it let the Continental troops march northward. However, Patrick Henry and the council, based in a now poorly defended Williamsburg, ordered a remnant minuteman battalion to

7. Though patriot leaders did not know it at the time, with Dunmore's departure from the Chesapeake the main theater of war moved decidedly northward, where it would remain for almost three years. See Don Higginbotham, *The War of American Independence: Military Attitudes, Policies, and Practice, 1763–1789* (New York, 1971), 148–162. When Congress asked for lead supplies from Virginia in late July, for example, the council politely turned it down, citing war with the Cherokees and Dunmore's forays. Page to John Hancock, July 27, 1776, McIlwaine, ed., *Official Letters,* I, 18.

8. Pendleton to Jefferson, July 29, Aug. 10, 26, 1776, *Papers of Pendleton,* I, 189, 199, 201; Page to the President of Congress, Aug. 3, 1776, McIlwaine, ed., *Official Letters,* I, 24; Aug. 6, 9, 10, 1776, McIlwaine et al., eds., *Journals of the Council,* I, 110, 115, 116.

the capital—insufficient in light of the number of troops leaving Virginia. Thus, they also ordered down another twenty-six companies of fifty militia each (or thirteen hundred men) to cover what the council called the "present naked and defenceless situation of this Country."[9]

This was one of the first times a large number of militia had been called out, and it was precisely what patriot leaders had wanted to avoid by first creating the minutemen and then an enlarged regular army. But, with the failure of the minutemen and the march of most of the Virginia regular troops northward, the militia was the only force available to the governor to counter any threats. Calling out the militia, however, was a political risk. Not only was it an indiscriminate imposition on freeholders at large, many of whom were politically active, but it was also a compulsory demand for military service. Whereas service in the minutemen and in the regulars was voluntary, armed service in the militia was mandatory. A mass call-out of the militia was, in short, a test of patriot support, allegiance, and authority in the new state.

Recognizing this, the council tried to tread lightly, asking for only one or two companies from a total of nineteen piedmont and southside counties. The council hoped that the reinforcement could still be made up of "Voluntiers" from among all of the militia in each of the counties. If not enough volunteers were forthcoming, however, the council ordered that the needed men be "draughted according to Ordinance." The county lieutenant would divide the militia into so many divisions as the number of men needed and draft a militiaman from each to serve for the duration of this particular call-out.[10]

Militia in the affected areas immediately showed their disapproval. Not all were convinced that the occasion demanded the expense and time of such a march. Most, too, were far enough removed from the more vulnerable areas nearer the coastline to think twice about the need, particularly given that no British troops had yet appeared off the shores of Virginia. Moreover, an epidemic that had swept the lower counties in late summer had also added to the outcry against the militia orders, and few militia were inclined to venture eastward in such an environment. Significantly, they made their case loudly enough that their legislative representatives took note. Just as the call went out for the militia, many representatives began their journey to Williamsburg for the fall session of the General Assem-

9. Sept. 26, 1776, McIlwaine et al., eds., *Journals of the Council,* I, 176.
10. Ibid.

bly on October 7, less than two weeks after the executive order had been signed. The newly gathered delegates immediately rescinded the order and turned the militia back home. Within a few months of creating a new government, then, legislators demonstrated the power and responsiveness of an elected assembly.[11]

⁕ ⁕ ⁕ In the same vein did representatives tackle mobilization problems in general at this same session in the fall of 1776. First, they bowed to popular pressure and shored up their support among the middling classes. Then they turned up the heat on disenfranchised and disloyal groups to meet their defensive needs. In some sense, their reforms continued the previous convention's bid to restructure social alliances within Virginia.

Most important, the delegates bolstered their support by finally exempting Dissenters from taxes to support the established church. The Virginia Declaration of Rights had given all men a right to the "free exercise of religion" but had stopped short of disestablishing the Anglican Church. Dissenters throughout the new state, while praising Article 16, immediately went on the attack and demanded the complete disestablishment of the church and freedom from paying taxes for religion. Both supporters of the establishment and Dissenters played on patriot leaders' fears of the Revolution. On one hand, Dissenters claimed that eliminating church taxes and a state church would gain patriot leaders many more adherents at a time when they needed unanimity. Supporters of the establishment countered that disestablishing the church would anger more people than it would placate. They warned patriot leaders to avoid a measure "by which the greater and more orderly part of the state will be aggrieved and may be sickened" of the Revolution. Disestablishment might even lead to further civil war, which would be "a little unseasonable."[12]

In the end, popular petitions helped sway the assembly in the Dissenters' favor. At least ten different petitions in favor of disestablishment

11. *Journal of the House of Delegates* (Williamsburg, Va., 1776), 8. For the sickly conditions among troops stationed at Williamsburg, see Oct. 10, 1776, Diary of Robert Honyman, Jan. 2, 1776–Mar. 11, 1782, Alderman Library, UVa (microfilm).

12. *Va. Gaz.* (Purdie), Oct. 11, Nov. 1, 8, 1776; *Va. Gaz.* (D and H), Dec. 13, 1776. One reluctant supporter of the established church noted that Dissenters were dangerous, particularly Dissenters who preached pacifism and a leveling spirit. The established church was necessary, he wrote, to help restrain these dangerous notions (see *Va. Gaz.* [Purdie], Dec. 13, 1776). Cf. Thomas E. Buckley, *Church and State in Revolutionary Virginia, 1776–1787* (Charlottesville, Va., 1977), 21–37.

reached the assembly in the fall of 1776, including one signed by almost ten thousand people. In the face of these arguments, the number of petitioners, and the need for more support for the war, the legislature could not ignore the issue any longer. Despite opposition from powerful conservatives like Robert Carter Nicholas and Pendleton, Thomas Jefferson engineered a compromise that at least temporarily satisfied the Dissenters. Though the Anglican Church was not disestablished, compulsory taxation for its support was ended. In fact, no one would be taxed for the support of any church, and contributions would be voluntary. Though the legislature kept control over the licensing of both meetinghouses and preachers of Dissenting sects, few people believed such laws would be strictly enforced, given the present climate. Some of the details had yet to be worked out, and full disestablishment lay in the future, but Dissenters had scored a major victory principally as a result of the Revolutionary war.[13]

Tenants also weighed in to demand justice in the midst of sacrifice. In the fall of 1776, when rents were due, trouble began again in the heavily tenanted Prince William and neighboring counties. Henry Field, Jr., the collector of quitrents for Lord Fairfax in Prince William, Fauquier, and Culpeper Counties, complained that many tenants had taken advantage of "the Times" and had withheld their rents. As in Loudoun the previous year, many had incited their neighbors to do the same. All attempts Field had made at collecting the rents were "without Effect." One group of renters sent in a petition to the General Assembly in November 1776 to demand changes in the law. More than one hundred people in Prince William County—or just more than 15 percent of the adult white male population—complained that, since the beginning of the war, they had considered themselves and all of the community there "equally interested" in the contest. Yet, since their trade had come to a halt, an "evident inequality" had hurt mainly the tenants and the debtors in the state. In remarkably explicit class terms, they claimed that, though the "landlord and Tenant, the Creditor and Debtor, the Gentleman and the Peasant" ought to bear a "just proportion" of the expenses of the war, the stoppage of trade had invariably hit tenants, debtors, and poor people hardest. Landlords and creditors benefited because their rents and debts accumulated from year to year regardless of the state of trade or crops. But, during the war, the tenants and debtors had no possible way to make money from their "Honest In-

13. Buckley, *Church and State*, 21–37; Hening, comp., *Statutes at Large*, IX, 164–167.

dustry" and discharge their rents and debts. They did not want such rents and debts totally abolished, but, rather, wanted the assembly to force landlords and creditors to accept such debts and rents in the form of the "produce of the earth" at "reasonable" prices. Offering what they believed to be a fair deal, the petitioners also made clear the consequences of continuing the present unjust policy. "Thousands" would end up "in utter ruin," but, equally important, the problem might create "a dissatisfaction in the minds of many of the Zealous Friends to liberty."[14]

The General Assembly also had to face the same problem that the executive had struggled with: balancing Virginia's defensive needs with those of the Continent. By the end of August, the British had begun to move against General George Washington and his dwindling army in and around New York. By November, Washington had been pushed out of the New York area altogether and was soon in full retreat across New Jersey. With the situation in the North rapidly deteriorating even as they sat, the General Assembly could not remain immune to pleas for help from Congress. Specifically, Congress asked Virginia for another six battalions of regular soldiers, on top of the nine new regiments Virginia had raised earlier in the year. Moreover, the terms of service for the original two regiments raised in the fall of 1775 were about to expire, and they would have to be reenlisted, or new recruits found in their place. In responding to Congress, Virginia's policymakers continued the same strategy that they had employed previously and in creating a new government. They tried to leave middle-class Virginians alone and put more pressure on lower-class Virginians to do the fighting. They found an ally in Washington.[15]

14. Henry Field, Jr., to the General Assembly, [Nov. 18, 1776], Prince William County Petition, [Nov. 2, 1776], Virginia Legislative Petitions, LiVi. Jefferson, using military returns from 1780 and 1781, estimated that the militia from Prince William at that time numbered 614 (see Thomas Jefferson, *Notes on the State of Virginia,* ed. William Peden [Chapel Hill, N.C., 1954], 89). Though the assembly failed to act positively on the petition, it ignored the demands of landlords as well. Henry Field had told Lord Fairfax about his problems collecting rents. Fairfax in turn told Field to write to the assembly. Fairfax was convinced that the assembly would regard the "protection of his property" in the most serious light and with equal attention as "the Welfare and Interest of any other Individual belonging to this State." However, the assembly was not able, or willing, to do anything about the problem. Collective action by tenants—and the threat of the loss of their support for the patriot movement—had proved more intimidating than the threat to property.

15. Higginbotham, *War of American Independence,* 148–162.

The congressional request for more Continental troops marked a turning point for Washington and the main army. For some months, Washington had been pressing Congress for a longer-term, more professional army. In his eyes, short-term recruits were rapidly proving more of a nuisance than a help, providing no continuity or stability in the ranks. This became patently clear to officers at the battle of Quebec in December 1775, when short-term enlistees began leaving in the midst of the campaign. In the end, Generals Philip Schuyler and Richard Montgomery and Colonel Benedict Arnold were forced to attack Quebec hastily, and unsuccessfully. To avoid a repeat of this debacle, in which Montgomery was killed, Washington and others wanted more reliable, longer-term recruits. Not only would less time be wasted in training new troops for each campaign, but they could instill better discipline. Washington had found that, to encourage and keep new short-term recruits, he and his officers had to relax their discipline. With a longer-term army, Washington could worry less about mollifying the troops and discipline them into becoming a more effective fighting force—at least in his eyes.[16]

In the end, despite some mild protests over creating a larger army, Congress accepted Washington's proposals to new-model the Continental army mainly because of the immense British buildup of troops in New York in the summer of 1776, to counter which Washington would need an army to match the British. Accordingly, in December 1776 Congress not only authorized a huge increase in enlistments—by the end of the year, it had called for more than one hundred battalions of troops, or almost seventy-five thousand recruits—but also recommended to the states that these troops be raised for a minimum of three years or, better, for the duration of the war. Congress also gave in to Washington's demands for more discipline in the ranks and put greater teeth into the articles of war.[17]

Patriot leaders in Virginia, already relying on regular troops for the mainstay of their defense, readily acquiesced in the recommendations of Congress. The assembly ordered six new battalions raised, called for enlist-

16. Ibid.

17. George Washington to Hancock, Dec. 16, 1776, *Papers of Washington,* Rev. War Ser., VII, 351–352; James Kirby Martin and Mark Edward Lender, *A Respectable Army: The Military Origins of the Republic, 1763–1789* (Arlington Heights, Ill., 1982), 73–77. The new articles of war raised the limit of lashes from thirty-nine to one hundred for certain offenses and raised the number of crimes for which the death penalty could be imposed.

ments of three years or the war, and adopted the congressional recommendation for what Washington called a "large and extraordinary bounty" for the new troops. Washington believed that patriotism would not motivate the kind of people who would likely serve for three years or for the war. "To expect such People, as compose the bulk of an Army," to be motivated by "principles other than Interest, is to look for what never did and . . . never will happen." Congress in September thus offered each new recruit a twenty-dollar joining bonus and promised an annual set of clothes. For those men staying on for the duration of the war, Congress promised one hundred acres of land.[18]

Though responding to the congressional recommendation, the assembly must have realized the implications of such a measure. Given that the new Constitution maintained suffrage qualifications of a minimum of fifty acres of land, the assembly, in effect, promised full political citizenship in return for hard service for the state. In principle, then, poor and landless white Virginians could literally fight for their political liberty if they chose to. Desperation and the exigencies of war had thus forced the hand of the General Assembly after it had failed to change the suffrage in June.

At the same time, the General Assembly was shoring up its own defense. With all available Continental recruits being commandeered for service in the North, the assembly in October created three full-time battalions of infantry for state service only, subject to the same regulations and pay as the Continental soldiers. The state troops, enlisting for three years, would also receive an immediate twenty dollars bounty plus a new set of clothes each year. Unable to now use the Continental regiments for state defense and unwilling to depend on periodic call-outs of the militia, the assembly officially dissolved the virtually defunct minute service—instead of relying on eight thousand part-time citizen-soldiers, Virginians would now call on two thousand of their own full-time professional troops.[19]

In turning to an increased reliance on a more permanent army, represen-

18. Washington to Hancock, Sept. 20[-21], 24, 25, 1776, *Papers of Washington*, Rev. War Ser., VI, 351–353, 387–388, 394; Hening, comp., *Statutes at Large*, IX, 179–184; Sept. 16, 1776, Worthington Chauncey Ford et al., eds., *Journals of the Continental Congress, 1774–1789* (Washington, D.C., 1904–1937), V, 762–763.

19. Hening, comp., *Statutes at Large,* IX, 192–198. The assembly also took measures to protect Virginia's vulnerable coastlines. To pay for all of this, the General Assembly also raised a new tax on tithables, carriages, and land but ameliorated the burden by allowing the payment of the tax over eight years, until 1784 (219–225).

tatives also made it clear what kind of men they expected in the new armed forces and what other purpose the armed services might perform for them. The assembly, clearly shaken by the rising disorders over the previous year and a half and cognizant of the economic ill effects of its measures, took steps toward clearing their town streets and country lanes of the victims of its policies and those taking advantage of them. Noting the "great increase" of "idle and disorderly persons" in the state, the assembly decided to do something about such "rogues and vagabonds." Struggling to raise men for the new Continental regiments and now the state forces, the assembly took more severe measures to deal with both problems. If vagabonds could not give security for their good behavior or future job prospects, the assembly gave justices of the peace and the governor wide powers to imprison and ultimately impress such people into the armed services. Vagabonds were defined quite broadly as any able-bodied men who neglected or refused to pay their county and parish levies and who had no visible estate.[20]

The assembly also strengthened its hand against enemies within the state. It first defined treason—punishable by death—specifically as an act of war against the commonwealth, adherence to the enemy, or giving aid or comfort to the enemy. But the assembly also targeted any other resistance to the state. Aiming new legislation at those bent on the "destruction of good government" or obstructing the laws of government, the assembly outlawed the public assertion of the power, jurisdiction, or authority of the king or Parliament of Britain. Also outlawed were encouraging resistance to the laws of the state, persuading others to return to a dependence on the crown, and "rais[ing] tumults and disorders in the state," including those who "maliciously and advisedly terrify and discourage the people from enlisting into the service of the commonwealth, or dispose them to favour the enemy." Anyone convicted of such disaffection could be fined up to twenty thousand pounds and imprisoned for up to five years.[21]

Finally, near the end of its session in December, the assembly received news that Washington was in full retreat and Congress had fled from Philadelphia just ahead of the British army. Shocked and worried still about their own defense, the House of Delegates formed a committee of the whole, and George Mason offered a solution. Less than six months after Virginians erected a new constitutional government, Mason proposed to suspend that government and give greater emergency powers to Governor Henry,

20. Hening, comp., *Statutes at Large,* IX, 216–217.
21. Ibid., 168, 170–171.

with the advice and consent of the council. Believing that the "present imminent Danger" called for the utmost exertion of strength, Mason's resolution advocated no less than a "Departure from the Constitution of Government." Extra power would be given to Henry until March 1777 (when the General Assembly would meet again) to meet Continental requisitions, to order the state battalions into service northward if needed, and to call forth any greater military force he and the council judged necessary. He was given great latitude to raise volunteers or even more battalions. The resolution, which passed the lower house, also recommended to Congress that it give Washington "more ample and extensive Powers for conducting the Operations of the War."[22]

• • • Thus, in a few deft strokes, the General Assembly had considerably enlarged the state's capacity to mobilize for war, yet made it clear who would now bear its burden. But, if patriot leaders were keen to push lower-class Virginians to fill the ranks of the army, lower-class Virginians had their own agenda. Many looked warily at entering the army for a minimum of three years, particularly when Washington made it clear that he wanted a more disciplined army. In general, enlistments for the Continental army, at least, were very slow. From early on, officers encountered problems recruiting men. In Loudoun County, for example, an unsympathetic Nicholas Cresswell reported that, at a militia muster of six hundred men in late October, officers pleaded for recruits, offering the generous bounty of money and lands, "but get very few men." Rather, Cresswell reported, there was only "much rioting and confusion."[23]

Even patriots had to admit that white Virginians were reluctant to join

22. The Senate succeeded in replacing the clause that "the usual forms of Government shou'd be suspended" with a more moderate stipulation that the governor and council be given "additional powers." "Resolutions Urging Recruitment and Conferring Emergency Powers on the Governor and Council," [Dec. 21, 1776], *Papers of Mason*, I, 325–327.

23. Oct. 28, Nov. 12, Dec. 14, 1776, Nicholas Cresswell, *The Journal of Nicholas Cresswell* (London, 1925), 166, 169, 176. Virginia's recruiting problems were widely reported, particularly by friends of the British. One Hessian officer, for example, had heard by then that "Virginia wants to hear no more of independence; her militia makes no haste to join the mob [i.e., the army]." Major Carl Bauermeister, Journal, Dec. 16, 1776, Bernhard A. Uhlendorf, ed., *Revolution in America: Confidential Letters and Journals, 1776-1784, of Adjutant General Major Bauermeister of the Hessian Forces* (New Brunswick, N.J., 1957), 140.

up, and reports from all across the new state brought bad news to the capital. In early December, John Smith of Frederick County admitted that officers in the Shenandoah Valley were experiencing severe problems recruiting men in the western regions. A few weeks later, Robert Honyman noted that, in the central piedmont area, "enlisting men for the new regiments meets with bad success; the people being much more backward than they were formerly." There was a brief flurry of enlistments near the end of December, as news reached Virginia of Washington's successes at Princeton and Trenton, but, when it became apparent that Washington's victories were only temporary successes, recruiting fell off once again. John Page wrote from Williamsburg at the end of February, "Inlistments . . . I fear will never be compleated—several Counties have not raised a Man."[24]

Many, of course, did take advantage of the liberal bounties and the promise of land. Daniel Trabue and his brother thought of enlisting in the army because there was little else to do to make money. The problem was that there was no market for their goods: "At this time no sail for produce." So he and his brother William "concluded we would Join a company that was a going to the North under General Washington." Daniel himself fell ill, so he did not enlist, but his brother went with a "number" of others. Daniel eventually enlisted with George Rogers Clark for his western expedition at the end of 1777 and subsequently used the army to prospect for land.[25]

Many other men were willing to exchange one kind of bondage for another, temporary kind of servitude. In 1775, the Third Virginia Convention had forbidden recruiters to enlist any servants at all except apprentices with the written consent of their masters. Yet desperation drove recruiters to enlist anyone that seemed willing to serve. Indentured and convict

24. John Smith, on behalf of the Frederick County Volunteers, to the House of Delegates, Dec. 12, 1776, in "Virginia Legislative Papers," *VMHB*, XVIII (1910), 29-31; Dec. 31, 1776, Diary of Honyman (cf. entries of Apr. 10, 30, 1777); Patrick Henry to R. H. Lee, Jan. 9, 1777, McIlwaine, ed., *Official Letters,* I, 90; Page to R. H. Lee, Feb. 27, 1777, Paul P. Hoffman, ed., *Lee Family Papers, 1742-1795* (microfilm) (Charlottesville, Va., 1966). Cf. Peter Grant to [Leven Powell], Apr. 9, 1777, Christopher Greenup to Powell, May 2, 1777, Granville Smith to Powell, Aug. 28, 1777, "The Leven Powell Correspondence, 1775-1787," *John P. Branch Historical Papers of Randolph-Macon College,* II (1902), 123-125, for reports of poor recruiting in Loudoun County and Williamsburg.

25. Chester Raymond Young, ed., *Westward into Kentucky: The Narrative of Daniel Trabue* (Lexington, Ky., 1981), 43.

servants took full advantage. By mid-1777, George Washington believed that the Virginia Line of the Continental army was full of convict servants purchased from their masters by recruiting officers. Cresswell thought that the only company that officers from Loudoun County could raise was full of "rascally servants and convicts most of them just purchased from their masters." Though such men might have been coerced into service by masters wishing to make a profit on their sale, no doubt many welcomed the bargain as a swift end to their servitude. Even if they stayed in the army for the length of service contracted, it was likely shorter than the time remaining on their indentures. Further, it was easier to escape the army than ever-watchful masters. Both Washington and Cresswell believed that most servants would "desert the first opportunity."[26]

Enslaved Virginians also took advantage of the desperate need for soldiers by offering themselves to recruiters under the guise of being freemen. The 1775 prohibition against enlisting servants presumably applied to enslaved Virginians, but, at some point between 1775 and early 1777, desperate recruiters began allowing at least free blacks into the Virginia Line. Many enslaved Virginians then presented themselves as free men to recruiters, who, desperate to fulfill their quotas in order to gain commissions, were quick to turn a blind eye to such subterfuges and happily accepted black Virginians, free and unfree. By May 1777, enough enslaved Virginians had run away and enlisted in the army to alarm the assembly. Legislators declared the practice of enrolling black or mulatto Virginians unlawful unless they produced a certificate affirming their free status from a local justice of the peace. In doing so, of course, legislators gave official sanction to the practice of enrolling free blacks into the army, a practice not adopted in Maryland until 1780 and not adopted at all south of Virginia. They also opened the door for enslaved Virginians to gain their freedom from their masters by serving as substitutes for them if they were drafted.[27]

The numbers of men who did step forward, however, were limited. In

26. Hening, comp., *Statutes at Large,* IX, 12; Washington to Hancock, May 13, 1777, *Papers of Washington,* Rev. War Ser., IX, 411; Dec. 14, 1776, Jan. 7, Mar. 3, 10, 1777, Cresswell, *Journal,* 176, 180, 186, 187. The assembly formalized the practice in May 1777 when it allowed recruiting officers to enlist servants and apprentices, apparently without their masters' consent (see Hening, comp., *Statutes at Large,* IX, 275–276).

27. Hening, comp., *Statutes at Large,* IX, 280; Benjamin Quarles, *The Negro in the American Revolution* (Chapel Hill, N.C., 1961), 56–57.

early April 1777, as far as Washington could ascertain, Virginia's nine old regiments did not exceed 1,800 effective men (when there should have been approximately 4,500 men in service), and Henry had told him that he did not think more than four of the six new regiments would actually be filled. As late as May 1777, only twelve battalions had joined Washington to the north, the largest consisting of only 326 men present and fit for duty. Full battalion strength was 738 officers and men. Of those twelve battalions, only 2,512 Virginia troops were present and fit for duty, or about a quarter of the total number Virginia had been asked to provide. Nor was there much chance of recruiting any more men. By the end of March, Henry had concluded: "Enlistments go on badly. Indeed they are almost stopped."[28]

• • • Though patriot leaders rarely reflected on the reasons for the poor enlistment rates, at least explicitly, there had been good reasons for a decline in the enthusiasm. In the first place, morale in Virginia was generally low as a result of the problems the state had experienced the previous fall. Though trade had been opened for several months, the flow of goods into Virginia was still extremely slow, and shortages of goods created more conflict. For example, salt was again in high demand in the fall of 1776. On September 12, the council paid a pound per bushel for eight hundred bushels of salt. By the end of September, Nicholas Cresswell noted that salt was selling for forty shillings a bushel when it normally sold for four. The demand for salt was so great that it again caused civil disturbances. When one trader brought a shipment of salt into South Quay in Nansemond County on the south shore of the James River, the locals "assembled in great Bodies and declared that the Salt should not be removed till they are furnished." They also wanted it on credit, or at the public expense, having no money to buy it. The importer, Richard Savage, was, given their

28. Washington to Hancock, Apr. 12[-13], 1777, *Papers of Washington,* Rev. War Ser., IX, 129; Henry to R. H. Lee, Mar. 28, 1777, McIlwaine, ed., *Official Letters,* I, 129. Cf. "General Return," Executive Papers, LiVi; Returns of the Eighth and Tenth Regiments, dated April 10, 12, 1777, Miscellaneous Revolutionary Collection, W. H. Cabell Papers, LiVi; Henry to Washington, Mar. 29, 1777, McIlwaine, ed., *Official Letters,* I, 130; Henry to Charles Lewis, Feb. 21, Mar. 15, 1777, Governor Patrick Henry Papers, LiVi; Charles H. Lesser, ed., *The Sinews of Independence: Monthly Strength Reports of the Continental Army* (Chicago, 1976), 46; Mar. 25, 1777, McIlwaine et al., eds., *Journals of the Council,* 375–376, and generally, March–April 1777.

temper, inclined to give it to them. Two months later, in early December, Cresswell reported from Leesburg that a "Dutch mob of about 40 horse-men went through the town to-day on their way to Alexandria to search for Salt." It was widely believed that, if they found any, they would "take it by force." "All of them," Cresswell noted with alarm, were "armed with swords or large clubs." Cresswell again worried that worse was to come. If more did not come in, "the people will revolt." "They cannot possibly sub-sist without a considerable quantity of this article."[29]

Salt was not the only item in demand; Cresswell thought that short-ages were widespread. By early 1777, Robert Honyman noted, because of shortages, the prices for all goods, and especially basic goods, had risen sharply. He believed that many merchants from Maryland and Pennsylva-nia had sent immense quantities of paper money to Virginia to buy up to-bacco as well, to insulate themselves from the public credit if the currency should fail. However, for Virginians it meant that even more money was in circulation, which drove up prices for everything. The inflation exacer-bated relations between the states, as many Virginians believed that Con-gress was at the root of their problems. In January 1777, Governor Henry told Richard Henry Lee that some of his countrymen "perceive errors in Congress." Henry thought that the situation was not helped by the "prac-tice of engrossing all foreign goods and Country produce." At the end of March 1777, he reported that most corn flour and meat in Virginia had been bought up, so it was impossible to supply the army. Even Henry believed that a partner of Continental agent Robert Morris was in Virginia and had "speculated very largely in such articles as the army wants." Such activity, if not stopped, would have "fatal consequences."[30]

29. Sept. 12, 30, 1776, McIlwaine et al., eds., *Journals of the Council*, I, 156, 180; Oct. 1, 1776, Cresswell, *Journal*, 164. Cf. Sept. 17, 1776, Diary of Honyman. Two days later the group returned from Alexandria, "without doing the least mischief." They had been given three pints of salt each and told that there would be much more soon. Dec. 4, 6, 1776, Cresswell, *Journal*, 173-174. For the ethnic composi-tion of Loudoun County, which was diverse, see James Chapin Bradford, "Society and Government in Loudoun County, Virginia, 1790–1800" (Ph.D. diss., Univer-sity of Virginia, 1976), 15-20, 26-31.

30. Henry to R. H. Lee, Jan. 9, Mar. 28, 1777, McIlwaine, ed., *Official Letters*, I, 90, 129; Jan. 16, 1777, Diary of Honyman. In early July, the council noted that it had received "credible Information" that several people were moving around the country in the guise of officers "ingrossing the Commodities of the Country at the

Yet poor trade and speculation had already begun to have "fatal consequences," at least regarding recruitment. Potential recruits were promised
a good bounty and land after the war, but they got little to start with. There
were several reports that Congress could not deliver on the promises of
their generous bounty. In Loudoun, where recruits were particularly hard
to find, Cresswell reported that the Continental paymaster in Virginia again
could not even advance the bounty money for new troops and that the state
was in no position to help. Many men who might have been enticed by the
new bounty refused to budge on mere promises. Such news "greatly im-
peded" the "progress of recruiting." The House of Delegates finally had to
ask the governor to write to Congress to forward money as quickly as possible. At times, recruiters could not deliver even the basics. In early 1777,
Henry thought that enlistments were slow because they had no blankets
or even clothes to give to the new recruits.[31]

Shortages not only affected recruiting directly: they also hit hard at wartime morale in general. Cresswell wrote in January 1777, "This is a most
unhappy country." The biggest problem was that "every necessary of life is

---

most extravagant prices." The council assumed they wanted to depreciate the currency and also accused the same men of spreading "false and injurious Reports" of
the condition of the army and of the general state of affairs with a view to "discouraging people" from "engaging in the American Service" (July 8, 1777, McIlwaine
et al., eds., *Journals of the Council,* I, 450–451).

The council thought such speculation dangerous too. In early September 1776,
on the recommendation of the naval board, the council had authorized and encouraged a "scheme of trade" using all available ships, wanting to export as much as
possible in return for "Salt, clothing, arms, and other necessaries for the army" that
might be had in the West Indies or continental Europe. It was a risky business, but
the executive felt desperate enought to underwrite the venture on the public expense. Six ships were ordered off to the West Indies after a full cargo of tobacco and
flour had been purchased at public expense, with a wish list of goods that included
fifty-four hundred bushels of salt. The executive also ordered blankets, osnaburgs,
woolens, linens, sail duck, medicines, powder, and arms and swords. It estimated
the entire order would cost the public £11,325. It also began authorizing private
ventures. Sept. 12, 13, 1776, McIlwaine et al., eds., *Journals of the Council,* I, 156,
158–159; cf. Nov. 20, Dec. 9, 10, 16, 1776, McIlwaine et al., eds., *Journals of the
Council,* I, 246, 270, 273, 284.

31. Nov. 12, Dec. 14, 1776, Cresswell, *Journal,* 169, 176; Journal of the House of
Delegates, Nov. 16, 1776, McIlwaine, ed., *Official Letters,* I, 63, and Patrick Henry
to R. H. Lee, Jan. 9, 1777, I, 90. Cf. Jan. 12, 1777, Cresswell, *Journal,* 180.

at an extravagant price, some of them indeed is not to be had for money." The least well off were the hardest hit. "Poor people are almost naked." Cresswell, hardly impartial or optimistic, lamented that poorer Virginians were suffering. More was in store: "I am persuaded there will be a famine very soon as well as a War."[32]

With shortages worrying many, lower-class Virginians had good reason to forgo service in the Continental army, particularly if even the promise of a bit of cash and a steady income was not so certain. However, they had other reasons for not joining up, perhaps the most important being that service in the Continental army now meant service outside the state. The men recruited in the winter and spring of 1775–1776 had enlisted believing that they would serve locally, or at least within Virginia. At first, they had been stationed locally, usually within a few counties of their homes. But, once Dunmore had left the state, most of Virginia's regular regiments were ordered northward to join Washington's army, and other troops were ordered south to North Carolina and Charleston.

The movement of these troops caused problems. Even when the council ordered one group of soldiers to move from Hampton several miles across the James River to Portsmouth, there were widespread complaints. Some of the soldiers worried about getting ill on the epidemic-ravaged Portsmouth side of the river, and others about the families they would have to leave behind. Complaints were more acute among those ordered out of the state altogether. Indeed, one group of Continental recruits, who had enlisted in Northumberland County in the Northern Neck in the spring of 1776, took the ultimate step when Congress ordered their company northward. They mutinied and risked a punishment of death rather than obeyed the order to march out of the state.[33]

32. Jan. 8, 1777, Cresswell, *Journal,* 180. At the same time, the British decided to try to capitalize on the problem by ordering a specific blockade of the Chesapeake (see J. A. Robinson, "British Invade the Chesapeake, 1777," in Ernest McNeill Eller, ed., *Chesapeake Bay in the American Revolution* [Centreville, Md., 1981], 357). Cf. Jan. 16, 1777, Diary of Honyman.

33. So too did Virginia troops who were ordered southward. When some had been ordered into North Carolina to help General Robert Howe defend against a landing of up to three thousand British troops at Cape Fear in May, many were reportedly "discontented at Marching farther" than Halifax, in Virginia. Charles Lee, also at Halifax, could not believe the "disorderly mutinous and dangerous disposition" of these soldiers, among whom the "spirit of desertion . . . is so alarmingly

Potential recruits were not stupid. Whereas many earlier recruits had been enticed into the Continental army in the belief that they would be used for home defense, it was clear by the end of 1776 that regular troops would be sent elsewhere. Candidates were under no illusion about where they were to serve if they enlisted, and many recruiting officers in 1776 and 1777 complained that Virginians were loath to enlist for service outside the state. In the summer of 1777, Granville Smith reported from Williamsburg that, though there were many militia in town, he could not recruit a single one—"They seem much averse going to the Northward." Some recruiting officers lied to get around local fears. Near the end of 1777, Governor Henry told Washington that there were a "great many" deserters who were "skulking on the Eastern Shore" because, when they were recruited, "their officers took up the general opinion that their service would be confined to that shore, and promised to remain there." "Their desertion," he acknowledged, "followed upon orders to march away."[34]

Prospective recruits who refused to serve out of state were only looking after their own interests. Prepared to make some sacrifice for long-term economic gains, they hesitated when the risks became higher, as when sol-

———

great." If the desertion continued, they might not be able to hold the field, Lee warned, and the army might become "one mass of disorder, vice and confusion." Robert Howe to Pendleton, May 24, 1776, Charles Lee to Pendleton, May 24, 1776, *Rev. Va.,* VII, 247, 248–249.

Sept. 13, 1776, McIlwaine et al., eds., *Journals of the Council,* I, 159–160, and cf. Nov. 13, 1776, 236–237. Also cf. Apr. 10, July 17, Aug. 15, 1776, Diary of Honyman; *Va. Gaz.* (Purdie), Sept. 27, 1776; *Rev. Va.,* VI, 70; Richard C. Bush, "'Awake, Rouse Your Courage, Americans Brave': Companies Raised in Northumberland County for the Virginia Continental Line, 1776 and 1777," *Bulletin of the Northumberland County Historical Society,* XXIX (1992), 11; Selby, *Revolution in Virginia,* 90–91, 124, 126–127, 128.

34. Other officers deliberately kept back their new recruits from marching northward, and Henry thought that the officers were deliberately obstructing the march of the new recruits. Whether they did so in order to keep the troops nearby for their own protection or because of opposition among the troops themselves, he did not say. However, delaying the troops from marching served both officers and men. Granville Smith to Leven Powell, Aug. 28, 1777, "Leven Powell Correspondence," *Historical Papers of Randolph-Macon College,* II (1903), 125; Henry to Washington, Dec. 6, 1777, Henry to R. H. Lee, Mar. 20, 1777, McIlwaine, ed., *Official Letters,* I, 126, 211.

diers began serving out of state. One big risk associated with service away from home was disease. Even within Virginia, dying from disease was common. After the fighting at Gwynn's Island in July 1776, one officer reported, "We are in but a bad state . . . our men are sickly and die but too fast." A little later in the year, Robert Honyman noted that "the troops in the lower parts of the country have been extremely sickly these two months past, especially at Williamsburgh." The regiments that had been ordered northward "were exceedingly thinned by sickness and death."[35]

With new enlistments still faltering in the winter of 1777, a smallpox epidemic in the army exacerbated problems. As early as February 1777, Pendleton had heard that the "small Pox rages so violently in our Camp" to the north. He believed that it would "much retard our enlistments." Moreover, as officers and soldiers returned to Virginia to recruit new men, return home, or enjoy furloughs, they brought the disease into the heart of Virginia. Pendleton believed that returning soldiers had "dropped it" in several parts of his home county of Caroline, as well as "others that I have heard of." At least some of the reports were true. Some 37 percent of 163 recruits from Northumberland in 1776–1777 died from various diseases at camp, whereas only 3 percent had died from wounds received in battle. Concern over the spread of smallpox became so great that an inoculation program was begun for soldiers leaving the state, which only exacerbated fears that the army was a death trap. By the spring of 1777, the effect of disease and tales of disease had helped cripple recruiting. Henry noted in March 1777 that the "terrors of the smallpox, added to the lies of deserters and the want of neccessarys, are fatal objections to the continental Service."[36]

35. George Johnstone to Leven Powell, Aug. 6, 1776, Robert C. Powell, ed., *A Biographical Sketch of Col. Leven Powell, Including His Correspondence during the Revolutionary War* (Alexandria, Va., 1877), 37–38; Oct. 10, 1776, Diary of Honyman.

36. Pendleton to R. H. Lee, Feb. 8, 1777, *Papers of Pendleton,* I, 205; Bush, "Companies Raised in Northumberland," *Bulletin of the Northumberland County Historical Society,* XXIX (1992), 16–18; Apr. 30, 1777, Diary of Honyman; Henry to R. H. Lee, Mar. 28, 1777, McIlwaine, ed., *Official Letters,* I, 129. Cf. Henry to Adam Stephen, Mar. 31, 1777, and Henry to Washington, Mar. 29, 1777, McIlwaine, ed., *Official Letters,* I, 130–131, 133. Though Henry thought these tales were exaggerated, the numbers afflicted in the army were staggering. More than 25 percent of recruits in the Continental army were listed as sick at any one time during

Given the widespread anxiety about Continental military service outside the state, officers had a hard time persuading Virginians to join up for the regular service. Yet ordinary citizens now also had more choice about what they might do for a bit of extra money. For one thing, white Virginians at loose ends could more easily make money outside military service during the war. Recruiting did help cause a manpower shortage in the state, as elsewhere. The shortage drove up prices for laborers generally, making civilian life more profitable than the military for some—especially important with prices for goods on the rise, too. One skilled laborer from Maryland suddenly found himself beset by new opportunities. He had initially served an apprenticeship in one of the large sailcloth factories in Hull, England. He had then contracted as an indentured servant in Maryland and had finally been released just as the war began. Footloose and without employment, the man thought he would try to board a privateer at Alexandria and seek a fortune on the seas, but George Mason, who knew his former master, stopped him. Mason knew that he was too "useful to the public," and Mason encouraged him to "lay aside his privateering Scheme," promising him "good wages" and some "fu[r]ther reward" if he could help with the manufacture of sailcloth in Virginia. Mason wrote Governor Henry to employ him immediately and on good terms. Such opportunities drove up prices for badly needed workers, skilled and unskilled. Early in 1777, the council offered two pounds per month for laborers to work on military fortifications at Portsmouth. By June, savvy laborers forced the council to abandon its wage control policy and find men on the best terms possible instead.[37]

But footloose white Virginians who thought that the army might yet be the best way of making money had more choices available to them. For ex-

---

the fall of 1776. Sickness peaked at 35 percent in December (Lesser, ed., *Sinews of Independence,* xxx–xxxi; cf. Elizabeth A. Fenn, *Pox Americana: The Great Smallpox Epidemic of 1775–1782* [New York, 2001]). Cf. R. H. Lee to Jefferson, May 20, 1777, Hoffman, ed., *Lee Family Papers.*

37. Mason to Henry, Apr. 6, 1777, *Papers of Mason,* I, 336 (the workman's name was not given); June 26, 1777, McIlwaine et al., eds., *Journals of the Council,* I, 441. On labor shortages in the mid-Atlantic region during the war, see especially Michael V. Kennedy, "The Home Front during the War for Independence: The Effect of Labor Shortages on Commercial Production in the Mid-Atlantic," in Jack P. Greene and J. R. Pole, eds., *A Companion to the American Revolution* (Oxford, 2000), 332–341.

ample, potential soldiers could now choose to serve with other state lines of the Continental army. The Virginia council, under pressure from Congress, had permitted officers from South Carolina and Georgia to recruit in Virginia, heightening competition for increasingly scarce manpower. Though the bounties and pay were the same from line to line, recruiting officers, whose very commissions depended on their speed in raising a full quota of recruits, often competed for enlistees and at times offered their own incentives. Governor Henry thought that, in the end, the "enlistments for Georgia . . . have greatly hurt ours" and that, by the end of March, as many as two battalions of men had been poached.[38]

Service in the new *state* regiments also offered another choice to potential soldiers. Indeed, the assembly of the fall of 1776 had undermined recruiting for the Continental army when it called for state regiments to provide for the primary defense of Virginia. Recruiting for this service began in earnest in February 1777. In return for joining on for three years' service, a recruit would receive twenty dollars plus a new hunting shirt, a pair of leggings, and a blanket, or ten dollars per year in lieu thereof. Moreover, the act for raising the state regiments, acknowledging the complaints of soldiers, specifically protected them from being ordered out of the state by Congress "on any pretence whatever," without the consent of the General Assembly. Though they would not receive a bounty of land as did soldiers who signed on in the Continental army for the duration of the war, such soldiers were still promised a decent joining bonus and a secure job close to home for three years. The state also undertook to care for the soldier and his family in case of disability; if he was killed in service, his family would be supported. In contrast to the Continental regiments, the two state regiments were recruited relatively quickly.[39]

38. Henry to R. H. Lee, Mar. 20, 28, 1777, McIlwaine, ed., *Official Letters,* I, 126, 129, and Henry to Washington, Mar. 29, 1777, I, 130; Hening, comp., *Statutes at Large,* IX, 192-198, 213-214. The Georgia officers at least, were limited to three hundred soldiers. See Proceedings of the Fifth Virginia Convention, June 6, 14, 20, 1776, *Rev. Va.,* VII, 371, 372, 488, 557; "Resolution Allowing Georgia Recruiting Officers to Seek Enlistments in Virginia," [Dec. 18, 1776], *Papers of Mason,* I, 324. Cf. *Rev. Va.,* VII, 705-706.

39. Hening, comp., *Statutes at Large,* IX, 192-198. In part because of these many choices, some Virginians believed that likely recruits were growing scarcer and that any further demands would hit the agricultural industry hard, worsening shortages. See, for example, Mar. 22, 29, 1777, Cresswell, *Journal,* 189-191.

Young men with a penchant for military service and in need of ready cash could also choose to stay at home and make money from shorter-term militia service. Any man who was called out for service could hire and send a substitute in his stead. This regulation provided a lucrative black market for short-term soldiers who could sell themselves to the highest—and most desperate—bidder. Though the pay was not constant, soldiers had more flexibility and opportunities to demand more cash. In late 1776, there were certainly opportunities.[40]

The different choices, combined with the emerging labor shortages, gave many potential recruits some leverage in return for their service, and the choices were important. Indeed, potential recruits made it clear that they would not be dragged off to fight in just any army. Four men serving on board a merchant vessel recently arrived from Saint Eustatius jumped ship when they got to Virginia, and they took up offers from desperate recruiting officers on board armed vessels belonging to the state. James Richey also knew a bargain when he saw one. Epaphroditus Rudder, a recruiting officer, had promised Richey higher pay, if he enlisted in the state line with Rudder, than what the law allowed. When the inflated pay was not forthcoming, Richey discharged himself from Rudder's command and enlisted with another officer, Edward Ragsdale—presumably for a better deal.[41]

Yet some men made clearer political choices, especially about whom they would serve under if they did serve. One important reason for the decline in enlistments over the fall and winter of 1776–1777 was the resignation of the popular Patrick Henry as the commander of the Virginia Line of the Continental army in March 1776, which had caused widespread consternation. Many patriot leaders believed that morale in general had been hurt, and his resignation also caused problems within the existing regiments. When Henry's troops in the First Regiment were asked to reenlist a few months later in the summer of 1776, they announced they would not serve under their current officers. Andrew Lewis, who had replaced Henry at the

40. Hening, comp., *Statutes at Large,* IX, 89–90; Nov. 21, 1776, McIlwaine et al., eds., *Journals of the Council,* I, 246–247. Militia call-outs continued throughout the winter of 1776–1777, mainly in response to rumors and reports of British ships in the Chesapeake Bay or on their way to it (see, for example, Feb. 5, 1777, McIlwaine et al., eds., *Journals of the Council,* I, 326).

41. Dec. 7, 1776, Mar. 13, 1777, McIlwaine et al., eds., *Journals of the Council,* I, 269, 367.

head of the Virginia troops, was particularly unpopular. He was central in trying to get the men to reenlist but had apparently rendered himself "obnoxious" because he had "maltreated" the troops.[42]

William Woodford, colonel of the Second Virginia Regiment and one of the more conservative military leaders, had also angered the troops who served under him. His dispute with Henry was widely known, and he had made himself more unpopular in the summer of 1776. After the Fifth Convention elected Henry governor, the First and Second Regiments sent a joint message of congratulations. Woodford announced in the *Virginia Gazette* that the address of his men did not reflect the "sentiments of the colonel." He eventually lost control over his troops, considered "the most profane and disorderly of any" of the Virginia regiments. When he tried to persuade his men to reenlist in August 1776, they refused to follow him. Woodford, in disgust, resigned.[43]

On the other hand, soldiers were willing enough to serve under popular officers. William Christian, Henry's brother-in-law and successor as commander of the First Regiment, was one such leader; he was able to retain and re-recruit his men. When he appealed to his men of the First Regiment, they "almost to a man swallowed the bait," according to one cynic, and reenlisted. The First Regiment was apparently so popular that the troops were commended by the council for their good "spirit" in reenlisting for three years and agreeing to "march to the support of our Friends of New York." In the end, when Congress asked Virginia to send the First and Sec-

42. Pendleton to William Woodford, Mar. 16, 1776, *Papers of Pendleton,* I, 158; Page to [R. H. Lee], Apr. 12, 1776, Hoffman, ed., *Lee Family Papers;* July 27, 1776, McIlwaine et al., eds., *Journals of the Council,* I, 97; Washington to John Parke Custis, July 24, 1776, *Papers of Washington,* Rev. War Ser., V, 441–442. Lewis had been an unpopular military leader in the backcountry during the Seven Years' War. See Albert H. Tillson, Jr., "The Militia and Popular Political Culture in the Upper Valley of Virginia, 1740–1775," *VMHB,* XCIV (1986), 295. Cf. *Rev. Va.,* II, 325–326.

43. Woodford's soldiers made it known that they would reenlist only under Colonel Charles Scott, the popularly elected commander of the volunteer companies assembled at Williamsburg in the summer of 1775 who had been accused of being too lenient with his men. *Va. Gaz.* (Purdie), Aug. 9, 1776; George Johnstone to Leven Powell, Aug. 6, 1776, Powell, ed., *Biographical Sketch,* 37–38; Selby, *Revolution in Virginia,* 127–128; Pendleton to Woodford, Oct. 11, 1776, *Papers of Pendleton,* I, 203.

ond Regiments northward, the council had to send the Third Regiment under George Weedon instead of Woodford's Second, because the officers had failed to recruit, or re-recruit, enough men.[44]

• • • Caught between choosy lower-class Virginians and politically vocal middle-class militia, state leaders were forced to take alternative, and often divisive, measures. When Washington pressed Henry to send up the newly recruited troops as reinforcements in the desperate days of December 1776, the governor could think only of resurrecting the idea of calling for volunteer companies. By March, when even Henry had to concede there was "little prospect" of reinforcing Washington with new recruits, Henry again told him that he could hope to reinforce him only with volunteers. He doubted he could persuade the state regiments to march beyond the borders of the state, even with his new powers to order them to, and was pessimistic about the idea of sending militia, because they too would resist. Henry thought he could raise enough volunteers to help, even while enlistments for the regular army had virtually come to a stop, because volunteers would be drawn from an entirely different class of men from those expected to join the regulars. They would serve for only six to eight months, and Henry thought they would come mainly from the "upper parts" of the country and be wealthy enough to find their own arms, clothes, and blankets; they would also be headed by officers of their "own choosing."[45]

But Henry's solution, based upon his experience at the head of volunteers in Virginia in 1775, found little favor among now professional officers like Washington, who quickly turned down Henry's offer and repeated arguments about the need to recruit a full-time professional army instead. A short-term army was destructive to the cause. The recruit that joins

44. George Johnstone to Leven Powell, Aug. 6, 1776, Powell, ed., *Biographical Sketch,* 37–38; Selby, *Revolution in Virginia,* 127–128; Aug. 5, 1776, McIlwaine et al., eds., *Journals of the Council,* I, 108.

45. Henry to Washington, Mar. 29, 1777, McIlwaine, ed., *Official Letters,* I, 130; Washington to Henry, Apr. 13, 1777, *Papers of Washington,* Rev. War Ser., IX, 146–148. Henry and the council actually tried to raise volunteers in late December but had to stop because they had only contributed to the "ill success" of recruiting for the regular troops. Henry to Cornelius Harnett, President of the Committee of Safety, North Carolina, Dec. 23, 1776, McIlwaine, ed., *Official Letters,* I, 84, and Proclamation by the Governor of Virginia, Dec. 27, 1776, I, 85–86; Dec. 26, 1776, Feb. 19, 1777, McIlwaine et al., eds., *Journals of the Council,* I, 300, 350.

a volunteer company was "uneasy—impatient of Command—ungovernable"; Washington and his officers wanted men that they could discipline properly. But Washington's new model army reexposed the central contradiction in the patriot cause and efforts to mobilize for war. People had to choose between being respectable citizens and staying in the militia and volunteer companies, and selling themselves into the more disciplined army, whose key was discipline and subordination to officers. Thus those with more of a stake in society were less likely to join the army, and those without a stake had less reason to support the patriot cause. Ultimately, Washington believed that a good bounty would entice needy men to come forward and subject themselves to the discipline necessary to face up to the British army. But lower-class Virginians and potential recruits for the army showed that, though the economic incentives were important, they were interested in more than just money.[46]

When a good bounty proved insufficient, some of Washington's officers proposed an alternative to Henry's initiative. While Henry wanted to call forth volunteers, some recruiting officers wanted to compel men to serve. Some were already doing so in an effort to claim their commissions. Nicholas Cresswell reported in March that recruiting officers in Loudoun, perhaps hoping that the new vagrancy law had established a precedent already, had begun "pressing the young men into the Army." Anti-British patriot rhetoric, of course, had vilified the British navy for doing exactly the same thing, and the laboring poor around the colonies had long been irritated by the illegal seizure of persons. In the face of such seizures, the people of Loudoun fought back. Cresswell reported that, in defiance of the attempts to impress potential recruits, there were "Great tumults and murmurings among the people" of Loudoun. The only reason that there was not further resistance and violence was that the people were "in general disarmed." Cresswell noted the irony: in such circumstances people could do little but "groan" under the "effects of an Independent Government."[47]

46. Washington to Henry, Apr. 13, 1777, *Papers of Washington,* Rev. War Ser., IX, 147.

47. Mar. 22, 29, 1777, Cresswell, *Journal,* 189–191. On impressments, see especially Jesse Lemisch, "Jack Tar in the Streets: Merchant Seamen in the Politics of Revolutionary America," *WMQ,* 3d Ser., XXV (1968), 371–407, and, more recently, Peter Linebaugh and Marcus Rediker, *The Many-Headed Hydra: Sailors, Slaves, Commoners, and the Hidden History of the Revolutionary Atlantic* (Boston, 2000), esp. 228–229, 235–236.

Frustrated by their neighbors' unwillingness to step forward, officers in Loudoun had begun compelling some of their less fortunate neighbors into service. When they faced concerted resistance, they looked to the state for help. Peter Grant, for example, an officer trying to recruit in the spring of 1777, had used his "utmost endeavors" to enlist men but had secured only four. He wanted more coercive powers, as he believed the country was "full of young Men" who were likely recruits. If they would not come into the army willingly, he hoped that measures would be soon taken to "force them into the Country's Service."[48]

In response to pressure from Washington and other Continental army officers like Grant, Congress finally recommended to the states that they take more coercive measures to procure men, suggesting on April 14 a series of measures designed to fill up their assigned quotas. Congress first proposed that the states allow any two militia to exempt themselves from all further military service upon the provision of one able-bodied soldier who would serve for three years or for the duration, the militia's exemption lasting as long as the soldier served. It also suggested that the legislators force any exempted men, like Dissenters, to furnish a set number of long-term recruits. Then, if the state quotas were not filled by May 15, Congress recommended that the states pass still more coercive measures and make "indiscriminate draughts" from their respective militia "without regard to Rank, Sect of Religion or other Privilege whatsoever."[49]

Once Congress had given its assent to drafting men for the army, Virginia officers in the Continental army pleaded with legislators at home to carry out Congress's recommendations to make up embarrassing deficiencies. George Weedon asked councillor John Page to round up deserters and spur enlistments but by mid-April felt that "the backwardness of the

48. Peter Grant to Powell, Apr. 9, 1777, "Leven Powell Correspondence," *Historical Papers of Randolph-Macon College,* II (1902), 123–124. Cf. Christopher Greenup to Leven Powell, May 2, 1777, 124–125.

49. Ford et al., eds., *Journals of the Continental Congress,* VII, 262–263. Most states were experiencing recruiting problems similar to Virginia's. The strength of the Continental army did not reach a peak in 1777 until October, when there were 39,443 men in the ranks, including more temporary militia reinforcements. This was only just more than half of the number Congress actually called for, or a shortfall of 35,000. It was also 8,000 short of the peak strength the army reached in October 1776, when far fewer battalions were in existence (Martin and Lender, *A Respectable Army,* 89).

recruiting Service" was "a little alarming." For Weedon, it was clear that "nothing but a draft will effect the Quotas of the states."[50]

Though his subordinate officers were keen to draft men in order to sustain their commissions, Washington was more cautious. Though he believed that a draft was necessary, it needed to be done carefully. He had seen firsthand that even a highly selective draft that targeted "vagrants" during the Seven Years' War had produced much resistance and at least two riots. The quality of the soldiers produced by the draft was also questionable in his eyes. He saw two alternatives at this point. Virginia could either draft men indiscriminately from the people at large, or it could rely on self-interest by allowing richer men to exempt themselves from any further military service by finding a long-term recruit. Perhaps the best way was "making it in the Interest of the Timid, the Rich, and the Tory to furnish Soldiers, at their own Expence, in ease of themselves." In spite of potential abuses, Washington told Henry that he favored this latter option, believing that it would produce more willing soldiers because the highest bidder would, in effect, hire them. The recruits would then be at least serving for money and not against their will. Drafting men indiscriminately might "produce Convulsions in the People and their Opposition, by the manner in which it is conducted."[51]

Ultimately, if Continental officials were convinced of the need for more coercive measures and possibly a draft, many were equally sure who ought to be targeted. Richard Henry Lee, a congressional delegate, had told Jefferson at the end of April that Virginia must institute a draft as the only way that Virginia could fill its quota. "I realy believe that numbers of our lazy, worthless young Men will not be induced to come forth into the service of their Country unless the States adopt the mode recommended by Congress of ordering Drafts from the Militia." Washington was more explicit about who ultimately ought to fill the ranks, whatever method was chosen: the army could be filled only with "the lower Class of People."

50. George Weedon to Page, Apr. 15, 1777, Papers of George Weedon, 1776–1779, 1789, LiVi (photocopies of originals at the Chicago Historical Society). Cf. Weedon to Page, May 31, 1777, Papers of Weedon, and John Chilton to his brother [Charles Chilton?], Aug. 11, 1777, in Keith Family of Woodburn, Fauquier Co., Papers, VHS.

51. James Titus, *The Old Dominion at War: Society, Politics, and Warfare in Late Colonial Virginia* (Columbia, S.C., 1991), 63–65; Washington to Henry, May 17, 1777, *Papers of Washington*, Rev. War Ser., IX, 452.

Though he had hoped they could hold out sufficient inducements for "the lower Class of People" to enlist voluntarily, Washington believed that they would inevitably be unable to avoid the "necessity of compelling them to inlist."[52]

• • • In May Virginia legislators began to discuss a coercive draft from the militia as they gathered for their spring session, keenly aware of the sentiments of the people out-of-doors. Jefferson, for example, noted: "In this country it ever was the most unpopular and impracticable thing that could be attempted. Our people even under the monarchical government had learnt to consider it as the last of all oppressions." Though most patriot leaders close to the executive—like Pendleton and councillor John Page— had become convinced of the need to draft men, the more popularly elected members of the House of Representatives were not so sure; it dragged its feet over the issue. A month after the assembly convened, Pendleton reported that it had still "finished little." At about the same time, John Banister, a prosperous delegate from Petersburg who also supported a draft, noted that legislators were wasting much time trying to come up with schemes to avoid one. Conceding that a draft "ought to be the last resource," he shared his colleagues' uncertainty about how other Virginians would react. But Banister thought the situation was serious enough to warrant an attempt: the "experiment must be made at every hazard."[53]

Banister revealed various proposals that had been put forth, all "calculated to supercede the necessity of a draft." But it was Pendleton, recovering at home from a fall from a horse, who revealed the outline of the most radical proposal: that the assembly had called for all exempted men from the militia owning more than one thousand pounds of property to pay what would have amounted to a surcharge of five pounds each. This additional tax on the wealthy—and those not actually responsible for defending the country—would go directly toward an extra bounty to encourage men to

52. R. H. Lee to Jefferson, Apr. 29, 1777, *Papers of Jefferson,* II, 13–14; Washington to Henry, May 17, 1777, *Papers of Washington,* Rev. War Ser., IX, 451.

53. Jefferson to John Adams, May 16, 1777, *Papers of Jefferson,* II, 18; Pendleton to Woodford, June 14, 1777, *Papers of Pendleton,* I, 214; John Banister to Theodorick Bland, June 10, 1777, John Banister Papers, VHS. Pendleton seems to have been convinced of the necessity of a draft by May 1777; see Pendleton to Woodford, May 3, 15, 1777, *Papers of Pendleton,* I, 206–207, 209. Cf. Page to R. H. Lee, Feb. 27, 1777, Hoffman, ed., *Lee Family Papers.*

enlist. The measure, which took to heart the complaints of many poorer Virginians about who should bear the burden of war, was ultimately defeated. Divided over means, legislators were desperate to avoid a draft, but even the popularly elected delegates were not prepared to go so far, at least not yet.[54]

In the end, Virginia legislators compromised. In the first instance, legislators did all they could to encourage recruits to fill the state's quota of Continental troops. They took up congressional recommendations and offered exemptions to any two men in the militia who procured a third for regular service. They officially, and publicly, sanctioned the enlistment of free blacks so long as they could prove they were free. Adopting Congress's recommendations, they sanctioned the enlistment of apprentices and indentured servants by army recruiters (but not by other militia)—with or without their masters' consent—and offered immunity to recruits against prosecution for debts up to fifty dollars. Additionally, the assembly offered to make public provisions available to the wives, children, and aged parents of any poorer soldiers who could not support themselves in the soldier's absence.[55]

If the county quotas were not full by August 10, the civil and military leaders of each county were to implement a second measure. The militia would be divided into as many divisions as men were needed, each nearly equal in men and property, and each responsible for raising one recruit voluntarily. The divisions were expected to pool their resources to try to induce or entice a man to enlist. If they did not procure a soldier within fifteen days, a draft would take place. Contrary to suggestions made by both Washington and Congress to draft men indiscriminately, the assembly targeted the more vulnerable in society. Draftees would be picked, not by open lottery, but by the opinion of the field officers and "four first magistrates" of the county. From the ranks of the delinquent divisions, these officials would "fix upon and draught one man, who, in their opinion, can be best spared, and will be most serviceable." The new recruits, or picked draftees,

54. Pendleton to Woodford, June 14, 28, 1777, *Papers of Pendleton,* I, 214; John Banister to Theodorick Bland, June 10, 1777, John Banister Papers, VHS. Pendleton thought the tax on exempts had actually passed and reported it as such to Woodford on June 28. However, there is no mention of it in the final act; it must have been dropped at the last minute (see Hening, comp., *Statutes at Large,* IX, 275–280).

55. Hening, comp., *Statutes at Large,* IX, 275–280.

were to serve for a full three years and receive the same bounty and pay as voluntary recruits.[56]

• • • Though legislators believed that a draft would be unpopular, they eventually took the chance because many worried that commitment to the patriot cause among ordinary white Virginians was not secure enough. As Edwin Gray put it, it was not simply the "Spirit of Inlistment" that was missing in Virginia, but rather "the spirit of patriotism" that seemed "at this period to be smother'd in some measure." In these circumstances, a draft designed to draw out and target the socially marginal was the answer to both of Virginia's pressing problems: sustaining morale and commitment and providing an effective defense. Indeed, Banister's comments help us understand one of the main reasons why the General Assembly in May 1777 went ahead with the draft in spite of its worries. Though middling farmers would be responsible for procuring recruits, propertied farmers were unlikely to be targeted in the draft. Despite the divisions in the assembly, few doubted who would ultimately serve in the army: apprentices, servants, free blacks, vagabonds, and debtors. Draft officials were to pick out only those they felt expendable, or, in the words of one recruiting officer, all "Lazy fellows who lurk about and are pests to Society." Most would have no political rights. The fact that draftees would be picked, not by lottery, but by the field officers and four leading magistrates of each county ensured that only the troublesome or powerless would be chosen. Indeed, in this respect the draft would also allow legislators to deal with the vagrancy problem that concerned them the previous summer and fall. Legislators hoped targeting only the "expendables" in society would alienate only those who were already alienated—those who stood outside or at the margins of political life.[57]

At the same time, the erection of a permanent and prominent army

56. Ibid.; Aug. 29, 1777, Diary of Honyman; Pendleton to Woodford, June 28, 1777, *Papers of Pendleton,* I, 215. The field officers and justices were also responsible for pooling their own money and raising a man themselves.

57. Pendleton to Woodford, May 3, 1777, *Papers of Pendleton,* I, 206–207; Edwin Gray to James Gray, May 10, 1777, Ridley Family Papers, VHS; John Chilton to his brother [Charles Chilton?], Aug. 11, 1777, Keith Family of Woodburn, Fauquier Co., Papers, VHS. Cf. Pendleton to Woodford, May 15, 1777, *Papers of Pendleton,* I, 209; R. H. Lee to Governor Patrick Henry, Apr. 15, 1777, Executive Papers, LiVi; George Johnston to Leven Powell, Mar. 29, 1777, Powell, ed., *Biographical Sketch,* 59; Dec. 14, 1776, Cresswell, *Journal,* 176; Apr. 10, 30, 1777, Diary of Honyman.

would bolster the confidence of middling farmers and encourage a greater attachment to the cause. Men like Banister believed that a show of strength and authority was vital to shore up patriot support. A vastly augmented army on the scale that Washington and Congress envisioned, even if raised by coercion, would actually help convert many to the cause. A large army once raised, which was "capable of acting with advantage against the enemy, would be a means of *confirming the minds of the common people,* who always judge by events." Once patriot leaders could prove that the war was winnable, the "augmentation of the forces" would be "no difficult matter." Only the "éclat of victories," Banister argued, "strikes the gross of mankind." For Banister the recruitment of soldiers, by any means, became the paramount objective. An army superior to the British would soon give "reputation to our arms, *increase our adherents at home,* and procure us allies abroad."[58]

In one stroke, then, legislators could fulfill their Continental obligations, strengthen their own defense, and consolidate the support of the middling classes by isolating and exploiting a supposedly powerless group. Rather than force citizens to become soldiers, patriots forced noncitizens (or those without a vote) to become soldiers, giving citizens more incentive to commit to the new states. Thus the draft law of May 1777 was designed not only to further remove the burden of service from respectable, propertied, and enfranchised middling farmers and planters in Virginia; it was also de-

58. Banister might have been swayed by reports that in early January, after Washington's victories at Princeton and Trenton, enlistments were temporarily boosted. Nicholas Cresswell, among others, noted that, in the wake of Washington's victories, "the minds of the people are much altered." Only "a few days ago they had given up the cause for lost," but "their late successes have turned the scale and now they are all liberty mad again." Whereas recruiting officers could not get a single man a week before, Cresswell reported, "now the men are coming in by companies" (Jan. 7, 1776, Cresswell, *Journal,* 179). The flurry of activity was only short-lived. John Banister to Theodorick Bland, June 10, 1777, John Banister Papers, VHS (emphasis added); cf. Sept. 8, 1777, Diary of Honyman; Jefferson to William Fleming, July 1, 1776, Fleming to Jefferson, July 27, 1776, *Papers of Jefferson,* I, 412, 474–475.

As if to test this experiment, legislators also instituted an oath of allegiance: citizens must renounce any allegiance to Great Britain and pledge to inform the government about any acts of treason. Those who refused to take the oath would be disarmed, prohibited from holding any office, serving on juries, suing for debts, voting, or buying lands or tenements. Hening, comp., *Statutes at Large,* IX, 281–283.

signed to help fortify a patriotic alliance between those same farmers and their wealthy officeholding neighbors and leaders. As they had in the past, patriot leaders hoped that the poor, the unpropertied, and the expendables of Virginia society—those who, in the opinion of local leaders, could "be best spared, and will be most serviceable"—would provide the cement to bond that alliance.[59]

59. Hening, comp., *Statutes at Large,* IX, 275–280. In this, legislators did have their experience in the Seven Years' War in America to guide them, when they originally targeted "vagrants"—those "who have no visible Way of getting an honest Livelihood." Indeed, in the previous war, the Burgesses were explicit about their motives for recruiting this group when they exempted "any person to serve as a soldier, who hath any vote in the election of a Burgess" (Titus, *Old Dominion at War,* 59–60).

CHAPTER 9 *The Politics of Lower-Class Draft Resistance, 1777–1778*

Despite the best efforts of patriot leaders, many of the "lazy, worthless young men" in Virginia in the summer of 1777 did not sit back and wait to be targeted by draft officials. Instead, they resisted coercion to push them into the army, sometimes violently. If the army did tempt lower-class Virginians, they at least extorted great bounties from desperate farmers in return for their service. Finally, when lower-class Virginians could not resist the laws, they often evaded them, crippling recruiting efforts.

Though the first draft law was designed to bond propertyholding Virginians together, the actions and reactions of the so-called expendables began to create new alliances. Indeed, such resistance had rippling effects on Virginia's wartime politics. With Congress and officers in the Continental army pushing from above for more soldiers and lower-class Virginians resisting from below, the assembly was caught in the middle. As delegates struggled to balance these competing interests, new cracks began to emerge, particularly when propertyholding freeholders were mobilized in the militia to serve in place of those badly needed recruits. In return for their service, and their votes, the assembly had to make concessions to ordinary Virginians. Most notably, freeholders demanded and got a new and revolutionary tax system. Lower-class Virginians, then, in resisting efforts to coerce and entice them into the army, created new divisions—and alignments—among patriot leaders especially, but throughout Virginia society too.

• • • Initially, it looked as if legislators' draft plans might work. With the prospect of a draft, a desperate search for recruits helped squeeze more enlistees onto the parade ground. At the same time, the new law created opportunities for poorer Virginians to get something in return for their now badly needed service. The law made it especially easier for the very lowest classes in Virginia to seek a form of freedom in the army. Not only were recruiting officers now desperate to find and accept anyone who might show a willingness to serve, but so too were the divisions of militia who wanted to avoid a draft and individuals who wanted an exemption. Servants and slaves now had even greater leverage to convince others that they were free.

Enslaved Virginians certainly continued to take advantage of the desperation of recruiters and potential recruits alike. Just before the draft took place, Joe ran away from his master, Charles Jones, in Alexandria. Joe was about twenty-one years of age and could "read and wright" according to his owner, who understood that Joe wanted to "enlist as a freeman." And because recruiting officers could enlist white servants, many servants sought them out. Several owners believed that their indentured servants were headed straight for nearby recruiting officers. John Holladay from Spotsylvania County reported that his English servant, thirty-five-year-old Matthew Fright, ran away and would probably enlist with a recruiting officer, pretending he was free. Samuel Love of Loudoun County lost two convict servants in the early summer of 1777. Love also thought that twenty-year-old London-born George Dorman (alias Holderness) and David Hinds, a thirty-five-year-old Irish ropemaker and sailor, would try to pass themselves off as soldiers and enlist "at the first opportunity."[1]

The new law also provided many opportunities for recruits in need of cash. The law stipulated that the Continental bounty would be given to recruits in addition to any "private gratuities" they might receive from other militia to serve in their stead. The evidence suggests that many strove to get as much money as they could for their now desperately needed services. Even before the draft began, bidding for potential recruits had begun driving up prices. Some recruiting officers had to resort to offering additional incentives to potential recruits, often out of their own pocket. One officer complained that such men had "spoilt the recruiting Service" by offering up to fifty dollars per man. Yet officers were at the mercy of the men they were trying to recruit. Raleigh Colston, the captain of the sloop *Liberty,* learned this lesson when he tried to invoke patriotism as a good reason for his crew to take lower wages. The crew made it clear on what terms they

1. Owners, at least, believed that their bondsmen were not fussy about what service they joined. Edward C. Travis of Jamestown thought that Jesse, a seventeen-year-old who had run away in August, would either enlist in the army or join a ship and pass as a sailor and freeman. *Va. Gaz.* (Purdie), Aug. 8, supplement, Sept. 12, Oct. 31, 1777; cf. Sept. 5, 1777.

would serve, their spokesman declaring, "Country here or Country there, damn my Eyes and limbs but I'll serve them that give the best wages."[2]

Showing a sensitivity to the power of contracts, potential recruits were often in a strong enough position to strike different deals with those who wanted their services, deals that did not always involve more money. Some wanted to secure some status. Louis Charles, Jr., of Brunswick County claimed that he had made a conditional "Contract" with Lieutenant Philip Mallory of the Fifteenth Virginia Regiment. Charles explained that he had already served as a minuteman and a regular soldier. When asked to enlist again, Charles extracted a promise from Mallory that he would gain a sergeant major's place in the company. When Mallory failed to deliver the promotion, Charles refused to serve. Another man, James Skelton of Charlotte County, also struck a deal with an officer, William Dickson, over his leadership of the company he was raising. Not wishing to risk service with another, unknown officer, Skelton claimed that he had enlisted only on the condition that Dickson himself continued in the Continental service. When Dickson "threw up his commission," Skelton claimed his discharge.[3]

Once the militia had been split into divisions in early August in prepa-

---

2. Col. Digges to Theodorick Bland, Sept. 16, 1777, Charles Campbell, ed., *The Bland Papers: Being a Selection from the Manuscripts of Colonel Theodorick Bland, Jr.* (Petersburg, Va., 1840, 1843), I, 69; Granville Smith to Leven Powell, Aug. 28, 1777, "The Leven Powell Correspondence, 1775-1787," *John P. Branch Historical Papers of Randolph-Macon College,* II (1902), 125; Raleigh Colston to William Aylett, Oct. 24, 1777, as cited in John E. Selby, *The Revolution in Virginia, 1775-1783* (Williamsburg, Va., 1988), 172. The aggrieved captain, Raleigh Colston, thought the crew was a "a sett of unfeeling animals."

Still other men made extra cash out of bounty jumping. John Thomas, for example, a blacksmith from Amelia County, enlisted with two or three officers, received a bounty from each, and promptly deserted each time. One man from the Eastern Shore became a sailor on the frigate *Virginia,* deserted, and had allegedly "taken several unlawful bounties" (*Va. Gaz.* [Purdie], Oct. 3, Aug. 8, 1777). Other whites also enlisted in the army for traditional reasons. John Douding, for example, enlisted for three years' service to escape an unhappy domestic situation. Douding said his wife Lucy had behaved in a very "unfriendly manner" to him. In going northward with the army, Douding warned anyone that she should not be trusted on his account as he would pay no debts she might contract in his absence (*Va. Gaz.* [Purdie], Oct. 10, 1777).

3. *Va. Gaz.* (D and H), Aug. 8, 1777; *Va. Gaz.* (Purdie), Nov. 28, 1777, supplement.

ration for the draft, the frantic search for soldiers gave lower-class Virginians even greater bargaining power. Robert Honyman in Hanover County reported, "Large sums of money have been collected by the divisions in many Counties to hire a man, but without effect." He opined that "50, 60, and 70 pounds have been offered and no more to be had." Each division of militia was eager to avoid a draft, so potential recruits hired themselves out to the highest bidders. Landon Carter, one of the four first magistrates of Richmond County, grumbled that he and his colleagues could hire a man only for twice the stipulated rate.[4]

Moreover, anyone drafted could still hire a substitute up to the moment of marching, so many potential recruits waited to see whether they could extort even more money from those who wanted to avoid service. One officer reported that some domestic militia were paying up two, three, or four times as much as they might have paid if they had hired someone before the draft took place. He had even heard of some militia paying one hundred pounds for a man to enlist in their stead. William Harris from Culpeper County and two brothers from Carolina had purposely waited until after the draft to come forward and offer their services. They had in the end received "very considerable sums of money" to take the place of men who had been drafted.[5]

Lower-class Virginians at risk of being drafted who could not afford to pay such sums for substitutes resorted to other means to try to avoid service. Even before the draft, some men tried to disrupt the recruiting service, perhaps to sabotage the act altogether. Landon Carter in Richmond County complained in early July of problems they were having implementing the new recruiting law. The other magistrates in the county were having little success in "restoring the County to good order, Particularly in Suppressing the attempts making to Prejudice the recruiting Service."[6]

4. Aug. 29, 1777, Diary of Robert Honyman, Jan. 2, 1776–Mar. 11, 1782, Alderman Library, UVa (microfilm); Sept. 2, 1777, Jack P. Greene, ed., *The Diary of Colonel Landon Carter of Sabine Hall, 1752–1778* (Charlottesville, Va., 1965), II, 1128.

5. Col. Digges to Theodorick Bland, Sept. 16, 1777, Campbell, ed., *Bland Papers,* I, 69; Granville Smith to Leven Powell, Aug. 28, 1777, "Leven Powell Correspondence," *Historical Papers of Randolph-Macon College,* II (1902), 125; *Va. Gaz.* (Purdie), Oct. 3, 1777.

6. July 7, 1777, Greene, ed., *Diary of Carter,* II, 1107.

As the day of the draft approached and fewer and fewer potential recruits stepped forward, militia who felt themselves under threat of being picked out stepped up their general resistance to the act. Again in Richmond County, Landon Carter had attended court only because a "worthy member begged I would come to give weight and order to the Proceedings." Then, just after the actual draft took place, two men, John Jones Griffin and William Sutton, were summoned to answer a charge of "Contempt offered by them to the Officers of this State." In Loudoun County also, eight men were brought before the court just after the draft law went into effect, charged under it with resisting the government and raising "Tumults and Disorders in this State." Under the same law and immediately following the draft, at least two men were brought before the Mecklenburg County court.[7]

Those who could not stop the draft could at least sometimes evade it if they were actually picked out for service. Many of those targeted for the draft were footloose, so they sought fortunes in other states. Robert Honyman later wrote that he thought not half of the conscripts ever joined the army. Most deserted and ran off to the Carolinas, Georgia, or the Ohio backcountry. From Hanover County alone, twenty of twenty-seven drafted men had deserted. Nor was this unusual. In the aftermath of the draft, the newspapers were full of advertisements for deserters. In one issue of the *Virginia Gazette* in October, five separate advertisements sought aid in rounding up deserters, including sixteen who had disappeared from Fairfax County alone.[8]

7. Sept. 1, 1777, Richmond County Order Book, no. 18, LiVi; Aug. 8, 1777, Greene, ed., *Diary of Carter*, II, 1121; Aug. 12, Sept. 9, 1777, Loudoun County Court Records, 1776–1783, LiVi; Sept. 8, 1777, Mecklenburg County, Order Book 4, 1773–1779, LiVi.

8. Six men from the Charles City County militia who had been drafted ran away. Five were still "now lurking about" in the county, and the sixth—Perkins Thomson, Jr., a shoemaker—reputedly went off to Brunswick County. Two other draftees had also not yet come in. Seven other men from Prince George County were also deemed deserters, including three described as "mulatto." Five men who were drafted in James City County—virtually that county's entire quota—failed to appear at their rendezvous. Lieutenant John Tankersley also lost virtually the entire quota drafted in King George County. He advertised the loss of fourteen drafted men, including Evan Payne, a mulatto, from that county. Lieutenant Samuel Baskerville lost four drafts from Powhatan County and eight drafts from Cumberland

Ironically, advertisements for deserters might also have contributed to faltering voluntary enlistments in the army. Though patriot leaders had made it clear among themselves whom they wanted to target for service in the army and were more explicit in the provisions for drafting men in 1777, the advertisements for deserters painted a more public picture of the kinds of men who were compelled and coerced into the army. Advertisements are a particularly rich source of information about soldiers in Virginia, telling us much—not just about the kinds of men that joined or were picked out to join—but also about officers' perceptions of them. Patriot officers were often scathing about the quality of the recruits. In turn, advertised as they were in the public papers, such descriptions also helped shape public opinion about just who ought to be in the army.

Significantly, advertisements for deserters were very similar to advertisements looking for runaway servants and slaves—a fact that did not escape the notice of both readers and deserters alike. Officers gave names, a short description, and any distinguishing characteristics of the deserters. In tone, too, officers were as disdainful of the objects of their notices as were masters who were furious at their slaves for running away. In early September, for example, Alexander Spotswood, colonel of the Second Virginia Regiment, put a notice in the *Virginia Gazette* advertising thirteen deserters from his regiment who were then in service in New Jersey. They included thirty-five-year-old Francis Dryskil, an Irishman who chewed tobacco and was "very fond of Liquor," and Joseph Bryant, who was also "fond of Liquor" and had a "remarkable scar on one of his lips." William Denny had also deserted, another Irishman, about thirty years of age who was "much pitted with the Smallpox" as well as being "fond of Liquor." His younger countryman, John Sanders, was only about eighteen and "smooth faced." Thomas Trap was a thirty-year-old sergeant in the army who was also "pitted with Smallpox" and "talks in a whining Manner." Trap had

---

County, and Ensign Isaac Holmes lost seven men from Mecklenburg County. Jan. 6, 1778, Diary of Honyman; *Va. Gaz.* (Purdie), Oct. 3, 31, Nov. 1, supplement, 28, 1777; *Va. Gaz.* (D and H), Sept. 26, 1777; *Papers of Mason*, I, 373n; cf. *Va. Gaz.* (D and H), Oct. 3, 1777.

Lieutenant David Walker also lost twelve men raised or drafted in Dinwiddie County (*Va. Gaz.* [Purdie], Nov. 14, 1777). The *Virginia Gazette* (Purdie), of Nov. 28, 1777, contained an advertisement for twenty men from Hanover, "draughts from the *Hanover* militia" for the Fourteenth Regiment, who had failed to appear at the appointed time.

left the army with his wife—"heavy with Child"—who had been with him during the campaign. Finally, the deserters included brothers Philip and Brice Ragan, who were twenty-two and twenty years old, respectively. Philip, a corporal, "speaks fierce" and had a "dark Complexion"; Brice was of a "fair Complexion" and a more "agreeable look." In a similar vein, two weeks later, Captain William Murray complained of two runaways from his artillery company. Edward Sage had lost one of his "under Eyelids" and had a scar on the same side of his nose; John Freeland was much marked by smallpox. Both, the captain warned, had been "bred to the Sea."[9]

Given their status as deserters, the men described in these advertisements might be a particularly exceptional group. Yet at the very least such descriptions would have had an impact on public opinion in Virginia. Indeed, if, like Nicholas Cresswell, more middling Virginians did not already think of the army as a "ragged crew," they could have only recoiled at the thought of joining such a motley crew as described by Spotswood and Murray. Most of the deserters were described as either "fond of liquor" or ravaged by smallpox or both. Of the thirteen, four were described as Irish, one as English, and only one specifically as a "Virginian." Five (three of whom were foreigners) were between the ages of 30 and 35, and the four others whose ages were given were between 18 and 22. None seemed to have a home to speak of. Spotswood thought Benjamin James would flee to Baltimore, where his parents lived, and Joseph Bryant might try to go to King George County, where his parents lived. Richard Lewis the twenty-five-year-old Englishman, "formerly" lived in Loudoun, and of course Trap and his wife presumably had made a home anywhere on the road.[10]

Descriptions such as these, taken together with the combined effect of the market in soldiers, resistance, protest, and desertion, rendered the draft a failure. Pendleton's experience in Caroline County was probably typical. Noting that they needed four recruits to complete their portion of the quota, he wrote that one division paid a recruit eighty pounds to serve for them, a sum that put it out of the power of the other divisions to procure their men. The field officers and justices, who were ordered by law to pay fifty shillings each to hire a man to exempt themselves, could not match the market. They paid in the full twenty pounds and "offered it for a man, but in vain." They had drafted men from the remaining two divisions, but

9. *Va. Gaz.* (D and H), Sept. 5, 19, 1777.
10. Ibid., Sept. 5, 1777.

Pendleton was sure they would never join the army; they "will probably hide."[11]

At best, perhaps fewer than a thousand men ultimately enlisted or were drafted into the army. In May 1777, a total of 3,561 men were listed in the ranks of the Virginia Line, including those sick and on furlough. By December, there were at most just more than 4,000 Virginia troops with Washington at Valley Forge, including hundreds of men who were listed as sick, on furlough, or "wanting shoes, etc." The Seventh Virginia Regiment, for example, headed by Colonel Alexander McClanachan, listed a total of 427 men in the battalion. However, 80 were missing shoes and thus out of action, 139 were on furlough in Virginia, 104 were sick and not present, and another 10 were sick at camp. This left only 46 men present and fit for duty as well as another 48 on duty elsewhere. Altogether, the number of men from Virginia who were present and fit for duty by the end of the year was at best about 1,500, or almost 1,000 fewer than in May.[12]

• • • Quite apart from the crippling effects of draft resistance on the Continental war effort, opposition to the laws had wider ramifications. Far from cementing an alliance with middling farmers, patriot leaders' efforts, combined with lower-class resistance, created further divisions among Virginians. As some of the advertisements imply, for example, draftees dodging the army often found support and sympathy in their own communities. Even before men were coerced into service, regular military officers complained of the countenance that was given deserters from the army in Virginia. George Weedon felt, "Desertions have been to frequent and to much Encouraged by the reception they meet with in this Country." When the draft was introduced, patriot leaders had tried to prevent desertions by passing an act at the same time authorizing the county lieutenant to appoint militia to search out and deliver suspected deserters before the county court. Those who harbored deserters or aided them in any way faced fines of up to five pounds. Moreover, the government promised a bounty of three pounds to anyone who would turn in a deserter.[13]

11. Edmund Pendleton to William Woodford, Sept. 13, 1777, *Papers of Pendleton*, I, 224.

12. Charles H. Lesser, ed., *The Sinews of Independence: Monthly Strength Reports of the Continental Army* (Chicago, 1976), 46–47, 54–55.

13. George Weedon to John Page, Apr. 15, 1777, Papers of George Weedon,

Most ignored the reward and instead flouted the laws. For some, it was a family affair. James Patterson, a twenty-year-old, deserted when his captain was "decoyed off by his Father." For others, friends and neighbors often helped. Pendleton complained shortly after the draft that in Virginia there were "a great many" deserters who found sanctuary among friends and neighbors. He despaired over the effect on patriot authority. "Friends Secrete them and the Neighbours connive at it, and what is every one's duty becomes Nobody's."[14]

Where local officials tried to enforce the law, they sometimes incited violent resistance. In piedmont Cumberland County in 1777, a general fistfight broke out when one county official attempted to apprehend a drafted deserter. On October 4, 1777, Warren Walker, a planter and successful tanner, grand juryman, and owner of up to thirty-nine slaves, unsuccessfully attempted to take Isham Brown into custody, "knowing him to be a Deserter." The propertyless Brown was probably one of the eight draftees from Cumberland who deserted. When Walker tried to apprehend him, Brown went for help and returned with James Corley, a propertyless "carpenter." Brown then attacked Walker with a chair. When Walker called upon Corley to aid him in taking Brown, he found only another antagonist. Corley, described by Walker as being "stript'd farther . . . having his Sleeves and Collers open," appeared to be "very angry by rubbing his fist together." According to witnesses, Corley declared that he "swore he wou'd see fare play. and that he woud strike any man that interfered." Stephen Lockett, a planter from nearby Prince Edward County who witnessed the events, said nobody moved, and Brown went free.[15]

1776-1779, 1789, photocopies of originals at the Chicago Historical Society, LiVi; Hening, comp., *Statutes at Large,* IX, 289-290.

14. *Va. Gaz.* (D and H), July 25, 1777; Pendleton to Woodford, Nov. 29, 1777, *Papers of Pendleton,* I, 238.

15. The account is taken from an "Information," Oct. 6, 1777, Cumberland County Court Records, Suit Papers, box 1, 1770s-, LiVi. For the deserters from Cumberland, see *Va. Gaz.* (Purdie), Oct. 31, 1777. Neither Corley nor Brown appears in the 1782 tax records; Walker does not appear in the land tax records but is listed as owning a substantial 39 slaves, 8 horses, and 72 cattle in 1782 (Cumberland County Personal Property Tax Records, 1782, LiVi). For Walker's status in the county, see May 26, 1777, July 30, Sept. 27, 1779, Cumberland County Court Records, Order Books, 1779-1784, LiVi.

Apprehending deserters could be a lucrative business. See, for example, Sept. 11,

The practice of rescuing deserters was widespread. Jacob Hoveaker and David Huffman of Loudoun County, for example, rescued Henry Boyd, a deserter from the Continental army, and hid him from two men who had apprehended him. When patriot authorities tried to intervene, violence could result. When Henry Peyton, cornet of a troop of horse, tried to take up a deserter in Loudoun County, he was "shot through the body."[16]

Sometimes, then, lower-class Virginians like Isham Brown and James Corley banded together along class lines. Equally often, the new laws divided communities along kinship or family lines. Still other communities conspired against patriot authority itself and complained more generally about the unjustness of the laws. Later in the war, men from Charlotte, Buckingham, and several adjoining counties petitioned the assembly about the 1777 draft. They felt that it was too arbitrary, and they had always looked upon it "as hard and bearing on Individuals whom Caprice whim or Opinion should discriminate." Men chosen by this method were of little service to their country: "Some have gone unwillingly, others deserted and little benefit arose from the whole, but a Considerable injury . . . from driving into refuge men who might otherwise Serve the Country." Because of the way they had been picked, no "Conscientious persons" could fail to empathize with those that deserted. They acknowledged that the law had "nearly spent its force yet they Could wish it intirely repealed" and "the Striking bad policy and hardship of The measure" recognized. Thus, while patriot leaders hoped to build a wartime alliance with their more respectable neighbors, the draft sometimes turned whole communities against patriot authorities.[17]

But what might have been more worrying for patriot leaders at the state level was the fact that community feeling often forced the hands of local patriot officials. Such was the case in Hanover County, where twenty drafted men had deserted and the county lieutenant did little to enforce the law. He openly tolerated those who had evaded the draft of 1777, declar-

1777, H. R. McIlwaine et al., eds., *Journals of the Council of the State of Virginia* (Richmond, Va., 1931–1982), I, 487.

16. Nov. 12, Dec. 14, 1776, Nicholas Cresswell, *The Journal of Nicholas Cresswell* (London, 1925), 169, 176; May 11, 1778, Loudoun County Court Records, 1776–1783, LiVi.

17. Charlotte County Petition, [Oct. 15, 1779], LiVi; Buckingham County Petition, [Nov. 23, 1780], LiVi.

ing in 1781 that the recruitment act of 1777 was "a Law, that I never could Consider, but in an unjust Light."[18]

Significantly, the effects of the resistance of many white Virginians trickled further upward and also led some patriot leaders to question publicly the authority of the assembly. In Prince William County, for example, Cuthbert Bullitt, a justice and member of the assembly, told his constituents that he was "greatly concerned to hear that the Draught has given uneasiness to many." Bullitt's neighbors had complained about the fact that the draftees could be dragged away and forced to serve outside the state. Bullitt took up their cause and declared his agreement publicly: men drafted could not lawfully be forced to serve outside the commonwealth. He would inquire into the matter on behalf of the draftees and gave his word, "If the Law is in their favour, they shall return to their Homes."[19]

Such divisions among Virginians worried many patriot leaders. One patriot, calling himself "A Virginian" in the *Virginia Gazette,* acknowledged that there was much "discontent" because of the draft. He asked for a ready obedience to the new state laws and looked for deferential behavior in the face of the new coercive measures: "Anticipate the draught; enlist cheerfully, or at least submit to be draughted without murmuring." He believed that the willingness of people to submit to the laws was linked to their commitment to the new independent government. He pleaded with other Virginians to shun "the reproach of being disobedient to the sacred laws of your country." If they obeyed the law, they would show a determination to "preserve your present constitution inviolate."[20]

The anonymous writer was especially worried that such resistance would weaken them more generally. Intimating that their problems were worse than most would admit, he noted that loyalists, enslaved Virginians, and the British would all be watching for any opportunity to capitalize on the problems within the state. Fence-sitting Virginians would also take

18. John Syme to William Davies, Mar. 7, 1781, John David McBride, "The Virginia War Effort, 1775–1783: Manpower Policies and Practices" (Ph.D. diss., University of Virginia, 1977), 255.

19. "Address to the Inhabitants of Prince William County," Oct. 6, 1777, Executive Communications, box 1, LiVi. Bullitt was subsequently corrected about the laws and forced by the county court to sign a retraction, which he did, but not without upholding his right to criticize the government (see accompanying documents, ibid., for the full case).

20. *Va. Gaz.* (Purdie), Aug. 1, 1777.

their cue from the success or failure of such efforts. He concluded by emphasizing the importance of maintaining a front of unanimity. If that front were broached, their enemies would invariably triumph, because Virginia would be "weak through discontent and divisions amongst ourselves."[21]

• • • Reports of "large Fleets" on the coasts of Virginia in mid-August sent the state into a panic, within two weeks of the Virginian's public warning that the British, loyalists, and enslaved Virginians might capitalize on divisions among whites. When Admiral Richard Howe's fleet sailed into the Chesapeake on August 16, white inhabitants were "exceedingly terrified" at the spectacle. Though mainland Virginia was spared a repeat of the events of 1775–1776, enslaved Virginians once again took advantage of the presence of the British fleet. Though the invasion scare lasted only a few short weeks, it took a heavy toll on Virginia's slaveowning planter class in particular. The council reported that "many Negroes" had absconded from Northampton and Accomack Counties and had joined the enemy. They believed "many more" would follow their example.[22]

21. Ibid. The Virginian might also have been worried because of reports that the administration of the oath of allegiance was not going down well among Virginians either. For examples of resistance to it, see F. L. Lee to R. H. Lee, Aug. 17, 1777, "Selections and Excerpts from the Lee Papers," *Southern Literary Messenger,* XXVII (July–December 1858), 260; Hening, comp., *Statutes at Large,* IX, 281–283; *Va. Gaz.* (D and H), Aug. 22, Sept. 19, 1777; Loudoun County Court Records, 1776–1783, LiVi; Brunswick County Petition, [Oct. 10, 1778], Virginia Legislative Petitions, LiVi. Prince William Tax Commissioners, [Oct. 14, 1779], Prince William County Petitions, Virginia Legislative Petitions, LiVi; Robert Kinkade Petition, [June 2, 1779], Rockbridge County Petitions, Virginia Legislative Petitions, LiVi. For the other counties, see Virginia Legislative Petitions, LiVi; *Va. Gaz.* (D and H), Aug. 29, 1777; Emory G. Evans, "Trouble in the Backcountry: Disaffection in Southwest Virginia during the American Revolution," in Ronald Hoffman, Thad W. Tate, and Peter J. Albert, eds., *An Uncivil War: The Southern Backcountry during the American Revolution* (Charlottesville, Va., 1985), 188–189.

22. Benjamin Quarles, *The Negro in the American Revolution* (Chapel Hill, N.C., 1961), 117; Sylvia R. Frey, *Water from the Rock: Black Resistance in a Revolutionary Age* (Princeton, N.J., 1991), 146; Sept. 5, 1777, McIlwaine et al., eds., *Journals of the Council,* I, 483. Even before the British came into the bay in numbers in the fall of 1777, patriots had a taste of what they could expect when almost three hundred enslaved Virginians from coastal counties like Northumberland, Gloucester, and Lancaster joined British ships blockading the bay.

They did, and not just from the Eastern Shore counties. Thirteen enslaved Virginians belonging to Major Thomas Smith of Gloucester County took advantage of the occasion to flee their bondage. Though most enslaved Virginians who tried to reach the British were from eastern or bayside counties, some ventured from much farther. Twenty-year-old Tapley from Richmond made a run for it when the British came into the bay. His owner, George Kelly, believed he would make straight for Portsmouth and try to escape to a British ship of war. Lewis and Prince—who ran away from Nelson Anderson, Jr., of nearby Hanover County—might have joined Tapley. Anderson worried that both of the runaways were capable of acting like freemen, and Prince, who was "much used to the tending of gentlemen," had acquired an acquaintance with "most of America" while he served Mr. Brown of King William County. Anderson feared that Lewis and Prince would head for the Chesapeake to try to join Howe, as Prince had at least once tried to join Dunmore. One enslaved Virginian, James, tried to reach the British from as far away as Pittsylvania County.[23]

Though white Virginians despaired over the loss of their valuable prop-

23. Sept. 25, 1777, McIlwaine et al., eds., *Journals of the Council,* I, 496. *Va. Gaz.* (Purdie), Sept. 12, 19, Nov. 21, 1777. Newspaper advertisements also make clear that many enslaved Virginians took off when the British were in the bay (see, for example, *Va. Gaz.* [D and H], Oct. 3, 10, Dec. 5, 1777). Cf. *Va. Gaz.* (D and H), Aug. 1, 1777; Feb. 13, 19, 1778, McIlwaine et al., eds., *Journals of the Council,* II, 82, 86.

As British ships lingered in the Chesapeake during the fall, enslaved Virginians throughout the eastern counties continued to take to the waters. One report, from the Northern Neck, noted that "Many Negroes" had allegedly joined the British because it was not in the militia's power to "guard the whole river." The *Virginia Gazette* warned patriots to be more vigilant. A correspondent noted that "the Gentlemen" in the area in particular had contributed to problems. Instead of destroying their boats and preventing any slaves from reaching the enemy, they had tried to preserve all of their property. As a result, they and others lost "some hundred pounds" worth of both property and slaves. In one instance, a Captain Townsend Dade had locked his boat in a barn. The next night, up to ten enslaved Virginians from several different plantations banded together, took his oxen and broke open the door, and carried the boat to the riverside to effect their successful escape (Dec. 23, 1777, Diary of Honyman; *Va. Gaz.* [D and H], Dec. 19, 1777). Enslaved Virginians took the risk despite white propaganda that the British were only too happy to give them refuge in order to sell them in the West Indies (see *Va. Gaz.* [Purdie], Sept. 26, 1777). For other runaway attempts, see *Va. Gaz.* (Purdie), Oct. 10, 17, 1777.

erty, they were also constantly in trepidation about the threat their property posed to them the former masters. In preparing Virginia's defense, for example, the council feared most that, if the British invaded, newly freed black Virginians would terrify their former masters as in 1775. Former slaves would be used as "Instruments in the Hands of our Enemies," because they would no doubt set about "committing Robberies and other Depredations on their former Masters." Certainly, escapees were already being used on board the British ships in the bay. Yet, on this occasion the council worried about the possibility of white and black cooperation, betraying its lack of faith in the patriotism of many white Virginians. Anxious that many whites would also join the enemy, the council ordered the immediate removal of anyone suspected of holding loyalist beliefs to the interior of the state.[24]

The council also ordered all the county lieutenants along the bay and the navigable rivers to collect and secure all boats or other vessels that might help "our internal Enemies or Slaves" escape to the enemy. With the two groups easily lumped together, the concern of the council turned out to be well founded, as blacks and disaffected whites took the opportunity of the alarm to make their escape. On August 21, Governor Henry got word that four white men, including John Goodrich the elder, in jail in Albemarle County for their loyalist activities, had escaped. They had since been spotted making their way down to the James River with "four Negroes." Whites and blacks did more than escape together, however. At least one group of eight sailors and five "stolen Negroes" led by a Captain Dunbar of Gloucester County sailed on one of the enemy's tenders and plundered up and down the coastlines during the invasion scare. The *Virginia Gazette* reported that Dunbar had been "a long time in company" with the motley crew.[25]

Moreover, the council had received reports that the disaffected had begun to stage another uprising in the Norfolk area in order to encourage the British to help liberate them. Many had allegedly "openly avowed" an

24. Sept. 5, 1777, McIlwaine et al., eds., *Journals of the Council*, I, 483. For escaped Virginians and their service on board ships, see *Va. Gaz.* (Purdie), Oct. 10, 24, 1777.

25. Aug. 16, 21, 27, 1777, McIlwaine et al., eds., *Journals of the Council*, I, 466, 472, 475; *Va. Gaz.* (Purdie), Aug. 22, 1777; *Va. Gaz.* (D and H), Oct. 3, 1777. Goodrich had been named as one of the ringleaders of a conspiracy in the Norfolk area "to foment a Dangerous Insurrection" there in June. See June 20, 1777, McIlwaine et al., eds., *Journals of the Council*, I, 435–436.

intention to assist the enemy when the opportunity came, and others had already begun to do so by giving the British intelligence. Still others had raided the homes of patriots in the area and disarmed them. Worse, the council believed that many more inhabitants "are Suspected of having Intentions to assist the Enemy."[26]

The effect of so many reports took its toll on the nerves of the council. By the end of the first week of September, the council gave the same powers to the officers of Norfolk and Princess Anne Counties on the south side of the James River that it had given to the commanders of the Eastern Shore. The council was even worried about Williamsburg as well. It ordered all military officers to be particularly attentive to the conduct of all those in Williamsburg who had as yet refused to take the oath of allegiance. It then ordered the mayor and commanding officer at Williamsburg to work together to do all they could to "preserve the internal Peace and Security of the City." At the very least, resistance from within Virginia again helped tie up the resources available to patriot authorities, even in the midst of the invasion scare. Disaffected whites and rebellious blacks exacted a costly toll from patriot leaders.[27]

The council also turned its hand to motivating the militia. Even before the British had signaled their intention to come into the bay, the council panicked and within days called out almost four thousand militia all over the state and even ordered a regiment of Continentals on their way to Washington to stop and await further orders. The invasion scare lasted only until mid-September, when firm news arrived that the British had indeed landed on the Eastern Shore in Maryland and were headed northward rather than toward Virginia. The brevity of the scare, however, was overshadowed by the lessons learned during mobilization for it.[28]

On one hand, patriot leaders in Virginia had cause for hope. When the council called for help from almost all of the counties east of the Blue Ridge Mountains, the militia responded, in the words of Governor Patrick Henry,

26. Sept. 6, 1777, McIlwaine et al., eds., *Journals of the Council,* I, 484.

27. Aug. 16, 27, Sept. 6, 1777, ibid., I, 466, 475, 484; *Va. Gaz.* (Purdie), Aug. 22, 1777.

28. Aug. 15, 16, 19, 28, Sept. 1, 9, 13, 30, 1777, McIlwaine et al., eds., *Journals of the Council,* I, 463–464, 467, 470, 476, 479–480, 486, 488, 499 (but see Sept. 15, 17, 1777, I, 489, 491); John Page to George Washington, Aug. 15, 1777, to Governor Caswell, Aug. 16, 26, 1777, H. R. McIlwaine, ed., *Official Letters of the Governors of the State of Virginia* (Richmond, Va., 1926–1929), I, 176–177, 179–180; *Va. Gaz.* (D and H), Aug. 15, 22, 1777.

with "great alacrity." Within a week of the initial call for militia, the news-papers reported that more than six hundred militia were camped in and around Williamsburg. By the end of August, virtually all the militia had arrived in the lower counties. One report put the number of men embodied at nearly five thousand.[29]

Patriot leaders, embarrassed over the past year by their inability to raise recruits for Washington's army, were thrilled at the response, and several wrote immediately to their congressional delegates to boast about their suc-cess. Edmund Pendleton, responding to news that General William Howe had evacuated New Jersey, enthusiastically told Richard Henry Lee that Virginians were also playing their part in the conflict. The numbers of mili-tia called for by the council during the invasion scare were easily made up in each county, and there were more than enough: "In most Counties the whole declared themselves ready, if wanted." Mann Page, Jr., also boasted about the militia's enthusiasm for service against the threatened British in-vasion. He told Richard Henry Lee that the militia's "zeal to assist their country was so great in many [upper] counties, that the numbers which were required of them . . . were readily made up."[30]

Both Pendleton and Page were especially pleased with the militia turn-out because, they claimed, in most counties the militia had not waited until they were drafted into service, but had instead turned out voluntarily. The council had called for between fifty and one hundred men from each county, and the new state law had stipulated that county commanders could draft the militia in rotation to serve during emergencies like this one. However, if enough volunteers stepped forward for service in any given county, the county lieutenant need not coerce anyone into service. Pendleton told Lee that in Caroline County not one militia had had to be drafted; they were all "Volunteers." Page also told Lee that in most of the counties he knew about the needed militia contingents were also made up of volunteers.[31]

29. Patrick Henry to George Washington, Sept. 5, 1777, McIlwaine, ed., *Official Letters*, I, 184; *Va. Gaz.* (D and H), Aug. 22, 1777; John Parke Custis to George Washington, Sept. 11, 1777, *Papers of Washington*, Rev. War Ser., XI, 201–203. Cf. Sept. 2, 1777, Diary of Honyman.

30. Pendleton to R. H. Lee, Aug. 30, 1777, *Papers of Pendleton*, I, 221; Mann Page, Jr., to R. H. Lee, Sept. 2, 1777, "Selections and Excerpts from the Lee Pa-pers," *Southern Literary Messenger*, XXVII (July–December 1858), 260. Cf. Mann Page, Jr., to R. H. Lee, Sept. 23, 1777, Paul P. Hoffman, ed., *Lee Family Papers, 1742–1795* (microfilm) (Charlottesville, Va., 1966).

31. Pendleton to R. H. Lee, Aug. 30, 1777, *Papers of Pendleton*, I, 221; Mann

Patriot leaders were also convinced that these volunteers were different from the men targeted for service in the recent draft. Mann Page told Lee that the militia were generally "fine looking Men . . . well armed" and in "high Spirits." John Parke Custis concurred. He told George Washington that the militia who had turned out were, indeed, "very fine men." Thomas Nelson, Jr., in charge of the militia during the invasion, was also pleased. Reviewing his forces in Williamsburg, he publicly declared that he was "much satisfied" with their appearance.[32]

Perhaps most important, the turnout of the militia during the British invasion scare helped mask the discontent and divisions within Virginia caused by the first draft for Continental soldiers. Under threat from British forces, patriots within Virginia were clearly focused on state defense. That the first draft for Continental soldiers had gone horribly wrong receded quickly in importance. Virginia might have trouble filling its Continental quota of troops, but were they really necessary for the preservation of the state? Certainly, Edmund Pendleton believed that the militia's turnout during the invasion scare went some way toward redeeming Virginia for its poor recruiting record. By implication, he also revealed his priorities concerning state versus Continental needs. "However difficult it may be to raise a regular Army," Pendleton told Lee, the militia were, in the end, more important. "Our resources in that way are infinite." John Harvie concurred, telling Jefferson after the invasion scare that, despite the poor recruiting for the Continental army, "a well Regulated Militia may be our Salvation."[33]

• • • But, as much as patriot leaders were excited by the militia turnout, militia themselves demonstrated the limits to their commitment. Some volunteers, for example, made it clear that they would serve only under particular terms, thereby attempting to distinguish themselves from their lower-class neighbors who might serve in the regular army. Captain Wil-

---

Page, Jr., to R. H. Lee, Sept. 2, 1777, "Selections and Excerpts from the Lee Papers," *Southern Literary Messenger,* XXVII (July–December 1858), 260; Mann Page, Jr., to R. H. Lee, Sept. 23, 1777, Hoffman, ed., *Lee Family Papers.*

32. Mann Page, Jr., to R. H. Lee, Sept. 23, Oct. 14, 1777, Hoffman, ed., *Lee Family Papers;* John Parke Custis to Washington, Sept. 11, 1777, *Papers of Washington,* Rev. War Ser., XI, 201–203; Selby, *The Revolution in Virginia,* 134.

33. Pendleton to R. H. Lee, Aug. 30, 1777, *Papers of Pendleton,* I, 221. Cf. Pendleton to R. H. Lee, Oct. 11, 1777, *Papers of Pendleton,* I, 229; John Harvie to Jefferson, Oct. 18, 1777, *Papers of Jefferson,* II, 34–35.

liam Fontaine of Hanover County raised one of those volunteer companies of militia in August 1777. While on duty, he and the men serving with him came up with a plan to help defend the state on future similar occasions. Fontaine told Governor Henry that he was willing and able to keep a company of militia ready for duty at any time. They would be a "Select Body" and would serve for home defense whenever the government called upon them. Unlike the regular militia and the troops in the Continental army, however, Fontaine explained that the terms of service for his men would have to be—in one important respect—different. Though subject to the same military regulations as other militia, Fontaine's volunteers demanded that they be allowed "such officers as would be agreeable to them." Fontaine reassured his fellow Hanover countyman Henry that this would be no ordinary group of militia or troops. Indeed, Fontaine explained, the volunteers under his command could actually be trusted with this responsibility. The volunteers would be "young Men of the better Sort of people."[34]

And if patriot leaders were fixated on state defense, militia showed they were even more so. Indeed, in August 1777 many Virginians made a clear distinction between service in the Continental army and service in the militia, but they also made it clear to patriot authorities that there was a vast difference between service in the militia for the defense of the state, and service outside the state. In the midst of the British invasion scare, Congress, facing the desperate state of the Continental army, asked Virginia for reinforcements from the militia for service in Pennsylvania: a third of the militia from the northwestern counties of Prince William, Fairfax, Loudoun, Berkeley, Frederick, Dunmore, Fauquier, and Culpeper as well as a state regiment as a temporary relief force, to march to Frederick Town in Maryland and await General Washington's orders. The Virginia council, upon that request, ordered the militia to serve until November 30, or a maximum of two months.[35]

In contrast to the "alacrity" and "zeal" in the face of the British invasion scare in Virginia, the militia ordered northward did not go readily. In fact, several individuals, including James Reach of Loudoun County, tried to

34. Aug. 27, 1777, McIlwaine et al., eds., *Journals of the Council,* I, 475.

35. July 8, Aug. 15, 30, Sept. 1, 1777, ibid., I, 451, 464, 478, 479; *Va. Gaz.* (D and H), Oct. 24, 1777; General Orders, Oct. 7, 1777, *Papers of Washington,* Rev. War Ser., XI, 415–416; Selby, *Revolution in Virginia,* 134; James Kirby Martin and Mark Edward Lender, *A Respectable Army: The Military Origins of the Republic, 1763–1789* (Arlington Heights, Ill., 1982), 82–83.

stop the militia from marching. Other militia banded together in defiance of the call-out. Militia from Culpeper would not march without some guarantee that they would not have to serve as late as November. In order to get them to march, the colonel of the contingent had to promise them that they would be relieved at the end of October, not November, as Congress had requested. Learning about the locally negotiated contract after the fact, Governor Henry was forced to comply with it and asked General Washington to discharge them, unless they themselves "chuse to serve longer." Finally, militia from Dunmore County also refused to march farther than Frederick Town.[36]

Real problems arose among the state regular troops, too, when they were called northward at the same time. Following the orders to reinforce Washington, the papers were filled with notices advertising deserters from the state regiments. Some of them specified that the soldiers had absconded just before they were to go northward. At least one man claimed he had made it an explicit condition of his enlistment that he would not be sent out of the state. Adam Cousins of Fluvanna County was happy to serve in the army, but he wanted to ensure that he stayed close to home. He enlisted only on the "express condition" that, if his state regiment was ever ordered out of Virginia, the lieutenant, George Thompson of Albemarle, would immediately discharge him. When his regiment was ordered to join Washington, Cousins claimed his discharge. Having enlisted for service close to home, even many Virginians in the regular state forces decided that they would not fight outside their own borders.[37]

• • • Problems in the militia and state forces only reinforced the new alignments emerging in Virginia. Indeed, as resistance to militia call-outs increased and draft resistance became widespread, local officials were forced to adapt and temporize state laws, often allying themselves with their neighbors rather than the state government. Though some patriot leaders

36. Aug. 30, 1777, McIlwaine et al., eds., *Journals of the Council,* I, 478; Aug. 22, 1777, Worthington Chauncey Ford et al., eds., *Journals of the Continental Congress, 1774–1789* (Washington, D.C., 1904–1937), VIII, 667; Apr. 14, 1778, Loudoun County Court Records, 1776–1783, LiVi (there was no record that Reach was ever brought to trial); Henry to Washington, Oct. 23, 1777, McIlwaine, ed., *Official Letters,* I, 198; John Harvie to Jefferson, Oct. 18, 1777, *Papers of Jefferson,* II, 34–35.

37. *Va. Gaz.* (D and H), Nov. 7, Dec. 19, 26, 1777; *Va. Gaz.* (Purdie), Nov. 28, 1777, supplement.

in the state were buoyed by the general turnout of the militia in defense of the commonwealth, others, like Patrick Henry, were increasingly frustrated, particularly by the power of local officials to hinder mobilization at all levels.

Local militia officers especially exercised a great deal of control over the administration of state laws and executive demands. They could, in the first instance, simply resign their commissions if they did not want to carry out state orders, as some had done when forced to conscript their militia. Officers who sympathized with their men could also decide not to prosecute delinquent or offending militia to the full extent of the laws. But what worried the executive most was the fact that militia officers themselves were often implicated in the recalcitrance of their militia.[38]

When these transgressions came to light—and it is clear that only the most flagrant violations did—the executive could do little about them. The council could order a county court-martial, but, since colleagues and neighbors of the accused usually sat on these courts, few officers were ever prosecuted. Local officials had a clear monopoly over county affairs.[39]

38. For poorly timed militia resignations, see Nov. 21, 27, 1776, June 19, 1777, McIlwaine et al., eds., *Journals of the Council,* I, 246–247, 254, 435; Sept. 5, 1775, Feb. 17, 1776, Greene, ed., *Diary of Carter,* II, 938–939, 984–985. For officers who refused to prosecute their militia, see Court Martial for the County of Prince William, Oct. 17, 1776, Prince William County Petitions, Virginia Legislative Petitions, LiVi, and T. Blackburn to Jesse Ewell and Cuthbert Bullitt, Oct. 25, 1776; Sept. 18, Dec. 6, 1776, McIlwaine et al., eds., *Journals of the Council,* I, 166, 267. See McBride, "Virginia War Effort," 59–61, for the lenience of the Augusta County court-martial. For officers' encouraging disobedience, see Dec. 4, 1776, Jan. 1, 24, Mar. 4, 1778, McIlwaine et al., eds., *Journals of the Council,* I, 262–264, 303, II, 73–74, 97.

39. For the council's frustration at local court-martials' exonerating officers, see Dec. 4, 6, 1776, Jan. 1, 23, Feb. 18, 20, Oct. 28, Dec. 6, 1777, Feb. 27, 1778, McIlwaine et al., eds., *Journals of the Council,* I, 262–264, 266–267, 303, 318, 348, 351, II, 18, 42, 93.

Henry wanted more power over the militia. In theory, the governor, with the advice of council, had constitutional power over the militia. The executive had the authority to embody the militia, to direct it, and to replace officers for misbehavior or inability. In practice, however, the militia laws of the state, which the assembly alone had authority to change, limited the governor's power.

In response to militia insubordination throughout 1776, Henry had convinced the assembly of the need to make some important changes to the militia laws in May 1777. An officer who resigned when called out for duty could be sent out as

Governor Patrick Henry was agitated about his lack of authority over such officers. When local officers delayed or refused to send their recently recruited troops to rendezvous points on their way northward in early 1777, Henry was furious over his lack of authority to punish them. There was, he complained to Richard Henry Lee, a "remissness among the officers," as they "do not in general exert themselves as they ought." Henry had sent expresses to every county colonel and had printed public advertisements in the papers on several occasions. "All won't do," Henry complained. "The executive of this country can exercise no command" over these officers "in the opinion of most people."[40]

If the draft in August 1777 had signaled the tendency of ordinary Virginians to close ranks at the county level against intrusive state legislation, the problem was heightened when freeholding voters in the militia were involved. Henry saw for himself how local officers had helped their militia obstruct the council's orders to march northward to help Washington in the fall of 1777. Not only had they countenanced their militia's foot-dragging, but some officers had led the opposition to the order. In the case of the Dunmore County militia, even the field officers were involved. The officers had told authorities that they could not be supplied properly on the road to Maryland, so they suspended their march. John Harvie, Virginia delegate to Congress, reported that he had firsthand information that their excuses were without foundation. Harvie was furious that the field officers of the militia were involved; two of them, Harvie reported with disgust, were assembly delegates for the county.[41]

------

a private in any case and suffer punishment for disobedience. The assembly also beefed up the punishments for mutiny, desertion, and disobedience while the militia were out in service. Finally, it changed the composition of the courts-martial to comprise at least seven officers, captains or higher, including the county lieutenant or at least a field officer. These new rules applied when the militia were called out against an invasion or insurrection. They helped but did not solve all the problems Henry had encountered in the militia. Even though local courts-martial might be presided over by persons of higher rank than previously, they remained the final arbiter of any wrongdoing, and punishments were still light. An officer could be demoted only for disobedience. Privates could be fined and imprisoned, but only up to two months' pay, or one month's imprisonment. Act for Providing against Invasions and Insurrections, Hening, comp., *Statutes at Large,* IX, 291–297.

40. Henry to R. H. Lee, Mar. 20, 1777, McIlwaine, ed., *Official Letters,* I, 126.

41. Aug. 30, 1777, McIlwaine et al., eds., *Journals of the Council,* I, 478; Aug. 22, 1777, Ford et al., eds., *Journals of the Continental Congress,* VIII, 667; Apr. 14,

As Harvie's complaints show, Henry's problems with the militia and his efforts to enforce executive directives could put him into direct conflict with the legislature. The Dunmore County militia field officers were not the only senior militia officers who sat in the assembly. Indeed, traditionally, the highest-ranking field officers were often the most prominent citizens of the county. This arrangement worked well when the interests of the state government were the same as those of the local government. However, when ordinary Virginians exerted pressure on their militia officers and challenged state directives, those officers were often and increasingly forced to close ranks with their neighbors instead. When Patrick Henry tried to assert authority over the militia, he sometimes challenged the authority of elected representatives of the people.

Henry had had firsthand experience of this problem in the fall of 1776 when the legislature overruled the executive's call for militia to come to Williamsburg. As demands mounted on the militia, such clashes became more frequent. Problems came to a head in the fall of 1777, in the aftermath of the British invasion scare and Henry's attempts to reinforce Washington with militia. When the assembly convened, it immediately questioned the executive's actions. The delegates debated the propriety of the council's order to remove all suspicious persons from coastal areas during the invasion scare. They then questioned the order to send militia out of the state. Perhaps led by the delegates from Dunmore County who had been involved, the delegates debated whether Henry's actions were actually legal. In the end, a committee of the whole house resolved that, because Pennsylvania had actually been invaded, the governor and council had in fact "acted according to the laws of this Commonwealth." Because the matter had become so divisive both within the assembly and out-of-doors, the legislature printed its resolutions in the newspapers.[42]

Pressure from below, then, created cracks at the top. Henry, caught between the demands of Washington and Congress on one side, and the assembly and reluctant patriots on the other, grew increasingly irritated with his colleagues. His reaction to the assembly's debate is not known, but two days later he complained about the assembly to Richard Henry Lee in Con-

1778, Loudoun County Court Records, 1776–1783, LiVi; Henry to Washington, Oct. 23, 1777, McIlwaine, ed., *Official Letters,* I, 198; John Harvie to Jefferson, Oct. 18, 1777, *Papers of Jefferson,* II, 34–35.

42. *Journal of the House of Delegates* (Williamsburg, Va., 1776–), Dec. 16, 1777; *Va. Gaz.* (D and H), Dec. 19, 1777.

gress. Though the delegates had been sitting for almost two months, they had done nothing: "Not one law of importance is passed." Henry wanted Lee to come home to help invigorate the assembly. "The general interest of America, and the welfare of this state, call you here." Henry, the former populist, wanted people in the legislature who might be less responsive to the people, hinting that "the Era of calamity" might date from the absence of people like Lee from the assembly.[43]

• • • If Henry clashed swords with the assembly over his power over the militia, he need not have worried about their inclination to beef up the recruiting laws. Most delegates knew as well as Henry that, if the state could not reinforce Washington with more regulars, more call-outs of the militia would be necessary. It was because Washington had too few Continental soldiers in the late summer that Congress had asked Henry to reinforce the army with militia. Henry didn't trust his power over the militia to want to repeat the experiment; many delegates to the assembly wanted to avoid angering their constituents with further call-outs.

Besides, most delegates were in a buoyant mood. Though the dramatic fall of Philadelphia at the end of September darkened expectations, especially when followed with news of Washington's defeat at Germantown, patriots in Virginia could only celebrate when news reached them at Williamsburg by the end of October that General John Burgoyne and his entire army had surrendered at Saratoga. Impatient patriots called for a holiday, military parade, and a grand party, all before official word from Congress had reached the capital. When the official reports arrived, the government celebrated for another two days, culminating in a lavish ball given by the General Assembly as the delegates convened in Williamsburg for their fall session.[44]

Though many legislators, including Edmund Pendleton, hoped that

43. Henry to R. H. Lee, Dec. 18, 1777, McIlwaine, ed., *Official Letters,* I, 219–220. He also told Washington that a "hint" from the general might "lead to something important, at a time like this, when most people seem at a loss to fix on the most effectual means of prosecuting the war vigorously." Henry to Washington, Oct. 30, 1777, McIlwaine, ed., *Official Letters,* I, 199. Cf. Henry to R. H. Lee, Nov. 10, 1777, I, 202, Henry to Washington, Dec. 9, 1777, I, 213.

44. Martin and Lender, *A Respectable Army,* 83–87; *Va. Gaz.* (D and H), Oct. 31, Nov. 7, 14, 1777; Pendleton to R. H. Lee, Oct. 25, Nov. 8, 1777, to William Woodford, Nov. 8, 1777, *Papers of Pendleton,* I, 230, 233, 235–236; Selby, *Revolution in Virginia,* 135.

Burgoyne's surrender might alone be sufficient to push Britain into suing for peace, delegates had little choice but to press on with plans for war. At the battle of Germantown, what was left of the Virginia Ninth Regiment was virtually wiped out. Not only did representatives face repeated demands from Washington and Congress to recruit and replace Virginia's quota of soldiers, but they also had to face up to the worsening financial situation. The costs of the war were skyrocketing while the unsupported currency that the assembly kept printing slid ever downward in worth. These two demands weighed heavily on the representatives and caused much debate. In early January 1778, Edmund Pendleton began to think that the session "hath been the most tedious I ever experienced." Much time had been spent on heated discussion and debate over two crucial questions: "the difficulty and Novelty of drafting men to recruit the Army, and the mode of taxation."[45]

The assembly first turned to the question of the army, which took until the beginning of January 1778 to resolve. Virginia needed at least eight thousand new recruits or reenlistees to fulfill its quota. Delegates still believed that enticements were the best way to recruit the majority of the men needed. They also hoped they could again lean on the same men that had already joined up and, thus, held out good inducements for men to reenlist. To those men already enlisted in the first nine regiments whose terms of service would expire at the end of 1777 or in the spring of 1778, the assembly first thought about offering a bounty of ten dollars on top of the Continental bounty to those who enlisted for three years or the war, later raising it to twenty dollars. New recruits to the army would get ten dollars over the Continental bounty (of money and land) if they enlisted for at least three years. Finally, despite a congressional request that the states raise troops only for a minimum of three years, or for the war, the Virginia General Assembly allowed recruits to enlist for just one year. If they did, they would still get twenty dollars total.[46]

45. *Va. Gaz.* (D and H), Oct. 24, 1777; July 8, Aug. 15, 30, Sept. 1, 1777, McIlwaine et al., eds., *Journals of the Council,* I, 451, 464, 478, 479; General Orders, Oct. 7, 1777, *Papers of Washington,* Rev. War. Ser., XI, 415–416; Selby, *Revolution in Virginia,* 134–135; Martin and Lender, *A Respectable Army,* 82–83; Pendleton to R. H. Lee, Oct. 25, Nov. 8, 1777, to Woodford, Oct. 25, Nov. 8, 1777, Jan. 2, 31, 1778, I, 230–233, 235–236, 240, 246.

46. Pendleton to Woodford, Nov. 29, 1777, Jan. 2, 1778, *Papers of Pendleton,* I, 238, 240; Nov. 26, 1777, Ford et al., eds., *Journals of the Continental Congress,* IX, 967; Hening, comp., *Statutes at Large,* IX, 337–338, 342. Washington told Custis,

Invariably, however, most delegates believed that enticements would only help, but not solve, the recruiting crisis. Though the last draft had engendered so much opposition, most legislators believed that another draft was the only way to complete their quota. However, there was less agreement on what kind of draft there ought to be. Discussion was again heated. Edmund Pendleton outlined the different proposals. Significantly, none of the alternatives discussed replicated the experiment of "picked" men tried by the previous assembly. Perhaps overawed by the popular outcry against and resistance to the previous draft, swayed by the arguments of sympathetic representatives like Cuthbert Bullitt, who had publicly opposed the last draft, or convinced by a combination of the two, the assembly abandoned the idea of picking men out arbitrarily altogether. It never repeated the expedient.[47]

Instead, the delegates discussed three alternatives. One group was of the mind that they ought to target "Vagabonds" more specifically. If vagabonds could not be had, then "those who approach nearest to them" should be picked. Pendleton, already uncomfortable with how men had been chosen in the last draft, thought this unworkable for two reasons. "To point out any men and condemn t[hem] as Vagabonds or worthless without a Regular trial . . . appears very exceptionable." The idea was particularly dangerous, given that they might be charged by "a Spiteful neighbour." But Pendleton also harbored other concerns about this method, as an aside: that it was dangerous to trust "our defence to such people." In the end, his colleagues agreed.[48]

The assembly considered the two other alternatives. One was to draft men from the whole militia "indiscriminately," or regardless of economic or family status. This, of course, was the most equitable manner. However, it was also too radical for some. Pendleton objected on the grounds of the damage to established families; it would be "cruel to force men from their Families to a distant Countrey for two or three years."[49]

Finally, the assembly also considered a third proposal—a "middle way"

---

for example, that, whatever plan George Mason or others came up with for filling the deficient Virginia quotas in the Continental army, it was "a measure that cannot be dispensed with, nor ought under any pretext whatsoever" (Washington to Custis, Nov. 14, 1777, *Papers of Washington,* Rev. War Ser., XII, 249).

47. Pendleton to Woodford, Nov. 29, 1777, *Papers of Pendleton,* I, 238–239.

48. Ibid.

49. Ibid.

—between the two other measures proposed, to draft men by a fair lottery but only between "the Single men." Pendleton believed that most would agree that "the young men are properest to go, and then it follows that all of them should take a fair and equal Chance." Eventually, the assembly decided to draft only single men, whether officers or privates, above eighteen years of age who had no children. Pendleton thought this was the best possible choice in the circumstances. "It is every way disagreeable," he acknowledged, "but being of absolute necessity, we must take a mode the least exceptionable."[50]

Having agreed on a method of drafting, anxious legislators did all they could to minimize the upheaval it might cause by making it as palatable to the people as possible. Congress, Washington, and other Continental officials wanted the soldiers recruited in 1778 to be for the long term; ideally, for the duration of the war, or at the very least for three years. Some in the Virginia assembly argued that they ought to stick to these recommendations. Original proposals called for drafts for a minimum of two or three years' service. Because he thought draftees would be forced to serve for two or three years, Pendleton dismissed the idea of making family men serve in the Continental army. Others argued for a term of a mere six months— only a little more than extended militia duty. Finally, all sides reached a compromise of a one-year term of service for those drafted into the army, much to the bitter disappointment of Washington and other proponents of a strong and more permanent army.[51]

For those who were drafted, there was some compensation, too. Drafted men would still receive the full Continental bounty of fifteen dollars. Moreover, once drafted, a man could enlist instead for three years or the war and get a further ten dollars above the Continental bounty of money and land. Significantly, those who had been drafted and served for one year would then be exempted from any further drafts and military service for a full year after discharge. Most important, the assembly also extended the practice of allowing substitutes for service. Though all single men would be subject to the draft, anyone with money could buy his way out. Eligible young men could hire substitutes ahead of time and thereby exempt themselves from

50. Hening, comp., *Statutes at Large,* IX, 339–340; Pendleton to Woodford, Nov. 29, 1777, *Papers of Pendleton,* I, 238–239; *Papers of Mason,* I, 365, 369–372.

51. Hening, comp., *Statutes at Large,* IX, 337–349; Pendleton to Woodford, Nov. 29, 1777, *Papers of Pendleton,* I, 239; Col. William Cabell to Col. John Cabell, Dec. 22, 1777, Hugh Blair Grigsby Papers, VHS.

the draft altogether. Or single men could wait to see whether they were picked as a draftee and then hire a substitute to go in their place. Such a loophole meant that, though the draft gave the appearance of being fairer than the previous one, the burden would still fall upon the worse-off.[52]

The assembly continued to try to drive a wedge between potential recruits and more middling militia in other ways, too. The new recruiting act stipulated that militia could avoid military service by turning in deserters. If single men apprehended a deserter, they would be exempt from the draft if the deserter had at least one year still to serve. If the community turned in deserters, their county's quota of recruits would be reduced accordingly. Moreover, those harboring deserters were now put at risk. Anyone concealing a deserter would be punished by military service for the time the deserter himself still had to serve. Finally, to help try to fill and keep filled Virginia's quota, deserters would have to serve double the time of their absence from service.[53]

Most significantly, and perhaps inexplicably, Virginia legislators limited the draft to a maximum of 2,000 men. Though Congress had asked Virginia for 8,160 to refill Virginia's Continental regiments, the assembly ordered only 2,000, proportioned to each of the counties in specified quotas. Not willing to risk the social upheaval and conflict that the previous attempt to draft militia had foreshadowed, the delegates simply refused to order the drafting of so many white Virginians. Instead, they hoped reenlistments and volunteer reinforcements would make up the majority of their quota.[54]

Buoyed by the turnout of the militia in August, the assembly also resurrected the idea of a volunteer plan, much to Washington's disgust, authorizing just more than five thousand volunteers to serve with the Continental army for six months. The terms of service were generous and clearly aimed at a different group of men than was expected to fill the ranks of the regular army. The volunteers, for example, could elect all company-grade officers. Significantly, in a bid to widen support for the war, the law was also designed to attract religious Dissenters. Recognizing that members of

52. Hening, comp., *Statutes at Large,* IX, 339–340.

53. Ibid., 342–348.

54. Ibid., 339–340; Pendleton to Woodford, Nov. 29, 1777, *Papers of Pendleton,* I, 238–239; *Papers of Mason,* I, 365, 369–372. Any county that had failed to raise its quota from the previous draft also had to add that number to the number to be drafted in 1778.

the Baptists and other Dissenting groups might be "averse to serving in the same companies . . . with others, and under officers of different principles," the volunteer plan allowed religious groups to form their own companies. They could even elect their own field officers if enough men volunteered to make a full regiment. Moreover, each volunteer would also get ten dollars bounty, and the assembly hoped to entice them to stay after the six months and join the regular army for another ten dollars, plus the Continental bounty. Importantly, anyone who volunteered for this temporary reinforcement would gain an exemption from further military duty for six months after his return. From the perspective of the delegates, the volunteers would serve two beneficial functions. They would relieve the pressure on Virginia to raise its share of Continental recruits, and they would also take the pressure off the militia, circumventing the further need for disruptive calls on them as they had experienced in August and September.[55]

• • • Part of the reluctance to pressure their constituents with a new draft was that legislators were also struggling to control state finances. The costs of the war were spiraling, and the General Assembly had issued more and more paper money over the past few years. However, in order to curry favor with their constituents and to give time to establish the authority of the new government, the collection of taxes to support the repeated emissions of money was put off to a future date. By the end of 1777, most legislators agreed that an immediate and heavy tax was necessary. The money in circulation was depreciating quickly because of the quantity of it, and its depreciation jeopardized the public credit of Virginia. Most believed that, by taxing back the currency and taking it out of circulation, the depreciation could be halted. By the end of August 1777, Richard Henry Lee was arguing that the "most extensive and vigorous taxes should immediately take place." Now was the time to do it, he asserted, because the sum in circulation was "immense" and the "vast plenty of money" rendered the collection of a heavy tax "more easy." Yet, despite general agreement among delegates to the assembly on the need to tax, debate over the means was again heated. Pendleton observed that the tax plan had occasioned "much Altercation" and "long debate."[56]

55. Hening, comp., *Statutes at Large,* IX, 348–349; Pendleton to Woodford, Nov. 29, 1777, *Papers of Pendleton,* I, 238.

56. R. H. Lee to Jefferson, Aug. 25, 1777, *Papers of Jefferson,* II, 30; Pendleton to Woodford, Jan. 16, 1778, *Papers of Pendleton,* I, 246.

Debate on a new tax plan was heated because legislators were already sensitized to the demands of their constituents. Indeed, debate in the General Assembly only echoed the discussion that had been going on out-of-doors for the past year or two, which had been inflamed by years of unequal tax laws. Before the Revolution, revenue in Virginia was generally raised by taxes on tobacco exports, supplemented by quitrents and occasional minor poll taxes that paid the ordinary running costs of the colony. When the government needed more money, as at the start of the Seven Years' War, it turned to a new and heavier poll tax and later a land tax based on acreage owned, not on the actual value of land, thereby protecting the wealthier lands of the propertied interests of the assembly. After the Seven Years' War had been paid for, legislators returned to a reliance on tobacco export taxes, along with imposts on foreign rum, brandy, and other spirits.[57]

Thus, when the Virginia conventions turned to the difficult task of raising money for the defense of the colony against Britain, as in military matters, they turned to traditional methods of raising revenue. The first taxes they laid were poll taxes and taxes on the acreage of land owned, in an effort to raise £350,000 in the summer of 1775. The Fifth Convention wanted to raise another £100,000 the following spring, but it deliberately postponed the collection of the taxes, first until 1777, then—with a new Constitution and a new legislature—until 1778, explaining that people in many parts of the state would be "unable to pay" if collections began in 1777 as scheduled. In the same session, the legislature also decided to emit another £400,000, but the collection of the taxes to sink *this* emission would not start until 1784. Then, in May 1777, in part to pay for the new recruits, the assembly authorized borrowing another £1,000,000 and committed the state to pay by December 1784. It made no specific provisions for funding this loan beyond a promise to levy property taxes sometime in the future.[58]

Anxious freeholders watched the mounting costs and emissions to support the war with alarm. With such heavy demands, taxpayers began to demand more accountability in return for their material support of the war. Indeed, the war brought the previous inequities of the tax system to the fore and gave freeholders the leverage to demand real changes. Worried free-

57. Robert A. Becker, *Revolution, Reform, and the Politics of American Taxation, 1763-1783* (Baton Rouge, La., 1980), 78-79. See Chapter 1 for a summary of taxes laid to pay for the Seven Years' War.

58. Ibid., 83-84, 194.

holders throughout the state had petitioned the assembly since the spring of 1776 about using new methods to pay for the increasingly costly war. As we have seen, the first salvo in this all-important internal conflict came at a crucial moment, in a significant form, when the county committee for Cumberland sent its two delegates to the Fifth Convention with very specific "Instructions" in April 1776. They wanted their delegates to lay an immediate tax in goods needed to supply the army. Farmers had a great quantity of provisions on their hands, which they needed to get rid of because of the "Stoppage of Trade." The army needed those supplies, and the Cumberland committee proposed providing them directly.[59]

In May 1776 Henrico and Hanover Counties followed suit and also asked the Fifth Convention to consider allowing freeholders to supply goods and provisions directly to the army in lieu of taxes. The land and poll taxes levied by the Third Convention were first due on June 10, 1776. The petitioners worried that the "immediate demand" for their taxes would cripple them, because many of them had no cash on hand to pay the taxes. To pay for supplies and provisions for the army, the convention had ordered the emission of more paper money, which was used to pay army suppliers who, by purchasing goods, were supposed to spread the paper money throughout the colony. In practice, however, as the petitioners from Hanover pointed out, the paper money was not circulated equally throughout the state. Suppliers spent the paper money wherever they could get the cheapest goods. As a result, paper money by the spring of 1776 was in very short supply in many places. The freeholders of Henrico County, then, wanted an opportunity to pay their portion of taxes with their produce. They even offered to provide arms, ammunition, clothing, or field equipment if it was necessary. Those from Hanover County thought the convention could do even better and could make assessments on each county according to what kind of provisions each could supply. Moreover, such a scheme would also prevent a "few from ingrossing the very profitable business of supplying the Army."[60]

By the fall of 1776, freeholders demanded more radical changes to the tax system. Inhabitants from the southside counties of Brunswick, Lunenburg, and Mecklenburg, for example, petitioned for a wholesale revision of

59. Cumberland County Committee Instructions to John Mayo and William Fleming, Apr. 22, 1776, *Rev. Va.*, VI, 434.

60. Proceedings of the Fifth Virginia Convention, May 13, 27, 1776, ibid., VII, 105, 270.

the laws. The petitioners wanted land taxes laid on the value of land, rather than the acreage owned, and property taxes assessed in the same manner. The problem, they claimed, was that the current tax laws, which stipulated a tax of four shillings on every hundred acres of land, favored those who owned rich lands. Those possessing poor lands "are obliged to contribute equally with the owners of rich lands." They wanted a more "equitable mode" of taxation, either by making everyone pay in proportion to the value of his land or by an assessment on real and personal property. The House referred the petition to a committee on Propositions and Grievances and asked it to "enquire into the allegations thereof." The committee reported that the petition was reasonable, but the assembly took no further action in that session.[61]

Frustrated with the lack of action, freeholders from other counties added their voices to those of the southside counties when the new assembly met in May 1777. Freeholders from the piedmont counties of Orange and Culpeper each sent in petitions for a more "equitable" system of taxes. Almost seventy inhabitants of Culpeper were explicit about the class implications of the existing land taxes. They were most concerned about the divisions between subsistence farmers and those who raised crops for a profit. When taxes were laid "indiscriminately," they complained, the less wealthy were usually most affected. "Lands of the meaner Quality," they asserted, "are Generally Peopled by the Poor." Even untaxed, the lands they owned required their "utmost Efforts of Industry and Labour" to eke out even a "bare Subsistence." On the other hand, those possessing rich lands obtained more plentiful crops, which meant they should pay more taxes. Those owning richer land actually benefited twice: in addition to allowing them to "enjoy all the Comforts of Life," their profits allowed them to make "annual additions to their Estates." In this light, the land and poll taxes were simply unfair.[62]

The General Assembly finally responded to these petitions in the new tax act created in the fall of 1777. In it, the poll tax, the mainstay of the colonial taxing system, remained, but it became less important. Each poll over the age of twenty-one would pay five shillings, but soldiers, sailors,

61. *Journal of the House of Delegates,* Jan. 3, Nov. 15, 1776.

62. Culpeper County Petition, [Nov. 4, 1777], Virginia Legislative Petitions, LiVi. Orange County farmers also took up the pen in the fall of 1777 to again demand a tax on the value of land rather than the acreage. See Orange County Petitions, [Nov. 3, 1777], Virginia Legislative Petitions, LiVi.

parish poor, and anyone on a public disability allowance (because of war-time service) was exempted. The bulk of taxes would be raised through a more revolutionary tax system based on the amount and value of property owned. For the first time in Virginia's history, lands would be taxed on the basis of their value, not simply acreage. Moreover, most other forms of property would be valued and taxed accordingly: ten shillings on every one hundred pounds of property, including land, slaves, mulatto servants under thirty-one years of age, horses, mules, and plate. The tax would be collected on August 1 and continue for six years. The new tax base was more complex, but it was progressive and would place the heaviest burden on the wealthy. Any cash on hand over five pounds would be taxed at the same rate of ten shillings per every hundred pounds. Salaries and profits from business dealings would also be taxed. Thus, men of commerce and trade would have to pay for the war as inventories and incomes were assessed. Creditors had to pay two shillings per pound of any annual interest on debts, and on quitrents received. Gentlemen wishing to show off their wealth in carriages would now have to pay ten shillings per wheel on all riding carriages. Cattle were charged at fourpence per head. There was also a tax on marriage and ordinary licenses. Finally, the assembly imposed a ten-shilling tax per hogshead of tobacco exported and six-pence per gallon of spirits distilled in the state or imported. Anyone who had not taken the oath of allegiance to the state by May 1, 1778, would have to pay double taxes. Significantly, the assembly also repealed all the former poll taxes and taxes on acreage of land that were due to be paid before 1784.[63]

If the new tax plan was a radical, even revolutionary innovation, the assembly sweetened the pill even further by calling for the *popular* election of the tax commissioners who would value the property. "Freeholders and housekeepers" would annually elect the tax commissioners, who themselves had to be landholders, possess the right to vote, and own visible property worth at least eight hundred pounds. These elected commissioners would then appoint two men per every hundred to value all the property. These appointed men, also landholders and voters, had to apply to everyone in their hundred for an account of taxable goods. The assessors, using this information and any other information that they "by any other

63. Hening, comp., *Statutes at Large,* IX, 349–368. Becker asserts that no one had tried even to argue for a tax in proportion to wealth since 1645 (Becker, *Politics of American Taxation,* 78–79).

ways or means discover," were then to assess the value of the property, "having regard to the local situation of lands and other circumstances."[64]

The assembly also made some concessions to other citizens, to tenants, for example, and made a move to abolish "feudal tenure" and stop the payment of quitrents. It also began recognizing the claims of the western inhabitants, moving to fulfill the promise made by the convention on June 24, 1776, to recognize the preemption rights of all settlers upon unappropriated lands. The new tax act acknowledged that there were "great numbers" of people who had settled on waste and ungranted lands on the western waters who had been unable to procure legal titles to the land. The assembly also saw that it would have to give legal title to the settlers there in order to tax that land. Thus, anyone who had moved west and settled before June 1776 would be given legal title to up to four hundred acres of land, which was then liable to be taxed as in eastern Virginia. In one stroke, the General Assembly attempted to secure the allegiances as well as the taxes of the "great numbers" of people in the western counties.[65]

• • • Thus did the assembly enact the most liberal and progressive tax law in Virginia's history. Legislators had taken so much care over the new tax act for several different reasons. First, they had numerous petitions from freeholders in Virginia on the subject, demanding fairer assessments. But these petitions were given particular force by recent events. Not only had the turnout of the militia prompted a greater appreciation of the importance of that body and the necessity of relying on it for the state's defense, but the recent draft and the need for new recruits made it imperative that some concessions be made. Amid the furore over the summer's attempt to draft men for the army and congressional demands to raise even more, the assembly needed to do something to secure the loyalty of its citizens to the new and now more burdensome state.

Jefferson later wrote that getting the state tax system changed was one of the more "remarkable alterations" he had wanted to introduce to make the principles of the new state less "inconsistent with republicanism."

64. Hening, comp., *Statutes at Large,* IX, 349–368.

65. *Papers of Mason,* I, 386–387, 388–390; Hening, comp., *Statutes at Large,* IX, 349–368. The assembly also signaled its intention to create a sinking fund for the public debt out of the still-unappropriated western lands, thus helping spread the tax burden further. See Resolutions, [Jan. 24, 1778], *Papers of Mason,* I, 424, 425n.

Though some legislators thought that there might be problems with the new tax act, most agreed with John Parke Custis when he told George Washington the plan would work because the "Valuation of Property is very low, which will render his Plan very agreable to the People." In the end, the new tax plan *was* designed to be "agreable to the People" by distributing the burden of the war more equally. It was also a concession in light of the need to draft more and the complaints that move might raise. Indeed, Pendleton linked the two issues throughout his descriptions of the assembly's activities. Moreover, at one point during the debates over the new recruiting laws he made the link between defending the state and paying taxes more explicit. He noted that some legislators thought it would be "prudent" to "exempt our Soldiers from taxes altogether," implying that they had, in fact, paid their dues through their personal service. Ultimately, Pendleton foresaw success, because they had taken "much care to make it as Palatable as possible."[66]

66. Thomas Jefferson, *Notes on the State of Virginia,* ed. William Peden (Chapel Hill, N.C., 1954), 136–137; Custis to Washington, Oct. 26, 1777, *Papers of Washington,* Rev. War Ser., XII, 12; Pendleton to Woodford, Nov. 29, 1777, Jan. 31, 1778, *Papers of Pendleton,* I, 239, 246. In the end, both soldiers and sailors were at least exempted from the five-shilling poll tax introduced in that same session. Pendleton to Woodford, Nov. 29, 1777, *Papers of Pendleton,* I, 239; *Papers of Mason,* I, 380.

CHAPTER 10 *Paralysis and* Division,
1778-1780

Though the assembly hoped its new tax laws would sweeten the bitter pill of another, more general draft in 1778, ordinary Virginians were having none of it. Their reaction to the new measures was even more divisive than to the previous draft and only reinforced the new and more local political alignments that were emerging. Indeed, because the new draft cut across class lines by targeting all single men, resistance to it followed ties of kinship and community and reinforced an emerging and stubbornly defiant localism.

As patriot leaders fought among themselves over who was to blame for Virginia's failing mobilization, lower-class and middling Virginians quickly turned their attention to reviving trade, capitalizing on the lull in the war effort, and demanding more concessions. With mobilization virtually paralyzed, recriminations among patriot leaders—and ordinary Virginians alike—grew apace as resistance from below forced further divisions above.

• • • As legislators retired to their homes in early 1778, they carried the call for recruits and news of the new draft and taxes with them. Early reports of popular opposition to the draft in particular disturbed some. Edmund Pendleton had heard that the draft law was "generally execrated and that the young men would not submit to a draught." Patriot leaders' anxiety led some of them to seize upon early reports as proof that their fears were unfounded. A few days after the draft in his home county of Caroline, for example, Edmund Pendleton was visibly relieved that there had been no outright resistance to it. "When the time came, nothing like Opposition appeared." John Parke Custis also told General George Washington on February 12 that the draft had already taken place in most counties, with little resistance. Legislators were particularly relieved because they felt the new draft would be a good indication of the extent of popular support for the new government. Custis in particular thought that the lack of opposition demonstrated that "our Government is well establish'd in the Minds of the People."[1]

Custis, Pendleton, and others spoke too soon. Within days, reports began to circulate that there were actually widespread problems with the draft. With the draft scheduled for the second Monday of February, ordinary Virginians rose to challenge it. Robert Honyman got wind of the problems early. About a week after the draft, he commented, "It was very generally disagreable to the people, and in some counties occasioned considerable disturbance." His own county of Hanover was spared any violent "disturbance," but locals paid an expensive price. The militia of Hanover raised "large sums" of money by subscription and offered it to those who would enlist voluntarily. Recruits there were thus paid almost sixty pounds each. With the bounty allowed by law, new enlistees were paid a joining bonus of sixty-nine pounds.[2]

In other counties, however, the draft produced swift and bloody resistance. In the lower Northern Neck, reaction was dramatic. At least four men tried to disrupt the draft in Westmoreland County. In neighboring Northumberland County, at least five men led a protest against the draft that brought proceedings to a halt. The county court there charged them for "behaving in a riotous manner on the day of the Draught." Several of these men were confined and put under guard by local militia officers, but others organized a rescue mission. Problems were not confined to the Northern Neck. Thomas Jefferson reported problems in Fluvanna County in the piedmont as well. Even in counties that had previously produced many willing recruits and full support for the patriot cause, there was vocal opposition. Two men from Culpeper County, for example, complained pub-

1. Edmund Pendleton to William Woodford, Feb. 15, 1778, *Papers of Pendleton,* I, 250; John Parke Custis to George Washington, Feb. 12, 1778, *Papers of Washington,* Rev. War Ser., XIII, 513; cf. Jefferson to Isaac Zane, Feb. 26, 1778, *Papers of Jefferson,* II, 175; Feb. 2, 1778, Diary of Robert Honyman, Jan. 2, 1776–Mar. 11, 1782, Alderman Library, UVa (microfilm). Similarly, Jefferson also struck a tone of self-reassurance. He was relieved that in Albemarle County, too, the "draught went down very easy."

2. Feb. 2, 22, 1778, Diary of Honyman. The inhabitants also took full advantage of the laws allowing counties to turn in deserters as part of their quota. Altogether, they apprehended ten men and actually exceeded their quota through voluntary enlistments and deserters.

licly and found themselves in prison. They had, they claimed, voiced their concern "against unjust discriminating draughts."[3]

Others made similar complaints, backing up their concerns with force of arms. In Loudoun County, "the People" prevented the draft from taking place with "violent and riotous behaviour," according to one report. Lund Washington noted a great deal of confusion about the draft in Loudoun and that the people were in arms over it. On the first attempt to make the draft, the militia mutinied and successfully prevented it from taking place. In the confusion, however, "one of the Mutineers got shot," though not fatally, probably by one of the field officers of the militia. Already angry, the militia then threatened to kill the county lieutenant, Colonel Francis Peyton, in reprisal. Shaken but undeterred, Peyton ordered another draft for March 11. However, he was pessimistic whether he would fare any better. He believed that they needed to be more forceful but needed state help. "Without some exertions of Government," he complained to the council, "there was little reason to expect a more successful Issue than before." The county was in a state of suspense and civil disorder for at least two months. In the end, officials in Loudoun brought a total of fourteen men to court in April and tried them in May. These were only the ringleaders, whom the court charged with "Riotous and disorderly behaviour in withstanding the draught."[4]

Where the draft was not stopped by collective and active opposition, draftees themselves either opted out or banded together to bid defiance to local officials. Forty-seven men were drafted in Fauquier County, for example, but only just more than half reached the army. Twenty-six men were actually delivered to the army, two men moved to other counties, and nineteen others stood their ground. They "alledged the Law was partial and would never join." Similarly, Lund Washington noted that, even if there had not been a riot in Loudoun because of the draft, they would have to do it over again anyway, as "the men who were draughted cannot be found." Other men waited for a better opportunity to escape, and many deserted en

3. Feb. 24, 1778, Westmoreland County Court Orders, 1776–1786, LiVi; Mar. 9, 1778, Northumberland County Order Book, 1773–1783, LiVi; Jefferson to Zane, Feb. 26, 1778, *Papers of Jefferson*, II, 175; *Journal of the House of Delegates of Virginia* (Williamsburg, Va., 1776–), Nov. 18, 1778, f. 70.

4. Feb. 27, 1778, H. R. McIlwaine et al., eds., *Journals of the Council of the State of Virginia* (Richmond, Va., 1931–1982), II, 93–94; Lund Washington to George Washington, Mar. 11, 1778, *Papers of Washington,* Rev. War Ser., XIV, 151; Apr. 14, May 12, 1778, Loudoun County Court Records, 1776–1783, LiVi.

route to the army. Up to the middle of May 1778, only 799 men marched from Virginia, of whom 41 had been left on the road for various reasons and another 42 deserted. Officials reported that men were leaving daily, draftees particularly. Of 28 drafts one Lieutenant Campbell escorted northward, 22 deserted.[5]

Thus, opposition to the draft again short-circuited recruiting plans. Unable to afford substitutes and unhappy with the discriminatory application of the law, many ordinary Virginians fought back against what they perceived to be an unjust law. Their strategy worked. By late May 1778, only 716 men of the 8,000 men asked for had been raised through the draft or through substitutions. George Washington wrote in late May 1778 that, even of the 1,500 recruits requested from the previous draft, together with the 2,000 men the assembly ordered drafted in February 1778, the Continental army had received only 1,242. Washington lamented that this was "so horrible a deficiency." Of all the drafts and volunteers ordered raised, Patrick Henry thought that "not one half of the Number voted by the Assembly have got to Camp." "Virginia," wrote one army chaplain definitively, "makes the poorest figure of any State in the Recruiting way."[6]

5. "Abstract of Men Raised under the Former Laws Passed for Raising Soldiers for the Continental Service—November 1782," *Virginia Military Records: From the Virginia Magazine of History and Biography, the William and Mary Quarterly, and Tyler's Quarterly* (Baltimore, 1983), 661–662; Lund Washington to George Washington, Mar. 18, 1778, *Papers of Washington,* Rev. War Ser., XIV, 221; John Robert Sellers, "The Virginia Continental Line, 1775–1780" (Ph.D. diss., Tulane University, 1968), 291. Still others found more creative ways to avoid the draft altogether. See Custis to Washington, Feb. 12, 1778, *Papers of Washington,* Rev. War Ser., XIII, 512–513.

6. Washington to R. H. Lee, May 25, 1778, John C. Fitzpatrick, ed., *The Writings of George Washington from the Original Manuscript Sources* (Washington, D.C., 1931–1944), XI, 452 (cf. 438n); Patrick Henry to Henry Laurens, June 18, 1778, *Papers of Madison,* I, 245; David Griffith to Leven Powell, June 3, 1778, Robert C. Powell, ed., *A Biographical Sketch of Col. Leven Powell, Including His Correspondence during the Revolutionary War* (Alexandria, Va., 1877), 79; R. H. Lee to Jefferson, May 2, 3, 1778, *Papers of Jefferson,* II, 176–177. Cf. Baylor Hill to Theodorick Bland, May 5, 1778, Bland Family Papers, VHS. The draft also short-circuited the volunteer scheme. In particular, the high prices paid by many counties and individuals to induce men to serve in their stead or as part of the county quota drove up bounties generally. Potential recruits simply refused to volunteer for the armed forces when they could sell their services to their neighbors for much higher

• • • Ordinary Virginians' resistance to the draft had important social and political consequences. Perhaps most significantly, the draft in Virginia helped reinforce new local, social, and political alignments. In some places, like Hanover County, the provision allowing men to turn in deserters worked the way legislators intended—it helped open divisions within communities that had heretofore blocked state attempts to enforce the laws. In many other counties, though, whole communities closed ranks against state legislation or any local officials who tried to enforce it. Indeed, though the draft law was designed to isolate single if not poorer men, opposition often came from all quarters. Lund Washington believed that the mutiny in Loudoun County "was begun by a Married Man." Washington, like other patriot leaders, thought that, because only single men were targeted, others would stay out of the opposition to it. "I expected they wou'd have been Silent, as the draught did not extend to them, but some people must do wrong." In his neighbor's challenge to the draft, Washington did not quite understand why communal interest had triumphed over self-interest.[7]

Local officials were once again key players in the unfolding drama. Though the state legislature stipulated the terms of the draft, local militia officers and justices of the peace were left to interpret the law as they understood it. This precipitated problems in some counties. Indeed, the anger of the militia in Loudoun stemmed in part from local officials' interpretation of the drafting law. According to Lund Washington, they had decided to exempt themselves and other "favoured" elites from the draft. "The Court who presided over our Draughtg Law in this Cty, was so exceedingly complisont that they woud not Suffer me to take a Chance for a prize," even though "there was no law to exempt me, and they were sworn to do the worck impartially." In Loudoun, the local board of magistrates and field officers took it upon themselves to judge "that it never was intended that the judges shoud judge themselves." They therefore exempted themselves, officers, and others they deemed important, like Lund Washington, from the draft. Thus, even within the militia, the board exempted at least two captains and one colonel in the county, though they were single men and should strictly have been included. Lund knew that this was not fair to the

prices. Robert Honyman noted in mid-March 1778 that recruiting for the volunteer scheme "scarce advances at all." There were "none at all offering for that service" (Mar. 15, 1778, Diary of Honyman).

7. Lund Washington to George Washington, Mar. 11, 1778, *Papers of Washington,* Rev. War Ser., XIV, 151.

other single men whose chance of being picked was further increased. He also knew that, in other counties, "officers as well as men drew" lots for the draft. He noted that his countrymen were also aware of the unfairness of the proceedings: "The people murmur and say our Draught was not agreeable to the letter of the Law."[8]

In Loudoun County, local officials were in part responsible for creating resistance to the draft. In other counties, their inaction helped mute outright resistance to it. Anticipating opposition because of their past experiences and because of the new rumors of opposition that many heard before the draft, some local officials simply refused to act. Some were paralyzed with fear. One officer in Loudoun County, perhaps mindful of the protesters' death threats to his commanding officer, "refused to act as Captain" in the middle of the crisis that engulfed his county. Still others sympathized with their neighbors. When protesters shut down the draft in Fluvanna County, even the county lieutenant—who was also a delegate to the House—might have played a role. The state council later accused Thomas Napier of "obstructing the Draught." The council ordered a court martial of Napier, but his own colleagues and subordinates acquitted him of the charges. A subsequent recruiting act acknowledged that many local officials had simply not carried out the law.[9]

Whatever the reasons for local officials' unwillingness to carry out the draft, their actions or inaction did signify that draft resistance had induced a general insubordination and disorganization in the militia that resonated throughout the ranks. The resistance of ordinary Virginians to the draft forced local officials to back off, sympathize, or risk a violent confrontation with their neighbors. Unlike in sprawling Loudoun County, most officials were not prepared to take the latter course. Instead, they chose disobedience to the state laws, happier to take their chances against the state government than against their own neighbors, often risking punishment and their state reputations for the sake of local harmony. As the example of Thomas Napier shows, however, with the backing of colleagues in the militia and on the county court bench, most local officials were prepared to

8. Ibid., Mar. 18, 1778, XIV, 221.

9. Mar. 9–10, 1778, Loudoun County Court Records, 1776–1783, LiVi; Sept. 2, Oct. 16, 1778, McIlwaine et al., eds., *Journals of the Council,* II, 183, 197. The 1778 draft law, legislators noted, had "not produced the end proposed," because many officials had not even laid out the divisions required for recruiting and drafting men according to their quotas. Hening, comp., *Statutes at Large,* X, 82–83.

take that risk. Draft resistance led to a breakdown of state authority. Local officials who could not command obedience from their neighbors in turn disobeyed state laws with impunity.

State officials and Virginians in the Continental service, like General George Weedon, understood that the draft had been defeated in large measure by the failure of those responsible for implementing it to carry out their orders—to deliver their recruits, whether volunteers or draftees, according to the law. "Every County almost, that have sent forward their men," Weedon complained, "have been short of their Quota." George Washington wrote in late May 1778, "Something has been wrong in conducting the draughts." Governor Henry claimed that the executive had done its "utmost" to raise Virginia's quota of troops, but they were unable to do more. "Very few more of the Drafts will ever be got into the Service."[10]

• • • If state officials like Henry were frustrated by the new alliances and the new mood of local defiance, state legislators were in for a bigger shock. The draft took place in February 1778. New elections for the General Assembly took place in late March and April. If the now annual elections provided a convenient barometer of the mood of the people, they proved that the mood had soured toward the government. John Parke Custis had in February thought that popular acceptance of the draft and new taxes showed that "our Government is well establish'd in the Minds of the People"; he was forced to admit he was wrong in March. As elections began, he wrote to George Washington of his earlier remarks, "I am now to contradict that assertion, and to assure you they are the reverse."[11]

Custis's assessment of the mood of electors translated into a high turnover of representatives. In the elections of 1778, Virginians returned an extraordinary number of new people to the assembly. A total of fifty new faces appeared at the session that began in May, not counting the new counties established in the west. This amounted to 36 percent of the House. Twelve counties changed both their delegates, and forty-three changed one of their

10. George Weedon to John Page, Mar. 31, 1778, Papers of George Weedon, LiVi; Patrick Henry to Henry Laurens, June 18, 1778, *Papers of Madison,* I, 245; Washington to Richard Henry Lee, May 25, 1778, Fitzpatrick, ed., *Writings of Washington,* XI, 452.

11. Custis to Washington, Feb. 12, Mar. 26, 1778, *Papers of Washington,* Rev. War Ser., XIII, 513, XIV, 316.

delegates. In only sixteen counties were both members who served the previous year returned. Significantly, in all the turbulent Northern Neck counties, either one or both of the representatives did not make it back.[12]

Patriot leaders were taken aback by the election results. John Page, Sr., was in a state of disbelief and could not understand what had happened. He thought that so many new and untested people had been elected because the "Freeholders" were in a "torpid State." "So few of them attend at Elections now," Page concluded, "that any Man may get into either House." Yet disgruntled electors in Virginia had not just elected "any Man"—they had elected men who would represent their interests.[13]

Though details of the reasons for the changes are scarce, one account of a by-election in the fall of 1777 reveals much about the volatile nature of popular politics during wartime. In Caroline County, an election had been called in the fall of 1777 to replace Thomas Lowry, who had accepted an appointment as sheriff after the spring session of the assembly. James Upshaw, Thomas Lomax, and John Page, Jr., all declared themselves interested in replacing Lowry. "The people," thought Pendleton, were most interested in Lomax and Upshaw and were apparently "much divided" between them. Page, on the other hand, was popular only with the wealthier

12. These figures are drawn from an analysis of the members of the General Assembly from each county and each year, listed in Cynthia Miller Leonard, comp., *The General Assembly of Virginia, July 30, 1619-January 11, 1978: A Bicentennial Register of Members* (Richmond, Va., 1978). In deducing whether representatives were "new" or not, membership was checked back to the elections of 1771. Thus, there may be a few in this category that had seen legislative service, but before 1771. Changes due to death, moves by members into the senate, Congress, army, or other public offices have not been accounted for.

Such a turnover matched the upheaval of the previous year, when 38 percent of the House had changed. Yet many changes in 1777 could be explained by patriot leaders by the opening of new positions in the Senate, council, and Continental services. Fewer of the changes in 1778 could be as easily explained. When taken together with the results of the previous year's elections, the scale and pace of change became apparent. Indeed, these two years saw the influx of a total of ninety-three new people into the House. In addition, eleven new counties began sending people to the assembly in 1777-1778, eight of whom were from newly created backcountry counties. Such a change in the composition of the House was unprecedented.

13. John Page to R. H. Lee, May 6, 1778, Paul P. Hoffman, ed., *Lee Family Papers, 1742-1795* (microfilm) (Charlottesville, Va., 1966).

gentlemen of the county. He would get some votes, thought Pendleton, but not enough, despite the fact that the "Gentlemen of Interest should Assist him."[14]

By mid-July, Upshaw began to think he would not stand. However, military affairs had a direct impact on the election. In mid-August 1777, as a result of the first draft, the Caroline County militia was reorganized and split into two battalions when it was found to be more than one thousand men. The county court was then responsible for choosing new field officers for the new battalions and chose Walker Taliaferro for colonel of the First Battalion, Upshaw for lieutenant colonel, and Richard Buckner for major. For the new Second Battalion, the court chose Lowry, Anthony Thornton, Jr., and John Minor for the same positions. The new appointments caused great discontent, and many of the captains who were not picked as field officers "are Offended and say they will give up their Commissions." In response, though, the captains apparently persuaded Upshaw to run for the assembly. He had reputedly voted to make the militia promotions by "merit" rather than "antiquity" (that is, seniority), as Pendleton called it. John Page, Jr., on the other hand, had voted for the promotion of the officers by rotation, or seniority, alone. As a result, he lost some ground. The third candidate, Lomax, had taken a quiet route since August and had declared that he would serve only if the freeholders chose him, and would not do any electioneering. Pendleton thought that, with such an attitude, Lomax would lose the election and Upshaw would almost "certainly succeed."[15]

Yet, if Upshaw had succeeded in wooing the militia officers of the county to his side, he still had to gain, and retain, the support of the militia themselves. When in early September—during the invasion scare—Upshaw was called to York to serve as lieutenant colonel of the battalion of militia there, Pendleton thought that this would "rather Assist than hurt his election which they say is sure." But Upshaw ran into trouble at Yorktown, which directly influenced the election race. With little to do at the garrison, the militia Upshaw commanded had allegedly complained that they wanted to go home, "to se[e] and take care of their wives and Children." Upshaw reportedly "treated it lightly" and replied that he too wanted to go home, "to se[e] his Mares and Colts," but that they all had to stay and do their

14. Pendleton to Woodford, June 14, 28, July 19, Aug. 15, 1777, *Papers of Pendleton,* I, 214, 216, 218, 220.

15. Ibid.

duty. Upshaw enraged the militia, and reports flew that Upshaw had insulted them by comparing *"His Mares and Colts to their wives and Children."* The story quickly made the rounds back in Caroline, and most of the militia involved and from the same side of the river then declared for John Page, Jr., though Upshaw "had several warm friends there before." As a result, Pendleton told William Woodford, "Electioneering . . . has taken a surprising turn in the County." Pendleton had not yet seen Upshaw to get his version of events but thought he could somehow "lessen the weight of the Offence, if not wholly remove it." Whatever the reality, Pendleton and others thought that it would have an immediate impact. "It is now said Mr. Page will have a great Majority."[16]

Upshaw somehow clawed back some ground, so that by the end of October the race was "daily fluctuating" between Upshaw and Page. Pendleton thought Lomax could still take it from both, "tho' that at present seems improbable." In early November, a week before the election, Pendleton believed that Upshaw had indeed regained the confidence of the electorate, at least in part because he had convinced some (including Pendleton) that there was "no foundation" for the militia reports. Upshaw had admitted that "Wives and Children, Mares and Colts were mentioned in the Conversation" but had argued that they had been raised "with no more connection or comparison with each other, than between things the most remote." Pendleton thought Upshaw would carry the election.[17]

The election race in Caroline County is revealing on several fronts. Not only did Pendleton now expect Lomax to campaign for his own election, but he was almost certain that, if he did not, he would have no chance with the voters. Perhaps most important, though, military service was central. Upshaw had made himself popular among the officers of the militia by declaring that he would actively seek a change in the promotion rules if he was chosen as a representative. His leadership of the militia during the British invasion scare was a further opportunity, according to Pendleton, for Upshaw to gain votes—not just among the admiring and patriotic voters he left behind but with the men with whom he would have inevitably come into close contact while in service. Yet, if Upshaw lived by the sword,

16. Aug. 28, 1777, McIlwaine et al., eds., *Journals of the Council,* I, 476; Pendleton to Woodford, Sept. 13, Oct. 11, 1777, *Papers of Pendleton,* I, 223, 228.

17. Pendleton to Woodford, Oct. 25, Nov. 8, 1777, *Papers of Pendleton,* I, 231, 236. In the end, both Lomax and Upshaw made it to the next assembly, because Pendleton stepped down in the spring.

he could also die by the sword. In this case, close contact with the electorate/militia had actually triggered the "surprising turn" in the fortunes of the candidates. Upshaw had stepped out of line in the eyes of his men. Not only did he appear to be insensitive to the real needs of the men he led, but he also showed a contemptuous arrogance that—in a society in which horse ownership was by no means universal—could have been interpreted only in class terms. Finally, in the face of a now volatile electorate sensitized to their own status in the county through their participation in the militia, it is significant that Upshaw felt compelled to publicly defend himself and explain his conduct. Ultimately, he was able to reconcile himself with the voters, but only by actively seeking to heal or at least explain away the rift between himself and the group of men that followed him into combat.

Not all election races were so intimately and directly tied to militia service, but the war overshadowed many platform issues. According to some patriots, voters in the spring of 1778 had elected representatives who promised to prosecute the war with less vigor and coercion than the former government. In some cases, this meant that voters elected disaffected candidates. John Page was particularly troubled about elections in Middlesex County. There, voters elected Philip Grymes, a noted tory. There were also reports that Middlesex almost chose Ralph Wormeley as well. Wormeley, a notorious and outspoken tory, came "within a few Votes of being sent" to the assembly with Grymes. Wormeley had already been banished to the backcountry early in the war because of his tory sympathies. Both Grymes and Wormeley would again land themselves in trouble with patriot authorities before the war was over. Page was frustrated and furious with the voters. Yet, by electing tories and tepid patriots to the assembly, Virginians sent a clear message—and new representatives—to the government.[18]

Though discussion of the reasons for these legislative changes was limited, the actions, or inaction, of the new representatives shed light on the mandate. The assembly met for only a short time and did little to further the war effort. Virginia's preparations for a summer campaign, Honyman reported, even in the face of "formidable" accounts of the enemy's preparations, were "rather languid." Legislators might have been further lulled

18. John Page to R. H. Lee, May 6, 1778, Hoffman, ed., *Lee Family Papers;* Leonard, comp., *General Assembly of Virginia,* 130. See Wm. P. Palmer et al., eds., *Calendar of Virginia State Papers and Other Manuscripts, 1652–1781, Preserved in the Capitol at Richmond* (Richmond, Va., 1875–1893), II, 279–280, for the suspicions they aroused later in the war.

into inaction by talk of peace. Since General John Burgoyne's surrender at Saratoga, many Virginians were hopeful. As the delegates convened in May 1778, rumors of a peace commission from Britain helped magnify these hopes. But it might have been confirmed reports of the long-awaited and hoped-for treaty of alliance with France that put delegates in a "languid" mood. With the promise of more foreign aid and even soldiers in the air and the barbs of still-angry constituents ringing in their ears, legislators sat on their hands—despite pleas from Washington, Congress, and Patrick Henry to support the war effort more vigorously.[19]

Most important, reflecting a sudden turnaround in attitude, the assembly refused to entertain the idea of further drafts for soldiers. Mann Page summed up the mood in a letter to Continental Congress delegate Richard Henry Lee in mid-May: most people in the assembly agreed on the need to

19. Diary of Honyman, May 2, 1778. In late April Pendleton reported news that another peace commission had been sent from London, on its way to treat with Congress: it was going to acknowledge the independence of the colonies. Pendleton worried about the effect that it would have on an already recalcitrant people and thought the report was another ruse to lull people and put them off their guard. The British could not lose with such a venture, knowing it would be a propaganda victory, thought Pendleton, even if they knew the peace commissioners would fail. A failed commission would help persuade most of the British people and "timid Americans" that the want of peace was the fault of Congress. Pendleton to Washington, Apr. 27, 1778, *Papers of Pendleton,* I, 255; cf. Pendleton to Woodford, June 27, 1778, Pendleton to Washington, Dec. 22, 1778, I, 261, 276.

To prevent Pendleton's prediction from coming true, patriot leaders at the congressional and provincial level worked hard to counter widespread notions that the war was just about over. Virginia's delegates in Congress, embarrassed by the dearth of recruits Virginia was able to muster, also tried to convince their colleagues in the assembly that the state would have to do better. *An Address of the Congress to the Inhabitants of United States of America, May 9, 1778* (broadside printed by Alexander Purdie) (Williamsburg, 1778), LiVi; R. H. Lee to Jefferson, May 2, 3, 1778, *Papers of Jefferson,* II, 176–177. Cf. R. H. Lee to Jefferson, May 11, 1778, II, 177–178.

Governor Henry, in part responding to such Continental pressure, prepared a long message for presentation to the Virginia assembly when it met in May, pressing it to take immediate steps to continue and even step up its preparations for war. Patrick Henry to Benjamin Harrison, [May 13, 1778], Henry to R. H. Lee, May 15, 1778, H. R. McIlwaine, ed., *Official Letters of the Governors of the State of Virginia* (Richmond, Va., 1926–1929), I, 270–273, 274. Cf. May 12, 31, June 6, 1778, Diary of Robert Honyman.

help strengthen the Continental army; they would "do their part towards it." However, he himself had "great hopes" that the troops could be raised "without our being reduced to the necessity of a draught." Six days later, he told Lee that little would be done during the legislative session. "Our people are too desirous of Peace."[20]

The assembly did pass a new recruiting law to try to fill its quota of Continental troops, but it watered the bill down and pointedly refused to try another draft. Instead, the new act was designed specifically to prevent the "inconveniency of draughting men" by "giving encouragement to soldiers." Accordingly, any man that would engage voluntarily for three years would receive a full $150 and a new set of clothes each year. Those who enlisted for the duration of the war would receive the same bounty and additional incentives and, most important, would be exempted from the payment of public taxes for the *rest of their lives*. Those disabled in service would be entitled to full pay for the rest of their lives as well. The few other measures passed by the assembly all tended to undermine even this weak effort at recruiting regular troops. For example, the assembly called for 2,000 temporary volunteers to immediately reinforce Washington for the coming campaign. Any volunteers would get a new set of clothing and $30 each, in return for about six months' service. Volunteers would also be free from taxes for a full year, and their wives and families would get public relief if they needed it. Finally, the legislators also ordered a new battalion of infantry raised for state service as well as a troop of 350 cavalry. Recognizing that the governor's orders to march the previous state regiments northward had put many Virginians off from enlisting for the state service, the new act stipulated that any order to march out of the state would constitute an automatic discharge.[21]

Thus, legislators in Virginia refused to budge in the face of repeated pleas by Continental officials for Virginia to implement more coercive and effective measures to recruit its complement of Continental troops. John Parke Custis, so optimistic about the success of the draft in early February, finally had to tell Washington that another one was no longer an option in the assembly. The new bill for recruiting men for the army held out

20. Pendleton to Woodford, June 6, 1778, *Papers of Pendleton,* I, 257; Mann Page, Jr., to R. H. Lee, May 15, 21, 1778, "Selections and Excerpts from the Lee Papers," *Southern Literary Messenger,* XXVII (July–December 1858), 261–262.

21. Hening, comp., *Statutes at Large,* IX, 445–449, 452–456; John A. Washington to R. H. Lee, June 20, 1778, Hoffman, ed., *Lee Family Papers.*

"every inducement to the men to enlist" voluntarily. Though many agreed that drafting men might be cheaper and more successful, it was now "the most disagreeable" option. Honyman also noted the change in mood in the assembly. In March, before the elections, he reported that recruiting had again deteriorated so much that it was "expected" that, when the new assembly met, "another draught must take place to raise a sufficient number of men." After the meeting, Honyman was surprised that there were to be no further drafts.[22]

Ardent patriots were bitterly disappointed with the measures taken by the assembly, and few believed that they would be very helpful. After watching his fellow legislators do little to further the patriot effort, Richard Lee (1726–1795) told Thomas Adams, then in Congress, that his fellow Virginians "seem to be asleep" and had elected representatives who would let them lie. "I think our Government wants energy." Jefferson believed that the measures proposed were "worse than ridiculous," because they would fool their friends into thinking help was on the way. "There will not be a company raised."[23]

But the legislation brought in by the new assembly reflected the changes in the composition of the House—and the response of legislators to the election upheaval. Many believed that the pressure on the militia only endangered the very tenuous alliance that patriot leaders had constructed with middling farmers in Virginia. That alliance had already been shaken by the recent elections, which brought in more legislators who were less willing to push their constituents too far. Thus members of the new assembly were either those sufficiently shaken by the 1777–1778 draft and ensuing

22. John Parke Custis to Washington, June 17, 1778, George Washington Parke Custis, *Recollections and Private Memoirs of Washington, by His Adopted Son . . . with a Memoir of the Author, by His Daughter; and Illustrative and Explanatory Notes, by Benson J. Lossing* (New York, 1860), 548; Mar. 15, June 6, 1778, Diary of Honyman. In the middle of the legislative session, perhaps having received reports from Henry or the Virginia delegates that the assembly was in a dovish mood, Congress approved a letter to the Virginia executive on June 10, 1778, urging the state to "adopt the most effectual and vigorous measures for speedily reinforcing the continental army with your quota of troops" (see Worthington Chauncey Ford et al., eds., *Journals of the Continental Congress, 1774–1789* [Washington, D.C., 1904–1937], XI, 583–584).

23. Richard Lee to Thomas Adams, June 29, 1778, Adams Family Papers, VHS; Pendleton to Woodford, June 6, 1778, *Papers of Pendleton,* I, 257; Jefferson to R. H. Lee, June 5, 1778, *Papers of Jefferson,* II, 194.

election to rule it out for the next year, or those chosen specifically to vote against putting more pressure on the militia.

That feeling was reinforced by the delegates' unwillingness to change substantially the militia laws themselves. When it became clear that local opposition had obstructed the 1778 draft, Henry again pressed his case for more authority over the militia. This time, Henry had more pressing arguments. In late February 1778, the council received news from the western and northwestern frontiers that Cornstalk and other Shawnee Indians at Fort Randolph might spark a war in that area. They believed "large Draughts" of militia might be needed for a possible war on the western frontiers, so they pleaded with all militia officers throughout the state to use their most "Strenious Exertions" to equip their militia and get them ready to march "at a moments warning." But problems arose on Virginia's eastern border too. In January 1778, Josiah Philips, a laborer, declared an outlaw the previous June for his treasonous behavior, had been captured and brought in to Williamsburg. By the end of April, he was again on the loose, and the council had word that he was again busy creating an "Insurrection" in Princess Anne County, with fifty other men. This time, the council ordered out one hundred militia from neighboring Nansemond County, along with a party that Colonel Thomas R. Walker was raising, to quell the insurgents. Local officers, however, had trouble enlisting help. Part of the problem, one officer thought, was that punitive fines in the militia were so low that his men thought it cheaper to pay up than turn up. They could afford to pay the fines "by earning more at home." The insurrection continued unopposed through April and May.[24]

When the new assembly convened in May, Henry wrote to the House of Delegates and the speaker that he was powerless to do much against the insurgents without more authority. They could not rely on the militia in Princess Anne or Norfolk Counties, because they were ill disciplined, and many were disaffected. The militia in neighboring counties, like "too many other Militias in the State," suffered from an almost "total want of discipline," which rendered them useless. Using this latest crisis as a stick

24. Jan. 3, 1777, Feb. 19, Apr. 11, May 1, 1778, McIlwaine et al., eds., *Journals of the Council,* II, 58, 86, 121, 127; Governor Henry's Circular Letter, Apr. 12, 1778, McIlwaine, ed., *Official Letters,* I, 265. Cf. John Alonza George, "Virginia Loyalists, 1775–1783," *Richmond College Historical Papers,* I (1916), 199–200; John Wilson to Henry, May 20, 1778, Executive Communications, LiVi; May 27, 1778, McIlwaine et al., eds., *Journals of the Council,* II, 140.

with which to extract more coercive power over the militia from the assembly, Henry asked it to reform the militia. Perhaps thinking of the conduct of the militia ordered northward in September 1777, Henry told Benjamin Harrison, speaker of the House, of "several Instances of refractory and disobedient Conduct" that had gone unpunished. The militia were generally happy to flout the laws, because the fines for delinquency of all kinds were "esteemed of so little Consequence." Offenses were "common." The militia thus needed more discipline, and fines for disobeying the militia laws had to be increased.[25]

The assembly only reluctantly agreed to put more teeth into the regulations governing the militia. In An Act to Amend an Act for Providing against Invasions and Insurrections, the assembly recognized that the existing punishments for mutiny, desertion, disobedience, and cowardice were insufficient to deter delinquents. Courts-martial could now inflict any fine they determined reasonable in the particular case, but local courts-martial would still determine the verdicts. Neither the governor nor the council was given any further power or authority. In the end, even the new powers of the courts-martial were limited to inflicting a punishment of no more than six months' pay.[26]

Moreover, the assembly made it clear that it had no sympathy with Henry's efforts to use the militia to reinforce Washington to the north. Only very reluctantly, over great opposition, did delegates agree to extending the governor's temporary authority to march militia out of Virginia into neighboring states. Supporters of more vigorous activity just managed, "with great difficulty," to get the measure passed.[27]

Henry was furious that the assembly had not passed stronger militia and recruiting laws, increasing his irritation with the representatives. He was

25. Henry to Harrison, May 21, 28, 1778, McIlwaine, ed., *Official Letters,* I, 277–278, 282–283. Phillips was back in jail in Williamsburg by mid-July (July 20, 1778, McIlwaine et al., eds., *Journals of the Council,* II, 169). A group of militia in Frederick County who were supposed to help guard suspected Quakers told their commanders that they were going home. When their commander told them they would be fined, they said they were "able to pay it, and went away" (Thomas Gilpin, *Exiles in Virginia: With Observations on the Conduct of the Society of Friends during the Revolutionary War . . .* [Philadelphia, 1848], 174). Cf. Henry to Harrison, Dec. 11, 1778, McIlwaine, ed., *Official Letters,* I, 337.

26. Hening, comp., *Statutes at Large,* IX, 458.

27. Custis to Washington, July 15, 1778 (John E. Selby, *The Revolution in Virginia, 1775–1783* [Williamsburg, Va., 1988], 136).

pessimistic about the new legislation. In a letter to Henry Laurens, president of Congress, the governor laid the blame for Virginia's poor recruiting squarely on the shoulders of the assembly. It had failed to help, he said, and made any further effort by the executive useless: there was "too little reason to expect any success" in recruiting men in Virginia or reinforcing Washington with militia. He was more explicit about his anger with the assembly to Richard Henry Lee. The measures they had taken to try to recruit men for the army, the governor confided, would only "expose our State to contempt." "Let not Congress rely on Virginia for soldiers." In the end, Henry believed that a "different spirit prevails" in Virginia. Referring mainly to the assembly, Henry told Lee, "Public spirit seems to have taken its flight from Virginia."[28]

Finally, the new mood among legislators might also be measured by one extraordinary step they took. The General Assembly became one of the first governments in the modern world to abolish the slave trade. Originally the idea had come before the assembly in the spring of 1777, when it had been tabled. With several important amendments, the bill was revived in the spring of 1778, when it passed into statute. The new law declared that all slaves imported into Virginia would be freed. As radical as the move was, legislators narrowly missed out on attacking the entire institution of slavery. The original bill called for permitting private manumissions of slaves as well as an implication that the legislature intended to restrict slavery even more at a later date. As it stood, the new law fell far short of such lofty goals, for it carefully excluded slaves brought in by their owners, slaves brought into the state by owners who were only passing through the country, and slaves belonging to newcomers planning to settle permanently in Virginia. The law also excluded slaves that Virginians inherited or obtained outside the state by marriage. Only the commercial slave trade was forbidden.[29]

Though Jefferson might have husbanded the bill through the assembly,

28. Henry to Henry Laurens, June 18, July 8, 1778, Henry to R. H. Lee, June 18, 1778, McIlwaine, ed., *Official Letters,* I, 289–292, 298; July 25, 1778, Ford et al., eds., *Journals of the Continental Congress,* XI, 721. Patriots outside the state were equally disappointed with Virginia. See, for example, James Duane to George Clinton, Mar. 21, 1779, Paul H. Smith et al., eds., *Letters of Delegates to Congress, 1774–1789* (Washington, D.C., 1976–2000), XII, 216.

29. Selby, *Revolution in Virginia,* 158; Hening, comp., *Statutes at Large,* IX, 471–472; James Curtis Ballagh, *A History of Slavery in Virginia* (Baltimore, 1902); Bill to Prevent Importation of Slaves, *Papers of Jefferson,* II, 22–24.

he could have counted on support from three diverse and perhaps over-lapping quarters. For one thing, there had been a sudden influx of new representatives from farther-flung western counties, where slaveholding was not as widespread or as sought after as in eastern areas. Representatives from eastern areas might have joined with their western colleagues in stopping the importation of slaves in order to increase their profits on the sale of slaves they already owned. Finally, legislators might also have been pushed into adopting this extraordinary measure by another group of Virginians in 1778. Enslaved Virginians themselves helped persuade planters throughout Virginia that stopping the slave trade was in their best interests. Indeed, though the desire for greater profits among planters undoubtedly contributed to the move to abolish the slave trade, enslaved Virginians had reminded whites throughout the war that they were a dangerous presence. Not only did rebellious slaves keep more hands at home—and out of the army—to supervise them, but they also took advantage every time the British came into the bay. The most recent invasion scare, in August and September of 1777, was no exception.

• • • The actions and reactions of the legislature reflected a new mood among ordinary Virginians. Freed from the worry of an impending draft, whites, for example, began putting their farms back in order. With the new taxes scheduled by the previous assembly soon due, it was in fact imperative they do so. It was an opportune moment, too, because, for the first time in months, the bay was clear of the enemy, and trade ships began arriving in the state. Moreover, a "seasonable" spring and summer promised good crops with which to trade.[30]

Patriot leaders inadvertently encouraged a brisk trade in the spring of 1778 because of their desperate efforts to help supply Washington's army in the shadow of the winter of Valley Forge. Both the state and Continental governments had authorized and commissioned purchasers to supply the army. With prices in the northern states already high, these purchasers converged on Virginia in early 1778, in competition with private purchas-

30. Sept. 21, Nov. 2, 1777, Diary of Honyman. George Webb believed the wheat harvest had been the best in many years but that many growers had turned back to tobacco because it kept better when trade was stopped (Webb to Thomas Adams, June 26, 1778, Adams Family Papers, VHS). Even as August brought heavy rains that damaged crops, the prices of foreign commodities continued to drop because of increased trade activity (see June 26, Aug. 20, 1778, Diary of Honyman).

ers. In late May, the first of several large French ships arrived in Virginia loaded with goods. The state bought everything, but as a private purchase and thus at an inflated price of 6s per livre (it had been 1⅓s the previous year). In order to pay for the goods, the state began buying up vast quantities of tobacco—two thousand hogsheads (or two million pounds) of it—to send back with the French ships. Such were the rush and the logistical difficulty of supplying the ships at Alexandria and Yorktown that all other operations came to a halt during June, July, and August. Just as the French ships were leaving, Congress then ordered a convoy of tobacco for its own agents in France. With so many buyers in the state, speculators and small farmers alike finally had an opportunity to demand what they wanted for their goods, particularly tobacco. By the time this convoy was complete at the end of October, the price of tobacco had risen to almost £5 per hundredweight.[31]

Almost at the same time, Congress authorized a new commissary general, Jeremiah Wadsworth of Connecticut, to purchase twenty thousand barrels of flour for the French fleet under Admiral d'Estaing, who arrived in early July. Wadsworth was told to buy it in the South because prices were already so high in the northern states. As Continental agents tried to buy as much as they could, prices soared. The assembly in the fall of 1778 tried to prevent hoarding and banned private exports of grain, but the prices kept rising. In December, Congress asked for another eighteen thousand barrels of flour. The state agent for the Continent, William Aylett, managed to scrape most of it together, but he warned Congress that farmers had become "extortionate" in their sales and that Virginia could no longer be relied on for it.[32]

The state assembly was reluctant to interfere with the newfound enthusiasm for trade, and efforts to curb the burgeoning appetite for trade were stifled. Custis told Washington that a bill had been brought into the House for regulating trade in the spring of 1778, but the assembly failed to pass it. Custis was angry that the new assembly had once again put the interests of people of the state ahead of Continental demands. Knowing Washington's army was still suffering from a want of supplies, the bill would have helped divert needed goods northward. Instead, the assembly preferred to let market forces work toward the benefit of its constituents. Custis was

31. Selby, *Revolution in Virginia,* 181.
32. Ibid., 180–181; *Papers of Mason,* I, 459–464. Cf. June 4, 1778, McIlwaine et al., eds., *Journals of the Council,* II, 143.

confident that the bill for regulating trade would have been "productive of good consequences." However, it was "thrown out" in the end, because trade "had too many friends in the house to let it be injured."[33]

As a result of the demands, many Virginians took advantage, and all sectors of society were able to capitalize on the short boom. As farmers found fresh markets for their crops and charged ever-increasing prices for them to keep up with the depreciating currency, laborers in turn demanded more for their services. In fact, with the premiums laid out for military service in all branches of the armed forces, workers finally began to enjoy the benefits of their labor. Advertisements for both skilled and unskilled workers began appearing in the newspapers with much greater regularity in 1778. A desperate adventurer in North Carolina advertised for seamen in the Virginia papers, for example, offering a twenty-dollar bounty plus an expenses-paid trip to New Bern. Ropemakers, cardmakers, coopers, wire-drawers, scythe- and sword-cutters, and general laborers were desperately needed at Hunter's Iron Works in Smithfield, and Joshua Storrs promised "extraordinary Wages" and "proper Dwelling Houses" to a manager and two or three good spinners if they came to work at his ropery in Richmond.[34]

The demand for workers, combined with the pressure on the labor force exerted by military service, meant that wageworkers commanded new power over prospective employers. Even early in 1778, Lund Washington noted that it was difficult to find seamen to outfit a privateer in his possession because they were in such high demand. They were no sooner hired than they would be lured off with promises of higher wages. The same was true of carpenters. Only two weeks later, Lund told his cousin the general of one weaver employed at Mount Vernon who suddenly found himself in high demand in 1778. He had somehow managed—"contrived," in Lund's words—to turn in a deserter from the army, which exempted him from military service himself. Now on the open market, the weaver grew

33. J. P. Custis to Washington, June 17, 1778, G. W. P. Custis, *Recollections and Private Memoirs,* 548.

34. *Va. Gaz.* (D and H), July 25, Aug. 1, 29, 1777. Thomas Nelson, Jr., complained in June that almost everyone in Virginia was consumed with making money through trade. "Almost every Man," he believed, was "engag'd in accumulating Money." Nelson to Washington, June 30, 1778, in John Robert Sellers, "The Virginia Continental Line, 1775–1780" (Ph.D. diss., Tulane University, 1968), 321. See Selby, *Revolution in Virginia,* 163–183, for an assessment of the economy during wartime. The boom of 1778 was short-lived and never on a solid foundation.

bold and told Lund that he would no longer work at Mount Vernon for less than one hundred pounds a year. The weaver was confident of his value and told Lund that, if he did not pay him that rate, he would leave, "saying he cou'd get it" elsewhere. Lund had hoped to pay him less than half this sum. Though he questioned the weaver's real value, he could do little in the circumstances. He needed help on the estate but did not know where to turn for it. Such demand must have been a liberating experience for many laborers of the day, who now would have some economic, and hence social, freedom and leverage.[35]

Those who labored for a living continued to find good wages in the military as well. Many jumped at the attractive—and rapidly increasing—bounties. Those in a position to do so could and did manipulate the recruiting laws to their own advantage. Indeed, potential recruits often found ways to capitalize on the desperation of patriot leaders to raise new troops. They took advantage of the already generous enlistment schemes to give themselves maximum benefit and return on their risk. In part, they took advantage of spiraling inflation, and, in part, they contributed to it. As the Virginia legislature continued to print money to pay the large bounties it promised and other wartime costs, prices for goods, but also for military labor, rose quickly.[36]

When the assembly made economic enticements the sole inducement to join the army in 1778 and 1779, the inflation of bounty rewards grew. Though members of the militia were no longer quite so desperate to recruit men in their places to avoid being drafted, recruiting officers, who could not secure their commissions without the full complement of new recruits, *were* desperate. By early 1779, Robert Honyman reported that recruiting officers were paying up to $450 more than the prescribed bounty of $300 to

35. June 6, 1778, Diary of Honyman; Lund Washington to George Washington, Mar. 18, Apr. 1, 1778, *Papers of Washington,* Rev. War Ser., XIV, 220, 382. Cf. Lund Washington to George Washington, Sept. 2, 1778, LiVi; Mar. 7, 30, 1778, McIlwaine et al., eds., *Journals of the Council,* II, 99, 112–113. On labor shortages in the mid-Atlantic region during the war, see especially Michael V. Kennedy, "The Home Front during the War for Independence: The Effect of Labor Shortages on Commercial Production in the mid-Atlantic," in Jack P. Greene and J. R. Pole, eds., *A Companion to the American Revolution* (Oxford, 2000), 332–341.

36. As early as January 1777, Robert Honyman reported that "every thing rises exceedingly in price, owing to the immense quantity of paper money, and likewise to the precariousness of its credit" (Jan. 16, 1777, Diary of Honyman; cf. Apr. 10, 1777).

procure recruits. Neighboring North Carolina helped drive up prices too. One report stated that North Carolina was offering an extra $50 bounty but also an extra $1 per day—and enticing a number of men out of the Virginia Line into their own. By the fall of 1779, the sums given to recruits for the army had reached critical proportions. Pendleton thought that almost every man enlisted had cost, on average, about £5,000.[37]

Though army life was generally unattractive, new recruits could and did find some benefits amid the harsh discipline, neglect, and poor pay. Some enlistees tried to bring along their own comforts. Quite a few men brought their wives, and some their families. Washington complained in 1777 that the "multitude of women . . . especially those who are pregnant, or have children, are a clog upon every movement." Though disparaging, Washington gradually came to accept the presence of soldiers' wives, who often performed valuable services, including nursing, cooking, and cleaning. Other soldiers learned to cope by forming new and rewarding relationships with their fellow recruits. Many units formed an important esprit de corps based on their short but intense experiences in the war. But, if their situation became intolerable, soldiers could and did rebel by deserting or mutinying. Thus, perhaps because it was relatively easy to desert and find sanctuary at home, few soldiers resorted to mutiny to remedy their condition.[38]

Generally, however, potential recruits found the perquisites of civilian demand for their labor more attractive than the army. As a result of the "rage of amassing," as Honyman put it, far fewer whites joined the army.

37. Mar. 12, 1779, Diary of Honyman; Arthur Campbell to Henry, Mar. 15, 1779, Palmer et al., eds., *Calendar of State Papers,* I, 317; Pendleton to James Madison, Sept. 25, 1779, *Papers of Pendleton,* I, 308–309.

38. See Don Higginbotham, *The War of American Independence: Military Attitudes, Policies, and Practice, 1763–1789* (New York, 1971), 389–419, quote on 397; Robert Middlekauf, *The Glorious Cause: The American Revolution, 1763–1789* (New York, 1982), 496–510; Middlekauf, "Why Men Fought in the American Revolution," *Huntington Library Quarterly,* XLIII (1980), 135–148; Holly A. Mayer, *Belonging to the Army: Camp Followers and Community during the American Revolution* (Columbia, S.C., 1996), 122–191; Charles Royster, *A Revolutionary People at War: The Continental Army and American Character, 1775–1783* (Chapel Hill, N.C., 1979), esp. chap. 5; James Kirby Martin and Mark Edward Lender, *A Respectable Army: The Military Origins of the Republic, 1763–1789* (Arlington Heights, Ill., 1982), esp. chap. 4; Charles Patrick Neimeyer, *America Goes to War: A Social History of the Continental Army* (New York, 1997).

By June, Honyman thought that most people's attention had been diverted from the war effort. In part, many likely candidates for service had already "experienced the dangers and hardships of military service" and had had enough while others, though not disaffected, were reluctant because "the dangers of their situation is not so imminent from the successes of the last campaign." Yet Honyman also believed that "every class and rank of people are so totally engrossed with schemes and projects for making money." "Every other consideration," Honyman complained, "holds but an inferior place." The problem was exacerbated by the fact that, increasingly, the army was poorly supplied. Moreover, new recruits could never be sure when they might get paid, whether they would receive the promised bounty of land at the end of the service, or how much their fixed wages would finally be worth because of the rapidly depreciating currency. Given the rewards at home and the risks in serving, poorer Virginians were more likely to take their chances at home.[39]

The lack of recruits to the army did mean that other, previously excluded groups could take advantage of the shortages in the military. For example, a growing number of apprentices and indentured servants found their way into the ranks. Beginning in the summer of 1777, servants and apprentices could legally leave their masters without consent. Some of those enlisted with their master's consent. Most did not. Abraham Leafman, a fourteen-year-old apprenticed to Francis Lockett, ran away in late 1777 and joined the newly formed state artillery company. Life in the army could promise more freedom and, especially, a better start than an apprentice could normally look forward to. So many apprentices joined the army over 1778 and 1779 that groups of masters complained to the assembly. Military service could be of benefit to those already in some form of coercive and exploitative situation.[40]

39. June 6, 1778, Diary of Honyman. Cf. J. P. Custis to Washington, June 17, 1778, G. W. P. Custis, *Recollections and Private Memoirs,* 548. The poor supply of the army had become so critical that the new recruiting law stipulated that new soldiers would not have to march out of the state until they were provided with the bounty of new clothes that they were promised for enlisting (Hening, comp., *Statutes at Large,* IX, 454–455). Cf. E. Wayne Carp, *To Starve the Army at Pleasure: Continental Army Administration and American Political Culture, 1775–1783* (Chapel Hill, N.C., 1984); Erna Risch, *Supplying Washington's Army* (Washington, D.C., 1981).

40. *Va. Gaz.* (D and H), Sept. 19, 1777; *Journal of the House of Delegates,* June 14, 1779, Nov. 24, Dec. 5, 1780. Cf. Neimeyer, *America Goes to War;* and *Va. Gaz.*

Of course, many enslaved Virginians also saw new opportunities in the army—any army. Because the British were no longer close enough to attract runaway enslaved Virginians, some took advantage of labor shortages to work within the system to gain their freedom. By 1778, enslaved Virginians knew that, in the face of falling white enlistments, recruiters were more likely to enlist blacks, enslaved or free. Whereas, for most of Virginia's history, whites had been collecting rewards for catching and returning runaways to their masters, the new recruiting law meant that whites could make money by helping enslaved Virginians find freedom. It stipulated that recruiting officers would get ten dollars for each recruit they brought into the army. Blacks knew that recruiters would be happy to accept their claims to freedom. In June 1778, one master believed that one of his runaways was "smart enough to go off and [en]list." Hundreds of others were too. Lewis, an enslaved Virginian, obviously knew what he was doing when he passed himself off as a free black called Lewis Roberts and made it clear that he would "take a man's place" to go to the northward. By the middle years of the war, blacks constituted a significant minority in the Continental army.[41]

(D and H), Dec. 19, 1777. Citizens in Frederick County complained in the summer of 1779 about the large number of apprentices and servants who had joined to serve as substitutes for other militia. By the fall of 1780, enough apprentices had run away to join the army that a group of mechanics from Winchester made another official complaint.

The best account of the effect of the Revolution on the apprentice-master system is W. J. Rorabaugh, "'I Thought I Should Liberate Myself from the Thraldom of Others': Apprentices, Masters, and the Revolution," in Alfred F. Young, ed., *Beyond the American Revolution: Explorations in the History of American Radicalism* (DeKalb. Ill., 1993), 185–217.

41. Petition of Thomas Walker, Jr., Oct. 23, 1779, Virginia Legislative Petitions, LiVi. William Beck, who belonged to Thomas Walker, Jr., served with Walker and under Colonel Charles Lewis in "several Campaigns" in the northern states and got his freedom that way. Walker admitted that Beck had "during his servitude behaved in a most exemplary manner." In return Walker petitioned the assembly to give Beck his freedom. Some men, like Anthony Ferriah, a mulatto, enlisted, received a big bounty, and promptly deserted. Ferriah and others like him could use the bounty money to finance a flight to freedom. Hening, comp., *Statutes at Large,* IX, 454–455; Gerald W. Mullin, *Flight and Rebellion: Slave Resistance in Eighteenth-Century Virginia* (New York, 1972), 133; Higginbotham, *War of American Independence,* 395–397.

While those who had something clear to gain joined the army, most white Virginians simply ignored the renewed calls for service. Pendleton wrote hopefully in mid-June that the "Military Spirit seems reviving" when he heard that recruiting officers in his county had procured almost thirty men, but his optimism was short-lived. The rumor proved unfounded. Only a week later he noted, "The recruiting for [the] line goes on slow or rather not at all." Colonel George Carrington of Cumberland County reported retrospectively that a recruiting officer was appointed under the new act of spring 1778, but not a single man was raised. When Henry called for the state recruiting officers to make returns of their enlistments at the end of October 1778, the council reported that "few Men" had been recruited, and immediately discharged nine recruiting officers for failing to produce any new soldiers. Thomas Nelson, Jr., at the time attempting to raise a cavalry unit in Virginia, wrote bitterly: "So great is the aversion of the Virginians to engaging in the army that they are not to be induc'd by any method."[42]

• • • Many patriot leaders believed there was a link between trade and poor recruiting and that profits were more important than patriotism. From Mount Vernon, John Parke Custis complained to Washington in mid-June about the lack of commitment to the cause. "Our countrymen appear to be totally changed," as all "military ardour" appeared to be "almost extinguished." The "little paltry trade among us" has "engrossed the attention of all orders of men." It had also increased the price of labor to such a degree that no soldiers could be enlisted. But patriot leaders were also concerned that the "rage of amassing" indicated a still more general indifference to the patriot cause.[43]

Indeed, in the midst of the "rage of amassing," new reports of a possible rapprochement reached Virginia. Early in the summer of 1778, General William Howe withdrew from Philadelphia and returned to New York, fueling speculation that the British would soon withdraw from the conti-

42. Pendleton to Woodford, June 20, 27, 1778, *Papers of Pendleton,* I, 259, 261; "Abstract of Men Raised," *Virginia Military Records,* 671; Oct. 31, 1778, McIlwaine et al., eds., *Journals of the Council,* II, 207; Thomas Nelson, Jr., to Washington, June 30, 1778, quoted in Sellers, "The Virginia Continental Line," 321. Cf. June 26, 1778, Diary of Honyman.

43. J. P. Custis to Washington, June 17, 1778, G. W. P. Custis, *Recollections and Private Memoirs,* 548; June 6, 1778, Diary of Honyman.

nent altogether. At the same time, patriot leaders sensed that some of their neighbors were indifferent about the French alliance. Henry thought that, despite the French help they had already received, some "prefer the offers of Britain."[44]

Pro-British sentiment grew when the economy began to falter in the fall of 1778. Persistent rains in the latter half of the summer had ruined many expectations of good crops, prices of foreign goods had begun to rise again (although the bay remained free of the enemy), and supplies from France were thought "insufficient and indifferent to our needs." As planters began to hoard tobacco as insurance against the depreciating currency, many people wished for a stable trade—with any suppliers. Thus, "All ranks of people," claimed Honyman, "wish earnestly for a renewal of the British trade."[45]

Patriot leaders in northern Virginia got a shocking demonstration of the sentiments of ordinary Virginians in the summer of 1778 when they tried to mobilize the militia. The governor had, in April 1778, asked all county lieutenants to step up the training of their militia and get one-third of them ready for marching, in case they were needed. John Augustine Washington, the county lieutenant in Westmoreland County, called his militia together for June 2. On that day, however, Washington found the militia in a rebellious mood. To Washington's "great surprise," he found that the call-out had "created so much warmth in the minds of the people" that it was impossible to carry out his orders. Washington wisely postponed the call-out of the militia, but the militia themselves did not wait for a second muster. Taking extralegal action against Washington and the executive order, they secretly circulated a "Subscripsion" that bound them together to prevent the call upon the militia. The associators were specific about their aims. They had heard rumors that they, the militia of Westmoreland, were being called together to march northward to help reinforce

44. Henry to R. H. Lee, June 18, 1778, McIlwaine, ed., *Official Letters*, I, 292.

45. The poor weather continued into October, flooding the rivers and destroying yet more property and stock, and was climaxed by a whirlwind. And prices of foreign goods continued to rise "amazingly." Sept. 29, Oct. 21, 1778, Diary of Honyman. Cf. Bruce A. Ragsdale, *A Planter's Republic: The Search for Economic Independence in Revolutionary Virginia* (Madison, Wis., 1996), 257. Some patriot leaders in Virginia also began to wonder whether peace might not be the best option, at least for the moment. See Mason to R. H. Lee, July 21, 1778, *Papers of Mason*, I, 430; Jefferson to R. H. Lee, Aug. 30, 1778, *Papers of Jefferson*, II, 210–211.

General Washington, and the association bound them to "stand by each other and oppose any attempt that may be made to march them out of this State." Altogether, at least forty-eight men (or almost 10 percent of the militia in the county) signed the subscription and also gathered together on June 21 to oppose the call-out again. Washington believed that the associators had the support of the majority of the community and that the mood was widespread, noting a "most uncommon backwardness towards the service among the people" in the early summer. Worse, he thought that the people in neighboring counties were also in a state of rebellion. He believed "Richmond and Northumberland is going on in the same way."[46]

The same fears that plagued recruiting for the Continental army also played on the minds of the associators of Westmoreland. John Augustine Washington admitted that most of the rebellious militia were adamantly opposed to marching northward. He thought they might have feared smallpox or other "dangerous disorders" that they were told prevailed in the main military camp to the north. Smallpox and what Washington called "camp-fever" were, he concluded, far more alarming to his neighbors than "any dainger they apprehend from the arms of the enemy." Washington's militia also worried about leaving their own homes defenseless. But Washington was also concerned that the militia insurrection was due to a lack of commitment to the patriot cause, which, in turn, was linked to lingering class resentments. He told Lee that "the situation of our affairs and the nature of the contest" was being misrepresented to the "ignorant, uninformed people." Those stirring up trouble, Washington claimed, played upon existing class resentments in the lower Northern Neck. Washington thought that the persons misrepresenting the patriot cause had considerable influence on the people, "making them believe that it was produced by the wantonness of the Gentlemen, and that the poor are very little, if any, interested."[47]

46. John Augustine Washington to R. H. Lee, June 20, 1778, Hoffman, ed., *Lee Family Papers*.

47. Ibid. Under the circumstances, Washington tried to tread carefully. Rather than assert his authority, he tried to reason with his rebellious neighbors. He "assured them" that the executive council could not have meant to order them away from their homes when they were as exposed to British depredations as they were. But Washington was actually at a loss about why the governor had ordered him to get the militia ready in the first place; all he could do was guess. The governor's intention, he told his recalcitrant militia, "must have been" to put them in a posture of defense in case they were invaded. But Washington's speculative arguments

Well aware of such sentiments to sway their constituents, legislators gathering for the fall session of the General Assembly were again unwilling to take much effort to carry on the war. Despite dwindling enlistments falling far short of their Continental quota and further direct pleas from Washington, the assembly refused to enact or enforce any kind of draft for Continental soldiers. Popular opposition to the previous two drafts had scared many legislators off from thinking of another. Pendleton told Washington, "Drafting in any Shape is so unpopular a measure, that our Assembly have laid it aside." He believed that the assembly would continue to depend on "high bounties only" to secure its quota, which he held out little hope for.[48]

So, partly owing to pressure from Washington, the assembly did at least order a new contingent of 2,216 troops raised, requiring that 1 in every 25 militia be enlisted into the Continental army for either eighteen months, three years, or the war. The assembly also called for each county to provide any and all deficiencies in quotas from the previous years but failed to prescribe a method for raising the men or for punishing counties that failed to do so. As Pendleton predicted, the assembly relied instead on further incentives and high bounties in trying to compete with the economic benefits of life outside the army: a gill of spirits every day, exemption from poll taxes for life, half-pay for widows, disability pay, and necessities provided by a public store that would sell goods to the soldiers at 1774 rates. And, much to the frustration of Washington and other patriot leaders who desperately

---

rang hollow in the face of worries about farms and families and class resentments. "Nothing seam'd to convince," he complained to Richard Henry Lee.

48. Concerned that the assembly might continue to neglect the Continental establishment, Washington sent Colonel James Wood of the Eighth Virginia Regiment to make it clear to the assembly that the reinforcements were still urgently needed. Wood despaired at what he found. He told Washington that all the talk in Williamsburg in October was of peace. The "whole legislature," he wrote, "were highly pleased, with a thorough persuasion, that the war was at an end, that the British troops were embarking, and that there was not the most distant probability they would again return to the Continent." Only a letter from Washington that Wood presented to the House on November 2 helped rouse them, temporarily, from their "lethargy." See Col. James Wood to Washington, Nov. 12, 1778, McIlwaine, ed., *Official Letters,* I, 320n; Selby, *Revolution in Virginia,* 137; Pendleton to Washington, Dec. 22, 1778, *Papers of Pendleton,* I, 276–277. Washington complained to Henry about Virginia's quota in October, noting that some of the Virginia regiments were only the size of a company or two (see Washington to Henry, Oct. 7, 1778, Fitzpatrick, ed., *Writings of Washington,* XIII, 46).

wanted to build a long-term professional army capable of matching the British, the assembly also left the door open for short-term recruits. Men who enlisted for eighteen months only would still get a generous bounty of three hundred dollars. Those who enlisted for three years or the duration were promised four hundred dollars and one hundred acres of land for three years' enlistment and two hundred acres for the duration (the Continental bounty). The assembly also set aside lands in the western backcountry for soldiers and their officers.[49]

As legislators struggled to come up with the right formula for attracting new recruits, one thing was certain: "There was to be no draft." Delegates even publicly acknowledged that the previous draft had been a failure and that they ought to correct the situation, yet they refused to put any teeth into their efforts. Many counties, delegates noted, had failed to furnish their quota as directed by the act of October 1777. They had either failed to draft the men or neglected to secure their drafts and forward them to Continental officials. Instead of drafting the men now, the assembly told county officials to try to make up this deficiency over and above the new quota. They were given no explicit instructions how to, nor any additional legal or coercive powers. Clearly, the responsive assembly wanted to avoid any further confrontation with its constituents.[50]

• • • The fruits of the assembly's inaction soon became apparent. A few short months after the assembly adjourned in the winter of 1779, the British struck Virginia in a ferocious lightning raid. On May 8, a fleet of about 30 British ships came into the bay and made for Hampton Roads. The British were led by Major General Edward Mathew, with strong naval support from Commodore Sir George Collier. They first attacked Portsmouth, and then Suffolk, which they burned. About two thousand troops landed and burned as much stock as they could get their hands on. They captured or destroyed more than 130 vessels, three thousand hogsheads of tobacco, and other supplies worth an estimated two million pounds. Enslaved Virgini-

49. The House also debated whether to offer new recruits even more land for their services, over and above the Continental bounty. Hening, comp., *Statutes at Large,* IX, 565–567, 588–592; *Papers of Mason,* I, 465–466.

50. Feb. 15, 1779, Diary of Honyman; Hening, comp., *Statutes at Large,* IX, 588–592. To pay for the new recruits, the assembly tried to remedy some of the defects in the old tax law. See Hening, comp., *Statutes at Large,* IX, 547–552; Pendleton to Washington, Dec. 22, 1778, *Papers of Pendleton,* I, 277.

ans flocked to the British in the hundreds, taking advantage of the first presence of a large force in the heart of Virginia since 1776. Estimates of the number of enslaved Virginians who sailed away with the British ran from five hundred to fifteen hundred. The British withdrew on May 24, before any effective resistance could be mobilized.[51]

Patriot leaders did what they could to defend themselves against the British, but it had little effect. The House of Delegates, which had just reconvened, immediately ordered a volunteer force of militia raised, to serve for the duration of the invasion, and Governor Henry on May 15 issued a proclamation asking all county lieutenants to put their militia in a state of readiness and then ordered almost five thousand militia down to the lower counties. They arrived too late to be of any use and, as Honyman noted, were dispersed to different places so that any one group would not have been enough to defend any county against the full force of the British. Honyman chose to serve in the militia and see the war for himself, even though it was not his turn. He thought that the British generally went unmolested for almost two weeks and could have easily burned Hampton, York, and Williamsburg as well.[52]

Though some in the state believed that the turnout of the militia had been strong, quick, and adequate to prevent the British from attacking other ports like Hampton, the raid and the state's response only embarrassed most Virginians. Pendleton was ashamed of Virginia's defense. Acknowledging that the militia had turned out with speed, he complained that there was little in the way of a permanent defense force that could counter the British. Nor did Henry lead the troops personally, as his term as governor was expiring, Pendleton noted, and "his thoughts turned the contrary way." The virtually unopposed invasion would be a "great blotch in our Annals."[53]

51. Perhaps not all went willingly. Pendleton thought that privateers chased down enslaved Virginians by adopting "the old African Mode" of hunting them and rewarding those who brought them in. June 1, 1779, Diary of Honyman; Pendleton to Woodford, May 24, June 21, 1779, *Papers of Pendleton,* I, 285, 290; Henry to John Jay, May 11, 1779, to R. H. Lee, May 19, 1779, McIlwaine, ed., *Official Letters,* I, 366–367, 371–372; *Va. Gaz.* (Dixon and Nicolson), May 15, 1779; Sylvia R. Frey, *Water from the Rock: Black Resistance in a Revolutionary Age* (Princeton, N.J., 1991), 150–151.

52. *Journal of the House of Delegates,* May 14, 1779; *Va. Gaz.* (Dixon and Nicolson), May 15, 1779; June 1, 1779, Diary of Honyman.

53. William Fleming to Anne (Christian) Fleming, May 20, 1779, Hugh Blair

• • • Remarkably, even this humiliating raid failed to energize Virginians; instead, it exacerbated existing divisions and created new ones. Throughout the rest of the year, with the war effort paralyzed by lower-class Virginians, trade once again at a standstill, and peace talks stalled, the only thing that was moving was the ever-spiraling inflation of the currency. Virginians of all ranks, as Honyman noted, stood "amazed and confounded." They also stood very much divided. The inability of Virginians to contribute to the Continental effort, to control inflation, and now even to defend themselves led to many recriminations and divisions among patriots in Virginia. Virginians with sympathies for Washington and Congress grew angry at more state-minded patriot leaders, who themselves grew irritated by continual demands and requisitions from Congress. Within Virginia, middling and wealthy Virginians grew frustrated with the rising inflation and criticized patriot leaders, while others began to speak out against their lower-class neighbors.

Continental officials, for example, grew increasingly irritated with their fellow Virginians, and the Virginia delegates to Congress were particularly scathing. Some of them blamed ordinary Virginians. William Fleming thought that the desire for peace and more trade had overwhelmed patriotism. He complained to Jefferson, the new governor, "The bulk of

Grigsby Papers, VHS; Pendleton to Woodford, May 24, June 21, July 26, 1779, *Papers of Pendleton,* I, 285, 290, 293. Henry officially resigned four days after the British withdrew.

The language used by patriot leaders to describe the raid emphasized their deep-seated humiliation. Governor Henry's proclamation in the midst of the raid told of "horrid ravages and depredations" that included "plundering and burning houses, killing and carrying away stock," and "other abominable cruelties and barbarities." Privately, he spoke in less inflamed terms, but in a letter to Richard Henry Lee he felt humiliated. To add to Virginia's humiliation and Henry's disgust, the assembly had also asked for aid from Congress and neighboring states. The Virginia delegates asked Congress to take note of the "most unnecessary, wanton, and outrageous barbarities" committed on the citizens of Virginia, and the new governor, Thomas Jefferson, followed up with a letter to John Jay, complaining of the "ravages and enormities, unjustifiable by the usage of civilized nations, committed by the enemy on their late invasion." Proclamation, *Va. Gaz.* (Dixon and Nicolson), May 15, 1779; Henry to Jay, May 11, 1779, to R. H. Lee, May 19, 1779, to Harrison, May 28, 1779, McIlwaine, ed., *Official Letters,* I, 366–367, 371–372, 377; *Journal of the House of Delegates,* May 20, 1779; May 24, 1779, Ford et al., eds., *Journals of the Continental Congress,* XIV, 640; Jefferson to Jay, June 19, 1779, *Papers of Jefferson,* III, 5.

the people thro'out the states, seem to have lost sight of the great object for which we had recourse to arms, and to have turned their thoughts solely to accumulating *ideal* wealth, and preying upon the necessities of their fellow citizens." Others blamed state leaders. Richard Henry Lee pressed George Mason to take the lead in reforming Virginia's war effort: "There never was a time when the fullest exertion of ability and integrity was more necessary to rescue us from impending ills." Lee hinted that the new delegates elected to the assembly were responsible for the want of "wisdom and integrity, and industry" that prevailed in government, as many men sought public office merely "for getting into wealth on public funds and to the public injury." "Extreme mismanagement" had prevented Virginians from taking more effective measures against the British.[54]

Continental officers, too, such as George Washington, complained about the leadership of the state. He wanted Mason to push the assembly to take stronger steps to prosecute the war. At no time in the war had he so strongly felt America's "liberties in such eminent danger as at present." People felt the war was at an end, and they wished only to make money and to "get places" in the new administrations. "Friends and foes seem now to combine to pull down the goodly fabric we have hitherto been raising at the expence of so much time, blood, and treasure." Washington pointed his finger at men in the states in particular, though, and asserted that, unless the "bodies politick exert themselves to bring things back to first principles . . . inevitable ruin must follow." He even pointed the finger at Mason himself, Jefferson, and others in Virginia who seemed to think "we are about to set down under our own Vine and our own fig tree."[55]

Continental army officers in the Virginia Line also resented the efforts of their state-minded colleagues. Officers had watched from the sidelines as their fortunes at home went from bad to worse. As early as 1777, some officers had complained that they were suffering from the rapidly depreciating currency while forced to pay high taxes in Virginia for lands that they were unable to cultivate in their absence. When the economy improved temporarily in 1778, Continental officers watched anxiously as their compatriots made big profits. Thomas Nelson, Jr., believed that many officers re-

54. June 1, 1779, Diary of Honyman; William Fleming to Jefferson, May 22, 1779, Jefferson to Fleming, June 8, 1779, R. H. Lee to Jefferson, Mar. 15, 1779, *Papers of Jefferson,* II, 236, 269, 288; R. H. Lee to George Mason, June 9, 1779, *Papers of Mason,* II, 513–515.

55. Washington to Mason, Mar. 27, 1779, *Papers of Mason,* II, 492–493.

signed after they came home on furloughs in early 1778 because they could not resist the temptations of trade. With a fixed income from their wages, the possibility for making more was irresistible. He told Washington that officers returning home invariably found that "every Man who remains at home is making a fortune, whilst they are spending what they have, in the defence of their Country." By 1779, the mood had turned darker, especially among those who had stayed in the army. While many in Virginia amassed fortunes and contributed to the depreciation of the currency, those who had "devoted their lives and Fortunes to the Salvation of America" were in "distress," according to Pendleton, who hoped that the government of Virginia would not allow such a "piece of Injustice and ingratitude."[56]

Continental Virginians were angry at their state-based colleagues, and vice versa. Though Henry while governor had often fought with the General Assembly to fulfill Virginia's Continental obligations, the sympathies of the new governor, Thomas Jefferson, seemed to lie with the state. Within a month of taking office, Jefferson protested to John Jay that Virginians felt neglected by the Continental naval forces. The whole of the Chesapeake Bay, he claimed in June 1779, was blockaded by a "parcel of trifling privateers" under the protection of two or three larger ships that Virginia's naval force could not oppose. Jefferson complained that the American fleet had never been sent to Virginia, though it had consistently protected other states. Even British ships captured off the capes had been taken away from Virginia for use by other states. The next month, Jefferson was more explicit with Richard Henry Lee, Virginia's congressional delegate: he could only hope that Congress would "correct their long continued habits of neglect to the trade of these Southern states, and to send us some aid."[57]

But not all Virginians blamed Congress or other states. Some prominent

56. John Cropper, Jr., to Jay, Aug. 16, 1777, Palmer et al., eds., *Calendar of State Papers,* I, 325; Thomas Nelson, Jr., to Washington, June 30, 1778, quoted in Sellers, "Virginia Continental Line," 321; Pendleton to Woodford, Apr. 26, 1779, *Letters of Pendleton,* I, 279.

57. Jefferson to Jay, June 19, July 17, 1779, *Papers of Jefferson,* III, 5, 39. Jefferson, sympathizing with the hardships of his neighbors, also told William Fleming that he ought to do everything in his power to push Congress to conclude a peace treaty. There was a general feeling that peace and Independence were within their power, but Congress had delayed and frustrated British overtures, Jefferson told him. "It would surely be better to carry on a ten years war some time hence than to continue the present an unnecessary moment." Jefferson to Fleming, June 8, 1779, *Papers of Jefferson,* II, 288.

gentlemen believed other wealthy Virginians were behind their troubles—at least their financial woes. Some thought that the rising prices were a result of a few speculators who engrossed goods ahead of the state and Continental agents and, in turn, demanded much higher prices from desperate purchasers. One agent, Thomas Smith, was exasperated by some of the wealthier Virginians in the state. He told a colleague, Benjamin Day, in the fall of 1778 that most of his problems stemmed from elites in the state. "I have such a dislike to the Speculating Gentry that I have sometimes as Cruel thoughts as ever Caligula had."[58]

Yet some patriot leaders were most exasperated by their less wealthy neighbors—laborers demanding high wages for their work, recruits demanding high prices for their service, farmers exercising the upper hand in negotiations over trade. Honyman noted, "The Planters keep back their Tobacco, and will not sell it under extravagant prices." When Thomas Smith tried to find agents who would help him make state purchases, few volunteered. One merchant replied, "The buying of Tobacco, formerly no very difficult task to those who had been sometime established in the business, as the Planters came to their Stores, or were to be met with at stated times and places, has now got into quite a different channel—You must look for them at the back County Courts, Musters or go to their Houses, and then probably fail in persuading to sell at any price."[59]

Many gentlemen were furious that ordinary Virginians could and would protect their own interests. Pendleton, disgusted by the "Spirit of Avarice" besetting many in Virginia by 1778, cited the problem to Washington. Paper money was eagerly sought after by most white Virginians "as if it contained in itself the essence of meat, drink and cloathing or even of all the virtues" while those same people—"graspers," as he called them—were deliberately undermining the credit of the paper money. They "affect to decry it, as of no more value than Oak leaves." For Pendleton, the "Spirit of Avarice" was directly linked to Virginia's inability to raise an army: the "demon of avarice, and spirit of extortion," he exclaimed to Washington, "seem to have expelled the pure patriotism from the breasts of those who usually compose armies."[60]

58. Selby, *Revolution in Virginia,* 180.

59. Sept. 29, 1778, Diary of Honyman; Charles Yates and Archer Payne to Thomas Smith, Mar. 30, 1778, quoted in Selby, *Revolution in Virginia,* 180.

60. Pendleton to Washington, Apr. 27, Dec. 22, 1778, *Papers of Pendleton,* I, 255, 276–277, and May 21, 1778, quoted in Sellers, "Virginia Continental Line,"

Ordinary Virginians, however, had their own reasons for acting as they did. Farmers, for example, held back their tobacco for good reason. As demand for goods and services pushed prices up through 1778, they were desperate to keep pace so that they would not be caught short. Eager to take advantage of the demands for their goods and labor, many farmers and laborers were extremely anxious about the depreciating currency. The growing quantity of paper money from the state and Congress meant that any money they had on hand was quickly becoming worthless. Farmers either had to amass enough paper money to keep up with the rising prices of goods and labor, or stockpile enough tobacco to act as insurance against an increasingly worthless currency. Either option contributed to inflation.

The financial situation grew worse for ordinary Virginians. By Christmas 1778, the prices of all commodities had been "prodigiously enhanced," especially the "necessaries of life." By February, British ships had again laid a blockade on the coasts, prohibiting the arrival of any friendly ships. Prices thus rose enormously again. Honyman believed that the "poor suffer extremely, and the prospect of their farther distress is most alarming." Even food was scarce. The shortages occasioned a "most eager desire in all ranks of people of peace, and surely no country ever wanted that blessing so much as this miserable impoverished ruined land."[61]

In increasingly dire straits, many ordinary Virginians who had looked forward to peace in 1778 began to demand it in early 1779. When new reports hit Virginia that the British were ready to recognize American Independence, it was "greedily received by the people," according to Honyman, "as the certain Harbinger of peace, for which we all pray most devoutly, as the only thing that can save us from impending ruin." These hopes were

---

289. Cf. June 6, 1778, Feb. 15, 1779, Diary of Honyman. Tobacco prices rose constantly through 1778. After selling for 30s a hundredweight during 1777, tobacco rose to about £3 early in 1778, and then to £5 by the fall, and up to £10 by early 1779 (Selby, *Revolution in Virginia*, 180).

Other gentlemen did not specifically condemn potential recruits, but instead indicted Virginians more generally for their inability or unwillingness to make the effort to raise an army. John Banister at once blamed legislators for their reluctance to press more vigorously to fill the army, and their constituents for not pushing their representatives. John Banister to Theodorick Bland, June 19, 1778, Charles Campbell, ed., *The Bland Papers: Being a Selection from the Manuscripts of Colonel Theodorick Bland, Jr.* (Petersburg, Va., 1840, 1843), I, 86–87.

61. Dec. 25, 1778, Feb. 3, 1779, Diary of Honyman.

dashed by the British raid in May and the arrival of the king's speech to Parliament the previous November, and Honyman reported, "The people are much disappointed and dejected." The "minds of many are changed, and they are of opinion if we could have peace on good terms by giving up independence we should do very well." Those suffering the most were the most ardent advocates of peace, and, when push came to shove, ordinary Virginians knew whom to blame. The "lower class of people execrate their leaders, who have led them on by fine promises to utter ruin."[62]

Virginians who could vote continued to express their frustration at the polls. High turnover in the legislature continued in the spring of 1779 when George Dabney thought he saw a further erosion in the membership of wealthy and traditionally prominent men in the legislature. He wrote in the midst of the 1779 elections, "Alas how are the mighty fallen!" George Mason was pleased that some talented men had made it into the legislature, but by the middle of the session he was not so sure that they were using their abilities to advance the patriot cause. Many representatives, he worried, represented the pro-British sentiments of an increasing number of Virginians. "The last Elections have mended our House, in Point of Abilities, but I fear not in sound Whigism and Republican Principles."[63]

62. Ibid., Feb. 24, 1778, Feb. 15, June 1, 1779. Cf. Pendleton to Woodford, Apr. 26, 1779, *Papers of Pendleton,* I, 278; Ragsdale, *Planter's Republic,* 257. As late as Jan. 5, 1780, William Fitzhugh found widespread concern among "very sound Whigs and sensible Politicians" that Virginians retained too great a partiality "in favor of the Mother Country and Her Manufactures" (Fitzhugh to Arthur Lee, Jan. 5, 1780, quoted in Ragsdale, *Planter's Republic,* 257).

63. George Dabney to Charles Dabney, Apr. 18, 1779, Charles W. Dabney Papers, LiVi; Mason to R. H. Lee, June 4, 1779, *Papers of Mason,* II, 508. At the very least, the new elections only strengthened the hands of planters not from the tidewater or connected to it. The strongest testimony thereto was the renewed effort to move the capital away from Williamsburg. By 1779, the strength of the western counties and the composition of the House was such that supporters of a move had the upper hand in the General Assembly. The recent invasion only confirmed the necessity of such a move. Still, debate was divisive. Honyman noted that the proposal was met with "great opposition from the low land gentlemen," but he thought that the "up landers" now had the "upper hand" in the House and would be able to carry the measure if they could only agree on where exactly to move the capital. Indeed, the success of the bill was jeopardized only when supporters of a move divided over how far it should be. Members of the House proposed, in turn, Richmond, Fredericksburg, Charlottesville, and even Staunton. Richmond won. An attempt to

But, besides asserting themselves at the polls, some ordinary Virginians also asserted their general frustration with the war effort through vociferous petitions to the legislature, revealing further divisions and forcing delegates to take a closer look at their recruiting laws. In the spring session of 1779, for example, at least seventy-eight men from Orange County and seventy-two men from Culpeper County petitioned the General Assembly for a more equitable recruiting system. Those from Orange County claimed that, in the previous drives for recruits, people in their community contributed unequally toward raising recruits. The main problem was that the onus for fulfilling obligations for military service invariably fell upon individuals, whether through actual military service or by purchasing a substitute. Laws that placed the burden or obligation of service on the individual invariably favored the wealthy. So too did those laws that allowed men to purchase exemptions from military service by buying substitutes. William Allason, for example, a wealthy merchant living in Falmouth, was drafted for militia service during the invasion scare of September 1777. Allason hired a substitute, John Rankin, and told the county lieutenant, Colonel Humphrey Brooke, that he couldn't serve himself because he was "absolutely unfit for the Task from a Lameness in one foot." Allason also told Brooke that he had a "poor little Daughter and no white person to take care of her who I shou'd be extremely unwilling to leave." Allason, unlike many less wealthy militia, was in a position to do something about his situation. Yet Allason also claimed an exemption based on his status. He thought it beneath him to serve in the militia as anything less than an officer, as a "soldiers duty would also go exceedingly hard with me never having been accustomed to that way of Life that renders a man fit for common service."[64]

On top of all of this, as the petitioners from Orange County pointed out, many older and wealthier men like Allason had been invalided off the militia payrolls altogether. The cumulative effect of this system meant that, by 1779 and 1780, many wealthier men were no longer obligated to contribute toward finding recruits, and didn't.

------

reconsider the move in the fall session revealed how close it was. In a rare roll call vote, the motion to reconsider failed on a vote of forty to forty-five. June 12, 1779, Diary of Honyman; Selby, *Revolution in Virginia*, 236. Cf. Pendleton to Woodford, July 26, 1779, *Papers of Pendleton*, I, 294.

64. William Allason to Col. Humphrey Brooke, Sept. 9, 1777, "Letters of William Allason," *Richmond College Historical Papers*, II (1917), 168–169; Hening, comp., *Statutes at Large*, IX, 275–280, 339–342, 588–592.

The petitioners from Orange County asserted that in previous recruiting drives many of the militia had gone to "much trouble" and contributed "large sums" of money above the state bounty to entice soldiers. The "poor Militia" were particularly "liberal in their contributions"; their patriotic actions were in contrast with wealthier men in the county, not on the militia rolls, and uninterested "by a desire of serving their Country." Referring to Scripture, the petitioners compared the efforts of the "poor Militia" in the County with the wealthy: "It may be truly said they were like the widow in the parable who threw in all she possessed, when many that possess great estates . . . refused to contribute one farthing." As "injurious to the community" as this was, it was also "highly unreasonable," because the wealthy were "so materially interested" in the outcome of the cause. The poor, who had the least to lose, bore the biggest burden and had to make the biggest sacrifices to try to raise men while some of the wealthiest men stood by and watched them scramble for recruits and substitutes.[65]

One illuminating exception to this problem helps prove the rule. Carter Braxton of King William County had recently run into trouble with his colleagues for what was called his "Mercantile rapacity." As a delegate from Virginia in Congress, northern newspapers accused him of abusing his post for personal profit. The rumors and reports of his trading activities, which even fellow conservative Pendleton thought had gone beyond all "reasonable and proper bounds," had also landed him in trouble with elites in Virginia. In 1778, the assembly had turned him out of his post in Congress and would not even let him defend himself before it. According to Pendleton, he was "driven" away from the assembly by a "Party" who made out that his "political sentiments were either bad, or pretended to be so." Despite trading activities that helped drive up prices in general, Braxton was able to maintain his popularity in his county with an exceptional effort in helping to raise recruits. Braxton's neighbors reported he had done some "generous things." More specifically, he had over the past winter recruited —at his own expense—one of the men needed for King William's quota of Continental recruits. Thereby he exempted an entire division from find-

65. Orange County Petition, [May 13, 1779], Virginia Legislative Petitions, LiVi. Of course, poorer militia were also materially interested in procuring recruits under this voluntary system of raising soldiers because it meant that they would also be relieved of future, perhaps more coercive calls on them to fill the army. If the assembly instituted another draft, individuals might have to stump up far more money in order to avoid service.

ing and paying for one. This was generous enough, thought Pendleton, but especially because Braxton was under no obligation to do so. Braxton had "before purchased his exemption from Military duty by finding a Man to serve for three years." His help in finding and paying for yet another recruit earned him considerable kudos at home, according to Pendleton in neighboring Caroline County. The freeholders of King William elected him to the assembly in April 1779.[66]

Other wealthy men were not so generous, and infuriated petitioners from Orange County advanced a solution. The "obligation is equal on all men, to defend their liberty and property," even though they might not be able to do actual "bodily service." Accordingly, any money raised for bounties in the previous and any future drive for recruits ought to be collected from everyone, not just those in the militia, through a tax on *all* property. Petitioners from Culpeper County were explicit about what form that tax should take. In a novel argument that for the first time advocated a common solution to the two major problems facing Virginia—high inflation and manpower demands—the Culpeper petitioners demanded high and specific taxes (of actual goods, not money) in order to pay much larger bounties. Like the petitioners from Orange, a large proportion of the militia had recently paid more money to raise soldiers than their taxes would have amounted to, a fact they had a "just right to complain of." Not only did the active militia alone suffer, but the increasingly exorbitant bounties contributed further to depreciating the currency, as more and more emissions of paper money were needed to cover them. The Culpeper petitioners proposed an interesting solution: that the bounties be paid directly by higher taxes, which would help to redeem a great deal of the currency, to raise a more permanent army, and to stabilize the economy. They argued— perhaps overly optimistically—that, if potential recruits saw that the state was reducing the amount of money in circulation and they thus had some guarantee that their bounties would not be worthless within months, they would demand less to serve.[67]

Tying the two problems together would make higher taxes more palatable, the petitioners asserted. Most people agreed that there were only two ways to raise an army: through high bounties and coercive drafts; and all

66. Pendleton to Woodford, May 10, 1779, *Papers of Pendleton,* I, 282.

67. Orange County Petition, [May 13, 1779], Virginia Legislative Petitions, LiVi; Culpeper County Petition, [May 18, 1779], Virginia Legislative Petitions, LiVi.

those who "delight in freedom and an equality of Justice, must prefer the former." Higher taxes to pay for these bounties would be acceptable only if, they claimed, they were based on the same principle as the new tax system of 1777: the bounty money must come "out of the common stock," from taxes paid in proportion to the value of everyone's property. "Every person contributes (as of right they ought) in proportion to their taxable property." If the tax was fair, paid by everybody (even invalids and exempts), and put directly toward paying bounties, even the poor, who could ill afford higher taxes, would accept the plan, suffering proportionately less. Where there was "but Little given, their will be but Little required." Most people, and especially poorer Virginians who believed they might be targeted in a draft, would choose higher taxes over a draft, which would shift to individuals the full burden of hiring a substitute or actually serving themselves. Eventually even the poor would more cheerfully pay "in proportion to their Estates," the petitioners insisted, any tax found necessary to support the credit of their money ("when rightly informed") and thereby "fill up our Army by Voluntary enlistments rather than the disagreeable alternative of draughts or any mode similar theirto."[68]

Ultimately, the two petitions called for a more communal approach to raising recruits and stipulated that all members of the community should pay according to their means. But the petitions also marked a new assertiveness on the part of freeholders. Not content with airing their grievances against existing policies, petitioners now claimed a right to suggest alternative policies and practices. Though still cloaked in a thinly veiled language of deference, freeholders were less reluctant to recommend or demand a particular change in the laws. In this particular case, they also stipulated who ought to benefit and suffer from the law. Increasingly frustrated by a war that they thought was draining their strength and resources, ordinary Virginians began to voice more class-based arguments to distribute the burden of war more evenly. The petitions, as it turned out, only foreshadowed a new kind of thinking among freeholding Virginians—thinking that would produce deeper divisions.[69]

68. Culpeper County Petition, [May 18, 1779], Virginia Legislative Petitions, LiVi. In the end, the petitioners called for a further tax of at least twenty shillings on every one hundred pounds worth of property.

69. Freeholders could also rant about their worse-off neighbors, however. Charlotte County petitioners, for example, later complained that many lower-class Vir-

• • • The assembly actually did incorporate the most substantial part of the petitioners' demands in a law for raising four new state regiments in May 1779. The militia was to be divided into groups of twenty-five men, and each division was responsible for enlisting a soldier. In addition to the twenty-five able-bodied militia, *all* persons liable to pay tax (male and female) were to be added to each division in equal proportions. Each division would then be responsible for contributing $750 for a volunteer's bounty, to be raised within the division in proportion to taxable property. Thus the new law included everyone who had property to defend, not just those on the militia rolls, as the petitioners from Orange demanded. Everyone paying in toward the bounty would also now get credit for doing so in a discount from the next year's taxes. Thus poorer militia would not have to scramble to come up with cash to pay for a substitute or recruit and then pay taxes on top of this.[70]

In an important sense, the assembly moved the responsibility for paying for a recruit to the community and away from the individual. Wealthy individuals could still buy themselves out of service, but those who could not afford to would not be individually responsible for raising a recruit or face a disproportionate burden of the expense of doing so. Obviously, the new recruiting law was of considerable benefit to many militia.

The law also demonstrated that the General Assembly was ever more preoccupied with provincial defense. In light of the recent British raid, the assembly again put state needs ahead of Continental concerns. With bounties to match those offered for Continental service, recruiting for the state regiments, combined with the request for the short-term volunteer defense force, would inevitably undermine efforts to raise the Continental quota. State service was made more attractive to potential recruits, too, because the law stipulated that the provincial regiments could be ordered to serve only in neighboring Maryland, North Carolina, and western Pennsylvania in the case of the western regiments.[71]

---

ginians had taken the large bounties offered, deserted, and then prospected for land (see Charlotte County Petition, [Oct. 15, 1779], Virginia Legislative Petitions, LiVi).

70. Hening, comp., *Statutes at Large,* X, 32–34.

71. Because of the recent raid, legislators had also immediately passed a law for raising a body of volunteers for the state during the most current British invasion. Hening, comp., *Statutes at Large,* X, 23–27, 32–34.

Legislators all but ignored the Continental army. The assembly certainly refused to try to coerce men into its ranks. Publicly acknowledging that the last act "hath not produced the end proposed," the assembly extended the deadline for providing recruits to August 2. But there were no fines or punishments compelling local officials to enforce the law or any fines or punishments for those who ignored, evaded, or obstructed the draft. Instead, the assembly again offered high bounties and other incentives: $750 over and above the Continental bounty to anyone who would enlist or re-enlist for the war, pay and clothes, one hundred acres of land at the end of the war, and exemption from taxes during the service.[72]

Significantly, new tax laws introduced in the spring of 1779 also targeted wealthier Virginians. The General Assembly reformed the land valuation procedures but also adopted freeholders' suggestions to levy a five-year "specific tax." Beginning in March 1780, every man, free or slave, and every female slave over sixteen would owe one bushel of wheat; two bushels of corn, rye, or barley; ten pecks of oats; fifteen pounds of hemp; or twenty-eight pounds of tobacco. Most payments were expected to be in tobacco or corn. Yet, most significantly, and reflecting the new composition of the House, Mason pushed through Jefferson's earlier idea of reimposing a poll tax, but only on enslaved Virginians. This five-pound-per-poll levy, which would "run high" among the slaveholders, as Pendleton noted, targeted the wealthy. All other regulations, according to an irritated Pendleton, were made with a "view to preserving equality."[73]

New laws to finally settle the western lands were also a victory for less wealthy Virginians and those with western interests. In the first place, title was given to squatters who had actually settled on western lands be-

72. Ibid., 23–27, 82–83. Cf. "Form of Recruiting Commission," Nov. 28, 1779, *Papers of Jefferson,* III, 203, for the extent of promises held out to recruits.

73. Dec. 25, 1779, Diary of Honyman; Pendleton to Woodford, May 24, 31, June 21, 1779, *Papers of Pendleton,* I, 286, 290, 291. Cf. Culpeper County Petition, [May 18, 1779], Virginia Legislative Petitions, LiVi. Though the tax on slaves was welcomed by nonslaveholders, many people complained about the commodity tax Mason introduced this same session, which was more like a poll tax. The new commodity tax also meant that the "poorest man in the state is Compelled to pay as much as those of the most opulent fortunes, that do not Consist in Servants and Slaves" (Amherst County Petition, [Oct. 15, 1779], Virginia Legislative Petitions, LiVi; cf. Rockingham County Petition, [Nov. 9, 1779], Virginia Legislative Petitions, LiVi).

fore January 1, 1778, of up to four hundred acres. George Mason success-fully reintroduced a land office bill that validated old headrights, treasury rights, and military bounties for colonial troops issued before 1778; but the act canceled the large, not-yet-surveyed grants to speculating compa-nies that the colonial council had authorized. Upon the opening of the land office, anyone could purchase western lands for forty pounds currency per hundred acres. As important, the statute gave preemption rights to older settlers at the same price, up to one thousand acres in addition to their original four hundred. The law also laid out the provisions by which sol-diers could claim their land bounties and new settlers could purchase land. Finally, land companies had to sell to settlers at the price at which they originally offered the land even if the sale was delayed and inflation oc-curred in the meantime. Thus, the laws eliminated about half of the colo-nial land companies' claims, leaving the state of Virginia with a virtual mo-nopoly over the western lands. The laws also satisfied both existing settlers and speculators. It was believed that the western lands would solve a great many of Virginia's wartime debt problems, and the bills passed easily.[74]

The land office act proved a boon to both existing settlers in the west and to restless Virginians in the east. Perhaps predictably, Continental offi-cials, and particularly army officers, were angry about these new laws, which encouraged western migration and speculation. William Woodford was concerned that recruiting for the Continental army would plummet even further while desertion rates would soar, as were Washington and other Continental officers. To them, the personal dependence of unlanded Virginians in the army was preferable to their finding independence in the form of land and property in the west.[75]

Pendleton, on the defensive, told Woodford that the damage had already been done: many unpropertied and poorer Virginians had long since made their bid for independence, and the legislature was only responding to this flood of Virginians to the western lands. Tenant farmers, owners of poor and marginal land in the east, the landless, and deserters had been mov-

74. Hening, comp., *Statutes at Large,* X, 35–65. For an explanation of the new laws, and Mason's own stake in them, see Selby, *Revolution in Virginia,* 229–232; Jack M. Sosin, *The Revolutionary Frontier, 1763–1783* (New York, 1967), 154–155; Thomas Perkins Abernethy, *Western Lands and the American Revolution* (New York, 1937), 218–222; Edmund Randolph, *History of Virginia,* ed. Arthur H. Shaf-fer (Charlottesville, Va., 1970), 272–273.

75. Pendleton to Woodford, July 26, 1779, *Papers of Pendleton,* I, 294.

ing out west since the convention in 1776 had promised that a future land office would favor the claims of squatter-settlers. "The Natural Spirit of removing from paying rent for poor lands," Pendleton argued, "to fresh Rich lands without paying anything for them drew our people out there fast." That resolution "afforded equal Temptation to your Officers and Assylum to your deserting Soldiers." If the General Assembly had not acted now to establish a land office, the continued flood of people out west would eventually cause chaos—squatters were settling the country "Irregularly" and laying the foundation for "much dispute." Legislators were concerned that, "above all" other reasons for establishing the land office, the land "would have been ingrossed by Settlers and none left for Sale," and they feared they would lose a valuable source of revenue for paying off their war debts. At forty pounds Virginia currency per hundred acres, the income would be "considerable," and this was the "most powerful" motive of the assembly, according to Pendleton.[76]

However many Pendleton thought had moved out west already, plenty more still wanted to go. The law was passed just as news of Lieutenant Colonel George Rogers Clark's recapture of Vincennes trickled back into eastern Virginia. Troops returning home brought tales of rich western lands for the taking. Daniel Trabue was one of those soldiers. On his way back to eastern Virginia, he ran into several poor families who were already very interested in any stories he had about Kentucky. They asked a "bundence of qustions about kentucky and the Indians." After hearing his story, "they was astonished and much gratified," particularly when he showed them the plunder he had brought back from the Indians. Then, when Colonel Richard Calloway returned from the legislature, everyone insisted upon seeing him—"They thought it was a great affair," Trabue recalled. Yet, if Trabue's Chesterfield County neighbors were impressed by the no-doubt-exaggerated tales of Indian conquests, they were more impressed by the stories of Trabue and other veterans about the lands available in Kentucky. In this case, the result was direct: "Several of these neighbours Did buoy land warrents and got land in Ky."[77]

News of the land office act spurred on potential migrants, and many of Trabue's neighbors wanted to accompany Trabue back to Kentucky "as they wanted to see the country and get land when the office was to be

76. Ibid.

77. Chester Raymond Young, ed., *Westward into Kentucky: The Narrative of Daniel Trabue* (Lexington, Ky., 1981), 67–68.

opened the next spring." Upward of forty men volunteered to help Trabue take back powder and lead. So, too, did many of Trabue's own relations. By the fall of 1779, Trabue noted, more people than ever had moved to Kentucky. "Their was so many people had come and was a coming" that his commanders decided not to keep up the soldiery at the forts any longer. One newcomer estimated that nearly three thousand people arrived in Kentucky during the fall of 1779 alone. Trabue himself was surprised to "see the quantity of people that had recenty moved out to Kentucky, and they weare more yet a coming."[78]

• • • In the end, the new land office act certainly did not help recruiting for the Continental army; the new legislation to recruit the state's quota turned out to be as ineffective as previous attempts, and new recruits were

78. Ibid., 67–68, 70, 73, 74–78, 174n. Cf. Mar. 16, 1780, Diary of Honyman. Local militia officers believed that they could use western lands to entice volunteers for western expeditions; see The Officers of the Berkeley County Militia to Jefferson, Jan. 25, 1781, *Papers of Jefferson*, IV, 451–452. The land office act stimulated further speculation. Honyman said in early 1780 that the "greatest part of the people" were taken up in "schemes of interest of several kinds" and "immence fortunes have been made by trade, or speculation as it is called." Having bought up three thousand acres, Honyman boasted that, with such a landgrab at stake and good quantities of currency in circulation, there was a "wonderful passion" among almost "all ranks" to engage in some sort of trade or speculation.

The act provoked greater division, as the legislators' concession to speculators did not please everyone. Indeed, more than 130 people from Albemarle County complained that there were no limits to how much land could be bought and no stipulation that it had to be settled. They wanted to limit the amount of land that speculators could buy up in the Kentucky region, proposing that a "White free Man" had to be settled on every four or five hundred acres of land within two or three years of purchase. On a very practical level, if speculators were allowed to buy up large tracts of land, the actual settlers would be too thinly settled to establish schools and churches and, most important, to provide an able defense against Indian attack. The petitioners were also angry that the poor would then do all the difficult work. It was "extreamly unjust" that "those who are poor . . . Shou'd be at the Expense of perhaps, both Blood and Treasure, to defend the Country for those who are at ease and Safety at Home, their Lands growing in Value for them and their so many Generations, They never having done an equal Part in Settling or defending the Country." Selling large tracts of land to "Opulent Individuals" was simply unnecessary as well as unjust. Petition of Albemarle County Inhabitants, Oct. 14, 1779, Virginia Legislative Petitions, LiVi.

scarce in 1779. In Cumberland County, for example, nineteen men were required. Despite the increased bounties and perquisites, the county lieutenant, Colonel George Carrington, was unable to procure all the men through voluntary enlistments. He would have drafted the men according to the law, he stated, but, because there were no penalties, he could do nothing more. Officials from Southampton also complained that they could not raise their full quota, because the law prescribed "no mode of compulsion against the delinquent divisions." Richard Henry Lee, back in Westmoreland County in the Northern Neck, also revealed that officers had made little progress recruiting there. As late as October, "Such is the tardiness of people to engage in the Military that we have yet obtained but two men in Westmoreland."[79]

The returns of the First Virginia Regiment, probably the strongest regiment at any moment during the war, showed the shortcomings of Virginia military policy in the middle years of the war. In September 1776, 590 men were enrolled in the regiment (406 were present and fit for duty). By the end of 1779, even after being reinforced with remnants of the Ninth and Tenth Virginia Regiments, the First consisted of only 295 men, most of whose terms were expiring. Finally, just before its capture at Charleston, South Carolina, in May 1780, the strength of the regiment was listed at just 195 effective men. Jefferson had wearily summed the situation up in a letter to Washington in November 1779: the government was doing all it could, "but we find it very difficult to procure men."[80]

79. "Abstract of Men Raised," *Virginia Military Records,* 671; Hening, comp., *Statutes at Large,* X, 32–34; R. H. Lee to Jefferson, Oct. 13, 1779, *Papers of Jefferson,* III, 106. In November, Jefferson confessed to John Rutledge, "It has been a matter of real mortification to me that the whole of the troops ordered from this state on the Southern service under Genl. Scott have not yet been marched on." Even the recruits they had scraped together could not yet be marched out of the state, because the assembly had declared that new enlistees should receive every article of clothing promised as bounty first. If ordered to march before fully equipped, the men could claim a discharge—and Jefferson could not find adequate clothing. The state had offered a "liberal compensation in money" but had been able to march only one division in June, and to equip one other division that had marched in October. Those remaining were as yet unequipped. Jefferson to Rutledge, Nov. 11, 1779, *Papers of Jefferson,* III, 180.

80. Charles H. Lesser, ed., *The Sinews of Independence: Monthly Strength Reports of the Continental Army* (Chicago, 1976), 33; Lists of Officers of the First

The continued poor recruiting reflected wider problems in Virginia during the middle years of the war. At root were the increasing costs of the conflict that had contributed to spiraling inflation and an increased yearning for peace on any terms. Many prominent gentlemen, including Patrick Henry, despaired. Though most of their problems, he confided, stemmed from the depreciation of their money, this only reflected deeper concerns. The state of the currency could be likened to the "Pulse of the State." In this light, he observed: "I have feared that our Body politic was dangerously sick. God forbid it may not be unto Death." He then talked about the growing avarice of people, the "wicked" attempts to raise prejudices against the French, and the treachery of supposedly good whigs keeping company with "the Miscreant Wretches who I am satisfy'd were laboring our Destruction." He was troubled by the inability or unwillingness of his colleagues in the assembly to do anything about the disaffected among them, which brought the "Virtue" of his "Country men" into question. He hoped his own health would soon allow him to return to public affairs, before it was too late. He concluded: "Tell me do you remember any Instance, where Tyranny was destroyed and Freedom established on its Ruin among a people possessing so small a Share of Virtue and public Spirit? I recollect none; and this more than the British Arms, makes me fearfull of our final Success."[81]

Henry seemed unsure about whom exactly to blame for the current malaise, but like many other patriot elites he had a general sense that it was the fault of the "people" and their elected representatives. Yet ordinary Virginians had their own ideas about who was to blame. Some were angry that the promised rewards of foreign alliances were yielding only limited results. Others blamed Congress and Continental officials. Still others, like the Westmoreland associators, blamed the "wantonness" of patriot leaders for fighting a costly war on traditional terms while the poor were "very little, if any interested." And, while some elite and middling Virginians lashed out at the apathy of lower-class Virginians or their avarice for de-

Virginia Regiment, June 1, 1777, Dec. 9, 1779, May 1, 1780, Miscellaneous Revolutionary Papers, box 3, LiVi; Jefferson to Washington, Nov. 28, 1779, *Papers of Jefferson,* III, 204–205. In May 1779, Washington was forced to consolidate eight thin regiments from Virginia into four (see Robert K. Wright, *The Continental Army* [Washington, D.C., 1983], 147).

81. Henry to Jefferson, Feb. 15, 1780, *Papers of Jefferson,* III, 293–294.

manding higher wages and bounties, others complained that the wealthy were not contributing their fair share to the war effort. In the midst of these divisive sentiments, the assembly stood divided and paralyzed.

Indeed, even as the British were carrying through plans to bring the war to the South, Virginians were preoccupied with internal affairs as they went again to the polls early in 1780. Perhaps the most pressing issue was the effect a new congressional plan for reforming currency might have in Virginia. On March 18, 1780, Congress had proposed a scheme to reduce the national debt from two hundred million dollars down to five million by revaluing the outstanding Continental currency at a rate of forty to one in specie. The plan was designed to stabilize the currency and halt the spiraling inflation that plagued all the states. Honyman reported an increase in interest in the elections in Virginia, mainly among those who were unhappy about the high taxes and the high prices of all goods. The previous December, he had noted that people were very "alarmed" at the rise of all prices and the depreciation of the currency, and he believed more people were interested in the elections than ever before.[82]

That interest concerned Honyman. They "choose those who make fair promises of altering things for the better," and he thought "many of those chosen are men of mean abilities and no rank." But Honyman was not the only one who complained. Almost as soon as the assembly convened, some delegates made an unsuccessful move to regulate the election of members of the General Assembly. George Mason, who might have been behind the move, thought that recent General Assemblies had been filled with "ignorant or obscure" men "so unequal to the Office." Whereas Honyman in part believed that the quality of the legislature was due to too many people actually voting in the elections and voting according to their own interests, Mason believed that not enough people voted, or at least not enough of the right kind of people. Mason thought that "a factious bawling Fellow, who will make a Noise four or five miles round him," could "prevail upon his party to attend" and "carry an Election against a Man of ten times his Weight and Influence in the County." Men of greater stature and more "Modesty and Merit" were thus not only discouraged from offering themselves as candidates but also could not compete if they did.

82. Dec. 20, 1779, Apr. 15, 1780, Diary of Honyman; cf. July 4, 1780. Congress wanted the states to tax in the outstanding currency, which they could then trade in to Congress for new money.

Signifcantly, both Mason and Honyman were disturbed by the fact that voters conceived their interests carefully and chose men that they knew would represent them. Thus the "Body politic" was not dangerously sick, as Patrick Henry put it; it merely reflected the first fruits of republican government.[83]

83. Ibid.; see "Remarks on the Proposed Bill for Regulating the Elections of the Members of the General Assembly," [ca. June 1, 1780], *Papers of Mason,* II, 629–631, 631–632n. Mason proposed some Draconian remedies; see 630–631, 632n. Significantly, Mason also had to account for the disaffected within Virginia, a timely reminder that the state's internal foes were not often far from the consciousness of patriot leaders. Mason thought more people would vote if elections were held on a single day in April, but, having experienced at first hand the wrath of the disaffected and enslaved when the state's collective attention was diverted, Mason believed that the strongest objection to holding elections on the same day throughout the state came from the "Danger of Insurrection of the Slaves, or disaffected." Voters wanted their representatives to actually represent them, not, as Mason envisaged, to *virtually* represent them.

PART FOUR

Revolution of Fools and Knaves

CHAPTER 11 *Revolutionary* Demands

WAR COMES TO THE SOUTH

While Virginians divided and waited for peace, the British moved to bring the war to the South and open up a new front, believing themselves at a stalemate in the North. By 1778 and 1779, the southern states were looking more inviting to the British: more thinly settled than the northern states, more vulnerable by sea, more dependent on foreign markets for imports and their exports, and arguably much more valuable. Moreover, intelligence reports of loyalist support encouraged the British to think that they might make more progress in the southern states than they had hitherto made in the North. These reports, combined with the knowledge that enslaved Americans might help make up a fifth column, or at least keep vulnerable whites at home from battle, supported the British in thinking that they could more easily subdue the South than the North.[1]

The British campaign in the South began in late 1778 against Georgia, the newest and weakest of the former British colonies. By the end of January 1779, both Savannah and Augusta were in British hands. After unsuccessfully trying to lure General Washington into a decisive battle around New York in 1779, General Henry Clinton also turned to the South. In December 1779, Clinton sailed for South Carolina with almost ten thousand troops, landing thirty miles south of Charleston in February 1780. In response, Washington ordered all of Virginia's remaining Continental troops under General William Woodford southward from the Continental camp in New Jersey to Charleston. Woodford's meager remnant group of about seven hundred troops was joined by General Charles Scott and another contingent.[2]

1. Don Higginbotham, *The War of American Independence: Military Attitudes, Policies, and Practice, 1763-1789* (New York, 1971), 352-354.

2. Ibid., 356-357; John E. Selby, *The Revolution in Virginia, 1775-1783* (Williamsburg, Va., 1988), 211-213.

The Virginians entered Charleston in early April 1780, unfortunately walking into a British trap. Within days, General Clinton's forces had encircled and cut off all routes into and out of the city. On May 12, the British forced several thousand American troops under General Benjamin Lincoln into an unconditional surrender. By the end of May, Lieutenant Colonel Banastre Tarleton and the British cavalry effectively wiped out most of the remaining troops in the Virginia Line, who had marched late under Colonel Abraham Buford, at Waxhaws, South Carolina. As many as four hundred men were killed, some massacred after they had surrendered.

The War for American Independence had entered a new phase. If Virginians had struggled through the first half of the war, the British turn to the south stretched all their resources to the breaking point. The fate of the Virginia Line at Charleston and at Waxhaws foreshadowed greater problems to come. In March 1780, Robert Honyman worried that, even in the face of the new British campaign in the South, the attention of most people in the state was still "very little taken up with the war at this time." The only people who were disturbed about it were those who suffered most by it and "who ardently long for some change." The fall of Charleston would force change. For many in Virginia, the Revolution was about to begin.[3]

• • • The new Virginia assembly that met in May would be slow to react to events in the South, and delegates would continue to bicker, even more divided than previously. On six separate occasions during the session, delegates demanded roll call votes. Most measures designed to put Continental defense on the best footing ran into vocal opposition from delegates concerned about their own constituents. The high legislative turnover that had marked annual elections of the previous four years and renewed interest in elections had ensured that Continental demands were tempered by local concerns, particularly in the face of the British shift of strategy.[4]

Thus, almost immediately, the assembly composed an address to the Continental Congress that tried to deflect responsibility for southern defense from Virginia. Acknowledging presciently after the fact that Charleston appeared to be about to fall to the British, the assembly conceded that the rest of South Carolina and North Carolina likely could not be defended.

3. Higginbotham, *War of American Independence,* 356–357; Selby, *Revolution in Virginia,* 213; Mar. 16, 1780, Diary of Robert Honyman, Jan. 2, 1776–Mar. 11, 1782, Alderman Library, UVa (microfilm).

4. Selby, *Revolution in Virginia,* 251.

Worried about discontent among their own people, the assembly told Congress that the progress of the British would invariably be accompanied by an increase in disaffection, which would "extend with their success." The total effect of the British campaign might produce "the most fatal consequences to the American cause." Given this, the assembly felt compelled to look after the interests of the state. It would do as much as it could and would raise and send forward a body of militia to help, but Congress could not expect much from the state. Virginians already feared an attack by the British on their eastern frontiers and by the Indians on their western. The militia would be too slow in reaching Charleston and might have to be diverted because of Virginia's own defensive needs. In a thinly veiled rebuke, the assembly proclaimed it its duty to "call the attention of Congress to this important object" and to "conjure them without delay, to adopt the most effectual means of defending and maintaining the southern States." The assembly called upon Congress to send more Continental troops and arms for the North Carolina militia, Virginia having already furnished as many of the latter as "it is able to spare."[5]

Before Congress could reply, legislators did order 2,500 militia to the defense of South Carolina, ordered 10,000 stand of arms (or muskets) to neighboring North Carolina, and granted the governor power to impress horses and wagons to facilitate the movement across the state of 1,400 Continental troops from Maryland and Delaware to the South. The 2,500 men were to come mainly from southside and piedmont counties, from the bor-

5. Address of the General Assembly of Virginia to the Continental Congress, [May 24, 1780], *Papers of Mason,* II, 623-624. The assembly seemed keen to ensure that rumored French help would also make it down to the southern states. See Samuel Huntington to Thomas Jefferson, May 19, 1780, *Papers of Jefferson,* III, 378-380; May 29, June 13, 1780, Diary of Honyman.

Congress's carefully worded and equally thinly veiled reply warned the legislators that they could not "rely too far, on the assistance which may be drawn from the army of the United States." Instead, "much will depend on their own vigorous efforts." If Virginia did become the main seat of war, Congress was sure the state militia would respond. Just more than a week later, Congress asked Virginia to send five thousand militia to South Carolina and to keep five thousand more ready to march. June 5, 7, 1780, Worthington Chauncey Ford et al., eds., *Journals of the Continental Congress, 1774-1789* (Washington, D.C., 1904-1937), XVII, 487, 493-494. Cf. James Madison to Jefferson, June 6, 1780, *Papers of Madison,* II, 39; May 29, 1780, Diary of Honyman; June 17, 1780, Ford et al., eds., *Journals of the Continental Congress,* XVII, 523-524.

der with North Carolina to as far north as Orange and Spotsylvania Counties. The assembly ordered no militia from the troubled backcountry or from the vulnerable tidewater region. Legislators also ordered the governor to be ready to call out an additional 5,000 militia if necessary.[6]

The move to order the militia to serve outside the state did not go unopposed, both within the assembly and without. Honyman reported that the resolution "met with great opposition in the assembly" and almost failed to pass. Moreover, the assembly continued to refuse to heed a congressional recommendation that it order five thousand militia out and keep five thousand on standby, despite Congress's offer to pay for the militia in service.[7]

In voicing their opposition to the march of so many militia, many legislators were concerned about the political costs. Even as the march was debated in the assembly, militia out-of-doors grew uneasy. Reportedly, a "very great and general discontent" arose among them as soon as rumors circulated that the assembly would order a march. Honyman had heard that "numbers protest loudly that they will not go" and thought the feeling was widespread. Going ahead with the plan, Honyman warned, "will occasion great confusion," and probably fewer than half of the men called for would actually go down to South Carolina.[8]

As delegates wondered how many militia they could send southward, they heard from those wondering whether they would be forced to go. In the midst of debate, Charlotte County militia reminded representatives that the pool of available militia was dwindling, with call-outs increasingly falling on the shoulders of the poor. The petitioners asserted that they had supported government so far and had contributed their "just proportion of the expence" of the war as well as "personal service when required." The petitioners laid bare the class-based injustice of military service and summed up the arguments of a growing number of complaints of freeholders that had been accumulating since the beginning of the war. "In the personal services expected from the Citizens of this Commonwealth, the poor among

6. June 13, 1780, Diary of Honyman; Hening, comp., *Statutes at Large,* X, 221–262, 309–315.

7. May 29, 1780, Diary of Honyman; June 17, 1780, Ford et al., eds., *Journals of the Continental Congress,* XVII, 523–524.

8. May 29, June 13, 1780, Diary of Honyman. Even the shocking news of the capitulation of Charleston, which reached Virginia while the assembly was still sitting, failed to provoke an order for more militia to march. Though the fall of Charleston "has given great alarm to our Leaders," they were not yet ready to risk sending more militia.

us who scarce obtain a precarious subsistence by the sweat of their brow, are call'd upon as often and bound to perform equal Military duty in defence of their little as the great and oppulent in defence of their abundance." They were angry that many wealthy Virginians were able to avoid even an equal amount of service. The "great and oppulent," the petitioners asserted, "who contribute very little personal labour in support of their families, often find means to screen themselves altogether from those military services which the poor and indigent are on all occasions taken from their homes to perform in person." What was worse was that slaveholders in particular benefited twice over. While nonslaveholding whites risked their lives, their families, and their estates through their personal service in the militia, slaveholding planters exempted themselves and grew rich on the back of their slaves' labor.[9]

The legislature had exacerbated the problem the previous session by reintroducing a poll tax. Building on complaints heard about the relationship between taxes and military service over the previous year or two, the petitioners represented military service as a form of taxation and ingeniously linked the two. They first claimed that, despite the injustice of military service, the new tax system introduced in 1777 at least ameliorated the disproportionate demand that military service made on less wealthy Virginians. The "just and rational mode of Taxation by the Assessment of property" meant that wealthier Virginians would at least have to shoulder their fair share of the cost of the war. The petitioners recognized problems in assessing such property, but they were angry that the assembly had simply reintroduced the poll tax rather than fixed the assessment tax. The new poll tax meant that poorer nonslaveholding whites would have to pay the same tax as a wealthy slaveholding planter, despite the fact that the poorer white was probably already paying more through his personal service in the militia. Yet, in criticizing the reintroduction of the poll tax, the petitioners indicted not just the wealthy in Virginia but also slaveholders. Now, poorer whites who labored for their own and their family's subsistence while juggling the demands of the state in the militia would be taxed not just as much as the wealthy planter but also almost as much as the planter was charged for each slave who labored for him. The poll tax on whites was three pounds, whereas slaveholders had to pay only four pounds per enslaved Virginian. The reintroduction of the poll tax fell "indiscriminately

9. Charlotte County Petition, [May 26, 1780], Virginia Legislative Petitions, LiVi.

on all" and thereby compelled "the poor who bear the heat and burthen of Military duty to pay nearly an equal proportion of Taxes with him who labours only to support the extravigance of a Voluptuous master." They demanded an immediate repeal of the tax and a reform of the tax assessment system to correct such a glaring injustice. They wanted to ensure that the "poor and labourious may be altogether exempted from any tax on their persons, which with the other services expected from them, they are in fact unable to pay."[10]

The Charlotte County petitioners had chosen the moment carefully for presenting their petition. They used past military service to justify their claims, and future service and allegiance to press their argument. Knowing that the crisis at Charleston would probably engender ever-greater demands on the militia, they made no bones about what they wanted. They tied their complaints directly to the current crisis: thinking themselves "entitled on the present great and pressing emergency to be heard."[11]

The assembly did not reply specifically but did take the petitioners' concerns into consideration in debating both the terms of the militia call-out and the new recruiting laws for the Continental army. The assembly thus authorized an increase in the pay of the militia, offering $7\frac{1}{2}$ pounds of tobacco per private for each day in service and reduced the pay disparity between officers and privates. The assembly also explicitly made provision for the families of poorer militia sent southward, empowering the commissioners of the tax to dip into the stores of the commodity tax to give corn or grain to the needy.[12]

But it was in the new recruiting law for the Continental army that demands for reform were more clearly felt. Chastened by complaints like those of Charlotte County citizens, the legislature expressed a preference not to rely too much on the militia. And, once it learned about the fall of

10. Ibid.

11. Ibid. The petitioners reminded delegates that they were "their Representatives."

12. Hening, comp., *Statutes at Large,* IX, 10, 21–23, 34, X, 223, 226. In 1775 a colonel in the militia received one hundred times more per day than a private, and a captain's pay was twenty-four times that of a soldier in his company. In 1780, the assembly offered a captain just more than five times as much as a private per day and a colonel just eight times as much.

The assembly also tried to beef up the laws against disobedient militia in anticipation of trouble. See Hening, comp., *Statutes at Large,* X, 225, 310.

Charleston as well as the capture of most of Virginia's line, most legislators realized that they would have to take stronger action to re-recruit their quota for the Continental army. On top of their poor recruiting figures over the past few years, most Virginians who had enlisted in the army had been captured or killed at Charleston. Even before the fall, there was some talk of the need for an additional eighteen hundred regular troops at least. Afterward, legislators talked about raising five thousand more.[13]

Though legislators had been reluctant to put teeth into their efforts to recruit for the Continental army since 1778, the British move to the South forced the assembly to choose between raising an army (which would now presumably be closer to home) and calling on the militia. It was an easy decision, but the wary assembly also watered down the provisions for re-recruiting the Virginia Line, whittling the figure down to three thousand, about one-fifteenth of the available militia, or only half of what Congress had fixed as Virginia's quota for the Continental army. Recruits were also asked to serve only until the end of 1781, or about eighteen months, destroying the hopes of many Continental officers, especially Washington, that the army could finally be raised on a more permanent footing.[14]

Legislators did, however, dare to impose another draft, but this new call for recruits was an innovation, and very much based on persistent demands from below. For example, legislators adopted the previous assembly's reform of the bounty and tax laws for raising state troops and tied the two together in their new policy for recruiting Continental troops. Bounty money raised by militia in order to hire soldiers would be paid in proportion to taxable property and would contribute toward the militia's next tax assessment. But, like the last law for recruiting state troops, this new law for recruiting Continental troops stipulated that everyone with assessable wealth in the county had to be included in a division and contribute toward raising bounty money and a soldier. Each division had to have roughly equal amounts of property, too.[15]

13. May 29, July 4, 1780, Diary of Honyman.

14. July 4, 16, 1780, ibid.; Ford et al., eds., *Journals of the Continental Congress,* XVI, 150; Hening, comp., *Statutes at Large,* X, 257–262. The preamble to the act revealed the rationale behind yet another temporary measure: hope that the expected arrival of a French fleet and troops would help bring the war to an end quickly or at the very least relieve the demand on Virginians themselves.

15. Hening, comp., *Statutes at Large,* X, 257–262. The divisions were allowed thirty days to try to raise a recruit from their midst. The law allowed them to offer

Given this more equitable demand for bounty money, the legislators dared to impose another draft—but they also went to extraordinary lengths to ensure it would not actually take place. Most radically, divisions were each given the power to raise any amount of money—in addition to the state and Continental bounties—to try to recruit a soldier to exempt themselves from the draft. Any extra bounty money would come out of the pockets of everyone in the division and would have to be paid by everyone in equal proportion to his wealth. Every propertyowner was thus responsible for bearing the burden of the war and, in this case, of raising soldiers to fight that war for him in proportion to his means. Moreover, the group as a whole was responsible for finding a recruit. The new law had shifted the burden of the draft from the individual to the communal, and from persons to property. Thus, in reintroducing the draft in Virginia, legislators had given all active militia—rich or poor—the power and means to buy themselves out of service.[16]

• • • Before the legislature could see whether its gamble with recruiting proved popular, there were other challenges to face. The renewed British offensive in the southern states, followed by the moves of the legislature to call out the militia, contributed to fresh "discontents" in Virginia. Robert Honyman thought that the fall of Charleston could not have come at a worse time: it was "very dangerous" news, "when our army is so diminished, our Credit at its lowest Ebb, and the people weary, dispirited and discontented."[17]

Some of this discontent manifested itself in Virginians' reaction to the militia call-out. When the controversial order to march to South Carolina

------

any potential recruits state certificates for one thousand pounds net of inspected tobacco that they could redeem at the end of their service, above and beyond the Continental bounty. Impoverished recruits were assured that their widows or aged parents would be supported by the state if they should die in service, to the amount of one barrel of corn and fifty pounds of pork each year. They could recruit outside their own division only if the division in which the enlistee they wanted to hire lived had already procured a soldier. Divisions could, of course, recruit men from outside the state altogether if they had the means, or they could recruit the homeless or any transients not enrolled in the Virginia militia.

16. Ibid., X, 257–262. The legislature also came down hard on pacifists like Quakers and Mennonites, who were now expected to carry the full costs of finding substitutes.

17. June 13, 1780, Diary of Honyman.

finally did go out, Honyman reported "violent mutinies" in several counties and that many who were ordered to march simply "staid behind." Still others dallied. Two weeks after the order to march went out, he thought that most militia had not yet even left their homes and that many who did so did so "very unwillingly." Some then deserted along the way. Perhaps as many as eleven hundred of the twenty-five hundred militia ordered southward never made it to their rendezvous with General Horatio Gates in Hillsborough, North Carolina.[18]

The militia who actually turned out for the southern campaign only ran into further trouble. After joining Gates, they were fed little and were poorly outfitted. Gates then pushed his poorly trained troops several hundred miles into a confrontation in mid-August with a strong contingent of General Cornwallis's battle-hardened troops at Camden, South Carolina. The militia broke ranks and fled as soon as the battle began. From the reports Jefferson received, it appeared that most of the militia "ran like a torrent and bore all before them." Not long after the battle Honyman met with some of the deserters, as "numbers of them after they run away never stopt till they came home." When the battle began, Gates had about 1,000 regulars and about 2,800 militia from North Carolina and Virginia under his command. When he regrouped at Hillsborough two hundred miles away, he had only about 700 men left.[19]

The militia's response to the British invasion foreshadowed greater divisions within Virginia. For the southern invasion did help galvanize some Virginians into action. For disaffected and enslaved Virginians, the British offensive rekindled hopes that liberation was still possible. Trouble quickly broke out again in the turbulent southwestern corner of Virginia, for example. In Montgomery County, the disaffected formed an association reportedly to "disturb the Peace of this unhappy Frontier as soon as the season will permit." The county lieutenant, William Preston, told Governor Jefferson that British agents in Montgomery and Washington Counties were pushing people to take an oath of allegiance to the king and that they met with considerable success in some neighborhoods. They were spurred on by rumors that the British intended to attack the frontiers of the southern colonies, join with the disaffected and the Indians, and create a pincer

18. May 29, June 13, July 4, 16, 1780, ibid.; Selby, *Revolution in Virginia*, 214.

19. Aug. 31, Sept. 8, 1780, Diary of Honyman; Jefferson to George Washington, Sept. 5, 1780, *Papers of Jefferson*, III, 595–596; Selby, *Revolution in Virginia*, 215; Higginbotham, *War of American Independence*, 357–360.

movement with the British army in the eastern parts of the states. Actual Indian raids had already helped convince many that such a movement was under way. British agents also attempted to capitalize on divisions within patriot ranks by offering poorer inhabitants good pay and quitrent-free land if they joined with the loyalist forces.[20]

After Charleston fell to the British in May, the disaffected grew bolder. Patriot leaders in the area believed that two hundred men had gathered in June in Montgomery County and were planning to take the lead mines. More reports in July repeated these plans, but new rumors noted that ardent loyalists planned to join with and liberate the convention army imprisoned in Charlottesville (where it had been garrisoned since the surrender of Burgoyne at Saratoga) to help invade the east. This uprising was foiled, but there were repeated alarms over insurrections in the southwest counties throughout the summer and fall of 1780. Problems became acute when news of the battle of Camden began to spread. Honyman reported insurrections in several counties, especially those bordering North Carolina. He thought that two hundred men had gathered in Henry County, "considerable bodies" had gathered in Washington and Montgomery Counties, and a "great and dangerous conspiracy of Tories" had lately been discovered in Bedford County, much closer to his home county of Hanover. By the end of September, Jefferson believed that "many hundreds" had taken oaths of allegiance to the crown in the southwestern counties. More worrying to Jefferson, however, was the possible spread of such disaffection. "Other counties equally relied on may fail us in the hour of trial," he warned Congress in September.[21]

The problem of disaffection was exacerbated when the British actually invaded Virginia once again. On October 20, 1780, Major General Alexander Leslie sailed into the Chesapeake at the head of twenty-two hundred troops and several ships of war. The British force moved quickly, dividing

20. Emory G. Evans, "Trouble in the Backcountry: Disaffection in Southwest Virginia during the American Revolution," in Ronald Hoffman, Thad W. Tate, and Peter J. Albert, eds., *An Uncivil War: The Southern Backcountry during the American Revolution* (Charlottesville, Va., 1985), 195; Apr. 15, 1780, Diary of Honyman.

21. Aug. 31, 1780, Diary of Honyman; Jefferson to Samuel Huntington, Sept. 14, 1780, *Papers of Jefferson,* III, 647–648. Bedford County was supposed to provide more than two hundred militia for service in South Carolina, Henry just more than one hundred (Hening, comp., *Statutes at Large,* X, 221–226).

its force between Portsmouth and Newport News and Hampton. Within days, cavalry forces had taken Kemp's Landing and Great Bridge and had moved north from Newport News almost half the distance to Williamsburg.[22]

Jefferson tried to counter Leslie with further calls on the militia, but he seemed more worried that the British might have revived plans to liberate the convention army barracked near Charlottesville. He thought this not as unlikely as it seemed, because of "the extensive disaffection which has been lately discovered, and almost total want of arms in the hands of our good people." He confessed that the danger from the invasion on the eastern frontier was less than that of civil war in the interior part of the state. The fear that the British might head westward, and "the dangerous convulsions to which such an attempt wou'd expose us, diverts the attention of a very considerable part of our militia from an opposition to the invading army."[23]

Jefferson did not have to wait long before some of his fears were confirmed. The very next day he told Congress of new signs of disaffection. He had heard of a "very dangerous Insurrection in Pittsylvania" that had been discovered and prevented just three days before it was to take place. Relieved that this "dangerous fire" was "smothered," he worried about when it would again break out. He believed it would depend entirely on what happened in the eastern theater. Horrified at the extent of disaffection, he suspected the malcontents extended from Montgomery County all along the southern boundary of Virginia to Pittsylvania County, and as far north as the James River. It was rumored that there were disaffected as far north as Culpeper County. Even before the latest problems in Pittsylvania County, he had to admit that the "Spirit of disaffection" was wider-spread than he could have ever predicted.[24]

Yet, just as the tide of disaffected activity was cresting in Virginia, Jefferson received better news. A powerful patriot force had defeated a thousand-strong contingent of loyalists under the command of Major Patrick Ferguson at King's Mountain, South Carolina. About four hundred Virginians, including the commander of the American troops, Colonel William Campbell, were involved in the battle, which put an end to some of the most

22. Selby, *Revolution in Virginia*, 216.

23. Jefferson to Thomas Sim Lee, Oct. 26, 1780, *Papers of Jefferson*, IV, 71.

24. Jefferson to the Virginia Delegates to Congress, Oct. 27, 1780, to James Wood, Oct. 5, 1780, *Papers of Jefferson*, IV, 14–15, 76–77.

vicious partisan fighting of the entire war between whigs and tories in the southern backcountry. It also helped quell the activities of many disaffected in Virginia. Soon after the battle, General Leslie also pulled out of Virginia. In light of the defeat at King's Mountain, Cornwallis canceled his joint invasion of North Carolina and told Leslie to head straight for South Carolina, where they would set up winter camp at Camden. Leslie put out to sea in mid-November.[25]

As this new British threat subsided, the plots and actual uprisings in the southwest help put a face on the people that were often condemned as tories and dismissed. Some of the men involved, of course, were ardent "Tories." But, while local and state patriot leaders believed that ardent loyalists were behind the widespread disaffection, most people who got tangled up in the uprisings simply wanted to be left alone. When William Preston tried to reason with insurgents and convince them that they would be crushed if they persisted, one man, John Heavin, protested that all they wanted was to be left alone. Heavin and neighbors he had spoken with all said they simply wanted peace, and Heavin was planning to uproot and disappear in the face of patriot resentment. However, he claimed that his departure should be taken as a sign, not of his guilt, but of his regard to the "Internal peas of this State." Preston wanted him to swear allegiance to the state, but Heavin would not, because he had "never meddled with war from the first moment and Cant think of Intangling myselfe with it now."[26]

25. Evans, "Trouble in the Backcountry," in Hoffman, Tate, and Albert, eds., *An Uncivil War,* 196, 199, 204; Jefferson to the Virginia Delegates in Congress, Oct. 27, 1780, *Papers of Jefferson,* IV, 76–77; Aug. 31, 1780, Diary of Honyman; Selby, *Revolution in Virginia,* 215–216; Higginbotham, *War of American Independence,* 364. Significantly, after General Leslie's invasion of the Portsmouth area, in which the British did far less damage than the previous incursion, Leslie wrote to General Clinton urging that they take a more permanent post there, which was, in his opinion, "the Key to the Wealth of Virginia and Maryland." Leslie believed most of the people there were sorry to see him go and were tired of the war (*Papers of Madison,* II, 187).

26. Evans, "Trouble in the Backcountry," in Hoffman, Tate, and Albert, eds., *An Uncivil War,* 198. Certainly many in the east feared the insurgents were ardent tories willing to take up arms for the British. Jefferson thought that "many hundreds" had actually enlisted in the British army. Honyman thought that there were "many thousands" enlisting. Jefferson to James Wood, Oct. 5, 1780, to the Virginia Delegates in Congress, Oct. 27, 1780, *Papers of Jefferson,* IV, 14–15, 76–77; Aug. 31, 1780, Diary of Honyman.

John McDonald of Montgomery County found himself on trial for his part in the insurrection in his county that year. Yet his reasons for joining in with the disaffected were also invidiously simple. He was tired of the burdens imposed on him by the patriot government. He had declared that he would pay "no taxes and if they were Inforced Col. Preston might take care of himself and if any harm followed he might blame himself." The problem, as McDonald saw it, was that "he thought We had been fighting for Liberty but slavery was a consequence." Increasing taxes, money, and militia call-outs took their toll on the stretched resources of men who might well have formerly been patriots. The treatment of such men by local officials helped confirm that few were particularly dangerous, and local officials were eager to reincorporate them into the patriot fold. In the end, few people were actually tried for treason. Most who were punished, and they were a minority of those involved, were convicted of lesser crimes and generally treated as wayward patriots rather than outright loyalists. The legislature also generally responded by offering pardons to even the ringleaders of the uprisings.[27]

• • • Compounding the problems in the southwest, revealing trouble also broke out in the lower Northern Neck in the summer of 1780. Here, the draft of 1780 was the final straw. In both Lancaster and Northumberland Counties, large numbers of the militia assembled in opposition to the draft. In Lancaster, John Taylor, the county lieutenant, reported that the entire militia "asembled in a Mob," with few dissenters among them. Their "riotous behavour" prevented Taylor from carrying out the draft. In neighboring Northumberland, the county lieutenant, Thomas Gaskins, tried to push ahead with the draft in the face of widespread opposition. The results (highlighted in the Introduction) were fatal. One militia officer was shot dead by aggrieved militia, and "Almost the whole County was inflaim'd," according to Gaskins. When Gaskins tried to round up other militia, in-

27. Evans, "Trouble in the Backcountry," in Hoffman, Tate, and Albert, eds., *An Uncivil War,* 202–203, 205, 211. David Jameson, who was privy to the court-martial proceedings held in Pittsylvania County after the insurrection there was headed off, told Madison that it appeared that "many were privy to and aiding in the intended insurrectn. in that County, but they were chiefly if not altogether composed of the lower rank of the people." Jameson believed that more prominent men were suspected, and probably involved, but that it was difficult to prosecute such men. Jameson to Madison, Nov. 25, 1780, *Papers of Madison,* II, 201.

cluding officers, to subdue the insurgents, many of those he counted upon "appeared in arms against us." Gaskins finally had to back off to avoid further bloodshed. Perhaps as many as 150 men were involved in the standoff, or almost 30 percent of the county's active militia.[28]

Of the seventy-one men involved in the riot who were named, only twenty-eight, or just fewer than 40 percent, can be identified on the tax lists of 1782. Thus more than 60 percent of those involved had either moved, were still living in someone else's household, or were too poor to be taxed in 1782. The propertied men owned an average of eighty to one hundred acres of land, worth just more than twenty-two pounds. They were usually responsible for three tithables (perhaps oneself, two sons, two enslaved blacks, or a combination). They also owned on average eight cattle and one or two horses each. Some, like William Blackerby, had served on grand juries. Others, like John Humphries and Maximillian Haynie, had been trusted enough by local officials to act as guard to escort a loyalist to Williamsburg in 1777. Some of the rioters were local officials themselves—one man had recently acted as a constable, and three actually were or had been company-grade officers in the militia. By contrast, the militia officer shot dead during the riot, Edwin Hull, from a prominent and wealthy family in the area, owned three hundred acres of land, eleven slaves, thirteen cattle, and two horses. Though few of the rioters in Northumberland were as wealthy as Hull and many were landless or at least very poor, a sizable contingent of militia involved were still propertied farmers with a stake in society.[29]

The riots in the lower Northern Neck were a sign of deeper disaffection and discontent, much like the problems in the southwest. Throughout the war, this region had been quick to revolt against state laws and proclamations. George Mason believed that the riots in the lower Northern Neck were the fault of local leaders. He was "not at all suprized" by the violence of the draft resistance, he claimed, for it was inevitable where there was no respect for the government. "If such dangerous Mutinies are not affectually quelled, and the Ring-leaders punished, Government can't subsist.

28. See Introduction, n. 1, above.

29. See Nov. 13, 1780, Northumberland County Order Book, 1773–1783, LiVi; Proceedings of a Court Martial, Sept. 16, 1780, Executive Papers, LiVi; Northumberland Land and Personal Property Tax Lists, 1782, LiVi; Richard C. Bush, "Revolution and Community in Northumberland County, Virginia, 1776–1782," *Bulletin of the Northumberland County Historical Society*, XXX (1993), 25.

. . . If the truth cou'd be discovered, I doubt not but some of their princi-pal men are privately at the Bottom of it."[30]

But, if Mason pointed to the suspected complicity of local officials, he also underestimated the real grievances of his less wealthy neighbors. The lower Northern Neck had the greatest inequalities in wealth in Virginia. Many divisions might have been simply unable to raise enough money for new recruits without bankrupting themselves. By the fall of 1780, there were fewer potential recruits, and they usually came at a tremendous price. A division with little money would have been hard-pressed to find enough to raise a soldier. If the divisions were not made with due regard to the equality of property in each, the militia might have had a cause for com-plaint.[31]

Whatever the specific trigger, the problems in the lower Northern Neck —like those elsewhere in the state—were more properly representative of a growing disenchantment with the war effort and the specific policies of the patriot government. The numbers involved and the sentiments of rioters indicated a wider-spread dissatisfaction with the increasing burdens of war. As such, it was part of a larger network of problems that arose when the British began their southern campaign. But, while patriot leaders were often quick to condemn the disaffected as tories or loyalists, closer inspec-tion of the nature of such dissent almost always dissolved the artificial lines of "loyalty" imposed by those above.

• • • In this climate, patriot leaders might have expected the new draft law to provoke further trouble more generally. However, for the first time in the war, the loudest complaints about the new draft law came from the wealthy. Indeed, many wealthy Virginians—and particularly those who were ex-empted from actually serving in the militia—were angry that their prop-erty was now at the disposal of less wealthy Virginians to hire recruits and escape the draft. One of the wealthiest men in the state, David Jameson, complained that the recruiting act would prove a "heavy tax" for people like him. Few men, he believed, would take the risk of being drafted, so they

30. George Mason to Jefferson, Oct. 6, 1780, *Papers of Mason,* II, 676. Mason believed that, "where the leading Men" were "true Whigs, and possessed of com-mon Discretion," there was "little Danger of Resistance."

31. For economic stratification in the Northern Neck relative to the rest of the colony, see Norman K. Risjord, *Chesapeake Politics, 1781–1800* (New York, 1978), 1–68.

would try to raise as much money within their division as they could. Even before the draft took place, he had heard that some divisions had already pledged five thousand pounds to hire a soldier. Jameson thought, in such circumstances, the price could go as high as ten thousand pounds. "Who will run the risk of being drafted if he can by taxing his Neighbours procure a Man[?]"[32]

Jameson was, at least in part, right. Many men with little or no taxable property made sure that they did not fall prey, pushing up the bounty money in a desperate bid to avoid a draft in their division. With the extra money raised in proportion to wealth, the bounty tax fell heaviest on the wealthiest. Robert Pleasants, an immensely wealthy Quaker from Henrico County, complained about the militia in his division who owned *no* property. It was "highly unreasonable" that the men who were not liable to pay anything "should have it in their power, to hire a man on any terms they please at my expence, to screen themselves from a draft." When they themselves were safe from the possibility of a draft, they "don't . . . feel for others." He had heard that one of the men in his division had announced he would give fifty thousand pounds for a recruit "rather than submit to a draft." Of course, a huge proportion of the fifty thousand pounds would have to come out of Pleasants's pocket, as he noted.[33]

Theodorick Bland, Sr., another wealthy and prominent Virginian, also complained about the leveling effects of the new draft law. Bland owned property in at least two different counties and had thus been forced to pay out twice. Militia in his Amelia County division had demanded almost £525 from him alone, and his neighbors in his home county had run up a charge of £1,435. On top of this he had also paid £600 for his son's proportion toward a new recruit. With a total bill of more than £2,500, Bland was furious with the assembly's draft law. He expressed his disgust in clear class terms: the assembly had given too much power to the unpropertied, or lower, classes. Legislators had effectively "put the power of taxation into the hands of the very lowest class of people." Bland believed that there would be only one result in such circumstances: such laws would "reduce the most opulent fortune to a level with that of the inferior class of people."[34]

32. David Jameson to Madison, Aug. 13, 1780, *Papers of Madison,* II, 58.

33. Robert Pleasants to Col. Turner Southall, Sept. 3, 1780, Robert Pleasants of Curles, Henrico County, Letterbook, LiVi.

34. Theodorick Bland, Sr., to Theodorick Bland, Jr., Oct. 21, 1780, Charles

Bland was, in some sense, right. The actual burden of military service invariably still fell on the marginal, but they were now in an even better position to reap a more substantial reward in exchange for their risks. By mid-August, Honyman reported that the going price for a recruit was about £3,000 per division, though in some places potential recruits had driven the price up to £5,000. Honyman's own division ended up giving £3,500 for a recruit. After the time for recruiting had passed, Jameson noted that prices for recruits had not quite reached the sum of £10,000 that he had predicted. Most recruits, he asserted, had been hired for between £2,000 and £8,000. Edmund Pendleton concurred, claiming that the average price was about £5,000. Thus, Virginia's lower sort were again able to manipulate mobilization to serve their own ends during the war.[35]

Wealthy Virginians were particularly angry because they had to pay out so much for so little. Jameson complained that, though such exorbitant sums had been paid out to hire recruits, only a temporary army had been raised. Their bounty money, he grumbled, was more than enough to secure their services for the duration of the war, instead of a mere eighteen months; it was really enough "for-life." Edmund Pendleton also despaired that, by the time the new recruits became proficient soldiers, their terms of service would run out, and Virginians would again have to incur the "ruinous expence of recruiting." The bounties paid out during the summer of 1780, he claimed, were far too expensive. "At any rate of depreciation," the sums paid out "must exceed the ability of any Countrey frequently to repeat."[36]

Many middling farmers, however, appreciated the new law, because they no longer had to run the risk of paying quite so much to get out of serving as previously and everyone, including the wealthy, was helping to pay. More-

---

Campbell, ed., *The Bland Papers: Being a Selection from the Manuscripts of Colonel Theodorick Bland, Jr.* (Petersburg, Va., 1840, 1843), II, 37–38.

35. Aug. 14, 31, 1780, Diary of Honyman; Jameson to Madison, Aug. 13, Sept. 20, 1780, *Papers of Madison,* II, 58, 94; Pendleton to Madison, Sept. 25, 1780, *Papers of Pendleton,* I, 309. Though we know a great deal about the tremendous inflation that plagued Virginia—and indeed, all of the new states during the war—and the difficulties that each state had in raising men and money for the war, rarely do we know about the people involved in pushing up that inflation. The actions and choices of ordinary individuals determined wartime policy, either indirectly or directly, at least as much as if not more than the elite-dominated legislatures.

36. Jameson to Madison, Sept. 20, 1780, *Papers of Madison,* II, 94; Pendleton to Madison, Sept. 25, 1780, *Papers of Pendleton,* I, 309.

over, any money they actually paid in could be claimed as part of their tax assessment. A later petition from Hanover County asserted that the recruiting act of May 1780 had been the least objectionable of the draft laws enacted by the assembly. It had given "the most general satisfaction of any law that has been enacted for that purpose" and had "best answered the end for which it was designed." They dismissed the claims of many wealthy gentlemen that the law was open to many "abuses," except perhaps in "some few instances," but generally the law was administered fairly in their eyes. In any case, they claimed, such loopholes could be corrected. Most important, it was the "general principles" of the law that were so salutary and that they hoped would be retained in any future draft: "That all those who possess property in every district or division may be obliged to contribute as much, in proportion to their property, as will procure a soldier (let it be ever so much) in a limited time."[37]

By most accounts, the draft law was the most effective of the war and least opposed, which was testimony to how widespread the sentiments of those from Hanover were throughout the state. George Mason, even while acknowledging problems in the lower Northern Neck, concluded that the draft for the regular service had been carried out uneventfully. It was "not only quietly, but cheerfully executed" in Fairfax and "neighbouring Countys." Governor Jefferson reported that recruiting seemed to go well. "Our new levies," he claimed, "rendezvous in large numbers." Though Pendleton was a little less sanguine about the numbers they were actually able to recruit, he did think that "some very clever fellows" enlisted that would serve the state well.[38]

Despite the relative popularity of the recruiting law, however, it soon became obvious to legislators gathering in the fall of 1780 that the numbers raised were insufficient in several important respects. Though the battle of King's Mountain helped steady frayed nerves in Virginia, General Leslie's foray into the state, which actually delayed the meeting of the assembly, only reminded Virginians of just how vulnerable they still were. Moreover, with fewer than a thousand men, General Gates was all that now

37. Hanover County Petition, [May 24, 1782], Virginia Legislative Petitions, LiVi.

38. Mason to Jefferson, Oct. 6, 1780, *Papers of Jefferson,* IV, 18–19; John David McBride, "The Virginia War Effort, 1775–1783: Manpower Policies and Practices" (Ph.D. diss., University of Virginia, 1977), 110; Pendleton to Madison, Sept. 25, 1780, *Papers of Pendleton,* I, 309.

stood between the main British army and Virginia. Though some Virginians hoped that North Carolina would help bear the brunt of the continuing British offensive, it quickly became apparent that Virginia was on its own. Madison told assembly delegates in mid-December that the North Carolina legislature had done nothing that fall toward raising any levies for the Continental army.[39]

Moreover, further call-outs of the militia and the enormous cost of raising new recruits made some people reconsider the laws, especially the length of time for which recruits were raised. Because of the expense and the additional militia burden, by the fall of 1780 some middling farmers concurred with their wealthier neighbors and complained that the recruits should have been raised for a longer period than eighteen months. As the legislators gathered, farmers once again articulated their grievances and demands. As they did so, they pointed to their militia service and payment of taxes to legitimate their own claims to exemptions from more onerous wartime service. In doing so, they began to formulate an idea of citizenship in the new Republic that could simultaneously exclude the lower classes while using military service to claim rights.

Petitioners from Berkeley County, for example, were most concerned that the recruiting law passed in the spring increased their tax burden overall, without actually raising a more permanent army that would exempt most from further and frequent militia call-outs and future drafts. Though they were happy with the mode of raising the soldiers, they agreed with people like David Jameson that the soldiers ought to have been raised for the war. The petitioners from Berkeley County considered themselves "Greivously oppressed" by the draft. They complained that, for the money they had spent raising recruits under the previous draft law, they could have enlisted troops for the duration of the war. Distinguishing themselves from the kind of people most likely to join the army, they claimed that vol-

39. Madison thought that the exertions of the militia during the late British invasion would have helped spur them on, but he had heard that they were assigned as "the obstacle to its practicability." Pendleton to Madison, Nov. 13, 1780, *Papers of Pendleton*, I, 322; Madison to Joseph Jones, Dec. 19, 1780, *Papers of Madison*, II, 249. See Walter Clark, ed., *The State Records of North Carolina*, XIV (Winston, N.C., 1896), 378, 387, 390. Jones told Madison on November 5 that there were three big issues in front of the assembly—raising the army, supplying it, and supporting the currency. Jones to Madison, Nov. 5, 1780, *Papers of Madison*, II, 161–162.

unteers for the army were driven by profits, not patriotism. Such "Mersi-nary" soldiers used the laws to "make the best market" of themselves. Most potential recruits took note of the short enlistment periods and realized that they could easily take advantage of the laws. The Berkeley militia pointed to a deepening divide between themselves and those whom they expected to do their fighting for them. The present laws gave such men the "power" and encouragement to "Fleece from the virtuous and good part of our Citizens Whatever their avaricious inclinations may prompt Them to exact."[40]

In making their case for a more permanent standing army, the militia from Berkeley succinctly articulated the views of many of their counter-parts across the Atlantic. They pointed to the example of other nations, in fact, "all nations and Countrys but ours," who did not hesitate to take proper measures to keep "that Class of men, in the field as a standing army." Instead, the upstanding militia were "Haras'd" with call-outs, taking them away from their families and estates. They contrasted their situation with "that Class of men" who had come to "depend upon the field for his living," who "will not work." Discontent was growing. The more frequent calls on true citizens to act as soldiers "Causes great uneasiness and disquiet in the Country." Indeed, they raised the same warning that John Banister had in 1778: they were "much allarm'd" at the "Confusion and Disorder" that seemed to prevail. As "friends to our Country," the petitioners thought it time to speak out to prevent a more general insurrection. The only way to do so was by paying "proper and Vigorous attention to procuring a stand-ing army." Moreover, if they had a "standing Disciplin'd army, Something Decisive might be expected."[41]

The petitioners from Berkeley made it clear that full citizens of the new Republic had the right not to do actual service in the cause of the state, but to pay others to. Patriarchy was key. Once a standing army was raised, "Then would your Loyal and faithfull Citizens enjoy that Domestic Tran-quility which affords Contentment and Happiness even in the midst of Dis-tressing war." In doing so, they would be free to "struggle to maintain Their familys" and give "Support" to "the Glorious Cause in which they are en-gaged." Thus, they argued the next assembly ought to follow the same for-mula in drafting men, especially in "Proportioning the Wealthy and In-digent, as nearly as possible together" in each militia division, but that

40. Berkeley County Petition, [Nov. 18, 1780], Virginia Legislative Petitions, LiVi.

41. Ibid.

each division would have to raise a man for the duration of the war. Once the division had raised a soldier, it would forevermore be exempt from all future military service. Those divisions that did not or could not raise a recruit would be subject to future shorter drafts and call-outs of the militia. Such a provision, the petitioners claimed, would be "oppressive to none," as the draft would not be "Compulsitory, but will put it in the power of such as wish to Exert Themselves, to procure a standing Army, so to do."[42]

The demands of the Berkeley petitioners were accompanied by a torrent of complaints from militia who had broken ranks and fled back to Virginia after Gates's defeat at Camden. Despite a public outcry about their performance and wholesale desertion, many of the militia were unrepentant. Indeed, many were angry that they had been asked to serve for such a long time and at such a distance from the state. The assembly had ordered them to serve for three months, and their tour of duty did not start until they actually reached South Carolina. One group of deserters from Goochland County claimed that such a length of service brought uncommon hardships to their families, that most of them were "very poor Men, with Family's of small Children unable to Labour." They deserted because they feared losing a "great part of their Stocks, by the shortness of their present Crops." They appealed to Governor Jefferson to spare them from the eight months' service in the Continental army they were now required to do as punishment: "What then must be the distresses of their helpless families the ensuing Year, should they be deem'd Soldiers Eight Months longer[?]"[43]

But deserting militia even made claims to citizenship while justifying their actions. Amherst County militia, for example, based their case against serving another eight months on their rights as citizens of a new Republic. The militia reminded the assembly that they were first and foremost propertied citizens. Though they were "very poor and many of our Familys large tho' weak," they were landed farmers. Repeating the arguments of the Goochland militia, they reminded Jefferson that they had already sacrificed the present year's crops through their service, and their stocks and their families were likely to suffer much further distress. If made to serve another eight months, they would be "depriv'd of any possibility of making any the year to come." Service for another eight months would "Compleat our Ruin." If this reminder were not enough, the Amherst militia asserted

42. Ibid.

43. Hening, comp., *Statutes at Large,* X, 221–226; Petition of Certain Deserters, Oct. 7, 1780, *Papers of Jefferson,* IV, 20–21.

that they had not actually broken the letter of the law. Technically, they "never did Refuse" to march but had actually gone and served a considerable part of their tour of duty before deserting. Moreover, they were still ready to serve out their term. Indeed, they demanded another chance to "retrieve our own Reputations as Citizens of a Free State" and requested the pay that was owed to them. They would "Chearfully march On," if justice was done to them. They reminded the assembly that they were merely representatives. While they enjoyed the "inestimable Blessings of a free and frequent Representation," they expected that "Impartial Justice and Judgment" would be "dispensed (as far as is Consistent with the General Common-Weal) to every Individual Member of the State."[44]

The militia's reaction reflected a new and more assertive mood in Virginia: a mood that echoed the petitioners from Charlotte County in emphasizing past military service and contributions to the war effort as good grounds for challenges to new patriot measures. In some sense, military service, usually in the militia, legitimized citizenship in the new Republic. But, as the militia from Amherst pointed out, if military service helped legitimize claims to citizenship in the new state, it also legitimized their complaints and challenges to the authority of the new government. Farmers who had done some kind of service, however short the tour of duty might have been, expected "Impartial Justice and Judgment" from their representatives.[45]

• • • Caught between the demands of enfranchised and angry militia on one hand, and the insistent requests of Continental officials for more soldiers on the other, state leaders were presented with a Revolutionary dilemma. Their struggle to solve it reflected the centrality of both class and slavery in their thinking, but not entirely in the way we would expect. Indeed, the presence of enslaved Virginians had encouraged the British to continue their operations in the southern states. While at war, enslaved Virginians had more opportunities than ever before to run away or rebel against their masters. But, during the British invasions, enslaved Virginians also caused havoc for patriot mobilization efforts. The presence of a restive and opportunistic enslaved population deterred many farmers from joining the army or serving in the militia. Some farmers were afraid of

44. Petition and Memorial of Sundry Militiamen of Amherst County, Oct. 9, 1780, LiVi.

45. Ibid.

leaving their families and farms at the mercy of rebellious enslaved Virginians; others more simply worried that their own slaves might take the opportunity of their absence and run away. Even more worrying for state leaders, many western farmers and poorer Virginians who did not own slaves were reluctant to fight to defend slaveholders. At the very least, many of those who did not own enslaved Virginians believed that slaveholders had more at stake in the conflict and thus ought pay more for their defense. Moreover, many nonslaveholders were resentful that their personal service cost them much more than the service of slaveholders. They often complained that they were reluctant to serve for long terms, because they had no enslaved Virginians to labor for them in their absence, as others had. Because middling whites refused to serve in the armed forces and poor farmers and laborers resented slaveholders' wealth and, more generally, the cost of war, patriot leaders eventually came up with at least one ingenious—and Revolutionary—solution of their own.

Thus, in mid-November 1780, Joseph Jones revealed the outlines of a radical new plan to raise the army. It showed not just how far the representatives were prepared to go to avoid a draft but also how much legislators had absorbed class-based complaints that the wealthy in Virginia had not borne their fair share in paying for the war. The new plan thus also revealed the changes in the composition of the legislature that had taken place in the previous spring and also over the past few years of wartime elections. A committee, of which Jones was a member, had drafted a bill to raise Continental troops for the duration of the war. It believed that the best bounty it could offer potential recruits would not be cash, as previously, or even a generous amount of land. Rather, the committee suggested that in addition to the Continental bounty (which still included a parcel of land) it should offer new recruits an enslaved Virginian between the ages of ten and forty. As striking as this new policy was, the committee went further, suggesting that such enslaved Virginians should be taken (forcibly if necessary) from all slaveholders who owned more than twenty bondsmen, in the proportion of every twentieth slave.[46]

46. Jones to Madison, Nov. 10, 18, 1780, *Papers of Madison,* II, 168, 182–183; undated bill, Legislative Department, Rough Bills, LiVi (brought to my attention, with thanks, by Brent Tarter at the LiVi). Slaveholders would be given a fixed amount of time to bring forth the slave voluntarily, after which time the slave would be impressed and they would be compensated—the slaves taken from them would be valued in hard money, to be repaid within eight years. The slavehold-

Though Jones himself confessed to James Madison that he was "no great friend" to this plan, he had helped perfect it because the majority of the committee favored it. Jones was "determined to join in any scheme that shall be practicable for raising Men for the war." If they could make this scheme practicable, it would, he believed, produce the needed men for the duration of the war, as "the Negro bounty cannot fail to procure Men for the War."[47]

Critically, Jones told Madison that, if the plan could be made to appear practicable, it would also "be palatible to the Delegates whatever it may be to the Senate." There were "strong objections" that could be brought against it, and the "Negro holders in general already clamour agt. the project and will encounter it with all their force." "The scheme bears hard upon those wealthy in Negros," he admitted, "as that property is sacrificed to the exoneration of other property." However, in the present political climate, such opposition would come to naught. "You know a great part of our House are not of that Class or own so few of them as not to come within the Law shod. it pass." Indeed, one representative from the near western county of Botetourt, Thomas Madison, believed that the legislature introduced this scheme precisely because it wanted to make the wealthy pay their share of the war. Madison told William Preston of Montgomery County, "The principle on which this Bill was founded was . . . that Negroes were a desireable Property, and it would be obliging to the Wealthy, who perform little personal duty, to contribute largely." Thomas Madison's comments echoed the protests from freeholders in the numerous petitions from around the state over the previous several years protesting how little wealthier men actually contributed to the war effort.[48]

Slaveholders and those sympathetic to slaveholders fought back, however. After more than two weeks of discussion in committee, the whole House debated the bill heatedly for the next week. There was much discussion about the length of service of draftees. The "prevailing opinion" in the

---

ers would be paid back, with 5 percent interest, by deducting the value of the slaves from their taxes, starting five years from then. Those furnishing slaves would also be exempted from future drafts for men except in the case of invasion or insurrection.

47. Jones to Madison, Nov. 18, 1780, *Papers of Madison,* II, 183.

48. Ibid.; Thomas Madison to William Preston, Nov. 30, 1780, Preston Papers, VHS. Jones noted that it would actually be a loan to the state and would aid the public need for money, but he admitted that few affected by it would see it as coming under the "denomination of the ancient mode of *benevolence.*"

committee was to draft men for three years, but Jones thought that such a long period would be opposed in the House. But there were also "various opinions" on the subject of offering enslaved Virginians as bounties. At the very least, though, Jones thought they would still end up at least giving a bounty of a slave. Debate then seemed to center on who would provide the enslaved Virginians. Slaveholders appeared to have got an amendment that the enslaved Virginians to be used for the bounty would come out of a specific tax on slaves and plate.[49]

By December 2, the plan for giving enslaved Virginians as bounties seemed to have been laid aside altogether. Opposition to the "Negro scheme" arose, according to Pendleton, from various fronts. Some legislators considered it unfair to slaveholders, believing it was "unjust, sacrificing the property of a part of the Community to the exoneration of the rest." Yet not all legislators were worried about the justice of the bill to slaveholders. Pendleton hinted that more practical objections to the idea also helped kill the bill. Finally, Pendleton reported, some legislators also found the irony of providing enslaved Americans as incentives for soldiers too much to bear. The bill was "reprobated also as inhuman and cruel."[50]

James Madison, sitting as an observer in Congress, was one of those who thought the idea was "inhuman and cruel." It would be much better if patriot leaders in Virginia took the more obvious step and allowed enslaved Virginians themselves to serve. "Would it not be as well to liberate and make soldiers at once of the blacks themselves as to make them instruments for enlisting white Soldiers?" Madison thought that such a move would "certainly be more consonant to the principles of liberty which ought never to be lost sight of in a contest for liberty." He anticipated some of the objections of his countrymen. With white officers and mainly white soldiers, "no imaginable danger could be feared from themselves." Nor would it have an adverse effect on the remaining slaves, for experience had shown that "a freedman immediately loses all attachment and sympathy with his former fellow slaves."[51]

49. *Journal of the House of Delegates* (Williamsburg, Va., 1776-), Nov. 27, 28, 29, 30, 1780, 47, 49-52; Jones to Madison, Nov. 24, 1780, *Papers of Madison*, II, 198; Pendleton to Madison, Nov. 27, Dec. 4, 1780, *Papers of Pendleton*, I, 324, 325; Thomas Madison to William Preston, Nov. 30, 1780, Preston Papers, VHS.

50. Pendleton to Madison, Jan. 1, 1781, Jones to Madison, Dec. 8, 1780, *Papers of Madison*, II, 232-233, 268.

51. Madison to Jones, Nov. 28, 1780, ibid., II, 209, 210. The editor notes that

Madison might not have been the only proponent of such a move, for Jones immediately countered with some seemingly well rehearsed objections to arming enslaved Virginians. Jones worried that arming enslaved Virginians might encourage the British to do likewise, as they had done before. No doubt with the nearly anarchic conditions of the fall of 1775 in mind, he thought that the British would be tempted once again to arm enslaved Virginians and thus "fight us in our own way." The consequences would be disastrous. If the British armed the enslaved, "this wod. bring on the Southern States probably inevitable ruin." Apart from the civil war that might ensue, there were other, more practical reasons for keeping enslaved Virginians at home. Arming enslaved Virginians and giving them their freedom would draw away too many laborers from farms, so "as to ruin many individuals." As it was, what they helped produce was "but barely sufficient to keep us joging along with the great expence of the war." Though the freedom of enslaved Americans was an important object, it should be done gradually so that they could find laborers to replace them, "or we shall suffer exceedingly under the sudden revolution which perhaps arming them wod. produce."[52]

After the slave scheme had been laid aside, debate turned to other enticements that they could offer lower-class Virginians to serve for the duration of the war. One proposal would give recruits a bounty of £5,000 for three years or for the war. Jones hoped that the bounty could be reduced to at least £3,000, which would still be £9,000,000 for three thousand men, an "amazing Sum for a bounty." In such circumstances, the legislature still thought that hitting the wealthiest men in the state would be the best strategy, so they proposed that this bounty money be raised only from among all persons owning assessable property worth more than £300 specie, who would be taxed an additional 2 percent.[53]

Madison intended this part of his letter for publication. Maryland, in fact, did authorize the enlistment of enslaved men into the army in their legislative session in the fall of 1780. However, the following year they stopped short of raising an entire regiment of enslaved Marylanders. See *Papers of Madison,* II, 210n; Benjamin Quarles, *The Negro in the American Revolution* (Chapel Hill, N.C., 1961), 56–57.

52. Pendleton to Madison, Jan. 1, 1781, Jones to Madison, Dec. 8, 1780, *Papers of Madison,* II, 232–233, 268.

53. Jones to Madison, Dec. 2, 1780, *Papers of Madison,* II, 219. Jones himself thought that rotating the militia into and out of service would be the best solution. In order to reduce such an expense, Jones thought it best to draft militia for two years with a small bounty or even no bounty at all. Each group of militia would then

Legislators were so adamant about offering a huge bounty—and taking it from the wealthy—because they were desperate to avoid a draft. By now, most legislators realized that imposing a draft would at the very least be politically suicidal; at worst it could mean full-scale social upheaval. White Virginians' resistance to earlier drafts and more recent militia call-outs made legislators well aware of the potentially dangerous consequences of imposing an unpopular draft. Jones lamented, "Our Legislators are timid or affect many of them to be timid abt. a draft." Instead, they were much happier to raise the bounty and consider taking most of the money from those in a better position to pay.[54]

The problem was compounded by the fact that Washington, Congress, and even many freeholders within the state were now vehemently insisting that the new recruits or draftees be enlisted for long terms, so as to avoid the necessity for any further drafts. Most proarmy advocates—like the militia from Berkeley County—argued for enlistments for at least three years but preferably for the duration of the war. To enlist men for such a length of service, most legislators believed they had to offer a huge incentive, enough to persuade most potential recruits to enlist voluntarily. But they also had to find money for doing so in a way that would not anger their middle-class constituents.

Legislators thus debated the issues well into the new year. In the end, though, and despite the objections to the slaves-as-bounty scheme, proponents of the measure were still able to incorporate part of it into the final recruiting act. Of the three thousand new recruits to be raised, legislators proposed to entice as many as possible to enlist voluntarily, offering very generous bounties. Soldiers who enlisted for the duration of the war would get twelve thousand dollars; those who enlisted for three years would get eight thousand dollars. Recruits could also hold out and get extra bonuses from desperate divisions. Those enlisting for the duration of the war would also receive a "healthy sound negro" between the ages of ten and thirty, or sixty pounds in gold or silver, at the option of the soldier, at the end of his service. Finally, recruits for the duration would also get three hun-

---

be replaced by more militia for another two years. He also thought that, if they allowed an exemption from the draft or from militia duty out of the state to anyone who procured a soldier for the war, many would get one, and they could get soldiers for far less money. Jones thought, or hoped, that the property threshold for taxing for the bounty money would come down to one hundred pounds.

54. Ibid.

dred acres of land. Thus, lower-class Virginians were able to extract a huge windfall in return for their services to the state. Not only would they get enough land to vote, but they would also receive money enough to establish themselves and even an enslaved Virginian to make that land more productive.[55]

Middling Virginians, however, did not quite get what they wanted in the final settlement, though they did win a major concession. The bounty money, including the cost of the enslaved Virginians, would not come from the wealthy alone, but rather from all in proportion to wealth. Everyone with property was required immediately to pay the previously legislated 2 percent tax on all property, in specie, in bills of credit emitted under the resolutions of Congress of March 18, in any other paper money at the rate of forty to one, in crop tobacco, or in hemp. The money collected would then be put directly toward the cost of the bounty. Though the power of taxing wealthier neighbors to raise recruits was not, in this instance, given to the militia divisions, all taxpayers still had to contribute toward raising the bounty. The assembly thus continued the practice of making everyone—including invalids, exempts, and anyone with property—pay for the common defense.[56]

And legislators did take a chance on another draft. If, after fifty days, the divisions of militia could not entice a recruit, the county lieutenant would draft someone from the division by lot. Anyone drafted would still have ten days to procure a substitute, and he would be given an additional four thousand dollars to do so. Though ultimately ordinary farmers might be forced into compulsory service with the now dreaded Continental army, the

55. Even during debate over the extent of the bounty, most legislators seemed to believe that raising recruits for the duration of the war was actually out of the question. Pendleton complained that, though the assembly had been fighting over the final figure for a bounty, it appeared that it was still going to offer it only for three years' service at the most, not for the duration. As far as Pendleton knew, "I understand they have no hopes of Raising them for the War." After the assembly had adjourned, Theodorick Bland, Sr., also reported, "No arguments could prevail with them to raise men during the war." Pendleton to Madison, Dec. 4, 1780, *Papers of Pendleton,* I, 325; Pendleton to Madison, Jan. 1, 1781, Jones to Madison, Dec. 8, 1780, *Papers of Madison,* II, 232–233, 268; Theodorick Bland, Sr., to Theodorick Bland, Jr., Jan. 8, 1781, Campbell, ed., *Bland Papers,* II, 51; Hening, comp., *Statutes at Large,* X, 326–337.

56. Hening, comp., *Statutes at Large,* X, 327–328. Cf. Jones to Madison, Dec. 2, 1780, *Papers of Madison,* II, 219.

assembly tried to create several important loopholes to make it much less likely that men would actually be drafted.[57]

Finally, the assembly tried to strike a balance between those who wanted to raise a permanent army and those who wanted to avoid forcing men to serve in it. Though the assembly held out attractive bounties for those who would serve for three years or, especially, the duration, any draftees or their substitutes would have to serve for only eighteen months in the Continental army. A draft of the militia for three years' service was discussed, but the legislature did not even think of drafting them for the duration and ultimately settled for only eighteen months, much to the frustration of Continental officials and officers like Washington.[58]

• • • The plan to offer enormous bounties for soldiers had important implications—it helped foul up the congressional plan of March 18, 1780, to revalue Continental currency and stabilize the economy. The congressional plan, which had only just received the approval of the General Assembly the previous spring, had called for the redemption through taxes of all old currency and the emission of a new Continental currency at an exchange rate of forty to one. By the fall of 1780, however, the state was again in a financial crisis. The new and sudden demands of the southern campaign helped drain the treasury once more. So, contrary to the congressional plan, the assembly decided to emit a further ten million dollars in state currency, mainly to pay for bounties, and postpone its redemption until 1785. Moreover, the speaker of the House, Benjamin Harrison, appended an amendment to the emission bill that declared that both the new congressional currency and the two million dollars issued by the state the previous session would be legal tender in payment of any tax. Both measures would undermine the new congressional plan, which called for retiring all the old currency before accepting any of the new currency. A fear that Virginians would run out of cash, especially to pay the increasingly heavy taxes, forced the assembly to accept the amendment on a very close vote. Joseph Jones thought that the new emission and concessions on taxes (and he believed that the new ten-million-dollar emission would also be accepted for taxes) meant that the congressional plan of March 18 would be "in great measure defeated."[59]

57. Hening, comp., *Statutes at Large,* X, 326–337.
58. Ibid.
59. Selby, *Revolution in Virginia,* 248–251. See James Madison, Jr., to James

Continued anger at Congress and Continental officials helped convince many legislators that it would be better to look after their own citizens than uphold the plan of March 18. Jones told Madison that the state simply could not keep up with the payments it had to make. The bills already passed would soon exhaust the new emission of ten million dollars (or, as Jones seems to imply, six million pounds). Jones told Madison that many felt—and had actually been told by General Nathanael Greene—that Congress had let the "whole burthen of the Southern Army . . . fall on this State." There was also a critical shortage of arms. Jefferson begged the delegates to Congress to procure more cartridge paper, boxes, and muskets. All of their extra arms would soon be in the hands of the militia assembling against General Leslie. If anything happened to them, they had no others except "a few scattered Squirrel Guns, Rifles etc. in the Hands of the western People." Finally, Patrick Henry proposed that they send a special emissary to Congress and to General Washington to try to get more help from the Continent or at least to put pressure on Spain or France to help in the southern campaign.[60]

Madison, Sr., Mar. 20, 1780, *Papers of Madison,* II, 3, for a brief explanation of the congressional plan. Jefferson to Madison, July 26, 1780, Jones to Madison, Nov. 5, 18, 24, 1780, *Papers of Madison,* II, 49, 161–162, 183–184, 198. Jones told Madison that Patrick Henry led a group of his "auxiliaries" against Richard Henry Lee and his supporters over the question whether the new currency and the emission of two million dollars from the previous session ought to be allowed in payment of taxes. Henry, it seems, won the debate again (II, 199). Henry had opposed it because he feared that it would depress prices in the agricultural South and raise taxes to redeem a currency that, he believed, had already made its way to the more mercantile northern states. Henry first persuaded others to go along with his own plan, which proposed retiring the national debt in ten or fifteen years, which would moderate the rate of deflation and tax increases. The continuance of the specific tax would help with the immediate expenses of the state. However, when Henry left the House after gaining a successful vote, his opponents overturned the decision and gained approval for supporting the congressional plan. Worried that the plan might not be implemented by all the states, George Mason also proposed an emission of two million dollars of state money to cover emergency costs. The assembly hoped this would not affect the new plan by making it acceptable only for payment for specific taxes designed to redeem it and it alone. Cf. Pendleton to Madison, Nov. 27, Dec. 4, 1780, *Papers of Pendleton,* I, 324, 325.

60. Jones to Madison, Dec. 2, 1780, *Papers of Madison,* II, 219; Selby, *Revo-*

Significantly, though, while many legislators in Virginia blamed Congress for their woes, more-Continental-minded leaders inside and outside the state were disgusted by the assembly's conciliatory measures. Though many were upset that the state had undermined the congressional plan to stabilize the currency, their criticism focused on the main cause—the unwillingness of the assembly to raise a more permanent army except by offering huge bounties. Pendleton, among others, was incredulous. Shortly after enlistments began, he told Washington that, though the bounty was high, the bulk of the new soldiers would have to be drafted. Because the term of service for drafted men was only eighteen months, they would "as Usual" return home "as soon as they have learnt their duty." Pendleton was furious about the "Indigested distructive Measures" of the recent assembly. Instead of acting with "foresight" and "wisdom," the assembly once again lost the opportunity to create a more permanent army and, instead, "scrambled up" the present law "on the spur of Occasion." Pendleton had grown tired of the proceedings of his colleagues in the assembly. He told Washington that he had "long lamented the want of System and Stability in the Conduct of our Public affairs."[61]

Theodorick Bland, Sr., who had complained so vociferously about the previous recruiting law, was even angrier about the proceedings of the assembly in this session. He expressed his anger to his son that the assembly had given recruits the option to enlist for three years only. Moreover, draftees would have to serve for only eighteen months. The delegates to the assembly were to blame. "A majority" of them were, according to Bland, "enemies to America, or fools or knaves, or all three." Bland feared the consequences. The new recruiting law and the proceedings of the assembly generally were such that "God grant it may not bring on a revolution in this state." He feared that such a consequence was actually the "wish of a majority of the assembly."[62]

lution in Virginia, 255; Jefferson to the Virginia Delegates in Congress, Oct. 27, 1780, *Papers of Madison,* II, 153.

61. Pendleton to Washington, Feb. 16, 1781, *Papers of Pendleton,* I, 339.

62. Theodorick Bland, Sr., to Theodorick Bland, Jr., Jan. 8, 1781, Campbell, ed., *Bland Papers,* II, 51. Cf. A. Drummond to John Coles, Mar. 13, [1781], Carter-Smith Papers, UVa.

CHAPTER 12 *Asserting Fundamental Rights*

MILITIA SERVICE AND RESISTANCE, 1781

Even as legislators were putting the final touches on the much-debated bills for raising and supplying the army and raising a revenue, the British began a series of devastating incursions into the state in early 1781 that would eventually bring the state to its knees. Yet, even in the midst of these punishing invasions, white Virginians squabbled among themselves and tried to find appropriate scapegoats for their inability to effectively counter the British. Significantly, though, initial militia turnouts by middling Virginians helped validate the long-standing complaints and protests of many white Virginians. As state officials pressured the militia further, those citizens resisted with almost patriotic fervor, and petitions of protest grew more explicit, bold, and demanding. Their recalcitrance in turn severely strained political relations on a myriad of levels. Though militia resistance struck a blow against Continental harmony and unity, the ferocity of that resistance helped to cement more local alliances within Virginia, between middling whites and county officials and even between state leaders and their beleaguered counterparts throughout the country.

• • • The now infamous General Benedict Arnold, who entered the Chesapeake Bay with just fewer than twenty ships on December 30, 1780, headed the first British invasion. Within days, Arnold swept up the James River and landed about eight hundred troops at the Byrd plantation at Westover. He then marched unopposed to Richmond, reaching the fledgling city on January 5. Along the way the British destroyed a great deal of private property and the arms foundry at Westham. After ransacking as many public stores and records as he could find, Arnold withdrew to Benjamin Harrison's plantation, Berkeley, where he inflicted heavy damage to the rebel leader's estate and freed Harrison's entire enslaved population. Withdrawing on January 10, Arnold's force raided and plundered along the

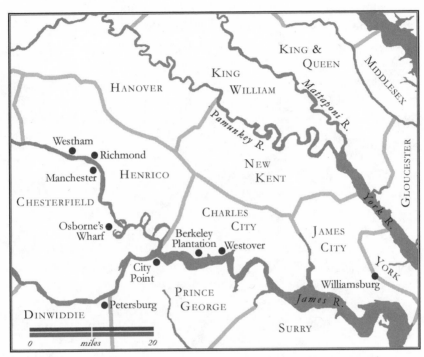

Map 3. The Upper James River

James River for more than a week, finally setting up quarters at Portsmouth.[1]

Though the actual damage Arnold inflicted was relatively small, the psychological damage loomed large. Arnold's raid shocked planters all along the James River, many of whom had never come face-to-face with the enemy. As shocking as Arnold's raid was to whites, it also served as a new clarion call for enslaved Virginians who lived along the route of the invasion. Many blacks who had waited impatiently for the British to make some kind of progress in the state used the opportunity to make their escape. The Reverend James Madison reported that many families along the route of Arnold's raid had "suffered greatly." He reckoned that some had lost as many as thirty to forty of their slaves, and "every one a considerable Part of their Slaves." By the time he returned to Portsmouth, Arnold had been joined by upward of three hundred enslaved Virginians. Countless others disappeared from plantations and farms in the confusion.[2]

In the face of the threat, propertied white Virginians along the riversides and in the invasion route did all they could—not to oppose Arnold, but to get their property, and particularly their slaves, out of the way. St. George Tucker, for example, helped his wife and child escape and then went back to help his neighbor Theodorick Bland do the same. Most other gentlemen living on valuable riverside estates followed suit. Bland felt that there was nothing to stop the British if they invaded up the rivers of Virginia. In such circumstances, Bland concluded, "I am determined to remove from this place immediately." One witness reported that the alarm was "so great and sudden, that almost every person in the neighbourhood was endeavouring to put some of his Property in a state of safety by removing it." Jefferson also fled. After directing the removal of public stores and records across the James River to Manchester, Jefferson left Richmond with his family in the early morning of January 5, when the British were approaching.[3]

1. See Theodorick Bland, Sr., to Theodorick Bland, Jan. 8, 1781, Col. John Banister to Theodorick Bland, January 1781, Charles Campbell, ed., *The Bland Papers: Being a Selection from the Manuscripts of Colonel Theodorick Bland* (Petersburg, Va., 1840, 1843), II, 50–52, 53–54.

2. The Reverend James Madison to James Madison, Jan. 18, 1781, *Papers of Madison,* II, 293; Sylvia R. Frey, *Water from the Rock: Black Resistance in a Revolutionary Age* (Princeton, N.J., 1991), 157.

3. Theodorick Bland, Sr., to Theodorick Bland, Jan. 8, 1781, Campbell, ed., *Bland Papers,* II, 51. See Depositions Taken in 1796 respecting Jefferson's Con-

While patriot leaders fled, ordinary Virginians actually earned praise for their role in this most recent invasion. Colonel John Banister believed that the turnout of the militia in his own county of Dinwiddie had prevented the British from coming there. Moreover, Banister thought, the militia had generally helped turn the British invasion force back to City Point and then to return to their fleet. Even in flight, the militia still gained the kudos of relieved planters. A grateful St. George Tucker related how the militia had run away "manfully" from the British after skirmishing with the enemy between Hood's and Bland's ordinary. Many believed that, had the government been more organized or had the British stayed longer, the militia would have been able to defend the country. While in flight himself, Theodorick Bland, Sr., asserted that, if the enemy invaded overland, he would meet with a "spirited opposition" from the militia.[4]

As Virginians were coming to terms with the new British invasion, more positive news arrived from southward, further elevating the status of the militia. Virginia General Daniel Morgan managed to almost completely destroy the reviled and feared cavalry legion headed by Banastre Tarleton at Cowpens, South Carolina, with a force largely composed of Virginia militia. With tactics that best utilized the inexperienced militia, Morgan cut down the eleven-hundred-strong British force, killing two hundred and capturing another six hundred. One Virginia officer described it as a "Glorious stroke" in which Virginia militia especially were "spoke of with the greatest applause for their behaviour that day." Edward Stevens, commanding the Virginia militia with General Nathanael Greene's army in the South, hoped that the performance of the militia would more than make up for the embarrassing performance at Camden the previous summer.[5]

The militia also earned praise a few weeks later when the southernmost counties were called upon in February 1781. By this time, General Charles Cornwallis was on the move against Greene's beleaguered southern army. Greene had continued to retreat across North Carolina before the British rather than risk another battle. As he crossed the Dan River, the threat to Virginia became acute. Governor Jefferson immediately issued orders

---

duct during Arnold's Invasion, Daniel Hylton's Deposition, Oct. 12, 1796, *Papers of Jefferson,* IV, 271–272. Jefferson's actions would, of course, come back to haunt him.

4. Col. John Banister to Theodorick Bland, Jan. 1781, St. George Tucker to Theodorick Bland, Jan. 21, 1781, Campbell, ed., *Bland Papers,* II, 53, 56.

5. Edward Stevens to Thomas Jefferson, Jan. 24, 1781, *Papers of Jefferson,* IV, 440–441.

calling forth the militia of the southern piedmont and southwestern counties, but many had already marched without waiting for his order. George Waller, major of the Henry County militia, told Jefferson that the county lieutenant had already ordered the militia out, in greater numbers than Jefferson requested. "The approach of the enemy Towards this state, Appeared to Alarming To await your commands." At least seven other counties did the same. Jefferson was jubilant and boasted to Congress: "The spirit of opposition among the people was as universal and ardent as could have been wish'd. There was no restraint on the numbers which embodied but the want of arms." Others were equally excited. The Reverend James Madison thought that the response of the militia did honor to the middle and backcountry counties: at no time, "not even the Year 75," did Virginians show more enthusiasm.[6]

Public praise for the militia on these several occasions early in 1781 had two important results. Not only was successful militia service testimony to ordinary Virginians' protests that they would actually serve if conditions were right, but it also forced patriot gentlemen to look elsewhere in their search for someone to blame for their renewed troubles. For example, both local and Continental critics could not believe how easily Arnold had raided as far inland as the Virginia capital. Some gentlemen, like St. George Tucker, blamed the problem on government, not the militia. Tucker thought that there were more men in the field than muskets to arm them and was furious at the government's inability or unwillingness to take effective preventive measures. He raged against the "obstinate, lethargic, [torn] Wretches" in power. Robert Honyman simply noted that the governor and council were "universally and heavily censured for their neglect and supineness on this occasion" and blamed for the insult of the invasion.

6. Jefferson to the County Lieutenants, Feb. 18, 1781, Robert Lawson to Jefferson, Feb. 16, 1781, George Waller to Jefferson, Feb. 21, 1781, Lewis Burwell to Jefferson, Feb. 15, 1781, Thomas Read to Jefferson, Feb. 15, 1781, Jefferson to Horatio Gates, Feb. 17, 1781, Jefferson to Thomas Read, Feb. 17, 1781, Jefferson to Nathanael Greene, Feb. 17, 1781, Jefferson to Samuel Huntington, Feb. 26, 1781, *Papers of Jefferson,* IV, 612–613, 619–620, 629–630, 637, 638, 641–642, 646–647, 682–683, V, 12; the Reverend James Madison to James Madison, Jr., Mar. 9, 1781, *Papers of Madison,* III, 10, 11–12n. Cf. James Madison, Jr., to Philip Mazzei, July 7, 1781, *Papers of Madison,* III, 177; Edmund Pendleton to James Madison, Jr., Mar. 5, 1781, *Papers of Pendleton,* I, 341; Feb. 24, 1781, Diary of Robert Honyman, Jan. 2, 1776–Mar. 11, 1782, UVA (microfilm).

Others blamed the assembly. The Reverend James Madison thought the poor quality of representation there had rendered the state incapable of defending itself. "Virginia still contains Citizens who are willing to risque all in the Cause, but the Assembly has lost its Respect." He claimed: "Iniquitous Laws produce Disgust. Disgust, Languor and Indifference. Thus many care not whether Arnold or Steuben are victorious."[7]

The state government was not the only target of censure. Feeling increasingly vulnerable, even patriot leaders increasingly lashed out at Congress, the northern states, and at times the French for failing to help them during the present crisis, while continuing to claim that Virginians themselves were doing all they could. John Banister, the county lieutenant of Dinwiddie, had seen at first hand the efforts of his neighbors during the invasion threats of January and February. The militia earned his respect. Banister thus thought the problems they still faced were due, not to the militia, but to the lack of arms in the state. The state government itself was partly to blame for not being better prepared, according to Banister, but the root of the problem was that arms taken by Congress earlier in the war had never been returned. Now, he could not believe "how unjust it is in Congress not to assist us with Arms when we have to contend singly with the greatest part of the british Army." He contrasted the militia's response with that of its supposed allies, noting that Virginians were flocking in from all quarters. "The people are entirely unanimous, and spirited on this occasion." On the other hand, he despaired, "the rest of the continent have totally abandoned us."[8]

Private sentiments concerning the lack of forthcoming help from Congress and the northern states made their way to the highest echelons of the state government. Even Jefferson complained that he could get no prom-

---

7. John Banister to Theodorick Bland, January 1781, St. George Tucker to Theodorick Bland, Jan. 21, 1781, Campbell, ed., *Bland Papers,* II, 54, 56; Tucker to Theodorick Bland, Jan. 3, 1781, Bland Family Papers, VHS; Jan. 29, 1781, Diary of Honyman; the Reverend James Madison to James Madison, Mar. 9, 1781, *Papers of Madison,* III, 10, 11-12n. Cf. R. H. Lee to Theodorick Bland, Jan. 26, 1781, Campbell, ed., *Bland Papers,* II, 57-58.

8. John Banister to Jefferson, Feb. 20, 1781, *Papers of Jefferson,* IV, 663-664; Banister to Theodorick Bland, [1781], Campbell, ed., *Bland Papers,* II, 67. Jefferson concurred with Banister (see Banister to Jefferson, Feb. 20, 1781, Jefferson to Greene, Feb. 10, 1781, Jefferson to Horatio Gates, Feb. 17, 1781, *Papers of Jefferson,* IV, 575, 637, 663-664).

ises of assistance from Congress during the crisis. He told Horatio Gates that he had been "knocking at the door of Congress for aids of all kinds, but especially of arms," since the middle of the previous summer, but to no avail. He strongly believed that Congress had a duty to help the southern states, and Virginia in particular. "Justice indeed requires that we should be aided powerfully." At the very least, Congress ought to "repay us" the arms that Virginia "lent" to Congress earlier in the war. With more arms, Jefferson, like Banister, believed that they stood a chance against the British, "tho' abandoned to ourselves."[9]

Public praise for the militia also helped legitimize complaints among the militia about doing further service. Only two weeks after he had praised the Virginia militia for their role in the battle of Cowpens, Edward Stevens was furious with the men under his command. Their term of service had come to an end, and they wanted to go home. Stevens needed them to stay on just a few days longer until Greene's main army could catch up with them. Stevens paraded his men and implored them to stay, but to no avail. "To my great mortification and astonishment scarce a man would agree to it," Stevens complained, "And gave for answer he was a good Soldier that Served his time out."[10]

But militia were just as apt to demand to return home before their official term of service expired. Many were happy to serve during an emergency like Arnold's raid or Cornwallis's advance, but few were happy to stay away from home for much longer than absolutely necessary. Within ten days of being called out following Arnold's raid, for example, militia from Hanover and Goochland Counties began to grow uneasy about staying out in service. They complained that few men had been left behind in the counties from which they were drawn. Many worried about their families, who were vulnerable not just to the British but also to the disaffected and to insurrections by enslaved Virginians.[11]

Bedford County militia also demanded that they be allowed to return home once they saw that Major General Alexander Leslie was safely back in Portsmouth. They told General Thomas Nelson, in command of the whole of the militia, that they had little food and few arms with them and that many of them had been in duty during the last invasion—and they had

9. Jefferson to Gates, Feb. 17, 1781, *Papers of Jefferson,* IV, 637.
10. Edward Stevens to Jefferson, Feb. 8, 1781, ibid., 562–563.
11. Charles Fleming to Jefferson, Jan. 17, 1781, ibid., 385–386.

a rightful claim to be relieved immediately. When the militia got no relief from Nelson, they pressed their own commander, county lieutenant James Callaway, to pursue their case with the governor. Callaway told Jefferson that the four-hundred-strong contingent "are Becomeing Very Uneasy for Relief." They were generally "Poor men, and many of them haveing large Familys, whose Subsistance Totally Depends on their Labour, and the Season of the year far Advanced."[12]

More seriously, perhaps, militia service helped give credence to complaints about the authority of commanding officers, particularly Continental army officers. In 1780, Jefferson began appointing supernumerary Continental army officers to command militia when they were called out in the field, in an effort to put a stop to the lenience of militia officers and the encouragement they sometimes gave to their men when disobedient. However, the plan backfired; many militia refused to serve if they were put under the command of regular officers. Bennett Goode told Jefferson in late 1780 that he could not raise a temporary detachment of guards for the magazine at Taylor's Ferry. No militia would step forward, because the previous officer there, Colonel Edward Carrington, a former Continental officer, treated the militia like regular troops. He had reportedly "caned a sarjent and Ordered two of the soldiers striped and whiped." Goode, a militia officer, believed that, if "such abuses" were allowed to go unpunished, "it will not be in the power of Your Officers to furnish a guard at that place."[13]

The Caroline County militia also had an unforgettable experience under a Continental officer during Leslie's invasion in the fall of 1780. They had, Edmund Pendleton claimed, turned out "with great alacrity and even ardour." However, the experience was soured for many of them when they came under the command of Major Charles Magill, a regular army officer, and were forced to obey the dictates of army rules, regulations, and discipline. Pendleton reported that the militia from Caroline returned from their tour of duty "with the most rivited disgust." At least eight men had died after falling ill. The militia blamed the deaths on the "Brutal behaviour of a Major Mcgill, a Regular Officer." "He wantonly drove them thro' Ponds of Water which might have been easily avoided, and would not allow

12. Thomas Nelson to Jefferson, Jan. 22, 1781, James Callaway to Jefferson, Mar. 11, 1781, ibid., IV, 426–427, V, 123. Cf. George Carrington, Jr., to Jefferson, Mar. 7, 1781, V, 82.

13. Bennett Goode to Jefferson, Dec. 15, 1780, ibid., IV, 208–209.

them time to eat, thus travelling in their wet cloaths, they contracted laxes and Pleurisies, which proved fatal." Pendleton sympathized with the militia and complained to James Madison (in the Continental Congress) that "forced Marches and too *Strict* Attention to Order" would "hurt raw Men." He wondered about the effect such treatment would have on recruiting for the Continental army, but he also worried that it might hurt their home defense as well. The militia involved, he said, had come back and spread the word about their experiences. It had a deleterious effect on the morale of the militia in general. A few months before the British invaded the state in earnest, the militia in Caroline went on strike. "It is announced in all Companies," Pendleton warned, "that they will die rather than stir Again."[14]

Many who did turn out in 1781 did not stay long once they were put under Continental officers again. During Cornwallis's advance against Greene in North Carolina in February, the same Major Magill told Jefferson that the Virginia militia were joining them daily. However, many of those who had enthusiastically volunteered to serve from the southside counties were already on their way back. Though Magill ridiculed them, the volunteers themselves believed they had good reason to go home. They claimed that "the burthen, and heat, of the Day was entirely thrown upon them, and that they were to be made a sacrifice by the Regular Officers to screen their own Troops." "Full of this Idea," Magill reported, "the greater number left."[15]

When they served under their own officers, militia were usually able to force them to comply with their demands, or at least demand, and get, their sympathy. If not, militia had other means for getting what they wanted. As a last resort, if their officers or local officials were not responsive, militia in service could and did also threaten mutiny. Such was the case with many of the militia on duty in the Portsmouth area. At the same time that Jefferson was sent glowing reports about the enthusiasm of the militia in turning

14. Pendleton to Madison, Oct. 30, Dec. 4, 11, 1780, *Papers of Pendleton,* I, 320, 325, 326.

15. George Lee Turberville to Jefferson, Feb. 12, 1781, Charles Magill to Jefferson, Mar. 10, 1781, *Papers of Jefferson,* IV, 594–595, V, 115–116. There is no reason to think that Magill was a particularly harsh officer, but rather typical of the type needed and often found in the regular Continental army. Jefferson during this period particularly recommended Magill's "zeal, discretion, and good sense" (Jefferson to Greene, Feb. 18, 1781, *Papers of Jefferson,* IV, 647–648; *Papers of Madison,* II, 68n, 234–235n).

out to oppose Cornwallis, James Innes told Jefferson that the troops under his command were on the verge of mutinying. They had been in service for several weeks and were beginning to tire of camp duty. They were, he told the governor, poorly clothed and, as a result, were "lousy dirty and ragged, and . . . becoming every day more sickly." In addition, Innes noted that poorer militia were anxious about their farms and families. "Such a spirit of disquietude prevails among the poorer Class, whose Corporeal Labours are necessary to sustain their families that I have been, and still am apprehensive of a mutiny, unless some assurances can be given of a speedy relief." Three days later, Innes wrote again, insisting that Jefferson send replacement militia in order to quell the "mutinous spirit" that prevailed among his troops.[16]

Even unsympathetic officers were often forced to adopt a more conciliatory tone soon after taking command. Innes was one. He finally told Jefferson that a full mutiny of his refractory militia would have "Evil consequences" in the present circumstances. He was forced, "contrary to my Ideas of military Discipline to adopt a temporizing Conduct." Two weeks later, he explained the problem of consent to one of the officers under his command. Innes needed more troops to join General von Steuben across the James River to help with his expedition against Portsmouth. Consequently, he asked one of his colonels to "Endeavor to persuade [the militia] to Cross the River," but only if it could "be effected without coercive measures." Innes hoped the colonel had enough "Influence" over the men to get them to cross. Should the militia still prove "Governable," he could reinforce Steuben with a sizable detachment. However, if they began to show signs of the "mutinous spirit" they had shown before, Innes simply planned to discharge them.[17]

As Innes's problems reveal, the demands of recalcitrant militia in Virginia ultimately contributed to deteriorating relations between the state and the Continent in two important ways. In the first place, the assertiveness of the militia frustrated Continental officers who were used to commanding more disciplined soldiers. But, in trying to get state officials to

16. James Innes to Jefferson, Feb. 21, 24, 1781, *Papers of Jefferson*, IV, 675, 699. Jefferson authorized Innes to call out reinforcements on February 24, but they were slow in providing relief.

17. Ibid., Feb. 21, 24, Mar. 6, 1781, IV, 675, 699, V, 73–74. Virginia leaders might have been sensitized by the reports from Philadelphia of the mutinies of the Pennsylvania and New Jersey lines. See Madison to Jefferson, Jan. 9, 1781, IV, 325–326.

do something about the militia, Continental officers ran into a further wall. State officials, anxious to preserve harmony within the state, proved unwilling to push the militia too far. Ultimately, the militia forced state and Continental leaders to change their plans.[18]

The most important Continental representative in the state was Steuben, who had recently arrived to take charge of military operations in Virginia. He was decidedly unimpressed by the Virginia militia. When Arnold fell back to Portsmouth, Steuben began to mount a campaign against him, particularly encouraged by the arrival of a French squadron under Captain Arnaud de Tilly in the bay. However, with Cornwallis's approach from the south draining men and arms in that direction, Steuben ran into numerous problems assembling his force for the campaign against Portsmouth.

At first, Steuben wanted to use the militia already on duty in the lower counties. Jefferson, apparently in response to Innes's reports, to memories of the insurrectionary activities of the disaffected the previous year, and perhaps to reports of Continental army mutinies in the North, told Steuben that he could not use these troops. He had no choice but to discharge the militia in the lower counties. "The precedent of an actual mutiny would be so mischevious as to induce us to believe an accomodation to the present temper most prudent." He told Steuben that, in the circumstances, he might not be able to use the militia for any offensive action against the British at Portsmouth.[19]

Nor did Steuben have much better luck trying to get reinforcements to assemble an expedition. At his request, the council ordered out one-quarter of the militia from Loudoun, Fairfax, Prince William, and Fauquier Counties to aid in the expedition against Leslie. General George Weedon, in command of this northern contingent, told Steuben that tardy militia had delayed his march southward to join him. Weedon told Steuben that 286 rank and file had come from Fairfax and Prince William to Fredericksburg but he had been assured by Jefferson that there should be at least 385. A week later, Weedon was still waiting for more militia to turn up. Those who had arrived were also proving refractory. When Weedon finally arrived at Williamsburg, he was only more disgusted at the "deranged situation of

18. Serious militia resistance forced Jefferson to change his plans on the western frontier as well. See The Officers of the Berkeley County Militia to Jefferson, Jan. 25, 1781, Jefferson to George Rogers Clark, Feb. 19, 1781, ibid., IV, 451–452, 653.

19. Jefferson to Steuben, Feb. 24, 1781, ibid., 700–701.

our defence in this Quarter." The militia from neighboring counties had not bothered to turn out, he reported, though men were desperately needed for the impending expedition.[20]

Steuben, awaiting reinforcements, was frustrated and furious with the militia. After it became apparent that the militia from the northwest would be slow in arriving, he finally persuaded the council to order out a further 1,100 militia from counties closer to Portsmouth. Among others, the council ordered out 104 men from New Kent County, of whom the county lieutenant could get only 28 to march, and he expected half would desert on the way to Williamsburg. The majority of the militia believed that others had deserted with impunity and insisted that they would not do any duty until the others were punished. The militia also claimed that they had been in duty on several occasions since the previous October, which they thought exonerated them from wrongdoing this time. Charles Dabney reported that it was the officers of the militia from New Kent who had promoted the mass desertions. "Unless some vigorous measures are taken to prevent such shameful proceedings," complained John Walker, serving with Steuben, "it will be utterly impossible to concert any Measures of offence or defence with any probability of Success."[21]

The following day, Steuben wrote to Jefferson, scarcely concealing his anger. Only 12 men had actually turned up from New Kent of the 104 expected, and they were unarmed. Steuben was unwilling to give them arms, or even take command of them. Moreover, his quartermaster had told him that government officials would give him no assistance in impressing badly needed horses. Furious, he told Jefferson that, because of the assurances from state officials, he had told Washington and Lafayette that everything would be ready for the expedition against Arnold. He was now embarrassed that he had placed so much confidence in the government of Virginia, and he wondered whether the powers of the government were ade-

20. Feb. 17, 1781, H. R. McIlwaine et al., eds., *Journals of the Council of the State of Virginia* (Richmond, Va., 1931–1982), II, 295; George Weedon to Steuben, Feb. 28, Mar. 8, 1781, to Jefferson, Mar. 3, 10, 1781, *Papers of Jefferson,* V, 28–29nn, 54–55, 122–123.

21. Mar. 1, 1781, McIlwaine et al., eds., *Journals of the Council,* II, 301; John Walker to Jefferson, Mar. 8, 1781, Charles Dabney to Jefferson, Mar. 23, 1781, *Papers of Jefferson,* V, 101–102, 214. In contrast, the local commanding officer of New Kent County, William Clayton, wrote to Jefferson in defense of his militia. See William Clayton to Jefferson, Mar. 16, 1781, *Papers of Jefferson,* V, 154-155.

quate to actually furnish the expedition. He warned Jefferson that he would issue no further orders until he had some response from him and that he would report the problems to both Lafayette and the commander of the French fleet. He told Jefferson that the defense of Virginia was in jeopardy. The French commanders might not want to "engage too far in an Enterprize which there is no prospect of carrying through."[22]

On the same day, Jefferson fired back at Steuben, revealing the extent of his dilemma. He could, he explained, do very little about the widespread disobedience, disregard for the laws, and breakdown in the chain of authority. "We can only be answerable for the orders we give, and not for their execution. If they are disobeyed from obstinacy of spirit or want of coercion in the laws it is not our fault." Yet Jefferson was also adamant that the people of Virginia deserved to be recalcitrant. The council had indeed refused to sanction an armed force to accompany the quartermaster when he impressed the horses, because they did not feel it necessary. So far, white Virginians had actually parted too easily with their horses by delivering them to every man who said he was riding on public business. Finally, the militia, Jefferson asserted, had enough "real Calls to duty" that it was not "proper" to "harrass" them further by putting them at the disposal of the quartermaster. Indeed, Jefferson noted, they suspected that they were not wanted by the quartermaster "as *Militia,* but as servants." Ultimately, the militia forced Steuben to abandon his attack.[23]

When Lafayette arrived in Virginia in early March to take command, Jefferson was more conciliatory but no more helpful. He could only apologize for the problems in Virginia. He hoped Lafayette would understand that it was not from a want of spirit among the executive of the state that they were suffering. Rather, "Mild Laws, a People not used to war and prompt obedience, a want of the Provisions of War and means of procuring them render our orders often ineffectual, oblige us to temporize and when we cannot accomplish an object in one way to attempt it in another."[24]

22. Steuben to Jefferson, Mar. 9, 1781, *Papers of Jefferson,* V, 106–107.

23. Jefferson to Steuben, Mar. 10, 1781, ibid., 119–120. See also Jefferson to the Speaker of the House of Delegates, Mar. 10, 1781, 114–115, for similar justifications.

24. Two days later, he wrote again to Lafayette. The breakdown in their mobilization, Jefferson explained somewhat disingenuously, was entirely due to the unpreparedness of Virginians, who had the war for the first time "seriously fixed in their Country." Two days later, he wrote again to Lafayette. Jefferson to Lafayette,

• • • The militia also used their military service in the early months of 1781 to justify their noncompliance with the new recruiting and draft law for the Continental army. Many county lieutenants wrote to Jefferson that they were unilaterally suspending the draft in their counties because so many of their militia were out in service. Most believed that, if they went ahead with the draft in the absence of the militia, they would risk outright rebellion. In Bedford County, where there had already been insurrectionary activity in the previous year, James Callaway thought that drafting militia while they were actually out serving as militia "would have Occasioned a General Disturbance." But officers in less turbulent areas were also forced to suspend the draft while the militia were out on duty. Officers in Powhatan County, for example, decided at a court-martial that the recruiting act should not be put into effect until the militia ordered to join General Greene returned. Other officers around the state followed suit. The militia also persuaded Jefferson. In early March, he called for more militia from Hanover, Caroline, Spotsylvania, and King William Counties to help on Steuben's expedition. In doing so, he gave the commanding officers in each county free rein to suspend the draft for regulars if they felt it was necessary.[25]

Many officers also used the disruption of the British invasions as a good excuse to unilaterally suspend the law. Colonel W. R. W. Curle told Jefferson that the field officers and magistrates of Hampton unanimously agreed that they could not go ahead with the draft in the county because of the "frequent Invasions" and the "great Distresses" to which those in Hampton in particular had been subjected. Those, along with the "dispersed Situation" of the inhabitants of the county, had stopped the tax commissioners from even making a start on their assessments, and the officers and magistrates would not budge until they had the tax assessment to hand. If they could not divide the militia properly or pay potential recruits, they refused to carry out the law. The field officers and magistrates of nearby Elizabeth

---

Mar. 10, 12, 1781, ibid., 113, 129. Cf. the second letter of the day written by Jefferson to Lafayette, 130–131.

25. Officers of the Greenbrier Militia to Jefferson, Jan. 29, 1781, Mosby to Jefferson, Feb. 24, 1781, James Callaway to Jefferson, Mar. 11, 23, 1781, Jefferson to the County Lieutenants of Hanover and other Counties, Mar. 12, 1781, French Strother to Jefferson, Mar. 28, 1781, John Page to Jefferson, Apr. 13, 1781, Sir John Peyton to Jefferson, May 3, 1781, ibid., IV, 469, 700, V, 123, 128, 212, 272, 436, 596.

City County also "declined" carrying out the draft because of the disruptions of the British invasions.[26]

Most militia officers "declined" to carry out state orders for drafting men because of popular pressure. John Syme of Hanover County told Jefferson that many of his militia refused to pay the taxes for the draft. He also claimed that the delays caused by the British invasions had nullified the draft law, arguing that the time allotted for collecting the bounty tax had expired, rendering the law obsolete. Syme also said that his militia had convinced many of his official colleagues, and even one of his own field officers had sided with the militia, publicly declaring that "He Will not Pay a Shilling, and intends to Plead the Laws not being in Time." Others feared popular resistance. Returning from the battle of Guilford Courthouse, Daniel Morgan told Jefferson he found "the people in a ferment about the Taxes" and thought that only a "small force" in each county would help compel obedience to the laws.[27]

Other local officials agreed that the only way to enforce the laws at this point was by coercion. George Corbin of Accomack County told Jefferson that, if he wanted to enforce the law in Accomack, he would have to find someone "powerful" enough "to force obedience to your Excellencys will; as I am well convinced that force alone can effect it." In that case, Corbin warned, he would have to resign, and the state would have to find someone else to do the job. But force, of course, was one thing that local officials did not have at their disposal. Civil authority in the counties was limited to a dozen or so justices (of whom usually only a handful were active at any one time, particularly during the Revolution), a sheriff, and several constables. Militia officers were most responsible for carrying out military laws, but there were only a handful of field officers (often the same men serving as justices) and company-grade officers. The militia themselves were the only force readily at their disposal to control or contain any collective action. In the face of widespread resistance, the militia as a source of authority was at best uncertain, at worst a source of lawlessness of its own, and local officials

26. W. R. W. Curle to Jefferson, Feb. 26, 1781, ibid., V, 11; "Abstract of Men Raised under the Former Laws Passed for Raising Soldiers for the Continental Service—November 1782," *Virginia Military Records: From the Virginia Magazine of History and Biography, the William and Mary Quarterly, and Tyler's Quarterly* (Baltimore, 1983), 661; cf. 671.

27. John Syme to Jefferson, Feb. 26, 1781, Daniel Morgan to Jefferson, Mar. 23, 1781, *Papers of Jefferson*, V, 14, 219.

were reluctant to press unpopular measures upon their neighbors. Caught between unpopular state laws and angry neighbors, many local officials were forced to abdicate their authority.[28]

Thus, in the midst of one of the worst military crises in Virginia, militia officers resigned in ever growing numbers. Of eight counties surveyed, either the county lieutenant or another field officer resigned in seven in the first half of 1781. Most of them resigned in late January and February, as orders went out to recruit and draft more soldiers. In Hampshire County, for example, the county court in mid-March replaced the county lieutenant, Enoch Innis, stating that he "refuses to serve." In Cumberland County, both the colonel of the militia and the county lieutenant resigned by the end of February. The latter claimed he had served for too long and was no longer willing to "go through the fatigue of it." Coming at this crucial moment, the effects of such key resignations were deleterious. Replacements for both officers in Cumberland were not sworn in until the end of April. And, of the thirty new recruits required of Cumberland County by the new law, only three or four men were raised, and officials later admitted that there was "No draft made."[29]

Some officers resigned because of popular pressure. Others sympathized

28. George Corbin to Jefferson, Feb. 28, 1781, ibid., 21–22. In the face of Corbin's letter and threatened resignation, Jefferson rescinded the order to collect the public arms (137).

29. See Executive Department, Governor's Office—Militia Commission Papers, box 3, LiVi; May 14, 1781, Northumberland County Order Book, 1773–1783, LiVi; Feb. 8, 1781, Southampton County Court Order Book, 1778–1784, LiVi; July 19, 1781, Lancaster County Court Orders, no. 16, 1778–1783, LiVi; Apr. 24, 1781, Westmoreland County Court Orders, 1776–1786, LiVi; Loudoun County Court Records, G, appendix. For Cumberland County, see Cumberland County Court Records, Suit Papers, 17802, LiVi; Jan. 22, Feb. 26, Apr. 23, June 16, 1781, Cumberland County Court Records, Order Books, 1779–1784, LiVi; "General Return of Recruits in Virginia Raised under the Act of October 1780," War Office Records, LiVi; "Abstract of Men Raised—November 1782," *Virginia Military Records,* 671. Two key field officers—the county lieutenant and colonel of the county—resigned in Albemarle County a little later as well, and in the summer of 1781 the field officers of Orange County were all replaced (see Apr. 16, Aug. 18, 1781, McIlwaine et al., eds., *Journals of the Council,* II, 335, 377). Cf. John Nash to the Executive, Apr. 21, 1783, Wm. P. Palmer et al., eds., *Calendar of State Papers and Other Manuscripts, 1652–1781, Preserved in the Capitol at Richmond* (Richmond, Va., 1875–1893), III, 470. Nash had taken over as county lieutenant in Prince Edward County at the end of May 1781.

with the complaints of their neighbors. Corbin's counterpart in Northampton County, Isaac Avery, thought that the orders to collect the public arms, together with the recruiting law, were simply intolerable. The recruiting law, which in his county meant drafting men, was "a mode of impressing more equal I confess, but far less politic, than that some times practiced in England." Avery told Jefferson that he always both "publicly and privately" professed that the drafting laws were "inconsistent with Liberty and free Government." Moreover, his neighbors also resented the recruiting laws, which "hath been always the Subject of great complaint." These new measures, combined with the inability of the people in the county to pay their taxes because of the embargo, he cautioned, were "such as greatly depress the Spirits of the People." "If no steps are taken to redress them," he concluded, they might "lead to events that will be productive of the most serious Consequences." With that warning, Avery himself also resigned his key post.[30]

• • • Where the draft was carried out, it followed now predictable patterns, in which the poor and vulnerable were most likely to end up serving. A sole surviving return of recruits and draftees from Loudoun County following the 1781 draft provides perhaps the fullest picture of how a wartime community dealt with a difficult and potentially divisive call for men. Loudoun, one of the largest counties in Virginia, was required to provide a contingent of 119 recruits. In the spring of 1781, a mere 14 men enlisted voluntarily, all landless laborers in their mid-twenties, including 1 sailor and 1 "waggoner." Volunteer laborers included Frederick Sexton, an eighteen-year-old from Loudoun, Robert Bryan, a thirty-six-year-old also from Loudoun, and James Smith, a twenty-five-year-old from Montgomery County, Maryland, who subsequently deserted. Most volunteers enlisted for the duration of the war, preferring to take advantage of the better bounty, an enslaved Virginian, and the promise of land. All, it can be presumed, were in need of money and land.[31]

Most of those who stepped forward to serve did so only as hired sub-

30. Isaac Avery to Jefferson, Mar. 16, 1781, *Papers of Jefferson,* V, 153–154.

31. Return of the Recruits raised for the County of Loudoun under the Act of Assembly for October 1780 . . . , [May 1, 1781], Auditor of Public Accounts Inventory, Militia Lists, 1779–1782, LiVi. Few documents like this list survive. The average age of the volunteers was 26, of the substitutes residing in Loudoun was 24, and of those living outside Loudoun was 27.

stitutes in the place of drafted men. With a draft looming, most potential volunteers would have made more money serving as substitutes. Forty-four drafted men hired substitutes after they were picked to serve. All of the substitutes waited until the draft took place to see whether they could secure even more bounty money from individuals desperate to avoid being dragged off for eighteen months of service. Seven men signed on as substitutes on the day of the draft. Thirty-nine men held out for longer and, because of the temporary suspension of the draft in the county, were procured between March 26 and April 30. Again, these were generally men in need of extra cash or a stake in society. Nineteen, or 43 percent, of these substitutes were listed as laborers. The rest were mostly low-skilled tradesmen, including four tailors, three weavers, three shoemakers, a sailor, a wagoner, a butcher, and a "distiller." From the more highly skilled trades, there were a single blacksmith, a cabinetmaker, two coopers, and two fullers. Significantly, only four of these substitutes listed themselves as farmers.[32]

Most middling farmers sought ways to avoid the draft. Some did all they could, for example, to find substitutes, who came from nearby counties like Berkeley and Stafford but were also found from further afield, like Pennsylvania or Maryland. John Jack, the thirty-one-year-old distiller, came all the way from Kentucky, and Robert Johnson, a twenty-six-year-old laborer, was a resident of North Carolina. They might have been transient workers in the county, or they might have made it known to friends or family of drafted men that they were available for hire. Though desperate, farmers in Loudoun did not turn to their sons or other kin to avoid the draft. Indeed, whereas farmers often sent relatives as substitutes for militia duty within the state, military duty in the Continental army appeared too risky to send close relatives. None of the substitutes listed in the return from Loudoun had the same name as him he replaced.[33]

Most often, of course, farmers continued to pressure local officials to find means to prevent the draft from falling on themselves, even if it meant exploiting others. In Loudoun County, 10 of the 119 recruits needed to complete Loudoun's quota for the Continental army came from the Quaker community. The draft law stated that, if Quakers were drafted, the com-

32. Return of the Recruits of Loudoun, LiVi. For an analysis of one group of recruits in neighboring Maryland in 1782, see Edward C. Papenfuse and Gregory A. Stiverson, "General Smallwood's Recruits: The Peacetime Career of the Revolutionary War Private," *WMQ*, 3d Ser., XXX (1973), 117–132.

33. Return of the Recruits of Loudoun, LiVi.

manding officer of the county had to find a substitute for each to serve for eighteen months. The substitute would get the same bounty as a draft. If any more money were needed to recruit the substitute, all the Quakers and Mennonites in the county would be charged in equal proportion to their property. In Loudoun, it appears that either 10 Quakers were drafted or that the local militia officers simply allotted ten divisions (or a quota of 10 men) to the Quaker population. Though no men appear to have been raised to serve as substitutes for the Quakers listed as drafts, approximately 125 Quakers were hauled into court in the spring of 1781, tried, and most fined heavily—in order to help pay for finding other recruits to go in their stead.[34]

The recruits Loudoun officers managed to scrape together with offers of large bounties or coercion were not unlike those from other places in the state. In Culpeper, for example, another large county (and, like Loudoun, situated far from the vulnerable coasts), only 7 men stepped forward voluntarily to fill the quota of 106. These included Enoch Cox, a nineteen-year-old shoemaker, and William Wedgroof, a nineteen-year-old free mulatto who lived in Culpeper town and who engaged for the war. John Tim, also a Culpeper town resident, was a carpenter. None of these men owned land or appeared in the property tax records. Because of the lack of volunteers, ninety-nine divisions were subject to a draft. Of these, 46 of the men drafted found substitutes, who were generally needy. Of the 14 who actually appeared in the property tax records, 9 owned no slaves, and none of them owned more than two horses. Though they earned less from the state for stepping in as substitutes, they earned rich and more immediate rewards from their neighbors. Moreover, by stepping in as substitutes rather than volunteers, they also had to serve only eighteen months.[35]

The Culpeper draft also shows the highly stratified nature of conscription in Virginia. The average number of slaves that militia officers of the county held was 12.5, and they also owned an average of 579 acres of land worth about £248. Seven colonels owned an average of 31 enslaved Virginians and 1,344 acres of land worth about £620 each, and nineteen captains owned an average of 8.4 slaves and 447 acres of land worth £184. They had similar holdings in horses and cattle, with the average for all officers at 6.5 horses and 20 cattle. Fifty-two draftees who do appear in later tax

34. Apr. 11, 1781, Loudoun County Court Records, 1776–1783, LiVi. Two women were also among those convicted.

35. John R. Van Atta, "Conscription in Revolutionary Virginia: The Case of Culpeper County, 1780–1781," *VMHB*, XCII (1984), 279.

records, on the other hand, owned an average of 3 slaves each, 3.1 horses, and 7.1 cattle. They also owned only about 253 acres of land worth about £116. Substitutes, of whom only fourteen (or 30 percent) could be found in the property tax records, owned an average of 1.3 slaves, 1.9 horses, 3.6 cattle, and about 172 acres of land worth only £62. Most striking, however, was the number of draftees and substitutes who were not listed at all on the tax records in 1782. Because of this, we can assume that perhaps as many as seventy-eight draftees and substitutes (or 68 percent of the total) owned no land at all. Draftees who did not hire substitutes were, predictably, the poorest of the group.[36]

Some substitutes, of course, continued to come from the very lowest class of Virginians. In Culpeper County, at least three black men joined as substitutes for whites. Twenty-two-year-old Philip Phillips, forty-year-old Thomas Shaw, and thirty-one-year-old Joseph Hughes preferred to take their chances in the army in return for some extra cash and perhaps a later favor or two from their neighbors. The three might have been free already, but they were most probably escaped slaves or even Virginians given their freedom in return for serving in the army. The newspapers again reported the unsettling frequency of enslaved Virginians' seeking freedom in the army. George and Tull, for example, ran away from Brunswick County in southern Virginia early in 1781. George, a twenty-three-year-old, had previously run away by joining the army under Colonel Buford and served with him southward to Hillsborough in North Carolina before he was found out and returned. Tull, a large twenty-seven-year-old mulatto man, had recently been seen near Richmond, where he said he was going to Fredericksburg to enlist in the service "or join a regiment." Enough black Virginians, free and unfree, showed a willingness to serve that recruiting officers were more than happy to take them on. White Virginians were also more than willing to send enslaved Virginians to the army as substitutes.[37]

36. Ibid., 279.

37. Van Atta, "Conscription in Revolutionary Virginia," *VMHB*, XCII (1984), 274–275; *Va. Gaz.* (Dixon and Nicolson), Mar. 24, 1781. For enslaved Virginians informally sent as substitutes, see Hening, comp., *Statutes at Large*, XI, 308, 309; Benjamin Harrison to the Assembly, Oct. 20, 1783, Executive Communications, LiVi. Joseph A. Goldenberg, Eddie D. Nelson, and Rita V. Fletcher, in "Revolutionary Ranks: An Analysis of the Chesterfield Supplement," *VMHB*, LXXXVII (1979), 184, 186, note the presence of many blacks in the army but do not give a number or percentage.

It was one thing to raise recruits; it was another altogether to get them into the army. The new levies from Culpeper County, the tax commissioner reported, would not budge from the county until they had received their full bounty money: they became mutinous and refused to march to their rendezvous. They complained that they had no money to leave with their families or to purchase goods for and along their march. Their opposition forced the commanding officer to extend their furloughs until the tax commissioners could collect enough money to pay them, and many deserted while waiting. Of the 53 draftees who did not find substitutes, 21 never made it into the army. Of the volunteers or substitutes, 11 also did not make it into the army, which meant that, of 106 men required from Culpeper, only 74 made it into the army, or 70 percent of the quota. Culpeper probably provided a higher proportion of its quota than most counties.[38]

Forty-two men, or 40 percent of the 106 men listed (and legible) in the Loudoun return, were drafted but listed as deserted. They probably never even appeared at the muster on the day of the draft, for no details apart from their names were ever recorded. Only 6 men were actually drafted and listed as present for eighteen months of service. They included twenty-one-year-olds Jacob Johnson and John Russell, both laborers, Cornelius Slacht, a twenty-eight-year-old weaver, and nineteen-year-old Job Warford and twenty-seven-year-old Joseph Watson, both listed as farmers. All resided in Loudoun. Though they stayed long enough to have their details recorded by military officers in the county, we can never be sure how long they stayed with the army. Draftees were not the only ones who deserted. Of the 14 voluntary enlistments, 3 deserted, presumably after they picked up at least part of their bounty. Of the 44 men hired as substitutes, 9 subsequently deserted, including John Jack, the distiller from Kentucky. Thus, of the county's quota of 119 recruits, local officials delivered at most only 49 men, or just more than 40 percent of the number asked of them.[39]

Many counties turned a blind eye to deserting draftees. William Davies at the war office thought that many of the divisions sent him recruits who had been only partially paid their bounty. The recruits came to the ren-

38. Tax Commissioners of Culpeper County to Jefferson, Mar. 29, 1781, *Papers of Jefferson,* V, 278; Van Atta, "Conscription in Revolutionary Virginia," *VMHB,* XCII (1984), 279. For other problems with the bounty money, see William Preston to the Governor, Mar. 15, 1782, Robert Jones to William Davies, Aug. 7, 1782, Palmer et al., eds., *Calendar of State Papers,* III, 100, 252.

39. Return of the Recruits of Loudoun, LiVi.

dezvous to register the fact that they had been raised, but they expected to be sent back home in order to collect the rest of the bounty, whereupon they deserted. The divisions that raised them were happy to look the other way, because they had already been given credit for raising the recruit, and they no longer had to pay the rest of the promised bounty. Some divisions found other ways to capitalize on deserters from the army. Davies told the governor that one man deserted from a division in Southampton and was then promptly turned in by another division in neighboring Brunswick County as a deserter from another engagement. The Brunswick County division claimed him in order to exempt itself from raising anyone else, even though, Davies claimed, it must have known he had enlisted in Southampton before it took him up.[40]

Davies was furious that so little could be done about the widespread violation of the laws and was particularly incensed at the widespread complicity of local officials in allowing deserters to remain at large. He was disgusted at the "open toleration, I might justly say, protection which is afforded to deserters." Combined with what he called the "ruinous fondness the Assembly have always shewn for short enlistments, enlisting and deserting have become the professed employment of numbers of men in this state." By the end of the year, he reported that it was well known that "numbers that have actually enlisted or drafted" had been "permitted by the indulgence or inattention of those in their counties to remain unmolested at home."[41]

Yet most local officials were actually forced to look the other way. Part of the problem was that the number of deserters was growing such that local officials were powerless to do anything about them. Davies admitted as much when he made his first report in March, worrying that each draft was producing two deserters for every recruit. This was the case with the last draft in 1780 and looked to be the case with the current draft. The numbers of deserters "will soon become too formidable to be meddled with."[42]

• • • The recalcitrance of the militia, both in resisting the draft and in resisting too many onerous demands upon them, finally forced Jefferson to call the assembly together for an emergency legislative session. In a circular

40. William Davies to Jefferson, Mar. 18, 1781, *Papers of Jefferson,* V, 173–175.

41. Ibid.; Davies to the General Assembly, Nov. 26, 1781, War Office Records, LiVi.

42. Davies to Jefferson, Mar. 18, 1781, *Papers of Jefferson,* V, 173–175.

letter to the delegates, he told the representatives that they were in urgent need of "Men and money." The treasury had already run dry because of the constant and massive demands made on it by suppliers and soldiers. He was also worried about keeping enough men in the field, both for Virginia's own defense and to fulfill Continental demands. The British invasions had already disrupted recruiting. Moreover, he thought that they could not rely on the militia for much longer. The general officers of the militia had told him that the militia felt themselves stretched and were growing dangerously impatient. Though the commanding officer, Thomas Nelson, Jr., had determined to reduce the militia to twenty-seven hundred infantry, Jefferson thought there would be "considerable difficulty" in keeping even that number in the field. He also sent information disclosing "the refusal of considerable numbers of militia within certain counties to come into the feild, and the departure of some others in defiance with their arms."[43]

Jefferson believed that the legislature needed to do two things: reform the militia laws and enforce the recruitment of their Continental quota of regular troops as soon as it could. Under pressure from Steuben, Jefferson asked the assembly to make some amendment to the invasion law or take some kind of action, warning, "The crisis at which these instances of disobedience to the laws have appeared, may bring on peculiar ill consequences." But Jefferson, perhaps sensing that the legislature might be loath to make the militia laws any more coercive, used the arguments of the militia themselves. He told the delegates that the militia complained about the number of times they had been in service and would prefer to raise an army properly, to exempt themselves from the fighting. The militia had claimed they "would give any consideration to raise regulars, rather than be kept in service themselves." Jefferson thus gave the assembly at least an option: it could enforce the recruiting laws and perhaps obviate the need for further calls upon the militia. Jefferson warned that they must do something. The state was under siege; it needed money and men "to enable us to meet our enemies in the north, south, east, and west."[44]

43. Circular Letter to Members of the Assembly, Jan. 23, 1781, Steuben to Jefferson, Mar. 5, 1781, Jefferson to the Speaker of the House of Delegates, Mar. 6, 9, 1781, *Papers of Jefferson,* IV, 433–434, V, 66–70, 76, 105.

44. Ibid. Steuben sent in his own proposal for a wholesale reorganization of the militia. Jefferson based his assessment of the militia's claims on Thomas Nelson's letter when he led militia against Arnold in January. Nelson told Jefferson that the militia had been "so much harassed lately that they would give nearly half they pos-

While Steuben pressed the legislature directly for militia reform and Jefferson pressed it to enforce the recruiting law, the militia itself also spoke up. Even as they took their seats, the delegates in the assembly faced a barrage of petitions from their constituents. Most petitions, drawn up in the midst of the British threats, focused on the draft and, in particular, the means by which the bounty money would be raised. But, in making complaints about the draft, petitioners were more vocal, careful to assert their citizenship in the new state—usually based on their past military service in the militia. Finally, petitioners were implicitly and explicitly concerned with the contributions of other members of society in Virginia. The middling farmers who bore the brunt of the new draft law lashed out at those both below and above them, challenging the very claims to citizenship of those who had not contributed fairly to the war effort in the new civil state.

Petitions from Cumberland County, in the heart of the piedmont, and Berkeley County, in the northwest part of the state, were among the first and most illuminating petitions to reach the assembly. The petition from Cumberland was the most explicit. More than 175 men put their names to an angry memorial against the draft law passed by the previous legislature. The petitioners began by invoking their interpretation of the very nature of the Revolution. They understood that it had been fought to guard against all "arbitrary and partial proceedings," and protection against such proceedings had been a "Fundamental right" since the beginning. The bill of rights, they claimed, specifically protected that right by requiring the assembly to act with the "publick liberty" in mind and guard against any infringements on it. However, "to the great Mortification" of the petitioners, the recruiting act passed by the last session of the legislature was "repugnant to the aforesaid principles."[45]

The petitioners felt most aggrieved by the mode of collecting taxes for paying the bounty money. Whereas the previous law had allowed divisions to raise as much money as they needed to hire a recruit and to deduct that money from their next tax payment, the new law had asked for the taxes up front. This raised several problems. First, if farmers paid the tax

---

sess to raise Regulars, rather than be subject to the Distresses they feel at leaving their Plantations and Families." Thomas Nelson to Jefferson, Jan. 22, 1781, *Papers of Jefferson,* IV, 426–427.

45. Cumberland County Petition, [Mar. 5, 1781], Virginia Legislative Petitions, LiVi.

up front, they would have little left to use to try to entice a recruit, either with the rest of their division or, in the most desperate scenario, after they were drafted. The problem was widespread. French Strother of Culpeper County also told Jefferson that many ordinary citizens were at risk of being drafted because they had no money left to hire substitutes. He noted that the 2 percent tax had "fallen Very hard in Many Instances" and many no longer had it "in their power to Extricate themselves."[46]

But the petitioners from Cumberland also complained that they had no time to prepare to pay the tax. The legislature had passed the law only in early January, and the tax had to be collected within forty days. This would have been difficult enough, but the British invasions and calls on the militia had made it almost impossible. "We consider the raising such an emence sum on a sudden demand," the petitioners claimed, "to be oppressive and wrong." Berkeley County citizens agreed and complained that the provision law had exacerbated the problem. That law, also passed in 1781, stipulated that commissary agents could seize provisions to supply the army in return for certificates, which meant that few farmers had any cash, and they had nothing left to sell. They were angry that the provision law had "extorted" all "the Commodities the farmer hath to sell" without any payment for their goods. They were issued certificates for their goods in lieu of paper money. For residents who lived far from the capital, these certificates were almost impossible to redeem for paper money. By the time they received certificates, they claimed, there was rarely any cash left to redeem them.[47]

Many farmers worried that they would not be able to pay the sudden taxes and that their property would be seized by the sheriff and sold to pay them—for less than it was worth, or "distress and disposing of property greatly under its real value." Berkeley County petitioners believed that seized property would sell for barely "one third its real Value." Thus, to pay

46. Ibid.; French Strother to Thomas Jefferson, Mar. 28, 1781, *Papers of Jefferson,* V, 272.

47. Cumberland County Petition, [Mar. 5, 1781], Virginia Legislative Petitions, LiVi; Berkeley County Petition, [Mar. 7, 1781], Virginia Legislative Petitions, LiVi. Accomack County citizens also complained that there was not enough money in circulation, mainly, they asserted, because the embargo law meant that they could not dispose of their grain (see Accomack County Petition, [Mar. 14, 1781], Virginia Legislative Petitions, LiVi). Cf. Mar. 12, 1781, Diary of Honyman.

a tax of ten pounds, farmers feared that they might end up losing as much as thirty pounds of property. Even worse, to Cumberland petitioners, the "most designing speculators" in the state who did have money might purposely buy their property at deflated prices.[48]

The thought of losing so much and then facing the draft distressed many farmers. But the petitioners were particularly angry because of the sacrifices they had already made on behalf of the war. The Berkeley County petitioners were angry that the provision law had already forced them to give their goods to the public. "What must be a mans feelings," they asked the legislature, "when he finds his Property Seiz'd and Sold," only to pay a "Tax Due to Government," when at the same time the public had already got the property that the farmer depended upon to pay that tax? The Cumberland County petitioners also claimed that they had made sacrifices and "freely" given their support to the war up to this time. To drive the point home, they contrasted their perilous situation with those who, instead of suffering, had actually made money from the war. Those "most designing speculators" would "make great advantages of the industrious Planter on whom we depend for the most essential necessaries for the support of the present war."[49]

The Cumberland petitioners also lashed out more explicitly at their wealthier neighbors in their protest against the draft. The previous draft law allowed the able-bodied militia in every division to demand extra recruiting cash from all propertied people in their division to go toward raising a recruit. Under the new law, able-bodied militia could raise extra cash to hire a recruit, but propertied people were exempt from this extra burden. Propertied people who were exempt from the militia had to pay only the 2 percent tax. Echoing the earlier complaints of their counterparts in Charlotte County, the petitioners from Cumberland were angry that invalids and other exempts from the militia were again allowed to escape the full costs of the war, how invalids especially had it "in their power" to withhold contributions for raising soldiers for each division. This was wrong, and not founded on the "true principles of equity." Invalids and exempts had their property "equally protected in comon with other Citizens" who were sub-

48. Cumberland County Petition, [Mar. 5, 1781], Virginia Legislative Petitions, LiVi; Berkeley County Petition, [Mar. 7, 1781], Virginia Legislative Petitions, LiVi.

49. Ibid.

ject to the draft "without an alternative." The most galling aspect of this legislation, they felt, was that invalids were often "the most wealthy part of the Yeomanry."[50]

Cumberland was not the only angry county. In other places, the militia did not bother to petition the assembly; they took the law into their own hands. In Richmond County, for example, the militia raised a cry when at least sixty men were left off the militia rolls, or 15 percent of the militia. The county lieutenant, Leroy Peachey, told Jefferson, "The People . . . murmur'd greatly at the number excus'd." The more men who were left off the militia rolls, the fewer men were left in the divisions who could pool their resources and hire a recruit. If they could not hire one, the more men left off meant that those still in the divisions had a greater chance of getting drafted. Richmond County militia were angry enough to force Peachey to include himself in one of the divisions of the militia. Even though he had classed himself as an invalid, Peachey told Jefferson that he felt obliged to put himself in one of the divisions and take "a Chance as the Rest" at being drafted, "in order to keep the People quiet." As in Cumberland, there was an implicit class division in the challenge of the Richmond militia. Peachey told Jefferson that he had the support of all of his genteel colleagues, but the militia forced him to put himself in the draft even though "the whole of the Gentlemen were of Opinion that I was not an able Body'd Man."[51]

Petitioners from Rockbridge and Orange Counties also remonstrated against the recruiting law, but they focused on the terms of the draft itself and also drew attention to their different socioeconomic position. Rockbridge County militia, for example, wanted the assembly to adapt the recruiting law to their particular circumstances, where, in the western backcountry, few people owned many slaves and the "daily exertions of a great majority of the inhabitants, are necessary to support their families." They could ensure the security of their families if called upon for terms of three months, but they would "inevitably be ruined" if soldiers were drafted away for eighteen. They thus offered to serve three months each in rotating groups, believing that such a frequent supply of new recruits would provide a more effective defense force.[52]

50. Cumberland County Petition, [Mar. 5, 1781], Virginia Legislative Petitions, LiVi.

51. Leroy Peachey to Jefferson, Mar. 23, 1781, *Papers of Jefferson,* V, 219–221; Return of the Militia, Nov. 21, 1782, Executive Communications (oversize), LiVi.

52. Rockbridge County Petition, [Mar. 9, 1781], Virginia Legislative Petitions,

In the end, all of the petitions contained thinly veiled warnings to the legislature that it could not take their support of the war for granted. The petitioners from Orange County cautioned that the present law "tends greatly to aggreive us." Drafting men for eighteen months' service would jeopardize their support for the war. The prospect of such a long time in service would "so depress our spirits as to Cool our Zeal." The Berkeley petitioners also were explicit. Their situation was a "melancholy consideration." "If not Redress'd," they warned, it "will in future we fear, create great Uneasiness and heart burning amongst our people." The petitioners from Cumberland told the legislature that the law as it stood had a tendency to "disturb the minds of the people and lessens their zeal for the cause for which they are now contending." The petitioners demanded that the assembly suspend the act until it could be "more finally and impartially examined." If the legislature did not take these warnings of internal discontent seriously, farmers from Orange County added another possibility. Knowing how important unanimity was to the patriot cause, particularly amid rumors and actual revolts of the disaffected, they claimed that the law had a "Manifest tendancy to Awaken regret and so produce re[misness] in the minds of the people towards the great Cause . . . and Consequently to Brake union therein."[53]

LiVi. Orange County citizens, and "more Especially the malitia," made the same proposal, and also were most concerned about the length of service required. They had tried hiring men, but to no avail. Now, facing a draft for eighteen months, they worried that such a long separation from their families would be a disaster. They would lose at least two crops, they explained, which would bring "misery and ruin" to their families. Orange County Petition, [Mar. 14, 1781], Virginia Legislative Petitions, LiVi.

The petitioners from Orange and Rockbridge Counties also carefully pointed out the benefits of their alternative proposals. If the tour of duty were shorter, Rockbridge petitioners claimed, they would have a much more "healthy and effective Army." The petitioners from Cumberland also pointed out that soldiers raised under the present law would hardly "exert themselves in defending their Country with the same Zeal and Ardour with those who are induced to step forth on more equitable principles." Orange County Petition, [Mar. 14, 1781], Virginia Legislative Petitions, LiVi; Rockbridge County Petition, [Mar. 9, 1781], Virginia Legislative Petitions, LiVi; Cumberland County Petition, [Mar. 5, 1781], Virginia Legislative Petitions, LiVi.

53. Orange County Petition, [Mar. 14, 1781], Virginia Legislative Petitions, LiVi; Berkeley County Petition, [Mar. 7, 1781], Virginia Legislative Petitions,

• • • Faced with this groundswell of protest, the emergency assembly vacillated over what to do. Ostensibly, Jefferson had called the assembly together to debate three issues—the extension of the provision law, the lack of money in the treasury, and recruitment. Jefferson believed that, in the dangerous military circumstances, it ought to have been a short meeting. However, the mood of the people and the fact that new elections were scheduled for April meant that legislators were forced to tread carefully. The session lasted for a full three weeks, and every item on Jefferson's agenda engendered heated discussion and debate.[54]

Once again, instead of facing up to their immediate problems, the delegates quickly lashed out at Congress and the northern states. They appointed Patrick Henry, John Taylor, and John Tyler to draft a complaint to Congress. The three brought together and articulated a growing critique of Congress that had been gradually generating support among patriot leaders in Virginia, reporting what was later called a "Battery . . . against the Northern States." The remonstrance was scathing and reminded the northern states of their obligations to Virginia, opening by noting that the northern states had, "in times of their own need, used the affectionate appellation of Brethren" but had now "forgotten the duties of such a relationship." Virginia had in the past given its full support to the war while it raged to the north, "but when we came to look for our Northern allies, after we had thus exhausted our powers in their defence . . . they were not to be found." "Impoverished by defending the northern department," Virginia

LiVi; Cumberland County Petition, [Mar. 5, 1781], Virginia Legislative Petitions, LiVi. See also H. R. McIlwaine, ed., "Journal of the House of Delegates of Virginia, March 1781 Session," *Bulletin of the Virginia State Library,* XVII (1928–1930), 8–9.

54. Proclamation Convening the General Assembly, Jan. 23, 1781, Jefferson to the Members of the General Assembly, Jan. 23, 1781, *Papers of Jefferson,* IV, 432, 433–434; John E. Selby, *The Revolution in Virginia, 1775–1783* (Williamsburg, Va., 1988), 260–262. The session was marked by tension. Though Jefferson only meant to press on with absolutely necessary measures in the emergency session, some representatives tried to press their own agenda. First, a move was made to move the capital once more. The motion was defeated by a thin margin of seven. Then another motion was mooted that called for the recording of votes on any motion at the request of two or more delegates. Sensing problems at the polls, those in favor of the motion wanted voters to be able to distinguish "virtuous conduct" among the delegates from "vicious, weak or wicked conduct." The motion was rejected without a division.

was now completely exhausted fighting the southern war, which fell almost entirely to it to support. The remonstrance reflected the concerns of many of Virginia's taxpaying militia. Virginia's only resource was paper money, the remonstrance explained, of which it had been forced to emit twenty-one million pounds over the past three months. The "enormous taxes" it was forced to lay on its citizens to redeem the currency were particularly distressing because so many of its citizens were in the field serving as militia rather than raising their crops. On the other hand, it accused the northern states of using the opportunity of the war's moving southward to shore up their depreciating currency instead of raising new troops with which they could help the southern states. Virginia, they argued, could do little more. It needed the assistance of the other states, especially for men, money, and other military supplies. The remonstrance concluded with a warning: "If they are denied, the consequences be on the heads of those who refuse them. The Assembly of Virginia call the world and future generations to witness that they have done their duty."[55]

In the end, the remonstrance was not adopted, because Benjamin Harrison returned from a special envoy to Congress with promises of assistance before the committee could report to the House. Edmund Pendleton downplayed the remonstrance as a rough draft penned by one person alone and not even considered by the whole committee charged with preparing it. However, even Pendleton saw fit to send it to James Madison, one of Virginia's delegates to Congress. He told Madison not to publish it, but he did think that members of the Congress ought to be aware of the strength of feeling reflected in the petition. "It may not be improper perhaps for Congress to pay attention to the Sentiments."[56]

Pendleton grew particularly frustrated about the lack of forthcoming help from the northern states especially. A few weeks after he sent the "Bat-

55. Rives Family Papers, Alderman Library, UVa. The document appears to be in the hand of John Taylor, with a note that it was sent to James Madison by Edmund Pendleton. It was reprinted by William C. Rives in the *History of the Life and Times of James Madison,* I (Boston, 1859), 276–279. I have followed the manuscript version here.

56. Pendleton to Madison, Mar. 26, 1781, *Papers of Pendleton,* I, 346; Washington to Jefferson, Aug. 26, 1779, *Papers of Jefferson,* V, 76–77. Other prominent Virginians also continued to write to Madison and others in Congress complaining of the lack of northern help, including David Ross and David Jameson. See David Jameson to Madison, Aug. 10, 15, 1781, David Ross to Madison, May 18, 1781, *Papers of Madison,* III, 125–126, 215–216, 227–228.

tery" to Madison, he told him that Virginia was suffering badly because the militia had so often been out in service, their crops in particular irreparably damaged. Not only were more men away from their farms, but more crops were needed to actually feed the men in service. Pendleton was also growing impatient with the delayed arrival of reinforcements from the North, irritably reporting that he had heard rumors that the Pennsylvania line had refused to march southward. He felt they needed those troops as well as those of Lafayette to help drive off the British. A little later, he heard a report that the Pennsylvanians were actually holding back their troops. Instead, "Our people are made very angry by a Report that the Pennsylvania[ns] . . . were throwing out Insulting speeches that Virginia was too grand—let her be humbled by the Enemy, and such like."[57]

Patriot leaders also used popular sentiment about the French to push their Continental colleagues for help. Sentiments in favor of peace with Britain over the past few years had already revealed a degree of anti-French feeling, and George Mason thought that the latest British incursions had sparked a new and more pervasive anti-French outburst. After further British plundering up the Potomac in March, Mason told the Virginia delegates in Congress that many were dissatisfied with the extent of help forthcoming and that many of his neighbors had focused their censure on the French and the Spanish. A "general Opinion" prevailed that "our Allies are spinning out the War, in order to weaken America . . . and thereby leave us, at the End of it, as dependent as possible upon themselves." Mason could only sympathize with his less fortunate neighbors. "However unjust this Opinion may be," he wrote, "it is natural enough to Planters and Farmers burdened with heavy Taxes and frequently draged from their Familys upon military Duty, on the continual Alarms occasioned by the Superiority of the British Navy." Mason doubted patriot leaders' abilities to keep "our People much longer firm, in so unequal an Opposition to great Britain."[58]

57. Pendleton to Madison, Apr. 23, May 28, 1781, *Papers of Pendleton,* I, 351, 359. Pendleton also asked Madison directly, "Do Congress mean to leave the Weight of this Southern War entirely upon Virginia?" Pendleton to Madison, Apr. 7, 1781, I, 349.

58. George Mason to the Virginia Delegates in Congress, Apr. 3, 1781, *Papers of Mason,* II, 680–683. Cf. Mason to George Mason, Jr., June 3, 1781, II, 693–694. Jefferson also tried to push the French into helping the Virginians, writing directly to the French representative, Anne César de La Luzerne, with an appeal for help. Thinking that La Luzerne's last letter, which held out the promise of aid from France, would help "inspirit" the people, Jefferson told La Luzerne that they were

Under the growing belief that their northern and French allies had abandoned them, the legislature then turned its attention to home defense, which had now become critical. First, Jefferson's call to issue more money ran into difficulties between the Senate and the House. However, after much discussion and consultation, the assembly agreed to issue another ten million dollars, and up to fifteen million if required, which would be redeemed by the end of 1792. The House also had a long debate about a bill to extend the time for impressing clothes, beef, and wagons and for recruiting the army. The main sticking point seems to have been whether to control the prices assessed for impressed goods, which the assembly ultimately did. As far as the army was concerned, the assembly acknowledged that officials in some counties had suspended the draft because their militia had been called out. In other counties, the draft had proceeded "under great doubts and obstacles," because the time limit had expired. The assembly did not change the draft law, but only extended the time for collecting the bounty tax. The assembly did give the governor power to suspend the act if necessary. Perhaps more significantly, the assembly forbade the distress of any property to pay for the 2 percent tax on anyone in military service, reassuring militia that they would not lose their property while they were out in service.[59]

The assembly then tried to amend the militia law in accordance with Jefferson's directions to more effectively discourage desertion and compel men to turn out, but in the end did nothing. Not trusting the one-sided complaints of Steuben, or even the worries of Jefferson, the assembly wanted to investigate the problems reported in the militia for itself. In a close vote of thirty-two to twenty-seven, delegates sympathetic to the militia managed to defeat an amendment of the invasion law on its third reading in the House. The assembly decided to obtain a full report for its next session so that it could consider what changes were strictly necessary.[60]

---

unable to cope alone with the combined armies of the British and that many were increasingly bitter that the northern states were not sending help. The Cherokees also threatened in the west and had tied up almost three thousand men on the Ohio River. The militia could contain these threats, Jefferson thought, but they were not armed properly. "Under such circumstances it is not easy to foretell events, and it is natural for our People to ask if they are to have no help from others." Jefferson to La Luzerne, Apr. 12, 1781, *Papers of Jefferson*, V, 421–422.

59. Hening, comp., *Statutes at Large*, X, 393–395, 399–400; Selby, *Revolution in Virginia*, 261.

60. Jefferson to the Speaker of the House of Delegates, Mar. 9, 1781, *Papers of*

The assembly did, however, try to raise troops for a more effective home defense. Continental army officers, including Steuben, wanted a plan much like the old minuteman system, whereby forty-two hundred men would be on call for a year. Unwilling to put more pressure on the militia, the assembly called for more volunteers. Patrick Henry and a committee he headed reduced the number to less than a third of that number and called for volunteers, who would be trained more than the militia and receive the same pay as Continental soldiers and half pay when not in service. To encourage enlistments, they would receive a bounty of two thousand dollars and be exempt from any other military service but not exempt themselves from the current draft for Continental soldiers.[61]

• • • The special session ended on March 22. As the assembly adjourned, events took a turn for the worse. A new British fleet under Admiral Marriot Arbuthnot skirmished briefly with the French fleet off the Virginia capes and forced the French to set sail back to Rhode Island. Arbuthnot's fleet sailed into the bay and delivered General William Phillips with more than twenty-five hundred reinforcements for Arnold, who was still at Portsmouth. With their arrival, Lafayette and Steuben abandoned plans to attack Portsmouth, and Lafayette actually returned to his troops in Maryland, who had been on the way to join the attack. At almost the same time, news began to reach Virginia that Cornwallis had beaten the American army under Nathanael Greene at Guilford Courthouse in North Carolina, though Cornwallis had also incurred heavy losses. Steuben, frustrated in his attempts to attack Portsmouth, concocted another plan to use some of the troops amassing for the attack on Portsmouth to help reinforce Greene to the south. He called for two thousand militia for an expedition to North Carolina, believing that, if they could put pressure on Cornwallis, Phillips and Arnold would shift from Portsmouth and come to his aid.[62]

With a reinforced British army in the state, only promises of help from Congress, and little will among assembly members to help reinforce the southern army, Jefferson and the council decided otherwise—to stay out

---

Jefferson, V, 105 (and see 76 and notes); Selby, *Revolution in Virginia,* 260. The assembly did, however, try to figure out how many militia there were in the state (Hening, comp., *Statutes at Large,* X, 396).

61. Hening, comp., *Statutes at Large,* X, 391–393; Selby, *Revolution in Virginia,* 260–261.

62. Selby, *Revolution in Virginia,* 269–270, 274.

of North Carolina. They felt they could do little but try to secure Virginia itself. First, the executive used its newly legislated powers and suspended the draft for regular troops in another thirty-seven counties, most of which had militia out on duty. Calls on the militia induced the suspension of the draft in more than half of Virginia's counties. Then the executive blocked Steuben's efforts for the militia who were already out in service south of the James River to be sent to reinforce Greene. Though it had Lafayette's endorsement, Jefferson and the council decided that Steuben's plan was too risky and unlikely to work, given the temper of the militia. Moreover, they felt it would be impolitic to send so many armed militia southward when arms were in such short supply in Virginia. Instead, they agreed to try to reinforce Greene with a quarter of the militia from eleven south-western counties—where the draft had already been suspended—who they hoped would be able to furnish their own arms. Steuben was so disgusted that he announced he was going to join Greene in any case, who himself railed against the "partial views" of state authorities and wondered aloud whether Congress ought to change the rules about who should govern the militia when called out. Other Virginia military leaders, like General George Weedon, also complained about the lack of support for the plan, but they too had Virginia's interest in mind. Weedon lamented that the executive "have not an Idea beyond Local Security," but he supported the plan mainly because he thought it was best to keep the fighting out of the state if they could.[63]

By this point, most militia shared the council's reluctance to worry about distant battlefields. On top of recent calls for their service and in contrast to their recent and voluntary turnout against Cornwallis, militia in the southwestern counties reacted to the new call for their services southward with threats and protest. The militia were particularly angry that the assembly had not abandoned the recruiting act altogether, as many worried that they could serve in the militia and still end up being drafted. Because they would not be able to get a crop planted, they would have difficulty raising the 2 percent tax and buying themselves out of service, if necessary. Militia in the southwest made it clear that they would serve in the militia or help raise a more permanent army, not both. George Skillern of Bote-

63. *Papers of Jefferson,* V, 212n; Mar. 22, 29, 1781, McIlwaine et al., eds., *Journals of the Council,* II, 316, 322; Steuben to Greene, Mar. 27, 30, 1781, Weedon to Jefferson, Mar. 27, 1781, Weedon to Steuben, Apr. 1, 3, 1781, *Papers of Jefferson,* V, 262–263, 276n, 277n. Cf. Selby, *Revolution in Virginia,* 270.

tourt County explained that nonslaveholders would be particularly hard hit: "The Season of the year is Such, that to Call on men, with Families, and who have no Other possible means to support themselves and Families but by their own Labour, no other alternative but inevitable Ruin, must be the Consequence, for before their Return the season for Sowing and planting will be over." He also told the governor that, if they could now stay at home, they would "Easely" complete their draft. If they went unmolested now, they could be counted on to help out later "Chearfully," when "the Season will admit, and Should Necessaty require it." In all, within weeks of Jefferson's call to reinforce Greene, seven of the eleven counties had asked to be excused from the service. Robert Lawson also noted that even the men who did march to aid Greene did so "with the greatest reluctance." Lawson thought that most of the counties asked to send men had not sent nearly enough men; others had simply sent none at all.[64]

The situation closer to home was also growing darker. Under the pressure of repeated call-outs, the draft, and the loss of their crops, militia began to protest serving even in the lower counties of Virginia against

64. Robert Lawson to Jefferson, May 1, 4, 1781, George Skillern to Jefferson, Apr. 14, 1781, *Papers of Jefferson*, V, 449–450, 583–584, 598. In the face of this new call on the militia, a new complaint arose. Many began to claim that they were doing more than their fair share of military service, especially when compared to other counties. The militia of Charlotte County, for example, complained that they were "too Sensible they have more men in duty than any of the Neighbouring Counties" and were satisfied that they had done enough. Samuel McDowell of Rockbridge County told Jefferson that his militia had protested for the same reasons. His militia were determined that they will have "Eaqual Justice done them." Thomas Read to Jefferson, Apr. 4, 1781, Samuel McDowell to Jefferson, Apr. 20, 1781, *Papers of Jefferson*, V, 344–345, 507–508. Cf. James Barbour to Jefferson, May 2, 1781, V, 587–588; Jefferson to Samuel McDowell, Apr. 23, 1781, V, 541–542; Apr. 23, 1781, McIlwaine et al., eds., *Journals of the Council*, II, 340.

Other local officials were powerless to enforce state calls for their militia even had they wanted to. William Preston of Montgomery County in the southwest thought that as many as one-half of his militia were "disaffected, and . . . cannot be drawn into the service either by threats or otherwise." If he tried to punish them by law, he feared "they would either withdraw to the mountains, or embody and disturb the peace of the county." The other half of his militia were not enough to defend such a large county from depredations by the Indians, and he believed he could not call out any militia to go to the aid of General Greene. William Preston to Jefferson, Apr. 13, 1781, *Papers of Jefferson*, V, 437.

the British, with greater vehemence. Throughout March and April, Jefferson tried to keep enough militia in the field in the lower counties to defend against any further incursions by the British stationed in Portsmouth under General Phillips. As the season grew late, farmers serving in the militia grew increasingly desperate to get home to plant their year's crops. William Constable, General Muhlenberg's aide-de-camp, told Steuben in early April, "The militia begin to be much dissatisfied." They had been asked by the governor to stay on until reinforcements arrived, but Constable believed they would not stay an hour beyond the term for which they were called. They had already begun to desert, and Constable feared, "If the other men do not arrive in a short time our numbers will be reduced to almost nothing."[65]

• • • As Virginia's defense collapsed, the new mood of the militia was troubling for many patriot leaders. Some, like George Weedon, continued to read such resistance as a symptom of the lack of authority the fledgling government enjoyed. Weedon despaired that the executive had no power or authority over the militia, or even its officers. Indeed, as Robert Wooding pointed out, even the "Gentlemen" of some counties sided with their militia in defiance of orders from the state government.[66]

But what figures like Weedon and Wooding seemed not to grasp was the fact that many militia protested the onerous demands on their time and property precisely because of their attachment to the new government, and their *own* reading of the principles of that government. As militia increasingly claimed in more frequent, explicit, and demanding petitions, they believed the Revolution had been fought to guard against all "arbitrary and partial proceedings." They claimed that the Bill of Rights, as they understood it, gave them a "Fundamental right" to protect their livelihood and their property. Moreover, their service in defense of the new state, however limited it might have been, gave them further cause to judge whether laws were "oppressive and wrong," to demand "Eaqual Justice," and to

65. William Constable to Steuben, Apr. 7, 1781, *Papers of Jefferson,* V, 295. Cf. French Strother to Jefferson, Mar. 28, 1781, William Call to Jefferson, Apr. 6, 1781, William Preston to Jefferson, Apr. 10, 1781, James Callaway to Jefferson, Apr. 11, 1781, James Slaughter to Jefferson, Apr. 11, 1781, Jefferson to Samuel Cox, Apr. 14, 1781, V, 272, 358, 398–399, 402–403, 407–408, 444.

66. Weedon to Jefferson, Mar. 28, 1781, Robert Wooding to Jefferson, Apr. 18, 1781, ibid., 273, 495–496. Cf. Jefferson to Wooding, Apr. 21, 1781, 530.

think themselves "entitled on the present great and pressing emergency to be heard." Indeed, militia were as quick to assert they would "Chearfully march On" if justice was done them as they were in predicting dire consequences if not. At stake was the fundamental nature of the new government. As Amherst County militia had pointed out, while they enjoyed the "inestimable Blessings of a free and frequent Representation," they expected that "Impartial Justice and Judgment" would be "dispersed (as far as is Consistent with the General Commonweall) to every Individual Member of the State." In their written complaints and their outright defiance of executive orders, of course, the militia were only putting truly democratic principles into practice.[67]

67. Cumberland County Petition, [Mar. 5, 1781], Berkeley County Petition, [Mar. 7, 1781], Charlotte County Petition, [May 26, 1780], Virginia Legislative Petitions, LiVi; Samuel McDowell to Jefferson, Apr. 20, 1781, *Papers of Jefferson,* V, 507–508; Petition and Memorial of Sundry Militiamen of Amherst County, Oct. 9, 1780, LiVi.

CHAPTER 13 *Defeat*

Perhaps aware of the divisions within Virginia, in mid-April 1781 the British began moving up the James River again and for the next two months ranged virtually unopposed across the heart of Virginia. Their advances culminated in a strike against Charlottesville—where the General Assembly had adjourned to for safety—and they came within an hour of capturing Governor Thomas Jefferson himself, who was forced to flee his hilltop home, Monticello. Taking advantage of the presence and ambitions of a restive enslaved population, the British were able to paralyze state defenses and encourage further disaffection.

Taking their cue from patriot leaders, most ordinary Virginians made the best terms they could in the circumstances. Even in the midst of the disintegration of Virginia's defense, militia still protected their interests, demanded concessions, and resisted all efforts to draft them into the army. When militia were forced to serve, they most often revolted. Panic-stricken leaders, unable to raise an army, call out sufficient militia, and protect themselves, increasingly lashed out at the northern states and called for a dictator within their own. With the arrival of Washington and Continental and French reinforcements later in the summer, Virginians were able to limp toward Yorktown, where allied forces forced the surrender of Cornwallis despite, rather than because of, Virginia's support.

• • • As had become usual, Jefferson heard that the British were on their way up the James River again only well after the fact. One detachment quickly overwhelmed the lower Peninsula and swept through both Yorktown and Williamsburg. It stopped at the Chickahominy River shipyard and destroyed all work in progress before sailing up the James again. Taking advantage of Virginia's largely undefended waterways, within a few days the British landed at City Point (about midway between Williamsburg and Richmond) but decided against another attack on the capital. Moving against Petersburg instead, the British ran into about one thousand militia under Baron von Steuben (who had remained in the state after all) at Blandford (on the Appomattox). After skirmishing with the militia — for which the militia earned praise—the British occupied Petersburg and initiated a series of devastating raids in the surrounding countryside. In one raid on Osborne's Wharf (above City Point) on the James, they burned or captured about twenty ships, the bulk of Virginia's fledgling navy, that had been gathering there to attack Portsmouth. The ships, like the army, were badly undermanned, with only 78 crewmen present of a full complement of 590. In another raid, the British attacked Chesterfield Courthouse (a little farther west of Osborne's Wharf), where some of the new Continental army recruits were gathering. They burned the barracks and hundreds of barrels of flour and other stores. At the same time that Generals William Phillips and Benedict Arnold began their push up the James River, the Royal Navy and many independent privateers began plundering the shores of the Chesapeake farther north, in Maryland and along the Potomac, spreading panic further afield.[1]

The British continued their punishing raids in the piedmont into early May, reaching as far as Manchester, where they destroyed more than a thousand hogsheads of tobacco. Upon learning of the return of Lafayette, who reached Richmond in late April with twelve hundred Continental troops detached from the northern army, Arnold and Phillips hesitated and began withdrawing back to Portsmouth. However, just as they began pulling back, Cornwallis sent word that he was on his way to join them from North Carolina. After the battle of Guilford Courthouse, a shaken Cornwallis moved eastward toward the coast, leaving the way open for General Nathanael Greene to make a move to recover South Carolina and Georgia for the patriots. As it turned out, though, Greene's southern focus also cleared the way for Cornwallis to move into Virginia. Contrary to all expectations, Cornwallis moved north and ordered Phillips to meet him at Petersburg. Phillips and Arnold immediately turned back up the James and were back in Petersburg by May 8. There they waited for Cornwallis, who finally

1. Apr. 19, 21, May 8, 1781, H. R. McIlwaine et al., eds., *Journals of the Council of the State of Virginia* (Richmond, Va., 1931–1982), II, 337, 339, 343; John E. Selby, *A Chronology of Virginia and the War of Independence, 1763–1783* (Charlottesville, Va., 1973), 42–43; Selby, *The Revolution in Virginia, 1775–1783* (Williamsburg, Va., 1988), 271–273; Sylvia R. Frey, *Water from the Rock: Black Resistance in a Revolutionary Age* (Princeton, N.J., 1991), 158, 160–161. For the militia engagement at Petersburg, see undated draft of Steuben's report of the Battle of Petersburg, *Papers of Jefferson,* V, 550n.

arrived on May 20. A few days later, more British reinforcements arrived from New York. With almost seven thousand troops in the middle of the state, the British now appeared unstoppable. The British raids brought the state to its knees.[2]

• • • Enslaved Virginians reopened the most glaring wound inflicted by the British incursions. The British had turned their attention to the southern states and Virginia in particular precisely because they had had first-hand experience and knowledge that many black Virginians would welcome their presence and aid them in the conflict. Enslaved Virginians did not disappoint them this time, either. Those in the central piedmont especially had previously never had much chance to take refuge behind British lines. When the opportunity presented itself, many did not hesitate to take advantage.

Some turned on their masters first. Jack of Botetourt County tried to poison a Captain Madison and Major Quirk when the British invaded the state. He then set about "Engaging and Enlisting several negroes to Raise in Arms and Join the British." Jack was to be their captain. After getting caught, Jack broke out of jail and helped free a number of deserters and the disaffected who were in chains with him, and hid out for weeks before being caught again. While in hiding, Jack must have struck fear into whites in the area. One man said he was at large, "behaving in the most Insolent and Daring manner—Sometimes armed with a gun, Pistol etc," and "Threatening Revenge upon those that apprehended him and the witnesses." He was well known to neighbors as a "rebellious Servant and corrupter of other Servants." They demanded that the court execute him and make him "an example of Justice and not of Mercy."[3]

Most enslaved Virginians, though, believed their best chances lay with reaching the British. Billy from Dittingen Parish in Prince William County took his chances when British ships headed up the Potomac, for example. In early April, he helped the enemy and joined a ship with others to wage

2. For a summary report of British movements and militia action, see Jefferson to the Speaker of the House of Delegates, May 10, 1781, *Papers of Jefferson,* V, 626; Selby, *Revolution in Virginia,* 273–275; Frey, *Water from the Rock,* 158–159.

3. Wm. P. Palmer et al., eds., *Calendar of Virginia State Papers and Other Manuscripts, 1652–1781, Preserved in the Capitol at Richmond* (Richmond, Va., 1875–1893), I, 477–478, and Patrick Lockhart to Governor Nelson, Nov. 16, 1781, II, 604–605.

war against the state. Patriot forces soon captured Billy, and, after a quick trial, the court found him guilty. Betraying their anxiety in the midst of the British invasion, the members of the court wanted to make a public example of Billy in order to try to deter other enslaved Virginians from following suit. On May 8, the court sentenced Billy to hang, and afterward his head would be cut off and "Stuck up at some Publick Cross Road on a pole." Not all attempts ended so disastrously for enslaved Virginians. As British and patriot forces sparred around Hanover County, for example, two enslaved Virginians stole a horse belonging to Robert Honyman's neighbor and made a bid to join the British. They were recaptured by a group of Virginia cavalry but in the confusion of the skirmishing escaped and joined the British again.[4]

The British army facilitated and encouraged such ventures. When the British left Manchester, for example, in early May, they reportedly carried off huge stocks of horses and cattle and many enslaved Virginians. Edmund Pendleton thought that the British plunder in slaves was "immence," noting that from Yorktown alone the British had shipped 360 enslaved Virginians. When Phillips and Arnold began their initial withdrawal along the James River, Pendleton said they were "sweeping all the slaves and other property and Pillaging and destroying Houses" in their path. Though white Virginians complained that the British took enslaved Virginians as plunder, most knew that blacks sought their own freedom when the British came calling. Robert Honyman admitted in May that the British troops, officers and soldiers alike, had "enticed and flattered the Negroes, and prevailed on vast numbers to go along with them, but they did not compel any." Indeed, thought Honyman, enslaved Virginians "flocked to the Enemy from all quarters even from the remote parts." Moreover, enslaved Virginians were willing to make a run for the British lines despite many rumors that the British were apt to sell them in the West Indies or make them labor for the troops.[5]

4. Extract of Court Records, Prince William County, [June 7, 1781], Virginia Legislative Petitions, LiVi; June 1, 1781, Diary of Robert Honyman, Jan. 2, 1776–Mar. 11, 1782, Alderman Library, UVa (microfilm). Cf. Frey, *Water from the Rock*, 156–157; *Journal of the House of Delegates* (Williamsburg, Va., 1776–), May 1781, 11; H. J. Eckenrode, *The Revolution in Virginia* (1916; rpt., Hamden, Conn., 1964), 259.

5. May 11, June 5, July 22, 1781, Diary of Honyman; Selby, *Revolution in Virginia*, 274; Edmund Pendleton to James Madison, May 7, 1781, *Papers of Pendle-*

The loss of their enslaved population took a devastating toll on Virginian slaveholders, particularly wealthy ones. Honyman thought that some planters had lost "20, 30, 40, 50, 60 or 70 Negroes besides their stocks of cattle, sheep and horses." The damage the British had done and the losses inflicted on white Virginians, claimed Honyman, were "unspeakable." St. George Tucker's wife lost her entire workforce. Thomas Jefferson lost twenty-three of his enslaved population. Along the Potomac and Rappahannock Rivers, planters also suffered. When the British raided Mount Vernon, seventeen enslaved Virginians fled, including some of Washington's most-trusted house servants and artisans. Richard Henry Lee's brother William Lee lost as many as sixty-five enslaved Virginians, including, according to Richard Henry, about forty-five "valuable grown slaves and useful Artisans." William Lee's neighbors also "lost every slave they had in the world, and Mr. Paradise has lost all but one," according to Richard Henry Lee, who concluded that this was the case "of all those who were near the enemy." John Banister lost eleven slaves in the first British raid on Petersburg; when the British suddenly returned in early May, the rest of his enslaved population vanished.[6]

Enslaved Virginians ran off in such numbers that propertied Virginians put the protection of their valuables ahead of the common defense. Many planters again moved their livestock and enslaved population "up the country" and out of the way of the British. Honyman believed that, during the enemy's advance in late May, many people were moving their

---

ton, I, 354. Pendleton lamented, "So infatuated are these wretches that they continue to go to them, notwithstanding many who have excaped inform others of their ill treatment."

6. May 11, 27, 1781, Diary of Honyman; Ira Berlin, *Many Thousands Gone: The First Two Centuries of Slavery in North America* (Cambridge, Mass., 1998), 259; Richard Henry Lee to William Lee, July 15, 1781, to George Washington, Sept. 17, 1781, James Curtis Ballagh, ed., *The Letters of Richard Henry Lee* (New York, 1911), II, 242, 256; John Banister to Theodorick Bland, May 16, 1781, Charles Campbell, ed., *The Bland Papers: Being a Selection from the Manuscripts of Colonel Theodorick Bland, Jr.* (Petersburg, Va., 1840, 1843), II, 68–70; Selby, *Revolution in Virginia,* 275; Frey, *Water from the Rock,* 159, 167. Cf. Cassandra Pybus, "Jefferson's Faulty Math: The Question of Slave Defections in the American Revolution," *WMQ,* 3d Ser., LXII (2005), 243–264. Pybus notes that Honyman and others probably exaggerated cases of slaves' running away but, by the time Cornwallis dug in at Yorktown, he had as many as two thousand escaped Virginia slaves with him.

"Negroes, Cattle, Horses etc. from the route which it is supposed they will take." Many patriot leaders also took flight. Pendleton, Richard Henry Lee, and eventually George Mason were among the more prominent Virginians who abandoned their homes when the British were in the piedmont. Even Thomas Nelson, who was at the head of the Virginia militia who had turned out, took the time in the face of Cornwallis's advance to return to his Hanover County plantation to pack up some of his property and his family and send them to safety. Some, like Pendleton, took as many enslaved Virginians and as much property as they could convey; others fled for their lives, presumably just as worried about the British as they were about the effect of the British presence on their enslaved population.[7]

• • • With wealthy white planters and patriot leaders on the run to protect their property, ordinary white Virginians also looked after themselves. In response to the British incursions, Jefferson ordered out as many militia as there were arms from as many as forty-four mainly piedmont and southside counties. Few counties could or did comply. The county lieutenant of Bedford, James Callaway, told the governor that he would get few men to comply with the order; he could send only about 130 militia. Callaway insisted that it was mainly poorer Virginians who refused to turn out, despite his best efforts. Many of the militia had refused to go because of the "Extreem Busy Season of the Year." He asserted that this reason was particularly strong "among the Common People" and "Exceeds their Conception of the Necessity of Turning out." Even despite the British presence a few counties away, Callaway said they were particularly adamant about not serving, "Especially as the enemy is not immediately Pressing upon them."[8]

But, as Phillips and Arnold made their way up the James River, militia in their pathway also stayed at home. Honyman thought that "numbers" who could not move themselves out of the path of the enemy hid in nearby woods instead. James Innes, leading the militia in the Williamsburg area

7. May 27, 30, 1781, Diary of Honyman; Frey, *Water from the Rock,* 166; Emory G. Evans, *Thomas Nelson of Yorktown: Revolutionary Virginian* (Williamsburg, Va., 1975), 100–101; Pendleton to Madison, July 6, 1781, *Papers of Pendleton,* I, 265, 267; Richard Henry Lee to Arthur Lee, May 31, 1781, Ballagh, ed., *Letters of Richard Henry Lee,* II, 230; Mason to Pearson Chapman, May 31, 1781, *Papers of Mason,* II, 688; Selby, *Revolution in Virginia,* 271–272.

8. Apr. 14, 19, May 7, 8, 1781, McIlwaine et al., eds., *Journals of the Council,* II, 335, 337, 343; James Callaway to Jefferson, May 21, 1781, *Papers of Jefferson,* VI, 3.

against the initial British thrust, could not raise any reinforcements as he fell back before the new invasion. He told Jefferson that he had "in vain called for the aid of the adjacent Counties." Though Jefferson tried to order out counties farther up the James River, even they were extremely tardy in assembling. After two days of waiting, Jefferson complained that no militia had yet shown up at the rendezvous. John Banister thought, "The people are tired of the war, and come to the field most reluctantly." Five days after the initial emergency call-out, only three hundred men had turned out.[9]

Ordinary Virginians were also worried about the ever-present threat from enslaved Virginians. Edmund Randolph later recalled that the poor militia turnouts in the face of the British raids in 1781 were due to enslaved Virginians. "The helpless wives and children were at the mercy not only of the males among the slaves but of the very women, who could handle deadly weapons; and these could not have been left in safety in the absence of all authority of the masters and of union among neighbors."[10]

In these circumstances, desperate recruiters resurrected James Madison's proposal to arm enslaved Virginians. Major Alexander Dick was one patriot who thought they ought to give it a try in the desperate days of the spring of 1781. Trying to recruit men for one of the three regiments for the new state forces in 1781, Dick suggested that Virginia formalize an already informal practice of allowing enslaved Virginians to enlist in the army. Dick was having trouble and believed that there was "no probability of recruiting the Regiment" with white Virginians. Echoing James Madison's suggestion, Dick argued that they should consider accepting "likely young negro fellow's" from planters who would then be given compensation. Anyone who would compel an enslaved Virginian into service would also gain a personal exemption from future military service, he contended. In turn, the enslaved recruit would "be declared free upon inlisting for the War at the end of which, they shall be intitled to all the benefits of Conl. Sol-

9. June 5, 1781, Diary of Honyman; James Innes to Jefferson, Apr. 22, 1781, *Papers of Jefferson,* V, 532–533; John Banister to Theodorick Bland, May 16, 1781, Campbell, ed., *Bland Papers,* II, 68–70; Jefferson to James Innes, Apr. 21, 1781, to George Weedon, Apr. 23, 1781, *Papers of Jefferson,* V, 521, 546. Cf. Jefferson to Benjamin Harrison, Apr. 22, 1781, to Steuben, Apr. 26, 1781, *Papers of Jefferson,* V, 532, 560.

10. Edmund Randolph, *History of Virginia,* ed. Arthur H. Shaffer (Charlottesville, Va., 1970), 285. Perhaps surprisingly, there were actually few contemporary accounts of ordinary Virginians' fears of slaves during the war.

diers." Dick believed that the plan would succeed because enslaved soldiers would make for good recruits and, without a trace of irony, felt that "the men will be equal to any." Perhaps because he had inadvertently pointed out the perils of such a plan, the legislature did not take up his suggestion. There were other obvious objections, but possibly one of the more important reasons more white Virginians did not support the move was that too many enslaved Virginians had, so far, shown little inclination to support their patriot masters.[11]

Instead, the government still relied on a people who were increasingly unhappy about supporting the war. By this point, many Virginians were reluctant to aid the patriot cause in any way. Many were tired of giving supplies—through both impressments and taxes—and getting little back. They also no longer trusted state agents who usually had to give out certificates instead of cash. Richard Claiborne, who was responsible for helping to supply the army, told Steuben that he could not procure any horses, despite his best efforts. He had employed "Gentlemen of interest and influence," but they had only told him that there was a "General dissatisfaction and Suspicion among the people that they are determined not to suffer themselves to be deceived any longer, by being connected with contracts on public account." Claiborne told both Steuben and Jefferson, "Faith in general among the people towards the Public is totally lost . . . nothing is to be had unless necessity obliges them to it, without the cash or some personal private obligation is rendered to them." Claiborne thought the point had been reached in which "the Citizen will do nothing without being compeled by Military force."[12]

George Mason revealed that few would stand for such compulsion either. Readying himself for a rapid departure from his home in Fairfax County, Mason said that his neighbors were angry, particularly about the latest order for seizing live cattle for the supply of the armed forces. It had produced, he said, "Confusion and Oppression in this Part of the Country." He believed the law had to be clarified, or there would be "most probably Violence." He warned Jefferson that citizens in the new Republic would not stand for new oppressions. "The People in this Part of Virginia are well disposed to do every thing in their Power to support the war; but the same

11. Alexander Dick to the Speaker of the House, May 11, 1781, box 2, Executive Communications, LiVi.

12. Richard Claiborne to Steuben, May 18, 20, 1781, *Papers of Jefferson,* V, 669–670, 667n. Cf. Matthew Pope to Jefferson, May 31, 1781, VI, 53–54.

Principles which attach them to the American Cause will incline them to resist Injustice or Oppression." Many did. Few seemed willing even to aid Lafayette, who was plagued with problems supplying and clothing his detachment on the way down from Maryland. His commissioners could find few goods for sale in the countryside, and he could not even impress goods. "On our Approach," Lafayette complained, "Waggons and Horses Have Been Sent out of the Way."[13]

Instead of sacrificing themselves and more of their property, in the extraordinary circumstances many ordinary white Virginians copied their black neighbors and sought the protection of the British. While in the state, the British offered paroles to any militia who would promise not to take up arms against the British any longer. The British justified this practice because it was common to offer paroles to captured prisoners, who would and could be returned on a promise that they would not return to fight. The British were happy to offer such paroles to anyone enrolled in the Virginia militia, many of whom were equally happy to thereby exempt themselves from further military service. With many wealthy Virginians already exempt, many militia seeking paroles felt justified in doing likewise. Moreover, whereas many propertied Virginians spent most of their time in flight with their slaves, cattle, horses, and other valuable effects, many Virginians less able to flee could only stand their ground. Taking a parole from the British was often the only way to stop the British from plundering a farm or taking away as captives the men in the household.

The British had begun to offer paroles the previous fall, in 1780, when General Alexander Leslie invaded the state. So many people had taken paroles that Governor Jefferson felt compelled to outlaw the practice. Jefferson thought that, though some Virginians had taken the paroles out of fear or ignorance, others had done so with a design to avoid any further military service. Jefferson also admitted that there were many who had "voluntarily gone in to the enemy and tendered such paroles." Yet, despite the governor's prohibition, militia continued to take advantage. When the British came calling at Hampton in Elizabeth City County in the fall of 1780, for example, they did so after militia officers told their men that "every man who had a Family" could retire and "do the best for them they could." The officers later told the assembly that they had been forced to put the "Personal welfare of their wives Children and themselves with

13. Mason to Jefferson, May 14, 1781, Lafayette to Jefferson, Apr. 17, 21, 25, 1781, *Papers of Jefferson*, V, 477, 523-524, 553-554, 647-649.

their property" first and make terms with the British. When the British invaded in 1781, Virginians again took advantage of proffered paroles. Robert Honyman reported in early June, in the midst of the most recent British invasion, that "many people seem very fond of these paroles," for they believed it would "hereafter secure them from military service." Many people had gone voluntarily to the British, requested their protection, and been given their paroles. The county lieutenant of Elizabeth City later reported that the British had issued paroles to "most of the militia."[14]

As Jefferson well knew, the parole issue showed just how blurred the lines were between the disaffected, the treasonous, and the farmer desperate to protect his property. Certainly the disaffected and disloyal among Virginians were getting bolder with the presence and success of the British. In Bedford County, for example, the leaders of the insurrection of the previous year threatened county leaders again early in 1781. They were only waiting for the right moment to rally others who were becoming more hostile. Though they had been officially pardoned, they felt little obligation to the state, the county lieutenant claimed, as they had been told by their attorneys "that they had done nothing Capitol for which they could be Punished, and that they were not in need of such a Law." By late May, problems in Bedford had become wider-spread. David Ross told the governor that his brother had told him that "a pretty general consternation has seized the people there." Ross thought it was because of the rapid progress the British had made. He told Jefferson that many people believed they could no longer oppose the British, so they were ready to make terms with them. One Williamsburg merchant was more explicit. John Greenhow told a militia officer to "lay aside his Sword because we were already conquered."[15]

As the British made progress through the state, more disaffected Virginians were exposed in their wake. During Phillips's invasion, many people in his path did more than just offer paroles, according to patriot offi-

14. Proclamation concerning Paroles, Jan. 19, 1781, *Papers of Jefferson,* IV, 403–404; Elizabeth City County Petition, [Mar. 8, 1781], Virginia Legislative Petitions, LiVi; June 5, 1781, Diary of Honyman; Colonel Roe Cowper to the Governor, Aug. 9, 1782, Palmer et al., eds., *Calendar of State Papers,* III, 253. Cf. James Innes to Jefferson, Oct. [21?], 1780, General Assembly of North Carolina to Jefferson, Feb. 14, 1781, *Papers of Jefferson,* IV, 55, 610–611.

15. James Callaway to Jefferson, Mar. 23, 1781, David Ross to William Davies, May 27, 1781, *Papers of Jefferson,* V, 213, VI, 23–24n; Evans, *Thomas Nelson,* 100.

cials. On the heels of the British departure, Jefferson wrote to James Innes, who was due to return to Williamsburg to reassert control over the area, giving him instructions on how to proceed. Jefferson was furious. He had received information that many citizens in James City and York especially had committed acts, "some of which amount to high Treason." Jefferson worried, though, that they would never be able to gather evidence against the offenders, because they were concealed by the British invasion.[16]

The people of the exposed Northern Neck showed just how difficult it would be to get convictions for high treason, for different reasons. Some simply refused to serve any longer. In Westmoreland County, William Holland, a militia captain, refused to turn out when called to guard against British plundering up the Potomac. Holland had had enough and was desperate to avoid losing his property. He was also more than a little resentful toward citizens in the northern states. He told his neighbors that the reason he would not turn out to act as a guard was that "the people in Boston, New York and Phil: that stay'd by their property rescued it, and those that flew into the Country and took up arms lost it totally." He "swore by God if the enemy came upon the spott, he would not take up arms in defence of his country, but would stay by his property and would make the best terms he could."[17]

Others curried enough support among their neighbors to gain sufficient protection. In Northumberland County, Thomas Gaskins, the county lieutenant, asked Jefferson for help against a certain Joseph Hurst, who had apparently "bid defiance against all men who are friends to the American cause." Gaskins said he could arrest Hurst but that there was little point in trying him in the county, for he had too much support. "The people are so much poisoned by him and others of the same stamp," Gaskins complained. It would be particularly bad if Hurst were taken up and released, for Gaskins feared that he would only mock the authority of the patriot leaders. Hurst would "boast more than ever and take up more of the people than before." His county was "much divided" already; Hurst thus had the potential to do much greater mischief.[18]

16. Jefferson to James Innes, May 2, 1781, *Papers of Jefferson,* V, 593–594.

17. Affidavits of Saunders, Harper, and Washington, June 25, 1781, Beesly Edgar Joel to the Governor, July 2, 1781, Palmer et al., eds., *Calendar of State Papers,* II, 183, 196. A few months earlier, Holland had been granted an ordinary license in Westmoreland (May 29, 1781, Westmoreland County Court Orders, 1776–1786).

18. Thomas Gaskins to Jefferson, Mar. 17, 1781, *Papers of Jefferson,* V, 165.

Still others banded together to act collectively in defiance of the state. In Richmond County, disaffected militia allied to oppose local authorities in the very midst of the British invasion. After suffering through the draft in March, the county had been continually alarmed throughout the spring as British privateers were plundering along the riversides. By the end of May, many militia believed it was time to bring their suffering to a halt. When the county lieutenant issued yet another call-out of the militia, a "conspiracy" was set on foot by Fauntleroy Dye and Edward Wright. Dye and Wright, hearing of the call-out, called a meeting of neighbors and friends to plan a strategy to disrupt the planned mobilization. They decided to hold a "Barbecue" at a Daniel Wilson's house, on the same day the first division of the militia was supposed to go on duty. The purpose of the barbecue was supposedly to "try the strength of their party and to take Men from Meeting to exercise."[19]

At their meeting, they appointed two men, Avery Dye (Fauntleroy's son) and James Jenkins, as sergeants and instructed them to mimic the mechanism for calling in the militia by getting them to "warn in" all the men from the militia. By the time of the muster, almost all of the first division of militia had been "warn'd in." Some of them had been approached surreptitiously. A short time before the barbecue, Dye quietly invited two men and told them "it was a Place for all such persons to come to, who did not want to serve their country." Those who came to the barbecue, Dye said, "would determine to oppose any call of the Militia." The conspirators were confident that they could get sufficient numbers out to their alternative to the muster. Jenkins allegedly boasted that they "expected in a little time they should be able to get a sufficient Number to Oppose sufficiently the Militia's going out against any Force in the country and nothing but a force from the Army could raise [resist?] them." Dye had also boasted earlier that he could "raise a considerable Mobb." Significantly, though, to protect the leaders Dye and Wright, they were to assume leadership only "when they had got Men enough." Dye later admitted that only when he had "got

19. This and the following paragraphs have been put together from the various depositions contained in the Proceedings of a General Court Martial held at Leeds Town, June 18–19, 1781, Executive Papers, LiVi. The record of the court-martial, complete with testimony from witnesses, is a rare surviving document from the period and is a fascinating (though sometimes frustratingly sketchy) record of the incipient uprising in Richmond and the contours of popular discontent in the war in general.

a sufficient Number" would he "head them and Oppose the Measures of Government." Few people involved, however, were in doubt about who was behind the conspiracy. Supporters of the revolt described Dye and Wright as "good Leading Men."[20]

The conspiracy provoked serious debate among the militia. Zachariah White later recalled a conversation with William Ryals, who tried to persuade White to come to the barbecue by saying they had "two very good backers." Significantly, White refused to join the conspiracy, in part because he believed it was illegal but also because he mistrusted Dye and Wright. White remonstrated with Ryals "against such conduct and . . . endeavoured to shew him that Dye from his infamous Character would be unable to do any thing and as Wrights Character was but bad 'twas probable that Ryals would be left in the lurch." White, however, could not stop Ryals from going, as the latter was confident that they would have enough men to oppose the militia call-out. The contours of the debate that raged among the lower sort at the time are only thinly masked by the simple report of John Faucet, who testified that he believed that the barbecue was made by "disaffected persons for bad purposes and therefore [I] purswaded many from going to it." Still, Dye and Wright managed to get together "a party of Torys" who pledged "sooner to die than perform their tour of duty."

Some of the men that Dye and Wright persuaded to join them were deserters from the Continental army who were drafted in March. Richmond County was required to raise thirty-two men. At best, only eighteen made it to the army, leaving perhaps as many as fourteen at large in the county. At least three men involved in the incipient uprising were deserters who had been drafted to serve eighteen months. One was Daniel Wilson, who hosted the barbecue. These men had most to lose, for they faced the possibility of the death penalty if they were caught. When Thomas Awsbury, employed as an express rider for Richmond and Westmoreland Counties, went to the barbecue "to see what they were about," he found Wright, Dye, and "three deserters, two of which had Guns," and "some other people." When he first got to the house, one of the armed deserters,

20. The practice of "warning in" militia for duty when called for was common. Usually, as in this instance, a sergeant was employed to call around to all those needed or involved and to notify them of when and where to meet (see pension application of Wright Bond, Cumberland County, John Frederick Dorman, comp., *Virginia Revolutionary Pension Applications* [Washington, D.C., 1958–], VIII, 35).

Griffin [Crank?], "put his Gun out of the Window and swore he would kill any damn'd raskill that came after him."[21]

The barbecue ultimately failed, and state forces crushed the incipient uprising. When local officials appealed for help, Colonel William Nelson sent Major Beesly Edgar Joel into the county, who late in the evening of June 11, with a Major Vincent Redman and a party of "mounted Volluntrs," seized one man named Telfin, "a most notorious promoter of sedition," and then proceeded to the house of Fauntleroy Dye. Joel's men surrounded the house and called for the occupants, "a party of men in the loft," to surrender. The men at first refused and called out to Joel, "Come on, we will have life for life by God—We have arms plenty." Joel then ordered his men to set fire to the house, upon which the men in the loft "call'd for quarter and gave up." In the house, Joel found "the Sons of old Die" and Wilson the draft dodger, all of whom had their "Musketts loaded, and Bayonets fixt in Bed with them." Dye himself escaped, and Joel thought he had gone over to the British. Many believed he would try to procure a ship and continue to harass patriots in his county by plundering. However, Dye was captured within a few days, having hidden out in a very thick wood. Joel also rounded up a number of others who he believed were involved.[22]

At the court-martial that followed, only Dye and Wright were actually tried. Dye was charged with aiding and assisting the enemy during an invasion, encouraging desertion, and dissuading and discouraging the militia from opposing the enemy. Wright was charged only with discouraging the militia. Significantly, both were convicted only of dissuading and discouraging the militia from opposing the enemy, and Wright was also convicted of encouraging desertion from the army. The court-martial sentenced both to imprisonment for the duration of the war, and they were sent to Richmond.[23]

21. Testimony of John Marks, Thomas Awsbury, and Daniel Connelly, Proceedings of a General Court Martial, June 18–19, 1781, Executive Papers, LiVi.

22. Major Beesly Edgar Joel to Colonel William Nelson, June 12, 1781, Palmer et al., eds., *Calendar of State Papers,* II, 155, 156. Cf. George Weedon to the Governor, June 22, 1781, II, 180.

23. Weedon to the Governor, June 22, 1781, with enclosures, Proceedings of the General Court Martial, June 18–19, 1781, Executive Papers, LiVi. On June 23, the council resolved that Dye was "disaffected to the Independence of the United States and attached to their enemies" and told the county lieutenant of Richmond to remove him from the county, to some place secure, distant from the tidewater, and

The convictions and sentence were light because, despite their bravado, Dye and Wright were not necessarily the determined disaffected ringleaders they had been portrayed as in some of the testimony given to the court-martial. Indeed, Wright in particular emerges from a careful reading of the testimony as a desperate man who was more concerned about how he would feed his family than the politics of the Revolution. Wright had originally grown anxious when patriot leaders imposed another draft in January. As the day of the draft approached, Wright warned a neighbor, Samuel Stowers, that the "Gentlemen in Richmon[d County] had better not put him upon the Muster Roll." In an angry outburst that betrayed his anxiety, Wright told Stowers that, if he was drafted, he would "run over to the Enemy and get on board one of their Ships, and as he knew the Rivers and the Channels all over the State he would conduct the Enemies Ships for them." Wright boasted that he had been taken off the muster rolls in Westmoreland, where he had lived previously, because "the Gentlemen knew his Design and were affraid of him."[24]

Wright's several references to the "Gentlemen" in Richmond and Westmoreland also revealed the way in which class continued to shape popular responses to the demands of the war, particularly in the Northern Neck. Throughout the war, many ordinary Virginians were suspicious of the motives of patriot leaders in bringing them into it. This suspicion turned into resentment as it soon became clear that the lower classes would have to bear the main burden of the actual fighting. But many middling Virginians also resented the tremendous cost of the war. These grievances most often came to an explosive climax when all of the militia were called out to serve. Knowing that gentlemen who sat as officers and magistrates had the power to exempt or invalid individuals off the muster rolls and thereby exempt them from the most onerous duties, ordinary Virginians often felt powerless. Wright could thus boast that he had forced the gentlemen in Westmoreland to take him off the militia rolls. However, he was not so lucky or forceful in Richmond County. With many wealthy citizens exempted or invalided out of the militia, the conclusion was obvious to most lower-class Virginians who had to take up the slack. Dye and Wright appealed to this attitude in their appeal for adherents to their insurrection. One man told au-

---

out of the enemy's route (see June 23, 1781, McIlwaine et al., eds., *Journals of the Council,* II, 351–352).

24. Testimony of William Bernard and Samuel Stowers, Proceedings of a General Court Martial, June 19, 1781, Executive Papers, LiVi.

thorities that the ringleaders of the conspiracy declared "the Rich wanted the Poor to fight for them, to defend there property, whilst they refused to fight for themselves."[25]

Wright was also irritated by the desertion laws, which encouraged neighbors to turn on each other and turn any deserters in for rewards. After the draft had taken place, Wright confronted a number of men who he thought had been issued warrants to collect deserters within the county. Wright told a Roger Beckwith after "some altercation" that "he or any Man that would take up a Deserter deserved to be scalped." Beckwith then taunted him by asserting that it might be Wright's turn next to be drafted for the regular army. Wright asked Beckwith whether he would take him up if he refused to serve, and Beckwith told him, "perhaps he might," upon which Wright declared angrily that "no such fellows as he was should do it, and after some dispute between them the said Wright struck him."[26]

Yet, behind Wright's "boasting," violent demeanor, a desperate, almost pathetic figure emerges from the testimony. William Bernard, a former justice and lieutenant colonel in the Westmoreland militia, described Wright as a "hard-working" but "illiterate" man, who, contrary to his assertions, "regularly did duty" in the militia when he lived in Westmoreland. Yet now, in 1781, Wright was having trouble making ends meet under the pressure of heavy taxes and frequent interruptions to the running of his farm. With another call of militia duty looming, Wright had gone to Bernard to seek advice on how to "get clear form Militia Duty as an infirm Man." Bernard told him that he thought he was "full able" to serve and advised him "to behave well and not run himself into Difficulty." But Wright told Bernard that he "never would do Militia duty again and would sculk and hide and live in the Woods before he would be compelled to it." Significantly, though, Wright also declared at the same time that "he never would fight against his Country." Bernard told him "that was not enough; that he ought to fight for it."[27]

<hr />

25. Testimony of Vincent Redman, ibid., June 18, 1781.

26. Testimony of Roger Beckwith, ibid., June 19, 1781. Wright also approached one John Crawdson and asked him whether he, like Beckwith and Nicholas Sotwers, had taken an oath to take up deserters. Crawdson (perhaps wisely) had told him he had not, and he knew nothing of such an oath, whereupon Wright replied that he "was glad of it" (testimony of John Crawdson, ibid.).

27. Testimony of William Bernard, ibid., June 19, 1781. For Bernard's status in Westmoreland, see Feb. 5, 1776, Richard Barksdale Harwell, ed., *The Committees of*

Wright grew more worried. He told another witness that, if he could get but six barrels of corn for his family, "he was willing and ready to turn out to serve his Country." Described by one witness as an "honest man," Wright also tried to think of ways out of his dilemma. If he could lessen his stock, he might be able to turn out for militia duty in the fall. By reducing his stock, not only could he free up food stores for his family's use, but he could also reduce his workload on the farm. On top of this, Wright told someone else just before making plans for the barbecue that he had been unwell, "but that he was getting stout and would turn out in the next division." The exigencies of the war, however, would not allow him to wait.[28]

Moreover, Wright, like many others, could be genuinely concerned and fearful of the prospect of military service. Edwin Conway of Lancaster County told the governor around the time of the planned barbecue that "the depredations of the Enemy is very Rapid." Lindsay Opie and James Ball of Northumberland County told the governor just before that "the Enemy are distressing the People upon the Water in this part of the Countrey exceedingly, by Robing them and Burning their Houses, and we have few good Guns, and little Amunition to defend ourselves with, which is Very dishartning." The presence of the British made many militia wonder what might happen to their families and farms in their absence. With their morale at a low ebb, many people found it easier to believe that resistance to local authorities would relieve them of greater hardships than would continued resistance to Britain.[29]

Wright, then, with not enough bread on the table, his health failing, and fearing British depredations, was told in no uncertain terms that he would have to take even more time out to serve once again, or come under censure and perhaps be condemned to serve for eight months in the regular army for disobeying orders. Given such a choice, Wright felt compelled to avoid service illegally. By encouraging others to, there was more of a chance that

---

Safety of Westmoreland and Fincastle: Proceedings of the County Committees, 1774–1776 (Richmond, Va., 1956), 46, and Dec. 9, 1776, Westmoreland County Court Orders, 1776–1786.

28. Testimony of George Muse, Edward Eidson, John Marks, and William Bernard, Proceedings of a General Court Martial, June 19, 1781, Executive Papers, LiVi.

29. Edwin Conway to the Governor, [June] 1781, Palmer et al., eds., *Calendar of State Papers,* II, 145; Lindsay Opie and James Ball to Jefferson, Apr. 12, 1781, *Papers of Jefferson,* V, 424–425.

local officials would not push the matter. The choice, however, must have been difficult. In the end, Wright, like many others throughout the state, rich and poor, was pushed into looking after himself and his family first.

• • • The growing resistance of the militia forced the governor to turn again to the regular army. If the militia could no longer be relied upon for the state's defense, the council believed that it was imperative that Virginia raise the recruits that the previous assembly had ordered. At the very least, the state might then have a body of troops who could be used for a primary line of defense against the British. Moreover, some of the militia themselves told Jefferson that they would more happily make an effort to raise regular soldiers if they could be relieved of the constant demands of militia duty. Accordingly, on April 12, and on the advice of the council, Jefferson lifted the suspension of the draft in those counties whose militia had returned from service. Then, on May 7, the council advised the governor to repeal the suspension of the recruiting act altogether. The following day, though, the council received word that Major General Phillips and Lord Cornwallis were on the move again and would probably try to unite their forces in Virginia. The governor ordered out as many militia as there were arms from another twenty-three mainly piedmont counties. The call-outs of the militia did delay and in some cases completely disrupt the reimplementation of the draft. Worse, though, when local officials tried to draft men, widespread unease, discontent, and in some cases collective and violent resistance followed. As the British made further inroads into the state, Virginians continued to fight among themselves.[30]

At first, some counties, divisions, and individuals evaded the draft in ways similar to previous acts of resistance, often with the voluntary or compelled complicity of company- or even field-grade officers. Some divisions in Fairfax County, for example, sent men who were, according to the county lieutenant, Peter Wagener, "Invalids and altogether unfit to do the duty of Soldiers." Wagener ordered another draft, but those drafted then prevailed upon a local court-martial to hear their case. The court ruled that the second draft was illegal, and Wagener was left with no new soldiers. The problem was more general. Steuben complained that too many counties had drafted and recruited "little dwarfs and children," knowing full well that they would be returned. Another Continental officer complained

30. Apr. 12, May 7, 8, 1781, McIlwaine et al., eds., *Journals of the Council,* II, 333, 343.

that drafting men "who are not proper persons to perform military duty" was a well-known practice.[31]

By late April, however, the intensity of resistance to the draft had risen dramatically. Henry Lee, an ex–Continental army officer and commander of the Prince William militia, was determined to carry out the draft in his county. He proceeded to recruit, draft, and round up the forty-eight new soldiers needed from his county. However, much to his frustration, many had taken drastic measures to avoid being sent to the army. Lee complained that, of those recruited, "2 of whom cut off their fingers after the draft, 1 was discharged as being a Lunatick, 9 deserted and 1 remains in the County armed." In James City County, which lay between the York and James Rivers, the county lieutenant, Nathaniel Burwell, confessed that the draft had been held on Tuesday, April 17, but three days later the British occupied Williamsburg and Yorktown. Most of the recruits took the occasion to flee. Some were captured by the British, others "through choice" joined the British.[32]

The lengths to which drafts in Prince William and James City Counties went to avoid serving in the Continental army presaged confrontation elsewhere in the state. Trouble began in the western part of the state. In Augusta, the county lieutenant, George Moffett, reported that he was forced to stop the draft because of threats from his militia. He had gathered together some field officers and magistrates at one of their houses to lay out the divisions for drafting the recruits. As they began, he told Jefferson, people crowded into the house, handed over a "paper" signed by a large number of people, and demanded that the officers stop laying off the divisions until they could again petition the assembly as they had done before. Moffett told them that "they had mistaken our authority, that what they Wanted was not in our power to Grant." The crowd seemed "very uneasy and much out of humour." The militia then proposed an alternative to the field officers and magistrates. Knowing that those officers would by law be

31. William Davies to Steuben, Mar. 10, 1781, Peter Wagener to Jefferson, Apr. 3, 1781, *Papers of Jefferson,* V, 178, 335–336; Major Thomas Posey to William Davies, Oct. 2, 1781, Palmer et al., eds., *Calendar of State Papers,* II, 521. Cf. William Davies to the General Assembly, Nov. 26, 1781, War Office Records, LiVi.

32. "Abstract of Men Raised under the Former Laws Passed for Raising Soldiers for the Continental Service—November 1782," *Virginia Military Records: From the Virginia Magazine of History and Biography, the William and Mary Quarterly, and Tyler's Quarterly* (Baltimore, 1983), 669; Nathaniel Burwell to William Davies, Feb. 1, 1782, Palmer et al., eds., *Calendar of State Papers,* III, 50.

fined for not executing the orders to draft soldiers, the protesters told Moffett that they would pay any fines that the officers incurred. "Otherwise," the protesters warned, "they were Determined" to prevent the officers from laying off any districts. The officers tried to reason with the crowd, but tempers grew thin, and the people gathered outside became impatient. The crowd grew increasingly belligerent until, as Moffet related it, "a number of armed men, who till then had not appeared in the House, rushed through the Crowd Come Round the table wher we Sat, Demanded the lists or Roles from the Captains, Snatching up Every paper on the table that they thought made for their purpose." The protesters were "Exceedingly Insolent" and "Effectually put a Stop to any farther proceedings."[33]

The draft riots of 1781 were the culmination of years of growing resentment, but they also marked the beginning of a new kind of resistance. Previously, collective action was limited to targeted groups and limited to the muster field. Now, farmers took their grievances directly to the courthouse and court officials. They also had very specific demands and often believed that they were acting within the bounds of the law. Indeed, despite their recourse to violence, Moffett explained, those in arms had specific and limited aims. They were willing to serve as militia in defense of Virginia, but they would not serve as Continental soldiers. They were indeed "Cheerfully willing to Spend their hearts blood in Defence of the Cuntery," but they had been "Imposed upon" by the new recruiting law. They declared that they would "Suffer Death before they would be Drafted 18 months from the families and made Regular Soldiers of." Moffett also defended his neighbors. He said they were "Good Soldiers" and "Good Whigs" and "in General Despize the name of a tory." They had had some "Ill advice and are out of their proper Reason" and would regret their actions after they had had some time to think about what they had done. They would, Moffett warned, also petition the next assembly for a redress of their "Supposed Grievance." Significantly, it later emerged that two company-grade officers—Captain Wililam Ward and Lieutenant Lewis Baker—were most prominent among the leaders of the Augusta protest.[34]

The contagion of violence against the draft laws spread through the

33. George Moffett to Jefferson, May 5, 1781, *Papers of Jefferson,* V, 603–604. Cf. 605n.

34. Moffett to Jefferson, May 5, 1781, Samuel Patteson to William Davies, May 27, 1781, *Papers of Jefferson,* V, 603–604, VI, 2; Sampson Mathews to Thomas Nelson, July 7, 1781, Palmer et al., eds., *Calendar of State Papers,* II, 207.

western counties. After hearing about the success of the Augusta protest, militia from Rockbridge also put a violent end to local officials' attempts to draft them. Already angry that the governor had tried to force them to do more militia service than other counties, the Rockbridge militia were furious when they found out that Jefferson had canceled the latest militia call-out only to reinstate the suspended draft for Continental soldiers in the county. As many as one hundred men invaded the county courthouse and disrupted the proceedings of the officers and justices preparing for the draft. They "Seased the table" the officials were working on and "carried it off in a Roiatous manner," declaring that "no Districts Should be laid off there." Echoing the complaints carefully laid out in their petition that had been ignored by the General Assembly in March, the Rockbridge rioters reiterated that they would "Serve as Militia . . . and make up the Eighteen Months that way, but would not be drafted for Eighteen Months and be regulars." If the protest against the laying off of divisions did not work, the rioters vowed to disrupt proceedings on the day of the draft as well.[35]

The rioters in both Augusta and Rockbridge believed that it was lawful for them to protest against the laying off of divisions. Samuel McDowell told Jefferson that his militia thought "they could not be hurt for Preventing the laying off the Districts, as the Law Stands, for it only Punishes those who make roiets or Stop the Execution of the Act, on the Day of Draft." Again, some local officials had weighed in and given moral support and perhaps some free legal advice to the militia. McDowell was furious that "Such Ideas" might have been circulated by a member of the House of Delegates to the people of Augusta.[36]

Farther north, in Hampshire County, different groups of the disaffected came together to settle their grievances. The catalyst for what local officials called a "dangerous insurrection" was the attempt of local officers to recruit and draft soldiers for the Continental army as well as to seize sup-

35. Jefferson to Samuel McDowell, Apr. 23, 1781, McDowell to Jefferson, May 9, 1781, *Papers of Jefferson*, V, 541–542, 621–622.

36. McDowell to Jefferson, May 9, 1781, *Papers of Jefferson*, V, 621–622. The editors note that Zachariah Johnston of Augusta was the member of the assembly suspected, but he was cleared of all charges in a House committee investigation reporting on June 14, 1781 (622–623n).

Though he was not sure, McDowell was anxious about the consequences of such activity. "If true I am Sory to know that any man who acts in a Publick Character Should by any means Excite the People to resist the Laws; for in that case all Government is destroyed and we are intierly ruined."

plies and provisions for it. At first, a group of men had opposed the tax collector and forced him to stop his collections. Then a group led by a man named John Claypool also stopped the collector of beef and clothes. When the county lieutenant tried to arrest the men, he succeeded only in inflaming the situation. His posse of 50 men was met by as many as 60 or 70 armed men opposing them. Most of Claypool's men capitulated, but Claypool himself refused to give himself up. However, the following day more than 150 men gathered in opposition, including "Eighteen months men" (those who had been drafted), "several" deserters, including some English prisoners, and some militia who had been condemned to eight months' service in the regular army for deserting while on militia duty. Within days, perhaps as many as 700 people assembled and bade defiance against local officials' attempts to impose the law. The county lieutenant, Garret Van Meter, told Jefferson that they were "determined to stand in opposition to every measure of Government," and they had tried to persuade everyone in their neighborhood to join them in what he called their "Treasonable and destructive measures." "For this purpose," he reported, "they swear fidelity to each other." Though Van Meter thought that the insurrectionists objected to every state law, they apparently had very clear objectives. "Their principal object is to be clear of Taxes and Draughts."[37]

In the southern piedmont county of Bedford, recalcitrant militia also banded together with draftees to defy local officials. James Callaway, the

---

37. Garret Van Meter to Jefferson, Apr. 11, 14, 20, 1781, *Papers of Jefferson,* V, 409-410, 455, 513-514; Lafayette to Nathanael Greene, June 3, 1781, Stanley J. Idzerda, ed., *Lafayette in the Age of the American Revolution: Selected Letters and Papers, 1776-1790* (Ithaca, N.Y., 1977), V, 162-165; Lafayette to James Wood, June 4, 1781, James Wood Papers, Alderman Library, UVa (photocopies). Cf. Petition of John Claypool, Thomas Denton, David Roberts, Jr., Mathias Wilkins, and George Wilkins, 1781, Palmer et al., eds., *Calendar of State Papers,* II, 624-625. Jefferson, fearing that such an insurrection might snowball, told Van Meter the best way to deal with the rioters was "not to go against the mutineers when embodied which would bring on perhaps an open Rebellion or Bloodshed most certainly, but when they shall have dispersed to go and take them out of their Beds, singly and without Noise" (Jefferson to Garret Van Meter, Apr. 27, 1781, *Papers of Jefferson,* V, 566). The insurrection continued for weeks, though. See Colonel Elias Paston to the county lieutenant of Frederick County, May 22, 1781, and Peter Hog to Governor Nelson, Aug. 2, 1781, Palmer et al., eds., *Calendar of State Papers,* II, 113-114, 284-285, and Garrett Van Meter to Governor Nelson, July 28, 1781, II, 262-263.

county lieutenant, told Jefferson that he initially had problems with militia who had deserted when called on duty. A court-martial had sentenced them to six months' service in the regular army, but Callaway could not make them serve. When some of them were thrown in jail, they broke out, and others escaped from their guards. These "Disaffected and Disobedient Wretches," he complained, stayed together and proved troublesome. After the draft took place in the county, nearly forty of the impressed recruits deserted and were hidden by the escaped militia, forming a kind of maroon community of reluctant rebels. Morale in Bedford was generally low. One man wrote pessimistically that a "pretty general consternation has seized the people" and that most had "lost much of their military ardor." Disaffection was not confined to the lower sort; men of property, including justices, were implicated in the resistance.[38]

Meanwhile, on the state's eastern frontier, riots also broke out in both Northampton and Accomack Counties. In Accomack, the tax commissioners stated that the people were upset, but not angry, about the new recruiting act until they heard that a riot against the draft in neighboring Northampton County had put an end to it there. After they received news of it, many people in Accomack first refused to pay their tax. Then, when officials tried to draft men on April 23, upward of 150 or 200 men "armed with Clubs" gathered to oppose local officials. George Corbin, the county lieutenant, had expected some trouble, so he had ordered a group of "chosen men" to stand ready with a small cannon, but ultimately thought it would be "impolitic" to use force, as there were too many men at the protest who he felt were honest patriots. He told the governor that many of the militia confronting him "had always been accounted honest good citizens" and were now "mislead by false representations from the disaffected." Corbin thus tried to reason with them but failed. He then asked the clerk to look on the list for a division who had come and brought a man they had hired for the war. Corbin then laid the division list on the table, whereupon "one of the Mob snatch'd up the list, put the same in his pocket, telling the others, who by this time had crowded into the Court house, that if they approved of what was done to signify the same by three Cheers which was accordingly complied with." Again, Corbin tried to reason with them, but

38. James Callaway to Jefferson, June 4, 1781, David Ross to William Davies, May 27, 1781, Recommendation of the Justices of the Peace for Bedford County, May 1781, *Papers of Jefferson,* VI, 23–24n, 55, 77.

he and the other officials finally decided to postpone the draft to the following Thursday, when they hoped that cooler heads would prevail.[39]

On that Thursday, another crowd appeared "armed with Clubs swords guns and pistols" and took possession of the courthouse. They placed a sentinel at the door and "unanimously declared they were determined to oppose the Draft at the hazard of their lives." Though the tax commissioners noted it was generally the "same set of men" who gathered again, they were also concerned that many "men of property" "pretended" to be convinced by Corbin's arguments because they were afraid of being prosecuted. The tax commissioners thought they were still involved, for, though they "did not apparently head the Mob," they "were generally believed to act behind the Scene." Corbin concurred, telling Jefferson that he believed that the two men heading the mob the first day were John Custis and William Garrison; they had "left the mob and seemed sorry for what they had done" after he had reasoned with them both. Yet Corbin was still suspicious. "However penitent they might be I yet view them as the most dangerous persons concerned being the only persons of property amoungst them."[40]

In the end, Corbin took down some of the rioters' names, and a court-martial the following day condemned the "most culpable" as soldiers, according to the law, but local officials were powerless to enforce the court order. Corbin told Jefferson that he was induced to adopt mild measures rather than force because of the county's isolation, the proximity of the enemy, and the activities of the many disaffected in the county and area. Nor did they have any arms or ammunition in their magazine. Moreover, the tax commissioners asserted that things had got worse in the civil arena as well. "These lawless proceedings have thrown the County into the greatest confusion imaginable," they said. "People begin to publish, propogate and avow the most dangerous doctrines, sentiments and opinions." Once again, men of property were cited as being involved: "Gentlemen from whom better things might be expected have gone so far as to tell the people they have no occasion now to pay the two [per] Cent Tax." The tax collectors were having a particularly hard time under popular pressure: "Some

39. The Commissioners for Collecting Taxes in Accomack County to Jefferson, May 15, 1781, George Corbin to Jefferson, May 31, June 17, 1781, *Papers of Jefferson,* V, 651–654, VI, 44–47. For Northampton, see "Abstract of Men Raised—November 1782," *Virginia Military Records,* 666. Cf. Proceedings of a Court Martial, Executive Papers, LiVi; Palmer et al., eds., *Calendar of State Papers,* II, 497.

40. Ibid.

Collectors don't chuse to collect and others are threatned if they attempt it." Even some of the collectors themselves had large sums of money in their hands but refused to pay it to the commissioners: they told the people that they would return their money. Other collectors had settled with them, and still others had paid a portion of their taxes. This created more problems, however, as those who had already paid their tax complained that others had not. "Anarchy, confusion and disorder reigns triumphant amongst us," the tax commissioners concluded. There was a petition afoot to be sent to the assembly, the tax commissioners believed, praying for relief from the draft. Meanwhile, the tax commissioners wanted to know what to do in this "very singular and extraordinary occasion."[41]

In the lower Northern Neck, where collective violence had broken out the previous fall, local officials did proceed to draft again—under the protection of a troop of cavalry that had been raised in each county. The assembly authorized this police force after the troubles of the last draft. The cavalry was apparently effective in quelling any collective resistance to the draft, but it could not compel complete obedience to the law. Of the 119 men needed from the four lower counties of the Northern Neck, local officials reported that only 66 (or 55 percent) were delivered, and even many of these men were able to avoid joining the army, at least temporarily. As had happened in Culpeper County, both Leroy Peachey of Richmond County and Thomas Gaskins of Northumberland told Jefferson that they had delayed sending the men to their rendezvous point with the army because their tax commissioners had not collected enough of their bounty money. Fearing problems if they sent the men on without first getting their bounty money, both commanders held them back. The recruits from Northumberland had still not left by August. With the violence of the previous fall still

41. The Commissioners for Collecting Taxes in Accomack County to Jefferson, May 15, 1781, George Corbin to Jefferson, May 31, June 17, 1781, *Papers of Jefferson,* V, 651–654, VI, 44–47; Palmer et al., eds., *Calendar of State Papers,* II, 497; Mar. 28, 1781, Accomack County Orders, 1780–1783, LiVi. George Corbin resigned a few months later the post that troubled him so much. His successor, his nephew John Cropper, a long-serving officer in the Continental corps, was disgusted with the state of the militia in the county. Cropper also complained to the governor that, under Corbin, only twenty-five of the seventy-four divisions in the county had actually provided a new recruit under the late law. Cropper to Thomas Nelson, Aug. 25, 1781, Palmer et al., eds., *Calendar of State Papers,* II, 359–361; cf. George Corbin to William Davies, Aug. 18, 1781, Levin Joynes to William Davies, Sept. 10, 1781, II, 339–341, 400.

fresh in their minds and new reports of uprisings around the state reaching their ears, local officials in the lower Northern Neck were reluctant to push their neighbors too far.[42]

Collective violence or the threat of it helped undermine the draft also in counties other than those that reported their problems to the state government. Major Thomas Posey reflected that it was "obvious to everybody" that many local officials had either been "prevented" from drafting men or refused to draft men because of "an opposition of men in arms." William Davies wearily pointed to the inaction of many county officials when he told the General Assembly in November, "In many counties nothing has been done in this business."[43]

In sum, resistance, evasion, collective violence, or the threat of violence crippled the search for soldiers in Virginia in the spring and summer of 1781. Even before the extent of recruiting problems had become clear, Steuben complained, "The opposition made to the law in some counties, the entire neglect of it in others, and an unhappy disposition to evade the fair execution of it in all afford a very melancholy prospect." He was correct. Later in the year, when asked to fill out returns of soldiers raised under the recruiting act, only fourteen of seventy-three counties bothered to. Still later in the war, the executive tried to compile another report. This time, twenty-eight counties replied, and twenty-four noted specifically whether the recruiting act of 1781 was ever complied with. Fifteen counties admitted that they had never carried out the law. At best, perhaps only as many as thirty-two counties (or 44 percent) might have tried drafting men in 1781, and even many of these fell far short of their quotas. Though Loudoun's and Culpeper's recruiting drives were hardly a complete success, they actually did well in relative terms. Patriot officials in Henry County in the south-

42. Jefferson to Henry Lee, Sr., Apr. 13, 1781, Leroy Peachey to Jefferson, Mar. 23, 1781, *Papers of Jefferson,* V, 219–221, 434; Jan. 8, 1781, Northumberland County Order Book, 1773–1783, LiVi; Thomas Gaskins to Jefferson, Apr. 13, 1781, Executive Papers, LiVi; "General Return of Recruits Raised under the Act of October 1780 in Virginia," 1782, War Office Records, LiVi; Certificate for Westmoreland, 1781, box 2, Misc. Revolutionary Collection, LiVi; "A List of Recruits and Drafts for the County of Westmoreland," [n.d.], Auditor of Public Accounts Inventory, Militia Lists, 1779–1782, LiVi.

43. Major Thomas Posey to William Davies, Oct. 2, 1781, Palmer et al., eds., *Calendar of State Papers,* II, 521; Davies to the General Assembly, Nov. 26, 1781, War Office Records, LiVi.

west of the state, for example, raised only three volunteers and drafted only one of the forty-nine men they needed to complete their quota. The following year, when pressed by the state legislature, they drafted another four men and enlisted two more. No explanation for their backwardness accompanied the return of their tax commissioners.[44]

As for the permanent army Washington wanted, Virginia managed to find just 248 men who volunteered for three years or for the duration of the war. Even of these men, 3 remained in their counties, 22 absconded at some point after enlisting, and 10 were refused by the Continental receiving officers, probably because they were unfit for duty. Officials reported that a total of 775 men were drafted into the service. Of these, at least 49 remained in their counties, 118 had absconded on the road, and 48 had been refused for service. Thus, 213 volunteers and 560 draftees made it to their rendezvous points within Virginia, whereas the state's recruiting act had called for the raising of 3,250 men. If all of the men who made it to their rendezvous points stayed with the army, Virginia contributed a total of just 773 men, or a mere 24 percent of what the state had wanted to contribute to its Continental quota. Pressure from below thus thoroughly disabled mobilization for the regular army in 1781. Though repeated British invasions helped undermine the draft in Virginia, the militia's sometimes intense, sometimes passive, but persistent local resistance to state laws had brought recruiting to a standstill.[45]

• • • For patriot leaders, the timing of the draft riots and militia resistance could not have been worse. They took place amid and sometimes in the face of the British invasions in the state. Instead of rallying together to counter the British threat, hundreds if not thousands of ordinary Virginians rose up against patriot authority. Some patriots believed the successes of the

44. "Representation of the State of the Virginia Line," [May 28, 1781], enclosure in Steuben to Jefferson, May 28, 1781, *Papers of Jefferson,* VI, 31; General Return of Recruits, Nov. 26, 1781, War Office Records, LiVi; "Abstract of Men Raised— November 1782," *Virginia Military Records;* A Return of the recruits raised for the County of Henry under the Act of Assembly of October 1780 . . . , Sept. 30, 1782, LiVi.

45. "Representation of the State of the Virginia Line," [May 28, 1781], enclosure in Steuben to Jefferson, May 28, 1781, *Papers of Jefferson,* VI, 31; General Return of Recruits, Nov. 26, 1781, War Office Records, LiVi; "Abstract of Men Raised— November 1782," *Virginia Military Records.*

British invasions and the uprisings in some places were not unrelated. As the British made easy progress through the state, patriot leaders reported that many Virginians were anxious and close to giving up the fight. David Ross, attempting to secure patriot supplies at Point of Fork (at the confluence of the James and Rivanna Rivers), wrote at the end of May that morale and military service went hand in hand: "The people at present are really panic struck and have lost much of their military ardor." He feared worse consequences: "I need not tell you the force of imagination. If an idea goes abroad that we are not able to oppose the British, it will have an unhappy effect." Ross thought this was at the root of the problems in Bedford County, and "this seems too much the case already" in that county.[46]

Whatever they believed was the root cause of their troubles, most patriot leaders were themselves in a state of panic by the end of May. Enslaved Virginians, disaffected whites, and British soldiers struck terror into the hearts of many of them. Reluctant neighbors did little to allay their fears either. George Mason, preparing to flee his plantation in Fairfax during the British push into northern Virginia, told a Maryland friend, "Our situation in Virginia is truly critical and dangerous." He believed it would be only a few weeks before Maryland was in the same boat if no help was forthcoming from the French fleet.[47]

Jefferson called the assembly together again for the end of May, diverting it to Charlottesville, where he hoped it would be out of reach of the British. As legislators fled their homes and made one last attempt to gather, they contemplated desperate measures. Jefferson pleaded with the assembly to create a stronger naval and cavalry force, to draft enslaved Virginians into military work forces, and to give the executive greater power to enforce government policy. Many wanted to go further than Jefferson, however. Indeed, less than six months before Yorktown, Virginia's patriot leadership was shaken enough to demand and vociferously debate the creation of a "dictatorship" in the state.

Jefferson, shaken by the realization that the British were maneuvering to effect a junction of forces within Virginia, began appealing to the assembly as early as May 10 to take immediate action. But, as reports of militia resistance to call-outs and the draft flooded into his office, Jefferson spoke of the need for stronger measures to prosecute the war. "Further experi-

46. David Ross to William Davies, May 27, 1781, *Papers of Jefferson,* VI, 23–24.n.

47. Mason to Pearson Chapman, May 31, 1781, *Papers of Mason,* II, 688.

ence," Jefferson told Harrison at the end of May, "convince me that something is necessary to be done to enforce the calls of the Executive for militia to attend in the field." Though he was not sure whether this recent wave of militia resistance was due to the "backwardness in the militia," the "want of activity in their principal officers," or a combination of both, the current laws "seem scarcely coercive enough for a state of war." But Jefferson was worried about not only militia resistance; he also focused on the loyalties of many white Virginians. Most, he believed, were much happier to protect their property than the state. Many others were plain unfriendly and had actively helped the British while they were in the state. The only answer he could come up with to curb the activities of both groups was to declare martial law within a given area around the two armies and subject the citizens to more aggressive and restrictive military regulations.[48]

Yet Jefferson felt Virginia needed even more than this. Distressed by the inroads the British had made in the state, the lack of authority over his fellow Virginians, and the persistent loss of property, Jefferson prepared to resign the office of governor and made an appeal to George Washington to come to their aid. Jefferson told Washington that Cornwallis and Arnold had successfully come together and threatened Virginia from both east and west. The British navy was "ravaging" the shores of their eastern counties and tying up militia there, and rumors flew of "powerful Operations meditated against our Western Frontier by a joint force of British and Indian savages." With so many discontented and disaffected Virginians in their midst, black and white, Jefferson hinted ominously that Washington would know what could be expected in his home state if this situation continued. Lafayette might survive, but the British could easily pin him down and wage a different kind of campaign. Jefferson feared that the British were happy to try to "waste an unarmed Country and to lead the minds of the people to acquiescence under those events which they see no human power prepared to ward off." Thus, Jefferson saw no choice but to ask for Washington's personal intercession as Virginia's "dernier resort in distress." Though the assembly had not yet reached a quorum, "many mem-

48. Jefferson to the Speaker of the House of Delegates, May 10, 28, 1781, *Papers of Jefferson,* V, 626–627 (the editors note the resolutions agreed to by the House in consequence of Jefferson's reports on 29 May [629n]), VI, 28–29. Cf. Jefferson to Washington, May 9, 1781, V, 624; Steuben to Jefferson, May 28, 1781, Jefferson to the Speaker of the House, June 2, 1781, Jefferson to Lafayette, May 14, 1781, V, 644, VI, 31, 72.

bers of weight" concurred with him in asking Washington to come himself to his beleaguered state.[49]

In his letter to Washington, Jefferson was unclear what exactly he wanted Washington to do, besides bolster morale. He thought that the mere presence of Washington would bring most Virginians into the field to serve under him, but other legislators were not so sure that Washington's presence would be sufficient. Many began to talk of the need for some kind of a "dictator." Advocates for a dictator were spurred on by the knowledge that Jefferson would resign in the midst of the worst crisis during the Revolutionary war. His term of office expired on Saturday, June 2, and he made it clear that he would not seek reelection. The assembly postponed the election of his successor until Monday, but on Sunday night the British raided Charlottesville and almost captured Jefferson and many other legislators, who seemed shocked by the advance of the enemy. The assembly adjourned to Staunton, in the Shenandoah Valley, leaving the state without any semblance of government for almost an entire week. Many of the delegates actually went home, "without expressing a thought about any future collection of the Legislature." Jefferson had fled both his house and his post, and, because of resignations and poor attendance, only one member of the council, William Fleming, remained at the head of the executive. Without a governor and without a quorum, Fleming had little authority, and he believed that he could not even call out the militia.[50]

Thus, when the assembly reassembled in Staunton on June 7, with a reduced quorum of forty members, former militant volunteer George Nicholas (the son of the deceased Robert Carter Nicholas) moved to appoint a military "dictator." Henry Young reported that, when the assembly had reconvened, Nicholas had told his colleagues that he would, on June 9, "move to have a Dictator appointed." According to Young, both General Greene and General Washington had been talked of as a likely candidate for the job. Though Young thought the move inappropriate and that neither Greene nor Washington would accept such a role, he believed the mood of the assembly had once again changed: it was "a thin House of Delligates, but they are Zealous." Young thought the new assembly would be "very strict."[51]

49. Jefferson to Washington, May 28, 1781, ibid., VI, 32–33.

50. Selby, *Revolution in Virginia,* 281–282; R. H. Lee to the Virginia Delegates in Congress, June 12, 1781, *Papers of Jefferson,* VI, 90–92.

51. Henry Young to Davies, June 9, 1781, *Papers of Jefferson,* VI, 84–85.

Legislators were serious enough about the issue—and sufficiently aware of the controversy that it would stir—that they concealed their deliberations. There was no record of Nicholas's motion in the *Journal of the House of Delegates,* but it sparked a bitter and divisive debate. The fullest account of the affair is in a letter from Archibald Stuart to Jefferson almost four decades after the war. Stuart, a native of Staunton, was not a member of the House, but he was privy to its proceedings. He told Jefferson that Nicholas spoke in favor of establishing "a Dictator . . . in this Commonwealth who should have the power of disposing of the lives and fortunes of the Citizens thereof without being subject to account." Nicholas proposed Washington for this position and "refered to the practice of the Romans on similar occasions." After Nicholas introduced the motion, Patrick Henry seconded it. Henry, referring to the wartime precedents of the assembly, said it was "immaterial to him whether the Officer proposed was called a Dictator or a Governor with enlarged powers or by any other name." What was most important to Henry, Stuart recalled, was that "an Officer armed with such powers was necessary to restrain the unbridled fury of a licentious enemy." The motion was opposed by Mann Page of Spotsylvania and others, and, after a lengthy and heated debate, it was defeated. Stuart thought that the people out-of-doors had also influenced the debate, for it was obvious to him that the proposal "was not relished by the people." One almost contemporary historian wrote: "The pulse of the Assembly was incidently felt in debates on the state of the Commonwealth, and, out of doors, by personal conversations. Out of these a ferment gradually arose, which fore[t]old a violent opposition to any species of Dictatorship, and, as in a previous instance of a similar attempt, the [a]pprehension of personal danger produced a relinquishment of the scheme."[52]

Though Jefferson later condemned the move, he must have had some-

52. Archibald Stuart to Jefferson, Sept. 8, 1818, ibid., VI, 85–86n; John Burk, *The History of Virginia, from Its First Settlement to the Present Day,* IV, cont. Skelton Jones and Louis Hue Girardin (Petersburg, Va., 1816), xi–xii. Stuart told Jefferson that this was ostensibly the account he had given the former governor shortly after the affair, probably in conversation. On the basis of this information, Jefferson wrote a long and bitter denunciation of Nicholas, Henry, and the attempt to establish a dictator in the state in his *Notes on Virginia* (see answer to query 13, Jefferson, *Notes on the State of Virginia,* ed. William Peden [Chapel Hill, N.C., 1954], 126–129), where he confided that the proposal "wanted a few votes only of being passed." Burk, *History of Virginia,* IV, appendix, xi–xii; John Beckley to Jefferson, June 12, 1781, *Papers of Jefferson,* VI, 88, and notes.

thing similar in mind when he asked Washington to come to Virginia. Certainly Richard Henry Lee believed that such a move was necessary. Lee, recently in command of a defensive force on the Potomac to counter British privateering there, wrote independently from his home at Chantilly to the Virginia delegates in Congress on June 12. He told them of the enemy's movements, Jefferson's resignation, the dispersal of the assembly, and the probable capture of all their military stores at Point of Fork. Believing Virginia to be leaderless in the midst of this crisis, Lee pleaded with the delegates for an "immediate and powerful interposition," or "all the country below the Mountains will be in the power of the enemy in a few months." He had become convinced that only Washington could save the state at this point. If Congress sent him to Virginia, with full "Dictatorial power," they might be yet saved. He should be given such powers until the assembly could reconvene and formally assign such powers, but Congress ought to recommend to the assembly that he be given dictatorial powers for "6, 8, or 10 months as the case may require." Though Lee might have exaggerated the crisis in the state, his letter "is an illuminating reflection of the near panic that gripped the minds even of some of Virginia's leaders at this time."[53]

Ordinary Virginians seemed less panicked. Some did concur with leaders' calling for a dictator. A petition from Caroline County headed by Edmund Pendleton also called for greater powers, particularly over dissent in the state. Haunted by the collapse of Virginia's defense, the petitioners attacked the disaffected, whom they defined broadly—ranging from those who openly complained about the misapplication of public money to those who opposed the drafts because they felt they were unconstitutional.[54]

Against such charges, however, petitioners from around the state did not hesitate to defend themselves. Indeed, if patriot leaders and other Virginians were obsessed with regaining control over the rapid deterioration of authority, many ordinary Virginians proposed their own solutions in the midst of the crisis. Militia from Augusta, who had brought a violent end to

53. R. H. Lee to the Virginia Delegates in Congress, June 12, 1781, *Papers of Jefferson,* VI, 90–92, 93n. Cf. Lee's letters to Washington and James Lovell, June 12, 1781, Ballagh, ed., *Letters of Richard Henry Lee,* II, 233–238, which were enclosed in this one and set forth Lee's plan for a dictatorship in similar terms.

54. Petition of People of Caroline County to the General Assembly Asking for Stricter Regulation of the Enemies of the State, [June 2, 1781], *Papers of Pendleton,* I, 363–364.

the draft in their county, were one of the first groups to again petition the assembly. A summary of their petition in the *Journal of the House of Delegates,* which is all that is left of their remonstrance, explained their reasons for rebelling. The petitioners complained that the draft law was "unequal and unjust," as they were compelled to make up the deficiencies from other counties that had previously failed to raise enough men. In other words, while militia from Augusta felt that they had generally fulfilled their quota of required soldiers over the years, other counties had not. Without recognizing previous contributions to the army, the assembly was asking more of Augusta than of those who had previously been remiss. The draft, then, was "unequal."[55]

But the petitioners also felt that the draft was "unjust" because the quotas created for the different counties in the state were based on the number of militia in each county. Though this practice might at first appear just, they argued that the quotas really ought to be based on the "amount of property" in each county. Thus, a wealthier county ought to contribute more to the raising of an army, because that county had more to protect. Augusta, a western county, had fewer enslaved Virginians to worry about and much less valuable property to defend. This thinking extended the idea of equality in the defense of the state to its logical extreme. Whereas previously freeholders had argued for progressive taxes and some kind of equality within counties in manpower policy, the Augusta petitioners wanted richer counties to contribute more. In effect, the petitioners were saying that one hundred poor nonslaveholders in Augusta should have to provide only as many men as perhaps twenty rich slaveholders in Gloucester. They realized what militia in Northumberland and Lancaster Counties might have discovered the previous fall. It was one thing to distribute the burden and expense of service among rich and poor in the same county in proportion to wealth. However, if there were fewer wealthy men in the county altogether, poorer militia would suffer accordingly. Augusta militia wanted the government to apportion quotas by wealth, not by numbers of men.[56]

More than two hundred freeholders in neighboring Rockbridge County also complained about military policy in class terms that reflected a regional bias. They began by stating that they were fully committed to supporting American freedom and Independence and were willing and ready

55. *Journal of the House of Delegates,* May 31, 1781, 8–9.
56. Ibid.

to sacrifice both their lives and property for the cause—but only when such sacrifices were "Equally proportioned with our fellow Citizens who have they're all Equally at Stake." Already aggrieved that the state seemed not to have noticed that their county had done one extra tour of militia duty, citizens of Rockbridge also thought that the present recruiting law weighed unevenly on militia like themselves. They were subsistence farmers who depended on family labor: "We Generally procure a Sustenance for our Selves and families by the Labour of our own hands and one days Labour is necessary for the Next days Support." Given such circumstances, those who were compelled to serve eighteen months in the army must "at once Subject their families to inevitable ruin." This would be considered more "Convincingly plain" when the legislature considered that there was no one to replace them and work in their place. "Neighther Labourers can be had for hire Nor Substitutes to fill up the Ranks." It was thus patently unjust that "one Should be devoted to Ruin by bearing a burthen" while the rest of the division to which the draftee belonged did not have to serve at all. They proposed a radical, more communal innovation. "If Equally devided amongst fifteen," the burden of service would be more bearable, and "Just." Instead of one man's serving for eighteen months, six men from the same division ought to serve for three months each. The six men who served in the regular service would then be exempted from militia service until each of the other nine men in the division had also served at least one tour of duty. Such a plan could only appear "Reasonable to Every honest man," and they were confident that the assembly would change the law. Not only would such a move strengthen the army, but it would also make the burden of service more tolerable for the poor, and "those Disagreeable Consequences which a Sense of impending Ruin will unavoidable produce [would] be hapily prevented."[57]

The Rockbridge County militia reminded the legislature that there were still many militia in the state who were willing to fight, but they wanted to on their own terms, and with their own interests in mind. The laws as they stood, they complained, simply did not take those interests into account. One of the biggest problems they saw was that the planter-dominated legislature did not understand how difficult it was for farmers without slaves to leave their farms for any length of time. Slaveholding, then, particularly in wartime, increasingly became the touchstone for class divisions

57. Rockbridge County Petition, [June 14, 1781], Virginia Legislative Petitions, LiVi.

among white Virginians. More than one hundred militia from Pittsylvania County made the point more explicitly. Like the Rockbridge petitioners, they claimed they had always contributed to the war with men, money, and materials, and they were still ready to serve the state. However, they were willing to do so only "in such a manner as would not totally ruin themselves, their Wives and Children." The present recruiting law would do just that, as many of the petitioners were "poor men without a single Slave, with a Wife and many small Children to maintain." Taking such men away from their families "would reduce them to the most indigent circumstances and hard grinding Want." Yet they would do anything in their power to contribute to the common defense and even help raise regular soldiers, but they would not stand for a draft.[58]

Other militia weighed in with similar sentiments. A group of men from Amherst, for example, noted that "for some time past" they had considered the "recruiting business to be in a great measure at an end." Instead, it was clear to them that the defense of the country really lay with the militia, and they wanted the legislature to change the militia laws. Militia service had now become "the most distressing" because "many helpless families are left without the necessaries of life, thereby to encounter every species of want and misery." They asked the legislature for more money, in order to properly compensate militia for the loss of their crops and to provide adequate relief for their families in their absence. They also wanted the legislature to regulate the terms of militia service, and particularly the length of service each tour of duty ought to be. Some tours were but a few days, but others lasted as long as three months, which proved "burthensome" to many poorer militia. They hoped the legislature would see that "matters of such Consequence, in a well regulated State," should not be left to "mere chance." They wanted "equal justice" established by law.[59]

In the end, the assembly tried to accommodate complaints from both above and below. It did not appoint a dictator per se, but it did give the newly elected governor, Thomas Nelson, more extensive powers than ever before. Nelson, who had been in command of the militia, thought he knew what powers might be needed. The assembly gave him the authority to call out all of the militia if necessary and send them wherever he chose and power to impress supplies, imprison suspected tories and create special courts to try them, and extend any recruiting or impressment laws. The

58. Pittsylvania County Petition, [June 19, 1781], ibid.
59. Amherst County Petitions, [May 29, 1781], ibid.

assembly also passed An Act for Establishing Martial Law within Twenty Miles of the American Army, or the Enemy's Camp, and passed stronger measures to suppress militia resistance and keep them in the field. To prevent riots like the one that happened in Richmond County, anyone opposing a call of men into the field would be considered "civilly dead" as to his property, which would descend to his next of kin immediately. Anyone who refused to serve when called out could be declared a regular soldier for six months. Anyone who deserted, once out, could be put to death. But An Act to Amend the Act for Regulating and Disciplining the Militia focused on the officers of the militia as much as the men, because, as the legislators stated, they had run into "many difficulties in bringing delinquent officers of the militia to punishment." Thus any officers could be arrested by the governor, while on duty or not, and any court-martial sentence on a field officer had to be submitted and approved by the governor. Moreover, the governor could also appoint officers over the militia, ensuring tighter control over them when out on duty.[60]

But, if the assembly pushed the militia to perform, it was also careful to make it clear for how long. Responding to the complaints of the Amherst County militia, the assembly stipulated that any militia tours of duty should not exceed two months of service, unless reinforcements were unavoidably detained. The assembly also ensured that Virginians' efforts would contribute only to state defense. On May 29, the House adopted a resolution demanding that no further supplies or men should be sent out of the state to aid either Greene or Washington. Then it amended the emergency session's act for raising two legions for the defense of the state so that, if anyone enlisted in the state forces, he would be exempted from being drafted into the Continental army. Moreover, any county producing recruits for the state forces would be credited as if it had actually produced a Continental soldier. To try to encourage people to turn in deserters, any militia who turned in a deserter would be credited with a tour of duty in the militia. Moreover, the assembly authorized the governor to appoint recruiting officers to raise up to three thousand men for the Continental army. They could be enlisted for as little as two years or for the duration of the war, and even those who enlisted for only two years would get as much as ten thousand dollars. Though the assembly did not specifically repeal the draft act passed

60. Archibald Cary to Jefferson, June 19, 1781, *Papers of Jefferson,* VI, 96–97; Hening, comp., *Statutes at Large,* X, 411, 413–416, 416–421. For more forceful antitory measures, see X, 414.

in the winter session, its actions effectively ended any further attempts to draft men that year.[61]

Finally, the assembly again lashed out at Congress and the northern states at the end of its legislative session. Indeed, with only a hint of French and Continental help over the past few arduous months, white Virginians' fury with their allies was undiminished from the last assembly. John Banister, for example, warned Theodorick Bland in mid-May that their situation wore "no favorable complexion." He compared the relative lack of help forthcoming from the northern states to Virginia's "conduct to them in their day of peril." Such sentiments found their way into another address, dated June 19, 1781, and drawn up and presented to the assembly by Patrick Henry. This new address repeated many of the same arguments as the earlier one. However, the new address paid more homage to the sufferings of the ordinary Virginians who, as militia, were "sent into long, expensive and painful service, in great numbers from time to time at seasons the most inclement and distressing to them under every discouragement arising from a general want of necessaries, a sickly climate and a series of Defeats and disasters." Even when they were busy assisting the North earlier in the war, Virginia had suffered under "frequent invasions by sea as well as hostilities on our Western Frontier" that had kept "our people in a constant state of alarm and have called for such frequent returns of military Duty as were distressing in the highest degree to a people whose commerce is destroyed while they are loaded with Taxes." Despite the widespread militia resistance and virtual lawlessness in the state, ordinary Virginians had earned the right now to demand help: "The suffering of a virtuous people who now feel every thing that a cruel, vindictive and enraged Enemy can inflict, compel us to make the Demand And Justice ensures a compliance with it on the part of Congress." Unlike the last address, drawn up in March 1781, the assembly adopted this one and sent it northward.[62]

61. Hening, comp., *Statutes at Large,* X, 410–411, 416–420, 433–434; Selby, *Revolution in Virginia,* 279. The council did not carry out its mandate until Aug. 23, 1781, when it decided to appoint district recruiting officers rather than county recruiting officers in order to save time and expense (Aug. 23, 1781, McIlwaine et al., eds., *Journals of the Council,* II, 378).

62. John Banister to Theodorick Bland, May 16, 1781, Campbell, ed., *Bland Papers,* II, 68–70; "An Address to Congress from the General Assembly of Virginia," [June 19, 1781], Executive Papers, LiVi (photocopy in Virginia Legislative Petitions, UVa).

• • • For once, by the time the assembly adjourned, the situation in Virginia had improved. On June 10, General Anthony Wayne finally joined Lafayette in Virginia, bringing about eight hundred Pennsylvania troops with him. Cornwallis, now facing almost four thousand troops, decided to retire eastward, thinking that he had shaken the Virginians and interrupted their supply lines. By June 16, Cornwallis had reached Richmond, and by June 25 he was in Williamsburg, keen to retire to the tidewater to await orders from General Clinton about what to do next. Expecting to be sent northward again in anticipation of an assault on New York by a combined force of Washington's army and a new French fleet under Admiral de Grasse on its way from France, Cornwallis had to wait until July 20 before learning that Clinton wanted him to keep hold of the lower Peninsula and occupy Hampton and Yorktown. Cornwallis thought that Yorktown was the only suitable deepwater harbor, and by early August he had begun to fortify the town and Gloucester Point across the River.[63]

Most patriots in Virginia believed that Cornwallis was in retreat and were cheered by the presence of more Continentals to help. Lafayette was puzzled by Cornwallis's movement, but relieved. Despite the British withdrawal, he had trouble keeping his militia force together, and Wayne's contingent had dwindled to nearly five hundred through sickness and desertions. Lafayette, thinking that some of the British would pull out and go to New York, was readying to leave Virginia altogether. Accordingly, he began planning to send Wayne southward to join Greene and appealed to Washington to transfer him to a theater where he could see more action. Virginia, he told Washington, was militarily "in a state of languor."[64]

Simultaneously, however, Washington contemplated moving on Cornwallis in Virginia, less and less convinced that an assault on New York would succeed. Perhaps also swayed by critical letters from his patriot colleagues in Virginia, Washington left it up to the French to decide where to attack by giving the new fleet free rein to choose where to land. The commander of the French forces, comte de Rochambeau, who had never been completely happy about the prospect of attacking New York, pushed comte de Grasse toward the Chesapeake. On August 14, Washington learned that de Grasse was indeed headed for Virginia. Almost at the same time, he

63. Selby, *Revolution in Virginia,* 286–291; Don Higginbotham, *The War of American Independence: Military Attitudes, Policies, and Practice, 1763–1789* (New York, 1971), 379.

64. Selby, *Revolution in Virginia,* 292–293.

heard from Lafayette that Cornwallis had begun digging in at Yorktown. Within five days, almost the entire Continental army under Washington outside New York had begun moving southward. The French fleet arrived in the Chesapeake Bay on August 30 and then chased off a smaller British fleet. Washington arrived in Williamsburg two weeks later. By the end of September, about 7,800 French troops and 5,200 Continentals began the siege of Yorktown.[65]

Virginians themselves, however, were slow to react to the sudden turn of events. As Cornwallis turned back eastward, Honyman thought "Great numbers of militia" had joined Lafayette, cheered by the apparent British retreat. However, in early July, Honyman also noted that many men were at home, "busily engaged in getting their small grain" during the "Fine dry harvest weather." Lafayette himself could not believe how many militia had disobeyed orders to turn out. Despite the new, heavy-handed militia laws, he complained that even the county lieutenants were complicit in the militia's disobedience. The local commanders shortened terms of service for their men, "against the law established by their Representatives," believing "no one will ever punish them."[66]

Problems were compounded by the fact that the governor and most of the council remained out of action until at least mid-July. The new governor, Thomas Nelson, fell ill shortly after his election and disappeared for two weeks, not taking command until mid-July. Even so, the council had persistent difficulties finding a quorum, and then Nelson fell ill again in mid-August. For several critical weeks the government was in disarray. Once Nelson recovered and it was clear that a major showdown was expected at Yorktown, he exercised his new powers with particular vigor from early September onward. He impressed grain, rounded up tories, and ordered out the militia. Nelson hoped that Cornwallis's withdrawal to Yorktown would inspire Virginians to turn out. He canceled the order to send southwestern militia to reinforce Greene, against which there were again many protests, and hoped that, now the harvest was in, the militia would turn out "with the greatest alacrity," for there "never was a Time when vigorous measures were more necessary, or when they promised greater Advantages." He thought a "successful opposition on our Part, which the

65. Ibid., 293–296, 303–304; Higginbotham, *War of American Independence*, 382.

66. June 14, 23, July 3, 1781, Diary of Honyman; Selby, *Revolution in Virginia*, 296.

Strength of this State is very capable of making . . . will in all Probability . . . Put a happy Period to the War."[67]

The end of the war did come, of course, but with an indifferent contribution from Virginians, despite the "Strength of this State." Only very late did Virginia militia begin to gather in any force. After noting the arrival of the French fleet in the bay, Honyman recorded that "Great numbers" of militia had been called down from most counties. A few days later, he could report that the militia were heading toward Yorktown "in great numbers." Caught up in the excitement, Honyman himself joined with the militia, but only as late as October 7, when he marched downriver to Yorktown. Within a week, he was back, "very much fatigued and indisposed," and disillusioned with the numbers of militia he found participating. He admitted that there were "but few" in the camp before York, and certainly no more than about 1,500 of the 15,000 troops that he estimated were employed in the siege were militia. Most, he reckoned, were French troops. Even the best estimates of the number of militia at Yorktown show that perhaps no more than 3,000 participated in some way, whereas 7,800 French troops, and more than 5,000 Continental troops—mainly from states north of Virginia—played the greatest role. This, of a militia estimated to number almost 50,000.[68]

Virginia also experienced problems supplying so many foreign troops in the state, even though, most commentators agreed, there were plenty of provisions available. As Honyman admitted, the troops at Yorktown were "much straitened for provisions, notwithstanding the great abundance in the country." Thomas Nelson, the governor and militia commander, also found "much Difficulty and Vexation" in trying to provision the allied armies at Yorktown. He thought it was in part due to the French agents in

67. Selby, *Revolution in Virginia*, 296–298; Evans, *Thomas Nelson*, 111; McIlwaine et al., eds., *Journals of the Council*, II, 369.

68. Sept. 3, 5, 15, Oct. 7, 15, 1781, Diary of Honyman; Evans, *Thomas Nelson*, 117–118. William Davies made the estimate of the total number of militia available based on returns at the war office, in July 1781. He included all militia east of the Allegheny Mountains (see Davies to David Jameson, July 14, 1781, Palmer et al., eds., *Calendar of State Papers*, II, 219). For militia not staying the course, see Evans, *Thomas Nelson*, 118; Davies to Thomas Nelson, Sept. 15, Oct. 10, 1781, War Office Orders [Letters], Aug. 15–Nov. 1, 1781, LiVi; Nelson to Davies, Sept. 19, 1781, H. R. McIlwaine, ed., *Official Letters of the Governors of the State of Virginia* (Richmond, Va., 1926–1929), III, 59; James Clay to Nelson, Sept. 13, 1781, Executive Papers, LiVi.

their midst and the desire for real specie but also due to a lack of confidence in government. The people were unwilling to sell supplies to Virginia officials because "former Treatment gives them perhaps too little Reason to expect Justice."[69]

Most people, however, wanted to sell only to the French, because they would get hard money in return for their goods. Virginians, rich and poor, held back from offering supplies freely. Pendleton was clearly piqued that not just ordinary Virginians were withholding supplies in order to sell to the French for specie. He told Madison that "some great men" were also trying to evade the seizure of grain and instead sell to the French agents. St. George Tucker, Nelson's own aide, was one of those "great men." Knowing of the arrival of the French agents, he told his wife to withhold provisions from the state commissaries until the French arrived.[70]

• • • In the end, the only Virginians who participated in the siege of Yorktown with any great enthusiasm were the hundreds of black Virginians who had joined the British.[71] Though there was little they or anyone else could do at that late hour, Cornwallis believed that "great numbers" of enslaved Virginians "have come to us from different parts of the country." Clinton thought Cornwallis had "thousands" of blacks in his ranks

69. Oct. 3, 1781, Diary of Honyman; Thomas Nelson, Jr., to David Jameson, Oct. 1, 1781, Autograph Letter Collection, 1771–1807, UVa.

70. Selby, *Revolution in Virginia,* 299; Evans, *Thomas Nelson,* 114–117; Pendleton to Madison, Sept. 10, 1781, *Papers of Pendleton,* I, 371; Sept. 26, 1781, McIlwaine et al., eds., *Journals of the Council,* II, 390.

71. George Corbin to William Davies, Aug. 18, 1781, Levin Joynes to Davies, Sept. 10, 1781, Palmer et al., eds., *Calendar of State Papers,* II, 339–341, 411. Enslaved Virginians were often only too willing to join the British, not just for freedom but to fight against their former masters. The summer of 1781 gave them plenty of opportunities. A short-lived period of peace in Accomack County on the Eastern Shore, for example, was shattered by the arrival of four barges on one of the outlying islands. A Captain Robinson with about one hundred men, "cheifly Negroes," plundered some of the inhabitants of the island, fired on others, and burned several houses. Though a party of militia gave chase for almost four days, the marauders escaped. The blacks among those who plagued the Eastern Shore for the rest of the summer, Levin Joynes reported, were mainly ex-slaves or those from Accomack who had made their way to freedom. They were more worrisome than other plunderers: "These fellows were really dangerous to an individual singled out for their vengeance whose property lay exposed."

at Yorktown. The service of former black bondsmen against patriot forces in Virginia infuriated and frightened men like Pendleton. When Continental forces began their siege of Yorktown, Pendleton told Madison that they were making headway against the British pickets but that they "keep their swarm of Negroes busily employed in intrenching and Fortifying" their position. Many black Virginians died defending their freedom while whites stayed at home to protect theirs. St. George Tucker believed that an "immense number of Negroes have died, in the most miserable Manner in York," mainly from diseases.[72]

Despite the desperate efforts of black Virginians, Cornwallis surrendered on October 17. Before he capitulated, he might have had as many as three thousand blacks with him. When he sailed from Virginia, he took only hundreds, rather than thousands, with him. Most were abandoned, with many sick and dying from diseases. They were simply left behind to shift for themselves. Among them was a group from among the eighty-two enslaved Virginians belonging to John Banister who had fled to the British earlier in the year. When Cornwallis surrendered, Banister, like other slaveowners, came looking for his property. One group of Continental soldiers had taken custody of some of his former slaves, but they were unsure of what to do with them. The group of black Virginians faced reenslavement and feared harsh and punitive retribution from their former owner. Among the Continental soldiers guarding the enslaved Virginians was a battle-hardened veteran called Joseph Plumb Martin. He and his northern colleagues might have had some moral qualms about returning the black Virginians to a life of slavery. More likely, they could not but empathize with the plight of these former slaves who had only tried to fight for their freedom. Given the numbers of blacks who joined the army, Martin and his colleagues might have even fought alongside formerly enslaved Virginians. When the captured Virginians told Martin of their plight and their worry of retribution, Martin and his colleagues intervened. Acting as intermediaries, the soldiers told Banister of his former slaves' fears and said that they would not turn them over to him without some kind of guarantee of their safety. Frustrated by both the soldiers' interference and the continued intransigence of his enslaved population, Banister finally relented. He gave

<hr>

72. Tucker's journal of siege of Yorktown, *WMQ,* 3d Ser., V (1948), 387, 392–393; Frey, *Water from the Rock,* 171; Pendleton to Madison, Sept. 10, 1781, *Papers of Pendleton,* I, 371; Sylvia R. Frey, "Between Slavery and Freedom: Virginia Blacks in the American Revolution," *Journal of Southern History,* XLIX (1983), 376, 383.

his former slaves a choice whether to return with him or stay where they were. To entice more to return with him, Banister had to promise that he would punish none of them for their own unsuccessful declaration of independence. It was, perhaps, a fitting end. For, when Cornwallis and his troops sailed from Yorktown, their departure marked the success of one rebellion and the end of another.[73]

73. Pybus, "Jefferson's Faulty Math," *WMQ*, 3d Ser., XLII (2005), 243–264. Pybus notes that there might have been another fifteen hundred enslaved Virginians in Portsmouth when the British evacuated. Berlin, *Many Thousands Gone,* 263–264; Frey, *Water from the Rock,* 171; Pendleton to Madison, Sept. 10, 1781, *Papers of Pendleton,* I, 371; Frey, "Between Slavery and Freedom," *Journal of Southern History,* XLIX (1983), 376, 383; Joseph Plumb Martin, *Private Yankee Doodle: Being a Narrative of Some of the Adventures, Dangers, and Sufferings of a Revolutionary Soldier,* ed. George F. Scheer, rev. ed. (n.p., 1998), 241–242.

Toward the New Republic

THE REVOLUTIONARY LEGACY OF THE
WAR FOR INDEPENDENCE

For most Virginians, black and white, Yorktown marked the end of the War for Independence. But, if the war was over, the Revolution continued for many. In the years following Yorktown, both in war and peace, Virginians continued to act out the drama initiated in 1775, drawing on lessons learned in the great conflagration. The experiences of Virginians in the immediate postwar years not only show the extent to which wartime experiences shaped postwar life but also give us a glimpse of how the Revolution and the war had changed and were changing Virginians. But, as messy, divisive, and ambiguous as the Revolutionary war was, so too was its legacy. We cannot easily find the "roots of democracy" or the fundamental social and political changes we might commonly associate with the Revolution. Yet, in looking at both the direct and indirect consequences of wartime conflict in the postwar period, we can begin to understand the nature and magnitude of the changes that were wrought.

Put simply, blacks and poor whites ultimately gained very little from their often heroic efforts in the name of liberty during the war. Instead, middling whites claimed most of the immediate fruits of the Revolution. They cited wartime service and sacrifices, for example, in a tenacious attempt to hold on to their remaining property, even if that "property" had recently risked its life serving in the armed forces in place of its owner. But middling whites also lashed out at their wealthier neighbors, making claims on those who still presumed to rule. They did so by employing wartime strategies of resistance in closing ranks at the local level and by forcing state legislators to put provincial interests first. All of this, of course, had a ripple effect at the Continental level, as more nationalist-minded men sought ways to overcome local resistance, the more democratic tendencies of state legislatures, and, more generally, the factious political culture that had so frustrated them during the war and beyond.[1]

• • • As hostilities came to an end after Yorktown, Virginians of all persuasions began to take stock. Poorer white Virginians, at best, found that the end of the war brought mixed but mostly disappointing results. Those who had joined the Continental army, for example, received few of the rewards for which they had often been fighting, both during the war and after. Very few soldiers were paid regularly, and most were paid in certificates, or promises to pay. But as little as regular soldiers received for their efforts, they invariably lost what they got. In the midst of an immediate postwar economic depression and as the state began to collect heavy taxes, most veterans quickly either redeemed their certificates by paying their taxes with them or, particularly in the case of their congressional final settlement certificates, sold them to speculators at a greatly discounted price. Anticipating Congress's later decision to pay interest on the certificates, a relatively small number of speculators were only too happy to buy up certificates. Soldiers desperate for cash immediately sold their certificates—some to their own officers—simply to return home. Captain Thomas Hamilton told William Davies in March 1782 that many of the regular soldiers got certificates from the auditors but were "selling them for mere nothing." One of them sold a certificate worth forty-eight pounds for four pounds "paid in hand." Unless some step was taken to prevent "such base advantages," he thought the soldiers would be ruined. He even suggested that the auditors stop issuing them.[2]

1. On these developments more generally, see Allan Kulikoff, "Revolutionary Violence and the Origins of American Democracy," *Journal of the Historical Society,* II (2002), 229-260; Michael A. McDonnell, "National Identity and the American War for Independence Reconsidered," *Australasian Journal of American Studies,* XX (2001-2002), 3-17.

2. Beginning in 1780, the states assumed the costs of paying their soldiers. Most states paid their troops in money and certificates in 1781 and 1782. Of Virginia's debt of $2,766,000 specie in 1792, certificates issued to soldiers in the Continental Line accounted for $1,754,000 of this amount, mainly for back pay and depreciated wages accrued beginning in 1780. Virginia paid its troops up to the beginning of 1782, when Congress again assumed the final settlement of soldiers' accounts. Congress mainly issued certificates for commutations of pensions and other items not covered by the state. In total, Congress issued military certificates amounting to nearly $11,000,000. However, $5,000,000 was earmarked for the commutation

Even if soldiers held on to their certificates in the short run, Congress did not redeem them until the 1790s, by which time almost all soldiers had sold them. So too had most civilian holders of certificates for supplies given the Continent during the war. In addition to issuing $11,000,000 in military certificates, Congress also issued another $6,000,000 worth of certificates to civilians. By 1786, only one or two years after the bulk of public securities had been issued by Congress, more than 65 percent of the public securities held by Virginians had passed out of the hands of the original holders. By the early 1790s, when these securities could be exchanged for new bonds expected to trade near their face value under the new government framed by the Constitution, only a tiny proportion remained in the hands of the original holders.[3]

Moreover, very few soldiers actually received the promised bounties of

---

of pensions for officers in the Continental Line, a result of the Newburgh affair. On average, soldiers got only up to $200–$300 in satisfaction of all their claims, whereas officers received between $1,500 (for lieutenants) and $10,000 (for generals). Virginia received a total of $1,129,000 of the Continental sum of $11,000,000. E. James Ferguson, *The Power of the Purse: A History of American Public Finance, 1776–1790* (Chapel Hill, N.C., 1961), 180–181, 187–188, 252, 254–255; Don Higginbotham, *The War of American Independence: Military Attitudes, Policies, and Practice, 1763–1789* (New York, 1971), 412; Thomas Hamilton to William Davies, Mar. 7, 1782, Wm. P. Palmer et al., eds., *Calendar of Virginia State Papers and Other Manuscripts, 1652–1781, Preserved in the Capitol at Richmond* (Richmond, Va., 1875–1893), III, 87; Joseph Plumb Martin, *Private Yankee Doodle: Being a Narrative of Some of the Adventures, Dangers, and Sufferings of a Revolutionary Soldier*, ed. George F. Scheer, rev. ed. (n.p., 1998), 279, 282, 284–287. Cf. ——— to Captain Benjamin Walker, Jan. 10, 1782, Revolutionary Government, War Office Letter Book, 1781–1786, LiVi.

3. In neighboring Maryland, for example, the state owed $900,000 to about 318 people by 1790. However, a mere 16 people owned $455,000, or more than 50 percent of this debt. A total of 48 percent of all holders, who were owed sums of less than $500, held only $28,600—or just more than 3 percent of the debt. The 8 people who owned more than $25,000 each of the debt had almost no original holdings, more than 97 percent of the certificates they owned having changed hands. In contrast, subscriptions of between $1 and $100 had changed hands at a rate of 33 percent. The rate of transfer for the entire debt in Maryland was 81 percent. Thomas Hamilton to William Davies, Mar. 7, 1782, Palmer et al., eds., *Calendar of State Papers,* III, 87; Higginbotham, *War of American Independence,* 412; Martin, *Private Yankee Doodle,* ed. Scheer, 279, 282, 284–287; Ferguson, *Power of the Purse,* 252, 254–255, 275–277.

land. The state laws promising Virginia soldiers land above and beyond the Continental bounty of land appear never to have been enforced. Further, any certificates for land were, like the final settlement certificates, sold off to speculators for desperately needed cash in hand. For its part, Congress did not begin the legislative process to grant veterans land until the ordinance of 1785, and there was little money for the costly enterprise of surveying and disbursing the land. Congress did not grant the first titles to bounty lands until almost fifteen years later. Again, most soldiers had by that time sold their land certificates. Even disabled soldiers struggled to find justice in the postwar world. While Congress granted officers five years' full pay in return for their wartime services, disabled veterans had to wait years for their five dollars per month compensation. Needy veterans were not given a pension until 1818, and it took another ten years for Congress to grant all soldiers a compensatory pension equal to their former pay.[4]

Of course, many soldiers, along with many other poorer whites, did end up moving out west in search of land anyway. Some, as we have seen, had gone to escape military service, or even taxes in eastern Virginia. The newly opened backcountry was a particular draw for men trying to evade the draft and also deserters, especially at the end of the war. As the fighting came to an end in eastern Virginia, hundreds more Virginians began moving west, despite gloomy reports of renewed hostilities with the native American communities who were desperately trying to stop the flood of people onto their lands.

By 1790, fifteen years after the first settlers arrived in Kentucky, there were more than seventy thousand people in the area. Almost half came from Virginia—the majority poor and landless. But most white dreams of a more secure landed future to the west went unfulfilled. Few found prosperity, especially in the near west. One study of Russell County in the far southwest of present-day Virginia shows that 5 percent of landowners

---

4. See Hening, comp., *Statutes at Large,* XI, 565; Higginbotham, *War of American Independence,* 412; Martin, *Private Yankee Doodle,* ed. Scheer, 283. Martin wrote bitterly of his experiences following the war and complained that, though Congress did, in the end, provide lands for the soldiers, "no care was taken that the soldiers should get them." Instead, speculators, "who were driving about the country like so many evil spirits," endeavored to "pluck the last feather from the soldiers." For one detailed analysis of the fate of soldiers from New England who served in the Continental army, see John Resch, *Suffering Soldiers: Revolutionary War Veterans, Moral Sentiment, and Political Culture in the Early Republic* (Amherst, Mass., 1999).

owned more than one thousand acres, and half had only between one and three hundred acres of land. They were the lucky ones. There were huge numbers of landless Virginians who were probably squatting on estates of nonresident speculators. More than 60 percent of taxpayers owned no land. In Fayette County (present-day northeastern Kentucky), too, 63 percent of the population were landless, and 9 percent of heads of households owned fewer than one hundred acres. In Kentucky generally, just more than a third of residents owned land by 1792.[5]

William Burnett, a native of Prince Edward County, puts a human face on the plight of many Virginia veterans. Burnett escaped from servitude during the war by running away and joining the army at age fifteen. He served in various roles for about eighteen months in 1780–1781. When the war ended, he drifted west, first to Henry County, then Wythe County, then Kentucky, and finally Tennessee. Burnett seemed to have no luck secur-

5. Dec. 5, 1781, Diary of Robert Honyman, Jan. 2, 1776–Mar. 11, 1782, Alderman Library, UVa. One officer trying to recruit a state defensive force after Yorktown complained that he needed to pay recruits their bounty money up front to entice them into the service. Eight months later he complained that many young men had taken the bounty he had fronted and promptly headed west to prospect for land. Alexander Spotswood to the Governor, Feb. 12, 1782, Palmer et al., eds., *Calendar of State Papers,* III, 60; Spotswood to John Tyler, Oct. 20, 1782, Executive Communications, LiVi; Fredrika Johanna Teute, "Land, Liberty, and Labor in the post-Revolutionary Era: Kentucky as the Promised Land" (Ph.D. diss., Johns Hopkins University, 1988), 62–64, 143, 160, 185; Elizabeth A. Perkins, *Border Life: Experience and Memory in the Revolutionary Ohio Valley* (Chapel Hill, N.C., 1998), 29–30, 54–55, 83, 84–85; Allan Kulikoff, *Tobacco and Slaves: The Development of Southern Cultures in the Chesapeake, 1680–1800* (Chapel Hill, N.C., 1986), 77. There were 73,677 people in Kentucky by 1790, including some 12,430 enslaved Americans, and 114 free blacks (Perkins, *Border Life,* 54). Norman K. Risjord, *Chesapeake Politics, 1781–1800* (New York, 1978), 45–46; Lee Soltow, "Kentucky Wealth at the End of the Eighteenth Century," *Journal of Economic History,* XLIII (1983), 617–633. Cf. Col. J. Parker to Governor Harrison, Mar. 10, 1782, Palmer et al., eds., *Calendar of State Papers,* III, 91–93; *Va. Gaz.,* May 11, 1782, in Hazel Dicken-Garcia, *To Western Woods: The Breckinridge Family Moves to Kentucky in 1793* (Rutherford, N.J., 1991), 75; Lee Shai Weissbach, "The Peopling of Lexington, Kentucky: Growth and Mobility in a Frontier Town," *Register of the Kentucky Historical Society,* LXXXI (1983), 115–133; Thomas L. Purvis, "The Ethnic Descent of Kentucky's Early Population: A Statistical Investigation of European and American Sources of Emigration, 1740–1820," *Register of the Kentucky Historical Society,* LXXX (1982), 253–266.

ing land or a competency. When Congress finally allowed needy veterans to apply for a pension in 1818, Burnett jumped at the chance. Congress turned his application down.[6]

The movement of so many whites westward had a significant impact in eastern Virginia. Some local leaders in eastern Virginia worried that the war and westward migration were contributing to the rapid drain of the white population from the eastern counties, leaving them more vulnerable to both internal and external enemies. Josiah Parker of Isle of Wight County took note that many of the young militia in his county had been lost during the war—some of them never returned from the army, many had been "swallowed" by the sea, and "some has gone to the back country." Moreover, so many whites had moved out west in the years during and

6. See John C. Dann, ed., *The Revolution Remembered: Eyewitness Accounts of the War for Independence* (Chicago, 1980), 371–373. John Shy speculates that veterans in particular might have been in a better position to move westward in the postwar years because of their experiences during the war: "The so-called Indian barrier was now breached and crumbling, and the prewar migratory trends simply accelerated. . . . Uprooted once by the war, veterans were ready to move again when conditions at home disappointed them." Shy, "The Legacy of the American Revolutionary War," in Shy, *A People Numerous and Armed: Reflections on the Military Struggle for American Independence,* rev. ed. (Ann Arbor, Mich., 1990), 258.

If dreams of landownership eluded many, so too did dreams of a more just society. Unable to secure title on lands monopolized by speculators ahead of their movement west, petitioners to the Virginia legislature and Continental Congress complained that, while they were actually defending the country against the British and Indians, "numbers of monied Gentlemen in the settlement, who lived in security and affluence and no ways contributed towards the defence or settling of this Country, monopolized great part of the most valuable lands in their hands to the great discouragement and hindrance of the equitable settlement thereof." As they had done in eastern Virginia, propertied Virginians protected their property—and particularly their enslaved population—first and foremost while allowing others to provide the first line of defense. See Fredrika J. Teute, "From Modern History to the End of History; or, Reconsidering the Narrative Links between the Antient Cultivation Law and Tenants of the Log Cabin," paper delivered at the conference "Class and Class Struggle in North America and the Atlantic World, 1500–1800," Bozeman, Mont., Sept. 20, 2003, 13. Cf. Petitions from Kentucky residents, Papers of the Continental Congress, no. 48, fols. 237–244, 247–248; *Journals of the Continental Congress* (Washington, D.C., 1904–1937), XVII, 760, XXIII, 532; Paul H. Smith et al., eds., *Letters of Delegates to Congress, 1774–1789* (Washington, D.C., 1976–2000), VI, 456–459.

immediately following the war, for example, that some eastern taxpayers, who suspected that their neighbors had moved west to avoid paying taxes, began to worry that their own tax burden would be increased immeasurably. A petition by inhabitants of Caroline County in the piedmont in late 1784 complained that the public revenue would soon be "greatly diminished by the emigration to the Western Country taking place this fall." They wanted the assembly either to ensure that taxes were laid in the Kentucky region as they were in eastern Virginia or that some provision was made for the collection of the taxes from those who had moved.[7]

Perhaps the greatest impact of the movement of so many whites westward was the entrenchment of slavery in eastern Virginia as a greater proportion of whites who stayed were or became slaveholders and the proportion of black Virginians to whites also rose. Only in western counties, however, was this a result of an absolute increase in the number of enslaved Virginians available. In most eastern counties, like York and Amelia, the enslaved population held steady, but the number of nonslaveholding whites in the counties diminished because of out-migration westward. White immigrants in the new states to the west outnumbered blacks by four to one. Whites who left were generally poor, with few or no slaves. The white population shrank, but the proportion of slaveholders increased: the whites who stayed behind got access to a larger local supply of enslaved labor. In post-Revolutionary Virginia, then, more and more whites who stayed had a direct personal stake in the system. As a result, by 1810, blacks outnumbered whites in fifty-two of eighty-two counties in the Chesapeake, and

7. Col. J. Parker to Governor Harrison, Mar. 10, 1782, Palmer et al., eds., *Calendar of State Papers*, III, 91–93; Teute, "Land, Liberty, and Labor," 143; Caroline County Petition, Nov. 16, 1784, Virginia Legislative Petitions, LiVi. Moreover, because so many poorer tenants in Virginia left to migrate westward in search of land that they could own outright, some planters were forced to change their agricultural practices. In Elizabeth City County, for example, propertyholders tried to stop the out-migration of tenant farmers and use their enslaved population to better effect by hiring out their slaves to poorer neighbors on yearly contracts. Slaveowners could thus gain rental income on both slaves and land, and poorer whites could aspire to some measure of respectability and maybe a stabler future. Richard S. Dunn, "Black Society in the Chesapeake, 1776–1810," in Ira Berlin and Ronald Hoffman, eds., *Slavery and Freedom in the Age of the American Revolution* (Charlottesville, Va., 1983), 77–78; Sarah S. Hughes, "Slaves for Hire: The Allocation of Black Labor in Elizabeth City County, Virginia, 1782 to 1810," *WMQ*, 3d Ser., XXXV (1978), 260–286.

blacks constituted more than 60 percent of the population in twenty-one Virginia counties.[8]

• • • For most of these African Americans—the very lowest class in Virginia—the Revolutionary war brought few positive changes. Some black Virginians eventually found freedom. Many others, however, died seeking it. As with whites who joined the army, postwar life did not bring to black Virginians the benefits they expected and for which many of them had made such mighty sacrifices. Many people—blacks and poor whites— were forced to move west; the former with their masters, the latter seeking greater freedom than they could find in the east. Both lost friends, family, and established kin networks. Neither found the Promised Land.

Many enslaved Virginians did literally fight for their freedom. Just how many found freedom within the British lines or by running away during the war we will never know. When Cornwallis left Yorktown, he probably took hundreds rather than thousands; they joined almost a thousand black Virginians and Marylanders who had escaped earlier in the war in the exodus from New York at the end of the war. Modern conservative estimates put the number of enslaved persons from Maryland and Virginia who escaped at about six thousand. Perhaps only two thousand of these actually found eventual freedom. The majority either died (usually from diseases) or were recaptured by their former owners. We cannot know how many might have died while trying to escape or who never made it to British lines.[9]

At least hundreds more enslaved Virginians fought for their freedom in the patriot forces. Conservative estimates of the number of blacks who

8. In nine Virginia counties between 1782 and 1810, the number of slaveholders rose from forty-three hundred to sixty-two hundred. In 1782, 46 percent of families held enslaved Virginians; by 1810, 54 percent of families did. Dunn, "Black Society in the Chesapeake," in Berlin and Hoffman, eds., *Slavery and Freedom*, 59–62, 66–67.

9. Cassandra Pybus, "Jefferson's Faulty Math: The Question of Slave Defections in the American Revolution," *WMQ*, 3d Ser., LXII (2005), 243–264; Ira Berlin, *Many Thousands Gone: The First Two Centuries of Slavery in North America* (Cambridge, Mass., 1998), 263–264; Allan Kulikoff, "Uprooted Peoples: Black Migrants in the Age of the American Revolution, 1790–1820," in Berlin and Hoffman, eds., *Slavery and Freedom*, 144; Sylvia R. Frey, "Between Slavery and Freedom: Virginia Blacks in the American Revolution," *Journal of Southern History*, XLIX (1983), 376.

served in Virginia forces during the war put the combined total of free and enslaved blacks at five hundred. Given that enslaved Virginians were often used as substitutes for white men in both the militia and the Continental army, and that recruiters were more than eager to accept enslaved Virginians, that figure is probably too low. Enough enslaved Virginians served for their white masters for the issue to come to the attention of the governor at the end of the war. Benjamin Harrison had heard that "many persons" had reenslaved blacks returning from service who had fought for them as substitutes. Even the conservative Harrison could not tolerate such injustice. Harrison felt compelled to give them "that liberty which they have contended for and which they have been in some measure instrumental in securing to us." Harrison's exhortations helped get a law passed in 1783 compelling slaveowners to free any slaves who had served as substitutes. The law recognized that many enslaved Virginians had indeed "contributed towards the establishment of American liberty and independence" and thus "should enjoy the blessings of freedom as a reward for their toils and labours." Some enslaved Virginians used the law to petition for their freedom in later years, claiming their masters held them illegally.[10]

The legislature also recognized that many enslaved Virginians might have earned their freedom in more private ways. During the war, the council and assembly manumitted numbers of enslaved Virginians who had, one way or another, performed "meritorious services" in the eyes of their masters. To reward such services, however, owners had to apply to the government to free their slaves. In recognition of this obstacle and also of the growth of sizable evangelical communities, the assembly repealed a fifty-nine-year-old prohibition on private manumissions in the state in 1782.[11]

The manumission law was a significant new avenue to freedom and

10. Kulikoff, *Tobacco and Slaves,* 419; L. P. Jackson, "Virginia Negro Soldiers and Seamen in the American Revolution," *Journal of Negro History,* XXVII (1942), 247–287, esp. 257 (Kulikoff uses Jackson's number of five hundred total black military men to conclude that fewer than one hundred slaves served in Virginia during the war); Frey, "Between Slavery and Freedom," *Journal of Southern History,* XLIX (1983), 374–398; Benjamin Harrison to the Assembly, Oct. 20, 1783, Executive Communications, LiVi; Hening, comp., *Statutes at Large,* XI, 308, 309.

11. Hening, comp., *Statutes at Large,* XI, 39, XII, 53, 182; Benjamin Quarles, *The Negro in the American Revolution* (Chapel Hill, N.C., 1961), 194; Berlin, *Many Thousands Gone,* 278. For wartime manumissions, see, for example, May 27, July 5, Nov. 14, 1777, H. R. McIlwaine et al., eds., *Journals of the Council of the State of Virginia* (Richmond, Va., 1931–1982), I, 418, 449, II, 28.

facilitated the rapid expansion of the free black population in Virginia after the war. Some whites proceeded to free enslaved Virginians because of their religious beliefs. In Southampton County, where one cluster of Quakers resided, almost twenty immediately began proceedings in court to free their bondsmen. Altogether, within the space of a few months, 106 enslaved Virginians found freedom in Southampton. Other whites freed their slaves for different and diverse reasons. Madison ended up freeing one of his enslaved Virginians, Billy, because he believed that he had been "thoroughly tainted" when he ran away to the British. Though he was recaptured, Madison thought he was no longer a "fit companion for fellow slaves in Virga." However, Madison also recognized the paradox. Billy only wanted "that liberty for which we have paid the price of so much blood, and have proclaimed so often to be [the] right, and worthy the pursuit, of every human being." Many other whites on the exposed Virginia coastlines also took advantage of the law and emancipated their slaves, perhaps for reasons similar to Madison's. By the end of the century, there were significant clusters of free blacks in counties along the lower James River and on the Eastern Shore, the areas hardest hit by the presence of the British. The towns of Richmond, Norfolk, and Petersburg also had sizable populations of free blacks. The law also helped free blacks purchase and emancipate other enslaved Virginians. Graham Bell, for example, freed five enslaved children whom he had bought three years earlier. Nine years later, he bought and manumitted an enslaved woman who paid him fifteen pounds. In 1802, he emancipated two more enslaved Virginians, declaring, "God created all men equally free," and in 1805 he freed his own brother.[12]

12. Dunn, "Black Society in the Chesapeake," in Berlin and Hoffman, eds., *Slavery and Freedom,* 50, 74, 75, 77; Kulikoff, *Tobacco and Slaves,* 433; Kenneth L. Carroll, "Religious Influences on the Manumission of Slaves in Caroline, Dorchester, and Talbot Counties," *Maryland Historical Magazine,* LXVI (1961), 176–197; Nov. 14, Dec. 12, 1782, Feb. 13, 1783, Southampton County, Order Book, 1778–1784, LiVi, fols. 248–250, 255; Louis Morton, *Robert Carter of Nomini Hall: A Virginia Tobacco Planter of the Eighteenth Century* (Williamsburg, Va., 1941), chap. 11; *Papers of Madison,* VII, 304; Berlin, *Many Thousands Gone,* 259; Mary Beth Norton, Herbert Gutman, and Ira Berlin, "The Afro-American Family in the Age of Revolution," in Berlin and Hoffman, eds., *Slavery and Freedom,* 189. Cf. Martin, *Private Yankee Doodle,* ed. Scheer, 242–243.

Perhaps more dramatically, Robert Carter of Nomini Hall arranged in 1791 to free all 509 of his enslaved population over a twenty-two-year period. Though not

Manumission activity surged in the years immediately following the end of the Revolutionary war and diminished somewhat until the number of emancipations leveled off at about 100 per year between 1787 and 1806. Altogether, the number of free blacks in Virginia and Maryland multiplied more than six times between 1780 and 1800. Manumissions created a substantial class of free blacks in the Chesapeake for the first time. Along with natural increase, the manumission law meant that, by 1810, the total free black population in the Chesapeake was 60,000, of whom 31,750 lived in Virginia. In all, one-third of free blacks in the United States lived in the Chesapeake by 1810.[13]

Despite the large number of enslaved Virginians who found freedom, the war left perhaps a more pervasive negative legacy for black Virginians in two important ways. Black activism during the war, for example, might have curtailed the number of postwar manumissions. Even as legislators contemplated the manumission law, enslaved Virginians continued to act against patriot whites. On the Eastern Shore, militia officers reported in May 1782 that they had suffered from "horrid dangers" for the past twelve months from privateers, refugee loyalists, and enslaved Virginians who had formed "bloody plots" against the chief patriots in the county. They had plundered families, turned women and children out of their homes, and induced more enslaved Virginians to join them, arming them with *"ropes as instruments of death."* One master discovered his slave in the midst of a plot, then foiled the scheme, and yet was still murdered. Enslaved Virginians posed such a threat to Eastern Shore inhabitants that local militia officers pleaded with the government to leave regular troops there, lest "general Anarchy" follow. Fearful that legally freed Virginians would offer a refuge for escaped and rebellious ones, more than sixty men from Accomack petitioned the assembly against the manumission law.[14]

Given enslaved Virginians' activities during the war, many whites

---

all of his slaves were freed by 1810, the Westmoreland census that year showed there were 621 free blacks in the county, one of the highest county totals.

13. Dunn, "Black Society in the Chesapeake," in Berlin and Hoffman, eds., *Slavery and Freedom,* 50, 62; Kulikoff, *Tobacco and Slaves,* 432; Ira Berlin, *Slaves without Masters: The Free Negro in the Antebellum South* (New York, 1974), chaps. 1, 2.

14. John Cropper to William Davies, May 2, 1782, George Corbin to Davies, May 2, 1782, Palmer et al., eds., *Calendar of State Papers,* III, 149, 166; Accomack County Petition, [June 3, 1782], Virginia Legislative Petitions, LiVi.

throughout the state were angry about the new manumission law. More than 1,200 white Virginians signed antimanumission petitions between 1784 and 1785. More than 110 people in Henrico County alone signed a petition that revealed that black Virginians were still using the war—and its lessons—as a means to gain their freedom. The petitioners believed that many newly freed black Virginians were aiding enslaved Virginians in evading capture. They were convinced that a great number of enslaved Virginians who were thought to have gone off with the army were still in the state. Not only did the increase in free blacks make it easier for such men to pass as free men, but freed blacks were also serving as "agents, Factors, and carriers" for escaped slaves. The petition also reflected a wider-spread concern among white Virginians about a postwar increase in black commercial autonomy, as more and more enslaved Virginians used valuable wartime skills and hired themselves out and traded on the black market.[15]

The mixed and often bitter legacy of black involvement in the War for Independence was one reason why abolitionist sentiment in Virginia was limited in intensity and short-lived. By the end of the 1780s, few whites crusaded for black emancipation. Within a generation, the manumission law had been repealed. And fewer than 10 percent of the black population found freedom during this period. Moreover, these freedmen lived precarious and marginal lives, in an increasingly racist society.[16]

15. Kulikoff, *Tobacco and Slaves,* 433; Henrico County Petition, Nov. 16, 1784, Virginia Legislative Petitions, LiVi; Sylvia R. Frey, *Water from the Rock: Black Resistance in a Revolutionary Age* (Princeton, N.J., 1991), 223-224. Cf. Fredrika Teute Schmidt and Barbara Ripel Wilhelm, "Early Proslavery Petitions in Virginia," *WMQ,* 3d Ser., XXX (1973), 133-146; Jon Kukla, "The Irrelevance and Relevance of Saints George and Thomas," *VMHB,* CII (1994), 261-270; Henrico County Petition, June 8, 1782, Virginia Legislative Petitions, LiVi.

16. More significantly, perhaps, within a generation of the end of the conflict, more blacks were enslaved in Virginia than ever before. More than 90 percent of blacks in the state were still enslaved, and the enslaved population had nearly doubled since 1776. Dunn, "Black Society in the Chesapeake," in Berlin and Hoffman, eds., *Slavery and Freedom,* 50, 52, 59, 62, 80; Kulikoff, *Tobacco and Slaves,* 434. Even during the war, the enslaved population actually grew because of natural increase from 210,000 at the beginning of the war to 236,000 in 1783. Despite the number of enslaved Virginians who found freedom, whites collectively did not lose slaves. In fact, the growth in numbers helped encourage them to ban the importation of more slaves in order to capitalize on the internal slave trade. Berlin,

Directly or indirectly, black activism during the war also caused thousands of white Virginians to move or sell their slaves farther westward, disrupting long-established and complex family and kinship networks. Forced migrations began when the British invaded the state, particularly under Cornwallis. Because white masters could not trust their black workers to remain on the plantation or avoid capture by the British, they often moved them out of the way of the enemy. Eleven tidewater counties, most of them in the immediate vicinity of Yorktown, reported a loss in the black population in 1782. Among them, they had twelve thousand fewer slaves than in 1755. Many, of course, had fled. Owners forcibly removed most others to counties in the southside and piedmont. The westward movement of enslaved Virginians began a general pattern of forced migration and greater increases in the interior counties that foreshadowed a much larger and longer period of migration westward into Kentucky, Tennessee, and beyond. For patriots, the Revolutionary war sanctioned the exploitation and appropriation of all lands west of Virginia, regardless of any remaining native American claims. By 1790, there were as many as fifteen thousand enslaved people in Kentucky alone. Many blacks had not fled toward freedom behind British lines during the Revolutionary war, because of their extended connections in the community. They now faced involuntary separations on a scale they had never experienced before.[17]

For black Virginians then, the Revolutionary war was indeed a crucial but also ultimately disappointing moment. On one hand, the Revolution helped foster a climate in which blacks could make a legitimate claim for freedom. On the other hand, the institution of slavery became wider-spread and more deeply entrenched in most places east of the Blue Ridge Mountains after the war. Thus it might have been no accident that black rebelliousness continued—and grew more violent—in the postwar period as enslaved Virginians grew increasingly frustrated with the lack of movement in southern emancipation and angry at the prospect of being forced to move westward. Between 1785 and 1794, the number of deadly assaults by blacks on whites rose dramatically, with 148 blacks convicted of mur-

---

Many Thousands Gone, 263–264; Allan Kulikoff, "Uprooted Peoples," in Berlin and Hoffman, eds., *Slavery and Freedom,* 144.

17. Dunn, "Black Society in the Chesapeake," in Berlin and Hoffman, eds., *Slavery and Freedom,* 58–62, and Kulikoff, "Uprooted Peoples," 143–171; Berlin, *Many Thousands Gone,* 264–265.

dering whites, another 24 convicted of attempted murder, and 10 executed or transported for assault. This rise in violence coincided with a number of insurrection scares and actual uprisings. St. George Tucker, who lived long enough to see the disruption of the war as well as Gabriel's Rebellion in 1800, thought he saw a difference between the slaves who responded to Dunmore's Proclamation in 1775 and those who took part in the plot in 1800: those who rose up in 1775 fought for freedom as a good, and those who rose up in 1800 claimed freedom as a right.[18]

• • • Unfortunately, black claims to freedom as a right ran headlong into the increasingly assertive claims of an aspiring white middling class to uphold their rights to preserve their property. Indeed, proslavery petitions written to protest any embryonic moves toward a general emancipation of enslaved Virginians in 1784 and 1785 indicate that many slaveholding whites linked their own participation in the war with their right to hold others in bondage. More than 160 petitioners from Lunenburg County, for example, asserted that they had broken from Britain, "sacrificed our Ease, Lives and fortunes, and waded thro' Deluges of civil Blood" for their right to their property. They had "seald with our Blood, a Title to the full, free, and absolute Enjoyment of every species of our Property." Equally did almost 300 petitioners from the counties of Amelia, Mecklenburg, and Pittsylvania assert that the new state Constitution was established in order to secure property and that they had "risked our Lives and Fortunes, and waded through Seas of Blood" to defend it.[19]

18. Frey, *Water from the Rock,* 225; Philip J. Schwarz, *Twice Condemned: Slaves and the Criminal Laws of Virginia, 1705-1865* (Baton Rouge, La., 1988), 231, 247; Dunn, "Black Society in the Chesapeake," in Berlin and Hoffman, eds., *Slavery and Freedom,* 81, and Benjamin Quarles, "The Revolutionary War as a Black Declaration of Independence," 294; Gerald W. Mullin, *Flight and Rebellion: Slave Resistance in Eighteenth-Century Virginia* (New York, 1972), 157. In the heart of the piedmont, Cumberland County resident W. J. Moulson wrote to the governor in early May because he had had word that "a dangerous insurrection is among the Negroes meditated, and a little after Harvest they mean to put it in Execution." Moulson refused to disclose any further details, for fear of fanning the fires. W. J. Moulson to Patrick Henry, May 6, 1786, Palmer et al., eds., *Calendar of State Papers,* IV, 132.

19. Dunn, "Black Society in the Chesapeake," in Berlin and Hoffman, eds., *Slavery and Freedom,* 81, and Benjamin Quarles, "The Revolutionary War as a Black

The proslavery petitions of 1784-1785 represented a marked change in the attitudes of many freeholders and middling men in the postwar period. Indeed, in many freeholders' eyes, military service and wartime sacrifices, however extensive or limited, legitimized *several* key postwar demands. Those included their right to hold others in bondage as property, their right to property more generally, and a right to local autonomy and limited outside interference in their affairs.

Freeholders' concerns over their right to their property were expressed most acutely in their resistance to postwar taxes. The huge cost of the war had yet to be paid, as many taxes had been deferred during the conflict. But, by the end of the war, if not before, many freeholders believed they had already paid their fair share of the cost of war through service in the militia, onerous high prices, and impressments of their produce to feed the armies. They also believed that the enormous expense of raising a more permanent army had been a significant sacrifice. In the end, mobilization had taught freeholders that military service and the payment of taxes were one and the same thing. Thus, when patriot leaders began pushing for the collection of regular taxes starting in 1782, they ran into massive opposition among people who protested paying even more for the war. But the experience of war and wartime military service now both validated postwar tax resistance and taught successful strategies of resistance.

These links between military service, taxes, and resistance were made patently clear in 1782, when Governor Harrison tried to reinstitute the failed 1781 draft for Continental soldiers. After Yorktown, the war was not yet officially over, and it was not yet clear that Cornwallis's surrender was decisive. Congress was still intent on keeping the Continental army together, and Washington was keen to maintain and possibly increase his scant numbers. Both sent letters to the Virginia government in late 1781 demanding that it fulfill its Continental obligations. When the assembly failed to act decisively, William Davies, the commissioner of war, managed to persuade the council to push ahead and issue an executive order calling for all counties to complete their previous drafts if they had not already done so.[20]

Declaration of Independence," 294; Schmidt and Wilhelm, "Early Proslavery Petitions in Virginia," *WMQ*, 3d Ser., XXX (1973), 138-143.

20. See Address of Congress to the States, Dec. 17, 1781, George Washington to the Governor, Dec. 19, 1781, Hening, comp., *Statutes at Large*, X, 499-500, 578-579, 581-582; Nov. 9, 1781, McIlwaine et al., eds., *Journals of the Council*, II, 399.

The executive order provoked an outburst from both outraged militia and weary officers who knew they could not enforce it. The responses reflected the lessons learned throughout the war. Some officers went ahead with the order but looked the other way when their draftees deserted. Other officers and militia responded forcefully but peacefully, usually citing their military experience as an excuse not to go ahead with the order. Increasingly, the militia were quick to assert that they had actually done more than their fair share of the fighting, contrasting their wartime service with that of Continental soldiers. If passive resistance and peaceful protest were not sufficient, the militia resorted to illegal and violent measures. When the officers of Greenbriar County tried to draft their militia, they were opposed by a large number of people who would not, according to the county lieutenant there, "suffer us to proceed." Just the threat of violence also forced the hands of militia officers. In Augusta County, scene of one of the riots in the summer of 1781, local officials feared a resumption, and the county lieutenant thought it highly "probable" that the day of the draft would "begin with tumult and End in some thing worse."[21]

As they had begun to do during the war, the militia put the assembly squarely between themselves and the executive. Acutely aware of their new

---

Davies, trying to take stock of Virginia's contributions, reckoned that the state had raised only about a quarter of the men Washington had asked for.

But the assembly, still reeling from the near catastrophic events of the summer, only passed a weak law calling for the voluntary enlistment of up to three thousand soldiers for two years' service or the duration of the war. The recruits were not to be drafted, but, rather, enlisted by recruiting officers, who were given generous bounties in specie to entice men.

21. Recounting their troubles throughout the war, Josiah Parker of Isle of Wight County concluded that, even in the past year alone, "we have all actually been Soldiers more than Twelve months, maintained ourselves, and did as labourious and dangerous duty as any Soldiers in the Continental Army." Col. J. Parker to Governor Harrison, Mar. 10, 1782, Palmer et al., eds., *Calendar of State Papers,* III, 91–93. Cf. Anthony Thornton to the Governor, Feb. 25, 1782, 77, William Davies to Benjamin Harrison, Mar. 5, 1782, 84, William Edmunds to the Governor, Apr. 2, 1782, 465, John Harmanson to William Davies, May 14, 1782, 164, Thomas Newton to William Davies, Mar. 17, 1782, 101, Thomas Gaskins to William Davies, Apr. 30, 1782, 155, Samueal Brown to William Davies, Apr. 14, 1782, 130, George Moffett to the Governor, Mar. 20, 1782, 104, William Edmunds to the Governor, Apr. 2, 1782, 465.

constitutional rights, both officers and ordinary militia questioned the executive's right to reinstate these drafts. Militia from Augusta County, for example, told the county lieutenant, George Moffett, that the order was contrary to the spirit of the last recruiting law passed by the assembly in November, which mentioned no drafts. To ensure that the executive order was contrary to the mind of the assembly, militia across the state also petitioned their elected representatives in an effort to override it. Employing numerous and well-rehearsed arguments against the draft, militia called for property-proportioned contributions toward bounties for volunteers. Further drafts, many claimed, were—in light of their wartime sacrifices— "cruel, oppressive, and highly derogatory to the heaven born Freedom for which we have so bravely struggled (by spilling our Blood and exhausting our Treasure)."[22]

Significantly, the assembly responded with a new law that tied wartime mobilization directly to the collection of taxes. The militia were to be divided into classes, but only those militia who had not paid one-eighth of their taxes would be liable to be drafted. The new law, then, entrenched the wishes of many middling militia that the payment of taxes should be sufficient to exempt them from active military service. Conversely, anyone who could not contribute to the public defense through his financial contributions, the law implied, would have to do bodily service.[23]

In tying together military service and taxes, the law not only reflected years of wartime development and the logical culmination of militia demands throughout the crisis, but in practice it also pointed toward a new and widespread phenomenon in postwar Virginia: tax resistance. At first, it seemed that the law was working as it should. In many counties, from tidewater Elizabeth City, to southside Lunenburg County, to previously troubled areas like Westmoreland County in the Northern Neck, and to Augusta County in the Shenandoah Valley, the commanding officers re-

22. Samueal Brown to William Davies, Apr. 14, 1782, ibid., 130, George Moffett to the Governor, Mar. 20, 1782, 104, William Edmunds to the Governor, Apr. 2, 1782, 465; Hanover County Petition, [May 24, 1782], Virginia Legislative Petitions, LiVi; Augusta County Petition, [May 30, 1782], Virginia Legislative Petitions, LiVi. Cf. Culpeper County Petition, Oct. 23, 1782, Virginia Legislative Petitions, LiVi.

23. Hening, comp., *Statutes at Large,* XI, 14.-20. The new law pleased few Continental officials. See, for example, Nathanael Greene to Governor Harrison, July 25, 1782, Palmer et al., eds., *Calendar of State Papers,* III, 229-230.

ported that virtually every militia man had paid his proportion of the taxes.[24]

As much as it seemed that militia were only too happy to do their patriotic duty by paying their taxes, it soon became clear that many militia were taking liberties with the new law and forcing their officers to cover for them. In some places, militia who were actually exempt from service were very slow to pay their taxes. In many places, militia had made only promises to pay the tax. Because the assembly had made the link between wartime service and the payment of taxes explicit, some militia began to demand retrospective recognition of their previous military service. In Botetourt County, George Skillern told the governor there were many men who had served in the militia, endured the hardships of the previous year, and never been properly paid what they had been promised. Now these same men could not pay their taxes. Skillern was surprised to find that his militia were not only applying to him for relief from the soldier's tax, but some were threatening to sue him for what they were owed. Little money was actually collected. In November 1782, only fifteen county lieutenants of seventy-two counties had sent a return of the money they had collected under the new act or the men they had raised.[25]

24. Roe Cowper to the Governor, Sept. 6, 1782, Palmer et al., eds., *Calendar of State Papers,* III, 290, Richard Henry Lee to Benjamin Harrison, Sept. 6, 1782, 291, John Coleman to the Governor, Sept. 13, 1782, 306, Nicholas Hobson to the Governor, Sept. 17, 1782, 313, John Bott to the Governor, Sept. 20, 1782, 315, George Moffett to the Governor, Nov. 8, 1782, 367. Cf. John Nash to the Governor, Sept. 20, 1782, 315, Abraham Green to the Executive, Nov. 11, 1782, 368, Thomas Fox to the Governor, Nov. 15, 1782, 372.

25. Leighton Wood, Jr., the new attorney general responsible for enforcing the collection of the soldier's tax, reported as late as July 1784 that forty-seven counties were delinquent for various sums. The larger counties appeared to be the worst offenders, with Dinwiddie still owing £815, Fauquier owing £641, and Berkeley still owing £398. In total, the counties still owed the state £7,515 for the 1782 soldier's tax alone. Roe Cowper to the Governor, Sept. 6, 1782, Palmer et al., eds., *Calendar of State Papers,* III, 290, Richard Henry Lee to Benjamin Harrison, Sept. 6, 1782, 291, John Pierce to the Governor, Sept. 27, 1782, 329; George Skillern to the Governor, Apr. 29, 1783, 473; William Davies to Nathaniel Greene, Sept. 22, 1782, Revolutionary Government, War Office Letter Book, 1781–1786, LiVi, and Circular Letter to the County Lieutenants and Recruiting Officers, Nov. 8, 1782; "List of Balances Due from the County Lieutenants, or Commanding Officers, under the Act of Assembly for Recruiting the State's Quota of Troops, to Serve in the Army

• • • As the war came to an official close, there were many reasons why ordinary Virginians found it difficult to pay their mounting taxes. A lack of ready cash—exacerbated by the withdrawal of the Continental and French forces—was one of the biggest problems facing farmers in Virginia. Complaints continued well into the late 1780s. But the lack of cash was compounded by a series of poor harvests, particularly of wheat and of corn. Many sheriffs and local officials worried that, quite apart from paying their taxes, many of their neighbors were suffering from a lack of basic necessities, and they were reluctant to press claims for taxes.[26]

The lack of cash combined with the poor crops meant that many white Virginians refused to pay their taxes because of their "distressed situation." But impoverished Virginians were quick to use their wartime sacrifices to legitimate their opposition to postwar taxes. Some claimed or demanded relief on the basis of their direct participation in the war effort. Gray Briggs of Dinwiddie County told the governor in the spring of 1782 that his neighbors were angry about the last tax act because, they claimed, they had been out on militia service for most of the previous year rather than get-

_____

of the United States, Passed in May Session, 1782," Palmer et al., eds., *Calendar of State Papers,* III, 600. Cf. John Banister to Benjamin Harrison, Apr. 14, 1783, Revolutionary Government, War Office Letter Book, 1781–1786, LiVi.

When militia could not pay their taxes, they offered up their property in lieu, but maybe because they knew no one would purchase their distrained property. Anthony Thornton to the Governor, Nov. 18, 1782, Palmer et al., eds., *Calendar of State Papers,* III, 373, John Coleman to the Governor, Sept. 13, 1782, 306; cf. Joseph Holmes to ———, Dec. 4, 1782, 389, James Holt to the Governor, Jan. 27, 1782, 422; Governor to the County Lieutenant of Fauquier, Nov. 9, Dec. 30, 1782, Revolutionary Government, War Office Letter Book, 1781–1786, LiVi; William Edmunds to the Governor, Apr. 2, 1782, Palmer et al., eds., *Calendar of State Papers,* III, 465.

26. On lack of cash, see, for example, Petition of Geddes Winston, February 1786, Leighton Wood, Jr., to the Governor, Feb. 11, 1786, Palmer et al., eds., *Calendar of State Papers,* IV, 87, William Grayson to the Governor, Jan. 22, 1785, 7, and 77–78. For local officials' reluctance to press claims, see William Grayson to the Governor, Jan. 22, 1785, 7, Sheriff of Nansemond to the Governor, Sept. 10, 1786, 168, John Berryman to the Governor, Sept. 24, 1786, 174, William Ronald et al. to the Executive, Nov. 26, 1786, 185, William Ronald to the Executive, Apr. 10, 1787, 264–265, William Boyer to the Executive, Oct. 15, 1784, 617; William White to the Governor, July 21, 1785, Governor's Office, Militia Commissions, Louisa County, LiVi.

ting their crops in. Significantly, they contrasted their military service with the actions of the magistrates in the county with whom they were supposed to lodge their list of taxable goods. They claimed, and Briggs agreed, that most of the magistrates were in hiding during the military crisis. By the time the magistrates "ventured home," according to Briggs, many taxpayers were out on active duty.[27]

Many others also protested against postwar taxes because of their wartime losses. In Dinwiddie, Briggs claimed that the 1782 tax assessed people on the basis of the numbers of enslaved Virginians they held in 1781. Given the great losses of both forms of property in the face of the British invasion, he thought their complaints were just, because the assessment subjected "great numbers of people to the paiment of a tax on slaves that are dead or shipped beyond sea by the British." Many in the lower counties of the tidewater claimed to be particularly hard-hit by the war. John Peyton, for example, told the governor as late as 1787 that he and his deputy sheriffs had not been able to collect any taxes since the war ended. There was no money in the county, nor any tobacco. More than one hundred inhabitants then blamed the war for their problems in a petition. On one hand, the armies on both sides had exhausted Gloucester, which had been completely stripped of any livestock. On the other, their lands had been ravaged sufficiently to prevent them from cultivating any tobacco. They were thus unable to pay "such heavy taxes, as at present they are loaded with, without selling Lands or Negroes." They would do even this if, through selling such property, they could get anywhere near their value. But few people had any money to purchase anything.[28]

27. Tax collectors in Cumberland County failed in 1785, they said, because of the "hardness of the times." A list of sheriff's petitions in 1785 and 1786 asking for relief from prosecution for the taxes owed to the state cited the scarcity of money and the general "poverty of the people" as the principal reasons why they were in arrears. Anthony New and L. Temple to Patrick Henry, Apr. 2, 1786, Palmer et al., eds., *Calendar of State Papers,* IV, 111, and 77–78; Petition of Joseph Carrington, Robert Anderson, and John Lee, Nov. 5, 1788, Virginia Legislative Petitions, LiVi; Gray Briggs to the Executive, May 16, 1782, box 23, Executive Papers, LiVi. Cf. Petition of Thomas Hughart, July 30, 1788, Palmer et al., eds., *Calendar of State Papers,* IV, 468, Petition of Jonathan Patteson, Apr. 23, 1787, 271, William Augustine Washington to the Governor, Nov. 7, 1788, 509, Nick Cabell to Patrick Henry, Jan. 17, 1786, 82.

28. John Peyton to the Executive, Feb. 21, 1787, Palmer et al., eds., *Calendar*

Lurking behind the farmers' complaints was a deep bitterness that the promise of the Revolution had gone unfulfilled and their wartime sacrifices had been in vain. The petitioners from Gloucester found themselves "short of that happiness, ease and plenty, so much Boasted of upon an establishment of our Independence and peace." The least the governor could do was recognize their contributions to the war effort and grant them some relief from taxes now.[29]

Most local officials were sympathetic to the plight and complaints of their neighbors. However, beginning in 1782, Wood, as the new attorney general, began pressing tax officials in general, and sheriffs in particular, for the taxes owed by their counties. Tax collectors were personally liable for the money owed to the state. Pressed by Wood, some local officials took a chance and began putting pressure on their neighbors. Ordinary Virginians reacted in different ways but generally avoided paying taxes by a variety of means. The most successful strategies of tax resistance in the postwar period owed a lot to the lessons learned about obstructing unpopular state laws during the war.

In many cases, people tried to manipulate the laws. Believing the law on their side, they were often prepared to back up their position by force of arms. In Richmond County, for example, two men, Robert Mitchell and Robert B. Carter, owed just more than two pounds each for the soldier's tax in 1782. The county lieutenant, Leroy Peachey, had apparently allowed the two men to go without paying the tax when it was due in 1782, even though he was supposed to draft delinquents. When the state attorney pressed Peachey for full payment, he, in turn, began pressing his neighbors by authorizing the distress and sale of the goods and property of the delinquents. Mitchell, a militia officer and justice of the peace, took advantage of Peachey's failure to draft delinquent taxpayers and claimed that the reason he never paid the tax was that he was willing to serve in the military. He then told the collector that, if "I seas'd any of his property he blow my brains out or any other man that come in an arbitrary way as he look'd upon that to be as such." The other tax delinquent took heart from

---

of State Papers, IV, 246, Petition of the inhabitants of Gloucester County, Apr. 17, 1787, 270–271. Peyton owed £4,851 for taxes and interest for 1783 alone (see III, 591).

29. Thomas Nelson, Jr., to Governor Randolph, Mar. 22, 1787, ibid., IV, 260, Petition of the inhabitants of Gloucester County, Apr. 17, 1787, 270–271.

Mitchell's position: he would not pay, as he believed Mitchell "understood the law better than he did."[30]

Many taxpayers could rely on their neighbors to help exonerate them. Though sheriffs could seize property and sell it for the nonpayment of taxes, they had to bring to court those who refused to give a list of their taxable property. Gray Briggs of Dinwiddie County explained the peril for many sheriffs. Though the sheriff might be able to persuade enough members of the grand jury to make appropriate presentments in the court, he could not count on the support of petit juries to uphold their claims against delinquents, particularly when they had public support.[31]

Juries also protected ordinary Virginians in postwar debt cases. During the war, as a concession to those fighting for Independence, no British creditors could collect debts in the courts, and few domestic creditors were able to use the courts either. Beginning in 1782, both domestic and British creditors began pushing to collect their now years-old debts. Though the assembly did not stand in the way of the domestic creditors, it did make concessions to debtors. It suspended any executions for debts until December of 1783, and, in recognition of the shortage of specie, it allowed payment of debts in hemp, tobacco, and flour and gave the county courts freedom to fix the value of such goods in debt cases. Worried that the debtors would pay up in produce the creditors did not want and that the courts would value the produce too high, Virginia creditors delayed action on their suits.[32]

Creditors had reason to be terrified of taking their suits before juries.

30. Warrant, *Commonwealth v. Mitchell and another,* Leroy Peachey to ———, Oct. 18, 1783, Miscellaneous Revolutionary Collection, box 1, LiVi. Peachey, now liable for the money, claimed in the General Court that he could do nothing more to collect the tax in the face of such threats. Cf. John Pierce to the Governor, and John Pierce to William Davies, Sept. 27, 1782, Palmer et al., eds., *Calendar of State Papers,* III, 291.

31. Briggs believed that most people owing money would point to their militia service the previous year and contrast it with the flight of the magistrates and tax commissioners of the county: "We shall never get a petit jury to find guilty those who can prove that the magistrates with whom they were to enlist [their tithables], were hiding from the enemy great part of the summer." Gray Briggs to the Executive, May 16, 1782, box 23, Executive Papers, LiVi.

32. A. G. Roeber, *Faithful Magistrates and Republican Lawyers: Creators of Virginia Legal Culture, 1680–1810* (Chapel Hill, N.C., 1981), 171–172; Charles T. Cullen, *St. George Tucker and Law in Virginia, 1772–1804* (New York, 1987), 32, 35.

John Hook, a partner of David Ross in one of the largest mercantile firms in Virginia, complained that most of the debts owing to them would have to be collected in the courts, as most debtors seemed happy to "stand out in hopes if juries will acquit them of Interests." Most did. Though creditors won a substantial majority of their suits, juries had the power of awarding damages, or interest. If a plaintiff sensed he might lose the case or that the jury was hostile, he often withdrew the suit in order to prosecute at a later date. Of those who won, few won back the damages, or interest, that they had declared, and most had to settle for reduced damages. Out-of-court settlements also usually involved dropping the interest that had accumulated over the wartime years. Creditors, frustrated by the slowness of the courts and the power of local juries to acquit defendants of the lion's share of their interest-laden debts, could do little except agitate for a reform of the courts.[33]

Sheriffs, if distraining property, also ran into local and collective opposition. Most often, neighbors of delinquent taxpayers simply refused to purchase any seized property. Geddes Winston of Hanover County told the attorney general that popular opposition to his efforts made his job impossible. He and his collectors had seized a great deal of property in lieu of unpaid taxes and appointed proper days for the sale of the goods, but "nobody would purchase" the seized property. Taxpayers in Mecklenburg County had employed the same strategy the same year. So too had Gloucester County citizens in 1782 and 1783 when, according to John Peyton, they agreed among themselves not to purchase one another's estates when they were seized. The sheriff of Princess Anne County had also "repeatedly seized the property of those who were in arrears and advertized it for sale, but such was the scarcity of money and the temper of the People,"

33. F. Thornton Miller, *Juries and Judges versus the Law: Virginia's Provincial Legal Perspective, 1783-1828* (Charlottesville, Va., 1994), 35-37, 46. Collective and passive resistance at the local level and in the local courts was repeated in later agrarian uprisings. See Mary K. Bonsteel-Tachau, "A New Look at the Whiskey Rebellion," in Steven R. Boyd, ed., *The Whiskey Rebellion: Past and Present Perspectives* (Westport, Conn., 1985), 97-118; Barbara Karsky, "Agrarian Problems in the New Republic," paper, European Association for American Studies Annual Conference, Bordeaux, April 2002, 7. Debts owed to British creditors were even more difficult to collect. At Independence, Virginians owed their British creditors close to two million pounds. See Bruce A. Ragsdale, *A Planter's Republic: The Search for Economic Independence in Revolutionary Virginia* (Madison Wis., 1996), 262; Risjord, *Chesapeake Politics,* 110-115.

he complained, that "in many cases no persons would bid." Tax resistance of this kind continued through the mid-1780s. A note, probably written by the attorney general at the end of 1787, detailed the many ways in which citizens formed "combinations to defeat the coercive measures adopted by the sheriffs to collect delinquent taxes."[34]

In places where "combinations" were not formed to prevent purchases of distrained goods, citizens took more drastic action. In Louisa County, for example, the sheriff noted that the property he had seized was sold at auction but "went exceedingly low" because of the scarcity of specie and the poverty of the people. One gentleman testified that he bought a large tract of land at two shillings per acre when it was actually valued at twenty shillings. Incensed at the prospect of selling their property "to suffer for a trifle," some taxpayers in Louisa quietly moved out of the county. Others in Louisa stole back their distrained property under cover of night. Finally, some farmers threatened to shoot the sheriff if he tried to seize their property.[35]

The pressure that sheriffs came under in the postwar period was reminiscent of the threats militia officers faced during the war. Squeezed on one side by angry and resistant neighbors and on the other by anxious state leaders keen to collect badly needed revenue, sheriffs were often forced onto the defensive. With few coercive resources, they more often than not ended up on the side of their neighbors. Indeed, judgments against sheriffs for delinquent taxes turned many prominent citizens into debtors of the state. Attorney General Wood told the governor in the spring of 1783 that he had a list of judgments against fifty-three delinquent sheriffs that he had obtained in the general court. The sheriffs collectively owed the state £53,385. In 1785, Wood again made a list of delinquent sheriffs against

34. Petition of Geddes Winston, February 1786, Palmer et al., eds., *Calendar of State Papers,* IV, 94, John Peyton to Edmund Randolph, July 29, 1788, 467–468, Petition of Reuben Vaughan, July 19, 1786, 154, Petition of the Sheriff of Nansemond County, Sept. 10, 1786, 168, Petition of the Sheriff of Princess Anne County, Apr. 26, 1786, 121, William Ronald et al. to the Executive, Nov. 26, 1786, 185, 280. Cf. William Augustine Washington to the Governor, Nov. 7, 1788, 509, Daniel Herring to Beverley Randolph, Dec. 20, 1788, 534; Petition of Joseph Carrington, Robert Anderson, and John Lee, Nov. 5, 1788, Virginia Legislative Petitions, LiVi.

35. Thomas Johnson to the Executive, Jan. 19, 1786, Palmer et al., eds., *Calendar of State Papers,* IV, 82. Johnson claimed that his neighbors were not opposed to the payment of taxes, but were angry at having to sell their property at such low prices. Many wanted a chance to sell their tobacco before they paid up.

whom he had obtained judgments. Forty were delinquent, representing almost three-quarters of the counties in the state. The amount outstanding totaled nearly £40,000. Thus, in diverse ways, ordinary white Virginians were able to maintain some semblance of control over the local institutions of government that affected them most directly, as they had done in the militia. As state officials tried to tighten control over the counties by making local officials more responsible for their neighbors' obedience to the laws, they succeeded only in humiliating some of their most respected citizens.[36]

Because of this, fewer people stepped forward to undertake the once-cherished position of sheriff. Some were unable or unwilling to give sufficient security for the collection of taxes; others simply resigned. Robert Taylor of Norfolk County complained that the office of sheriff, traditionally a reward for long service as a justice, was now almost impossible to fill. The present state of the country, he asserted, meant that the office would bring ruin on anyone who took it up. Just as the militia had forced many field officers into an early retirement during the war, taxpayers helped discredit and dissuade many gentlemen from taking up the once-lucrative and status-reinforcing post of sheriff.[37]

• • • Middling Virginians also managed to retain local control over the institution that was most central to their lives for the eight long years of war—the militia—much to the frustration of reform-minded nationalists. Just after the war ended, George Washington and nationalist-minded men in Congress, anxious that the dissolution of the Continental army would leave the fledgling Confederation without adequate protection from both internal and external enemies, moved to tighten up control over the state

36. Leighton Wood, Jr., to the Governor, Apr. 23, 1783, ibid., III, 473, to Patrick Henry, Feb. 17, 1785, IV, 9.

37. Robert Taylor to Andrew Ronald, Mar. 26, 1788, ibid., IV, 416. Cf. Archibald Cary to the Governor, Mar. 3, 1784, III, 567, Robert Ewing to the Governor, Mar 24, 1783, III, 459, 621. Jean B. Lee talks about this kind of problem in Maryland in her fascinating essay, "Lessons in Humility: The Revolutionary Transformation of the Governing Elite of Charles County, Maryland," in Ronald Hoffman and Peter J. Albert, eds., *The Transforming Hand of Revolution: Reconsidering the American Revolution as a Social Movement* (Charlottesville, Va., 1996), 90–117, in which she concludes that almost all local elites lost wealth, power, or status in the 1780s (92). Cf. Kulikoff, "Revolutionary Violence," *Journal of the Historical Society,* II (2002), 251.

militias. Washington, like many other Continental officers, was frustrated by the militia, owing to what he thought poor leadership. He thus asked the separate states to "put the National Militia in such a condition as that they may appear truly respectable," the best way being to give commissions in the militia to retiring Continental army officers. The idea was that these Continental officers would replace the existing militia officers, who had all too often been a source of opposition to Continental and state directives rather than a support.[38]

What Washington and others were concerned about was the apparent breakdown in the chain of authority during the Revolution. When the war began, many militia officers were also local justices of the peace, and the highest-ranking ones also usually served as burgesses. The interests of the commanding militia officers and the province were thus often one and the same. Those interests had been diverging since the beginning of the war because of the terrific demands put on local officials and their constituents, the introduction of a new focus of authority (and demands) in the form of the Continental Congress, and the steady attrition of militia officers by death, promotion, or resignation.

Generally, the war—and Independence—opened up hundreds of new positions, and mobility was high, owing to death and promotion. At the regimental level, the changes in personnel were perhaps most pronounced and certainly the most damaging. County lieutenants, colonels, and majors —many of whom were also county leaders and burgesses—deserted their posts in droves during the war. Resignations at the regimental level had a ripple effect and accelerated the changes that were taking place at the company-grade level. In most counties, few officers who held posts at the beginning of the war were in post, or even a higher post, by the end of it. In Cumberland County, for example, there were eight militia companies. Only one, created in 1777 when the county was divided, led by Joseph Carrington, retained the same commander throughout. Six others saw two captains, and the last saw three different officers take the lead during the war years. Of those changes, two can be accounted for by promotion; the fate of the rest is unknown, but none of them died. Most probably resigned under the wartime pressures of office. And in most counties militia officers who held posts at the company-grade level at the end of the war were significantly poorer than their counterparts. Perhaps most significantly, few

38. Harrison M. Ethridge, "Governor Patrick Henry and the Reorganization of the Virginia Militia, 1784–1786," *VMHB*, LXXXV (1977), 427.

militia officers in post at the end of the war were also part of the county political elite. Of the eight captains nominated in Cumberland County in 1775, four were justices or would become ones by the end of the war, reflecting the prewar trend that militia officers were an integral part of the county elite. None of the eight serving as captain in 1783 served on the bench. Clearly, as the war ground on, the county turned to less wealthy and connected men to fill the vacancies created by war.[39]

These changes helped bring a fresh style of leadership to the militia. New officers might have responded better to their neighbors' demands in the militia than gentlemen imposed upon the militia from the top. Indeed, some officers were clearly as happy to challenge gentlemen in the county as they were to defy state laws. Militia officers mediated between their men, local planters, the state, and the Continental Congress and army throughout the Revolutionary war. As the war ground on, local militia officers across the state increasingly negotiated subtle but crucial accommodations that helped their neighbors evade unpopular legislation. Often, local officials adopted a "temporizing Conduct," much to the frustration of some local gentlemen, but more especially of state officials like Patrick Henry. They ignored laws or evaded them. They "encouraged," "tolerated," and

39. Of course, the more ambitious were promoted, elected, or appointed to new positions in the state and Continental governments. But the demands of wartime service helped persuade many to resign. Isaac Dabney to William Davies, Aug. 28, 1782, Palmer et al., eds., *Calendar of State Papers,* III, 273, Thomas Butler to the Governor, Aug. 4, 1782, 249, Charles Lewis to the Governor, Aug. 19, 1782, 262, Lewis Burwell to Patrick Henry, Aug. 3, 1786, IV, 162. Cf. John Nash to the Executive, Apr. 21, 1783, III, 470, James Barbour to Benjamin Harrison, Feb. 23, 1784, 562.

Looking at tax lists from 1783–1784 for both groups in Cumberland, one finds a significant difference in wealth between the captains of 1775 and of 1783. The average acreage owned by those serving as captains in 1775 was 676 acres, compared to 463 acres in 1783. The average landed wealth of those appointed in 1775 (or 1777) was £361, compared to £271 for those serving in 1783. Similarly, the average captain in 1775 owned about 24 slaves, 6 horses, and 33 cattle, but the average in 1783 was only 13 slaves, 7 horses, and 21 cattle. Statistics based on an analysis of the Cumberland Land and Personal Property Tax Records, 1783–1784, LiVi, and an extended analysis of militia and justice of the peace appointments during the war years, as recorded in the Cumberland County Court Records, Order Books, 1774–1778, 1779–1784, LiVi. The median ratios were as follows: acreage, 528:410; land value, £290:£237; slaves, horses, and cattle, 25:13, 5:4, and 33:20.

"protected" deserters. They "countenanced" resistance to militia call-outs and were "backward" in carrying out orders to march. Or, if their orders were simply too intolerable, they resigned rather than carried them out.[40]

By the end of the war, local officials could no longer be counted upon to carry out provincial laws impartially. The alternative to such disobedience among the militia officers, local officials continually reminded state officials, was a far worse breakdown in order and authority. They refused to execute draft laws, they claimed, because "it would have Occasioned a General Disturbance" or simply because of the "general unwillingness of the people." In making such claims, of course, the militia officers brought the principles of republican government full circle. Though the elected legislature was supposed to rule on the basis of the consent of the people, local militia officers, especially during the war, reminded state leaders that most power now rested directly in the hands of those people. In the face of any kind of popular opposition to the laws, militia officers usually backed down. Ordinary Virginians thus forced local officials to challenge state authorities and defeat laws imposed on them from above. The most frequently challenged laws were the ones so ardently desired by Washington and other Continental officials.[41]

40. For challenges to gentlemen, see Landon Carter to the Worshipful the Court Marshal of Richmond County, October 22, 1777, Sabine Hall Papers, UVa; Sept. 4, 1775, Jack P. Greene, ed., *The Diary of Colonel Landon Carter of Sabine Hall, 1752–1778* (Charlottesville, Va., 1965), II, 937. Cf. Shy, "Legacy of the American Revolutionary War," in Shy, *A People Numerous and Armed,* 251; George Weedon to John Page, Apr. 15, 1777, Papers of George Weedon, LiVi; William Davies to Thomas Jefferson, Mar. 18, 1781, *Papers of Jefferson,* V, 173–175, Jefferson to the Speaker of the House of Delegates, May 28, 1781, VI, 28–29; Board of War to Jefferson, Apr. 5, 1780, Executive Papers, LiVi, and Lafayette to Thomas Nelson, Aug. 16, 1781; War Office to Colonel Isaac Dabney, Oct. 16, 1782, Revolutionary Government, War Office Letter Book, 1781–1786, LiVi.

41. "Abstract of Men Raised under the Former Laws Passed for Raising Soldiers for the Continental Service—November 1782," *Virginia Military Records: From the Virginia Magazine of History and Biography, the William and Mary Quarterly, and Tyler's Quarterly* (Baltimore, 1983), 661, 666; James Callaway to Jefferson, Mar. 11, 1781, Mar. 23, 1781, *Papers of Jefferson,* V, 123, 212; George Moffett to the Governor, Mar. 20, 1782, Palmer et al., eds., *Calendar of State Papers,* III, 104. Cf. Albert H. Tillson, Jr., *Gentry and Common Folk: Political Culture on a Virginia Frontier, 1740–1789* (Lexington, Ky., 1991), esp. 162, and Tillson, "The Militia

The attempt to reform the militia in 1784, then, was part of a broader national effort by men like Washington to regain control over the only defense forces now available. The militia act designed by the assembly in Virginia attempted to implement the main recommendation, by directing all current militia officers to resign their commissions on April 1, 1785, when the county lieutenant and his field officers would be replaced by men already commissioned by the governor, with the advice of his council. The new county lieutenant would then summon equal numbers of field officers and senior magistrates to form a board for dividing the county and appointing company-grade officers. These recommendations would then be sent back to the governor, to reject or accept. Significantly, the act implied that those without extensive wartime service would be replaced with officers with Continental army experience—the "most expert and fit" for such duty. Washington and other nationalists pushed for this measure not just because it would provide a job and some status for returning colleagues in the Continental army officer corps but also because it would finally put the control of the militia firmly in the hands of men more committed to the preservation of the Union than to their own communities. Virginia legislators passed the measure in part because of their unease over their lack of control over the militia. Patrick Henry and others in the state government could also view it as an opportunity to build a new system of patronage throughout the counties, especially important in the new but debilitated state government.[42]

But the difficulties in enforcing this militia reform only highlighted the changes that had been taking place during the war and reflected the

---

and Popular Political Culture in the Upper Valley of Virginia, 1740-1775," *VMHB,* XCIV (1986), 297.

42. Ethridge, "Reorganization of the Virginia Militia," *VMHB,* LXXXV (1977), 428-429, 430; Hening, comp., *Statutes at Large,* XI, 477-482; Circular Letter from Patrick Henry to Gentlemen in each County, Jan. 22, 1785, Revolutionary Government, War Office Letter Book, 1781-1786, LiVi; Horatio Gates to the Governor, Apr. 5, 1785, Governor's Office, Militia Commissions, LiVi. Other prominent war veterans agreed with Henry and Washington. Thomas Nelson thought that the only way to make the militia "truly respectable and useful" was to get rid of all the "civil-military officers" and replace them with "such Gentlemen as have distinguished themselves in the service of their country in the last war" (Thomas Nelson to the Governor, Mar. 1, 1785, Governor's Office, Militia Commissions, King William County, LiVi).

changed political landscape at the local level. The new militia act met with resistance from all sides. Field officers themselves were uneasy about the manner in which they might be replaced. In Buckingham County the law failed when John Nicholas, Jr., who had been chosen as a field officer, declined his commission because he thought the mode of choosing officers disgraced "at a single stroke both the good and bad servants of the State." Other gentlemen showed their sympathies for their existing militia officers. A rump group of gentlemen in Bedford County decided among themselves that, as none of the county field officers had been "guilty of any Acts of infamy," they would keep them as they formerly stood. In other counties, the gentlemen asked to make the nominations simply got together and decided not to have anything to do with the process. Such gentlemen in Cumberland County told the governor that they were too well aware of the "warmth which a business of this kind may possibly occasion in the county, should we adhere to the spirit of your letter."[43]

Though local networks among elites and questions of honor among officers dictated the reactions of many gentlemen and militia officers, the worries of the gentlemen from Cumberland show that many also weighed popular opinion. Lieutenant Alexander Doran of Washington County refused to accept a commission under the new militia act: not only were the appointments unconstitutional, but the "obligations" under it did not "coincide with the principals of the Constitution." But his main concern was popular resentment of the act. He told the governor, "Such a Spirit of resentment Seems to have taken place in the minds of the Citizens that it is become Contemptable." Given his belief and the widespread popular sentiment against the act, Doran thought it important to take a stand against

43. See John Nicholas, William Miller, and Charles Patt[orn], Apr. 12, 1785, Governor's Office, Militia Commissions, Buckingham County, LiVi; John Nicholas, Jr., to the Governor, undated, Governor's Office, Militia Commissions, Buckingham County, LiVi; Thomas Lumpkin to the Governor, Mar. 27, 1785, Governor's Office, Militia Commissions, LiVi; Archibald Stuart to the Governor, Feb. 22, 1785, Governor's Office, Militia Commissions, LiVi. Cf. William Darke to Colonel Thomas Meriwether, Aug. 9, 1785, Governor's Office, Militia Commissions, LiVi; Edward Stevens to the Governor, Feb. 22, 1785, Governor's Office, Militia Commissions, Culpeper County, LiVi; French Strother to the Governor, Feb. 28, 1785, Governor's Office, Militia Commissions, York County, LiVi; Henry Skipwith to the Governor, Mar. 1, 1785, Governor's Office, Militia Commissions, Cumberland County, LiVi. Cf. Ethridge, "Reorganization of the Virginia Militia," *VMHB*, LXXXV (1977), 431.

it and "defend the rights and priviledges of the Virginia Constitution or declaration of rights which has lost her Citizens such an Immence Sum of Blood and Treasure."[44]

Doran's concerns were probably not too far off the mark. Popular protests against the militia act emphasized the unconstitutional nature of Henry's move to appoint new field officers. The Virginia Constitution stipulated that all militia officer vacancies should be filled by appointment of the governor with the advice of the council, on the recommendation of the respective county courts. Instead of asking for the recommendations of the county courts as was the custom, Patrick Henry deliberately circumvented their control by soliciting the opinions of "respectable characters" in the counties "with whom the members of the Executive may happen to be acquainted." Washington County militia were not the only ones to note that Henry's actions were unprecedented. "Sundry Freemen" from Mecklenburg County also thought that the new militia act was "unconstitutional and oppressive" and would "eventually endanger our Liberties," and demanded that either the governor ignore it or the legislature change it. In these protests, ordinary Virginians began for the first time to make use of the written constitution to protest unjust laws.[45]

Much popular resistance to the militia act was also directed at the attempt to reassert military authority over the state. William Bentley had been appointed a major in the Amelia County militia but refused to accept the governor's commission. He was worried about popular sentiment: "from the Vague state of our Militia, and their backwardness to remedy it, together with their aversion to Regular Officers being in Commisn. wou'd render the Task, if at all practicable, exceedingly tiresome and disagreeable." His colleague Colonel Eggleston, Jr., also declined to serve, mainly because of the "odium and ridicule attending the recommendation business" but also his belief that the "temper of the people and their jealousy of

44. Alexander Doran to the Governor, Oct. 22, 1785, Governor's Office, Militia Commissions, Washington County, LiVi. The Governor's Office, Militia Commissions, are littered with resigned or refused commissions and reports of resignations. See, for example, Anthony Thornton to the Governor, May 12, July 12, 1785, Caroline County, LiVi.

45. Hening, comp., *Statutes at Large,* XI, 481; Circular Letter from Patrick Henry to Gentlemen in each County, Jan. 22, 1785, Revolutionary Government, War Office Letter Book, 1781–1786, LiVi; Virginia Constitution, *Rev. Va.,* VII, 652; Petition of Mecklenburg County, [1785], Palmer et al., eds., *Calendar of State Papers,* IV, 76.

any exertion of military authority in time of peace" would make the commission untenable.[46]

Many local officials and Continental army officers knew the reappointments would not go down well with a people who had grown accustomed to more popular officers. Robert Porterfield, who had recently moved to Augusta County and been issued a commission in the militia, refused to accept it because he felt he could not serve "without subjecting myself to a train of disagreeable circumstances," since he was unknown in that county and the people there appeared to "detest the Idea of serving as Militia under, what they call, regular officers." Porterfield thought the militia would not serve under even "the most respected of their inhabitants" if they had been at all associated with the Continental army. From the same county, Robert Gamble also thought that his being in the regular army would be a "powerful objection" rather than a "recommendation" with the people. Citizens had already been "so exceedingly clamorous and violent in their expressions" merely in expectation of Gamble's appointment. He thought the governor ought to ask militia colonel Sampson Mathews for nominations of officers, as he was "well acquainted with the genius and disposition of the people in this county as well as the abilities of the officers." Gamble thought Mathews could nominate men who could do the job and "please the populace."[47]

The need to please the people became a common refrain for those seeking a commission or offering support for a candidate. Archibald Stuart told the governor that the incumbent county lieutenant of Botetourt County, George Skillern, not only was able and experienced but his "Popularity in his County" ensured Stuart's recommendation of him. The gentlemen in Campbell County told the governor that they were renominating the old militia officers, as they had already given "universal satisfaction" in their posts. Major John Roberts refused to accept a commission in Culpeper County and, instead, recommended Henry Hather, who Roberts said "wood be agreeable to the Militia." Robert H. Saunders of Goochland County told the governor that he had served in different capacities, from

46. William Bentley to the Governor, May 20, 1785, Col. Eggleston, Jr., to the Governor, May 1, 1785, Governor's Office, Militia Commissions, LiVi. Most of the officers of Amelia refused to accept their commissions.

47. Ethridge, "Reorganization of the Virginia Militia," *VMHB,* LXXXV (1977), 436, 437; Robert Gamble to the Governor, Apr. 25, 1785, Governor's Office, Militia Commissions, LiVi.

"that of a common soldier to that of a Captain," which made him believe he could "Claim" the appointment of major. However, Saunders was also careful to assert that his rise in the ranks helped rather than hindered his claim. "Such an appointment would be Very agreeable to that Part of the People that is acquainted with me." It was precisely this popularity that advocates for militia reform wanted to circumvent.[48]

In the end, the attempt to reform the militia raised some important issues, particularly about representation. Officials in Middlesex County— one of the more politically divided counties in the war—warned the governor that the militia of their own and "the neighboring Counties" were "by no means reconciled to the Militia Law." They wanted to make the militia appointments "more agreeable" to the "wishes of the People." As a result, Middlesex officials took the unprecedented step of allowing the militia themselves to choose their field officers, on the grounds that this was more in tune with the new Constitution as well as the most popular method. They explained to Henry that they had taken that step, "supposing this to be the mode most conformable to our Democratic Constitution, as we were sure it was the most proper one to avoid any censure upon our Recommendations."[49]

Short of allowing the election of officers, most officials conceded defeat in the face of popular opposition. The "respectable Characters" of Caroline County refused to act, because they thought their recommendations "would be highly unpopular and invidious because we are unknown under the law." In Chesterfield County, most of the men recommended as subordinate officers had refused their commissions, and most of the militia felt that the new law was unconstitutional. St. George Tucker told Henry that the "general clamour against the principles of the Bill convince me that the

48. In Governor's Office, Militia Commissions, LiVi: Archibald Stuart to the Governor, Feb. 22, 1785; Edmund Winslow, John Quarles, John Ward, and Robert Adams to the Governor, Mar. 1, 1785, Campbell County; John Roberts to the Governor, Sept. 19, 1785, Culpeper County; Robert H. Saunders to the Governor, Mar. 2, 1785, Goochland County. Cf. Burr Harrison to the Governor, July 1, 1785, Prince William County; J. Briggs and Thomas Edmunds to the Governor, May 1785, Sussex County.

49. Francis Corbin to Patrick Henry, Mar. 1, 1785, Executive Papers, LiVi; F. Corbin, William Curtis, Edm. Berkeley, Overton Cosby, and G. Bird to the Governor, Mar. 15, 1785, Governor's Office, Militia Commissions, Middlesex County, LiVi.

Act is but too generally considered as incompatible with the principles of our Constitution. The law had been "rendered abortive by the dissenting voice of the people."[50]

The militia act fiasco had also left the militia in disarray, with crisis the most immediate effect in the backcountry. In early 1785, Arthur Campbell complained to the governor from Washington County, "The temper of the people from the dislike they have of the new Militia Act and other measures of government is such that our defense may be very precarious in case of a general Indian war." Two months later, Campbell's prediction began to come true. Walter Crockett wrote from neighboring Montgomery County that, owing to renewed Indian attacks, his militia were using the militia act as an excuse not to serve. He had called for a draft of the militia, but "the men Refus'd to obay, Saying the Gen'l Assembly had brok' all the officers in the State, there was know others appointed, and of Corce none had a wright to Command them." In Rockingham County, local officials worried about the militia because they had received many complaints about good people suffering at the hands of "Negres and other Disorderly persons."[51]

Eventually, Henry admitted failure in October 1785 by requesting that the assembly amend the militia act. The assembly changed the militia act in early 1786, to reinstate all militia officers who previously held commissions. Thus the state's attempt to reassert its authority over the militia, led by nationalists like Madison and Washington, failed in the face of opposition born of wartime experience. The people retained control of their officers.[52]

50. Ethridge, "Reorganization of the Virginia Militia," *VMHB,* LXXXV (1977), 431; William Smith to the Governor, Sept. 9, 1785, Governor's Office, Militia Commissions, LiVi; St. George Tucker to Patrick Henry, Jan. 6, 1786, Palmer et al., eds., *Calendar of State Papers,* IV, 79. Cf. Cullen, *St. George Tucker,* 46–47, 79.

51. Arthur Campbell to Patrick Henry, Mar. 27, 1785, Executive Papers, LiVi; Walter Crockett to Patrick Henry, May 26, 1785, Palmer et al., eds., *Calendar of State Papers,* IV, 31; Benjamin Harrison to the Governor, Aug. 6, 1785, Governor's Office, Militia Commissions, Rockingham County, LiVi. Cf. David Shepherd to the Governor, Mar. 9, 1785, Governor's Office, Militia Commissions, Ohio County, LiVi.

52. Even reinstatement caused further problems. By 1787, few of the militia officers who had been reinstated had actually picked up their commissions. One state official complained that the militia were in a "general deranged state." An official "Report of the Condition of the Militia of the State" drawn up in November 1787 showed that a "large majority of the Counties" were neither "properly or fully officered," and few returns could be procured. These and other problems had

• • • The failure of the militia act of 1784 was a tangible reminder that the upheaval of the war had, perhaps paradoxically, put paid to the idea of national union and, instead, strengthened middling Virginians' hold on, and loyalty to, new local institutions. That these local institutions—the court, the militia, sheriffs, and tax commissioners—had hardly changed in structure mattered less to most farmers than who controlled them and how they were affected by them. In this respect, the war really did teach some important lessons about collective resistance and popular government. Moreover, wartime service and sacrifice, however limited, legitimated these lessons well into the postwar period, as small farmers continued to protest against heavy taxes and the imposition of unpopular militia officers. Taken together, these postwar developments showed the extent to which ordinary white Virginians had asserted control over local institutions and begun to significantly influence local politics, broadly defined.

Though the extent of any changes and the impact they had on ordinary Virginians' lives is difficult to measure, we can sense something of it by comparing two moments in the lives of residents of Cumberland County in the central piedmont. In 1775, as it geared up for war, the Cumberland county committee—consisting of many of the traditional county elite—had expected and demanded from their neighbors "the most implicit Acquiescence and Concurrence in whatever we recommended" as they tried to turn the county full face forward to join the burgeoning Continental movement to resist British measures. By the end of the war, however, the people of the county were quick to make demands of their own on those same local leaders. A troop of Continental soldiers was posted in the county when a smallpox epidemic broke out in 1782. The commander, Christian

---

still not been sorted out as late as 1789. Ethridge, "Reorganization of the Virginia Militia," *VMHB*, LXXXV (1977), 434-435, 438-439; Hening, comp., *Statutes at Large*, XII, 10; *Journal of the House of Delegates of the Commonwealth of Virginia* . . . (Richmond, Va., 1786), Jan. 16, 1786; Hening, comp., *Statutes at Large*, XII, 10; Cullen, *St. George Tucker*, 48; Patrick Henry to the Magistrates of all Counties, June 7, 1786, Revolutionary Government, War Office Letter Book, 1781-1786, LiVi; James Barbour to Patrick Henry, Aug. 29, 1785, Palmer et al., eds., *Calendar of State Papers*, IV, 51, and 283, John Hudson to Beverley Randolph, June 6, 1787, IV, 293, "Report of the Condition of the Militia of the State," Nov. 14, 1787, IV, 358, T. Meriwether to the Executive, Jan. 12, 1788, IV, 394, Thomas Claiborne to the Governor, May 15, 1789, IV, 616. Cf. Palmer et al., eds., *Calendar of State Papers*, IV, 402, 420, 469; Edward Booker to the Governor, Nov. 30, 1786, Governor's Office, Militia Commissions, LiVi.

Febiger, made plans to inoculate his men but hesitated when he found his civilian neighbors were "extreamly uneasy." They had drawn up a memorial protesting plans to inoculate the troops and warned that, if the smallpox spread, Feibiger wrote, they would "lay the blame entirely on me, Should any Misfortune happen to themselves or Familys." Rather than risk the wrath of the officer themselves, the local farmers had chosen to use the county lieutenant to make their demands known. He made it clear to the regular officer that his neighbors were serious and there was little he could do about it, that the inhabitants threatened to "withold all Supplies and cease all Communication with us." Worse, according to Febiger, the county lieutenant "Spoke also of loaded Guns and in Fact made use of some very imprudent Expressions" on behalf of his neighbors. In the realm of political life, broadly defined, the war did bring a subtle but crucial shift. The balance of power among white Virginians had changed.[53]

• • • In turn, this subtle but significant shift in power and orientation had direct and indirect effects ranging far beyond the merely local. Indeed, the "small" politics of war fundamentally shaped the nature of public debates at both the state and Continental level in the postwar period as much as they did during the war. Not only did state leaders learn valuable lessons from their neighbors about the limits of their authority, but they also began searching for new ways to reconstitute that authority. Some yielded to popular sentiment; others struggled to contain and control it. The result was "the beginnings of sustained conflict between legislative factions over public policy" at the state level, and the movement toward a stronger federal government at the Continental level.[54]

53. Historians, of course, have been far too focused on locating the formal roots of a more democratic political culture and fledgling national identity in the new Republic to notice that many people had had enough of the "union" by the end of the war and had "democratized" even the most undemocratic of local institutions. June 30, 1775, "Proceedings of the Committees of Safety of Cumberland and Isle of Wight Counties, Virginia, 1775–1776," Virginia State Library Board, *Fifteenth Annual Report* (Richmond, Va., 1919), 15–16; Col. Christian Febiger to Governor Nelson, with enclosures, Nov. 16, 1781, Executive Papers, LiVi. Cf. Lee, "Lessons in Humility," in Hoffman and Albert, eds., *The Transforming Hand of Revolution,* 116–117.

54. Herbert Sloan and Peter Onuf, "Politics, Culture, and the Revolution in Virginia: A Review of Recent Work," *VMHB,* XCI (1983), 279. Cf. Norman K. Ris-

Throughout the war in Virginia, contemporaries had observed what to many seemed a disturbing phenomenon: high legislative turnover in the annual elections. As we have seen, such turnover was often specifically attributed to discontent over military policies and led to bitter legislative contests and significant changes in wartime policy. The high annual legislative turnover slowed in the postwar period, yet the more conflict-ridden politics did not. As Herbert Sloan and Peter Onuf have noted, the "most striking thing about Virginia politics in the postwar period" is that "the harmony so characteristic of the prewar years is completely absent."[55]

Most of the conflict among state legislators centered on the same issues that divided Virginians most during the war: the payment of taxes to retire the state and Continental debts. In short, they were conflicts over who would pay for the war and how. After Yorktown, in an effort to get their finances under control, the General Assembly passed an act making state paper money no longer legal tender except in payment of taxes and fixing its value in Spanish dollars at 100:1. The outstanding paper money could be exchanged, at the rate of 1,000:1, for new loan certificates, bearing 6 percent interest and redeemable in specie on or before December 1, 1791. The result was rapid deflation: within a year, there was only £1,000,000 left in circulation, compared to £60,000,000 (in face value). Over the next couple of years, the assembly authorized the issue of perhaps as much as another £1,000,000 in certificates to pay the state's demobilized soldiers, but in 1782 the assembly allowed holders to exchange these for western lands. A year later, it made taxes payable in certificates, even making such payment compulsory for certain levies. Over the next four years, the assembly retired £625,000 in paper certificates through taxes, substantially reducing the state debt but badly contracting the money supply. A legislative committee report in 1784 calculated that the state was retiring its war debt at the rate of £207,700 per year. Since annual expenditures were estimated at only about £250,000, more than 80 percent of the annual budget was thus devoted to debt retirement. Since debt certificates were a major part of the circulating medium, the state's currency was reduced by that much

jord, *Chesapeake Politics;* Risjord, "How the 'Common Man' Voted in Jefferson's Virginia," in John B. Boles, ed., *America: The Middle Period: Essays in Honor of Bernard Mayo* (Charlottesville, Va., 1973), 36–64; Jackson Turner Main, "Sections and Politics in Virginia, 1781–1787," *WMQ,* 3d Ser., XXXV (1978), 455–476.

55. Sloan and Onuf, "Politics, Culture, and the Revolution in Virginia," *VMHB,* XCI (1983), 280.

each year, and the dwindling supply of money could not but aggravate the postwar price depression.[56]

Anxious letters from county sheriffs, along with angry petitions from freeholders, reminded the legislature of grievances out-of-doors. Petitioners listed the scarcity of money, the low prices of tobacco, the recent poor crops, and the poor roads in the state as good reasons why they could not possibly pay all the taxes expected of them. If they had to pay taxes, many citizens demanded, they wanted to pay them in various ways that were suitable to their local circumstances.[57]

Popular feeling against postwar taxes had a direct effect on electoral politics, at least according to contemporaries. St. George Tucker thought that during the elections of the spring of 1782 the voice of the people would carry too much weight in the assembly. He feared that the new tax law would be either repealed or watered down so much as to be rendered ineffective. One legislator had "caught the popular ear most astonishingly" in his arguments against the present tax, complaining that it was unequal because the assembly would not accept hard-earned certificates in payment. Tucker thought him "the oracle of the people," but the people needed no oracle. In Cumberland County, Tucker charged, "they were about instructing their delegates to move for an absolute repeal of that law." Repeal of the tax law was "cherished by the people" and thus "probably by their representatives."[58]

Most legislators, eager to curry favor among their more vocal constituents, favored debt and tax relief after the war. They were responsive to the complaints of their less wealthy neighbors, sympathetic to the problems encountered by county lieutenants, sheriffs, and tax collectors in trying to administer the laws, and aware of the popular clamor against British and other creditors trying to collect debts with wartime interest from an exhausted people. They closed ranks and gave as much relief as possible. The assembly first answered them in the fall of 1782 by passing an act to allow western residents to pay taxes in tobacco, flour, or hemp. The follow-

56. Risjord, *Chesapeake Politics,* 98–100.

57. Ibid., 101–102; Jackson Turner Main, *Political Parties before the Constitution* (Chapel Hill, N.C., 1973), 252.

58. St. George Tucker to Theodorick Bland, May 2, 1782, Charles Campbell, ed., *The Bland Papers: Being a Selection from the Manuscripts of Colonel Theodorick Bland, Jr.* (Petersburg, Va., 1840, 1843), II, 79–80; St. George Tucker to Theodorick Bland, May 2, 1782, Bland Family Papers, VHS.

ing spring, Patrick Henry sponsored a bill to postpone for several months the taxes due on June 1 and to add deerskins to the list of commodities. Neither measure raised much opposition, though state creditors grumbled privately.[59]

The economic depression that followed the war only solidified prorelief sentiment. By the spring of 1783, and under intense popular pressure, even fiscally conservative Virginians like Benjamin Harrison and George Mason supported tax relief measures. Mason advocated postponing the collection of taxes until the fall, fearing that planters would be at the mercy of merchants if they had to sell tobacco to pay taxes too early in the year. He hoped that by then enough competition would prevent merchants from manipulating prices. The assembly did grant relief and, subsequently, almost annually allowed sheriffs extra months before they took legal action. Twice the assembly postponed the collection of taxes for longer periods, usually under pressure from the petitions that flooded the legislature each year.[60]

Through deferrals, the Virginia assembly managed to walk a fine line between popular demands and the retirement of most of its paper money. Tax relief in the last years of the war was clearly aimed at the "ease and convenience of the citizens of this commonwealth in their present distressed state." As the *Virginia Gazette* noted in May 1783, legislators were indeed "attentive to the ease and convenience of their constituents." Too much so, according to James Madison. Tax relief might have helped most Virginians, but it increased friction between the state, and Congress and Virginia nationalists.[61]

Indeed, widespread agreement on debt and tax relief among Virginia legislators forced procreditor and pronationalist Virginians to mobilize and organize. Men more involved in Continental politics—often the same men who had tried to pressure the state into passing more effective recruiting laws—worried that relief would delay Virginia's payments in fulfillment of its Continental obligations. When the assembly again postponed the collection of taxes in the spring of 1784, for example, James Marshall grumbled

59. Risjord, *Chesapeake Politics*, 101–102; Main, *Political Parties*, 252.

60. Risjord, *Chesapeake Politics*, 102, 137–138, 160–161; George Mason to Patrick Henry, May 6, 1783, *Papers of Mason*, II, 772; Main, *Political Parties*, 252. "Economic questions dominated Chesapeake politics throughout the 1780s and provided a catalyst for the first party system," concludes Risjord (160).

61. Risjord, *Chesapeake Politics*, 103; Robert A. Becker, *Revolution, Reform, and the Politics of American Taxation, 1763–1783* (Baton Rouge, La., 1980), 203.

about the "strange figure" that the state cut in national affairs. Madison, who returned from Congress in December 1783, helped lead this emerging procreditor faction. He began putting together a comprehensive program of political reform backed and supported by early and ardent nationalists like George Washington, Joseph Jones, and James Monroe. They achieved a significant shift in Virginia politics. Only when the nationalists began to rally together to resist the prorelief consensus within Virginia did interest groups begin to replace personalities in the Virginia legislature and a protoparty system begin to form.[62]

At the same time, many state leaders were undergoing a crisis of confidence. Popular pressure on the legislature both during the war and immediately after triggered unease and deep-seated anxiety about the nature of the government among prominent Virginia leaders. Though Mason reluctantly concluded that tax relief was necessary in 1783, he harbored serious concerns about the future of their republican experiment. He warned Patrick Henry that they somehow needed to take control of the legislature in order to reestablish some semblance of "justice." Congratulating Henry on the late official peace treaty, Mason wrote: "We are now to rank among the Nations of the World; but whether our Independence shall prove a Blessing or a Curse, must depend upon our own Wisdom or Folly, Virtue or Wickedness; judging of the future from the Past, the Prospect is not promising." Writing along the same lines to William Cabell the same day, Mason believed the assembly had to abolish all laws "as are contrary to the fundamental Principles of Justice" and adhere "to the Distinctions between Right and Wrong for the future." Mason, looking around him in a legislative hall that contained only about 10 percent of his colleagues from 1771, was distressed that the representatives of the people were not adequate for leadership in the postwar era.[63]

62. Risjord, *Chesapeake Politics,* 72–73, 81–86, 102–103, 137–138. Allan Kulikoff also concludes: "Political parties emerged in the 1780s and 1790s in the assemblies of both Virginia and Maryland. Whereas colonial legislators had frequently voted in personal cliques, regional and ideological parties abounded after the Revolution: creditors and debtors, nationalists and localists, and Federalists and Republicans vied for support in both legislatures during the early decades of the Republic." Kulikoff, *Tobacco and Slaves,* 425; cf. Main, *Political Parties,* 212–267.

63. Mason to William Cabell, May 6, 1783, to Henry, May 6, 1783, *Papers of Mason,* II, 768–769, 770. K. R. Constantine Gutzman says Virginia earned a reputation as the home of second-rate men with second-rate agendas in the 1770s and

Jefferson, too, was concerned about the legislature and thought that more than just a restoration of "Justice and Virtue" was necessary. Not long after his governorship, Jefferson wrote that the Virginia Constitution had put too much power in the hands of the popularly elected legislature, and the result was an "elective despotism." The only way to change this imbalance was to overhaul the entire state Constitution, and he could count on people like Madison and Richard Henry Lee and their increasing frustration with the power of the Virginia legislature, particularly as it blocked attempts to support Congress. When in the spring of 1784 the collection of the land tax was postponed yet again, Madison, with Lee, moved to call a constitutional convention. His primary concern was to break the power of the lower house. Ironically, the move for constitutional reform within Virginia was quashed in part because conservatives like Mason feared that, in the present political climate, the result might be worse. In the spring of 1783, he had asked correspondents like Cabell, Would they not rather wait to reform the Constitution "until the present Ferment . . . has subsided, and Men's Minds have had time to cool?"[64]

Virginia's reluctance (according to men like Madison) or inability (according to men like Henry) to fill congressional requisitions for money and supplies convinced Madison that Congress must have the power to coerce the states. On the other hand, Governor Harrison spoke clearly from wartime experience when he conceded that Virginia had fallen far behind in meeting congressional requisitions but that local circumstances needed to be taken into account. Necessity, not intent, caused the shortfall, and the legislature had no choice but to attend to its constituents' needs when it drafted laws. As Harrison told Robert Morris in 1782, Virginia could meet congressional requisitions and impose crushing taxes on its people, or it

1780s. Gutzman, "Old Dominion, New Republic: Making Virginia Republican, 1776-1840" (Ph.D. diss., University of Virginia, 1999), 97.

64. Thomas Jefferson, *Notes on the State of Virginia,* ed. William Peden (Chapel Hill, N.C., 1954), 118-129; J. R. Pole, *Political Representation in England and the Origins of the American Republic* (London, 1966), 296-304; Lance Banning, *The Sacred Fire of Liberty: James Madison and the Founding of the Federal Republic* (Ithaca, N.Y., 1995), 88. Banning concludes that, like Jefferson, Madison wanted the Virginia Constitution to "be, at once, more democratic in its derivation, more equal in its principles of representation, but *less* responsive to the will of the majority as expressed by its immediate representatives in the lower house" (133; cf. 132-137); Mason to Cabell, May 6, 1783, *Papers of Mason,* II, 769.

could deal first with their needs. It was his "indispensable duty" as an elected Virginia official to do the latter.[65]

Conflict between provincial and Continental-minded factions increased through the 1780s as the legislature continued to adopt tax delays, remissions, and schemes for allowing payment of taxes in commodities. In mid-1786, for example, Edmund Pendleton, who had rarely left the state during the war, explained to Patrick Henry that, in response to riots, demonstrations, and waves of petitions clamoring for tax and debtor relief, the legislature needed to follow a consistent policy of tax relief—to try to remain "in the happy medium between that Rigor which borders on Oppression of the people, and a negligence which tends to injure the public revenue." Madison, frustrated, concluded a few months later: "There is no maxim in my opinion which is more liable to be misapplied, and which therefore more needs elucidation than the current one that the interest of the majority is the political standard of right and wrong."[66]

Madison garnered some support in the Virginia assembly, and he scored some important victories. In the spring of 1785, for example, the assembly refused to consider issuing more paper money and rejected the further postponement of taxes. However, when Madison tried to get the legislature to open the courts for the collection of debts, he again ran into heavy opposition. Pro–debt relief advocates tied the issue to the legacy of the war and blocked legislation by adding a proviso that the courts would open only if the British left their posts in the Northwest. In part because of Madison's progress, prorelief advocates rallied in the fall of 1785 to postpone the collection of taxes until the following March. Archibald Stuart complained to Jefferson, "The people begin to feel their power and I am afraid have not wisdom enough to make a proper use of it." A seesaw battle followed. George Mason succeeded in passing a resolution in the spring of 1786 that paper money was "unjust" and "impolitic," and nationalist-minded men also got a recommendation passed that endorsed a convention in Annapolis to revise the Articles of Confederation.[67]

65. Becker, *Politics of American Taxation,* 205.

66. Ibid., 224; Madison to Monroe, Oct. 5, 1786, *Papers of Madison,* IX, 141; Pendleton to Henry, July 31, 1786, *Papers of Pendleton,* II, 483.

67. Risjord, *Chesapeake Politics,* 149–151, 154; Archibald Stuart to Jefferson, Oct. 17, 1785, *Papers of Jefferson,* VIII, 644–646; Gutzman, "Old Dominion, New Republic," 98. Cf. Risjord, *Chesapeake Politics,* 174–178, for a discussion of paper

As the procreditor, pronationalist party began gathering adherents through the mid-1780s, it faced the power of the people on several fronts. Party leaders watched anxiously, for example, as prodebtor forces began organizing during the elections. "The debtors as usual are endeavoring to come into the Assembly and as usual I fear they will succeed," complained one procreditor. "Paper money or not seems to agitate the generality of the counties," reported Edmund Randolph, when the Hanover County delegate won reelection "after a positive and unalterable declaration in public of his affection for paper money." Almost everyone had to take a stand over paper money. Moreover, after this election, prorelief supporters began to organize better than ever before, and for the first time they seemed to form a coherent platform of policies linking British debts, domestic debts, and court reform. Both emerging parties had to appeal to the people, organizing popular meetings as an instrument of political pressure as they had done in the last years of British rule.[68]

Many ordinary Virginians also redoubled their efforts to weigh in on the debate through petitions. In the fall of 1786, for example, petitioners from Spotsylvania County demanded some kind of debt relief. Like those petitioning for tax relief, they listed the low price of tobacco, the low demand for wheat and flour, and the "prevailing embarrassments of Commerce." They also complained about the scarcity of money and the short crop the previous year because of the drought. Given also their "great burthen of debt both public and private," they were convinced of the need for "legislative interference" in the "rigorous and speedy execution of Justice." They suggested that the assembly either adopt the installment plan for paying

money support, which Risjord says was limited in Virginia, and limited to late 1785 through to about 1787—in part blunted by tax relief (179).

68. See Risjord, *Chesapeake Politics,* 154–155. Indeed, mass meetings and outbursts of popular political sentiment helped one advance in party organization. Drawing from the lessons of prewar political meetings and presumably wartime mass protests, George Nicholas suggested to Madison that organizing a petition campaign in favor of disestablishment could be an effective way of overcoming the majority in the House in favor of a general assessment. As Risjord notes, Nicholas clearly assumed that the legislature would actually respond to the voice of the people, "itself an indication of how contemporaries viewed Virginia's political system" (209). The move, which resulted in the petition of ten thousand names and the disestablishment of the church, put the parties on the road to mass meetings, widely circulated sets of resolutions, and newspaper contributions.

back debts or at least ensure that any property seized and sold to pay debts was sold at a fair price and thus in a manner "as shall be thought best calculated to prevent ruin to the debtor."[69]

Significantly, prorelief advocates out-of-doors still based their demands on their sacrifices during the war either directly or indirectly. A petition from Pittsylvania County in the fall of 1787, for example, invoked wartime contributions to protest against the high taxes they believed were going to pay off bond speculators. The petitioners asked the legislature to "look back and see what a large Quantity of monies have been Collected from the people" to pay for the war. They had been told at first that much of it was for the payment of officers and soldiers "who Shed their blood in the field of Battle for us" as well as to the French, who lent them money at a crucial moment. However, most people knew that speculators had bought up the soldiers' certificates, so their excessive taxes were now going toward paying off "a few Individuals in Luxery" who had contributed little during the war and "perhaps never shed one Drop of blood on our behalf." Indeed, the petitioners believed that these same speculators had most likely been "our worst Enemies" during the war. The fact that the petitioners had lost so much property through taxes was particularly galling, given these circumstances, and "distressing to minds of we a free people (who fought for freedom and Liberty and gained the Day [to be?] continually paying of Taxes and not lessning the Debts Due." If something was not done, they feared becoming dependents, as they would have to sell their lands "untill we shall become Tenants."[70]

Prorelief petitions did not hesitate to make class-based claims and to juxtapose their services and labor, in myriad forms, against those who did not earn their wealth. In the fall of 1787, they resurrected these claims in support of paper money. More than 150 men from Albemarle County, for example, petitioned the assembly in November 1787 asking for more paper money to help them pay their "Domestic Debt." Little cash was circulating among them, and thus they were forced to pay debts, taxes, and other demands by selling their property. Though paper money was not ideal, they admitted, and might depreciate a little in the first instance, it would do so only because of enemies to the state who would not honor it. In any case,

69. Spotsylvania County Petition, Nov. 10, 1786, Virginia Legislative Petitions, LiVi.

70. Pittsylvania County Petition, Nov. 5, 1787, Virginia Legislative Petitions, LiVi; cf. Albemarle County Petition, Nov. 3, 1787.

"it is better for a few to Suffer a little, than a majority of the State to become Servants to the Rest." This would happen if they had no cash and had to keep paying their annual taxes, along with the "canker of six per Cent Interest Warrents." They did offer an alternative. If the assembly would not issue more paper money, the petitioners from Albemarle wanted the legislature to make sure their property sold at just prices if it was sold to pay debts. "What heart can stand by and see his property that he has labour'd hard for," they said, "sell for one fourth of its value and in a few years perhaps not for over one Tenth of its value"? In these circumstances, "then power will naturly follow property, then god help the poor."[71]

Prorelief advocates also made their views known outside the assembly's doors. Indeed, though nationalists thought the legislature was too responsive to the demands of the people, many ordinary Virginians themselves still did not think the legislature was responsive enough to their demands and petitions. By 1787, tax and debt resistance in Virginia was increasing to the breaking point. In December 1786, Edward Carrington took note of Shays's Rebellion and wondered, to Edmund Randolph, how long it would be before "the contagion of Eastern disorders will spread." In March and April, farmers complained of their heavy load of debt and taxes and initiated their own version of Shays's Rebellion. They first sought relief through peaceful protest—by forming associations, by boycotting property sold at auctions, and by flooding the legislature with petitions for paper money and tender laws requiring creditors to accept paper money from debtors at face value. Angered by the actions of the previous assembly, some farmers "talk boldly of following the example of the insurgents in Massachusetts and preventing the courts proceeding to business," wrote John Dawson to James Madison. On the eve of the May court session in King William County, the courthouse—with all the records of the county—was burned down. In late August, hundreds of farmers from Greenbriar County stormed the courthouse and stopped the justices from proceeding. In Amelia County, "disorderly people of desperate circumstances" obstructed the proceedings of the county debtor court session. As James Madison reported, throughout the state in 1787, Virginia officials watched

71. Albemarle County Petition, Nov. 3, 1787, Virginia Legislative Petitions, LiVi. On the power of petitions more generally, see Kulikoff, "Revolutionary Violence," *Journal of the Historical Society,* II (2002), 249; Ruth Bogin, "Petitioning and the New Moral Economy of Post-Revolutionary America," *WMQ,* 3d Ser., XLV (1988), 391–425.

"prisons and courthouses and clerk's offices wilfully burnt." As David Szatmary has observed, such activities caused widespread concern. Richard Henry Lee, in Philadelphia, said, "Here all join in lamenting the riots and mobbish proceedings in Virginia." Archibald Stuart, who was actually in Virginia at the time, "trembled with apprehensions of a rebellion."[72]

• • • Thus the upheaval of the war fundamentally shaped political divisions in the postwar years and the very contours of the public debate that led to the creation of the Constitution. Not only did middling Virginians employ similar wartime strategies of resistance to oppose onerous taxes, but they also questioned the very nature of those taxes in light of their wartime contributions of "blood and treasure." Indeed, more broadly, while they resisted and manipulated the implementation of tax laws and evaded creditors at the county level, freeholders in the postwar years continued to assert themselves through petitions to the legislature. As they had done during the war, small farmers bombarded their delegates and the legislature with instructions and petitions on a huge variety of issues great and small. From the disestablishment of the church, to petitions for relief from taxes, to protests over militia appointments, to paper money petitions, middling Virginians expressed their demands. By linking their postwar demands to their wartime sacrifices, ordinary Virginians claimed a moral legitimacy for their demands. Thus by invoking their participation in the war, however little service it was, middling Virginians claimed the Revolution.

In turn, many leaders within the state also learned valuable lessons both during and after the war about the expectations and demands of their less

72. Edward Carrington to Randolph, Dec. 8, 1786, Palmer et al., eds., *Calendar of State Papers,* IV, 195; John Dawson to Madison, Apr. 15, 1787, *Papers of Madison,* IX, 381; David P. Szatmary, *Shays' Rebellion: The Making of an Agrarian Insurrection* (Amherst, Mass., 1980), 125–126. The most drastic solution to taxpayer delinquency was jailhouse breakouts. One justice from Hanover County resigned because he thought the justices would be held responsible for "every debtor who breaks Jail." He had argued for a stronger jail, but his colleagues refused to budge (William Johnson to the Governor, Sept. 14, 1786, Palmer et al., eds., *Calendar of State Papers,* IV, 170). Jackson Turner Main notes that some Virginians had used violent tactics as early as 1783, when inhabitants of Lunenburg destroyed the county tax records in an effort to prevent the collection of taxes (*Political Parties,* 252).

wealthy neighbors and were far more responsive to them after the war. Less likely were they to put their self-defined interests above the concerns of their constituents. Most gentlemen leaders were ultimately far more willing to jeopardize provincial, even national harmony and consensus for the sake of more local issues in the postwar period. Though the consequences of Revolutionary resistance are difficult to measure over the long term, a more responsive legislature was almost certainly a result of the years of challenge during the Revolutionary war.[73]

Of course, such developments troubled an increasing number of men and directly contributed to the rise of Federalist support for a new Constitution. Indeed, recognizing and acknowledging the conflicts that divided Virginians during and immediately after the war—and the extent to which these conflicts severely crippled mobilization and later the repayment of wartime debts—might also help historians to finally bridge the gap between stories of what John Shy has characterized as the *destructive* American War of Independence and the so-called *constructive* political revolution that culminated in the creation of a Federal Constitution. For, in the end, the divisive and crippling experience of the war helped produce a small group of committed nationalists who emerged from the patriot leadership. These men were generally those who had occupied important positions during the Revolution, but usually outside their own states. They had often served in the Continental Congress and served on committees responsible for the conduct of the war. They had also—like James Madison—had significant experience dealing with more popular and responsive legislatures in the postwar period. Significantly, this nationalist cadre also included Continental army officers such as George Washington who were frustrated by the conflicts at the local and state level that undermined a successful war effort and postwar attempts to rebuild a national militia. Such men were also deeply troubled by the lack of evidence of a commitment of others to the cause in which they were so engrossed: by the persistent localism of state militias, by a growing antagonism between the citizens

73. Just as Alfred F. Young has argued that the "ghosts" of Daniel Shays, Abraham Yates, and Thomas Paine were a radical presence in Philadelphia at the time of the framing of the Constitution, so too did the memory of small farmers' wartime resistance haunt Virginia's leaders during the Confederation period, reminding them where the limits of their authority truly rested. Young, "The Framers of the Constitution and the 'Genius' of the People," in "Moving Beyond Beard: A Symposium," *Radical History Review*, no. 42 (1988), 7–47.

of the states, and by an increasing antipathy among those people toward Continental institutions such as the Congress and the army. It is perhaps no surprise that almost every general in the Continental army supported moves to strengthen the powers of the federal government.[74]

Thus, precisely because so many ordinary people defended their interests and refused to fight the war on terms proposed by elites, elites themselves in turn began thinking about new ways of organizing society and politics to protect a notion of society that some at least believed was increasingly under threat. These new ideas became particularly evident in elites' responses to the massive tax resistance of the 1780s, in which thousands of farmers justified their refusal to pay taxes on the basis of their wartime services and material sacrifices. Just as the anxiety of some elites found expression in a heightening of postwar tensions among state legislators, it also pushed some to radically rethink the nature and structure of the government of the fledgling union. John Marshall supported a stronger central government because "the general tendency of state politics convinced me that no safe and permanent remedy could be found but in a more efficient and better organized general government." The political settlement of 1787 thus reflected the myriad conflicts that had been endemic throughout the war.[75]

The "national" legacy of the War for Independence, then, was a reactive, oppositional one as certain elites responded to the divisive and often violent forces of disunion that they saw throughout the war, and strove even harder to provide a more effective national government. What they were reacting to was the fractious popular political culture that had developed during the war. What common people saw as their newly won rights, for example—to ignore the Continental war effort and exploit new opportunities—commentators saw as moral and political degeneration. Likewise, what hundreds of thousands of ordinary Americans saw as the center of

74. The link between army officers and Federalists is an old one, but the reasons for this connection have been less well explored. See Stanley Elkins and Eric McKittrick, *The Founding Fathers: Young Men of the Revolution* (Washington, D.C., 1961), but for a more recent take on this idea, see Don Higginbotham, "War and State Formation in Revolutionary America," in Eliga H. Gould and Peter S. Onuf, eds., *Empire and Nation: The American Revolution in the Atlantic World* (Baltimore, 2005).

75. R. Kent Newmyer, *John Marshall and the Heroic Age of the Supreme Court* (Baton Rouge, La., 2001), 28.

focus of their lives and families, and worth defending—their immediate communities—more national-minded elites saw as provincial and narrow-minded selfishness and lack of foresight.[76]

At the very least, the divisive experience of war and the postwar period —the harsh realities of such a protracted war that clearly revealed divisions and internal conflict far more than any consensus and shared values—goes far in explaining the change of mood "between the euphoria at Philadelphia in 1776," as John Shy has written, "and the hard-headedness of many of the same men, when, eleven yeas later, in the same city, they hammered out a federal constitution." Wartime conflicts, then, helped produce a "new realism, almost a cynicism, about human nature that is one key to American political survival after 1783." Clearly, state and national leaders were affected not just by the arguments and debates of their colleagues in the legislative chambers but more fundamentally by the many voices and actions of those they lived with, listened to, and often struggled against. Recovering the complex nuances of those debates, dialogues, and struggles throughout this period not only enriches but irrevocably alters our understanding of the founding period.[77]

76. "Abuses" were "enormous and almost without number," William Gordon wrote to John Adams in 1777, and "instead of having our affairs conducted with economy, the Continent hath been plundered, and business carried on at the most expensive rate, that Jack, Tom and Harry might make a fortune and live like gentlemen." Gordon's worries were echoed by literate commentators and politicians alike, from David Ramsay and Mercy Otis Warren to George Washington and Thomas Jefferson (see Lester H. Cohen, "Creating a Usable Future: The Revolutionary Historians and the National Past," in Jack P. Greene, ed., *The American Revolution: Its Character and Limits* [New York, 1987], 309-330 [quote on 314]).

77. For John Shy's comments, see "American Society and Its War for Independence," in Shy, *A People Numerous and Armed,* 119, 132. For an extended rumination on this theme, see McDonnell, "National Identity and the American War for Independence Reconsidered," *Australasian Journal of American Studies,* XX (2001-2002), 3-17. For two other suggestive outcomes of tying the war years together with the postwar years, see Terry Bouton's superb piece, "A Road Closed: Rural Insurgency in post-Independence Pennsylvania," *Journal of American History,* LXXXVII (2000-2001), 855-887; and Saul Cornell's nuanced and class-based evaluation of Antifederalism, in *The Other Founders: Anti-Federalism and the Dissenting Tradition in America, 1788-1828* (Chapel Hill, N.C., 1999).

Index

Accomack County, 109, 147, 155, 163, 292, 475n; landholding in, 25; electorate in, 26; county committee of, 80; militia of, 412; draft resistance in, 457-459; petition of, 489

Adams, John, 220, 239

Adams, Samuel, 173

Agnew, Rev. John, 31

Albemarle County: independent company of, 45-46, 57, 61-62, 115; minutemen in, 109; petitions from, 359n, 522-523; convention army in, 376

Alexandria, 130-131, 137, 157, 188, 210, 263; mechanics of, 46

Allason, William, 351

Amber, Jacquelin, 78

Amelia County, 150, 382; landholding in, 25; petitions from, 227-228, 492; resistance to militia reform in, 509; tax resistance in, 523

Amherst, Sir Jeffrey, 71n

Amherst County, militia of, 387-388, 434, 469

Anderson, Nelson, Jr., 293

Anglican Church, 31, 241-242, 253-254

Annapolis, Md., 520

Apprentices, 337

Arbuthnot, Adm. Marriot, 430

Armed forces. *See* Continental army, Virginia Line; Military service; Militia

Arnold, Gen. Benedict, 256, 398-400, 402, 408, 430, 433-437

Articles of Confederation, 520

Asbury, Francis, 30

Assembly. *See* Virginia General Assembly

Association of Gentlemen, 40

Atkinson, Roger, 204

Augusta County: draft resistance in, 453-454, 494-495; petition from, 466-467; resistance to militia reform in, 510

Augusta County East, 122

Augusta West, military district of, 94, 106

Avery, Isaac, 414

Awsbury, Thomas, 447-448

Aylett, William, 204, 333

Bailey, John, 85

Baker, Lewis, 454

Ball, James, 451

Banister, John, 349n, 401, 403, 471, 476-477; and drafts, 276-280

Baptists, 29-30; petitions of, 226; and Declaration of Rights, 241-242; and disestablishment, 253-254; and military service, 307-308

Baskerville, Samuel, 285-286n

Beckwith, Roger, 450

Bedford County: disaffection in, 376, 444, 462; militia of, 404-405, 411, 440; draft resistance in, 456-457; resistance to militia reform in, 508

Bell, Graham, 488

Bellew, Capt. Henry, 162, 168-169

Bentley, William, 509

Berkeley, Nelson, 124

Berkeley County: petitions from, 385-387, 421-423

Bernard, William, 450

Bird, Thomas, 129n

Blackburn, Thomas, 202

Blackerby, William, 380

Bland, Richard, 32n, 89, 216

Bland, Theodorick, Jr., 400

Bland, Theodorick, Sr., 382, 397, 401

Blandford, 82

Boston, 88

Boston Port Act, 1774, 21

Boston Tea Party, 1773, 19

Botetourt County, 94; militia of, 431-432; postwar tax resistance in, 496

86-87, 145-146; and Dunmore's Proclamation, 144-146; and patriot army,
260-261, 282

Conway, Edwin, 451

Corbin, George, 412, 457-459

Corbin, Richard, 64, 79

Corley, James, 289

Cornstalk (Shawnee), 329

Cornwallis, Gen. Charles, 375, 378, 401-
402, 430; and Virginia, 436-437; and
Yorktown, 472, 475-477

County committees: elections for, 97-98;
fears of, 237. *See also individual counties*

County courts: closures of, 35, 192; reform
of, 236-237, 241

Cousins, Adam, 299

Cowpens, battle of, 401, 404

Cox, Enoch, 416

Creeks: Overhill towns of, 248-249

Cresswell, Nicholas, 48, 126n, 187, 192,
198-199, 259, 261-265, 273

Crockett, Walter, 512

Cropper, John, 459n

Crowds, 34; in Williamsburg, 52-54; in
Norfolk, 81n

Culpeper County, 254, 316-317; militia of,
299; petitions from, 311, 351, 353-354;
and draft of 1781, 416-418, 422

Culpeper district minuteman battalion, 132

Cumberland County, 2n, 179, 413, 516;
county committee elections in, 123-124;
instructions of, 205, 310; petitions from,
223-224, 229-230, 421-424; civil disturbance in, 289; recruiting in, 339, 360;
militia officers of, 504-505; resistance to
militia reform in, 508; local autonomy in,
513-514

Curle, William Roscow Wilson, 148, 411

Currency: scarcity of, 188-189, 192; deflation of, 304, 345; reform of, 362,
395-396. *See also* Depreciation; Paper
money

Custis, John, 458

Custis, John Parke, 297, 314, 315-316, 321,
327-328, 333-334, 339

Dabney, George, 350, 409

Dade, Townsend, 293n

Dalrymple, Sir John, 146, 172-173

Dan River, 401

Davenport, Thomas, 124

Davies, William, 418-419, 460, 493

Dawson, John, 523

Debts: prewar, 24; resistance to paying, 29,
189-190; need of relief from, 33; postwar
resistance to, 500-501; of state, 515-524

Declaration of Independence, 212-215

Declaration of Rights. *See* Virginia Declaration of Rights

Deference, 114-115

Delawares, 87

Democracy, 217-218

"Democraticus," 222-223

Denny, William, 286

Depreciation: of currency, 188-189, 308.
See also Currency; Paper money

Deserters, 286-287, 447-448, 450; and
local communities, 288-291, 418-419

Desertion: from army, 265-267, 285-288,
317-318; from state regiments, 299;
rules against, 307; threat of, 336; from
militia, 375, 387-388; and draft of 1781,
418-419; and disaffection, 447-448, 450,
456-457

Dick, Alexander, 441-442

Dickson, William, 283

Dictator, calls for, 462-466

Dinwiddie, Robert, 22, 38, 40

Dinwiddie County, 401, 497-498, 500

Disaffection, 3; and Virginia Constitution,
236-237; and internal upheaval, 294-
295, 375-379; and enslaved Virginians,
375; reasons for, 378-379, 380-381; in
1781, 444-452; and deserters, 447-448,
450; and the draft, 455-457

Disestablishment, 241-242, 253-254

Dissenters, 29-30, 253-254; petitions of,
226-227; and Declaration of Rights,
241-242; and disestablishment, 253-
254; and military service, 307-308

Divisions: among white Virginians, 2-3,

129, 133, 141-144, 162, 293, 343-344, 437-440; cooperation of, with whites, 118, 145-148, 178-179, 294; response of, to Dunmore's Proclamation, 139-144; as captives, 176; and Declaration of Rights, 242; and Continental army, 261, 282, 338, 417-418; and abolition of slave trade, 332; and mobilization, 388-389; offer of, as bounties, 389-394; proposals to arm, 391; and invasion of 1781, 400, 437-440; offer of, as substitutes for whites, 417, 487; uprisings of, 437; plans to mobilize, 441-442; and Yorktown, 475-477; in postwar period, 486-492; and manumission laws, 487-490; and western migration, 491; postwar rebelliousness of, 491-492
—alleged conspiracies of: in Lancaster County, 22; on eve of Revolution, 47, 49; in Chesterfield County, 47, 49; along James River, 49
—individual: Aaron (Charles City County), 118n; Aaron (King and Queen), 130n; Amy (York), 141; Anthony Ferriah, 338n; Billy (Orange), 488; Billy (Prince William), 437-438; Bristow (Lancaster), 177; Caesar (Isle of Wight), 141; Charles (Stafford), 178; Daniel (Princess Anne), 129; Frank (Middlesex), 177n; George (Brunswick), 417; George (Spotsylvania), 86; George (Suffolk), 143; Harry (Prince George), 141; Harry (Stafford), 178; Jack (Botetourt), 437; James (Pittsylvania), 293; Jesse (Jamestown), 282n; Joe (Alexandria), 282; Joe Harris (Hampton), 130n; Johnny (King and Queen), 130n; Jonathan (New Kent), 85; Kitt (Stafford), 178; Lewis (Hanover), 293; Lewis (Prince George), 141; Lewis [Roberts], 338; Mial (Southampton), 85; Michael (Charles City County), 118n; Ned (Essex), 130n; Ned (Norfolk), 143; Phil (Southampton), 85; Prince (Hanover), 293; Rachel (York), 141; Tapley (Richmond), 293; Tim, 87; Tom (Isle

of Wight), 129; Tull (Brunswick), 417; Will (Frederick), 146; William Beck, 338n
—insurrections of: in Norfolk area, 130, 165; white fears of, 208-209
Evangelicals, 29-30. See also Baptists; Dissenters
Exemptions from military service: of overseers, 119, 227-228; of Dissenters, 226-227; repeal of, 240; claims for, 351; and elections, 352-353; complaints about, 423-424; and disaffection, 449-450. See also Militia

Fairfax, Thomas, sixth Baron, 254-255
Fairfax County: tenants in, 26; electorate in, 26; independent company of, 41, 46; plan for "Embodying the People" in, 43; county committee elections in, 126n; county committee of, 157, 163; and deserters, 285; draft in, 384
Falmouth, Maine, 173
Faucet, John, 447
Fauquier County, 254, 317
Fayette County, 483-484
Febiger, Christian, 513-514
Ferguson, Patrick, 377-378
Field, Henry, Jr., 254-255
Fincastle County, 94, 147; petitions from, 225; lead mines in, 248-249
Finnie, William, 54-55
Fithian, Philip Vickers, 80, 88
Fleetwood, Isaac, 129n
Fleming, John, 86
Fleming, William, 345-346, 464
Fluvanna County, 299; draft resistance in, 316, 320
Fontaine, Peter, 29
Fontaine, William, 297-298
Foreign alliances: demands for, 206-208
Fort Fincastle, 94
Fowey, H.M.S., 65, 74, 77-78
France: and commercial alliances, 206-208; anti-French sentiment of Virginians, 428-429; and Yorktown, 472-473

suspension of drafts, 452; and calls for dictator, 462–466; near capture of, 464; resignation of, 464–466

Jenkins, James, 446

Joel, Beesley Edgar, 448

Johnson, Jacob, 418

Johnson, Robert, 415

Johnson, Thomas, 216–217

Jones, Charles, 282

Jones, Joseph, 182n, 389–392, 395, 518

Jones, Walter, 34, 126

Juries, 500–501

Justices of the peace: appointment of, 236–237

Kelly, George, 293

Kemp, Samuel, 118

Kemp's Landing, 131, 133, 143, 377

Kentucky, 358–359, 415, 482–484. *See also* Western lands

Killimare, Matthew, 129n

King and Queen County, 201

King's Mountain, S.C., battle of, 377–378

King William County, 352–353, 523

Laborers: demand for, 268, 334–335

Lafayette, marquis de, 410, 430, 443, 472

Lancaster County, 22; draft riot in, 379–380

Land office, 357

Laws: evasion of, 290–291, 299–303. *See also* Draft resistance; Militia; Virginia General Assembly

Lawson, Robert, 432

Leafman, Abraham, 337

Lee, Arthur, 23

Lee, Gen. Charles, 112, 159, 212–213, 248; and command in Virginia, 184–187; and Virginia preparedness, 185–186

Lee, Francis Lightfoot, 159, 201; and Independence, 208–212

Lee, Henry, 203n, 453

Lee, Richard, 328

Lee, Richard Henry, 137, 158, 183, 188–190, 210, 219, 239, 275, 302–303, 308, 346, 360, 466, 519, 524; constitutional proposal of, 220–221

Lee, Thomas Ludwell, 217, 234, 242

Lee, William, 36

Leesburg, 187, 192, 194, 263

Leighton, James, 146

Leitch, Andrew, 191, 195–196

Leslie, Maj. Alexander, 376, 378

Leslie, Capt. Samuel, 131, 161–162

Leveling, 83, 196, 236, 382

Lewis, Andrew, 249–250, 270–271

Lewis, Fielding, 106–107, 116, 119, 128, 181, 200

Lewis, Richard, 287

Liberty (sloop), 282

Liberty pole, 81

Lincoln, Gen. Benjamin, 368

Literacy, 3

Liverpool (frigate), 168

Local autonomy: growth of, 14, 315, 513–514; and effect on state politics, 514–524; and effect on Continental politics, 524–527

Lockett, Francis, 337

Lockett, Stephen, 289

Lomax, Thomas, 322–325

Loudoun County, 2n, 112, 223, 261, 264, 273–274; electorate in, 26; resolves in, 35–36; county committee elections in, 126; revolt in, 187–197; and *Common Sense*, 198–199; poor recruiting in, 259; draft resistance in, 285, 317, 319–320; militia resistance in, 298–299; draft of 1781 in, 414–419

Louisa County, 28, 50–51, 195; county committee elections in, 125; tax resistance in, 502

Love, Samuel, 282

Lower-class Virginians: demands of, 6; and Seven Years' War, 27–29; and mobilization, 259–262; and drafts, 274–276, 281, 284–288; and concessions, 393–394

Lowry, Thomas, 322–325

Loyalists, 3–4, 133, 142, 378; regiment of, 153–154. *See also* Disaffection

Lunenburg County: landholding in, 25; petitions from, 227–228, 310–311, 492; tax resistance in, 524

Lyne, William, 201

McCarty, Charles Barber, 202–203

McClanachan, Alexander, 288

McClurg, James, 186–187, 204

McDonald, John, 379

McDowell, Samuel, 432n, 455

McGill, Andrew, 86

Madison, James, 23, 45, 69, 84, 242, 441; and slavery, 391, 488; and debt and tax relief, 517–524

Madison, Rev. James, 400, 402–403

Madison, Thomas, 390

Magdelan (ship), 54

Magill, Charles, 405–406

Main, Alexander, 81

Mallory, Philip, 283

Manumission laws, 487–490. *See also* Enslaved Virginians

Marlborough Iron Works, 146

Marshall, James, 517–518, 526

Martial tradition: lack of, 21, 37

Martin, Joseph Plumb, 476–477, 482n

Maryland Council of Safety, 195

Mason, George, 43, 46, 92, 95–96, 102, 106, 120, 183, 203n, 218, 258–259, 267, 346, 350, 357, 380–381, 384, 428–429, 442–443, 462, 517–518, 520; and Independence, 209–210; constitutional proposal of, 233–235, 237–238; and suffrage reform, 235; and Declaration of Rights, 241; and elections, 362–363

Mason, Thomson, 178

Massachusetts: and Lexington and Concord, 19, 49

Mathew, Maj. Gen. Edward, 343

Mathews, Sampson, 510

Maury, Rev. James, 28

Mazzei, Philip, 206n

Mecklenburg County, 44; petitions from, 227–228, 310–311, 492; draft resistance

in, 285; tax resistance in, 501; resistance to militia reform in, 508

Mennonites, 374n, 416

Mercer, Hugh, 100

Merchants: and volunteers, 82; in Norfolk area, 154–155; antipathy toward, 202–203

Mercury (ship), 77

Methodists, 29–30. *See also* Dissenters

Middle-class Virginians: and farms and families, 6; and alliances, 6; complaints of, 7; declining opportunities for, 25–26; postwar rights of, 492

Middlesex County, 325; resistance to militia reform in, 511

Military districts, 93

Military service: resistance to, 3–4, 13–14; rules and regulations established for, 96; elections of officers in, 96; and chain of command, 97; appointments of officers in, 99–102; unequal pay in, 111–112; distinctions in, 112–113; and wider social issues, 113–116; expense of, 119–120, 122–123; effect of Proclamation on, 148–149; complaints about, 193–194; and substitutions, 270, 306–307, 351, 414–416; and recruiting, 353–354; and enslaved Virginians, 417; and citizenship, 421–425, 433–434; and slaveholding, 424, 468–469; equity in, 467–470. *See also* Continental army, Virginia Line; Militia; Virginia state regiments

Militia: officers in, 37; function of, 37, 39; pre-Revolutionary resistance to service in, 38–39; pre-Revolutionary condition of, 38–40; resurrection of, in Revolution, 92–93; terms of service in, 92–93; and patrolling, 149; control over, 299–303, 320–321, 329–331; and courts-martial, 300; and elections, 322–325; laws governing, 330, 429, 469–471; and disaffection, 379; and slavery, 388–389; and Continental officers, 405–406; and state and Continental officials, 407–409; petitions of, 421–425; and service outside the state, 431-432; response of, to British in 1781, 440-452; and paroles, 443-444; and drafts, 452; and postwar demands, 492-493; and postwar tax resistance, 496-498; and resistance to postwar reform, 503-513

—call-outs for: in 1776, 252-253; in 1777, 294-299; and volunteers, 296-297; and terms of service, 297-299; success of, 401-402; and legitimation of complaints, 404-405

—complaints about: enlistments of gentlemen, 119; exemptions from, 119, 149-150; training in, 229; slaveholders, 229; musters of, 229-230

—exemptions: 93, 149-150; and complaints about, 119, 149-150; and Dissenters, 226-227, 240; and overseers, 227-228, 240; from drafts, 276-280

—officers in, 299-300; resignations of, 300, 320, 412-414; attrition of, 504-505; and state laws, 505-506

—resistance to service in, 191-192, 298-299, 340-341, 369-370, 374-375, 406-407, 411-419; and politics, 201-202, 252-253; and citizenship claims, 385-388

Militia Act (1784), 507-513
Miller, Alexander, 122
Minor, John, 323
Minuteman service, 92, 94-96; and independent companies, 95; and recruiting, 106-107; failure of, 107-122; complaints about, 109-116; skirmishes of, 131-132; replacement of, 257
Mitchell, Robert, 150, 499-500
Mobilization: and politicization, 197-198, and Independence, 198-215. *See also* Continental army, Virginia Line; Military service
Mobs. *See* Crowds
Moffett, George, 453, 495
Monroe, James, 518
Montagu, George, 65
Montgomery, Richard, 256

Montgomery County: disaffection in, 375-379; militia of, 432n; Indian attacks on, 512
Morale: of white Virginians, 262-265, 361-363, 374; and drafts, 278-280
Morgan, Daniel, 401, 412
Morris, Robert, 263
Moseley, Edward Hack, 129
Mount Vernon, 128-129, 144-145, 194, 334-335
Mulberry Island, 143
Munford, Robert, 31-32n, 44, 237
Murray, William, 287
Muse, Hudson, 202-203
Mutiny: of Continental Line, 181-183. *See also* Militia

Nansemond County, 31, 152, 329; salt shortages in, 262-263
Napier, Thomas, 320
Native Americans, 19-21, 130-131, 512; white fear of attack from, 61, 87, 94, 247-248, 329, 369, 375-376, 463; and Independence, 209-210; and western lands, 482-483
Nelson, Thomas, Jr., 64, 99-100, 165, 204, 208, 297, 339, 346-347, 404-405, 420, 440, 473-474, 507n; and governorship, 469-470
Nelson, Thomas, Sr., 131, 243
Nelson, William, 448
New Kent County: militia of, 409
Newton, George, 86
Newton, Thomas, 170
New York, 250-251, 255
Nicholas, George, 54-55, 77, 464
Nicholas, John, Jr., 508
Nicholas, Robert Carter, 44, 62n, 64, 137, 158, 163, 188-189, 205, 242, 254; and Independence, 214-215
Nonimportation. *See* Economic boycotts
Norfolk, 78; slave conspiracy in, 49, 130; county committee of, 81; runaway slaves in, 85; skirmishes over, 131-132; loyalists in, 133; occupation of, by patriots,

Taxes: for Seven Years' War, 23–24, 28–29; poll, 24; for Revolution, 120; complaints about, 120, 371–372; resistance to, 190; proposals for, 224, 309–311; reform of, 281, 304, 308–314, 356; and military service, 353–354, 373–374, 394; and disaffection, 379; and draft resistance, 421–423, 455–459; and western migration, 484–485; postwar resistance to, 493–503, 515–524
Taylor, James, 125
Taylor, John, 379–380, 426
Taylor, Robert, 503
Taylor's Ferry, 405
Tenant farmers, 223, 254–255; shorter leases of, 26; revolt of, 187–197; protests of, 254–255; and quitrents, 313
Test oath. *See* Oaths of allegiance
Thilman, Paul, 124
Thomas, John, 283n
Thompson, Bartlett, 123–124, 213
Thompson, George, 299
Thomson, Perkins, Jr., 285n
Thornton, Anthony, Jr., 323
Tilly, Arnaud de, 408
Tim, John, 416
Todd, John, 50
Tomkins, Bennett, 141
Tories. *See* Loyalists
Trabue, Daniel, 31n, 260, 358–359
Trabue, William, 260
Trade: demands for, 206–208, 223–224; and Independence, 208; renewal of, 332–334
Trap, Thomas, 286–287
Travis, Edward C., 282n
Treason, 258
Trenton, N.J., 260
Triplett, Capt. Simon, 195
"True Patriot," 67, 70
Tucker, St. George, 400–402, 475, 492, 511–512, 516
Tyler, John, 426

Upshaw, James, 322–325

Vagabonds: impressments of, 258; drafts of, 305
Van Meter, Garrett, 456
Virginia conventions
—First, 36
—Second: and militia law, 43–44
—Third, 74, 75; and mobilization for war, 89–102; adjournment of, 102
—Fourth: summoning of, 158; offensive measures of, 161–166; and Continental troops, 163–164; and Congress, 163–165; unity of, 165; and internal enemies, 165–166; and destruction of Norfolk, 171; and opening of ports, 173–174
—Fifth: elections for, 200–204; delegates to, 203–204; and Independence, 214–215; and new president, 216–217; committee representation in, 218; petitions to, 223–231; debates in, 234–235
Virginia council: and disaffected, 294–295
Virginia Declaration of Rights, 241–242, 253; and militia service, 433–434
Virginia Gazette, 67, 69, 72–73, 131, 202, 285–287
Virginia General Assembly
—of 1776, 252–253; petitions to, 253–255; and mobilization, 255–259
—of 1777: and drafts, 276–280, 304–307; and Patrick Henry, 302; and volunteers, 307–308; and taxes, 308–314
—of 1778–1779: lassitude of, 325–329; and draft, 326–328, 342–343; and recruiting, 355–356; and taxes, 356
—of 1780: and Congress, 368–369, 396–397; and South Carolina, 369–370; and recruiting, 372–374, 388–395; composition of, 390; criticism of, 403
—of 1781, 426–430; and Congress and northern states, 426–427, 471; and militia, 469–470
—in 1780s: and postwar debt and tax relief, 516–524
Virginia Line. *See* Continental army, Virginia Line
"Virginian, A," 291